In the Vale of Tears

Historical Materialism Book Series

The Historical Materialism Book Series is a major publishing initiative of the radical left. The capitalist crisis of the twenty-first century has been met by a resurgence of interest in critical Marxist theory. At the same time, the publishing institutions committed to Marxism have contracted markedly since the high point of the 1970s. The Historical Materialism Book Series is dedicated to addressing this situation by making available important works of Marxist theory. The aim of the series is to publish important theoretical contributions as the basis for vigorous intellectual debate and exchange on the left.

The peer-reviewed series publishes original monographs, translated texts, and reprints of classics across the bounds of academic disciplinary agendas and across the divisions of the left. The series is particularly concerned to encourage the internationalization of Marxist debate and aims to translate significant studies from beyond the English-speaking world.

For a full list of titles in the Historical Materialism Book Series available in paperback from Haymarket Books, visit:
www.haymarketbooks.org/category/hm-series

In the Vale of Tears

On Marxism and Theology V

Roland Boer

Haymarket Books
Chicago, IL

First published in 2014 by Brill Academic Publishers, The Netherlands

Published in paperback in 2014 by
Haymarket Books
P.O. Box 180165
Chicago, IL 60618
773-583-7884
www.haymarketbooks.org

ISBN: 978-1-60846-378-7

Trade distribution:
In the US, Consortium Book Sales, www.cbsd.com
In Canada, Publishers Group Canada, www.pgcbooks.ca
In the UK, Turnaround Publisher Services, www.turnaround-psl.com
In Australia, Palgrave Macmillan, www.palgravemacmillan.com.au
In all other countries, Publishers Group Worldwide, www.pgw.com

Cover design by Ragina Johnson.

This book was published with the generous support of
Lannan Foundation and the Wallace Action Fund.

Printed in the United States.

10 9 8 7 6 5 4 3 2 1

Library of Congress Cataloging-in-Publication data is available.

For Christina

Contents

Preface

I have come to see the relation between Marxism and theology as a difficult and tempestuous love affair, with a good mix of lust, affection, argument and profound differences of opinion. Even though they may go their own way for years at a time, they always return to renew their engagement. This book is the last of a series of five that have explored, criticised and salvaged what is useful and promising in that long affair, which is really another way of speaking about a rich tradition. The first three books deal with a range of Marxists, twenty-four of them from Rosa Luxemburg to Antonio Negri, while the fourth is a comprehensive engagement with Marx and Engels. This, the fifth and final volume, is my own response to that tradition, largely for the sake of some clarity and because the various positions I had taken and insights I had gleaned required a reasonably systematic effort to see what might fruitfully be deployed in current and future debates concerning 'Marxism and religion' – and because I really want to finish this study.

More of that in the body of the book, but for now, let me reprise a story about Marx, heaven and hell.

When Karl Marx dies, he is met by Saint Peter at the gates of heaven.

'Name?', asks Peter.

'Marx, Karl Marx', replies the famous thinker.

'Hmm', says Peter to himself, 'why do I know that name?'

'I am Karl Marx', Marx says, beaming, 'a founder of modern socialism and a driving force behind the communist ideal'.

'I see', Peter says. 'I'll have to check with God'.

So Peter rushes off to confer with God. God hears the name Marx and immediately a look of disgust spreads over his face. 'Marx?', God says, 'He's nothing but a troublemaker. Tell him to go to hell!'

So Peter happily signs the appropriate forms and Karl Marx is banished to Satan's domain.

Some time later, a free-trade agreement is forged between Heaven and Hell. The deal is hailed by all to be a great economic leap forward that will revitalise both struggling economies. After all, Hell has plenty of heat to spare, while

Heaven produces an excess of manna. But soon after the treaty, God realises that Heaven is no longer receiving any products from Hell. So he sends Peter down to investigate.

'Well?', asks Peter of Satan, 'What's the hold-up? We have an agreement!'

Satan shrugs his shoulders, exasperated. 'It's that Marx fellow', Satan replies. 'Ever since he got down here, all we've had are strikes and labour demands. Productivity has dropped to zero!'

'So?', Peter asks, 'What would you have us do?'

'Take him back. Take Marx back to Heaven, and I guarantee productivity will skyrocket!'

So Peter agrees, on God's behalf, to accept Karl Marx back into Heaven.

Normality returns, for a while. But some time later Satan realises that Hell has not received any orders from Heaven. In fact, very little communication at all has leaked from Up Above. So, concerned for the economic welfare of Hell, he makes a trip to Heaven.

'Peter! Peter, are you there?', Satan demands.

'Yes, what is it?', Peter answers.

'What's the hold-up? What about the flow of trade?'

'Oh I'm sorry', Peter says, 'We have decided to adopt an isolationist stance. We are a self-governing commune that is now focused on the needs of the proletariat. It is our opinion that this free-trade agreement benefits only the bourgeoisie'.

'What?!' Satan is furious. 'I demand to speak to God!'

Comrade Peter raises one eyebrow: 'Who?'

Neither heaven nor hell is safe from Marxist criticism. But this is by no means the whole story, for that criticism prefers to direct its energy to the vale of tears in which we live. As Marx put it in one of his most well-known texts on religion, the Introduction to his *Contribution to the Critique of Hegel's Philosophy of Law*, 'The criticism of religion is therefore *in embryo the criticism of the vale of tears*, the *halo* of which is religion'.[1] The catch is that any thorough criticism of the vale of tears cannot avoid religion, since religion is, for better or (more often) worse, part of the picture. That is the underlying assumption of this study, if not the whole series of *The Criticism of Heaven and Earth*. Yet I do not privilege religion, as idealist arguments tend to do, for I prefer to see it as one element in the total picture. Rather than being reductive, a Marxist approach to religion will always seek to expand analysis to include economics, history, society and ideology. Or,

1. Marx 1844c, p. 175; Marx 1844d, p. 378.

as Engels put it in a letter to Ludwig Kugelmann in 1867, 'In the words of our old friend Jesus Christ, we must be as innocent as doves and wise as serpents'.[2]

Although writing is often a solitary affair, the practice of hermits and those comfortable with their own company, this book would not have been written without overlapping networks of people who gave advice, offered encouragement, showered me with criticism (happily, most of it has been constructive) and at least showed interest. I would like to thank David Roberts, who shares my interests in Marxism and religion and continues to give insightful and thought-provoking criticisms and suggestions. Peter Thomas and Sebastian Budgen, wearing their hats with the *Historical Materialism* book series, remain enthusiastic about the whole project, making sure I do not slip up too often. Among those involved in the Religion and Political Thought project, which spans four continents, I must at least mention Carsten Pallesen, Ole Jakob Løland, Mads Peter Karlsen, Ward Blanton and Sara Farris, as well as Kenpa Chin and Philip Chia, who have opened up China and Taiwan to me (and instigated a series of translations). Warren Goldstein, the anchor of the Critical Theory of Religion project,[3] has been a vital conversation partner. Members of The Future of Religion seminar at the Inter-University Centre in Dubrovnik, Croatia, have provided a vibrant forum for discussion and debate, especially Rudolf Siebert, Michael Ott, Tatiana Senyushkina and Evgeniya (Jane) Goryunova. More recently, the stimulating engagements over Marxism and religion with Alex Andrews and Anthony Paul Smith have come to my aid, especially via my blog, *Stalin's Moustache*.[4] I should also mention the old trade unionist from Norway, Odd Andreasen, and the Seattle activist, Matthew Hamilton, who push me to think further and write more clearly. Closer to home, the Bible and Critical Theory Seminar, meeting for a couple of days every year in a pub somewhere in Australia or New Zealand, has put up with earlier, half-formulated versions of some of the arguments in this book. Gathering from diverse backgrounds and disciplines, members of the seminar have questioned, encouraged and, when all else was lost, raised a drink to signal it was beer-o'clock. As always, an old colleague from Monash University, Andrew Milner, the Methodist Marxist, has pinpointed the part of my argument that was weakest and urged me to be sharper. And at the University of Newcastle (my current abode) Terry Lovat has shown himself to be a rare breed of mentor. As Pro-Vice Chancellor of Education and Arts with a passion for theology, Terry encourages me to get on with what I love to do, even if he finds the whole exercise somewhat strange (why would anyone be interested in Marxism

2. Engels 1867a, p. 467; Engels 1867b, p. 567.
3. <http://criticaltheoryofreligion.org>.
4. <http://stalinsmoustache.wordpress.com>.

and religion?). I trust I have reciprocated a little with this book and the series as a whole for his support. At least I hope he will see why one should be interested in these matters. Finally, Christina has shared the intensities, struggles and jubilations of the writing process, all while she was carrying on with her own projects. To her I owe endless thanks.

The Hill
New South Wales
February 2013

Introduction

> What a sublime and, at the same time, sordid vocation this theological discipline has.[1]

It has been a long journey, this study of the way Marxism and theology interact with one another. But now at last, after too many years working my way through the vast majority of significant Marxists who have engaged with theology, I offer my own response to their multicoloured arguments. As the conclusion to the series I have called *The Criticism of Heaven and Earth*, this book undertakes two overlapping tasks. One is to gather the various insights I have identified in the previous four volumes and weave them into a coherent whole,[2] while the other is to pursue their implications further and develop a few new ideas on the way. Let me say a little about each task.

As I undertook the job of reading, reflection and writing the earlier four volumes, certain themes began to recur. Sometimes an idea would cause me to lift my eyes from the page, a spark that would trigger a whole new train of thought. At other times – relatively rarely – those discoveries would be ready-made, a gem that needed no further work. More often, I would pick up an idea and draw out implications only hinted at in the original text. Occasionally this would require reading against the grain, teasing out a position that was at odds with the dominant position of the author in question. Through these processes of engagement I began, gradually, to gather a number of ideas which

1. Negri 2009, p. 58.
2. Boer 2007a; Boer 2009b; Boer 2010a; Boer 2012.

required some further work, linking them together and developing them further. So what I seek to do here is gather a motley collection of thoughts and arguments and stitch them into a whole – relativising theology, atheism and theology, political myth, political grace, the political ambivalence of Christianity, the perpetual need for economic history, kairós and ákairos, ethics versus an unethical and unmoral position, fetishism and idolatry, political iconoclasm, secularism and anti-secularism, transcendence and transgression, and the question of death. Many of these items have appeared in some form in the earlier books, usually as an identification of a useful idea and at times as a tool of analysis. Yet they remained scattered, brought into play when needed, mentioned in conclusions to the earlier books and tagged for further elaboration. However, this book is not merely a long summary of what has gone before, for in each case I take the argument a good deal further, opening up new angles for dealing with these topics. The act of collecting them in one place is the first step of such a development, for then new avenues of analysis have opened up, but it remains a preliminary move. More importantly, I have attempted to strengthen some arguments, reshape some others in light of an insight or two and produce a few new positions. So this work is both summary and development, collation and elaboration, conclusion and exploration of a new direction or two. Although both approaches characterise the whole work, the first four chapters – on atheism, myth, ambivalence and history – function more in terms of summary and conclusion, while the remaining three chapters – on kairós, ethics and idolatry – focus more on developing some new arguments. Needless to say, despite its close relation with the previous four volumes, this work stands on its own, backtracking and providing the necessary groundwork where needed in order to expand my thoughts a little further.

Of old timber and lovers

As is my wont, I will provide an outline of each topic and chapter of this book in a few moments, but before doing so I would like to comment on some preliminary matters: the problem of systems, the nature of theology, theological suspicion and the need to relativise theology. The first of these – concerning systems and their problems – is really an elaboration on the previous paragraph, for I make no pretentious claims to provide a comprehensive system here. Philosophers have a temptation to build systems, although periods of anti-systematic impulse recur from time to time; literary critics (among whom I may still be located) slip into perpetual searches for new methods; historians attempt wholesale reconstructions when they have the nerve and are not distracted by yet another pile of archives. I must admit to being fascinated by the daring of such efforts, as well as the risk and devotion they entail. For example, Badiou's single-handed recovery of grand systems is as riskily breathtaking as it leaves him open to attack. Platonic in its scale, it draws in a vast array of topics – Greek tragedy, poetry, Lacan, mathematics, the New Testament, theology (Pascal and Kierkegaard), politics, art, and on and on – in a way that leaves him open to criticisms where he falls short, such as the class associations and anti-democratic tenor of Plato's elitist thought, the untroubled classicism, the dismissive polemics against 'sophistry' and the Romanticism of the event and its truth. Yet the fidelity to his own philosophical event can only be admired, and I find myself drawn to his bemusement, the shy flicker of a smile at being 'discovered' so late, especially when he made a virtue out of his solitary extremity with respect to the fashions of French intellectual and political life. But I would find that a singular exploration of the vast territories opened up would become a drag in the long term. And there are too many systems that have collapsed before they were barely thrown together without adequate structure or mental fortitude. Dühring's effort in the late nineteenth century merely required Engels's firm shove and it came tumbling down in a pile of girders and dust. Many have been the apparent new ideas of a life's work that have deflated with one simple prick. I think of my Hebrew teacher, Barbara Thiering, who constructed a whole edifice concerning the origins of Christianity among the Qumran (Dead Sea Scroll) sectarians, only to find that carbon dating comprehensively removed the Dead Sea Scrolls from the first decades of Christianity (they were written much earlier). Some have shown distinct insight with a single idea, such as Girard's mimetic desire, only to founder with the effort to make it universally explanatory, along with the desperate attempt to include within that system his religious conversion with a 'miraculous' healing from cancer after prayer.

So I prefer the comments of Adorno and Bloch. Adorno was wont to quote Nietzsche's adage: 'I mistrust all systematizers and avoid them. The will to a system is a lack of integrity'.[3] Adorno goes on to characterise system-building as provincial, naïve and caught in the past. It is like a cottage industry in a village, where the village stands in for the whole world and the system produced can pretend to have comprehended all knowledge, or at least provided a key to it. Philosophers continue to feel that they can construct a theory of the universe with a pen, paper and their own thoughts while sitting by a cosy fire in a cottage in the woods, even though they have not noticed how stale the air has become.[4]

3. Nietzsche 1990, p. 35.

4. Adorno 2008, pp. 41–2; Adorno 2007, pp. 65–8. See also his comments on the efforts by philosophers to stuff the infinite into a small cottage, that is, to contain an infinite universe within a paltry, limited number of axioms, in Adorno 2008, pp. 78–9, 186–7; Adorno 2007, pp. 117–18, 231–2. See further Adorno 2000c, pp. 23–5.

Adorno is of course having a dig at Heidegger, but he has little time for the provincialism of philosophical systems. As for Bloch, he notes the fading dreams and perpetual retreats of the great planners of systems, preferring in their stead detours, offshoots and accidental discoveries: 'Just as a detour in life so often turns out not to have been one at all, just as a little offshoot can provide the revitalizing contribution, so does the plan resign and overgrow itself at the same time in many first (and many late) masterpieces'.[5] He gives the example of the small beginning of Cervantes, who wanted merely to mock chivalric romances in *Don Quixote*, only to find he had created a parody of humanity. Or Hegel, who set out to write a conventional textbook on philosophy and ended up with the *Phenomenology*. As for a grand system of life, history, the universe and everything, Bloch gives the example of 'someone who wrote a philosophy of the postal system in three volumes, which was certainly an epochal idea at the time'.[6]

I do not propose to write a philosophy of the postal system, nor perhaps of the bicycle plan of Sydney. Instead, I think of my project here in terms of two images. One comes from a scavenging pastime of my own, cultivated during a poor childhood and somewhat poor adulthood as well. As I walk about the streets, my eyes effortlessly spot discarded items that may be of some value, at least to me. Pieces of quality timber, hidden under a garish coat of paint, or beaten, chipped and tossed out. I gather a length here, a piece of furniture there, pull out odd nails, strip off the old paint, and ponder how I can put the pieces together into a bookshelf, or perhaps a desk or some other simple piece of furniture. And then, with the hand tools available, I saw, sand, hammer, dowel, sand again and treat with nothing more than linseed oil. I seek out quality hard and soft woods and the results may contain odd sections of floorboard, a piece from a bed, a sideboard and what have you. Nothing fancy, constructed out of found objects; but before someone suggests that my finished products – and by analogy this book – are jerry-built out of junk, I should point out that they are massively heavy, solidly constructed and built to last generations. But they do the job, usually more than adequately.

So also with this book, or at least I hope it does the job more than passably. It too has come together like a collection of odd pieces of timber, often stumbled upon on the detours of which Bloch speaks. Eventually I found myself, after the unexpected growth of this series of studies, with a collection of ideas, oddly shaped, picked up here and there. Once gathered I turned them over, pondered how they might fit together, cutting off a little in one place and building on an idea elsewhere, gradually working them into one another. Every now and then

5. Bloch 2006, p. 67; Bloch 1985d, p. 92.
6. Bloch 2006, p. 67; Bloch 1985d, p. 91.

a new direction or two has sparked in the process. But the end result is a whole that is, to re-use a well-worn observation, more than its parts.

A second image reveals not so much the provenance of this study and its mode of construction but the working method itself. Marxism and theology are like two lovers, rubbing up against one another, the blood rushing to crotches, touching, stroking, grasping one another, at times fucking furiously and yet at others argumentative, mutually annoyed, distant and estranged. Often it seems to me that they are like lovers who cannot resist one another and yet cannot avoid arguing either. I think of it as an intimate, dialectical interaction in which neither remains the same. So while there are surprising confluences and liaisons, more often theology comes under sustained criticism from a Marxist angle, being transformed in the process. But so also do the various elements of Marxism, which I take as a collection of problems rather than a coherent method or position (but is not any approach like that?), meet the critique that comes from theology. It too is not quite the same after the engagement, forced to rethink its own positions in the process. So this study offers a dialectic of sorts, seeking not merely to analyse theology from a Marxist position, nor to subject Marxism to critique from the perspective of theology, but to do both. That means that the various readerships may need to readjust their expectations: Marxists will want a fully-fledged Marxist theory of religion, while theologians would prefer to see some insights from Marxism incorporated within the framework of theology. Neither audience will find exactly what they are seeking, but my hope is that they will find the project fruitful in unexpected ways – as has indeed happened with earlier volumes in the series. The argument that unfolds below explores the different ways in which the intimate, mutual critique of Marxism and theology works itself out, a process in which neither remains the same. Each must face up to some insistent questioning, be prepared to come clean and not seek to block, obfuscate or hold ground at all costs.

On theology

Given that this study is a full-blooded exploration of Marxism and theology, a word on theology itself is in order. As a working definition, I understand theology in terms of a disciplinary intersection: it deals with the nature of mythology (the central stories with which theology deals), nature and the environment (creation), with the human condition (anthropology), why the world is the way it is (harmatology, or the doctrine of sin), the problem of suffering (theodicy), the nature of the human subject (via Christology), how human beings might live together (ecclesiology), and the nature of history and hopes for the future (eschatology). Add to this an enduring and undeveloped contribution of

Althusser, particularly in terms of religion as one of the ideological state apparatuses, or as a practice or instance that is part of a larger social formation.[7] As Burton Mack points out, despite the increasingly widespread use of Althusser's approach in social thought outside Marxism, it remains curiously under-utilised in the study of religion.[8] So I understand theology not merely as a collection of thoughts or system of ideas, but as a body of rather complex thought enmeshed with institutional, social and economic structures, as well as being the site of significant ideological struggle.

I will have more to say on Althusser later on, but now a question immediately arises concerning my definition: is it not wrong-headed? Is theology not defined by belief in and discourse upon God – theo-logos? The problem is that Christianity has this strange and quite unique obsession with defining the core of religion (itself a term applied from Christianity to other 'religions') as the belief in a superhuman being. To my mind, that definition camouflages the full range of theology, concealing its full possibilities. Once we shift perspective, putting aside the assumption that religious belief comprises the core or perhaps the overarching unity of theology and realising that it is but one small and by no means necessary part, theology shows all its other colours. Do not get me wrong; I do not wish to preclude belief, but simply point out that it is but one possible and not at all dominant element among many others. I will argue this position more fully in the first chapter, save for one point. In making this definition, I also assume a recasting of how we understand disciplines. All too often, a discipline is defined by a unifying methodological core. But instead of defining each discipline in such a way, we should think of disciplines as intersections and not as solitary castles. So theology is not defined by explaining belief in muscled fairies, but by intersections of precisely those items I mentioned – history, environment, the human condition, hope, social questions, mythology and so on. The same point applies to methods. Is there a unifying method to theology or, perhaps, biblical studies? The answer to that question will depend upon whom you ask. A quick survey would include historical methods, philosophical concerns, literary analysis, sociology, folklore, and so on. The catch is that each one of these disciplines also becomes a set of intersections or crossroads in their own right.

Relativising theology

In the next couple of sections, I outline two determining methodological assumptions: theological suspicion and the need to relativise theology. Let me begin

7. Althusser 1971, pp. 127–86; Althusser 1995, pp. 269–314. Althusser and Balibar 1979, pp. 182–93; Althusser, Balibar, Establet, Macherey and Rancière 1996, pp. 396–411.

8. Mack 2008, pp. 48–81.

with the second. With predictable frequency we come across variations on the argument that theology is the source of everything from the study of physics to the invention of the condom, or perhaps that the incarnation of Christ begins a tradition of 'personalism' that has its current perverse outcomes in everything from free expression, through sexual liberation and gender equality, to social mobility.[9] The examples soon pile up: the ability to think of communal life must take account of the church and the sub-discipline of ecclesiology; freedom must be understood in terms of the paradox that true freedom comes only with subservience; or the very possibility of disenchanting the world (the one in which we supposedly live now) relies on an earlier, enchanted one. Theology used to be – goes the argument – the determining worldview of Western society until relatively recently, so it is no surprise that all we now take for granted should owe its originating impulse to theology. Or, with more specificity, we can find the various modernist and postmodernist positions already foreshadowed in medieval theological debates, so all we need do is return to those debates to find our answers. If we go back far enough or dig deep enough we will find that theology is our intellectual and social ancestor or perhaps the bedrock of nigh-on everything. This argument has many forms, such as the widespread assumption (based on multiple repetitions rather than any firm evidence) that Marxism owes immense debts to Jewish and Christian schemas of history and salvation.[10] Or it may be argued that all political thought is ultimately theological thought (Schmitt),[11] or that modern political thought and social theory in its different shapes has a covert – at times partially overt – theological foundation, so much so that its errors may be determined and critiqued on the basis of perceived theological errors (Milbank).[12] Or indeed that the secular disciplines with which we now work initially took their leave, or were shoved, from the nest of theology.

Alternatively and in an effort at thorough encirclement, one begins with a current problem – Deleuze's philosophy, Marxist thought, capitalism – and then shows how the problem finds a proper resolution in theology. Deleuze's immanence requires a Christological ontology to solve its quandaries, the depredations of capitalism can be solved only through theology, and Marxism's truncated approach requires the completion of theological transcendence to make the required breakthrough. Or in an even more extreme form, only the correct theology offers the solution, so one must avoid heresies like the Protestant-capitalist

9. Milbank in Žižek and Milbank 2009, pp. 116–17.

10. Berdyaev 1937; Löwith 1949; see also Kolakowski 1981, pp. 372–5; Fischman 1991, pp. 94–108.

11. Schmitt 2005. See also, from a French phenomenological perspective, Lefort 2006.

12. Milbank 1990; Žižek and Milbank 2009, pp. 110–233.

one in favour of a 'Catholic' option. Theology as alpha and omega of all thought, providing both the ground and telos of philosophy and politics – a comprehensive strategy of containment and overcoming in the name of theology.[13]

In response to this absolutising of theology – behind, beneath, before and above any other thought – I shall argue for the unflagging programme of relativising such claims: theology is not the source or the basis, the solution or the end, but merely one form such thought may take. I first developed this argument in earlier treatments of Theodor Adorno, Georg Lukács and Raymond Williams, where we encountered Adorno repeatedly making the point that Christianity itself is a profound compromise and appropriation of pagan patterns of thought and practice without which theology would be unimaginable; Lukács trying with some futility to exorcise romanticist, idealist and theological elements of his thought, or what he calls his 'messianic utopianism'; and Williams treating the Baptist chapel of his native Wales as a vanishing mediator for the values of 'warm Marxism'. Do not get me wrong: Adorno, Lukács and Williams do not make this argument themselves, but it emerges from their thought.

With Adorno, the relativising of theology first appears in his study of Kierkegaard, itself a book that engages deeply with theology (that it was a second habilitation (the first was withdrawn) which was approved by Paul Tillich only enhances such a status).[14] Adorno reminds us time and again that Kierkegaard's theological constructions are bound up with – usually Nordic and thereby pagan or non-Christian – myths in the very act of attempting to block Christianity's inescapable mythological ties. In making this move, Adorno stresses the fact that Christian theology provides no unsullied origin, no fount from which all that followed was subsequently secularised, debauched and paganised. Instead, theology itself arises from this complex relation to what preceded it and what exists beside it, of which theology then becomes one more code.

In Lukács's case, his effort to eradicate any trace of theological thought is in fact mistaken, for instead of assuming that religious ways of thinking comprise the source that must be overcome, it seems to me that they should be understood as one moment of much deeper traditions of thought and action. A close look at Lukács's works reveals a tension: the form of argument that appears in *The Theory of the Novel* comes under fire in *The Young Hegel*.[15] So, in *The Theory of the Novel* he argues that the only way to overcome a world 'abandoned by God' (the context of the rise of the novel) is to seek for the lost and integrated classical

---

13. As a representative sample, see Davis and Riches 2005; Cunningham 2005; Bell 2005; Baker and Gangle 2005; Pickstock 2005; Blond 2005; Milbank 2005. See the excellent criticisms of such positions in Surin 2005, pp. 257–9; Surin 2009, pp. 226–40.

14. Adorno 1989; Adorno 2003a. As another example, see also Adorno 1992, pp. 56–7; Adorno 2003g, pp. 206–7.

15. Lukács 1971; Lukács 1994; Lukács 1975; Lukács 1966.

world, one that we find, for instance, in Dostoevsky. However, in his later *The Young Hegel*, Lukács attacks Hegel for a very similar argument: the alienating 'positivity' of Christianity must be overcome, suggests Hegel, by means of the recovered republican freedom of ancient Greece and Rome. Similarly, in the famous prefaces to his later works, especially when they were reprinted, Lukács tries to identify when he successfully rid himself of his romantic anti-capitalism, messianic utopianism, as well as the senses of divine abandonment and the age of absolute sinfulness.[16] The catch is that in attempting to excise the content of his older argument, Lukács has missed a crucial feature of the form of that argument, namely, the awareness of a longer tradition that includes a religious moment within it. Far better, I suggest, to understand religion and theology as passing moments in longer trajectories of thought and action.

In doing so, we begin to relativise the absolute claims that cluster around theology. It seems to me that Raymond Williams enacts such a relativising move, although it emerges from a careful reading of his work rather than any explicit strategy on his part. When I mention Williams and religion in various contexts, the response is usually one of surprise: Williams and religion? But there is more than first meets the eye, either as historicising comments when he deals with drama, education, literacy and other matters in *Culture and Society* and *The Long Revolution*, or in his novels, where the tension between the Baptist chapel and established Church of England appears quite often.[17] Here we find that the values of Williams's 'warm Marxism' – neighbourliness, community, humanity, working-class solidarity, trust, faith, and even socialism – often centre on the chapel, which is as much a religious as a social and political focus of the Welsh towns in his novels. By contrast, in his critical work, the chapel becomes a vanishing mediator of such values, for the sources upon which Williams calls are his autobiography, the innate tendencies associated with Welshness and the working class. The chapel itself has disappeared; once it has done its task, enabling Williams to espouse his 'warm Marxism', he dismisses it from the scene. However, in doing so Williams enacts a relativising of theology, for the theological content of the values he espouses turns out to be one moment in a much richer and longer history.

So Adorno, Lukács and Williams bring forth what I call a passing moment of theology, although that term does give the impression that theology is fading into the distance (not without a few gestures of good riddance or waves of tearful farewell). What I mean is that theology provides one language for voicing political thought. However, I do not assume some core idea that then has its

16. Especially the prefaces to *The Theory of the Novel* and *History and Class Consciousness*. Lukács 1971; Lukács 1994; Lukács 1988; Lukács 1968.
17. Williams 1958; Williams 1960; Williams 1961; Williams 1978.

various expressions – like water poured now into a cup, now a glass, saucepan or bowl – whether in sociology, philosophy, theology or what have you. There is no need to have a core, for the particular expressions are moments of their own creation, constructed ad hoc for the problem at hand, but they also become translatable or transcodable into other tongues without the need for a basic message.

In many respects, this study is precisely such an exercise in relativising theology, a point I will bring to the surface from time to time but which often, gliding by like a submarine, remains assumed as a strategy of thought. The other strategy is what I have called theological suspicion, of which the relativising of theology is one strategy.

Theological suspicion

I draw the practice of theological suspicion from Adorno, although he did not put it in precisely these terms. Theological suspicion obviously has a pedigree that runs back through the Marxist practice of ideological suspicion; it may be seen as a subset of ideological suspicion, albeit with its own tools and assumptions. But how does theological suspicion work? Let me give the specific example of Adorno's own practice before making some general comments. Adorno was deeply wary of both secularised theology and liberal theology,[18] the former showing up in the philosophical work of Heidegger and Jaspers, among others, and the latter the dominant form of progressive theology in his time, embodied above all in the work of his very close friend, mentor and one-time colleague, Paul Tillich. The problem for Adorno was not that theology had lost its way, but that its absolutes threatened to slip into the underworld of philosophy. One might argue that this particular system of thought was thoroughly 'secular' (at least in the popular sense of the term), that being, becoming, the uncanny, hope, or authenticity were divested of their former theological content and reloaded with thoroughly new meanings. But that only made Adorno suspicious. Not so easy, he would point out, to empty the container and fill it with a fresh theological drink, for the container itself bore traces of its former usage. That is to say, form always clings to content far more tenaciously than one might expect. But even more perniciously, form itself is the manifestation of the given structures of a socio-economic system such as capitalism, so all the limits and promises of that system would show up in the thought, texts and culture produced. When we get a situation like theology, which trails a long history of associations with former systems, and which was also the way in which structures of power were articulated in those systems, the older patterns of power would cling to the

18. See especially Adorno 1973a; Adorno 2003j.

thought-forms even when deployed in other fashions. In other words, although secular thought (and liberal theology, which was in many respects a half-way house to secular theology) may think it has dispensed with theology, what it has actually done is redeploy the forms of theological thought. However, instead of being overt in their arrangements of power and recourse to authority (God, the church, priests and so on), these thought-forms now go underground and serve to bolster the authority of the philosopher and his thought, or perhaps other institutions of the state, in a way that is even more dangerous. Adorno was far more comfortable with theology out in the open, striding along the street in full view, announcing its presence without a hint of embarrassment; he was deeply suspicious of covert theology, lurking in the quiet corners, camouflaging itself with urban grey or rural green. When theology was overtly present, at least you had some sense of where you stood; now that it has become covert, the ground is far more treacherous. And without a sense of their relative status, the absolutes of theology would, if not challenged, make a subterranean transition to the absolutes of philosophy.

Anyone with a smattering of familiarity will recognise that Adorno's suspicions owe much to the Marxist practice of ideological suspicion and criticism, although Adorno gives it his own twist through the *Bilderverbot*, the ban on images drawn from the second commandment and turned into a leitmotiv of his work.[19] In order to situate theological suspicion within that wider framework of ideological suspicion, let me offer a few comments on the key features of ideological suspicion I wish to appropriate and deploy in my own analysis (those who know the story may skip the next few paragraphs and pick up the argument in the conclusion to this section).[20]

Ideology begins its chequered career as a negative term, designating 'false consciousness',[21] a way of concealing oppression and exploitation. The task of ideological suspicion was then to unmask and uncover (the terms are quite deliberate) this ideology in order to show the truth of that exploitation. Clear the bells and whistles of the superstructure and the real exploitation at the base

---

19. See further Chapter 7 and Boer 2007a, pp. 391–445.

20. For an excellent snapshot of the issues in discussions over ideology today, see the collection edited by Žižek (1994), especially Žižek's effort in the Introduction to give ideology a Lacanian twist in which the very effort to step outside of ideology is the most deeply ideological act of all. Eagleton's much-read text on ideology is also worth consulting. See Eagleton 1991.

21. Much like the sense it still enjoys in popular conversation (which is itself a mark of the way Marxist terminology and thought have entered into everyday speech), ideology is something that you, my opponent, have: it is an uninformed and somewhat doctrinaire opinion that screens the truth. You may think it is true, that it explains the real world, but I know that you are kidding yourself. And so it is my task to show you why and how your ideology screens what is really true.

becomes all too clear. For example, when one group or class claims that a particular programme is good for you and me, ideological suspicion seeks to show that such a claim actually justifies oppression. Thus, the move to drive down wages, break the unions and improve profits for large transnationals is presented as providing the opportunity for an increase in wages and the power of individual workers to bargain with their bosses for better conditions. Or the assertion that freedom of choice should cover all elements of one's public and private life actually conceals all manner of shady practices, from monopolies that present little real choice (how many types of drink does Coca-Cola produce?) to heavy government subsidies for private businesses, whether in healthcare, telecommunications or transport. Once such ideologies have been unmasked, once the real conditions of oppression have been uncovered, one may then set about correcting and overcoming the real source of oppression. For Marxists and other sundry revolutionaries, the real causes of oppression lie in the economic base and in the class oppositions that mediate this economic foundation. Translated, this means that you do not merely toss out your boss; you also need to change the system that needs bosses in the first place. Or, as the slogan would have it (also with a good Marxist pedigree): it's the economy, stupid!

To sum up, according to this type of ideological suspicion, ideology is bad for you since it screens the real source of your troubles. It is a little like those toilet sprays with different scents: apple, pear, fruits of the forest, lavender and so on. All the mist from the spray-can does is mask the smell of your crap. In order to identify the problem, you need to get rid of that can of lavender spray so you can smell what is really going on. Only then can you solve it properly. So also with ideological suspicion: the way to get rid of the problem is to dispense with the ideology, find the real source of the problem and deal with it.

Now, if I were to take up this type of ideological criticism into my practice of theological suspicion, it would look something like this: theology would become a religious form of ideology, one that conceals in religious terms the real causes of exploitation. For example, the old reactionary role of the churches in urging people not to protest and revolt against exploitation, since they will be rewarded in heaven for their faithfulness, is actually a means of ensuring that the powers that be – of which the churches are all too often a part – remain untroubled. Or the claim by Christian teaching that we must accept each other in love (because God is love) may be a way of ensuring that nothing changes. We accept you as you are, says the church, but that means we do not have to do anything about the system that makes you poor or rich, sick or healthy, exploiter or exploited.

However, there is a catch with the term 'false consciousness'; or rather, it is somewhat ambivalent. Over against the need to clear away false consciousness in order to see the real source of oppression, the attack on false consciousness also implies that we seek to replace this false one with a true one. In other words, the opposite of false consciousness is not necessarily its absence; it may also be true consciousness. This ambivalence opens the door into the next episode in the narrative of the development of theological suspicion: the sense of ideology as false consciousness has been superseded by a more complex understanding. Rather than mere false consciousness, ideology turns out to be a good deal more ambivalent and slippery. If I return to the opposition between false and true consciousness, then ideology is not only the province of ruling classes, not only the means of keeping vast numbers of people in servitude, not merely one mode of keeping insurrection down. Rather, ideology also belongs to those who oppose and seek to overthrow the ruling class. In other words, ideology critique seeks to put a better ideology in the place of a worse one.

The shift is rather profound, although it is usually described in terms of the well-lubricated distinction between criticism and description. By 'critical' is meant the approach to ideology I have outlined above, as false consciousness that needs to be corrected, while 'descriptive' or 'functional' designates an approach in which ideology becomes an unavoidable and thereby necessary dimension of human existence.[22] Although Marx tends towards the critical side, there is enough in his work that opens out to a descriptive approach, which would then be taken up with some enthusiasm by, among others, Lenin, Althusser, Gramsci and Bloch. At a basic level, such an approach would mean that theology, as a component of ideology, is no different from art, popular culture, writing, metaphysics, politics and what have you. Indeed, these items constitute the various forms ideology may take. The situation is, of course, far more complex and conflictual than that, but in order to see how, I draw on Althusser, Gramsci and Bloch, for they effectively shift the descriptive sense of ideology away from its inherent functionalism.

For Althusser, ideology is eternal and not something we can dispense with; as the representation of our relationship to the real social and economic conditions of existence, ideology is an indispensable part of political and economic struggles. For Gramsci, ideology becomes hegemony, which is (contrary to its popular usage) not merely a constantly reinforced ideology of the ruling class, but also a means for overcoming that ruling-class ideology. Indeed, Gramsci's development of the concept of hegemony was intended to find a means for the communist agitation and opposition to get some grip in the struggles against fascism. And for Bloch, ideology is deeply conflictual, neither purely false consciousness nor necessary function. His great interest was religion, or rather the myths of the

22. See Barrett 1991, pp. 18–34; Kiernan 1983; Larrain 1983a; Larrain 1983b; Dupré 1983, pp. 238–44; McLellan 1995, p. 16.

Bible (which is not quite the same thing); in the Bible, he argued, the myths of rebellion are often part of the fabric of myths of domination and oppression. The two are inseparably entwined, and so to throw out one would also involve losing the other. In light of this situation, he calls for the discernment of myth.

It is from these understandings of ideology and ideological criticism that I draw the concept and practice of theological suspicion. In particular, there are three features of ideology that I wish to stress and appropriate for theological suspicion: ideology is unstable, it designates struggle, and in that struggle discernment is crucial; so also with theology. Let me say a little more about each point.

The instability of ideology comes via Gramsci, especially his extraordinarily useful idea of hegemony. In a nutshell, hegemony means that any effort at domination and control is bound to be uncertain and shaky. In fact, the classic formulation of the theory of hegemony was intended to find a way to overthrow those who oppress. Or to put it even more forcefully (a point Derrida was to repeat after Gramsci), the very act of asserting dominance is inherently unstable. Subversion lurks in every murky doorway and under every bed. This is of course not the popular view, or indeed the popular usage of the term. The widespread concept of hegemony, even among some Marxists, is that hegemony designates the dominant position – another version of the early and succinct comment by Marx and Engels: 'The ideas of the ruling class are in every epoch the ruling ideas'.[23] And it is reinforced by force (police, both secret and not-so-secret, law courts and army) and persuasion (propaganda in the media, education and argument). There is some limited truth in this perception. However, the problem with a ruling hegemony is that its position is chronically unstable. For all its apparent strength, a dominant hegemony is more often than not an ill-fitting and shaky thing. It is constantly undermined and must be asserted by as many means as are available and in whatever possible forum – such as culture, politics, religion and economics. These range from crude propaganda to subtle influence.

Let me take one example: hetero-normativity. If human beings are naturally heterosexual, if it were a secure social assumption, then there would be no need for constant efforts to assert heterosexuality's dominance. Whether it is in preserving marriage as an institution for heterosexual couples, with its financial and legal hedges, or in the endless stream of dating programmes on television, or songs concerning love and its loss, or the little homophobic comments

---

23. Marx and Engels 1845–6a, p. 59. 'Die Gedanken der herrschenden Klasse sind in jeder Epoche die herrschenden Gedanken' (Marx and Engels 1845–6b, p. 46). Or, slightly differently in *The Manifesto of the Communist Party*, 'The ruling ideas of each age have ever been the ideas of its ruling class' (Marx and Engels 1848c, p. 503); 'Die herrschenden Ideen einer Zeit waren stets nur die Ideen der herrschenden Klasse' (Marx and Engels 1848d, p. 480).

made in passing that are part of a culture of machismo, or the positions of so many churches regarding both the sexuality of their members and above all their leaders – all of these suggest the very instability of hetero-normativity. We could perform the same exercise with hackneyed terms such as freedom, or the need to have a job, or the Cold War hangover that shows up in continued rhetoric against socialism, and so on.

Even more, *hegemonia* in Gramsci's hands points to a mechanism for undermining and overthrowing those very ruling ideas and the ruling class that lies behind them.[24] Indeed, this was a major reason Gramsci adopted the term in the first place. Not only is the dominant hegemony unstable, but we need to study it closely to see how an alternative hegemony – an ideology or collection of ideologies that ties in with communist social and economic organisation – might make some headway. For this reason Gramsci was fascinated by the Roman Catholic Church and the Protestant Reformation.[25] For all its apparent siding with conservative and repressive forces, its dirty little deals with the fascists, Gramsci traces out the way the first truly global organisation has managed to persist for so long. The secret is that the Roman Catholic Church's primary concern is to look out for its own interests. If that involves deals with the Right, it also involves coming to terms with the Left. At times this self-concern may be purely earthly, such as the pope's efforts to resist the loss of papal lands, but at others it involves the preservation of the clergy from being absorbed into secular educational establishments, or indeed ensuring that the allegiance of the faithful is primarily to the church and that to any other organisation a distinct second.

If the Roman Catholic Church had an organisational lesson or two for the communists, then the Protestant Reformation gave a stunning example of how to shake and transform a society through and through. For Gramsci, the Reformation was the last time a thoroughgoing revolution had happened. He wished dearly that Italy, too, had undergone such a shift, rather than its half-starts and misdirected efforts that were restricted to the upper classes and intellectuals. He searched for an 'Italian Luther', suggesting it may well have been Machiavelli had he lived long enough. But how do you manage such a transformation? It is not merely a matter of the time being right, or even the good fortune of having a duke or two to protect your early agitators. Rather, it involves a complete

24. The theme weaves its way through, as Peter Thomas calls it, the 'riddle wrapped in a mystery inside an enigma' of *The Prison Notebooks* (Gramsci 1992; Gramsci 1996; Gramsci 2007). Also useful are the selections in Gramsci 1971 and Gramsci 1995, although the first, edited by Quintin Hoare and Geoffrey Nowell Smith, frustratingly does not provide what is now the standard system of reference for notebook and entry numbers. See also Fontana 1993 and Boothman 2008, who traces the sources for Gramsci's use of the term among circles around Lenin in the USSR, in Italian socialist and idealist uses (Croce) and in Machiavelli. For a comprehensive analysis and reassessment, see Thomas 2009.

25. For more detail, see Boer 2007a, pp. 215–74.

overhaul, an 'intellectual and moral reform'[26] that shifts the very roots of society and runs through all its nooks and crannies.

So far we have instability and revolution – both crucial dimensions of hegemony that apply just as well to theology. Althusser would provide some crucial refinements to Gramsci's arguments, the most usable of which is the point that ideology is a marker of struggle, especially class struggle. Now, Althusser was not always as clear as he might have been, precisely in those moments where he sought militant clarity. So, on ideology he fudges between ideology as falsehood and lies (when he makes the troubled distinction between ideology and science), that is, as false consciousness, and ideology as an inescapable element of the ideological state apparatuses. The latter is a far more fruitful and enduring development. On this score, the primary sites of struggle are his famous ideological state apparatuses – education, family, law, politics, trade unions, communications, culture, and religion – to be distinguished from the repressive state apparatuses of police, army and so on.[27] Ideological apparatuses are not merely the domains of ideas and beliefs, but also institutional forms which have their own patterns of social relations and economic structures. At each nodal point, battles are waged over different and usually opposed patterns of belief and practice, battles that have a distinct material register as well. For example, with the family we find struggles over what is accepted as the definition of 'family': is it hetero-sexual or homosexual? Is it nuclear or extended? Is the Oedipal conflict central? Is the family eternal or subject to the vagaries of history? Is it biological or social? Is the very idea of the 'family' problematic?

So also with religion: it too is a site of ideological struggle.[28] Religions are by no means monolithic, seamless structures, for they are riven with struggles,

---

26. Gramsci 1996, p. 244; Q4§75. The phrase 'intellectual and moral reform' is Gramsci's code for the Protestant Reformation, and one that he uses for the desired effects of a communist revolution. In this same entry he goes on to point out: 'Therefore historical mat.<erialism> will have or may have this function, which is not only totalitarian as a conception of the world but also in that it will permeate all of society down to its deepest roots'.

27. Althusser 1971, pp. 121–73; Althusser 1995, pp. 269–314.

28. I leave aside a discussion of the looseness of Althusser's terminology, in which religion is the system of the different churches (Althusser 1971, p. 143; Althusser 1995, p. 283). The specificity of his French, Roman Catholic situation shows through in such a definition, and it also reveals the specifically Christian nature of his definition of 'religion'. Such an overlap is in part due to the history of the term 'religion', which in its medieval European usage meant Christianity. However, when the evidence began pouring in during the colonial era of very different systems of belief, the term 'religion' began to shift in sense. In order to come to terms with and categorise all the new data, the first scholars (such as J.G. Frazer) made use of the template from Christianity – a religion concerns the interrelations of belief, practice and institutions. If the template fits – as Christianity did – then it must be a religion and it needs a name, such as Hinduism, or Buddhism, or animism and so on. It was a classic case of universalising from a specific

debates, disagreements and heretics. I do not mean the standard liberal position (and objection to the 'new old atheists') that we should let the field of religion bloom with many different flowers in a glorious, hand-holding act of tolerance, but that we need to apply a distinctly Marxist analysis to religions: they are conflictual zones in which vital struggles are fought. I think here not merely of the age-old differences between Orthodox, Roman Catholic and Protestant, or even of the many varieties of Protestantism, or indeed breakaway Catholic and Orthodox churches. What we see are struggles over gender, which manifest themselves in terms of the debates over the ordination of women, or over sexuality, with which many churches struggle today, or over the role of the various churches in colonial expansion and subjugation, or in the face of the increasing pressures on environmental systems from unlimited capitalist growth. We find such struggles also over the Bible: is it one element of the tradition (the Roman Catholic position), or is it the sole arbiter of truth? Is it inerrant or not? Is its message one of existential salvation or of political insurrection? Is it, in short, a multivalent document or does it speak with one voice? The older sign of such struggles was the category of heresy, for the very struggle for the definition of heresy was the struggle for power in the churches. Above all, a religion such as Christianity continues to manifest a deep struggle over reactionary and revolutionary tendencies. As I will argue in detail in Chapter Three, this political ambivalence is one of the constitutive features of Christianity, one that may be explained by the tension-ridden moment of its emergence.

The final contributor to theological suspicion is Ernst Bloch, whom I will discuss in detail in Chapters Two and Three.[29] The relevant piece of Bloch's vast project on utopia and hope comes from his insight into myth. His particular twist was to argue that all ideologies have a distinctly emancipatory and utopian element about them, even the most repressive. Just when it seems as though a particular ideology is at its most domineering and repressive, a utopian possibility opens up. So also with myth, argues Bloch. He is particularly interested in the myths of the ruling class, such as the story of the fall in Genesis 2–3, or the rebellion of Korah in Numbers 16, or indeed the murmuring of the sons of Israel against Moses and Aaron in the wilderness. For all their efforts to cast such rebellion as sin, as a challenge to the deity, and for all the dire punishments that might be meted out – expulsion from the garden, swallowing up by the earth or a collection of plagues, diseases and sheer divine destruction – these myths also preserve in their very structure the signals of subversion. In other words, the myths

situation. Religion thus came to perform a double service: it still meant Christianity, but it also designated the so-called 'world religions'.

29. See also Boer 2007a, pp. 26–36.

of control and suppression preserve and indeed encourage insurrection. We cannot have one without the other.

What is called for, then, is a discernment of myth. Such discernment is an effort to sort the wheat from the weeds, to find the moments of insurrection in the midst of reactionary oppression. All the same, it is easier than it appears to be. We cannot simply compile a list – progressive myths in the 'pro' column and reactionary ones in the 'con' column. The trap is, as I have just argued, that quite often myths of repression contain elements within them that are revolutionary, usually cast in terms of unsavoury rebellion, if not outright 'sin'. Further, not all revolutions are the same: a 'palace' revolution where one part of the ruling elite replaces another will hardly make any difference. And then revolutions have a knack of turning sour, for those who championed freedom turn with dismaying alacrity into oppressors themselves. The French Revolution became the Terror, the Bolshevik overthrow of the old order in Russia turned into Stalinist orthodoxy, and the freedom of the Jews after the genocide of the Second World War has become the systematic oppression of the Palestinian people. So what we seek are those moments of insurrection that come from the proverbial 'bottom up', from those who are themselves downtrodden and represented as the rabble, the mob, the uneducated and the poor.

One may wonder what all this discussion of Bloch's take on myth has to do with theology. It seems to me that while theology has its own distinct history, its various branches and emphases of careful thought, its creativity and passion for rigour, it also concerns myth. Indeed, the primary content of theology is inescapably mythical: the existence and nature of God; the concern with redemption and salvation; the narrative that moves from creation, through incarnation, death and resurrection, to the eschaton. For this reason, Bloch's concern with myth and its discernment is central to any rethink of theology.

In sum, I plunder and translate a number of key elements for a strategy of theological suspicion: the instability of dominant hegemonies and the insurrectionist drive of hegemony itself; the nature of theology as ideological struggle; and the need for discernment in the engagement with theology, in which patterns of subversion are inseparably tied up with those of oppression. In this respect, I do understand theology as a subset of ideology, and thereby theological suspicion as a subset of ideological suspicion. But theological suspicion also takes on a life of its own, as I hope to show in the rest of this study.

Synopsis

Two strategies, then, underlie my project, namely, the relativising of theology and theological suspicion, each of them the result of frank confrontation with historical materialism. But now, as is my custom, let me provide a synopsis of the chapters that follow, a map for those who wish to gain a sense of the whole and then locate whatever path they wish to follow through the book.

As I mentioned earlier, the book is structured in two sections. The first section covers Chapters One to Four, beginning with a scene-setting discussion of atheism and Marxism. From there I develop an argument that leads me to the matter of economic history. The history is an effort to account for two distinctive features of Christianity, namely that it has produced one significant political myth in the form of Christian communism (Chapter Two) and that it is characterised by a profound tension between reaction and revolution (Chapter Three). In order to make some sense of these two issues, I explore the economic situation in which Christianity first arose (Chapter Four). The second section of the book focuses its energy on a number of select forays, specific proposals to advance the discussion of Marxism and theology. To be sure, the first section also offers a number of proposals – the need for Marxism to rethink the issue of myth and the political ambivalence of Christianity, the importance of atheism for theology, particularly protest atheism, as well as the economic reconstruction itself – but its primary concern is analysis and explanation, especially in terms of economic history. By contrast, the second section, which runs through from Chapters Four to Seven, offers a select number of explorations on key topics: kairós, ethics and fetishism. In each case, I make a sustained argument for the importance of these categories, modes of undermining their dominant perceptions (especially with kairós and ethics) and then ways to sharpen them for use in a Marxist toolbox that is serious about religion.

In some more detail: the first chapter broaches the perennial and topical question of atheism and theism. It begins by asking why some of the leading thinkers in the Marxist tradition have been and continue to be interested in theology and why atheists cannot also engage with theology. In its first half, the chapter offers both a survey and critique of the dominant approaches to atheism and theology: the 'new old atheists' (Richard Dawkins, Christopher Hitchens and company) are found wanting for their crass materialism and unreconstructed idealism in which religion is the cause of all our ills; the 'death of God' theologians (Thomas J.J. Altizer and Mark C. Taylor) have a little too much confidence in the death of God as an objective fact and are tied up with apocalyptic visions; the furious attack by practitioners of 'studies of religion' on theologians, charging them with a distinct lack of objectivity and reason and seeking to ban them from reputable tertiary institutions, offers a minimal, cornered view of theology that is far from its actual practice. None of these positions on atheism and/in theology do I find persuasive, but this does lead me to develop my own position in some detail in the second half of the chapter. Assuming the definition of theology outlined earlier in this

Introduction, I take up Marx's point that atheism is the last stage of theism, pursuing his Aufhebung of religion, in which it is both annulled and raised to another level entirely. From here we move through Marx's initial enthusiasm for Feuerbach's argument that religion is a projection and then on to track Marx's leap beyond Feuerbach, which turns out to be not merely the argument that religion is a symptom of social and economic alienation, but also that Aufhebung refers to both religious and economic alienation. In one sense, the rest of the book is an exploration of what this transformation actually means. The remainder of the chapter deals with some early moments in that exploration, digging out a tradition of freedom of conscience within Marxism in regard to religion, distinguishing anti-clericalism from atheism and then arguing for a central role for protest atheism within any self-respecting theology.

The second chapter sinks into the question of myth, which is, or at least should be, a vital matter for the Left. The chapter marks a significant step beyond an earlier argument of mine,[30] developing Ernst Bloch's approach to myth. It begins by covering some traditional ground in the analysis of myth, namely the distinction between theogonic, cosmogonic and anthropogonic myths, but only to introduce a fourth category, political myth or 'poligony'. Immediately, I engage in the first of a number of etymological analyses, not so much to rest upon the knowledge of the ancient Greeks but to subvert from within the classicist assumptions of such moves. Here we find that the reign of logos (as reasoned speech) over mythos (as fabulous and fictional) is by no means certain. The reason: mythos turns out to refer to muscular, forthright, arrogant and heroic speech, while logos is the sly and subversive word of the weak. In the struggle over meaning and dominance, we witness an intermingling of senses, so much so that myth too becomes the alternative mode of subversion, just as much as it can be the story of the powerful. From there I note Adorno's wariness concerning myth, particularly in light of the Aryan myths of the Nazis, but pick up Bloch's crucial insight that we need to discern myths, to find the insurrectionary moment in the midst of suppression. But myth – or some elements of myth – is also utopian for Bloch. So I set out to strengthen this anticipatory feature, drawing together a motley collection of arguments: the irrefutable motivation of Georges Sorel; the early (and theological) Althusser's suggestion that myth is a totality which has not yet achieved its concept; the close connection between Althusser's argument and the ontological argument – as that than which nothing greater can be conceived – not so much for God as for utopia; Alain Badiou's suggestion – in the very different but overlapping realm of truth – concerning the forcing of a truth; Deleuze and Guattari's deployment of reverse causality; and then a retooled version of

30. Boer 2009d.

the analogical argument, in which the anticipated actually provides the terms for our own analysis. The chapter closes with three examples of political myth, two unintentionally so and one quite intentional: Roland Barthes's denotative myth of a signless world, Fredric Jameson's oblique engagement with apocalyptic and then the political myth of Christian communism, especially in the hands of Marxist authors such as Engels, Luxemburg and Kautsky.

Political ambivalence is the topic of the third chapter, which opens by offering three extended examples of the oppressive history of Christianity – the extraordinary rise and fall of papal power over the half millennium from 1000 to 1500 CE, the designation and treatment of heretics, and then the history of California missions. Before the 'black book' critics of Christianity can rush in, I counter with three instances of revolutionary Christian movements and figures, namely Wilhelm Weitling (the first German communist, according to Engels), Thomas J. Hagerty, a priest and founding figure of the Industrial Workers of the World, or the 'Wobblies', and biblical scholar Norman Gottwald. Not the usual examples, like Thomas Müntzer and the peasant revolution, Gerrard Winstanley and the Diggers, or liberation theologians-cum-revolutionaries such as Camillo Torres Restrepo. But since I have dealt with them elsewhere,[31] I dig out some of the lesser known and, to my mind, more interesting examples. The purpose of this first half of the chapter is obvious, for I seek to show that Christianity has significant revolutionary potential alongside its well-documented repressive side. The second half of the chapter focuses on Marxists who have shown some awareness of this ambivalence, all for the purpose of providing a more comprehensive picture of political ambivalence from within Marxist thought. Some are less conscious of such ambivalence than others, so I designate the first group 'the unwitting' – Luxemburg, Kautsky (in one incarnation), E.P. Thompson, Althusser, Eagleton, G.E.M. de Ste. Croix and Horkheimer – and the second 'the witting' – Marx and especially Engels, Horkheimer again (in rarer moments), Michael Löwy, Kautsky (in another incarnation) and above all Bloch. By the end of this exhaustive engagement, it seems to me incontrovertible both that Christianity is deeply ambivalent politically and that a reasonable number of Marxists have provided us with the basis for accounting for that ambivalence, if not multivalence.

By the fourth chapter an urgent question arises: why did Christianity both develop the political myth of Christian communism and bequeath to us a deep political ambivalence? In this chapter, I set out to answer that question through an exercise in economic history. Much of the attention focuses on the key theologian of earliest Christianity, the Apostle Paul, but not before I have explored a

31. Boer 2007b.

largely ignored but crucial section of Marx and Engels's writings – the long and detailed critique of Max Stirner in *The German Ideology*. In what is really the engine room of historical materialism, I am interested less in the specific categories that result than in the process by which they are generated, for Marx and Engels gradually develop the first rough outline of historical materialism through their engagement with Stirner. Using this model of working, I then engage with the Apostle Paul, focusing on the many oppositions and tensions in his thought. By widening the analysis in order to include economic and social matters, I argue that these literary and thereby intellectual contradictions are valiant efforts to deal with brutal tensions generated by the transition from an older mode of production to that brought by the Romans. However, since Paul's resolution is incomplete, since he does not offer a clear narrative of transition, he leaves room for both reactionary and radical possibilities in the very workings of Christianity. Paradoxically, this is the reason for Paul's success, for he laid the groundwork for both the enthusiastic embracing of empire under Constantine and the perpetual resistance to such accommodation. The chapter closes by comparing the success of Paul's ambivalent resolution with the fate of Christian communism.

Chapter Five begins the first of three deep forays, seeking to take the interaction of Marxism and theology a little further. In this chapter I focus on kairós, which is usually understood as the opportune time and the time of crisis – with a heavy debt to the New Testament. I begin by gathering some Marxist approaches that may be described as kairological, namely those of Benjamin, Agamben, Badiou, Žižek, Bloch, Jameson and Negri. The proposals vary – as blast, flash, time that remains, event, laicised grace, *novum* and *ultimum*, miracle, fulfilment, apocalypse, rupture, the creative tip of the arrow of time, the immeasurability of production – but they are all variations on kairós. However, since this sense of kairós owes much to New Testament eschatology, I move on to provide my most complete statement to date on the differences between eschatology, messianism and apocalyptic, before questioning the assumed meaning of kairós. It turns out that the term refers not merely to time, but also to place, and that the basis of its semantic cluster concerns measure and appropriateness. In short, it means what is timely and in the right place, which I then open out to moral, social and economic associations. Kairós, it seems, is more at home with the status quo and what is opportune and appropriate to the ruling class, so I seek out ákairos, what is untimely and out of place. After connecting this analysis with Negri's discussion of measure and immeasure, terms which overlap directly with kairós and ákairos (although Negri is apparently unaware of the connection), I close by arguing for an akairological position.

The next topic, in Chapter Six, is ethics, which I define as the effort to grease social relations so that they run more smoothly. The chapter is an effort to provide some systematic reflection on my persistent suspicion concerning ethics. After a brief but necessary discussion of the tensions inherent in any ethical reflection – between universal precepts and empirical particularity, between the inevitable moralising (that comes from an effort to link the universal and the particular) and the attempt to escape moralising through a retreat to pure reflection – I critique two prominent forms of ethics today, care of the self and concern for the other. Under these topics, I analyse some select but prominent proposals for ethics on the Left (broadly understood), especially those of Michel Foucault, Judith Butler, Terry Eagleton, Alain Badiou and Slavoj Žižek. The first three I find wanting, while the other two head in the right direction, which is to question the focus on the 'other'. I take this criticism further, asking whether the 'other' is a given category to which ethics responds or whether it is produced by discourses such as ethics. This production of the 'other' by ethics becomes even more problematic as its close association with the biblical notion of the chosen people becomes apparent, let alone the inescapable theological underlay of the opposition between good and evil (a distinction theology is singularly unable to maintain). I close with a similar move to the one in the chapter on kairós, digging out the subversive undercurrent of *ethika* through some etymological spadework. Here we find that ethics and morals are derived from the Greek and Latin words for custom and habit, *ethos* and *mos* (*mores* in the plural). Given that the customs and habits in question are those already in place (by definition!) and that ethics concerns training in such customs (as Aristotle makes perfectly clear), I seek a way to undermine what is assumed, namely the habits and customs of the status quo, especially since they are those of the ruling classes (once again, Aristotle is explicit on this matter). So I come out with what is *aēthēs* and *praeter morem*, unethical and unmoral. Not so much a refusal of ethics, this option seeks to undermine ethics from within. Of course, these terms join forces with ákairos.

The final chapter broaches the dual question of fetishism and idolatry, the ground of one of the most fruitful intersections between Marxism and theology. However, in order to avoid a facetious elision of idolatry and fetishism (as is too readily done in theological discussions), I undertake a careful analysis of Marx's appropriation, reshaping and thorough transformation of the category of fetishism. In order to do so, I distinguish between the idol link and the fetish transfer. The first operates in terms of a signifying link between a tangible item – statue, person, natural feature or what have you – and the god in whom one believes. The object points to the god, operating in terms of a signifying link. The critique of idolatry severs this link, arguing that the god does not exist and that therefore the worshipper bows down before a mere idol. In contrast to this 'vertical' relation, the fetish transfer focuses on 'horizontal' relations: in the relation between worker and commodity, the commodity saps the energy of the worker who makes it, waxing while he or she wanes. The shift from idol link to fetish transfer is a complex one in Marx's thought, so I trace the way he draws the idea of fetishism from the study of religions, especially the work of Charles de Brosses, where idolatry had already been subsumed as a subset of fetishism; show how we tantalisingly miss out on Marx's full elaboration of fetishism in relation to religion due to the loss of his *A Treatise on Christian Art*; explore the way the critique of idolatry operates undercover in Marx's work while it also undergoes a significant transformation; then trace the reworking of the idea of fetishism, through the alienation of labour, the mediation of money, commodities and then every feature of capitalism, until capital as a whole becomes a fetish. In the process, Marx brings about a shift from the idol link to the fetish transfer, from the signifying link characteristic of idolatry to the transferring relation of the fetish, although he does so by appropriating the logic of the critique of idolatry: in the same way that one seeks to sever the signifying link between idol and god, so also does the critique of fetishism attempt to break the fetish transfer. The outcome is what may be called political iconoclasm. From there I pass on to analyse liberation theology, which falls short since it assumes that fetishism in Marx's hands is a mere extension of idolatry and so may be reappropriated within the critique of idolatry. By contrast, Adorno takes Marx a step further, explicitly making use of a central feature of the critique of idolatry – the ban on images or *Bilderverbot* – and deploying it directly in relation to the fetish transfer. In other words, he makes explicit what was implicit in Marx's thought, thereby developing a more consistent and rigorous political iconoclasm.

Apart from wrapping up the book, with a retrospective look at the overlapping aims of *The Criticism of Heaven and Earth* series as a whole, the conclusion makes three final proposals. To begin with, I reprise an argument that secularism may be defined – based on *saeculum* and *saecularis* in another etymological undermining – as an approach that takes its terms, modes of analysis and way of life from this age and this world, without reference to a world above or one beyond. Since both Marxism and (some elements of) theology remain profoundly dissatisfied with this world and age, seeking a thorough transformation or revolution that dispenses with this world, the upshot is that both of them are secular and anti-secular approaches. Further, I argue in favour of transcendence, albeit not a transcendence of power, authority and suppression, but one that discovers a transgressive sense of transcendence. The basic sense of *transcendo* is to climb or pass over and thereby to transgress, meanings that overlap with *transgresso*, which has not had such an illustrious theological career. In light of these connections, transcendence becomes a mode of climbing the fence or transgressing between this secular world, and another, anti-secular one.

After drawing out the connections with the akairological, unethical, unmoral and a-theistic options I took earlier, I close, appropriately, with death. Unpopular among some of the most important thinkers on the Left today (Badiou, Negri and Jameson), I return to the significant engagements with death in the work of Horkheimer, Adorno and Bloch. Here we discover not only Bloch's arguments against dogmatic theological and materialist positions regarding death, but also an openness to the idea of death as journey, the destination of which remains unclear. He also distinguishes between the physical process of dying and the ontological status of death, the latter of which produces sheer horror. Above all, I am impressed with Adorno's argument that the consideration of utopia is not worthy of the name if it does not deal with the elimination of death, for the attachment to and identification with death is the clearest marker of what is. So, utopia must involve both the elimination of death and removing resistance to the idea of the elimination of death, by which of course I mean not the physical process of dying, but of annihilating terror of death.

I close these introductory observations with three comments, one concerning what this book is not, another the occasional use of classical – Greek and Latin – etymology and a third dealing with the changing contexts for this study. To begin with, anyone who has even passing familiarity with the earlier volumes in this series will know that my primary concern is the work of key Marxists and their engagements with theology. The same applies here, for I draw upon, critique and creatively rework the most fruitful elements of the thought of a range of Marxists, from Marx himself to Negri in our own time. In other words, this study is not a direct analysis of theologians who have encountered Marxism. I do draw on a considerable number of them, whether biblical scholars, liberation theologians or New Testament critics, particularly those interested in the epistolary scribblings of Paul, but you will not find a systematic treatment of theologians per se. One reason for not giving theologians a full-frontal treatment is that I am an enthusiastic proponent of looking awry, in this case of looking at Marxism for theological insights, especially since Marxists such as Adorno and Bloch and Negri have a unique and subtle contribution or two to make to theological reworkings. Another reason is simpler: the task of embracing theologians directly is one that requires, should I have the energy, another study.

Further, on a number of occasions, I resort to etymological explorations of some key terms, especially *mythos*, kairós, *ethos* and *mos* (*mores*), *saecularum* and *transcendo*. My argument does so not because it buys into the classicist assumption – ancient Greece and Rome lie at the bedrock of 'Western' thought and practice – that bedevils so much of what one reads with rarely a question raised about its problematic function. Again and again, one encounters a variation on the same move: a treatment of political thought must begin with ancient Greece, or a philosophical discussion must begin with Plato or Aristotle or perhaps the Presocratics, or the treatment of law cannot begin without consideration of the Roman jurors, or any discussion of ethics must begin at least with Aristotle, if not further back. And those on the Left are just as guilty of such moves as others.[32] I have encountered only occasional criticisms of this classicist move, one from Adorno, who stresses the abyss that separates Kant's idea of moral philosophy from that of the Greeks: for Kant one produced these ideas purely on the basis of a rational process, whereas for the Greeks one reflected on pre-given material.[33] Negri is more forthright:

> The history of philosophy... has the tendency to manipulate repeatedly the same conceptual heritage and to present it to us in a synchronic package. In this sense, Plato is just as modern as Hegel. In each and every epoch, you will always find the Aristotelian philosopher arguing with the Platonic philosopher about the question of ideal forms, and so on and so forth. Such is philosophy's extraordinary sleight of hand: the history of philosophy produces, reproduces, posits, and presents itself as eternal – and it is able to do so because its foundational categories, from the transcendent to the transcendental, are incredibly useful for the continued existence and exercise of sovereign Power.[34]

For both Adorno and Negri, the repetitive invocation – both venerable and polemical – of the ancient Greeks and Romans foreshortens the massive amount of historical time between then and now, giving the impression through an 'enormously mystificatory sleight of hand' that Plato, Aristotle and the others are our contemporaries without realising the vast differences between those worlds and ours. I would add a few points. These moves buy into the myth of origins, a myth with which I am thoroughly familiar from biblical studies, let alone my original disciplinary work in classics.[35] Further, one need only look at a map or travel to that part of Europe to become aware of a simple fact: Greece belongs to the ancient Balkan region in Eastern Europe, not Western Europe, and the Greek world that continued into the Byzantine era (as Ste. Croix would have it) was very much an Eastern phenomenon. The claim that it is the source of Western thought is as brazen an act of colonialism as one will find. So the constant repetition of the classicist move may be seen as an obsessive compulsive disorder that conceals the fact that the path from ancient Greece to Western culture is one full of ruptures, discontinuities and long detours.

---

32. For example, Badiou 2006a; Badiou 1988; Badiou 2009; Badiou 2006b; Wood 2008. On ethics, see MacIntyre 1998.
33. Adorno 2000c, pp. 114–15.
34. Negri and Casarino 2008, p. 189.
35. An assumption that lies behind Bernal's flawed effort to undermine Greek dominance in *Black Athena*: Bernal 1987–2006.

In light of my suspicions concerning such classicism, what is the status of my etymological forays? Rather than simply refusing to engage in this process, I prefer to exploit the cracks in the edifice, teasing out other senses of the words in question which undermine – at least in part – their received meanings. I do so in full awareness that the classicist assumption needs to be questioned, that there are too many unexplored corners in the received meanings of terms appropriated from Greek and Latin. An exploration of the semantic cluster surrounding the terms in question brings out with surprising frequency meanings that reveal the class, moral and economic assumptions behind some of the key terms from ancient Greece and Rome. So I seek out alternative senses (as with *mythos*, *saecularum* and *transcendo*) or challenge those terms where they give voice to ruling-class assumptions by means of their opposites (with kairós, *ethos* and *mos*).

Finally, the question of context: I began this project in a serious way a long decade ago. At that time, it was based on two very personal passions, Marxism and biblical studies (which came to include theology). It had been some time since extensive interest had been shown in the question of Marxism and religion, the accessible study by McLellan being the last engagement of any length and the Marxist-Christian dialogue of the 1970s a distant memory.[36] So I began work in a small and dusty corner. To be sure, Hent de Vries had at about the same time produced his study, *Philosophy and the Turn to Religion*, thereby providing a slogan – the 'turn to religion' – that has been invoked regularly since. But his analysis was more smitten with poststructuralist thought, especially Derrida, than Marxism, and he does not situate such a return within the necessary geopolitical context of today. However, since that time the question of religion has returned to the geopolitical stage, the sign (rather than the cause) of that return being the attacks on the World Trade Center, or 9/11 as it has been branded. The 'new old atheists', as I call them in Chapter One, have responded to that return with popular and often strident attacks on religion as the cause of all our ills, bringing to mind eighteenth and especially nineteenth-century attacks against the superstition and irrationalism of religion. Other signs of this return include the curious recovery of Christian identities by some countries (especially European ones) that have been deeply secular for some time, alongside claims that we are returning to age-old ideological conflicts between Christianity and Islam. However, for my purposes the most important factor has been the rise and persistent strength of the anti-globalisation movement, theorised best, although not without significant debate, by Antonio Negri and Michael Hardt.[37] On the more modest level of this project, I have found that an increasing number of those

36. McLellan 1987.
37. Hardt and Negri 2000; Hardt and Negri 2004; Hardt and Negri 2009.

involved in the anti-globalisation movement have sought to think through their activism from the perspectives of both Marxism and religion, not least because a good number of them come from a religious background. Others, steeped in traditions of the Left, both intellectual and activist, have confessed a complete ignorance of the long engagement with theology by Marxists. In other words, by the happenstance of historical events and changing economic circumstances, my personal passions intersected with the interests of others. Thankfully, it is less rare to find studies on 'Marxism and religion' appearing here and there, among which this book and the project as a whole may find a place.[38]

This study, however, does not seek a diagnosis and prognosis of our current ills, a snapshot of our zeitgeist; instead it offers an analysis of the key features that come out of the tradition of engagements between Marxism and theology. Indeed, if we look back to, say, the work of Locke and Hobbes as they drew heavily from biblical resources to deal with an era of profound transition, or the turmoil in Germany in the 1830s and 1840s when Marx and Engels first honed their skills, or the jurist Carl Schmitt (whose work is a feature of current discussions, especially in the writings of Jacob Taubes and Giorgio Agamben) who drew upon the categories of the exception and the miracle in order to shape a controversial political and judicial theory in the troubles of the 1920s and 1930s, or the work of Ernst Bloch during the same period, who debated with theologians such as Rudolf Bultmann and later Jürgen Moltmann over utopia and eschatology, we notice that at times of political, economic and social turmoil, the Bible and theology become favoured zones for debate. I would hazard the suggestion that it is not so much the case that theology reappears at times of turmoil and change, but that its return is a sure signal of such turmoil, the questions driven by the political concerns of the moment. For these reasons, it is important to provide some historical depth and thereby a greater sense of the long interaction between Marxism and theology, perhaps reshaping that tradition in the process. In this way, I hope that this study may make some contribution to the renewed debate.

38. For example, see Molyneux 2008; Roberts 2005; Roberts 2008a; Roberts 2008b; Toscano 2004; Toscano 2009.

Chapter One
Atheism

> It [socialism]... is no longer mediated through the abolition [*Aufhebung*] of religion.[1]

I have always been mightily puzzled by two questions in relation to theology. First, why is it that theology assumes belief in a god or gods? Although this is a widespread assumption held by believers and unbelievers, by acolytes and sceptics alike, it actually seems obvious to me that both atheists and theists should engage with and write theology. Second, why do a good number of Marxists – philosophers, historians, literary critics and sociologists – engage with theology? The easy answer is that they do so as philosophers, historians, literary critics and sociologists, drawing upon theology for reasons of their own. Yet my suspicion is that there is far more going on, for all too often they make distinct contributions to theology. In earlier volumes in this series – *The Criticism of Heaven and Earth* – I have explored these contributions in what is really a tradition of Marxist theological reflection. But I remain intrigued by why they engage with theology so consistently, what is going on when they do and what the implications are for both Marxism and theology.

This chapter is a systematic effort to traverse both – obviously related – questions, although that traversal will also unfold throughout this book as a whole. As far as this chapter is concerned, it falls into two main sections. The first explores four possible approaches to

1. Marx 1844g, p. 306; Marx 1844h, p. 546; translation modified.

theology, although with a unique twist: I do not follow the usual paths of trawling through recognised theologians, whether well-known or less so, for I approach the whole question by looking awry, drawing out the positions of those who at first seem to be outside theology. Why? I wish to stay focused on the question of atheism and theology. So, the first three positions come from the misguided effort by the so-called 'new atheists' to attribute all that is evil in the world to religion (a reverse type of theodicy), from the ongoing 'death of God' or a-theological project, and then from a furious disciplinary debate between scholars of religion and of theology. In each case we come across efforts to characterise theology from an atheistic position, some negatively and others with a more sympathetic touch. As I was working through these positions, they began to fall naturally into a semiotic square, taking up various positions in relation to the acceptance or rejection of theology. But that square – the distinct advantage of which (apart from being able to pull out a few sheets of paper and a pencil in order to doodle – à la Engels) is to offer a spatial and ideological analysis that overcomes the inevitable narrative sequence of argument – begs a fourth position, which turns out to be my own.

That fourth possibility opens the gate to the second half of the chapter, which introduces some of the key features of what happens when you begin to rub Marxism and theology up against one another. Or, to shift metaphors, I take theology on a somewhat wild dialectical ride through historical materialism in order to see what happens on the other side. On that ride we meet Marx's Aufhebung of religion, the breakthrough in relation to Feuerbach's argument that religion is a human projection, the question of a radical freedom of conscience in relation to religion, anti-clericalism and then protest atheism. That final point concerning protest theology leads me to conclude that the distinction between atheism and theism is a proverbial red herring, for it places the dividing line at the wrong point. The issue instead is whether both theism and atheism offer compliance with oppression or protest against it, are prepared to jump into bed with oily tyrants and CEOs or to tell them to bugger off. Initial items, if you will, of an engagement between Marxism and theology, laying out the groundwork for the remainder of the book.

Banishing the gods?

I begin with a particular example, not remarkable in itself, for this man's experience is one that has been repeated again and again since the introduction of critical study of the Bible. Bruno Bauer, Marx's one-time teacher, friend and collaborator, felt his faith slipping away the more he studied the Bible. Nietzsche too found that the study of theology was a sure path to atheism. And many a student of the Bible and theology has come across the same stumbling block. My example concerns a certain Gerd Lüdemann, until 2009 a professor of the New Testament in the theology faculty at the University of Göttingen. In February 2009, Lüdemann wrote a terse email message to many colleagues and friends, telling them that the German Supreme Court had decided to reject his appeal against the decision by the university to ban him from teaching. This was his last court of appeal and the decision saw the blogosphere running hot over issues such as academic freedom and church control over theology. But why was Lüdemann, a respected New Testament scholar and tenured professor in his early sixties, prevented from teaching students? The reason was that he had come to the conclusion that the claims of Christianity are a fabrication and have no basis in fact. Nothing new in that, but the catch is that Lüdemann was teaching students training for ministry in the Evangelical Church. Fearful that the frail faith of their students might suffer at the hands of such a scholar, the church leant on the university, and Lüdemann was axed. And this from a university that was established on Enlightenment principles, has prided itself on free inquiry unhindered by external constraints and has boasted some of Germany's leading theologians such as Albrecht Ritschl (at least when German theologians led the world).

Apart from issues of academic freedom, of which I am sceptical, or indeed tenure, which seems to have the reverse effect and squashes originality,[2] what emerges from the Lüdemann case is a crucial question. Can one be a student of sacred scriptures and be an atheist? Indeed, can one be a theologian (as distinct from a biblical critic) and an atheist at the same time? In other words, does theology require one to be a believer first, so that, in the words of Anselm, theology may defined as *fides quaerens intellectum*, a reasoned and systematic explanation of one's faith? Yes, yes and no are my answers to these questions, but before I lay out my reasons on the table before us, I need to position my approach in the context of three competing approaches to theology. I am thinking not of the believing theologians (of which there are too many) or of dismissive secular critics who are happy to leave theology to the fusty old cranks in churches and theological faculties, but of three groups: the 'new atheists', or 'new old atheists' as I prefer to call them, who see religion as inherently evil and for whom no haste in the banishment of religion is unseemly; the proponents of studies in religion, who regard theology as the Siamese twin of theism and therefore argue it should have no place in any reputable intellectual endeavour; and the 'death of God'

2. I am tempted to see the relation between originality and tenure as an inverse ratio: the higher the emphasis on the value of tenure, the less originality and innovation there is. The Germanic and American systems are cases in point. Scholars pursuing tenure spend so much time and energy watching their backs – will this help or hinder my tenure prospects? – that by the time they do get tenure, the last trace of originality or possibility of interesting work has well and truly been beaten out of them.

theologians who seek to undertake 'atheology'. I come closest to the last group, although the definition of theology I put forward differs markedly from theirs. A triangulation, if you will, between 'new old atheists', atheologians and scholars of religion which will lead me to identify my own position.

'New old atheists'

For these neo-atheists theology is a matter of belief, but both belief and theology, and indeed any religion as such, cannot be thrown out soon enough. The neo-atheists have been at the forefront of a very public and polemical recovery in the West of arguments against religion. They comprise a loose group of quite different thinkers who have all of late attacked religion as a fiction that is detrimental for us all – more simply, religion is bad for you and me. Richard Dawkins's *The God Delusion*, Christopher Hitchens's *Letters to a Young Contrarian* and *God Is Not Great*, Daniel Dennett's *Breaking the Spell*, Sam Harris's *The End of Faith* and *Letter to a Christian Nation*, as well as a run of lesser lights, have all presented variations on the same basic line.[3] Having provided the diagnosis of our social ills, their prognosis is simple: dump religion as quickly as possible. As a result of their works, the small bands of what until now were frail, grey and dispirited secularist, humanist, atheist and whatnot societies have been given adrenalin injections and are organising conferences, political campaigns and actually welcoming new members under sixty years of age.

While they might all agree on the basic point that religion is in many ways bad for human society, the way they go about the task varies. Dawkins, the award-winning evolutionary biologist, proudly wears the label 'atheist' and calls on like-minded people to be out and proud (the gay pride allusions are quite deliberate). For Harris, the public intellectual, atheism really means the destruction of bad ideas, of which religion tops the list. For the late, privately-schooled Hitchens, who was once a Marxist and for whom Johnny Walker was the 'breakfast of champions', atheism is too mild a term, so he prefers 'anti-theist' to describe his militant efforts to debunk religions, especially the 'Abrahamic' ones. But they all share three basic assumptions: the primary role of Enlightenment reason, progress and a reverse theodicy. Let me say a little more on each. Evidence, experience, science, independent and free minds – these catchwords appear again and again in their works. And before them religion simply does not stack up. Given a stark choice between religion and science, there is not even a contest. Religion misrepresents the origins of humanity and the cosmos, it suppresses human nature, is inimical to free inquiry, and above all postulates the existence of a being

3. Dawkins 2006; Hitchens 2001, 2007; Dennett 2007; Harris 2005, 2006.

for which there is simply no proof; which, in fact, the evidence suggests does not exist.

A number of objections may be marshalled against these arguments, although a whole new sub-genre, from both expected (church) and unexpected (Marxist) quarters, has sprouted seeking to refute their arguments.[4] I will run through the objections as I see them, but the more interesting question is why these arguments are being made now and in the West. I do not include the objection – entirely predictable and expected from those within churches, synagogues and (less so) mosques – that these neo-atheists have simply misunderstood the rich complexity of theology, or that they have failed to discern its liberating possibilities alongside its tendency to alienation and oppression. This objection holds some truth, especially since the neo-atheists take the fundamentalist version of religions – most notably Islam, Christianity and Judaism – as the central and defining characteristic of the religion in question. Indeed, in an effort to forestall objections from moderates, they argue that moderates act as pernicious covers for the extremists. While this approach has been a standard line from defenders of faith, particularly in the Christian churches, it also characterises the response of Mark C. Taylor[5] and even Terry Eagleton as he increasingly recovers his role as a somewhat amateur theologian of the Catholic Left and defender of the faith.[6]

To begin, the arguments against religion are not new. The 'new atheists' should really be called the 'new old atheists', for there is nothing novel in their arguments, which go back at least to the Enlightenment *philosophes* in France (Voltaire et al.), as well as the radical theologians – although a-theologians may be a better description – like Ludwig Feuerbach, David Strauss, Max Stirner and Bruno Bauer in early nineteenth-century Germany.[7] It could be argued that the situation we have now, in which religion has once again become a vital factor of public life, is analogous to those earlier situations in the eighteenth and nineteenth centuries. And as with those earlier situations, it seems to some that the most radical line is to attack religion itself.

Further, they are guilty of naïve materialism, arguing that the scientific evidence weighs so heavily against God that he cannot possibly exist. Dawkins (and Dennett following him) makes use of an earlier idea, first elaborated in

---

4. As samples of the former, see Haught 2007 and Hedges 2009; of the latter see Molyneux 2008. For a religious assessment that seeks to take seriously some of the criticisms, see Peterson 2007.

5. M. Taylor 2007.

6. Eagleton 2006, 2009a; Eagleton and Schneider 2009. As for his theological *re*-turn, compare Eagleton 2001, 2003a, 2003b, 2003c, 2007 with Eagleton 1966a, 1966b, 1967a, 1967b, 1968a, 1968b, 1968c, 1969, 1970. For a detailed study of Eagleton, see Boer 2007a, pp. 275–333.

7. Feuerbach 1989; Feuerbach 1924; Strauss 1902; Strauss 1835; Stirner 2005; Stirner 1845; Bauer 1838; Bauer 1840; Bauer 1841; Bauer 1842b; Bauer 1843; Bauer 2002.

The Selfish Gene, called the 'meme', the cultural equivalent of the gene. In what is really a sophisticated version of sociobiologism, the meme seeks to explain in Darwinian terms how ideas and cultural phenomena are maintained and spread from generation to generation. More specifically, a meme is a replicating cultural entity, passed on by human beings, who have become quite efficient at preserving, copying and passing on behaviour and beliefs. Now, these memes change over time, being combined, refined, transformed, and at times producing new memes. But the result is a theory of cultural evolution comparable to biological evolution based on genes. Little imagination is required to see how such a theory applies to religion, which becomes a cultural meme, passed on from one generation to the next, modified and reshaped, but remarkably persistent. This religious meme is perhaps slightly more sophisticated than the so-called 'God gene' proposed by the geneticist Dean Hamer, who argues that some of us are genetically and psychological predisposed to religious belief and others not.[8] But the difference is one of degree, for the arguments are strikingly similar. Scientific certainty is one thing, however; what can stand up in a court of law is another. In the famous London bus-poster saga of 2008, Dawkins and others who had organised the campaign had to agree to change the poster from 'There is no God' to 'There's probably no God. Now stop worrying and enjoy your life' – just in case those dreadful Christians might object to false advertising and take them to court.

But this naïve materialism carries within it a pernicious assumption of evolutionary superiority, especially by the likes of Dawkins. As scientific atheists, they are already at the next evolutionary stage, one that has passed beyond this dreadful meme. In short, one assumes a rosy picture of human progress in which science and reason are gradually leading us all to a higher and better stage. Religion becomes a barbaric meme, an impediment to an enlightened approach to the world. The occasional slips, such as world wars, concentration camps, genocide, global capitalism, widespread economic exploitation, environmental degradation and collapse, chronic poverty and disease, are merely temporary setbacks, slight pauses in the rosy march of progress. Nothing quite like such blinkered optimism has been seen since perhaps the nineteenth century.

Further, the 'new old atheists' ultimately hold to an unreconstructed idealist position that is really a reverse theodicy. They argue that religion, as a collection of ideas, is the cause of all that is bad in the world – wars, suffering, intolerance, racism, sexism, homophobia and what have you. If traditional theodicy sought to reconcile God's power and love with the existence of evil, this new theodicy argues that evil militates not merely against God's power and love, but against

8. Hamer 2005.

God as such. The catch is that they believe as much in the power of religion as its strongest proponents, arguing that religion has a power within itself to do the greatest harm. They are dazzled, as Engels put it with his characteristic clarity, with the power of ideas: 'It is above all this appearance of an independent history of state constitutions, of systems of law, of ideological conceptions in every separate domain, which dazzles most people. If Luther and Calvin "overcome" the official Catholic religion, or Hegel "overcomes" Fichte and Kant, or if the constitutional Montesquieu is indirectly "overcome" by Rousseau with his "Social Contract", each of these events remains within the sphere of theology, philosophy or political science, represents a stage in the history of these particular spheres of thought and never passes outside the sphere of thought'.[9] But it should be unnecessary in this day and age to make the simple point that ideas do not do anything on their own; they make nothing, produce nothing, and cause nothing. People do. People use ideas to justify action, to frame attitudes, and even to develop an overarching framework to make sense of life, but ideas do not act on their own. In case I should seem excessively individualistic, I would stress even more that such idealism misses entirely the crucial role of social and economic factors in any event, however great or small. To say that religion is the cause of all that is wrong with the world, is the cause of oppression, war, suffering and hardship, simply misses the vital role of an economics based on exploitation and the drive for profit.

Let me give one example: the current struggle between a supposedly Christian West and Muslim East.[10] Is this struggle due to irreconcilable differences between two religions, which are actually quite close to one another? Of course not, for the current form of Muslim opposition arises from a long history of capitalist imperialism.[11] Although I should add a caveat, for even though Muslim culture and religion offers an alternative paradigm to the liberal ideology that goes hand-in-hand with capitalism, Muslim-majority countries are thoroughly immersed – indeed they are aggressive players – within global capitalist economics. What we really have is competition within a capitalist framework – all of which makes sense of the apparent struggles between a 'Muslim East' and a 'Christian West'. The obvious example is that cheap energy source known as oil: since Muslim-majority countries happen to be located where most of the

9. Engels 1893a, pp. 164–5; Engels 1893b, p. 97.

10. I take this example from Molyneux 2008.

11. Immediately the objection springs to mind: what of earlier hostilities between Muslim-majority areas and Christian ones, as with the Crusades, or the Ottoman Empire, and so on? That is the topic of another study, which would consider the control exercised over vital trade routes to the 'East', which led not only to wars but also to the effort, first by the Portuguese, to circumvent Muslim-controlled areas and find a new way to the East – hence the slow process of finding a way around Africa to India, eventually achieved by Vasco da Gama in 1497–8.

world's oil happens to be, and since the overdeveloped West needs that oil, conflict is bound to arise. The potential for massive profits from oil-rich countries puts them in an enviable position within the global economy. However, if those areas had happened to be Buddhist, for instance, then any concerted opposition to capitalist exploitation would be viewed as a hostile response by an evil and militant Buddhism.

A number of counts against the 'new old atheism': it is unoriginal, committed to a rusty old belief in the superiority of reason, naïvely materialist, given to a belief in evolutionary progress in which they are at the peak, and distressingly idealist. Yet a more dialectical reading would want to argue at least two points: religion does not escape entirely from their charges; and the more interesting question to ask is why this movement is happening now. The first point picks up my discussion of religion in the Introduction to this book, where I offered a brief description that drew upon Althusser's proposal concerning semi-autonomous instances and ideological state apparatuses. In light of that approach to religion, it quickly becomes clear that religion is far more than a set of ideas and beliefs, for it includes the institutional forms of religion and their enmeshment with social, political and economic forces. Not an earth-shattering point, but it does have a number of ramifications for the arguments of the neo-atheists. Instead of focusing on the idealistic features of religion, its ideas and beliefs, let us consider it from an institutional, material perspective. In that light, the criticism of the neo-atheists may have some bite. As an autonomous apparatus and practice, religion may well be responsible for all manner of acts of oppression – gendered, economic, sexual, political and environmental. But the crucial question is one of agency. What is the driving force of such acts? Are those acts by churches, synagogues, mosques and so on driven by religious beliefs, or by the economic and political needs of those institutions? The neo-atheists would argue for the former, that belief in the gods and the attendant hocus-pocus is the root of all evil. But that is, even within the framework I have established, an idealistic option. In reply, I would stress the connectedness of religion (it is, after all, *semi*-autonomous) with its economic and political dimensions, indeed with the whole social formation of which it is a part. Now agency begins to shift, for the reasons why religions may have acted and continue to act in the way they do are part of a complex that includes economic, political and social reasons. Why does the church become a bastion of patriotism and nationalism during warfare? Why does it seek to do deals with the powers that be to ensure its survival? As Gramsci argued in his analysis of the Italian Roman Catholic church, the key for the church has always been its own survival and flourishing, and in order to ensure those ends, it will act as it sees appropriate.[12] In other words, there are

12. See Boer 2007a, pp. 215–74.

complex political and economic reasons for the church acting in the way it does that go well beyond matters of ideas and beliefs. The most that one can say is that religious beliefs and rationales may provide justifications for acts of oppression, but they do not cause them. Even more, as Marx pointed out, religion often functions as a symptom of the brutality of social systems for which it acts as ideological glue. Finally, given the enmeshment of religion with the whole social formation, religion on its own is not guilty of some of the most brutal acts in human history, for it is the whole social formation of which religion is a part that is guilty. But in order to make that argument, the likes of Dawkins and Hitchens would need to rewrite their books from scratch.

I am even more interested in asking why the 'new old atheism' has taken off at all. Obviously it has much to do with the well-publicised return of religion to the geopolitical stage. But at a deeper level I would suggest it signals a global shift on cultural, political and economic levels. As the United States becomes more and more bogged down in wars it cannot win – Iraq and Afghanistan – and as it staggers from one lame-duck president to another, as the economic crisis that first hit with force in 2008 continues to roll on, the political dominance of the West stumbles ever more noticeably. The threat may be articulated in terms of either Islam or even China, but the 'new old atheists' voice in their own terms an effort to restore the dominance of Western politics and culture. Hence the recovery of reason, science, and progress, dusted off from the nineteenth century and rearmed to do battle once again. At this level, their efforts are of the same ilk as those countries of Western and Northern Europe who have thrown up walls of immigration, culture and politics against what they feel are threats from the poor of the world. Once one feels that the golden age is under threat and in the past, the game is already up.[13] Economically, this rearguard action may be seen as a response to a shift from the dominance of Western economies to those of the East. One way of reading the economic crisis of 2008 and beyond is in terms of an earthquake as the economic tectonic plates shift yet again: with a dip in economic growth, China emerges, surpassing Germany and Japan in the process to find itself in second place behind the USA. And as economies recover from this latest crash, those of the West will painfully scrabble back to some semblance of growth, while those of China, India and others power ahead. In this light, the 'new old atheists' may be seen as both symptoms of the shift and as cultural warriors manning the crumbling battlements.

13. On a more personal note, I have been struck time and again by the experience of passing into Western and Northern Europe after spending time in the East: one gains a sense of quiet suspicion of outsiders, desperate defence of what is passing, and an inebriated escape from a world gone to pot. The contrast with the zest for life, energy and optimism in the East grows with each border-crossing.

But let me close on a slightly different point, one which I will pick up later. Rather than being outside theology through their own rejection of religion, I would argue not merely that the 'new old atheists' take up what is really a theological position – atheism – but that they do so within a wider debate. This point is based on the assumption that religion is a site of intense ideological and institutional struggles, of which these neo-atheists are a part. For religions are, to gloss Althusser, ideological apparatuses in which a range of factors play a role – ideas and beliefs, but also institutional forms which have their own patterns of social relations, economic structures, judiciaries and modes of enforcements. Above all, an apparatus such as religion is a site of ideological struggle. Religions are by no means monolithic, seamless structures, for they are riven with struggles, debates, disagreements and heretics. I do not mean the standard liberal position (and objection to the 'new old atheists') that we should let the field of religion bloom with many different flowers in a glorious, hand-holding act of tolerance, but that we need to apply a distinctly Marxist analysis to religions: they are conflictual zones in which vital struggles are fought.

The death of God?

A very different group are the atheologians, who argue that atheists should not reject religion as a barbaric hangover from an evolutionary stage, but that atheists should engage with and write theology.[14] There are some differences among the atheologians: for example, Thomas J.J. Altizer and Mark C. Taylor argue that theistic theology, based on traditional concepts of God as creator and redeemer, is an antediluvian discipline that should be put out of its misery and, therefore, that atheology is the way forward. For others, especially Richard Curtis, theology should have room for both theists and atheists. As far as Altizer and Taylor are concerned, I must admit to finding Altizer far more interesting than Taylor, who is really engaged in that cottage industry known as philosophical system building. They both draw heavily on the unlikely pair of Hegel and Kierkegaard,[15] and they are both stricken with a sense of apocalyptic crisis.[16] As I will argue in a moment with Taylor, this perception of crisis should be read less as an analysis of actual crisis and more as a symptom of radical economic changes.

14. I take atheology according to its common meaning and not in the sense of covert or secular theology, or the hidden theological presuppositions of secular theories, as propounded by Dixon 1999, who follows and renames the 'genetic' approach of Milbank 1990.

15. Altizer and Hamilton 1968; M. Taylor 1975, 2000. For a recent engagement on a different level, see Vattimo and Caputo 2009.

16. Altizer 1990, 1985; M. Taylor 2007.

Altizer, the most well-known of the loose group called the 'death of God' theologians who created a ruckus in the 1960s, sought to realise the full implication of Nietzsche's proclamation of God's death. For Altizer, this death is nothing less than the outcome of the incarnation. God began the process of kenosis, or self-emptying, at the moment of creation and finally died through Christ. Or, in the Kierkegaardian terms so beloved by Altizer, the radical subjectivity of faith means that historical or objective Christianity has died. True to the tradition of dialectical theology that runs from Kierkegaard through to Barth, Altizer stresses the coincidence of opposites: through radical subjectivity God's death becomes an objective, historical fact; the sacred becomes profane through God's death; the death of God in Christ means that the spirit is poured out into the world; God's absence means that God is present in all things.[17]

How are we to assess these arguments? A hint comes with the overwhelming sense of apocalyptic crisis (exacerbated by Altizer's two great personal epiphanies of Satan and the death of God).[18] And confirmation follows with the connections between the other 'death of God' theologians – Paul van Buren, William Hamilton (who famously published an article in *Playboy*), and Gabriel Vahanian. Their arrival at the death of God – the traditional, transcendent creator God – through theology and their sense of apocalyptic crisis reminds me uncannily of the Young Hegelians in the 1830s and 1840s. David Strauss's democratic Christ, Bruno Bauer's free self-consciousness (against the false particularism of traditional religion), and Ludwig Feuerbach's projections were all versions of the death of God more than a century before, but they were also radical efforts to recast and renew theology. Of course, the catch with being a Young Hegelian is that one comes before Marx's breakthrough.

Mark C. Taylor's starting point is similar to Altizer's, namely the incarnational death of the conventional creator God (with a heavy debt to Kierkegaard). However, this death actually means a hiding, a going underground and turning up in all manner of unexpected places – for Taylor, art, architecture, virtual technologies and more recently finance and the market. In exploring this line, Taylor takes a very different path from Altizer's deeply theological work, passing from an analysis of modernism to spend a good deal of time in the tents of deconstruction.[19] Apart from the banality of many of Taylor's statements (for example, God as the 'infinitely creative process' is not so original, and his forays into economics are decidedly amateurish), two aspects of his approach need more comment. The first is his sustained sense of crisis, which strikes any reader

17. See Altizer and Hamilton 1968; Altizer 1966, 2003.
18. Altizer 2006.
19. M. Taylor 1984, 1986, 1987.

of *After God*.[20] Here, we come across the argument that the world is in a dire predicament, that the maps we use do not fit anymore and that we desperately need a new way through. The solution: a grand system, a theory of everything – theology, philosophy, literary criticism, art, architecture, technology, economic systems, education, and biological systems. And all of them interconnect via Taylor's favoured complexity theory, leading to a relational network model.[21]

While I admire anyone brave enough to produce such a system, the pitfalls are immense (recall the half-baked effort of Dühring, mercilessly dissected by Engels,[22] or the bravely dreadful work of Régis Debray).[23] I cannot help thinking of Adorno's comment regarding the provincialism of such systems, in which one has the conviction that it is possible to 'go into [the] office and believe that [one] can comprehend the universe from that vantage point equipped only with paper, pencil, and selection of books'. In Taylor's case, of course, I would update that with computer and internet, but the point with regard to such a cottage industry remains valid, for 'we need to tear down that cottage as fast as possible'.[24] At a deeper level, however, Taylor's sense of crisis and effort at system building are symptoms of his own context, namely the vast shifts in global capitalism in which anticipation of the decline of the USA is met with an effort at proposing a new version of empire.

This sense of apocalyptic crisis does not afflict the urbane Richard Curtis, who argues for a 'reasonable religion', one in which both theists and atheists can engage in theological debate.[25] As should be obvious, I have much sympathy with this position, especially since Curtis is also informed by Marxist approaches in his work. Curtis is what many may see as an oxymoron: a member of a church, an atheist, a theologian, and one involved in social-justice causes. How does he hold these positions together? He begins with two premises: God does not exist but religion, as a generic feature of human existence, does. Why? Religion gives expression, he argues, to the poetic dimension of human existence, to senses of awe and wonder (aesthetics), it expresses the limits and possibilities of human beings as social creatures (the social), explores what it means to be human in the first place (the existential), and is a specific need of the human brain for forming a conscious self through mediating structures called culture (the cognitive). Above all, religion provides a way of understanding, a 'web of ongoing narration' regarding our place in the world and how we fit in with one another –

20. M. Taylor 2007.
21. See M. Taylor 2001, 2004.
22. Engels 1877–8a; Engels 1877–8b.
23. Debray 1983; Debray 2004.
24. Adorno 2008, p. 42; Adorno 2007, pp. 67–8. Or, as Nietzsche put it, 'I mistrust all systematizers and avoid them. The will to a system is a lack of integrity.' (Nietzsche 1990, p. 35.)
25. Curtis 2007.

in short, it fulfils a vital ideological function. Now, one could argue that Curtis is in fact engaged in the scientific study of religion rather than theology, bringing in insights from the philosophy of mind, cognitive science and the social sciences, but he argues that they all feed into what might be called atheology. Perhaps the most intriguing element of his work is the way he draws upon both Marxism and liberation theology (a liberation atheology), especially the work of Juan Luis Segundo, to give his work a distinct political edge.

As I pointed out earlier, in some respects my work comes closest to these atheologians, although I do not share the apocalypticism of Altizer and Taylor, or the all-too-positive view of human nature and religion by Curtis. But before I outline my position, let me set up the opposition between the evangelical neo-atheists and the atheologians with the first opposition of a semiotic square (whether we view that in terms of Aristotle's logical square of opposites or Greimas's famous re-vitalisation of the square). Briefly, the value of the semiotic square is that it enables us to map the full range of possible positions as well as the ideological limits of the debate in question. The square begins with a simple binary opposition or contrary relation, conventionally inscribed as S^1 and S^2, or sometimes as S and –S. Eventually it fills out with the contradictories, $-S^1$ and $-S^2$, or non S and non –S, which are simultaneously enlargements of and steps beyond the pair in the upper register. The full square goes as follows:

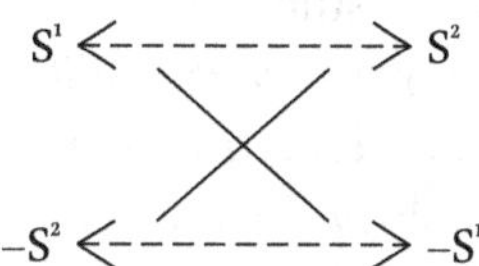

For now, I am interested in the first pair, for here we find the initial two atheistic approaches to theology: acceptance by the atheologians and outright rejection by the neo-atheists:

Acceptance (Atheologians) <---------> Rejection (Neo-atheists)

These are by no means the only options available, so let us explore yet another.

Theology versus studies in religion

By this stage, it should be obvious that I see little point in arguing – desperately and futilely, as the neo-atheists do – that religion should be abolished, or at least in trying to persuade people that they need to give it away for their own good. And I see no gain in arguing, with enlightened impatience, that the death of God is an objective reality and that theology should be undertaken with this in mind. I do agree, however, that there should be as much room for atheists as theists in theological writing, debate and struggle. Actually, I would suggest that the 'new old atheists' too should join the discussion once they have overcome their fundamentalist objections to religion and realise that they too make theological arguments. In other words, both neo-atheists and atheologians are really part of the struggles within religion, even within theology.

However, a further approach to theology within my mapping of positions remains – that of studies in religion. Even though I am further from this position than some of the atheologians, I deal with it here since it was the immediate trigger to the argument developed below. In the latter half of 2009, a furious debate erupted among bloggers concerning the relation between theology and studies of religion. It was initially a disciplinary debate focused on what is appropriate for universities: is theology a proper academic discipline or is that honour reserved for studies in religion? Soon enough it grew into a discussion around the nature of theology, theism and atheism. The trigger was a short piece in the *Chronicle of Higher Education* by Kurt Noll, a religion teacher at Brandon University, Manitoba.[26] Noll's argument was blunt and straightforward: theology is a pseudo-discipline since it involves apologetics for an assumed position of faith. A theologian takes as given a set of beliefs and does her best to defend them. By contrast, the study of religion is a genuine pursuit of scientific knowledge. In short: theology defends, the study of religion explains. At one level, this argument is obviously part of a larger turf war that has been going on since the establishment of studies in religion departments in universities. Keen to distinguish itself from its parents, theology departments and divinity schools, studies in religion has sought a method, disciplinary cohesion and a separate path, gradually developing strength as it learned to walk. And a key strategy, especially in North America where the debate is most heated, has been to reject the ways of its parent completely: theology is an academic charlatan, a quack peddling dubious products, which has no place in a university setting. For theology assumes belief in and wishes to defend what is patently beyond any reasonable inquiry – the gods. In sum, theology is by definition theist, while the study of religion is atheist or agnostic.

Many of the responses in the blogosphere[27] to Noll's argument were predictable: some approved, praising Noll for his straight talking and expressing a wish

26. Noll 2009.

27. As a sample from a much wider range, they came from colourful and less colourful blogs such as *Missives from Marx* (<http://missivesfrommarx.wordpress.com/2009/08/18/no-theology-in-religious-studies/>), *Camels With Hammers* (<http://patheos.com/blogs/camelswithhammers/2009/08/does-being-a-theologian-require-being-a-religious-believer/>), *Dr Jim's Thinking Shop* (<http://drjimsthinkingshop.com/2009/09/18/

to keep theologians away from any serious scholarship; others were more critical, pointing out somewhat predictably that he and his ilk have values too, that studies in religion has as many presuppositions as theology, so he had better be up front about them; or making ad hominem arguments against Noll without actually considering the detail of his argument. Invariably, those who dismissed Noll came from a faith position (mostly Christian and Jewish), while those who agreed with him were agnostics or atheists, some of them from studies in religion departments.

Now we can map onto our growing semiotic square these proponents of studies in religion who, following Noll, are happy to allow theologians to carry on with whatever mystifying arguments they choose, on the condition that they must do so outside the walls of reputable academic institutions – a position not unlike the neo-atheists, except that these religionists are perfectly willing to study religion but not permit anyone to do so from a theistic perspective. In other words, they fill the contradictory position on the square:

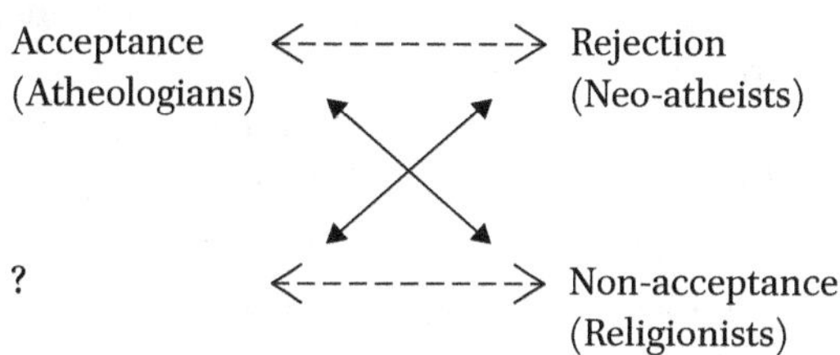

However, a more careful reading of the debate between the religionists and the theologians picks up two points that will take my discussion a step further. First, Noll himself admits openly that he is a theist outside his job as a religion teacher and an agnostic while on the job. In the debate, no-one seemed to pick up this crucial point: Noll himself is a believer in his private life, but when he walks through the front door of his religion department he is an agnostic teacher of religion who seeks to explain and advance knowledge rather than offer apologetics for his beliefs. In this respect, Noll has thrown a spoiler into the debates, for it is an opposition all-too common in biblical studies and occasionally theology, let alone the study of religion. For example, the methods of biblical criticism which have developed since the mid-nineteenth century in Germany (the context in which Marx and Engels did their own work) are actually methods that have

atheology-atheist-theology-atheist-religious-studies/>), *Targuman* (<http://targuman.org/blog/2009/09/17/atheology/>), *The Dunedin School* (<http://dunedinschool.wordpress.com/2009/08/23/religious-studies-versus-theology/>), *Higgaion* (<http://heardworld.com/higgaion/?p=1452>), and my own *Stalin's Moustache* (<http://stalinsmoustache.wordpress.com/2009/08/27/theists-and-atheists-and-theology-or-pinning-me-down/>).

bracketed the gods out. Analyses of biblical texts or the history of theology do not count God as a causal factor: He becomes a matter of belief for the actors in those texts or in that history, He may be a character in the stories, but God is not a causal factor per se. These methods are, in order to be 'scientific', agnostic or atheistic in the way they work (one reason for the opposition displayed towards them by conservative Christians and Jews). Yet, many of the scholars who practise biblical criticism and theology are believers, worshipping on Saturday or Sunday, at times leading worship, offering their critical skills for the building up of the faithful. Like Noll, they actually live double lives.

A second feature comes from an ignored response to Noll: he has defined theology into a corner where he can punch the living daylights out of it, at least when he walks through the doors of his university. Theology is, according to this definition, making sense of and defending a given set of beliefs, understood to have been revealed by God and, at times, mediated by the church. It is true that a good number of theologians with close ties to a church will agree, but the question that I raised in this debate was why anyone would allow conservative theologians to define the field in this way and why, on the other side, we would allow Noll and others to perpetuate this definition. My initial intervention generated a series of response, with *Missives from Marx* wanting to pin me down as to what I mean by theology.[28] For the anonymous author, who is a religion professor of Marxist persuasions awaiting tenure (hence the anonymity), theology involves 'discourses that advance claims about gods in a systematic or quasi-systematic way', or more specifically 'discourses about supernatural entities, discourses that mystify, or discourses that naturalize or reproduce the authority of religious traditions'. This is not quite the crass position of Kurt Noll, from whom theology boils down to unscientific apologetics, but it shares the puzzled assumption by many that theology is done by those who are theists and who wish to explicate and elaborate on the existence and nature of the gods. But *Missives* did challenge me to come clean, pinning me down (with a touch of homoeroticism) on the mat and asking, 'what sort of a theologian are you?'

Atheists and theology

My own response to the challenge began with the following, well-known argument and then pushed it to its logical conclusion. Christianity postulates the existence of God, heaven, hell (sometimes), an afterlife and so on. For many these do not exist, they are figments of the creative imagination, myths to live by. As a form of idealism, Christianity has no independent existence and thus

28. See the article 'Identifying Theology and Pinning Roland Boer' at <http://missivesfrommarx.wordpress.com/2009/08/23/identifying-theology-and-pinning-roland-boer/>.

does not have a history. Well and good, one might say, but this relatively common position has some curious ramifications.

We may respond and say that religion offers an erroneous belief about the world that needs to be corrected (the position of the neo-atheists, among others), or we can take, as I outlined in my discussion of ideology in the Introduction, a 'descriptive' or functionalist approach in which religion is a necessary and inescapable feature of human existence. If we follow this descriptive option, then religion is no different from philosophy, art, writing, politics, metaphysics and so on. In the same way that one holds a philosophical position or produces a plot for a novel, one also produces religious beliefs. This argument leads to the conclusion that, like art, writing, or philosophy, theology is worth studying as part of the creative activity of human beings.

However, another option is also possible, for it is perfectly logical to say: I know that God, the spirits, heaven and hell and so on are constructs of our imagination or characters in a story, but that is no barrier to belief, for I find the story as a whole provides a viable and largely positive myth to live by. This is actually close to Ludwig Feuerbach's position, except that he argued that these abstracted entities need to be returned to us as our own attributes in order to enhance our lives.[29] The number of people who actually hold to this position with regard to religion, however logical it might be, is rather small. Yet it is not uncommon to find it invoked in relation to a philosophical system, or even a novel or a complex computer game.[30]

However, the preceding argument will probably not persuade too many, so let me follow another line of argument, which elaborates upon some brief comments in this vein in my Introduction. In contrast to the many who still assume that theism and theology are the best of friends,[31] I would suggest that it is perfectly consistent to practise theology and not believe in a god. Theology is actually a system of thought, with its distinct terminology, modes of argument and lively debates that can operate quite well without any external reference point. In a sister discipline to theology – biblical criticism – this is a viable way to carry on one's work. As I pointed out earlier, for well over a century biblical criticism has operated with the assumption that one does not include the gods as causes of history or as those responsible for the production of the biblical texts (in their

---

29. Feuerbach 1989; Feuerbach 1924.

30. One or two religions have actually sprung up in response to novels, most notably Scientology after L. Ron Hubbard's woeful science-fiction writings, and the Church of All Worlds, explicitly based on Robert A. Heinlein's *Stranger in a Strange Land* (Heinlein 1991).

31. Marx was no exception in believing that the two are coterminous. As Janz 1998, p. 9, points out, Marx felt that once you exposed theistic belief as a fantasy, religion itself becomes obsolete.

writing, gathering and ordering into a canon). At most, the multiple personalities of God are actually characters in the story, as with any other literature.[32] The assumption that you need to believe in order to be interested in the Bible would have to be one of the strangest making the rounds today, shared by believers and non-believers alike. We do not expect an art critic to be an artist, a literary critic to be a novelist or a poet, a student of classical Greece to be a believer in Apollo or Venus, or a lecturer in Chinese to be a Chinese national.

If this is possible with biblical criticism, then why not with theology? Let me put it this way: biblical criticism is finally shedding the misleading attachment to intention. For too long it was assumed that the holy grail of interpretation was the intention of the author. So when scholars and readers came to the gospels, the aim was to find what Jesus himself intended – and thereby what God intended through these sayings. Biblical critics, or at least many of them, have realised that intention is but one small part of interpretation. Apart from the impossibility of finding out what the author(s) might have intended, or indeed accounting for the role of the subconscious in the production of texts, the search for intention relies on a relatively recent, bourgeois assumption, namely that thoughts are the possession of an individual mind, the private property of an owner who is thereby the arbiter of meaning.[33] However, even if we allow some space for intention (problematic as that might be), it needs to take its place beside many other factors. These factors are legion, including unconscious and unintended meaning, the sense provided by readers, the roles of social norms and cultural expectations, the intrusive roles of history and economics, the conflicting ideological voices in a text, or indeed the objective sense of the words on a page, the nature of the text itself and how it is structured. So also with theology: once we move past the assumption that religious belief constitutes the core or perhaps the overarching unity of theology and realise that it is one small and by no means necessary part, then theology shows all its other colours. It deals with nature and the environment (creation), with the human condition (anthropology), why the world is the way it is (harmatology), the problem of suffering, the nature of the human subject (via Christology), the nature of history, hopes for the future, how human beings might live together (ecclesiology), and the nature of mythology (the central stories with which theology deals).

---

32. In case there is a misunderstanding here, let me point out that I do not argue that biblical criticism is 'objective'; rather, it has replaced a particular set of theological assumptions with those of secular science.

33. Or, as Adorno puts it, 'I believe that in general it is a prejudice going back to what might be called the intellectual version of the middle-class parlour, according to which the products of the mind are the property of great thinkers, poets and composers, and so forth, whose plaster busts used to grace these parlours in the old days. They may have disappeared now, but may well survive in spirit, invisibly, and to even more disastrous effect because of that invisibility' (Adorno 2000c, p. 92).

Now, it might be objected that what I am actually talking about here is really a combination of 'ontology, anthropology, existentialism, and constructive social philosophy'.[34] For many, this really means studies in religion rather than theology,[35] especially if one removes that crucial element of theism from theology. As should be clear by now, that definition is to my mind wrong-headed and restrictive. Even more, it actually relies on the problematic idea that each discipline has its unifying core. As I argued in the Introduction, instead of defining each discipline by a core idea, I prefer to think of disciplines as intersections of various lines. So, theology is not defined by explaining belief in spirits on steroids, but by intersections of various roads that bear the signs of history, environment, the human condition, hope, social questions, mythology and so on. One could do similar exercises with each discipline – for example, literature, architecture or even physics – and come up with similar results, for they tend to be intersections rather than base camps.

In conclusion, let me make it perfectly clear that I do not wish to ban belief in God, but I do want to argue that there should be plenty of room for theologians who do not believe in God. After all, the discipline has a wealth of experience discussing and debating crucial issues central to human existence that it would be silly to discard. Atheism and theology are therefore as logically compatible as theism and theology; one can practise theology perfectly well without believing in the gods about which it speaks. It would seem that even the neo-atheists have their place around the theological table.

Marxism and theology

One of the major reasons for this lengthy discussion of some of the more important takes on atheism is that I seek a way to situate the Marxists who interest me, namely those who have engaged with theology and the Bible at some length. The list is quite long: Ernst Bloch, Walter Benjamin, Henri Lefebvre, Louis Althusser, Antonio Gramsci, Terry Eagleton, Slavoj Žižek, Theodor Adorno, Max Horkheimer, Lucien Goldmann, Fredric Jameson, Rosa Luxemburg, Karl Kautsky, Alain Badiou, Giorgio Agamben, Georg Lukács, Raymond Williams, G.E.M. de Ste. Croix, E.P. Thompson, Michael Löwy, Roland Barthes, Gilles Deleuze and Félix Guattari, Antonio Negri and, of course, Marx and Engels. An easy objection would be to say: yes, they might *deal with* theology, but they are primarily a mix

34. Comment from *Missives from Marx*, <http://missivesfrommarx.wordpress.com/2009/08/31/roland-and-theology/#comment-998>. See also <http://missivesfrommarx.wordpress.com/2009/09/04/cross-purposes/#comment-1146>.

35. So, for example, Chris Brady's article 'Atheology' at *Targuman*: <http://targuman.org/blog/2009/09/17/atheology>.

of philosophers, historians, and literary and cultural critics. In response, I would say: granted, but are not such disciplines really intersections of various paths? And what do we call it when they enter into theological debates and biblical interpretation? Is it philosophy, history, literary criticism, or is it also theology? My answer to that last question should not be difficult to guess.

Before I explore the ramifications of that answer, let me return once more to the semiotic square, for now it is possible to fill out the crucial last term. For that one, as Jameson has pointed out,[36] requires much blackening of pages with diagrams, erasures and rethinking, for it is the most difficult to identify and one that may well lead us beyond the ideological limits mapped out by the square.

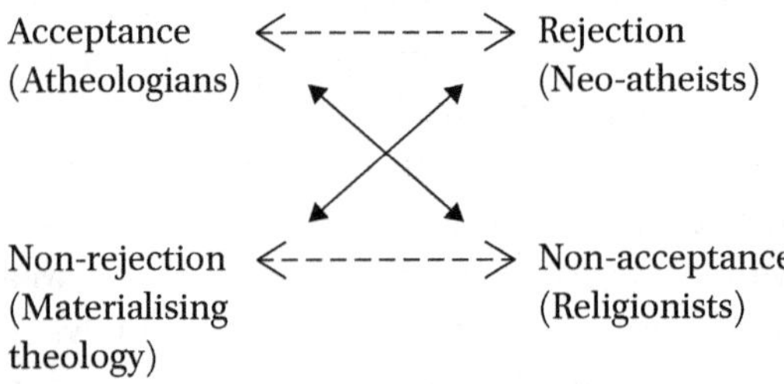

An obvious advantage of the square is that it shows up the possible allegiances along the different axes in way that a sequential narrative tends to obscure. So atheology and materialising theology (for want of a better term) join forces in what is technically called a lateral or deictic axis. Both seek to pursue a theology in which atheism has a perfectly valid place, although the way they go about the task differs. While the other lateral axis, between the neo-atheists and the religionists, shares the assumption that theology has no place in any serious discussion, they also differ as to how one excludes theology. Yet there is also a curious relation along the bottom axis, usually designated as the point of the neutral term, one given over to negation and privation. Precisely what negation means here is crucial: for the religionists it means that one banishes theology from intellectual pursuit, but for a materialising theology negation is a much more Hegelian term. It is an Aufhebung, designating both a negation but also a drawing-up to a new level. Theology is thereby negated, preserved and transformed, rather than simply banished.

But what exactly is a materialising theology? The term is (inadequate) shorthand for a dual dialectical process that I mentioned briefly in the Introduction. It is a theology that has run the gauntlet through historical materialism, not shying away from the tough questions and challenges. More fully, it follows a

36. Jameson 1987.

dialectical approach reminiscent of Adorno, in which theology stays the course until, sweating, filthy, worn out and hitting its wall, it arrives at its materialist 'truth content'. Conversely, one might take historical materialism and push it hard, untiringly and without mercy, until it too arrives at its theological truth content. But these are not dirty secrets to be uncovered, corpses beneath the floorboards whose stench has become unbearable, but theology transformed by its thorough immersion in materialism. To be precise and complete, I should speak of both 'materialising theology' and 'theologising materialism', except that the second term is quite an ugly and clumsy one, so I will stick with the first. I do so since the present participle stresses the process, rather than the finality of the somewhat popular 'materialist theology' touted by Žižek and others. For Žižek it is as much a desire to be as non-trendy as possible, but he does come close to what I seek, taking Ernst Bloch's axiom to heart: 'only an atheist can be a good Christian; only a Christian can be a good atheist'.[37]

Aufhebung

For the remainder of this chapter I shall outline some of the features of such a materialising theology, features that seek to lay the groundwork for the chapters that follow. To begin with, I pick up Aufhebung once again, that well-oiled and smoothly running term from the Hegelian-Marxist heritage. As for Marx himself, he may well have commented to Lasalle 'so specific is my aversion [*Widerwille*] to Christianity,'[38] but he also argued that atheism is a distraction from the real task of communist analysis and action.[39] His most astute reason for taking such

37. Bloch 1972, p. 9; Bloch 1968, p. 15.
38. Marx 1862a, p. 377; Marx 1862b, p. 627.
39. Most of Marx's discussions of religion appear in his earlier works, especially 'The Leading Article in No. 179 of the 'Kölnische Zeitung' (Marx 1842i; Marx 1842j), Debates on Freedom of the Press and Publication of the Proceedings of the Assembly of the Estates' (Marx 1842k; Marx 1842l), *Contribution to the Critique of Hegel's Philosophy of Law* (Marx 1843c; Marx 1843d), as well as the separate Introduction (Marx 1844c; Marx 1844d) and the 'Theses on Feuerbach' (Marx 1845b; Marx 1845c). Written during his early years of journalism and research, these are only the most substantial. Many of his other works contain comments and observations, but if I listed them here it would fill up the rest of the book. *Capital*, for example, is peppered with comments, allusions and references (often to Luther!). By contrast, Engels wrote a number of key texts on religion over his lifetime, including 'Letters from Wuppertal' (Engels 1839a; Engels 1839b), observations on religious life in Bremen while he was living there (Engels 1840a; Engels 1840b; Engels 1840c; Engels 1840d; Engels 1840e; Engels 1840f), three essays on Schelling's lectures in Berlin (Engels 1841c; Engels 1841d; Engels 1842c; Engels 1842d; Engels 1842e; Engels 1842f), a delightful satirical poem on the Bible (Engels 1842a; Engels 1842b), extended correspondence with his friends the Graeber brothers on matters theological and biblical (Engels 1839c; Engels 1839d; Engels 1839e; Engels 1839f; Engels 1839g; Engels 1839h; Engels 1839i; Engels 1839j; Engels 1839k; Engels 1839l; Engels 1839m; Engels 1839n; Engels 1839o; Engels 1839p; Engels 1839q; Engels 1839r; Engels 1839s; Engels 1839t; Engels 1839u; Engels 1839v; Engels 1839w;

a position appears in *The Holy Family* from 1845, particularly in his response to Bruno Bauer's atheistic programme. Atheism, Marx writes, is 'the last stage of *theism*, the *negative* recognition of God'.[40] In the larger context of the polemic against Bauer, the vociferous espousal of atheism turns out to be another sign that Bauer is still a theologian, for atheism is actually a theological position (the neo-atheists take note). One cannot be an atheist without having a God to lock-up, ignore, put to death or deny. Or, as Engels would put it much later (in 1884) with his customary clarity: '... that atheism merely expresses a negation is an argument we ourselves had already advanced against the philosophers 40 years ago, only with the corollary that atheism, as the *mere* negation of, and referring only to, religion, would itself be nothing without it and is thus itself another religion'.[41]

However, Marx takes what is by now a common argument (it was not so much then) a step further in a perceptive few comments in the *Economic and Philosophic Manuscripts of 1844*. Here, he starts with the same point concerning the theological nature of atheism, but then takes a huge stride forward to argue that we need to move well beyond the opposition between theism and atheism: '*Atheism*... has no longer any meaning, for atheism is a *negation of God* [*Negation der Gottes*], and postulates the *existence of man* through this negation; but socialism as socialism no longer stands in need of such a mediation.... It is man's *positive self-consciousness* [*Selbstbewußtsein*], no longer mediated through the abolition of religion [*Aufhebung der Religion*]'.[42] *Negation, Aufhebung, Selbstbewußtsein* – these are the key terms that spell a deep immersion in Hegelian thought (and, with *Selbstbewußtsein*, the residual influence of his one-time friend and colleague, Bruno Bauer). The gulf that separates atheism and socialism is that atheism is a mere negation while far on the other side stands socialism, which turns out to be an Aufhebung, a sublation, a preservation and lifting of

---

Engels 1839x; Engels 1839y; Engels 1839z; Engels 1839–40a; Engels 1839–40b; Engels 1840a; Engels 1841b; Engels 1840g; Engels 1841h) and then a series of major works: 'The Peasant War in Germany' (Engels 1850a; Engels 1850b), 'Bruno Bauer and Early Christianity' (Engels 1882a; Engels 1882b), 'The Book of Revelation' (Engels 1883a; Engels 1883b) and, towards the end of his life, the influential 'On the History of Early Christianity' (Engels 1894–5c; Engels 1894–5d). Engels never lost the habit of alluding to or quoting a Bible verse in the midst of his polemic to hammer home a point. They run into the hundreds if not thousands in his works. Two other joint texts are also steeped in religious matters, namely *The Holy Family* (Marx and Engels 1845a; Marx and Engels 1845b) and *The German Ideology* (Marx and Engels 1845–6a; Marx and Engels 1845–6b). Some, but by no means all of these works, have been gathered in various collections over time (Marx and Engels 1976; Marx 2002). For a detailed study of these texts, see Boer 2012.

40. Marx and Engels 1845a, p. 110; Marx and Engels 1845b, p. 116.
41. Engels 1884a, p. 173; Engels 1884b, p. 186. See further Moroziuk 1974.
42. Marx 1844g, p. 306; Marx 1844h, p. 546; translation modified.

religion to another level. Socialism does not kick away the ladder of religion, but pulls it up and then uses the wood to construct something quite new.

Atheism, it seems, has been left behind somewhat, dropped off the back of the field. It leads to the startling (it should not be, but for a variety of historical reasons it is) conclusion that atheism is not a prerequisite for socialism.[43] But armed with this opposition between negation and Aufhebung, I would like to read some of the most well-known of Marx's comments on religion from the 'Introduction' to his *Contribution to the Critique of Hegel's Philosophy of Law* (*Kritik* for short):

> For Germany, the *criticism of religion* is in the main complete [*im wesentlichen beendigt*], and the criticism of religion is the premise of all criticism [*die Voraussetzung aller Kritik*].[44]
>
> The evident proof of the radicalism of German theory, and hence of its practical energy, is that it proceeds from a resolute *positive* sublation of religion [*der entschiedenen* positiven *Aufhebung der Religion*]. The criticism of religion ends [*endet*] with the teaching that *man is the highest being for man*, hence with the *categorical imperative to overthrow all relations* [alle Verhältnisse umzuwerfen] in which man is a debased, enslaved, forsaken, despicable being.[45]

Let me exegete these passages for a few moments. Here, Marx dances rather deftly with two basic senses: the criticism of religion is 'complete', he writes, and it 'ends' – both verbs are variations on *enden* and *beenden* (*beendigen*), with the senses of finishing, completing, coming to the end of the line, a termination where it is 'all out and all change', as they would have it at my local railway station; but then he throws in a spoiler, writing now of the sublation or Aufhebung of religion, with the sense, as we saw above, of transition, suggesting that it is now time to move on, to change trains rather than come to the end of the journey. But are these two terms opposed, facing each other across a gulf, like negation and Aufhebung? We may well be tempted to opt for this conclusion, especially if we note that the criticism of religion is itself complete [*enden*], coming to a halt in the teaching that man is the highest being for man (Feuerbach had said as much, but then at one level these texts may be read as affirmations of Feuerbach criticism). By contrast, when it comes to the 'radicalism of German theory' we slip into Aufhebung. And not any Aufhebung, for it is a resolute one, a positive one. No negation here, for one moves well beyond religion through a process in 'which denial and preservation, i.e., affirmation, are bound up together [*worin die Verneinung und die Aufbewahrung, die Bejahung verknüpft sind*]'.[46]

---

43. See further the conclusion to Boer 2012.
44. Marx 1844c, p. 175; Marx 1844d, p. 378. See also Marx 1847.
45. Marx 1844c, p. 182; Marx 1844d, p. 385.
46. Marx 1844g, p. 340; Marx 1844h, p. 581.

If only it were so simple, but Marx is not one for comfortable simplicities. Note the crucial sentence: 'For Germany the *criticism of religion* is in the main complete, and the criticism of religion is the prerequisite of all criticism'. Here the two senses touch another: the criticism of religion is both 'complete [*beendigt*]' *and* a 'premise' or 'prerequisite [*Voraussetzung*]'. (I take *Voraussetzung* as another way of expressing Aufhebung, particularly since a prerequisite looks forward to what follows, is merely a first step, like a preliminary course of study in, say, Dutch or Danish that one must take before being able to make the leap to reading and writing in a new language.) So what Marx is really saying is that religion and its criticism must come to a completion, but only so that they may be sublated – negated, denied, preserved and affirmed – by a completely new stage.

Marx senses that this moment has arrived in his own time and indeed in his own thought (he was not one for lack of confidence in the face of almost insuperable odds). Much of this perception has to do with the tumultuous context in which he studied and lived in his youth: during his years in high school, university and as a journalist, essayist and radical critic, the dominant form of public and political debate in Germany was in terms of theology and especially the New Testament. In fact, Marx and Engels first honed their thought in response to a situation analogous with today, for it was dominated by the public role of religion. For a number of historical reasons, the various German states dealt with a whole range of modern issues through Christianity and the Bible.[47] While France had the radical atheistic criticism of Voltaire and company and while England had the deists, in Germany the debate was restricted to the nature of the Bible. Given the inseparable nature of religion and politics in the 'Christian state' (as the Prussian king, Friedrich Wilhelm IV, called it), to attack the Bible or Christianity was to attack the political status quo. So we find that the most controversial works in the early part of the nineteenth century were David Strauss's *Das Leben Jesu*, where he argued that the accounts of Jesus in the gospels are purely mythological,[48] or the arguments of the atheistic biblical critic Bruno Bauer against the oppressive particularism of religion and for a democratic self-consciousness,[49] or Ludwig Feuerbach's argument that religion is actually the projection of what is best in human beings, a projection that leads us to create an entity called 'God',[50] or Max Stirner's rambling criticism of everything that inhibits the individual ego.[51] Through these theological and often biblical works

47. See especially Breckman 1999.
48. Strauss 1902; Strauss 1835.
49. Bauer 1838, 1840, 1841, 1842b.
50. Feuerbach 1989, 1924.
51. Stirner 2005; Stirner 1845. Strauss, Bauer and even Feuerbach may be described as biblical, or at least theological writers, but Stirner? For that argument in full, see Boer 2012, pp. 109–25.

all of the central questions were debated, such as democracy, individual rights, freedom (of the press), reason, republicanism, parliamentary representation and so on. I cannot stress enough that these debates took place above all on the territory of the Bible and theology. So also Marx and Engels found themselves responding to and criticising theology.

The hints of this situation are not difficult to find in Marx's text – 'in Germany', he writes. But Marx wants to say that he will not be held back by those debates and struggles, at least in the form that they have taken up until that time. He and those like him will use that situation and those theological debates as a springboard, a crucible even, for his own agenda. They – Bauer, Strauss, Stirner, Feuerbach, or perhaps the early comrades who touted a Christian communism such as Wilhelm Weitling, Hermann Kriege, Karl Grün and Gottfried Kinkel – may want to carry on the criticism of religion but Marx has other interests.

One last phrase I have not touched upon until now: 'in the main [*im wesentlichen*]', or perhaps 'in essence'. I would like to read this phrase in two directions. One is to leave a gap for a little more criticism of religion, since it is not complete just yet. Engels would, of course, open up the gap in his later work, offering a series of influential if flawed assessments of the Peasants' Revolution in the sixteenth century, Bruno Bauer, the biblical Book of Revelation and early Christianity. And in many respects, my own project in *The Criticism of Heaven and Earth* has both traced and elaborated upon that opening. But another possibility may also be squeezed out of 'in the main' and that is in terms of the Aufhebung I have been tracing. The criticism of religion, as it has been practised up until now (Marx's 'now'), is passé, a thing of the past, as is the argument that atheism, or at least atheism as a mere negation, a living of one's life without the gods and a more-or-less evangelical assertion of such, is not a prerequisite for socialism. Instead, socialism means the sublation of religion – a very different type of atheism from that of negation. Perhaps we may distinguish between atheism-1 and atheism-2, where the former is the banal assertion that God does not exist (and is thereby still a theological position), while the latter involves the Aufhebung of religion. Unlike a string of atheists who have peremptorily declared the gods dead and religion now an interesting archaeological artefact, Marx is not quite ready to join the chorus of good riddances at the graveside. Not because he harbours some secret affection for religion; far from it, but he is ready to move on to what the Aufhebung of religion implies.

A little later in the same work (the 'Introduction' to the *Kritik*) he writes, 'The *Aufhebung* of religion as the illusory happiness of the people is the demand for their real happiness'.[52] Or as he puts it, with a Kantian flourish at the close of the

52. Marx 1844c, p. 176; Marx 1844d, p. 379; translation modified.

texts over which I have been obsessing, 'the *categorical imperative to overthrow all relations* [alle Verhältnisse umzuwerfen] in which man is a debased, enslaved, forsaken, despicable being'.[53] However, in order to see how that Aufhebung works, we need to pass through Marx's discussion of Feuerbach.

Feuerbach and beyond

The key, worn down with many uses, to that sublation of religion appears in the fourth thesis on Feuerbach – arguably the most concise expression of what Marx was thinking at the time concerning religion (and perhaps a summary of that thought in the tantalising absence of the lost manuscript *A Treatise on Christian Art*).[54] Alongside Strauss's *Life of Jesus*, Bruno Bauer's biblical criticism and Marx Stirner's *The Ego and His Own*, Feuerbach's *The Essence of Christianity* was one of the most significant texts of that turbulent era[55] – one we seem, for some strange reason, to be reliving in our own day. Marx felt that the argument that religion and the gods were projections of human beings was a huge breakthrough.[56] Feuerbach argued for an inversion: previous thought about religion began at the wrong point, namely somewhere vaguely in the middle; instead Feuerbach argued that God was not a pre-existing being who determined human existence, for human beings determine God's existence. Yet Marx also wanted to go beyond Feuerbach on two counts. First, since human beings project religion from within themselves, the place to begin analysis is not in the heavens, but here on earth with breathing, pulsing, loving, fighting, struggling and dying human beings. Second, the fact that people do make such projections is a signal that something is terribly wrong here on earth – why wish for something better from a super-human being if the life lived here is not out of joint? If we have our treasure in heaven, there our hearts will be, too, but that also means we do not have the treasure of life in the here and now. Thus, the presence of religion becomes a sign of alienation, of economic and social oppression. *That* needs to be fixed. As the fourth thesis puts it:

---

53. Marx 1844c, p. 182; Marx 1844d, p. 385.
54. See Chapter Five for a full discussion of the lost treatise.
55. Feuerbach 1989; Feuerbach 1924.
56. Bruno Bauer's influence should not be discounted, especially his argument that any religion suffers from a false particularism, claiming universal status on the basis of a particular person or group of people. See Bauer 1838, 1840, 1841, 1842b, 1843, 1850–1, 1852. The relationship between Bauer and Marx was extensive and complex, moving from a teacher-student relation, through a close friendship and collaboration, to sustained polemic. Yet many years later, Bauer and Marx met up again in London and renewed their acquaintance.

> Feuerbach starts out from the fact of religious self-estrangement, of the duplication of the world into a religious world and a secular one. His work consists in resolving the religious world into its secular basis. But that the secular basis lifts off from itself and establishes itself as an independent realm in the clouds can only be explained by the inner strife and intrinsic contradictoriness of this secular basis. The latter must, therefore, itself be both understood in its contradiction and revolutionised in practice. Thus, for instance, once the earthly family is discovered to be the secret of the holy family, the former must then itself be destroyed in theory and in practice.[57]

Projections, hypostases, returns – these are all very well, but it is the social and political reality of those people who make the projections in the first place that interests Marx far more. The burning question is not the fantastic projection but the person who makes such projections in the first place. For Marx, however, that person is not merely an individual, but one who is situated within a state and a society. What is it about such a society that generates such fantastic projections? Simply put, any society that needs and produces such religious projections is in a bad way.

So Feuerbach's projection leaves off the story half way, before it becomes really interesting; what counts is the need to consider social, economic and, I would add, the psychological and behavioural reasons for religion and religious belief. Yet with this conclusion most sociologists and historians of religion would agree (a sign of the continued influence of Marx). Marx goes one step further and argues that religion is in fact the sign of an alienated social and economic reality – and to that we need to direct our attention. Or, as Marx would put it in the famous and oft-read 'Introduction' to the *Kritik*, we live in an 'inverted world', in a 'vale of tears' of which religion is the 'halo'; it is, in short, a society riven with 'self-estrangement [*Selbstentfremdung*]'.[58] In the enthusiastic rush of his discovery, Marx does not tire of repeating the same call to action in slightly different ways: sublate illusory happiness to find real happiness; give up illusions in order to give up the situation that requires illusions; shake off the chain and its imaginary flowers in order to pluck the real flowers; religious disillusionment is a coming to one's senses and the basis for reason; establish the truth of this world once the world beyond has gone.[59]

One sentence succinctly sums up what I wish to draw from Marx, for it goes further than the points I have been covering until now. It comes from the

57. Marx 1845b, pp. 4–5; Marx 1845c, pp. 6–7.

58. Marx 1844c, p. 176; Marx 1844d, p. 379.

59. These phrases are drawn from those legendary sentences in Marx 1844c, pp. 175–6; Marx 1844d, pp. 378–9.

Economic and Philosophic Manuscripts of 1844, indicating precisely what Marx meant by the Aufhebung of religion: 'Religious estrangement [*Entfremdung*] as such occurs only in the realm of *consciousness*, of man's inner life, but economic estrangement [*Entfremdung*] is that of *real life*; its sublation [*Aufhebung*] therefore embraces both aspects'.[60] Aufhebung – negation, preservation, affirmation – of religion is not merely a *passing-through religion* with a whole new destination in mind; no, Aufhebung actually involves *both religious and economic alienation*, the one of consciousness, the other of the tough realities of life. Rather than passing from one to the other (here my train analogy breaks down), it '*embraces both aspects*'. We have come a long way from the atheologians, neo-atheists or even the religionists of my initial semiotic square. If this is atheism, then it is certainly a very different type compared to the atheism with which we are accustomed.

I am by no means the first to trek through these texts, so I have travelled lightly, not burdening myself with more than the bare necessities in order to identify what Marx means by atheism and the Aufhebung of religion.[61] By way of transition to the remainder of the chapter, let me close with an example of how that sublation works itself out in Marx's texts.[62] It comes from a barely used trail in his writing; not so much because it lies hidden in an out-of-the-way corner, drawing perhaps the occasional intrepid reader who is prepared to pull away the cobwebs and dust off the treasure. I speak of the vitally important yet dreadfully neglected third section of *The German Ideology* on Max Stirner. Here both Marx and Engels offer a page-by-page and often sentence-by-sentence critique of Stirner's effort to produce an entirely new world-historical narrative that turns on the radical individual human ego.[63] Patience has its own rewards, for what strikes the persistent reader is that the long struggle with Stirner is very much a theological struggle; one has only to look at the structure of Marx and Engels's criticism, moving through the major books of the Bible and quoting the Bible *ad nauseam*, criticising Stirner's prophetic role and theological dabbling, to see that what is at stake is religion. The outcome: out of that intense struggle with Stirner's theological residue the first clear statement of historical materialism arose. Marx and Engels cut, plane, sandpaper and shape the key pieces of what would become the comprehensive analytical tool of historical materialism, replete with its treatments of class, modes of production, a schema for world history and the lever of that history – the contradictions in class, economics and modes of production. As it is now, that statement turns up in the second and third sections of the first chapter on Feuerbach, where the most significant

60. Marx 1844g, p. 275; Marx 1844h, p. 515; translation modified.
61. For a much fuller discussion see Boer 2012, pp. 140–5.
62. I elaborate upon this example in the first part of Chapter Four.
63. Stirner 2005; Stirner 1845.

replies to Stirner were gathered in the second draft of the text. But my point is that it emerged through an effort not merely at countering, but through an Aufhebung of Stirner's theological and economic arguments, an Aufhebung, if you will, of religious *and* economic alienation.

Freedom of conscience?

All of these theoretical concerns did not merely arise out of Marx's head as he worked his way through mountains of tobacco and bottomless pots of coffee, for they were responses to immediate practical and tactical concerns. Two issues demanded attention from these struggles, the one concerning the policies of the First International and the other concerning freedom of conscience – the two are not unrelated. But what were those very practical struggles? They were part of Marx's experience while editing of the *Rheinische Zeitung* and its tussles with the conservative Protestant and Roman Catholic rags such as the *Kölnische Zeitung*, the *Rhein- und Mosel-Zeitung*, the *Münchener politische Blätter* or the *Trier'sche Zeitung*. Or they involved the heavily Christian nature of the early communism that infiltrated the Prussian borders from France, especially with leaders such as Wilhelm Weitling, Hermann Kriege, Karl Grün and Gottfried Kinkel.[64] Then again, there were intense struggles within the First International, where, apart from these religiously-inspired socialists (Weitling turns up as a signatory on the some of the early circulars from the executive), Marx and Engels often fought against two tendencies. So we find that in that intense altercation with Bakunin and the anarchists, the International steered clear of declaring an explicitly atheistic position. The reason: the trigger-happy Bakunin and company wanted to make atheism an article of political faith, dispense with all cults and replace it all with science. In response to the proposal by Bakunin – 'The Alliance declares itself atheist; it wants abolition of cults, substitution of science for faith and human justice for divine justice' – Marx observes, 'As if one could declare by royal decree abolition of faith!'[65]

The tousle-haired Bakunin might have wanted the International to pin an atheist label to all the coat pockets of members, but there were also former comrades such as Jules Favre or Mazzini who accused the International of precisely such a position. It seems as though the International could not win: it was either not atheist enough or it was too atheist. In response to the latter, Engels

64. Marx and Engels 1845–6a, pp. 484–530; Marx and Engels 1845–6b, pp. 473–520; Marx and Engels 1852a; Marx and Engels 1852b; Marx and Engels 1850a, pp. 528–32; Marx and Engels 1850b, pp. 459–63.

65. Marx 1868, p. 208. See further Marx 1872, p. 142; Engels 1872a, pp. 275–6; Engels 1872b, pp. 169–70; Engels 1870a; Engels 1870b; Marx and Engels 1873a, p. 460; Marx and Engels 1873b, p. 335.

observes: 'As to the charges against the International, they are either untrue or absurd, with regard to the first that it wants to make atheism compulsory, that is untrue'.[66] Add to all of this the accusations by frightened governments, their grovelling agents and the press that the International was a vast and monstrous conspiracy about to overthrow religion; or, as the interviewer from the *Chicago Tribune* put it to Marx, 'You and your followers, Dr. Marx, have been credited with all sorts of incendiary speeches against religion', so much so that 'you would like to see the whole system destroyed, root and branch'. To which Marx replies with a pause and a smile: 'We know... that violent measures against religion are nonsense; but this is an opinion: as Socialism grows, religion will disappear'.[67]

Aufhebung for popular consumption perhaps, but the refusal of the International to promulgate a decree in favour of atheism has at least two reasons: first, any campaign against religious belief is actually a diversion from communist agitation, for it slips into the idealist assumption that the cause of all our ills is religion, that it is evil number one against which we must engage in an almighty battle of beliefs; second, the International actually took up a position that can only be described as radical freedom of conscience. Freedom of conscience? Is that not a central plank of liberalism, in which I can have my beliefs in this corner and you can have yours over there (the need for a brick-veneer house, double-car garage, mortgage, sex toys, 2.4 children and so on)? Does it not presume the primacy of the sacrosanct and private individual – you're cool, I'm cool and we'll all sing Kumbayah? Let us see what Marx and then Rosa Luxemburg have to say.

In a revealing interview with *The World* newspaper, Marx was asked what he thought of religion. In reply, he distinguishes between the International and his own position. So he begins by saying, 'On that point I cannot speak in the name of the society'. But then he clarifies: 'I myself am an atheist.... It is startling, no doubt, to hear such an avowal in England, but there is some comfort in the thought that it need not be made in a whisper in either Germany or France'.[68] Is this a prosaic expression of freedom of conscience on matters of religious belief? I would suggest so, although Marx was ambivalent on the question of freedom of conscience. For example, in an early essay, *Comments on the Latest Prussian Censorship Instruction*, he makes the anti-censorship argument that religion is an inviolable 'subjective frame of mind [*subjectiven Gesinnung*]'.[69] As an argument against censorship, this position is perfectly understandable: at least some areas must be defended against the encroachments of the censor, particularly when

66. Engels 1871a, p. 608; Engels 1871c, p. 28; Engels 1871b, p. 164.
67. Marx 1879, p. 576.
68. Marx 1871c, pp. 605–6.
69. Marx 1843a, p. 121; Marx 1843b, p. 109.

the state is a conservative 'Christian state', with its deeply reactionary set of censorship laws (from the Federal Diet of 1835) that originally targeted revolutionary ideas from France (especially Saint-Simonism after the Revolution of 1830) but were soon extended to any criticism of the state or the church,[70] as well as an eager and snarling press pack ready to tear any dissenter to pieces. Indeed, the censor – with whom Marx had more run-ins than he cared to remember – was guilty of the worst hubris, shoving God off his pedestal and seeking to judge people's hearts in his place.

A hasty assessment of this argument by Marx would be to point out that he wrote it in 1843, when he was still burdened with a few too many liberal (and even Hegelian) assumptions. He did, after all, work for a newspaper, the *Rheinische Zeitung*, backed by the liberal burghers of Cologne. But that would be too hasty. Many years later (1875), when Marx came to write his *Critique of the Gotha Programme*, he attacked the platform of freedom of conscience [*Gewissensfreiheit*] as an old liberal watchword. But now his comments become exceedingly interesting, for while he blasts the hypocrisy of liberalism, he also hints at a more radical freedom of conscience. As for hypocrisy: 'bourgeois "freedom of conscience" is nothing but the toleration of all possible kinds of *unfreedom of conscience*'. Only some religions, or in fact the variations on one religion – Christianity – are free to worship. Jews may be tolerated, but only just. God forbid that one should want to choose Islam, or Hinduism or even atheism. The workers' party should have nothing to do with such a stance. But then, what it might want to do is take the slogan literally, to the immense discomfort of liberals: 'Everyone should be able to attend to his religious as well as his bodily needs without the police sticking their noses in'. And that includes the freedom to 'liberate the conscience from the witchery of religion',[71] should one so wish.

Pay close attention: Marx initially seems to dismiss the whole idea of freedom of conscience as a useless item of liberal ideology, but then he takes another step. A radical freedom of conscience is actually quite uncomfortable for bourgeois liberals, for it would thus entail being able to hold whatever religious, political or economic position one wished – which would thoroughly 'transgress' the bourgeois position. The word Marx uses here – *überschreiten* – is actually quite important. At the close of his comments he offers this sarcastic aside: 'But one chooses not to transgress the "bourgeois" level [*Man beliebt aber das "bürgerliche" Niveau nicht zu überschreiten*]'.[72] Now, *überschreiten* has the sense of crossing, exceeding, coming close to the sense of Aufhebung that I have been tracing in

70. See Rose 1984, pp. 5–23.
71. All quotations are from Marx 1891a, p. 98; Marx 1891b, p. 31.
72. Ibid.

this chapter. In other words, Marx is saying that a radical freedom of conscience passes well beyond, transgresses even its limited liberal sense.[73]

In order to gain a sense of what that radical freedom of conscience might mean, I draw on two elaborations, one from Žižek (with some significant help from Lenin and Claude Lefort) and the other from Rosa Luxemburg. From Žižek comes the distinction between actual freedom and formal freedom. Formal freedom is an apparent freedom, one where the range of choices seems open but they are in fact limited by the boundaries of a particular situation, of existing economic and political coordinates. In opposition to such limited freedom, Lenin would always ask whose interest is served by 'freedom': 'Freedom – yes, but for whom? To do what?'[74] And the purpose was to keep open the possibility of actual freedom, especially in the difficult moment of revolution when it was far too easy to back down and feel that one has gone far enough. Actual freedom, then, is the ability to transcend or transgress the particular context in question. It sees the various presuppositions and limits of a situation for what they are and undermines their claim to constitute the absolute horizon of thought and action. In other words, actual freedom is not the choice between two or more options – say, between two types of cheese at the shop (usually made by the same company) – within a limited situation, but the option of altering that situation. Žižek takes Lenin's distinction and goes on to apply it to Badiou's Being (formal freedom) and event (actual freedom), and the Apostle Paul's law and grace – the 'given coordinates' of a situation (Being, law or formal freedom) must be opposed by the effort to overthrow those coordinates (event, actual freedom and grace). However, I would like to apply them to Marx's comments on freedom of conscience: the bourgeois version is obviously formal freedom, for it sets up such freedom only within the limited possibilities of a capitalist situation. In this light, freedom of religion will only ever mean certain types of acceptable religions, or, for that matter, political options (existing political parties within a given system). By contrast, a radical freedom of conscience transgresses such a limited approach by asserting the full range of choices, above all the one that changes the coordinates of the situation in which freedom of conscience was initially promulgated.

The second elaboration comes from a far too neglected text by Rosa Luxemburg, *Socialism and the Churches*. Responding to the large number of recent recruits to the German Social-Democratic Party and the rabid vilifications of it at the hands of the clergy (nothing much has changed on that score), she writes: 'And here is the answer to all the attacks of the clergy: social democracy in no way

73. For a further discussion of Marx's idea of the communist 'association of free individuals', see Yu and Chu 2001.

74. See Žižek 2001b, p. 114; see also Lenin 1976, pp. 282–3.

fights against religious beliefs. On the contrary, it demands complete freedom of conscience for every individual and the widest possible toleration for every faith and every opinion'.[75] More is going on here than calming the consciences of new members with strong religious commitments, for Luxemburg sees that 'liberty of conscience' is a radical position – 'complete freedom of conscience', she writes, and 'the widest possible toleration'. She realises full well that she cannot attack the brutal censorship of the Czarist régime, which persecuted Jews, Roman Catholics, heretics and freethinkers in Russia and Russian-controlled Poland, and she cannot challenge the church's efforts to control people's beliefs by whatever means available, from state power to the Inquisition, and then argue that the socialists should act in exactly the same way with their members. Unlike all of them, she argues, we assert freedom of conscience.

However, there is a double paradox in freedom of conscience that shows up in both Marx's and Luxemburg's texts. The first is that the slogan of 'freedom of conscience' seems to produce the opposite in the limited form in which we know it today. So, when Friedrich von Hayek or Milton Friedman[76] argue for a link between freedom and capitalism, or freedom of conscience and freedom of speech with the so-called 'free market', it uncannily ends up being oppressive, producing widespread exploitation, poverty and environmental destruction. Or, in the hands of United States imperialism, 'freedom' becomes the ideological justification for invasion and occupation – without even seeing the contradiction, or perhaps in utmost cynicism, they seek to impose 'freedom' on countries (most recently Afghanistan and Iraq), with disastrous consequences.

There is, however, a second and far more interesting paradox – or rather, a properly dialectical point. As a movement that operates primarily from a collective perspective, one would expect that freedom of conscience would be far from such a programme – at least if one believes the critics of socialism such as Hayek, for whom collective will is actually a cover for the imposition of a dictator's will. By contrast, a fully collective programme is precisely one that does not seek to impose the will of one over the other. It involves, rather, a complex effort to allow each one in the collective to express his or her beliefs, foibles and obsessions without the imposition of control and censorship. As for the dialectical point: rather than throwing out the baby of freedom of conscience with the bathwater of liberal ideology, a fully collective programme will enable the full realisation of freedom of conscience. Or, to put it in the terms that Marx first suggested, a full freedom of conscience breaks through the confines of liberal ideology to a much more radical position.

---

75. Luxemburg 1970, p. 152; Luxemburg 1982, p. 46; translation modified.
76. Hayek 1960; Friedman 2002.

Anti-clericalism

Alongside freedom of conscience, another practical component of a materialising theology worth its salt is anti-clericalism, which must immediately be distinguished from atheism. A decent bout of anti-clericalism is always necessary and exceedingly satisfying, if not pleasurable. For example, Engels could, given his background and intimate knowledge of the church, produce some delightful observations. In bed with the ruling classes, whether the remnants of the older nobility or the new bourgeoisie, priests often join a list of the corrupt: 'Gendarmes, priests, lawyers, bureaucrats, lords of the manor in cheerful profusion and a total absence of any and every industry, so that one could barely conceive what all these parasitic plants live on, were there no counterpart in the wretchedness of the peasants'.[77] And in one of his engaging pieces on the military, Engels engages in a tally of available men for service, making the following delightful comment on the exemption of theologians from armed service in Prussia:

> Let us take this further. 1,638 men were deferred or exempted as theologians. Why theologians should be too grand to serve is incomprehensible. On the contrary, a year's army service, living in the open air, and contact with the outside world can only benefit them. So without more ado we will recruit them; 1/3 of the total number for the current year, with 3/4 unfit, still leaves 139 men to be included.[78]

Marx too could fire off a sharp remark, a skill he picked up when writing as a journalist and editor for the *Rheinische Zeitung* in the early 1840s. For instance, commenting on the Paris Commune and the clergy, he writes: 'The priests were sent back to the recesses of private life, there to feed upon the alms of the faithful in imitation of their predecessors, the Apostles'.[79] Or when he found himself on a train between Cologne and Frankfurt, he encountered a Roman Catholic priest (by the name of Mutzelberger), who loosened his tongue after Marx gave him a few swigs of his brandy bottle. At this point, 'the Holy Ghost came to my aid', for Marx was able to get quite a bit from him.[80]

Unfortunately, I can offer only a few out of a myriad of such comments, although one can find long hours of amusement reading them in the works of Marx and Engels, along with Luther and Calvin, Spinoza and Voltaire and many others. I long for a work that catalogues the best of them, especially since my

77. Engels 1856a, p. 49; Engels 1856b, p. 56.
78. Engels 1865a, p. 47; Engels 1865b, p. 47.
79. Marx 1871a, p. 332; Marx 1871b, p. 335.
80. Marx 1875a, pp. 84–5; Marx 1875b, pp. 8–9. See the full list of anti-clerical comments in the work of Marx and Engels in Boer 2012, pp. 37–9.

own background (Reformed or Calvinist, albeit of a wayward type) made anti-clericalism its bread and butter. And I know the church and its small-minded bureaucrats only too well: the smarmy bishop who leans back, resplendent in his purple, and smiles broadly while quietly inserting the knife; the petty power brokers, who make secular government look tame in their efforts, gain control over church coffers; the clerical apologist for the church's appropriation of the latest style of employer tactics, claiming that it will produce better conditions for all those who work for the church; the carer of souls who enacts endless emotional and psychic torture, all in the name of God's compassion. After all, the church has had a good two millennia to refine its skills, focusing on one's most sensitive spot, turning it on the rack and extracting grovelling obedience. Or, as Marx put it: 'General exploitation of communal human nature, just as every imperfection in man, is a bond with heaven – giving the priest access to his heart'.[81]

Yet, I should reiterate that anti-clericalism is not to be confused with atheism. Anti-clericalism is decidedly not the preserve of secular critics, especially on the Left, for it should also be very much part of any theological reflection. One should never tire of castigating, mocking and uncovering corrupt and venal clergy. But now I can also offer a re-reading of the neo-atheists, in part at least, for I read their works, despite the flaws and evangelical zeal, as the latest round of Enlightenment anti-clericalism: where they elide the two, I distinguish between attacks on religion in the name of atheism and criticisms of the clergy of mosques, synagogues and churches. The latter is by far the most productive. Yet, by reading these neo-atheists in this way I have tied them ever more closely in the web of a theological debate they so desperately wish to escape.

Protest atheism and theism

One item remains on my preliminary list for a materialising theology: what may be called protest atheism, which is where I would locate a viable role for atheism within any theology. In the face of all the abuses justified by theology, all the oppression for which theology is the theory, all the reactionary forms that system of thought has taken and all the craven bowing to power and wealth of which theologians have been guilty, atheism becomes a protest. The church can be a cruel institution, screwing up lives and perverting social relations, so much so that its various branches seem to have a reactionary default. In this context, atheism is a necessary protest. But I also suggest that such protest atheism is indispensable for any theology that is honest with itself.

This protest atheism has a long and venerable pedigree, although the operative term is protest. On that score, for any protest atheism one may also find a

81. Marx 1844g, p. 307; Marx 1844h, p. 547.

comparably protesting theism. As Marx observes in that oft-cited statement: '*Religious* suffering is, at one and the same time, the *expression* of real suffering but also the *protest* against real suffering [*Das* religiöse *Elend ist in einem der* Ausdruck *des wirklichen Elendes und in einem die* Protestation *gegen das wirkliche Elend*]'.[82] And Engels, too, with his argument that Christianity was originally a revolutionary movement that appealed to the poor, slaves and proletariat of the Roman Empire,[83] along with his efforts to claim Thomas Müntzer as a revolutionary precursor,[84] fills out this protest dimension of Christianity, so much so that he goes beyond Marx. Luxemburg (briefly) and Kautsky with his encyclopaedic predilections, would take Engels's arguments much further and create a militant tradition of religious protest,[85] and now these arguments reappear in our own time with the work of Alain Badiou and Slavoj Žižek.[86]

However, since I will have much more to say about these arguments in the chapter on ambivalence, I prefer to focus on two of the most articulate proponents of protest atheism. The first is Ernst Bloch, especially with his ingenious argument that Christianity has within it a tendency towards atheism.[87] He is, of course, fully aware of the anachronism – it would be like claiming that the dream of a suburban, brick-veneer home was something that we inherited from the Greeks – but Bloch takes the term in a distinctly political sense. Any protest against the oppressive deity of the Bible, the one who sanctions theocratic tyrants such as Moses, Aaron, David, Solomon or Herod, is an implicitly atheistic protest. In the various myths of the Bible, Bloch discerns an alternative tradition, one that challenges, at times wins over the oppressors, but more often suffers the punishment for rebellion or 'sin' – Eve in the garden, Cain, the builders of Babel, the murmurings in the wilderness, the revolts of Korah and Miriam, Job's cry for some justice, the Nazirites and their ascetic vows, the apocalyptic words of Jesus and the blood-curdling and lurid images of the apocalypse all give voice to an element of protest against the rulers and the God who would protect them. For Bloch this protest becomes a protest against a particular image of an all-powerful God, one of the secret police and white guards, and so one with whom we could well do without.

It seems to me that Horkheimer provides a step beyond Bloch, especially in his essay 'Theism and Atheism'.[88] Horkheimer traces the way *both* theism *and*

82. Marx 1844c, p. 175; Marx 1844d, p. 378; translation modified.
83. Engels 1894–5c; Engels 1894–5d.
84. Engels 1850a; Engels 1850b.
85. Luxemburg 1970; Luxemburg 1982; Kautsky 2007; Kautsky 1977; Kautsky 1947b; Kautsky 1947c; Kautsky and Lafargue 1977.
86. Badiou 2003b; Badiou 1997; Žižek 2000; Žižek 2001b; Žižek 2003.
87. Bloch 1972; Bloch 1968. See also Moltmann 2000a.
88. Horkheimer 1996, pp. 34–50; Horkheimer 1985g. See also Horkheimer 1989b; Bracht, Brückner, Horkheimer, Mitscherlich and Oxenius 1989.

atheism may form the substance of protest and the means of oppression. For Horkheimer, an atheism that resists a compromised religion which has done a deal with the devil of state power is a protest atheism: 'Atheism was once a sign of inner independence and incredible courage, and it continues to be one in authoritarian and semi-authoritarian countries where it is regarded as a symptom of the hated liberal spirit'.[89] What counts is resistance. Any political or social structure that follows the well-oiled groove of oppression must be opposed: religion may do so in the name of allegiance to a totally other, but so also may atheism, especially in light of ponderous cathedrals, prayers for kings, queens and tyrants, state services for the deaths of leaders, the all too common links between property, priests and ruling classes, and indeed church-inspired nationalism.

Horkheimer is fully aware that modern atheism has arrived late on the scene, struggling to gain imaginative traction.[90] So the metaphysical atheism of the Enlightenment or the replacement of God with nature did not get past the circles of cigar-smoking and wine-bibbing radical intellectuals. However, when the context changed, when nation-states came into being, scientific knowledge and technological know-how grew exponentially, populations exploded, world wars took us to new lows of depravity, and, above all, multi-national capitalism spread its web, then was atheism able to produce a historical narrative and gain the institutional power it needed. The catch is that when atheism did achieve its long-sought-after status, it betrayed its oppositional stance in the very same way that Christianity itself had done once it slipped into the seat of power. Now atheism became a state ideology, was institutionalised and became fat with the spoils of power. The manifestation of such a nightmarish outcome was for Horkheimer – at least in his time – fascism, but the point is that atheism, like theism, may easily become an authoritarian power.

The point of all this is that the line of opposition cuts not between atheism and theism, but between betrayal and resistance, oppression and protest. Atheism and theism may, at various times, end up on one or other side of that line. There is no doubt as to which side Horkheimer prefers: 'The idea of a better world has not only been given shape in theological treatises, but often just as well in the so-called "nihilistic" works – the critique of political economy, the theory of Marx and Engels, psychoanalysis – works which have been blacklisted, whether in the east or in the west, and provoked the wrath of the mighty as the inflammatory speeches of Christ did among his contemporaries'.[91] Therefore,

89. Horkheimer 1996, p. 49; Horkheimer 1985g, p. 185.

90. See Horkheimer 1996, pp. 41–5; Horkheimer 1985g, pp. 178–82.

91. Horkheimer 1996, pp. 48–9; Horkheimer 1985g, p. 185. Further, 'Those who professed themselves to be atheists at a time when religion was still in power tended to identify themselves more deeply with the theistic commandment to love one's neighbour

we need to read the situation carefully: when a religion becomes the ideology of a power structure, as we find in medieval states or in the long years of absolute monarchy in Europe, and when it actively sets out to pursue, round up, condemn, expel and execute those who do not toe the line, then atheism becomes an oppositional stand, along with those religions which have been proscribed. But if atheism succeeds in ousting all religion and becomes in its own turn the dominant ideology of a repressive state apparatus, then religion itself becomes a position of opposition to such a situation.

Perhaps the most significant ramification of Horkheimer's argument is that theism and atheism – as he tends to call the pair – may form what I have elsewhere called a politics of alliance.[92] While Horkheimer directs his comments at the historical alliance between atheism and the Left (at least from the time following Marx and Engels), my argument is directed at both the secular Left and the religious Left. Both may indeed find common ground in the struggle against forms of coercion and tyranny – as we find in the common struggle of some of the Christian churches and the Communist Party in South Africa during the apartheid era, or as we find today in the links between Christian, Muslim and Left groups in the Palestinian resistance against Israeli state oppression, or as we encounter in the anti-globalisation movement, where religiously-inspired radicals join with the coalition of the Left in opposing the depredations of capitalism and enacting the possibility of another world.[93]

Conclusion

I will keep this brief: out of the various possibilities for atheism and theology, the most promise lies in a materialising theology, in which theology, without shying away and becoming defensive, is taken all the way through historical materialism. This process provides us with what Marx called the Aufhebung of religion, the sublation of not only religion, but of both religious and economic alienation. And that led me to a reassessment of freedom of conscience, a call for the necessary role of anti-clericalism, as well as the realisation that the crucial opposition is not between atheism and theism, but between resistance and oppression, between protest and doing deals in the boardroom. Both theism and atheism have been and continue to appear on both sides, but I for one side with protest theism and atheism.

---

and indeed all created things than most adherents and fellow-travellers of the various denominations' (Horkheimer 1996, pp. 49–50; Horkheimer 1985g, pp. 185–6).

92. Boer 2007b, pp. 33–49.

93. See also Horkheimer's comments on the common ground of Marxism and Christianity in Horkheimer 1985m, p. 299; Horkheimer 1985o, pp. 312–13.

I close on a different note, one which uncannily illustrates my last point. In the first years of the early church, Christians were dubbed by the Romans *atheioi*, atheists. They were, in the eyes of the majority, suspicious characters, rumoured to engage in human sacrifice, anti-social activities, disrespect for civil order and insurrection. Above all, they did not believe in the gods, offer them sacrifices or show them any respect. Apart from the point that monotheism is closer to atheism than one might at first suspect (at one remove, in fact), what catches my attention with this polemic against the early Christians is a grain of truth: they were rabble-rousers, threats to good social order; in short, there is an element of resistance and protest that the Romans picked up. And that possibility may be found in either theism or atheism.

Chapter Two
Myth

> The question here is not of the death-of-fantasy as such, but of the destruction and deliverance of myth in a single dialectical moment . . .[1]

After the opening discussion of theism, atheism and theology, the next three chapters form a unit. I begin with the question of myth, especially what I call political myth, and then move on to political ambivalence, both of which are central features of the difficult affair of Marxism and Christianity. However, I am interested not merely in the workings of myth and political ambivalence, which I explore at some length in this and the following chapter, but also in the simple question of *why?* Why is Christianity given to political myths and why is that religious tradition torn so often between reactionary and revolutionary tendencies? In order to answer those questions, I turn in the fourth chapter to consider the question of history.

As for myth, it is not restricted to a religion like Christianity, for Marxism too has its share of political myths, although I have come across a good number of Marxists who react quite negatively to the suggestion. Indeed, myth is not an obvious topic for those accustomed to the firm ground of reason and rational political agents, the banishing of shadows with the Enlightenment or the staunch secularism of the Left. Nevertheless, as will become clear in this chapter, I do not argue a minimal position, namely that myth has a

---

1. Bloch 1972, p. 37; Bloch 1968, p. 67. Translation modified.

knack of appearing when theology and Marxism rub together, for I prefer the stronger position that myth is inescapable and even sorely needed within both. The subject matter of this chapter falls into three main sections: the political nature of myth, with a warning from Adorno and a bringing into relief of Bloch's discernment of myth for the sake of identifying the cunning of myth; a comprehensive strengthening of the anticipatory and utopian function of myth by means of a motley collection of arguments that runs all the way from Georges Sorel, through Althusser, Badiou, Deleuze and Guattari, to the analogical argument for God's existence; and then three examples, drawn from Barthes, Jameson and Christian communism, of the utopian drive of political myth.

This rather long argument requires a prolegomenon, largely because the chapter represents a significant development of an earlier argument concerning political myth.[2] In order to set the scene, I offer a brief sketch of that earlier argument, as well as situate what I call poligonic (or political) myth within the traditional designations of myth in terms of theogony, cosmogony and anthropogony. The final part of the prolegomenon draws upon the work of Bruce Lincoln, who identifies a deep ambivalence in the opposition between *mythos* and *logos* in the Greek heritage of those terms. In doing so, I engage in some subversive etymology in order to dig out alternative possibilities, an act that also undermines the classicist assumptions of such etymologies (as I mentioned in the Introduction).

Before I go any further, a brief word is needed on the relation between ideology and myth, between ideology critique and myth criticism. Is myth analysis really another version of the well-honed critique of ideology? At one level, it could be argued that myth is a subset of ideology, especially if we take Lincoln's definition of myth as 'ideology in narrative form'. Thus, myth in its various shapes takes its place alongside the other subsets of ideology such as literature, philosophy, religion, custom, and so on. Further, we could apply to myth the well-oiled distinction I mentioned in the Introduction, between 'critical' and 'descriptive' approaches, between the critique of ideology as false consciousness (which then needs correction) and the understanding of ideology as an inescapable feature of human existence. If so, then all we need do is apply to myth the various categories of ideological analysis – Marx, Lenin, Gramsci, Althusser, at least to begin with – and leave it at that. At this point theological suspicion, which I discussed at some length in the Introduction, comes into play: myth criticism is one form that such a suspicion may take. The upshot is that myth criticism has the same relation to ideology critique as theological suspicion, namely as a subset with its own particular identity. In other words, *Mythologiekritik* should occupy a

2. Boer 2009d, pp. 9–35. This chapter also draws and elaborates on scattered elements of Boer 2007a, Boer 2009b, and Boer 2010a.

separate seat from *Ideologiekritik*, even if they are within earshot of one another. Once given some space, myth criticism may pursue its own path, characterised in my own discussion by an astute cunning, by its nature as the powerful fiction of a completed truth and by the virtual power of its reverse causality. In what follows I explore these terms in much more depth to show how they work in developing the idea of political myth.

Prolegomenon

When it comes to definitions of myth, I prefer the shortest: myth is an important story. Sacrifice brevity and we enter the manifold and criss-crossing paths of valiant but desperate efforts to produce a catch-all definition.[3] But I do need to reflect on two common understandings of myth, one that myths are by definition false and simultaneously speak of a deeper truth and the other that myths are (usually) ancient stories that concern origins. I will have more to say on the fiction/deeper-truth dichotomy when I come to discuss the tension between *mythos* and *logos*.

Poligony

As far as ancient founding or origin myths are concerned, it is customary to distinguish between theogonic, cosmogonic and anthropogonic myths: stories concerning the origins of the gods, the cosmos and the human beings. The ancient Babylonian myth, *Enuma Elish*, contains all three in glorious detail, beginning with the generation of the gods, the conflict between them (especially Marduk's vanquishing of his mother Tiamat) and then moving on to tell how the world and then, as an afterthought, how human beings were created.[4] Or, to use an example with which I am extremely familiar (as a sometime biblical scholar), the creation myths of the Hebrew Bible forgo the theogonic element (although

---

3. Northrop Frye offers a refreshingly concise definition with which I can agree: 'myth is a form of imaginative and creative thinking' (Frye 1982, p. 35), which is slightly better than Lincoln's 'ideology in narrative form' (Lincoln 2000, p. 207). But then, a few years later, Frye succumbed to the temptation to be more encyclopaedic: myth tells a society 'the important things for that society to know about their gods, their traditional history, the origins of their custom and class structure' (Frye 1990, p. 30). Here Frye falls in with the crowd, which includes those dreadful followers of Mircea Eliade and the Chicago School of History of Religions, who seek an all-embracing definition that tries to cover narrative, subject matter, cultural status (myths as true for a distinct community) and social functions (ideology). See further Flood 2002, pp. 2–6.

4. Pritchard (ed.) 1955, pp. 60–72. See further Boer 2006c.

there are still echoes in the stories of Genesis and the poetic material of Job),[5] but the other two are present, famously in the two accounts of creation in Genesis 1 and 2.

What, then, of the poligonic? If we stay with the example of the Hebrew Bible, then, in order to see how a political tone enters the accounts of creation in the Bible, we need to move beyond the common assumption (at least for many biblical scholars) that myth is restricted to the first eleven chapters of Genesis. Instead, I suggest that the whole account from Genesis to Joshua, from creation through exile, exodus and on to the Promised Land, is a complex political myth.[6] At this level, the text resembles the political myth of *Enuma Elish*, the final concern of which is to indicate that Babylon has been established as the city of the gods and that the kingship flows in a direct line from the warrior god, Marduk. And when we consider the whole stretch of text from Genesis to Joshua, two features of the narrative become obvious. Firstly, the anthropogonic element of this myth ceases to be restricted to the male and female pair (a focus that smacks more of foreign heterosexual sensibilities and the bourgeois nuclear family) and becomes decidedly collective. Here, we find seemingly endless genealogies, the first beginning in Genesis and the last finishing in Joshua after passing through a book that is by and large devoted to genealogies, namely Numbers. Even the genealogies, overwhelming as they are in a way that often sends one off to sleep, are but one element in a far larger collective anthropogony. Once we have moved on from the descendants of Abraham, Sarah and Hagar in Genesis and open the pages of Exodus, the text deals not with individuals but a people, the children of Israel. And just when we think we have finally, after interminable delay, arrived at the point of the birth of the people, we are in for a much longer wait as this people gradually becomes a state.

By now we are in the midst of what I have called the poligonic. Cosmogony and anthropogony are also very much the concern of poligony and my efforts to separate the threads only show how closely they are wound together. Of course,

5. What seems to have happened is that the genealogies of the gods have become the genealogies of men (and I use the term quite deliberately): thus the phrase 'these are the genealogies of the heavens and the earth when they were created' at the beginning of the second creation narrative in Genesis 2:4 finds its echo in 'This is the book of the genealogies of Adam' (Genesis 5:1) that then winds its way through the narrative until Terah, the father of Abram in Genesis 11:24–6. Again and again we find 'these are the genealogies of…' in a way that purports to be about human beings and yet is saturated with the theogonic.

6. In this respect I follow Brenner, who describes it as an 'inauguration myth' or a 'liberation-cum-inauguration myth' (Brenner 1994, p. 11), and Lemche, for whom it is, along with the story of the Exile to Babylon, a 'foundation myth' (Lemche 1998, pp. 86–132). Even Dever can write, 'No scholar, revisionist or otherwise, thinks these materials anything other than "myth"' (Dever 2001, p. 98, n. 1).

the narrative of the birth of a people and then of a state is poligonic – this is stating the obvious. But let me outline the main themes of such a poligonic narrative. The first is the perpetually delayed double-promise to Abraham: in an increasingly frenetic tempo, God promises Abraham, the 'father of many', that a great people will issue from his loins and that they will have a land of their own. The first may, with much procrastination, appear with the arrival in Egypt (when they are without a land) and the second is realised only with the conquest of Canaan in the Book of Joshua. The other three themes are the escape from Egypt, wandering in the wilderness and conquest of the land. Fundamental themes of so many political myths that draw upon these texts, the escape from Egypt marks firstly the constitution of a people, with its own leadership, ritual and religious identity. The wilderness then brings about the birth of a state, landless, in exile, but a state nonetheless: here we have the law from Mount Sinai, of which most of the instructions (Exodus 23–7) concern the construction of the Tabernacle, priestly roles and vestments, the establishment of a judiciary (the 70 elders of Exodus 18), a body of religious professionals and an army. All of which puts them in a somewhat ready state for the third and final theme – the conquest of the land under Joshua. As many biblical critics have pointed out, the Promised Land permeates the text that precedes its narrative arrival, for many of the 613 laws make little sense except for a settled people involved in the annual cycles of agriculture.

The poligonic is, then, an inescapable feature of the long and multi-faceted myth in the Bible that runs from Genesis to Joshua; indeed, the poligonic permeates that text in a way that makes the theogonic, cosmogonic and anthropogonic subsidiary. And so it has been with the political myths that have drawn their inspiration from these texts, whether they were the myths of absolute monarchy in Europe, or the emerging nation-states after the French Revolution, or the underlying narratives of conquest and state formation from the Americas to Africa.

Yet, all of this merely situates my argument for political myth within the conventional understandings of myth as ancient and not-so-ancient tales of origin. In my *Political Myth*, I sought to go beyond such terms and develop, at least in preliminary fashion, a theory of political myth which might then be applied, critically, to situations in our own day, such as Australian and US foreign policy and the struggles over climate change. I do not wish to re-enter those debates here, save to summarise the theoretical argument, which acts a backdrop to the further developments of this chapter. In that argument, I sought to develop a dialectical theory of myth that is indebted to Marxist, feminist and psychoanalytic currents. Above all, I made extensive use of what may be called the constitutive exception, which owes significant debts to the psychoanalysis that comes to us through Lacan and has been mediated by Žižek, especially when he was more strictly Lacanian. I sought to give this constitutive exception a dialectical twist via Ernst Bloch, especially through what may be called the cunning of myth, in which subversive elements within myths have a knack of emerging out from beneath the hot blanket of repression. And so, as I engaged with both myths of reaction and revolution, I focused on two key phrases, facing the beast and the cunning of myth. By grasping the beast from one's shoulder and staring it in the face, I argued that the Left should call the bluff on political myths of reaction by forcing the constitutive exception, the unnamed and feared underside of such myths, to be revealed, which really means that the Left should ask what those myths might look like should they be realised. These myths of the Right always have an underside, so one task of the Left is to bring that repressed dimension to the surface, to tell the whole myth. So I pursued three closely related questions: what if we tell the full story? What if the Right should realise its political myth? What might be our response? In answering these questions, I brought the cunning of myth into play, arguing that however much the forces of political reaction may seek to impose their stamp on myth, there is always a subversive element that escapes such a stamp. Or rather, such reactionary myths produce subversion in the very act of mythmaking – hence the cunning of myth.

The outcome was a definition of political myth that went as follows: political myth involves the construction of labyrinthine eschatological worlds characterised by a dialectic of reaction and subversion. While reaction potently produces the opposition which it perpetually closes down, while reaction constructs fantasies that carefully conceal a horror that it has constructed, myth has a cunning knack of twisting out of such a stranglehold to hold out the possibility that myth is also the powerful fiction of a completed truth. In its various permutations, I traced the shape of such myth through the first six books of the Bible (Genesis to Joshua) and then criticised the way that such myths have been reappropriated, twisted and turned to new uses in our own day.

It will soon become clear that some elements of this approach to political myth may be found in the argument of the remainder of this chapter, particularly a dialectical reading of myth in light of that myth's cunning. However, as I worked at the previous volumes of *The Criticism of Heaven and Earth*, it became clear that my earlier foray into political myth fell short in a number of respects. So as I began developing the argument for this chapter, I left some of the psychoanalytic scaffolding behind and focused more resolutely on the Marxist permutations of political myth. So I return to Bloch and Adorno in order to offer a more extended reflection on political myth. But I also draw upon Althusser, Badiou and Deleuze and Guattari in that elaboration, before picking up some disparate examples from Roland Barthes, Fredric Jameson and the myth of Christian communism.

Mythos and logos

The final section of this prolegomenon constitutes one of a series of etymological forays, which function to undermine such an exercise in the very act of resorting to the ancient Greeks. It draws upon the ambivalence of the terms *mythos* and *logos*, especially in light the infamous 'Greek miracle' in which *logos* is supposed to have risen from the depths, clung onto a piece of dry earth and eventually ousted *mythos* from its throne. The catch here is that we assume we know what these terms mean: *mythos* is the fabled and fabling speech of poets and story-tellers, speaking of the gods and earth and men, of theogony, cosmogony and anthropogony, particularly in those texts of Hesiod and Homer from the 'heroic' age of Greek history; *logos*, by contrast is rational speech, the word of the philosophers such as Plato against the poets and dreamers. Not so, it seems, for *mythos* itself has always been a contested term, and *logos* has not always held the ground of straight, rational speech.

As Lincoln has persuasively argued,[7] contrary to what might be expected, *mythos* in the work of Hesiod and Homer is not the realm of fiction and fantasy, nor does it designate stories of the capricious gods, and it is far from the sense of a symbolic or sacred story, one with a deeper meaning than everyday language. *Mythos* is actually strong speech, muscular, forthright and brave. It is uttered by heroes and warriors, leaders among the ruling, propertied elite. Powerful males, arrogant and brutal, speak *mythoi* in the heat of battle or in struggles over opinion in the assembly. By contrast, *logos* is often laden with some telling adjectives and companions: seductive [*haimulios*], evil [*kakos*], falsehoods [*pseudea*] and disputes [*amphilogia*]. *Logos* turns out to be the weapon of the weak. Wily, deceitful, seductive and quarrelsome, it is the mode preferred by those without power, such as women, slaves, peasants, children and outcasts. Unable to match the brute force of powerful men, those who deploy *logoi* do so in order to win by other means. Needless to say, in the works of Hesiod and Homer *logos* does not have a good press, for in *logoi* the strong do not speak.

How then did Plato (and indeed Heraclitus) manage to sweep the field and bring about a complete revaluing of these terms? Lincoln traces in detail how the two terms were discursively contested over the centuries from Homer to Plato, how the supreme position of poetry in an oral culture held its place long in Greek history, and how *mythos* maintained its place as the weapon of the strong until quite late. But eventually, with the shift from an oral to a written culture, from an archaic economy to a slave-based one, from isolated city-states to modest empires, the *mythoi* of the poets came to be seen as deceitful, their words weaving spells rather than speaking the truth, and *logos* took its familiar place

7. Lincoln 2000, pp. 3–43.

(at least to us): the straight speech of truth, the voice of reason and thought, the preferred mode of speech of that new breed who called themselves philosophers. The first signs appear with Presocratics such as Heraclitus and Democritus, who favour *logos* and simply neglect *mythos*, but it is Plato who enables the significant if contested victory of *logos*. However, the fact that Plato had to banish poets and playwrights from his *Republic*, that Socrates (even if he was a construct of Plato's writing) was condemned for corrupting young wealthy men with his *logoi*, indicates that the terrain remained deeply contested.

Three points emerge that are important for my analysis of myth. As for the first point, let me put it this way: inevitably, in discussions over myth, one interlocutor will knowingly speak up and say that 'we' know that myth does not mean a fictional fairy tale, unlike the common folk. Instead, myth really designates a way of speaking about a deeper truth – usually these knowledgeable types are theologians. But that very objection actually narrates a historical progression in the understanding of myth, passing from the 'common' understanding of myth as fictional tale to one that has a deeper meaning, which is precisely the way myth was recovered in the eighteenth century. Not only is such an argument truncated, but it also misses a crucial ambivalence in myth, for it is not a case of either fiction or deeper truth, but very much both/and. When I come to the matter of Christian communism, I deploy this ambivalence to the advantage of such a political myth.

Second, *mythos* and *logos* are deeply political terms, not only in their usage in the texts, but in the struggles over the dominance of one over the other in the context of changing political and economic circumstances. This deeply political sense imbues my own reading of myth. Third, by the time the word was bequeathed to us, preserved in Plato's texts, it had a history that left it with an ambivalent, if not multivalent sense: language of both the strong and the deceitful, of both the brutal and the spinners of tales, of the forthright and the deceptive. I would suggest that what happened with the transition between the time of Homer and Hesiod and that of Plato is that we have not only a contested shift in the fortunes of *mythos* and *logos*, where they seem to exchange places and then mutate again, but also a mutual absorption of their contrasting senses within one another. Myth can be both truthful speech and wily tale, club of the strong and hidden weapon of the weak. My interest is in that wily, deceptive and subversive element of myth, either the *logos* of the archaic Greeks or the *mythos* of the arrogant Plato.

One last point: myth was finally recovered and Plato's championing of *logos* contested only towards the end of the eighteenth century in the wake of the Renaissance. In the intervening period, myths (Latin: *fabulae*) were treated as amusing, if somewhat childish stories, folktales of a dim and distant past, contrasted with both philosophy and the authoritative story of Christ. But the rediscovery of classical Greek and Roman texts produced some unexpected outcomes, one of which was the reshaping of the sense of myth as a valuable story of one's own past, none more so than that of Northern Europe. Now it becomes a symbolic and sacred story, one with deep import, expressing a truth as no other can. As economic and political power gradually shifted northward and as the shackles of the Mediterranean were thrown off, myth became tied up with the issue of the *Volk*, asserting an ancient superiority and power that eventually became the Aryan and then Indo-European hypothesis. Civilisation, argued the new narrative, began neither in the Mediterranean, nor in the ancient Near East, but further north or perhaps further east, anywhere from India to the Caucasus to the Arctic Circle (favoured by the Nazis). And a string of often venerable names are attached to this recovery: Herder, Grimm, Max Müller, Nietzsche, Edward Jones (the founder of modern linguistics and the Indo-European hypothesis) and Georges Dumézil.

I have recounted this brief tale of the changing fortunes of myth in order to situate the following discussion. It thus becomes easier to see why such a panoply of significant Marxists were and are suspicious of myth, including Adorno, Benjamin, Louis Marin[8] and Alain Badiou today. They respond to the baleful recovery of myth and its racist ties with the *Volk*, especially the appropriation by the Nazis and the outing of its deeply anti-semitic nature. Perfectly understandable is such an approach to myth, although it does stand in the tradition of Plato's valorisation of *logos* over against *mythos*. By contrast, Bloch offers a reading of myth that is fully aware of the ambivalence within myth, especially if we keep in mind the way *mythos* and *logos* swapped places and in the process mingled their meanings, being both the language of the repressively strong and wily weak, the preferred speech both of poets and mythologues and of calm rationality. Bloch opts, as we shall see, for a dialectical reading of myth that is fully cognisant of both senses within myth, albeit in a distinctly political register. But Bloch also challenges the recovered sense of myth that I have traced briefly above. All-too aware of its recent (in his time) baleful pedigree, it is as though Bloch has recovered the ambivalent and contested status of myth, with an eye out for its cunning, for the modes by which the weak challenge the rulers and even win through now and then.

8. Marin 1984. For Marin, myth and utopia are thoroughly incompatible, for myth blocks the way to utopia while utopia drops myth far behind.

Political myth

Now I turn to elaborate on the theory of political myth, doing so with a distinctly Marxist bent, seeking to go beyond my earlier study and keeping in mind the ambivalences within myth that emerged from those Eastern Europeans, the ancient Greeks. My closest conversation partners are Adorno and Bloch, the one profoundly suspicious of myth, the other a great champion of the political and utopian functions of myth. Beware of myth, Adorno warns us, for it provides one dreadfully gloomy narrative after another of domination, discrimination and repressive social order. Myth marks the moment when the tyrant bolts the gate, cracks his knuckles and sets to work, a sadistic smile on his face. Bloch, however, is not so sure that Adorno's account tells the whole story, for myth is too cunning to allow the tyrant to have the last word.

Adorno's wariness

Two charges may be laid at the feet of myth, at least according to Adorno: it is a narrative of oppression and it has left any subversive possibility well behind, perhaps in the realms of pre-mythical magic. In other words, Adorno is profoundly suspicious of myth, particularly in terms of the famed dialectic of myth and enlightenment. Nevertheless, it is worth listening to Adorno's reasons, in case we should be too bright and cheery about the subversive possibilities of myth. I begin with his most well-known argument, which appears in the discussion with Max Horkheimer that became the first two sections of *Dialectic of Enlightenment*, namely 'The Concept of Enlightenment' and especially 'Odysseus or Myth and Enlightenment'.[9] Here, Odysseus becomes the prototypical bourgeois, the prime instance of the way enlightenment – which Adorno and Horkheimer trace back to the Greeks – inevitably brings myth back in the very process of banishing it as so much superstition. Or, to put it in terms of the classic Adornoesque dialectic, if we push enlightenment far enough, dragging it to those murky places where it definitely does not wish to go, then myth turns up, blurting out the dirty secret that it is inseparable from the programme of enlightenment itself.

That myth Adorno finds unremittingly baleful.[10] It is synonymous with deception, false clarity, fixation, domination, exploitation (not least of women, but also

9. Horkheimer and Adorno 2002; Horkheimer and Adorno 2003. See also his suspicions of Wagner's wholesale and deadly recovery of a very political myth in Adorno 1981, pp. 114–24; Adorno 2003e, pp. 109–22; Adorno 2002a, pp. 589–90; Adorno 2003o, pp. 549–50.

10. Although he does, perhaps under the influence of theologians such as Paul Tillich and Rudolf Bultmann, consider what myth that has been thoroughly demythologised might look like. See Adorno and Benjamin 1999, pp. 127–8; Adorno and Benjamin 1994, pp. 168–9.

of nature) and the repression necessary for individual subjectivity to emerge. Myth must be uncovered and countered in whatever way possible; thus, to argue that myth is already enlightenment and that enlightenment generates ever more virulent forms of myth is a critique of enlightenment itself and not a retrieval of myth. Given the context in which Adorno did much of his work – the Nazi appropriation of myth in terms of the blond beast and of blood and soil – we can well understand the ideological suspicion that a Marxist of Jewish background would direct at myth, especially in light of the way the recovery of myth in nineteenth-century scholarship was connected so closely with the new-found nationalism and the Aryan/Indo-European hypothesis.[11] In this respect, Adorno shares the deeper wariness of myth that we find among Benjamin, Barthes and Badiou.

Is there any glimmer of insurrection? Not in myth, suggests Adorno, although we may find it in some pre-mythic moment. Let us see how his argument develops, particularly in the reading of the Sirens in Homer's *Odyssey*.[12] Here, Odysseus blocks the ears of his rowers with wax so they will not be tempted and seduced by the Sirens' song, but Odysseus himself orders the rowers to tie him, as tightly as they can, to the ship's mast so that he can hear the song but do nothing about it. Of course, Odysseus begs and cries out to his men to release him when he hears the song, but they calmly keep rowing, oblivious to their master's cries. For Adorno and Horkheimer, this is a prime instance of the dialectic of myth and enlightenment: here we find the simultaneous separation and subjection to one another of those who labour and those who do not (Odysseus bound to the mast and the men to the oars); the rationalisation and ordering of labour, which is now done under compulsion and without pleasure, becoming part of the machine while being unable to communicate; the parting of the ways between enjoyment of art and manual labour (while Odysseus can hear and contemplate the beauty of the song, the rowers do not hear it at all); the separation of intellect and sensuous experience in order to unify the former and subjugate the latter. In short, it is Hegel's master-slave dialectic *avant la lettre* – the proletarians who can no longer hear about their situation over against the immobile master trapped in the immaturity of domination. Odysseus is the proto-typical burgher.

However, the last point overlaps with the remarkably sympathetic reading of Polyphemous, the Cyclops.[13] Apart from the tension of subjectivity – Odysseus plays on his own name, responding to the Cyclops's question by saying that *Udeis*,

11. See especially Lincoln 2000, pp. 47–137.
12. Horkheimer and Adorno 2002, pp. 25–9; Horkheimer and Adorno 2003, pp. 55–60.
13. Horkheimer and Adorno 2002, pp. 50–4; Horkheimer and Adorno 2003, pp. 88–95.

Nobody, is there – that enables Odysseus's escape, Adorno and Horkheimer point out that the source of the remarkable power of the Cyclops is that they are older than the gods. That is, they come from before the law and social organisation, so whereas they seem to lack the laws of civilisation – they eat human beings and fend for themselves – they show compassion to their animals and to one another, a compassion lacking in Odysseus. For law and organisation are the objectifications of domination and what we find in myth is the exploration and establishment of law and organisation of society, as well as the patterns of the subjugation of women.[14]

I do not wish to dismiss Adorno's points lightly, for all-too often the great myths of formation of the state – poligonic myths, as I have called them[15] – spend a huge amount of narrative time on the suppression of rebellion, the delivery of the law, the emergence of a state, conquest of a land, the organisation of society and of the relations between the sexes. Any reading of, for example, the narrative from Genesis to Joshua in the Bible, or *Enuma Elish* from Babylon, will make this abundantly clear. In the *Odyssey*, the narrative shift that takes Odysseus from Circe (who tries in vain to get him to stay) to Penelope marks the transition from matriarchy to marriage: woman becomes both courtesan and wife.[16] Here, we find an assumed but never developed schema in which the first term marks something lost in myth: matriarchy to marriage, savagery to barbarism (Lewis Henry Morgan peeks over the page at this point),[17] animal to human individuation and subjectivity, magic to myth. The catch is that Adorno and Horkheimer refuse to explore what magic, matriarchy, human animality and savagery might actually entail.

Is it possible, in Adorno's account, to speak of a dialectic, not of myth and enlightenment, but of revolution and reaction in myth? Only if we widen our scope to include the pre-mythic or magical phase and myth itself; but even then it is less of a dialectic than a melancholy narrative of closure and oppression. Soon enough, I will turn to Bloch for a sense of that dialectic within myth, but

14. At this point Adorno shares an assumption concerning myth with Lévi-Strauss, particularly as we find it in his *The Raw and the Cooked* (Lévi-Strauss 1994). In an extraordinary *tour de force*, Lévi-Strauss relates 187 myths from South-American indigenous tribes to one fundamental structure, namely the passage from barbarism to society through the motif of food. The preparation of food, a process of moving from what is raw to what is cooked, marks the moment of social formation and ordering, in short, to culture. In contrast to the passage from raw to cooked, the other passage is from fresh to rotten, the mark of the lack of culture, of society and organisation. The difference from Adorno is that Lévi-Strauss's narrative is somewhat more benign, a necessary process rather than the imposition of an oppressive régime.

15. Boer 2005–6.

16. Horkheimer and Adorno 2002, pp. 54–9; Horkheimer and Adorno 2003, pp. 88–94.

17. Morgan 1877.

I am loath to dismiss too quickly the point that myth embodies rationalisation, social organisation, codifications of class, establishment of the law and so on. But what happens when myth does begin to look slightly less bleak? Is the inevitable recurrence of myth always such a bad turn of events? If not, then the eternal return of myth need not be a moment weighed down with foreboding. The dark alleyways and mythic slums of enlightenment become not so much the zones of barbarism into which enlightenment slips all too readily; instead, they may become possible zones of insurrection, the source of barricades and resistance. I would suggest, to begin with, that such a possibility emerges from within the dialectic of enlightenment itself. Initially, Adorno and Horkheimer operate with the assumption that enlightenment in its various historical moments is the realm of *logos* and reason, but that it always carries within it an oppressive *mythos*, not merely as an undermining feature of *logos*, but as constitutive of it. However, as the dialectic proceeds, they effectively absorb *mythos* and *logos* into one another in a way that I have sought to do earlier in my etymological foray into the shifts and ambivalences in the ancient Greek senses of the term. Once paired in this way, the terms and their senses begin to shift, exchanging positions and taking on one another's identities.[18]

Most importantly, I would suggest that myth does not merely justify repressive measures and thereby lock them into place; it explores the tensions and contradictions that make these problems in the first place.[19] To be sure, myth so often closes down the contradictions in the end, but not before it has given considerable space to them, and they are *precisely those contradictions that would render a social and economic order unviable*. Myth enables the airing of such contradictions because they cannot be entertained within certain social organisations. But I have run ahead of myself, for the possibility of reading myth in a slightly better light, of employing a dialectic that is not merely negative, requires Ernst Bloch to make an appearance.

Discernment

By this time, it has probably become obvious that I have a soft spot for the stern and prophetic Ernst Bloch. On this occasion, I wish to draw two insights from him concerning myth: the need for discernment and the anticipatory function

18. Or, to take an example from Adorno's formidable book on Kierkegaard, the tendency for Kierkegaard's efforts to avoid myth – through inwardness, history, the search for a mythless Christianity – to slip back into myth is not necessarily detrimental. See Adorno 1989; Adorno 2003a. See also Boer 2007a, pp. 395–421.

19. In this respect, Burton Mack is mistaken when he argues that such excesses in myths are the result of both compression and exaggeration, the concentration of the social roles and forces that structure a society as a whole. See Mack 2008, p. 79.

of myth. While Badiou, Adorno, Negri and even Benjamin, along with many others on the Left, are suspicious of anything that smells ever so slightly of myth, mysticism or theology, Bloch is one of the greatest proponents of myth for the Left. Rather than give myth a wide berth, casting distasteful looks in its direction, Bloch warns us against the knee-jerk mistrust of myth, for it can be revolutionary as well as reactionary. He understands all-too well the reasons why we should be 'wary of the mythical sphere in its entirety',[20] especially after the experience of fascist myths of blood and soil; yet he points out that the 'myths' so unceremoniously dumped by hard-nosed historical materialists also contain stories of murmuring, subversion and rebellion. Bloch is wary of proposing a wholesale recovery of myth, for this would open him up to charges of primitivism and obscurantism, of being a woolly-headed romantic who had thrown out all that was good about the Enlightenment. (Bloch was touchy about these matters, for he was often regarded with suspicion by fellow communists for precisely such leanings.) Yet if we ban myth, he argues, then 'the primitive, uncultured specters are thrown out, but the directives and announcements from on high remain to haunt as they always did'.[21]

The solution to this tension between discarding and preservation is the *discernment of myth*, which is really a dialectical reading of myth that neither throws myth out wholesale nor takes myth uncritically as a positive dimension of human culture. For Bloch, myth is neither pure false consciousness that needs to be unmasked, nor is it a positive force without qualification.[22] No matter how repressive, all myths have an emancipatory-utopian dimension about them that cannot be separated so easily from deception and illusion. In the very process of manipulation and domination, one finds a utopian residue that has not been entirely incinerated in the white heat of reaction, an element that opens up other possibilities at the very point of failure. Bloch is particularly interested in biblical myth, for the subversive elements in the myths that interest him are enabled by the repressive ideologies that show through again and again. If the Bible is not always folly to the rich, it is also the Church's bad conscience.

Bloch develops his position in debate, not so much with other Marxists (although they were certainly in his sights) but with an unexpected interlocutor: the great and very Lutheran New Testament scholar Rudolf Bultmann,[23] who proposed a programme of demythologisation of the Bible and theology. For Bultmann, the Bible contains the forms of thought, language and belief of the

20. Bloch 1998, p. 296; Bloch 1985c, p. 339.
21. Bloch 1972, p. 34; Bloch 1968, p. 64.
22. As may be seen in one of the best books I have ever read, the extraordinary but neglected work, *Atheism in Christianity* (Bloch 1972; Bloch 1968).
23. Bultmann 1984; Bultmann 1951; Bultmann 1952; Bultmann 1948. See also my extended discussion of this debate in Boer 2013c.

time in which its various parts were composed. In short, the dominant mode of expression was myth. However, for the *kerygma*, the message of the gospel, to be meaningful in the very different economic and culture situation of the early twentieth century, this mythological structure ought to be retired after many years of sterling service. Bultmann did not have in mind the accretions that had gathered over time – priests, pomp and hocus pocus – but the central features of Christianity that were drawn from the New Testament. So he proposed that the three-tiered cosmos with heaven above and hell below, the idea that Jesus descends from heaven to become a child and then a man, the virgin birth, the miracles of Jesus, especially the empty tomb, resurrection and ascension to heaven, the coming of the Holy Spirit and the return of Christ on the clouds at the end of history, should all be discarded as part of an outmoded mythic framework. But Bultmann did not stop there, for the demythologising was merely the first step; next came what might be called a re-mythologisation and he sought to accomplish this in terms of the existentialism that had swept through European philosophy. Yet, good Lutheran that he was, Bultmann argued that existentialism might be able to describe our status in sin, but that the ultimate word of salvation, addressed to us directly by God, could be found only the New Testament.

I sense some slight mischief in Bloch's engagement with Bultmann, for the surprise of this debate is that Bloch does not charge Bultmann with being too theological or too mystifying. No, Bultmann, the New Testament theologian, goes too far in the other direction. He has given in to the temptations of the age, conformed himself a little too much with the world (a charge that Horkheimer also would level at liberal theologians such as Paul Tillich)[24] and has all-too hastily hurled *all* biblical myth over the side. Instead, Bloch seeks discernment of myth, which involves differentiation in terms of the type of myth and its purpose (or message), which then leads him to a dialectical reading in which the cunning of myth comes to the fore. I take each one – type, purpose and cunning – in turn.

I am less taken with his effort to distinguish between different *types* or genres such as fairy tale, legend, saga and myth, and thereby in the argument that myth

24. Horkheimer 1978, pp. 219–20, 222–3; Horkheimer 1991a, pp. 389–90, 392–3; Horkheimer 1996, pp. 46–7; Horkheimer 1985g, pp. 183–4; Horkheimer 1996, pp. 154–6; Horkheimer 1985h, pp. 276–7; Horkheimer 1985q; Horkheimer 1985p, pp. 392–3. See further Boer 2010a. The complex and close relationship between Tillich, Horkheimer and Adorno still needs to be examined. Tillich supervised and accepted Adorno's second habilitation thesis on Kierkegaard, employed him as a research assistant during that time, invited him to give visiting lectures at Union Theological Seminary where Tillich had settled after fleeing Germany, and kept in contact with the Frankfurt School upon its return to Germany. In many respects, Tillich may be regarded as the theological member of the school. See, for example, the discussion in Adorno, Blum, Brunner, Dibelius, Frick, Horkheimer, Mannheim, Mennicke, Pollock, Rietzler, Schafft, Von Soden, Tillich and Zarncke 1987. See also Tillich 1951–63; Tillich 1952.

proper favours despotism and domination whereas fairy tale takes on a subversive nature.[25] However, the underlying reason for doing so is far more interesting, for Bloch is after the elements within myth that give voice to subversion and rebellion, against tyrants, despots and the odd repressive deity. And so we come to the more important matter of *purpose*, which focuses directly on the subversive elements within myths. Do they offer a repressive or a transformative story, one of oppression or liberation? Even if they seem to be overwhelmingly repressive, is there a moment of rebellion, however brief? Does someone trick the overlords even for a moment? Does a cunning hero win against the odds through a ruse? The story of Prometheus in Greek mythology, or the serpent in paradise in the Bible gives voice to this rebellious element in myth, even if they are punished in the end – the moment of insurrection has been preserved.

By now, we have already slipped into the *cunning* of myth: no matter how tight the security forces may be, how perverse the tyrant, how devastating the punishment, in some way the moment of rebellion slips through. Prometheus, Eve, murmuring in the wilderness, trick, devious hero – all these and more are signals of the cunning of myth. But – and here Bloch's dialectical approach to myth comes to the surface – it also operates at the far deeper level of the preservation of moments of rebellion in the first place. The very fact that so many myths deal with rebellion, even if they seek to close it down again and again, is the strongest mark of myth's cunning. That is to say, it is not merely the content of myth that reveals cunning, but the way that myths themselves preserve rebellion despite themselves. Thus, the exercise of discerning the subversive content and purpose of myth is also a recognition that the enabling conditions for subversive myths are precisely those myths that are not so, that through and because of the myths of dominance and despotism those moments of cunning and non-conformism can be there, too. Of course, by now we are in the midst of Bloch's dialectical approach to myth – 'destroying and saving the myth in a single dialectical process'.[26] The outcome is that often we need to keep both the oppressive and liberating elements of myth, since the utter banishment of myth discards that germ of a 'joyful message', of the 'deepest utopian theme'[27] within myth.

In sum, myth requires a decent dose of discernment, not so much to sort the wheat out from the thorns, but to identify the cunning process by which even myths of repression preserve a moment of rebellion. In that process, the politically emancipatory function of myth emerges.

---

25. See also the Bloch-inspired work of Jack Zipes (Zipes 1979, 1988).
26. Bloch 1972, p. 37; Bloch 1968, p. 67.
27. Bloch 1998, p. 300; Bloch 1985c, p. 343.

Anticipation, or utopia

Bloch's other major contribution, often regarded as his trademark, is the anticipatory, utopian function of myth. Both the seditious moments of myths themselves and the sheer cunning by which those moments are preserved in myths of oppression and white-guard terror are actually elements of the utopian drive. Eve's independent decision, the wily wisdom of the serpent, the surprising blessing which Cain extracts in the midst of his curse, the continual grumbling of the Israelites against Moses, Aaron and even Yahweh, the rebellion of Korah and company, the protests of Job, the uncompromising message of Jesus – all these and more are glimpses within biblical myths of an irrepressible desire for and anticipation of a better world. Bloch is, however, careful not to valorise myths of a past golden age, for these are reactionary utopias, constructed dreams of a world that never was, in order to justify the most repressive of measures today. Instead, he snatches these myths from the conservatives and reclaims them as expressions of hope for a future in which tyrants and the sundry despots – of capital as much as of the ancient world – have been deposed and banished. The vital point, then, is that myth is not necessarily a reactive genre, spinning its stories after the fact or in reaction to the world as it is; nor is it a reflective exercise, casting its eyes back in longing or relief to a bygone age.[28] For Bloch, myth anticipates, sometimes patiently and at other moments far more impatiently, what is to come.

For Bloch, myth is one of the great repositories of utopia, which really functions as code for socialism. To some extent, I want to follow his line in what follows, albeit with a twist: myths, including those of the Bible, are not merely huge storehouses of utopian themes, for myths, especially political myths, are active

---

28. This is in contrast to Lévi-Strauss, whose widely influential theory of myth assumes a reactive agenda – myth is a response to a social contradiction. As Csapo puts it, Lévi-Strauss understands myth as a 'cultural trouble-shooter' (Csapo 2005, p. 226). Lévi-Strauss's problem was that myth seems to run roughshod over the laws of logic and experience, following what he called a '*pensée sauvage*' or 'thought gone wild' in which all possibilities are open, and yet myths with the same patterns appear throughout the world (see Lévi-Strauss 1966; Lévi-Strauss 1968, pp. 206–31). His solution is not some recourse to a deep mythic consciousness or collection of archetypes, but the point that myth shares the common feature of a solution to a cultural contradiction. He would take this conclusion well beyond the study of myth – into art, the spatial arrangement of settlements, and so on – but the point is that the effort to solve the contradiction showed that myth is not so much a solution as a displacement. In other words, a social contradiction would show up as a formal contradiction in art and myth, as his example of Caduveo (a Brazilian tribe) facial art shows so well. In its formal tension between two axes in face painting, one along the natural lines of the face and another at an oblique angle, with no other means of dealing with social tensions within the tribe, the Caduveo used facial decoration to ameliorate and repress such tensions (Lévi-Strauss 1989, pp. 229–56; Lévi-Strauss 1968, pp. 245–68).

producers of utopian ideas and stories. Let me put it this way: if wily myths create possible worlds that impinge on our world, then they bend inexorably towards utopia. Myth and utopia, in other words, are the closest of comrades.

One of the best examples of Bloch's reclamation work appears with his treatment of Eden. All-too often, a regressive myth of some lost golden age, in Bloch's hands it becomes a basic motif that constantly reshapes itself and thereby 'comprehensively embraces the other outlined utopias'.[29] It may appear as the Promised Land or indeed the new Jerusalem, when Eden will be restored at the end, but above all Eden resiliently retains its physical, geographical and spatial configurations. The gate to the garden may remain locked, but that did not prevent generation after generation from searching for it and seeking to live in its proximity, seeking perhaps a utopian radiance from the blessed garden. Over time, Eden undertakes some remarkable travels, linking itself to other legends on the way. Bloch sees it in Jerusalem, which may itself now be in the antipodes (Dante), in India (which is often a moniker for Europe's persistent perception that the centre of the world lay 'east'), Prester John's mythical Indian kingdom, the voyage of St Brendan and St Brendan's Isle, in the Atlantic (which was again taken to be India), in what drove Columbus, who believed that close to his newly found 'India' was paradise, in the south land, Terra Australis, in the icy north of the kingdom of Thule, and then off Earth in the stars, or in the centre of the Earth.

Adorno once again

Once again, I must be wary of getting too enthused about the anticipatory, utopian possibilities of political myth, and once again the warning comes from Adorno, who is always useful to have around should the party get too wild. His scepticism regarding myth is as severe as that regarding utopia. So he adheres to 'the commandment not to "depict" utopia or the commandment not to conceive certain utopias in detail'.[30] The reason: the risk of idolatry, of setting up false hopes which will only come crashing down in disarray and with bloody consequences. Apart from Adorno's well-known pessimism concerning revolution (so much so that he consistently argued with the militant students in his classes of the 1960s),[31] the theoretical reason comes from his appropriation and extension of the first and second commandments in Exodus 20 and Deuteronomy 5 (see my fuller discussion in Chapter Five). In his hands, the ban on

29. Bloch 1995, p. 793; Bloch 1985a, p. 929. See the whole discussion in Bloch 1995, pp. 758–94; Bloch 1985a, pp. 887–929.
30. Bloch and Adorno 1988, pp. 10–11; Bloch and Adorno 1975, p. 69.
31. See, for example, Adorno 2008, pp. 47–54; Adorno 2007, pp. 73–84.

other gods blends into the prohibition on making any graven images in order to become the *Bilderverbot*. This extraordinarily fertile idea would make its way into Adorno's thought – as the Hegelian determinate negation – on philosophy (as non-conceptual and non-systematic), aesthetics, utopia, music and even theology itself. And so it becomes 'the prohibition on invoking falsity as God, the finite as the infinite, the lie as truth'.[32] In what is probably the most rigorous exercise in classic Marxist demystification, Adorno also puts a 'no road' sign over the track to utopia.

It would be too easy to say that Adorno is wrong, wheel out Bloch or indeed an Adorno-inspired Jameson to show why, and leave it at that. Instead, I prefer to work through Adorno himself, for he had a knack of allowing momentary glimpses – passing comments, turns of phrase, the ambiguity of a word, a convoluted dialectical sentence – of precisely those images he was so keen to block. The examples are scattered throughout his work, such as his effort to recover the old philosophical term, *restitutio in integrum*, 'of making whole once again the pieces into which it has been smashed',[33] but especially the comments on his music teacher, Alban Berg, whom Adorno described as 'the foreign minister of the land of his dreams [*Außenminister seines Traumlands*]',[34] and for whom the 'greatest works of art do not exclude the lower depths, but kindle the flame of utopia on the smoking ruins of the past'.[35]

But let me give two more extended examples, the first drawn from the early book on Kierkegaard, where Adorno unwittingly allows for the possibility that theology may have a genuine form, one that is allowed to take a very different path from the perpetual turn to myth in Kierkegaard's hands. We come across sentences such as these: Kierkegaard 'transforms [*wandelt*] the Christian doctrine of reconciliation into the mythical'; 'Thus the story is mythically reduced [*schrumpft*] to a sacrifice'; 'A border-guard mentality, unchallengeable discipline, the power of fascination – these the deluded Kierkegaard owes not, as he claims, to the purity of his Christian doctrine, but to its mythical reinterpretation [*mythischer Umdeutung*] in the paradox'. These terms – transform [*abwandeln*], reduce [*schrumpfen*], reinterpretation [*Umdeutung*] – suggest that there is perhaps a

32. Horkheimer and Adorno 2002, p. 17; Horkheimer and Adorno 2003, p. 40
33. Adorno 2008, p. 191; Adorno 2007, p. 237. See also Adorno 2008, pp. 113, 245; Adorno 2007, pp. 163, 315–16.
34. Adorno 1991, p. 33; Adorno 2003l, p. 366.
35. Adorno 1999, p. 79; Adorno 2003f, p. 96. See also the comments on Berg in Adorno 1991, pp. 8, 46; Adorno 2003l, pp. 334, 382; and on Mahler in Adorno 1992, pp. 17, 39, 145; Adorno 2003g, pp. 165–6, 189, 287. Note also: 'Is it not the case that in the final analysis Mahler has extended the Jewish prohibition on making graven images so as to include hope. The fact that the last two works which he completed have no closure, but remain open, translated the uncertain outcome between destruction and its alternative into music' (Adorno 1998b, p. 110; Adorno 2003i, p. 350).

more genuine theology, untransformed, not reduced or thoroughly reinterpreted, but only so that theology may be submitted to a dialectical search for 'truth-content'. Characteristically, this truth content may be attained only through theology and not by means of some import, all of which requires a deep engagement with theology in which one works through theology's contradictions.[36]

The second example appears in an essay, 'Sacred Fragment: Schoenberg's *Moses und Aron*'.[37] How can sacred art, he asks, possibly be made when such art is no longer possible? The only option is through the ban on images itself, through which the religious tradition, from which the ban originates, embodies the ban in its own artistic production. However, in a few key sentences Adorno offers the smallest possibility that myth itself, usually caught up in order, oppression and nature, may open up to something very different.[38] He observes that the ban on images is the central issue for both the text and the music in this (appropriately) unfinished fragment. As is his wont, in order to make this point he offers a thumbnail sketch of the history of music itself: music was originally the 'imageless art [*bilderlose Kunst*]' and, therefore, exempt from the ban on images. Gradually, especially in Europe, music became interwoven with the pictorial arts through rationalisation (a constant motif in Adorno's work) and the mastery of its materials. The outcome: music becomes part of that mythic sphere initially condemned by the ban. The catch is that the process of rationalisation enables the melding of music and pictorial art *and* condemns the process at the same time. Music is caught: the rationalisation of music generates the underside simultaneously condemned by rationalisation, namely myth (the dialectic of myth and enlightenment once again). How does one respond? One may either raise a protective zone around this mythic sphere or – Schoenberg's option – try to provide an 'image of the non-image [*Bild des Bilderlosen*]'. Schoenberg attempts this task through the tension between Moses and Aaron. The former, who is himself the bearer of the ban on images, does not sing but speaks, matter-of-factly, thereby undermining the binding status of the ban. And Aaron, the man of the image, the one who enables the construction of the golden calf, the man with the silver tongue, the priest in all his fine clothes – Aaron sings, but uses only language without images. In other words, Schoenberg attempts to embody the ban on images in a complex dialectic that recognises the entwining of both image and its ban; neither one without the other. But if image is inescapable, then so too is myth, the zone where music and image coalesce: it may

36. In order: Adorno 1989, pp. 110, 111, 119; Adorno 2003a, pp. 156, 158, 170. See further Boer 2007a, pp. 439–43.

37. Adorno 1998b, pp. 225–48; Adorno 2003i, pp. 454–75.

38. Adorno 1998b, p. 230; Adorno 2003i, p. 548. The remaining quotations in this paragraph are all drawn from this page.

be condemned again and again, but the mode in which it is condemned ensures that it is created and preserved. It is, to borrow a term from Bloch, an extraordinary example of the cunning of myth.

Are these moments when Adorno drops his guard, thereby requiring a more rigorous commentator to plug the gaps?[39] Not at all, for there is a logic to Adorno's own dialectical practice that enables precisely these glimpses. At least two relevant elements of his dialectic suggest that these openings are not mere slips, breaks in concentration in the difficult task of maintaining his negative dialectics. One approach is to see these utopian glimpses as the result of a classic Aufhebung (remember that we are staying within Adorno's own logic) in which the negative is both negated in turn and drawn up to a higher level – witness Adorno's own effort to produce an aesthetic theory and his troubled valorisation of avant-garde art, especially the 'new music', that escapes, however fleetingly, the pervasive effects of capitalism and reification – but this form of the dialectic is inextricably tied up with what it seeks to overcome. However, Adorno gave the dialectic his own characteristic twist, in which he immerses himself in the minutiae of a topic, an immanent micro-analysis that tracks down the contradictions until at last, panting and exhausted, they hand over their truth-content. That truth-content may be the complex connections with a class or social formation (as in Kierkegaard's status as a bourgeois *rentier* who tries to resist the inroads of commercialisation while embodying the deeper ideology of the private individual), or it may be the underside of a programme like enlightenment (in which myth turns up again and again), or it may be the glimpse of utopia in the midst of dystopia (especially in music). So also, I would suggest, with myth: here too, at the end of the run, panting, sweat-stained and ragged, it will finally need to pull a few utopian scraps out of it pockets.

Fragments: from motivation to analogy

So I would like to gather some theoretical scraps, the odds and ends of the utopian possibilities of myth that may be gathered, sorted, rearranged and reassembled. In doing so, I also seek to strengthen Bloch's somewhat vague anticipatory function of myth (what he tended to call hope). I have gathered six oddly shaped pieces of this utopian function of myth and assembled them into a picture of sorts, an argument, in other words, that seeks to go well beyond Bloch. Four come from erstwhile Marxist philosophers and two from theology itself (given that this book is a rubbing together of those two ways of thinking): Georges Sorel on the irrefutable motivational power of myth; Althusser (yes, even him) on the anticipated totality; Badiou on the future perfect; Deleuze and Guattari

39. So Wellmer 1997; Wellmer 1990, pp. 41–2.

on reverse causality; and nothing less than the ontological and analogical arguments for God's existence, which I will translate into utopia.

Sorel: irrefutable motivation

Georges Sorel was perhaps the first to argue for the importance of political myths for the Left, especially the myth of the general strike. The power of such a myth was to be found in its collective, irrefutable and motivational nature. It was to be a myth for the working class as a collective entity, providing the basis of belief for that class, or indeed the revolutionary group(s) in question. As a myth, however, it was not to rely on the empirical evidence of failure, of which there were many moments in the working-class agitations of the nineteenth and twentieth centuries. Instead, this political myth held its own in the face of disappointment, urging faithful militants to try yet again in spite of defeat after defeat. Finally, the purpose of the myth of the general strike was motivational: drawing on various images and metaphors of the efficacy of the strike, with its heroes and martyrs, the myth would encourage those who laboured to bring capitalism to its knees. In short, the myth of the general strike encapsulates the whole of socialism, which Sorel describes as 'a body of images capable of evoking instinctively all the sentiments which correspond to the different manifestations of the war undertaken by Socialism against modern society'.[40]

Althusser: a totality which has not yet achieved its concept

Anticipation, irrefutable motivation – still we are in the realm of hopes, dreams and stories. Is there something more that may be said about myth? Althusser provides one possibility, although not from the well-known scientific Marxism of the later writings, but the Hegelian and theological thinker of the early texts – a less than familiar Althusser, perhaps, but one who is there nevertheless. In an extraordinary long footnote in his Master's thesis, replete with the terminology and concepts of Hegel, the early Marx and theology itself, Althusser offers a reading of Genesis 1–3 – his only moment of direct biblical exegesis.[41] Above all, I am

40. Sorel 1961, p. 127.

41. Althusser 1997, p. 168, n. 252; Althusser 1994, pp. 244–5, n. 252. One footnote deserves another, so here is the full text of Althusser's footnote: 'The plunge of the product into Nature, which occurs as soon as the product escapes the producer's control and is no longer posited as being identical with him, gives us a better grasp of the creation myth. On the purest conception, God is the circularity of Love; he is sufficient unto himself and has no outside. The creation is literally a rupture in this circularity: God does not need the creation, so that it is, by definition, different from him. This non-identity of the Creator and his creature is the emergence of Nature. The product of the God-who-works escapes his control (because it is superfluous for him). This fall is Nature, or God's

interested in the last sentence: 'This deficiency explains why it is still necessary to revert to myth in order *to conceive a totality which has not yet attained its concept*; it is in the story of creation, on this view, that men contemplate the *reprise* of natural alienation'.[42] The second side of the semi-colon, with its ambiguous French word *reprise*, captures the dialectic of myth we have already found with Bloch, for it includes within its semantic cluster the senses of resumption, return, repair and then mending. In other words, myth involves the resumption or return (as from a journey) and mending (as of a bicycle) of natural alienation. *Reprise* enacts a dialectic within itself, for we find both recurrence and repair, perpetuation and overcoming, or (as I prefer) return and mending; myth may give itself out to narratives of the oppressive crushing of rebellion or to release from that oppression. Indeed, in Bloch's terms, myth cannot be understood without both elements in operation at the same time. But then, we may read it in Adorno's

---

outside. In the creation, then, men unwittingly repress the essence of work. But they do still more: they try to eliminate the very origins of work, which, in its daily exercise, appears to them as a natural necessity (one has to work in order to live, work is a natural law entailed by the fall – as appears in the myth of Eve: "you will earn your bread by the sweat of your brow"). Moreover, work is inherently conditioned by nature, since the worker transforms a nature that is given. In the creation myth, this natural character of work disappears, because the Creator is not subject to any law, and creates the world *ex nihilo*. In God the Creator, men not only think the birth of nature, but attempt to overcome the natural character of this birth by demonstrating that the creation has no origin (since God creates without obligation or need); that the fall has no nature; and that the very nature which seems to dominate work is, fundamentally, only as necessary as the (produced) nature which results from work.

'Developing and deepening this myth would perhaps enable us to anticipate what Marx means by "the identity of man and nature in work". Approached in this way, that identity would have two aspects. On the one hand, men are identical with nature in that they are identical with what they produce; their products become nature for them (this immediate identity through labour re-emerges in revolutionary action; one may therefore say that this alienation is already overcome in thought – men no longer need a myth to represent it, since it has become the object of economic science). On the other hand, men would also be identical with the nature that forces them to work, and which they transform through work; this second identity would be clarified through reflection of the first. Here, however, we would have only an embryonic anticipation, for, in the obvious, elementary sense, identity is still beyond men's grasp. Men see clearly enough that the natural world is given to them, and that they themselves exist because they exercise a measure of control over it, thanks to their knowledge and industry; however, they have not completely overcome natural alienation: they are subject to the elements, illness, and old age, and obliged to work in order to live. Moreover, if the work of scientific knowledge and of the transformation of the world is itself a recurrence of, and recovery from [*reprise*], natural alienation, the recovery is not complete: circularity is not re-established, and human circularity will no doubt be established before natural circularity (in a socialist world, say the Marxists, one will still have to overcome natural alienation). This deficiency explains why it is still necessary to revert to myth in order to conceive a totality which has not yet attained its concept; it is in the story of creation, on this view, that men contemplate the *reprise* of natural alienation'.

42. Ibid. First emphasis added.

fashion, pushing one term to its extreme so that it finally opens out to the other term: the possibility for repair or mending relies on the recurrence of alienation; only through the return of natural alienation is the repairing function of myth possible.

Even more weighty is the phrase that serves rather well as an alternative definition of political myth: 'a totality which has not yet achieved its concept [*une totalité qui n'est pas encore parvenue au concept*]'.[43] I read this phrase concerning the not-yet conceived totality of myth not so much as the description of the pre-scientific function of myth, in which we await the full concept with modern scientific thought, but as the utopian promise contained within myth. The realisation of the full concept of totality can take place only in utopia, so all we can do until that moment is deal in the language of myth. Indeed, as a genre of thinking and imagination that plunges into the labyrinth of language, that finds its foothold slipping at the edge of language (as Badiou would have it), I would suggest that myth offers a way to speak about an unutterable future.

Ontology

Those with ears to hear will have picked up a theological resonance in Althusser's comment concerning a certain totality that has not yet achieved its concept. Here, Althusser touches on the ontological proof for God's existence, which is by now impatiently waiting to have its say. But is Althusser's proposal for myth a secularised theological argument, an argument ruled out by the strategy of theological suspicion I outlined in my Introduction? No: we should see this argument, as well as the analogical argument that I will deploy a little later, not as primarily theological arguments that have been retooled for other uses; instead, their claims to be absolute and original need to be resolutely relativised. They are not inherently theological but have been used theologically in a phase that is impermanent and passing. That is, their theological use is but one use that may be made of arguments that are by no means necessarily theological.

The beauty of the ontological argument is its simplicity: that than which nothing greater can be conceived. The resonance with Althusser's totality which has not yet achieved its concept is not difficult to see. 'We have', as Adorno put it in a slightly different context, 'come strangely close to the ontological proof of God'.[44] But let us for a moment pick up the discussion in which that comment arises, a fascinating discussion between Adorno and Bloch on the contradictions of utopian longing. And I do so in order to show how the ontological argument might be reworked to strengthen the anticipatory function of myth. Adorno's

43. Althusser 1997, p. 168, n. 252; Althusser 1994, p. 245, n. 252.
44. Bloch and Adorno 1988, p. 16; Bloch and Adorno 1975, p. 74.

comment – that we have drawn nigh unto the ontological argument – is actually a response to Bloch's use of Brecht's idea of 'something's missing', from the play *Mahagonny*, to speak of utopia – 'one should not be allowed to eliminate it as if it really did not exist'.[45] This is an extraordinarily insightful comment by Adorno: utopia is, to gloss a phrase from Anselm's formulation in *Fides Quaerens Intellectum*, that than which nothing greater can be conceived. Indeed, all of Bloch's many categories, such as the 'not-yet consciousness', the 'life-force', the yearning for a better life, the criticism of imperfection and incompleteness that presupposes a possible perfection and so on, become various dimensions of that same ontological argument for utopia. Bloch will go so far as to characterise God as 'the problem of the radically new, absolutely redemptive, as the phenomenal of our freedom, of our true meaning'.[46]

Let me put it this way: Anselm's 'that than which nothing greater can be conceived' applies just as well, if not far better, to utopia, since it is an effort to deal with the connection between our world and utopia. It seeks, in other words, a bridge, a way of climbing or passing over, or indeed a way of transgressing the boundary between this world (the one of capitalism, for instance) and one that is beyond it. For in the effort to prove God's existence through rational thought, and not revelation, the ontological argument attempts to link reason and what is beyond reason. However, rather than the troubled notion of 'God', to which the ontological argument seems rather ill-fitted, it works rather well for the utopian function of myth. For in the image-ridden and metaphor-laden language of myth, often contradictory and ready to shift as the need arises, a recognition lurks that this language is inadequate for the task at hand. The ontological argument, at least in the way in which I have appropriated it, enables us to flush out that recognition: utopia is in some senses beyond thought, beyond the modes of discourse with which we are familiar. So what better way to speak of it than through myth?

Badiou: forcing a mythic truth

Yet we can still do better than Sorel, Althusser and the ontological argument, for I suspect that Alain Badiou's idea of 'forcing', or more completely, the forcing of a truth, may strengthen the anticipatory role of political myth. The idea of forcing comes out of Badiou's favoured zone of mathematics, specifically Paul Cohen, although I wish to apply it directly to myth. But – the close reader of Badiou may argue – Badiou deals with event and truth, with procedures of that truth (love, politics, science and art) and not those of myth and religion. The objection is fair, at least on the surface, for Badiou is, as he points out, an atheist by both

45. Bloch and Adorno 1988, p. 15; Bloch and Adorno 1975, p. 74.
46. Bloch 2000, p. 201; Bloch 1985b, p. 254.

heredity and conviction. He has little time for fiction, religion, God (whose death is synonymous with the end of the One at the hands of the set theory begun by Cantor and then perfected by Zermelo, Fraenkel, von Neumann and Gödel). So, in order to set up the possibility that Badiou's appropriation of forcing applies exceedingly well to myth, I need to take a small detour in order to show how his theory of truth cannot avoid the question of the fable.

Simply put, many of Badiou's arguments concerning truth also apply to myth, for myth is inextricably bound up with truth. A heretical reading of Badiou, to be sure, perhaps a conscious misreading to which he would object, but one that emerges from his own texts. However, since I have outlined that argument in detail elsewhere, here I offer a brief summary.[47] To begin with, in Badiou's perpetually recycled dealings with the four procedures of truth (science, politics, art and love) the ghostly presence of a fifth procedure appears from time to time. It may hover for a while in the background of his discussions of Pascal or Kierkegaard, or in occasional examples of truths and their events in which Badiou evokes the early church, but the ghost begins to firm in our gaze when we turn to Badiou's much-discussed book on Paul.

In the opening pages of this little book, *Saint Paul*, Badiou makes a telling observation that has drawn me back on more than one occasion. He writes: 'so far as we are concerned, what we are dealing with here is precisely a fable [*il s'agit pour nous, très exactement, d'une fable*]'.[48] What is a fable? For Badiou it is not merely the apparatus of the Christian faith, but above all the resurrection of Christ. This is a *point fabuleux*, a *point de fable*, he repeats with some force. The word 'fable' marks a deep and productive contradiction: it means both a fiction *and* the centre of Paul's message.

Badiou does not shy away from this contradiction, asserting the formal importance of the fable of the resurrection for Paul, indeed as an exemplar par excellence of the truth-event, and yet making it clear that he takes the event proclaimed by Paul as a fiction. Let us explore this contradiction further, for it opens up the possibility that Badiou has a contribution to make to the theory of myth I am developing here. For Badiou, Paul provides a paradigmatic case of the procedure of truth: he names an event, the resurrection of Christ, gathers a group of militants about him, a group characterised by fidelity, love and hope. For them, everything in the world has changed, so they live and act in accordance with that breakthrough. In other words, Paul's proclamation is an instance of the universal, not as a singular and absolute universal, but as one that is contingent, particular and available to all.

---

47. See, especially for detailed references, Boer 2009b, pp. 155–79.
48. Badiou 2003b, p. 4; Badiou 1997, p. 5.

It is not difficult to see how Badiou is caught: on the one hand, Paul presents an extraordinarily good model for the truthful identification of an event; on the other hand, the event in question is a fable. Badiou tries to get around the problem by arguing that religion belongs to the structure of fiction; for that reason, the event is fabulous and cannot be regarded as fact, unlike other events such as May '68, the Russian Revolution or the mathematical discoveries of Cohen or Gödel.[49] So, even though the resurrection is central to Paul's proclamation, even though the New Testament obsesses about this extraordinary claim, and even though, in Badiouese, Paul names it as an event, exhibiting all the procedures of truth including those who act in fidelity to the event, that event must be fiction. But that argument assumes some mode of verifying that an event has actually happened. Are there witnesses? Can it be registered in an objective fashion? Does one have incontrovertible evidence? Not so for the resurrection, it would seem.

The problem with this response is that it actually runs against Badiou's own stipulations concerning the nature of an event. For the event cannot be apprehended directly; its only 'proof' is that it has been declared and named by a subject who is constituted in the process of that declaration. All that we have is a witness who comes after the event. Had he or she not named it as such, altered the coordinates of his or her existence, and gathered a militant group faithful to that event, nothing would have happened as a result of the event. The reason: the event is supernumerary, unexpected, and inexplicable in terms of any known coordinates. Obviously, this approach to the event rules out any objective verification of an event, for that would be to use what is known – from the 'there is' – and thereby render the event numerary, expected and explicable.

Is there any way out of this dilemma? There is, but via the fable. It seems to me that Badiou has stumbled across a truth concerning the role of fable and thereby myth. In short, I would like to make the weakness in his argument a strength. Paul's fabulous event, named by him as the resurrection of Jesus, is not an embarrassing exception;[50] rather, it expresses the truth of the event itself. Any account of the event, any identification and naming cannot but be fabulous. Thus, the very strength of Paul's central claim that Jesus has been resurrected it that it is a pure fable. As Badiou points out, an event is not tied to any historical conditions or causes, is not falsifiable or verifiable in terms of the order of fact,

49. This is the gist of the response Badiou himself gave to a similar argument I made at the 'Singularity and Multiplicity' conference, held at Duke University on 26 March 2005.

50. Badiou has opined in retrospect that it would have been better if the book on Paul had not appeared so early in English, one of the first that introduced his system of thought to an English readership, for it has raised more problems for him than it has solved (personal communication from Ward Blanton at the University of Kent).

according to any of the canons of scientific or historical enquiry. How else to speak of an event that comes out of the blue except by fable or myth?

The same observation may be made about the other events that run through Badiou's texts – the poetry of Mallarmé, the statement 'I love you', the mathematical discoveries of set theory, the breakthroughs in science, or major revolutionary moments such as the communist revolutions of the twentieth century, both those that succeeded and failed. But it also applies to those other more theological examples, such as Pascal's miracle or Kierkegaard's leap.[51] One way, an exemplary way in fact, of speaking about such events at all is through the language of myth, especially when such an event is beyond the canons of science and history.

Two final observations on Badiou: I wrote above that my reading goes against Badiou in some respects. Yet, at times he makes observations that run alongside my own argument, whispering encouragement on the way. The first comes with his assertion that he is not interested in the content of Paul's fable, but in its form, for the form of Paul's truth claim – or, I would add, those of Pascal or Kierkegaard – exhibits a paradigmatic case of the procedures of truth.[52] Now truth itself, which is really the narrative concerning the event, takes on an even greater resemblance to fable. Paul speaks a truth concerning a fabulous event, but that truth can be described only in the terms of fable and myth. Formally, then, truth and myth begin to share the same space.

The second moment when Badiou comes close to admitting the inextricable presence of fable in the midst of the event and its truth is in the following: 'I have always conceived truth as a random course or as a kind of escapade, posterior to the event and free of any external law, such that the resources of narration are required *simultaneously* with those of mathematization for its comprehension. There is a constant circulation from fiction to argument, from image to formula, from poem to matheme – as indeed the work of Borges strikingly illustrates'.[53] Note what has happened: narration and mathematisation, fiction and argument, image and formula, poem and matheme begin to run into one another. So also with myth and truth, as indeed happens with Badiou's favoured philosopher

51. Badiou 2006a, pp. 212–22; Badiou 1988, pp. 235–45; Badiou 2003b, pp. 47–50; Badiou 1997, pp. 50–3; Badiou 2009, pp. 425–35; Badiou 2006b, pp. 447–57.

52. Badiou 2003b, p. 6; Badiou 1997, p. 6.

53. Badiou 2000, p. 57. See also his observation on Lacan: 'Far from opposing, as Heidegger did, the Pre-Socratic poem to Plato's matheme, Lacan has the powerful idea that poetry was the closest thing to mathematization available to the Pre-Socratics. Poetic form is the innocence of the grandiose. For Lacan, it even goes beyond the explicit content of statements, because it anticipates the regularity of the matheme' (Badiou 2006d).

Plato, who was not averse to reverting to myth when needed.[54] As is increasingly recognised, Badiou seeks to bridge and rework two linguistic registers, that of mathematics, especially formal language, and poetry. Central to his thought is the effort to link narration, fiction, image, poem and fable – all are necessary for dealing with the truth of an event, as much as argument, formula and matheme.

We should expect nothing else for what breaks into our mundane lives. The event is, after all, entirely extraneous, unexpected and undeserved – or to use terms that Badiou uses of the event, excessive, unassignable, unpredictable, indiscernible, and errant. For this reason, it operates at the edge of language. It should come as no surprise that Badiou has written poetry, plays and fiction – not only as a writer, but also in speaking of the event. As Badiou points out, the possibility of speaking about the event takes place when 'language loses its grip',[55] which is much like poetry, for it marks the moment when language begins to slip at the 'limits of language'.[56] At these moments, we begin to enter the realm of fable and myth.

Strikingly, Badiou himself comes close to making a very similar argument in a lecture, 'Politics: A Non-Expressive Dialectics', given at Birkbeck College, London, in November 2005. Towards the end of the lecture, Badiou considers the questions of politics and fiction. He begins by making a distinction between ideology and fiction, stressing the positive possibilities of the latter and then enlisting fiction on the side of truth with reference to Lacan's statement: 'truth itself is in a structure of fiction'. From here, he initiates a search for what he calls a new fiction, for the 'process of truth is also the process of a new fiction'.[57] In this case, I read 'new fiction', one without a 'proper name' and thereby generic, as a code for myth, especially a political myth as the source for renewed courage and hope. In Badiou's words: 'And in fact, when the world is dull and confusing, as it is today, we have to sustain our final belief by a magnificent fiction.... And the great fiction of communism, finally, the great fiction which goes from masses to proper names by contradiction of classes, is really a composition, a spatial composition of the political field, is the classical revolutionary composition of the political field'.[58]

---

54. For example, Badiou refers to Plato's myth of Er the Pamphylian at the end of the *Republic*. Badiou 2000, p. 57.

55. Badiou 2004, p. 109.

56. Badiou 2005a, p. 22.

57. Badiou 2005b, p. 12.

58. Badiou 2005b, pp. 12–13. This lecture was delivered a few months after I had first presented an earlier form of the argument of the preceding few paragraphs. At that gathering, a small conference called 'Singularity and Multiplicity', held at Duke University in March 2005, and which was devoted to Badiou's work, Badiou had been keen to resist my argument for the necessary role of a fictional, fabulous myth in the realm of truth.

My brief excursus has come to an end, although it has been necessary to show how and why Badiou's idea of forcing may apply to the anticipatory function of myth. Needless to say, forcing is deployed by Badiou to speak of truth, but since myth perpetually shadows these deliberations on truth, I will take the comments on forcing as applying to myth. What interests me is Badiou's suggestion that the form of speech proper to truth is the future perfect. Here is Badiou: 'Forcing is the point at which a truth, although incomplete, authorizes anticipations of knowledge concerning not what is but *what will have been if truth attains completion*'.[59] In short, truth now depends on a truth to come. In longer form, only in anticipation of its full realisation at some future point is it possible to speak of a truth now.

In order to see how that logic works, let me exegete this sentence from Badiou a little further. The last part is a conditional clause, which I can recast as follows: if truth attains its completion, it will have been. We may read the phrase 'it will have been' as either 'truth will have been' or 'it will have been true'. But there is a stronger sense to that phrase if we read it as it is, namely, with the intransitive form of the verb 'to be': it will have been. Now it becomes a statement concerning being, or rather, an ontological statement. For Badiou, the resolute Platonist and one-time Maoist, ontology is of course the domain of mathematics – one of his favourite intellectual and political places. But rather than charging ontology, or indeed Plato, with irretrievable idealism, for Badiou ontology is political.

What about the first part of our conditional clause? 'If truth attains completion', writes Badiou. There is no guarantee that truth will attain such a completion – hence the 'if'. No march of history here, no predestination, no history on our side. Such a truth may or may not attain completion, for it is thoroughly contingent, operating 'on the condition that that truth will have been'.[60] Further, what does it mean for us to say that truth may attain *completion*? We might understand Badiou's sentence as follows: truth has begun now, however partially and however dimly perceived, but at some future moment we will see it in its full light. Badiou's use of the pair incompletion-completion certainly lends itself to this sense – a partial truth in the present that will be completed at some moment in the future. If that is all Badiou can say, then it is not particularly stunning.

He replied that religion belongs to the realm of fiction, not fact, and was therefore not in the same zone as truth. By November of that year, in the lecture I have discussed briefly, he seems to have changed his tune somewhat.

59. Badiou 2004, p. 127; Badiou 2008, p. 138. This essay, 'Truth: Forcing and the Unnameable', appears in both *Theoretical Writings* and *Conditions* in slightly different translations. For all the technical detail, see Badiou 2006a, pp. 410–30; Badiou 1988, pp. 449–70.

60. Badiou 2004, p. 127; Badiou 2008, p. 138.

After all, Paul also wrote, 'For now we see in a mirror dimly, but then face to face' (1 Corinthians 13:12).

But there is a crucial twist in his schema. It is not so much a process of completing what is incomplete, of fulfilling what is promised; rather, the possibility of identifying and naming a truth now depends upon some future truth in all its fullness. In other words, the movement is from that future truth back to the present, and not the other way around. That truth yet to come generates the validity of the truth now, however partial it might be. The catch is that this truth of the future is contingent and not guaranteed. It remains unknown and uncertain and multiple, and so one has to wait and act in the belief that the future truth does indeed exist.

Or rather, it will have existed. This is where the future perfect comes into its own. The very possibility of saying anything about a truth relies on the fact that at some moment that truth *will have been* realised, *will have been* true. Thus, it is not that one awaits a truth in its completeness and in the fullness of time; rather, one anticipates a moment in history *after* that future truth, when one can look back and state that a truth has been. The future perfect anticipates (the future part) a moment when that truth is in the past and when we live with the effects of that completed truth (which is, after all, the function of the perfect).

This is the sense in which I would like to understand Badiou's idea of 'forcing a truth'. As I mentioned earlier, the idea of forcing comes from mathematics, specifically the work of Paul Cohen. The context is set theory, and the specific issue is the impossibility of naming a generic subset, which is both infinite (and therefore incomplete) and unidentifiable, since any description of any item in the subset is inadequate (or 'subtracted' from any predicate, in Badiou's terminology). What are we to do then?

> The crucial point, which Paul Cohen settled in the realm of ontology, i.e. of mathematics, is the following: you certainly cannot straightforwardly name the elements of a generic subset, since the latter is at once incomplete in its infinite composition and subtracted from every predicate which would directly identify it in the language. But you can maintain that *if* such and such an element *will have been* in the supposedly complete generic subset, *then* such and such a statement, rationally connectable to the element in question, is, or rather will have been, correct. Cohen describes this method – a method constraining the correctness of statements *according to an anticipatory condition bearing on the composition of an infinite generic subset* – as that of *forcing*.[61]

So also with the question of truth: strictly speaking, it is not possible to identify a truth, and yet through the idea of forcing a truth it does become possible.

---

61. Badiou 2004, pp. 127–8; Badiou 2008, p. 138. See also Hallward 2003, pp. 135–9.

One draws on the potential truth that may appear at some future point in order to 'force' that truth to make an appearance before its time. The very possibility of saying anything about a truth relies on the fact that at some moment that truth *will have been* realised, *will have been* true. So also with myth, I would suggest, especially since myth is inescapably part of the event and its truth. Myth offers an anticipation of worlds that will have been true, will have been realised. Or in a more prosaic sense, as the paint-store owner, Dan Fusco (Sam Coppola), says to Tony Manero (John Travolta) in *Saturday Night Fever*, 'you can't fuck with the future ... for the future fucks with you'.

Deleuze and Guattari: reverse causality

I have sought to bolster Bloch's utopian function of myth, turning it away from quiet dreaming on the front porch in the afternoon sun, or perhaps from the ramblings of the bore at the bar who has moved into her garrulously generous zone in which the world looks rosy for a while. Hope, irrefutable motivation, forcing of the world to come – to these I add reverse causality. An idea vital to Deleuze and Guattari, reverse causality is an argument that has been put to use fruitfully in physics, biology and economics.[62] For reverse causality, an event in the future can act on the present, or indeed the present may act on the past. More preferably, reverse causation challenges the linear perception of causality, in which an act now – say, my lighting a cigarette – becomes the cause of an event to come – relaxation, concentration, and then eventually lung cancer or any of the other myriad results of smoking. By contrast, reverse causality initially appears counter-intuitive. Let me give a few examples, the first drawn from mathematics and Henri Poincaré's recurrence theorem.[63] For Poincaré, any isolated dynamic system whose total energy is unchanged will over time return arbitrarily to one of its initial sets of molecular positions and velocities. In other words, no process is irreversible, no-one can tie a knot that cannot be untied. Thus, given an adequate (conceivably a long) time, the beer spilled on the table top will eventually return to the glass that held it, and the beer thus returned will eventually return to its components of barley, sugar, malt and hops. Not convinced? Let me take the example of 'swine flu' (or flu virus H1N1) in human beings in 2009: it produced a series of frenetic responses: quarantining of cases, slaughter of pigs, warnings of a pandemic, the rush to a vaccine and daily reporting on the news media. Nevertheless, swine flu turned out to be no worse than any other serious influenza virus that makes the rounds from time to time. However, what happened

62. See Surin 2009, pp. 274–6, whom I follow closely here. For a treatment of causality in Deleuze, see DeLanda 2002, pp. 117–22.
63. Poincaré 1892.

with swine flu was more than a simple pattern of prevention, for it fell into the logic of reverse causality: an anticipated threat that had not materialised as yet produces a string of responses as though the threat had materialised. One could go a step further and argue that swine flu brought about its own amelioration: by existing as a potential reality it brought about a number of actions that mitigated that reality. Even more, the example of swine flu structured reality – extensive health checks on arrival in countries such as China,[64] quarantines, a spike in doctors' visits, the employment of medical specialists in the rush for a vaccine, suspicions over sniffles – in response to an anticipated pandemic in a way that made the pandemic real.

One more example, now from the Bible: in Genesis 2–3, the so-called narrative of the fall, we have a comparable example of reverse causality, or at least the text may very well be read this way. The command from God not to eat from the tree of the knowledge of good and evil, indeed the very placing of such a tree in the garden, may be seen as an effort to prevent the dissolution of the moment in the garden itself (and 'garden' has here its myriad utopian associations). So the possibility of toil and sweat, of failing bodies and painful death, of antagonism and hatred between the man and woman, of constant war between man and beast – all these appear as threats to be thwarted. The command not to eat from the tree then functions as the effort to forestall such a reality. Yet by having the tree in the garden, the narrative makes that threat real. The flaw in the crystal becomes the reality it was supposed to prevent.[65]

Deleuze and Guattari invoke reverse causality in their argument concerning the (primitive communist) pre-signifying régime in relation to the despotic state. This régime is 'animated by a keen presentiment [*lourd pressentiment*] of what is to come',[66] a mode of resistance built into the system itself. So, through the régime's plural and segmentary nature it effectively blocks all that would

64. Indeed, that was my experience upon arrival in Shanghai in June 2009. Sterile white body suits, swimming goggles, face-masks, heavy boots and rubber gloves – six figures dressed as though they were entering a spacecraft or perhaps a laboratory with a highly contagious disease. They came on board after we had landed and passed through the plane in pairs. One zapped my forehead and, since doubt persisted, the other gently placed a thermometer in my mouth. I was cleared. But not so a grey-haired woman on the other side of the plane from where I was sitting; she gave a high reading. Immediately the white-suited disease troops sprang into action. Two rows on all sides of her were handed facemasks (three rows in Hong Kong). We had to wait half an hour for an official to come along; forms were filled out and signed and the infected party was marched off for quarantine.

65. I leave aside many other possibilities of interpretation, such as the argument for the narrative necessity of disobedience (what a boring text the Bible would be without it), or that the story is one of coming to maturity, or that the serpent is the only one who speaks the truth.

66. Deleuze and Guattari 1988, p. 118; Deleuze and Guattari 1980, p. 148.

abolish it – despotism, priesthood, the state apparatus, or, in the terms beloved by Deleuze and Guattari, the dominance of the signifier and a vicious circle of signs that have lost touch with their expressive contexts. In other words, the apparently barbaric ignorance of the pre-signifying régime is actually a mobilisation to resist the despotic state by anticipating what that state might be. But now the catch with the argument for reverse causality emerges. If we stay within the same logic, the very act of blocking such a possibility actually recognises its virtual existence in the here and now. The despot is coming; in a fashion comparable to the narrative of Genesis 2–3 with its trees, fruit and disobedience, the pre-signifying system gives birth to the signifying régime.

Yet reverse causality may apply equally well in reverse: the despotic régime, too, may be structured to prevent the disintegrating threat of the pre-signifying régime. Another example, drawn from the threat of the dissolution of capitalism, if not of communist revolution, illustrates my point rather well. In order to prevent such an event taking place, the various economic and state arms of capitalism are in a position of perpetual mobilisation: global summits to deal with economic crises (as with the rolling crisis that began with a credit crunch and stock market collapse in 2008, toppled a few major banks and made countries like Iceland and Greece bankrupt, and continues to cause havoc as I write); global controlling bodies such as the International Monetary Fund and the World Bank; the redefinition of 'terrorism' to include activists on the Left such as greens, anarchists and good old socialists; extensive surveillance of such groups by 'intelligence' organisations; and the perpetual ideological battle to discredit communism. An earlier instance of this effort to ward off communism comes from the 1960s and 1970s in Australia, when the liberal-conservative government (liberal in economic policy, conservative in social policy) sought to counteract a communist revolution, even though the Communist Party of Australia had perhaps at most a few thousand members who posed no apparent threat. Yet the government of the day (under Prime Minister Robert Menzies) operated an Australian version of American McCarthyism. ASIO, the Australian Security Intelligence Organisation, kept massive files on all members of the Communist Party, the government railed against the communist threat, and even attempted to have the massively threatening Communist Party banned (they failed). One might be forgiven for thinking that communism has been and still is a vibrant force, on the verge of taking over the world if it has not done so already. The point is by now obvious: an anticipated threat has a causal effect on the present in a way that makes that threat virtually present.

The implications for myth are not so difficult to see: with uncanny regularity myths tell stories of futile rebellion, usually for the ostensible purpose of showing why such rebellion is pointless. Think of Eve and the serpent, the murmuring of the Israelites in the desert against Moses and Yahweh, the insurrections of Miriam or Korah, the punishment of Prometheus, the narrative of the totalitarian evils of communism... Earlier, I argued that the preservation of these rebellious stories may be understood as the cunning of myth – a preservation through their reactionary closing down. But now I suggest that such mythic accounts might also operate in terms of reverse causality: they do not merely tell us why insurrection is futile, but in constructing these accounts in the first place they bring rebellion and an alternative world to life. In the very effort to block these possibilities, in shaping the status quo as one that must resist the threat, that threat becomes real. It is, if you like, a mythic example of Negri's *operaismo*, a constituent resistance to which power must constantly adapt and prevent from coming to be.

Analogy

As with Althusser's little gem of an insight, so also do Badiou's forcing and Deleuze and Guattari's reverse causality touch on a theological argument – the argument from analogy. They may well be slightly horrified at such a suggestion, muttering about my perversity to propose that they are in such company, although I would hope not. The reason: up until Althusser and the ontological argument, everyone remained true to Adorno's commandment not to depict utopia itself. But with Badiou and Deleuze and Guattari a switch began to take place. Instead of straining to catch a glimpse of utopia over the horizon or beyond the wall, instead of imagining ways to leap over the fence to the greener grass on the other side, instead of being content to wait and see what it might be like when we get there, instead of obeying the commandment not to speak of or depict utopia, we began to hear another question: what if utopia leaps over the wall and comes to us? Indeed, what if it already has arrived, affecting our world in so many ways that this world could not be imagined without such a utopia already amongst us? My terminology evokes the argument for reverse causality: it is not that we have suddenly made radio contact with utopia and can thereby corner the futurist market; rather, it is a shift in perspective that allows us to approach the whole problem anew.

Such a shift is the genius of the analogical argument for God's existence, but it also lies at the heart of the arguments for forcing and reverse causality. This argument for God's existence comes from the much-maligned Thomist tradition, refined as it was by Austin Farrer.[67] In its theological form, the analogical argument begins with the usual position that in order to understand God we project

67. Farrer 1979.

certain human traits, somewhat imperfectly, onto God. Thus, if we say that God is eternal, or that God is a loving, all-powerful and all-knowing being, we use these terms by analogy with human experience of these things. However, as a qualitatively different being, God's love is not human love; God's knowledge is not human knowledge, and so on. Yet these terms assist us in understanding God, albeit partially.

For the analogical argument, this is merely the first step, since it points out that this initial understanding of analogy has the whole relationship inverted. The true situation is that we can know what love, justice, power and knowledge might be only because they originate with God. As incomplete, contingent creatures we can know and experience these things only imperfectly, but their source is with God and only through God are they possible in the first place. The genius of the analogical argument is not that it discards the move from world to God, but that it uses that analogical move to open up the other possibility, namely that the analogical relationship moves from God to world.

This argument is, of course, dependent in some respects on the Platonic doctrine of the forms, and in that light it is clearly an idealist argument. And the analogical argument entails in its Thomist form an *analogia entis* which is problematically hierarchical.[68] Yet, to my mind, it is a highly intelligent form of idealism, to gloss Lenin, and the hierarchy is by no means necessary in my own reshaping of the argument from analogy. In fact, it dissipates when we move from an ontological form of the argument to a temporal one, for it is surprisingly easy to shift the argument from analogy onto a utopian register. Let me put it this way: it is not so much that the various terms from the present may be used in their imperfect way to give us a fleeting glimpse of that qualitatively different other world that goes by the name of utopia; rather, utopia provides the terms with which we might understand our present, although those terms are very imperfect derivatives of what that utopia contains. In other words, rather than taking terms from our present and projecting them into the future, we should, according to the analogical argument for utopia, work in reverse: the terms and concepts of an unknown future, no matter how degraded and partial they might be in our present perception and use of them, provide the way to think about utopia now. It is as though utopia has loaned them to us, however badly we might use that loan. Or, to return once again to myth, it is not that it uses another means, an alternative genre, to speak about a desired world (in itself, this is enough of a challenge to theories of myth that reiterate the crude designation of myth as circular and therefore locked into unchanging repetition), but that myth itself is an imperfect genre of thinking that derives its terms and very

68. See Surin 2005, p. 258, and Surin 2009, pp. 230–1, in his criticism of the effort to reclaim the *analogia entis* by the radical-orthodox school of theology.

mode of operating from that future, reaching across to grasp in a loose and slippery grip that yet-to-be-achieved totality.

The end of this long meditation on the anticipatory function of myth is at hand. As a result, political myth has gained some impressive credentials: binoculars turned to the future and armed with Bloch's discernment of myth, it has taken firm shape. Let me sum up the argument this far: the 'particularly sober and discerning mind'[69] identifies the repressive and subversive possibilities within the mythic labyrinth of language. All-too often, myth closes down moments of rebellion, trying to show how and why these options are not viable. Yet in doing so, myth both preserves such resistance and exhibits its own cunning. That is the task of discernment: espying the cunning of myth, anticipating the moment when the worlds that it creates impinge on the present. But myth is also deeply anticipatory and utopian; or rather, to give vague terms such as hope some much-needed muscle, political myth becomes a totality that has yet to achieve its concept, looking forward to that than which nothing greater can be thought, uttering a fabulous truth that will have been true, indeed, drawing terms from and speaking of worlds that directly affect the contours of our own in terms of reverse causality.

For example...

Enough, perhaps more than enough theory; it is time for some examples of utopian political myths that embody the theory at work, except that the linear progression of an argument on a page is unable to represent the fact that it was in interaction with examples such as these that I developed the theory in the first place. There are three, gathered from some likely and more unlikely corners. The first comes from Roland Barthes and his search for a realm of pure denotation. As a way to escape the clatter and clutter of signs and the pervasiveness of bourgeois myths, Barthes seeks the impossible – a world of pure denotation. The catch is that at the moment he finds that denotative utopia, he produces a striking myth or two of his own. The second example is drawn from Fredric Jameson, particularly his cautious comments on religious apocalyptic. Here, too, we find that a dialectical reading of myth rises to the surface. Each of these examples climbs in height and size: Barthes is the briefest and Jameson more extensive. The last example – Christian communism – is a fully built, hulking account, largely because I work my way through Friedrich Engels, Rosa Luxemburg and Karl Kautsky in order to outline the contours of a political myth central to Christianity.

69. Bloch 1972, p. 37; Bloch 1968, p. 67.

Barthes's denotation

Barthes? Is he not the smooth purveyor of semiology, the harbinger of poststructuralism before his untimely death, the aesthete interested in fashion, theatre and women's magazines? Of course, but he is also well known for the early collection of intuitive insights called *Mythologies* in which myth comes in for a sustained criticism as the parasite and distorter of language, the criminal figure who is familiar with alibis, changing identity and responsible for the dominance of bourgeois ideology.[70] No aspect of popular culture is free from myth's corrosive grasp, from steak and chips to the Tour de France, from washing powder to the Eiffel Tower. It hardly needs saying that Barthes had little time for myth when he wrote this work in the 1950s.

The catch, for Barthes, is that the moment he tries to break out of myth, he constructs his own myths with a distinct utopian tint. Let me backtrack for a moment: in his initial argument in *Mythologies*, especially in the essay that closes the collection, 'Myth Today', Barthes argues that myth is a second-order sign system, building upon (and distorting) the primary, denotative system (the apparently basic sense of a word, such as 'pig', which refers to an animal of whatever shape or size, in comparison to its secondary senses of glutton, pig-headedness and so on). Later, he would distinguish between two types of secondary systems – connotation and metalanguage – before going on to elaborate more and more levels. Later still, he would become suspicious of the claim to authenticity assumed by denotation – so much so that in *S/Z* denotation becomes as problematic as connotation, the last in a series of connotations which appears to present a simple truth, deceptively presenting itself as the first and primitive form of language. Indeed, Barthes now speaks of denotation as operating primarily as an archaic myth of the natural origin of language, as that 'old deity, watchful, cunning, theatrical, foreordained to *represent* the collective innocence of language'.[71]

At this point, a dialectic emerges in Barthes's thought, one not unlike that found in Bloch's thought on myth (although the tracks to the dialectic are quite different). Denotation may be a slippery beast, putting on an innocent appearance as the primal moment of language, but it may also take on a utopian function, presenting the possibility of the world of language that is beyond

70. Barthes 1993; Barthes 2002a. The original French edition contains more essays than those included in the English translation of *Mythologies*. The remainder, plus a gaggle of other essays, may be found in *The Eiffel Tower and Other Essays* (Barthes 1997); for the extra essays not in the original French version of *Mythologies*, see Barthes 2002b; Barthes 2002c; Barthes 2002d; Barthes 2002e; Barthes 2002f.

71. Barthes 1990, p. 9; Barthes 2002k, p. 126.

our own capabilities.[72] These hints at a denotative utopia bring to mind what is perhaps Barthes's most extraordinary book, *Empire of Signs*.[73] Here, Barthes constructs a semi-imaginary 'Japan' where the articulation of signs is so delicate that no meaning remains, where the fit between signifier and signified is so tight that nothing is left for any connotative system to gain a foothold. At all points where bourgeois myth does its most pernicious work – in language, food, games, cities, street signs, railway stations, faces, writing, the individual subject, theatre, poetry, bodies, and space – Barthes imagines a world where there is no meaning, where there is no reference to an ultimate signified. No soul, no God, no ego, no metaphysics, and so no myth. Pure denotation; is it not a complete absence of signs, a thorough 'semioclasm' of which Barthes dreamed in *Mythologies*? I would argue that Barthes goes beyond denotation, for his mythical Japan refuses even the initial connection between signifier and signified that produces the sign.

Here, Barthes has become his most dialectical. He admits that this type of project is thoroughly utopian,[74] indeed that it involves the application of semioclasm to the idea of the sign itself in a way that should resist myth[75] – at least as he understood such semioclasm in *Mythologies*. Is this what happens in *Empire of Signs*? Not at all, for Barthes has produced one of his most enticing myths – precisely at the moment that he constructs a utopia free of signs.

Jameson's apocalyptic

Now we can turn to Jameson, whose comments on apocalyptic I read – turning Jameson's own method loose on his work (somewhat like my reading of Barthes) – in a way that yields its mythic and utopian function. Jameson is, of course, one of the most important theorists on the Left today writing on utopia (which he insists on printing as 'Utopia'). I would suggest that Jameson, who has influenced my own thought in so many ways,[76] is the heir to Ernst Bloch on matters utopian, Jameson's *Archaeologies of the Future* being the unique successor to Bloch's *The Principle of Hope*.[77] But what has all this to do with myth, especially

72. Barthes 1983, p. 30, see also pp. 281–6; Barthes 2002g, p. 931, see also pp. 1179–84. See further Barthes 1985, p. 83; Barthes 2002l, p. 667; Barthes 1989, p. 77; Barthes 2002m, p. 801.

73. Barthes 1982; Barthes 2002h. See also his comments on the utopian form of *musica practica* where nothing is left over – Barthes 1991, pp. 265–6; Barthes 2002j, p. 450.

74. Barthes 1985, p. 97; Barthes 2002i, p. 678.

75. Barthes 1985, p. 85; Barthes 2002j, p. 669.

76. See especially Boer 1996.

77. Jameson 2005; Bloch 1995; Bloch 1985a. Although it has had less impact, at least as I write these lines, than some of Jameson's earlier works, *Archaeologies* is to my mind one of his most fascinating books.

political myth? Let us go back a little to an earlier piece of writing, a brief section at the close of *The Political Unconscious* called 'The Dialectic of Utopia and Ideology'.[78] I propose to read this dialectic – quite wilfully – as the dialectic of utopia and myth.

Any reader of these final pages in *The Political Unconscious* soon picks up on the fact that Jameson's dialectic is a reworking of Paul Ricœur's theologically inspired hermeneutics of suspicion and recovery.[79] Working his way through Ricœur's early *Freud and Philosophy*,[80] Jameson seeks to turn this double hermeneutics into a distinctly Marxist one, that is, in terms of ideological and utopian hermeneutics. In fact, Jameson argues that the equivalent to Ricœur's hermeneutics of recovery may be found within the Marxist tradition, for apart from Bloch's 'principle of hope', there is Bakhtin's notion of the dialogical and the carnival and then the Frankfurt School's concept of *promesse du bonheur*. I would add to this collection Adorno's appropriation of the term *restitutio in integrum*, a term now restricted to medicine and referring to full recovery after illness or surgery, but originally used much more widely in philosophical and theological circles to refer to the restoration of the world after some cataclysm or other.[81] As for Ricœur, the key with such a hermeneutics is not to dispense with the long moment of suspicion once it has done its work but to identify within suspicion the seed of what is positive in order to move onto recovery.[82] A comparable move applies in Jameson's reworking: utopian interpretation searches long and hard to locate the utopian dimensions of even the most corrupted and reactionary material, identifying where the wish for something vastly new and better shows through. In Jameson's words, '*all* class consciousness – or in other words,

78. Jameson 1981, pp. 281–99.

79. Jameson 1981, pp. 282–6. Jameson has been drawn to Ricœur for most of his intellectual life, although he admits to never having met Ricœur. For Jameson, who gave a course on Ricœur's *Time and Narrative* at Duke University in 2004 (which I had the good fortune to attend), Ricœur is a conservative old fogey, but a very polite and intelligent one. Indeed, Jameson opined in his usual way, the only way one knows that Ricœur has inserted the knife is when the blood begins to flow.

80. Ricœur 1970.

81. Adorno 2008, pp. 113, 191, 245; Adorno 2007, pp. 163, 237, 315–16.

82. Ricœur frames his discussion in psychoanalytic terms – the initial, negative moment unmasks the repressive surface and the subsequent moment releases the fantasy – yet Jameson is all too aware that theology is never far from Ricœur's thought (see also Badiou 2006c). Despite Jameson's admission that he is little interested in religion, he has in fact engaged with it on a number of occasions. These include the background of medieval biblical allegory and Northrop Frye for his own three-level method of Marxist interpretation, which he explores in *The Political Unconscious* (Jameson 1981, pp. 69–74; see my discussion in Boer 1996, pp. 3–41, and Boer 2005a), the engagement with Walter Benjamin in terms of the same allegorical schema in *Marxism and Form* (Jameson 1971, pp. 60–83), the historicising of religion as the ideology or 'cultural dominant' of that imprecise period known as 'precapitalist formations' in Jameson 1986 (see also Boer 1996, pp. 58–68), and a study of Augustine and heretical sects in Jameson 1996.

all ideology in the strongest sense, including the most exclusive forms of ruling-class consciousness just as much as that of oppositional or oppressed classes – is in its very nature Utopian'.[83]

A dialectic worthy of Bloch at his best, although it has brought Jameson his fair share of criticism, particularly when he suggests that even fascism, sexism, or racism have their utopian moments. Now myth takes its seat in my discussion, for Jameson's primary concern is with form rather than content: the act, so often collective, of presenting an ideal – or at least a 'better' (in the eyes of its proponents) – future that has not yet been achieved is in itself a utopian gesture. This point actually applies to any myth, whether of the Right or the Left, or anywhere in between. We may find some content more appealing that others, but that does not diminish the formal point. Even the most retrograde myth – of Nazism, say, or slavery or sexual oppression or a theocracy as we find in the biblical text of Chronicles[84] – still presents an image of what the desired, ideal or better society might look like. In other words, it becomes possible to interpret myth in light of his hermeneutics of ideology and utopia, to locate the utopian possibilities of myth from within the negative, ideological moment. In this sense I re-read Jameson's directive: 'a Marxist negative hermeneutic, a Marxist practice of ideological analysis proper, must in the practical work of reading and interpretation be exercised *simultaneously* with a Marxist positive hermeneutic, or a decipherment of the Utopian impulses of these same still ideological texts'.[85]

Out of a number of possible examples – such as the utopian possibilities of medieval theology, the revolutionary novum of the Reformation and its rediscovery of Hebrew, and the suggestion that heretical groups during Augustine's era are analogous to far-left groups today[86] – I restrict myself to one telling

83. Jameson 1981, p. 289. This approach to religion and myth stands in some tension with Jameson's other approach in which religion is relegated to a bygone era or reduced to a code for other issues, whether cultural, political or social. This approach is best encapsulated in his observation that 'religion is a figural form whereby utopian issues are fought out' (Jameson 1996, p. 161).

84. See Boer 2006b, pp. 136–68; Schweitzer 2007.

85. Jameson 1981, p. 296.

86. A few words on each instance: Jameson showers unexpected praise on medieval theology – 'unique conceptual resources', he writes, 'remarkably sophisticated', 'an extraordinarily elaborated and articulated system of thought', and a 'remarkable language experiment' (Jameson 2005, p. 61). As for Thomas More's monastic asceticism and enthusiasm for the Reformation (Jameson 2005, pp. 25–33), Jameson observes that asceticism becomes a utopian expression – in form at least – of a collective life, the face-to-face community and its inherent egalitarianism (here Jameson follows unwittingly in Kautsky's footsteps). For its part, Protestantism gives voice to the revolutionary excitement of the novum, most notably in the rediscovery of the Hebrew of the Old Testament (I must admit that this is the first time I have ever come across classical Hebrew described as a utopian motif – all the better!). Finally, in his study of Augustine – which is really a tough encounter with Foucault, who comes off the worse for it – Jameson

example of this hermeneutic, applying it to Jameson's own troubled effort to deal with religious apocalyptic in *Archaeologies of the Future*. Let us take it as a given that apocalyptic, with all its fevered speculation and anticipation of God and his chariots coming to vanquish one's opponents, is saturated with the language of myth, and that apocalyptic refers both to the narrative of catastrophe-cum-renewal and the ideology of a collective for whom that narrative is vital. But is it utopian? Initially Jameson is not quite sure about apocalyptic, offering a passing comment with the hope that it will be enough: 'The stars in the night sky are just such an apparition suspended in time, a multiplicity stretched immobile across space, whose other face is that firmament as the scroll of which the Apocalypse tells us that it will be rolled up in the last days'.[87] Soon enough, Jameson realises that he will not get off so lightly, particularly with Ernst Bloch peering over his shoulder (Bloch was quite enamoured with apocalyptic firebrands such as Joachim de Fiore and Thomas Müntzer). So Jameson seeks to distinguish between apocalyptic today – 'the increasingly popular visions of total destruction and of the extinction of life on Earth'[88] – and the 'original Apocalypse': 'Yet this new term oddly enough brings us around to our starting point again, inasmuch as the original Apocalypse includes both catastrophe and fulfilment, the end of the world and the inauguration of the reign of Christ on earth, Utopia and the extinction of the human race all at once. Yet if the Apocalypse is neither dialectical (in the sense of including its Utopian "opposite") nor some mere psychological projection, to be deciphered in historical or ideological terms, then it is probably to be grasped as metaphysical or religious, in which case its secret Utopian vocation consists in assembling a new community of readers and believers around itself'.[89]

Instead of making the most of the two extremes of this original Apocalypse (the Revelation of John) – between complete obliteration and inauguration of a new age – Jameson, at least in this quotation, attempts to shift the dialectic to another level: instead of concerning himself with the cataclysm and renewal afterwards, he argues that the utopian import lies not in the content but in the new community that takes shape around the apocalyptic vision (this image has more than a passing likeness to Badiou's militant band acting in fidelity to the mythical event). Now, although this alternative dialectical move is a good example of Jameson's hermeneutics of ideology and utopia, replete with his usual ability to look awry and find an alternative utopian reading, I wonder why he needs

---

argues that the early Christian sects may be read as the equivalent of far-left groups for whom Augustine is then the social democrat who seeks to negate and annihilate them (Jameson 1996). For a more detailed treatment, see Boer 2009b, pp. 53–8.

87. Jameson 2005, p. 94.
88. Jameson 2005, p. 199
89. Ibid.

to do so. I am perfectly happy to grant the collective point, but why not also engage directly with the tension between catastrophe and renewal, the end of history and the new age, or, in terms Jameson likes to use, between anti-utopia and utopia? Indeed, why not include the new community of readers, both agents and the faithful within this dialectic?

Yet when we turn to the long and somewhat rambling footnote that is attached to this afterthought on apocalyptic, Jameson attempts precisely the dialectic in which I am interested.[90] He speculates that 'the end of the world may simply be the cover for a very different and more properly utopian wish-fulfilment: as when (in John Wyndam's novels, for example) the protagonist and a small band of other survivors of the catastrophe go on to found some smaller and more liveable collectivity after the end of modernity and capitalism'.[91] Here is the collective, which now operates within the apocalyptic novel as the mark of a new age and is thereby a signal for the function of such literature itself, namely, to gather and foster a community for whom the literature itself is vital. Apart from John Wyndham, I would suggest that Philip K. Dick might want to make an appearance (for some reason that is beyond me, he does not do so at this moment, although he certainly does so elsewhere),[92] for Dick is certainly one who made extensive use of the narrative of catastrophe-cum-renewal, even if the grim life on the other side of the catastrophe is hardly one to write home about. Surely Thomas More should make an appearance here, too, for his founding text of the modern genre of utopia may be read as a sustained and largely successful effort to secularise the genre of apocalyptic and free it from the weight of its religious associations.

Despite my misgivings concerning apocalyptic, with its history of deluded crackpots leading bands of equally deluded followers to grisly ends, we cannot deny that it is a mythic genre of the first order. The basic feature of apocalyptic – the dialectical play between catastrophe and renewal – has all the hallmarks of fable or myth. In the effort to speak of new utopian reality, myth offers a vast collection of images, metaphors and ways of speaking. Yet apocalyptic indicates that myth is far more than language and narrative: in the same way that apocalyptic is simultaneously a genre of literature, an ideology of politico-religious

90. I have argued that the structure of this paragraph on apocalyptic and its heavy footnote is symptomatic of the side-stepping of questions of religion that runs through Jameson's discussions of utopia. See Boer 2009b, pp. 31–58.

91. Jameson 2005, p. 199. Its historical conditions, he suggests, may give voice to 'the expression of the melancholy and trauma of the historical experience of defeat', which is how he suggests we 'interpret the immense eschatological jouissance of the greatest of modern apocalyptic writers, J.G. Ballard (1930–), as the expression of his experience of the end of the British Empire in the Second World War' (ibid.).

92. Jameson 2005, pp. 57, 64, 69–70, 80–3, 96, 99, 263, 287, 288, 312, 343, 345–8, 363–83.

movements (or 'worldview' as the more timid might describe it), and an active force in forming and sustaining a collective experience, so also is myth.

Early Christian communism

Barthes and Jameson: two writers, two examples of the utopian impulse in distinctly political myths. Yet, my final example is perhaps the best of all, namely Christian communism. And who better to introduce it than Jameson, who observes that what was felt to be the rediscovery of the spirit of early Christianity during the Renaissance and Reformation was nothing less than a cultural revolution. A utopian excitement runs through this rediscovery, a 'new intellectual enthusiasm' that was deeply utopian and even revolutionary.[93] I would suggest that this impulse comes from what I call the political myth of early Christian communism, a remarkably resilient, if often marginalised, political myth that makes a reappearance from time to time, reshaped and reclaimed by yet another group seeking to shake the cultural and social foundations of the time.

Stemming from a couple of crucial verses in the biblical book of the Acts of the Apostles, Christian communism remains a classic political myth. Acts 2:44–5 reads: 'And all who believed were together and had all things in common; and they sold their possessions and goods and distributed them to all, as any had need'. Or more fully in 4:32–5:

> Now the company of all those who believed were of one heart and soul, and no one said that any of the things which he possessed was his own, but instead they had everything in common. And with great power the apostles gave their testimony to the resurrection of the Lord Jesus, and great grace was upon them all. There was not a needy person among them, for as many as were possessors of lands or houses sold them, and brought the proceeds of what was sold and laid it at the apostles' feet; and distribution was made to each as any had need.

More than one reader has detected in these verses a loud echo of the famous slogan, 'from each according to his abilities, to each according to his need!'[94] Add to this the practices of having meals in common and the abolition of family life, as well as the story of the rich young man from the gospels, where Jesus tells him, 'You lack one thing; go, sell what you have, and give to the poor, and you will have treasure in heaven; and come, follow me',[95] and a theme emerges that has become a powerful current in Christian political thought and practice.

93. Jameson 2005, p. 24.
94. Marx 1891a, p. 87; Marx 1891b, p. 21.
95. Mark 10:21; see Matthew 19:21 and Luke 18:22.

Before I draw upon four of the major exponents of this political myth – Engels, Luxemburg, Kautsky and Kristeva – let me state at the outset why it is important for my argument. To begin with, the core of this myth is collective. The very construction and retelling of the myth may have a collective impact, but this effect is redoubled by the fact that the content is itself collective. Further, this myth has an enabling and virtual historical power; in other words, the myth of Christian communism may initially be an image, using figurative and metaphorical language that expresses a hope concerning communal living, but once it becomes an authoritative story, appropriated into the material lives of communities, it gains a historical power of its own with historical consequences. Finally, this argument relies on the position that the story is by and large fictional (playing on the inevitable double sense of myth), for no biblical scholar worth a damn will argue that the Acts of the Apostles is at all reliable in regard to historical reconstruction. In what follows, I provide the groundwork for these positions.

Engels sowed the seeds for this extraordinarily fertile theme in 'On the History of Early Christianity'.[96] Throughout his life he was quite ambivalent about Christianity; having been devoutly committed to the Reformed tradition in his youth, from his early twenties he could voice both the strongest condemnations of religion and an awareness that Christianity has a revolutionary strain.[97] The latter theme comes to the fore in a series of studies in which Engels gradually came to terms with Christianity – 'The Peasant War in Germany, Bruno Bauer and Early Christianity, The Book of Revelation', and 'On the History of Early Christianity'.[98] I will have more to say on these texts in the next chapter, but the relevant points here are that Christianity was for Engels originally a revolutionary movement, that it drew its initial members from the lower levels of society in the Roman Empire, and that there are numerous parallels with the communist movement in Engels's own day.

Relying on the biblical research of Bruno Bauer, which Engels had come to appreciate after the earlier polemic of *The Holy Family* and *The German Ideology*, he pushes the point that earliest Christianity appealed mostly to slaves and poor free men and women. Bauer had argued that Christianity's appeal lay in its overturning of Hellenistic assumptions, stressing poverty against wealth and weakness against power; Engels took the argument further, suggesting that Christianity was actually made up of the poor and weak, or, to draw on terms I will explore in my sixth chapter, from the ill-born, ugly, unjust and evil, in short, the

96. Engels 1894–5c; Engels 1894–5d.

97. See Engels 1844a, p. 462; Engels 1844b, p. 544; Engels 1843a, p. 380; Engels 1843b, pp. 451–2.

98. Engels 1850a; Engels 1850b; Engels 1882a; Engels 1882b; Engels 1883a; Engels 1883b; Engels 1894–5c; Engels 1894–5d.

scum of society. Or in Engels's words, 'Christianity was originally a movement of oppressed people: it first appeared as the religion of slaves and freedmen, of poor people deprived of all rights, of peoples subjugated or dispersed by Rome'.[99] How does he know? He suggests that Roman imperialism crushed older social structures of clan and polis, imposed a new juridical system, exacted punishing tribute, and exacerbated the hopeless state of the vast majority of slaves, impoverished peasants and desperate urban freemen. To this situation, Christianity offered a radical response. However, since there is little evidence apart from the notoriously unreliable texts of the New Testament, Engels bolsters his reconstruction by making parallels with the communists he knew. Both early Christianity and communism appeal to the oppressed classes, both are afflicted by sectarian squabbles and endless splits, have countless false prophets who arise and lead people astray, suffer from a tension between ascetic self-denial and libertinage, endure persecution and ostracism, and they both hope for a better world, a hope that keeps them struggling despite numerous setbacks.[100]

From Engels, then, we have the appeal to the poorer classes, the revolutionary origins and the endless comparisons with communism of his own day. He does not, however, cite the Book of Acts concerning the nature of those early communities – for a very good reason. Engels followed the scepticism of biblical scholars such as Bauer and David Strauss (of *Das Leben Jesu*[101] fame) concerning the sheer unreliability of the New Testament for any historical reconstruction. Acts in particular, with its glorious march of the gospel from Jerusalem to Rome under the guidance of a ghostly Holy Spirit, full of magic, raisings from the dead, impossible rescues from prison and snakebite, is a wonderful and entertaining piece of literature, but it is not history.[102] I will return to this vital point concerning Acts when Luxemburg and Kautsky join the discussion.

---

99. Engels 1894–5c, p. 447; Engels 1894–5d, p. 449. Engels is actually the source of this idea in New Testament studies and church history. For more than half a century it became the consensus view among biblical scholars (see, for instance, Deissman 1978, 1929) and sociologists such as Troeltsch (Troeltsch 1992), until challenged by more conservative scholars who reclaimed and refined an older argument that preceded Engels, namely that Christianity as an urban movement attracted members from the middle and upper strata of Roman society (for a survey, see Stark 1996, pp. 29–48). Needless to say, the evidence is decidedly slim.

100. In fact, the likenesses between schisms and petty squabbles in both Christianity and the communist movement were often noted by both Marx and Engels. See the full collection of what is a multitude of references in Boer 2012, pp. 44–6, 279–81, 297–305.

101. Strauss 1902; Strauss 1835.

102. Another reason for Engels's studied avoidance of the Acts of the Apostles must be his and Marx's long-standing opposition to the first socialists, especially those from France who provided the initial inspiration for the German socialism of Moses Hess, Wilhelm Weitling and others. For instance, in his discussion of Étienne Cabet, Engels notes that French communists tended to be Christian, in contrast to the English socialists. Cabet's slogan was, after all, *le christianisme c'est le communisme*, and he explicitly

The next step in the political myth of Christian communism comes barely ten years after Engels published his 'On the History of Early Christianity'. In 1905 Rosa Luxemburg produced her long essay, *Socialism and the Churches*,[103] forcefully arguing that the first Christian communities were communist, even though it was a communism of consumption rather than production. Three years later, Karl Kautsky published the much more substantial *Foundations of Christianity*.[104] Both works make largely the same points, so I take them as a pair, although for some reason that is beyond me these one-time collaborators do not refer to each other. Luxemburg's and Kautsky's arguments may be seen as a confluence of two streams. One obviously comes from Engels, for they pick up his suggestions that the early Christians came from the slaves and impoverished free men – the proletarians – of the Roman world and that there are many parallels with the workers' movement of their own day. Kautsky strengthened the former point by arguing that Christianity was a militant proletarian response to Roman rule, an urban movement that mediated between the militancy of the anarchistic and disorganised Zealot liberation movement and the communist escapism of the Essenes who retreated to the countryside.[105] For her part, Luxemburg ingeniously turned the latter point – the parallels with her own day – to the workers' advantage, arguing that genuine Christianity was at one with the aspirations of those who were joining the Social Democrats.

The other stream actually comes from the first socialist movements in France and then Germany, precisely those 'utopian socialists' whom Marx and Engels castigated time and again. Filtering over the border from France, these early socialists were of a distinctly Christian stripe, arguing that the original Christian communities were communist and attempting to convert the teachings of Christianity into a code of ethics minus the supernatural rubbish. Like Engels – indeed like so many movements for reform within Christianity – they felt that they had rediscovered the original form of Christianity, a form that had been distorted by the later church, whether Roman Catholic or Protestant (forgetting of course Orthodox Christianity). It hardly needs to be said that this search for origins was really a way of playing out political struggles of the time. Yet what strikes any student of the period is how these struggles took place on the terrain of the Bible, particularly the New Testament. So Saint-Simon's criticism of capitalism was meshed with his argument that early Christianity was actually a religion of brotherly love and not a dualistic one with Heaven above and

---

drew upon the image of Christian communism in the book of Acts of the Apostles as a model for his own 'Icarian' communities. See Engels 1843a, pp. 399, 403; Engels 1843b, pp. 471, 475; Engels 1888a, pp. 234–5; Engels 1888b, pp. 117–18.

103. Luxemburg 1970; Luxemburg 1982.

104. Kautsky 2007; Kautsky 1977.

105. Kautsky 2007, pp. 167–9; Kautsky 1977, pp. 338–43.

Earth below. The faithful communities which formed after Saint-Simon's death constituted themselves as 'churches', throwing in a priesthood for good measure and declaring that Saint-Simon was the messiah. Despite their best efforts at self-destruction – schisms in the movement, defections to Fourier's phalansteries, an embarrassing venture to the Middle East to find a female messiah – this type of socialism spilled over the border to Germany and inspired a number of German radicals. Heinrich Heine, August von Cieskowski and Moses Hess, an early collaborator with Marx and Engels, were swept up by the moral vision and fervent anticipation that human society was moving forward to an era of brotherly love.[106] More significantly for my argument, leading figures in the early German communist movement were also deeply influenced – Wilhelm Weitling (whom we will meet again in the next chapter), Hermann Kriege, Karl Grün and Gottfried Kinkel. Marx and Engels worked until they dropped to excise this rather Christian element from within communism.[107] Marx was often at his most scathing when dealing with these erstwhile comrades: Hermann Kriege is the 'apostle of love [*Liebesapostel*]';[108] Gottfried Kinkel, leader among the German refugees in London, is the 'theologising belletristic Kinkel';[109] French socialism 'sentimentally bewails the sufferings of mankind, or in Christian spirit prophesies the millennium and universal brotherly love, or in humanistic style drivels on about mind, education and freedom'.[110]

Yet, despite all the hard work of Marx and Engels, this stream of Christian communism – which has a long, long history that precedes them[111] – would not exit the scene, tail between its legs. Instead, I would suggest that it shows up in Luxemburg's argument in *Socialism and the Churches*, profoundly modified and reshaped in light of Engels's reconstruction of the revolutionary origins of Christianity. As I mentioned earlier, Luxemburg and Kautsky (like these early socialists) took the description of the early Christian communities in the Acts of the Apostles as historical reports of real communal practice.[112] I will not dwell here on their efforts to reconstruct the economic and social situation of the first

106. See especially Breckman 1999, pp. 131–76.

107. Marx and Engels 1846a, p. 46; Marx and Engels 1846b, p. 12; Marx and Engels 1845–6a, pp. 484–530; Marx and Engels 1845–6b, pp. 473–520; Marx and Engels 1852a; Marx and Engels 1852b.

108. Marx and Engels 1846a, p. 50; Marx and Engels 1846b, p. 17.

109. Marx 1851a; Marx 1851b.

110. Marx 1852a, p. 142; Marx 1852b, p. 153. In the widely read *Socialism: Utopian and Scientific* Engels argued that this Christian-inspired socialism was a necessary but preliminary, and therefore crude, stage on the way to full socialism. See Engels 1880a, especially pp. 285–97; Engels 1880b, especially pp. 189–201.

111. See the extensive survey by Kautsky 1947b, 1947c; Kautsky and Lafargue 1977, as well as the excellent recent studies by John Roberts (Roberts 2008a, 2008b).

112. In this respect Luxemburg merely follows a long tradition within Christian thought. She cites some of the 'Church Fathers', Saint Basil and John Chrysostom in the

Christians within the Roman Empire, which is an effort to build on Engels's brief comments. They also expand on his attempt at parallels by arguing that the economic situation of the early Church is analogous to the situation in which they write.

But what of that early communism? Here, both Luxemburg and Kautsky agree on the basic details. Driven by dire poverty and atrocious economic conditions, a basic stipulation of the early community was a communistic structure and organisation. As Kautsky puts it, the first Christian community 'had been permeated by an energetic though vague communism, an aversion to all private property, a drive toward a new and better social order, in which all class differences should be smoothed out by division of possessions'.[113] In fact, this 'communistic mutual aid society'[114] was the secret of its success beyond the untimely death of its founder.

Nonetheless, there is a problem, since early Christianity operated according to a communism of consumption, not production. For Kautsky, the key issue was the urban nature of Christianity and its lack of an agricultural base; it had no internal means to sustain itself. It is all very well for people to aspire – based on the stories in Acts – to sell all they have and give what they gain from such a massive garage sale to the community of which they are a part. But that does nothing to change the way such things are produced. What happens when the goods run out? Do people go back to their various jobs and professions in order to produce or buy more goods so that they can sell them again or share them once more? Indeed, for Kautsky a communism of consumption needs the larger economic system to continue, for the commune's members would need to keep on generating some income in order to distribute it to each other.[115] Or, as Luxemburg puts it:

> But this communism was based on the consumption of finished products and not on the communism of work, and proved itself incapable of reforming society, of putting an end to the inequality between people and throwing down the barrier which separated rich from poor. . . . Suppose, for example, that the rich proprietors, influenced by the Christian doctrine, offered to share up between the people all their money and other riches which they possessed in the form of cereals, fruit, clothing, animals, etc. What would the result be? Poverty would disappear for several weeks and during this time the people would be able to feed and clothe themselves. But the finished products are quickly used

fourth century and then Gregory the Great from the sixth century, as well as the church historian Vogel from 1780.

113. Kautsky 2007, p. 217; Kautsky 1977, p. 433.
114. Kautsky 2007, p. 196; Kautsky 1977, p. 403.
115. Kautsky 2007, p. 221; Kautsky 1977, p. 442.

> up. After a short lapse of time, the people, having consumed the distributed riches, would once again have empty hands.[116]

Apart from the Christian communities themselves, nothing has in fact changed within the economic structures as a whole. So we find that early Christianity had no effect on the economic system based on slavery. In fact, it would rely on the rich producing more, by means of their slaves, so that they could once again share their wealth with the Christian community. Should they also sell their means of production, then the Christian communities would quickly starve. Already within early Christian communism, the logic of giving alms to the poor arose, for such a system could be maintained only if the rich kept making surpluses and kept on giving them to the poor.

Now Kautsky and Luxemburg diverge. Kautsky picks up the point concerning alms-giving by the rich and traces the way in which this initial Christian communism dissipates. The commune becomes a community that is increasingly attractive to the rich; the common meal (a real vestige of primitive communism) was divided into the symbolic Eucharist and a meal for the poor members who receive alms; as the community grows it develops its own administrative hierarchy of bishop, apostle and prophet. So great was the change that by the time Christianity was adopted by Constantine and became the religion of the Roman Empire, it had become yet another mechanism for exploitation. Yet Kautsky suggests – in line with his search for a tradition of pre-Marxist socialism – that the communist drive could not be eradicated entirely, so it was shunted off into monasticism. Here, we find an obverse of the urban-based communism of consumption, for the rural basis of the monasteries lent themselves to a communism of agricultural production rather than one of consumption. For all the expansions of the monasteries, their latifundia and concentrations of wealth, for all the exploitation of slaves and unpaid workers, they maintained 'uncommon resistance and capacity for development'.[117] All of which was to lead into the Middle Ages and its religiously-driven communist movements.[118]

By contrast, Luxemburg presses the point that modern-day socialists differ from early Christian communism, for socialists demand a more fundamental change in the means of production. While the Christian communists 'did not demand that the land, the workshops and the instruments of work should become collective property, but only that everything should be divided up among them, houses, clothing, food and finished products most necessary to life', the socialists seek to make into common property the actual 'instruments of work, the means of

116. Luxemburg 1970, pp. 137–8; Luxemburg 1982, pp. 26–7; translation modified.
117. Kautsky 2007, p. 241; Kautsky 1977, p. 488.
118. Kautsky 1947b.

production, in order that all humanity may work and live in harmonious unity'.[119] In other words, socialism will complete what Christian communism began. The latter's intention may have been in the right place – an ardent belief in communism – but it needs to go a step further: not only do the products of an economy need to be held in common, but so also do the means of production. Her rather arresting conclusion is then that socialism is the logical outcome of Christianity: 'What the Christian Apostles could not accomplish by their fiery preaching against the egoism of the rich, the modern proletarians... can start working in the near future, by the conquest of political power in all countries by tearing the factories, the land, and all the means of production from the capitalists to make them the communal property of the workers'.[120]

It is almost time to stand back and ask what we can do with these arguments. Before I do, however, let me bring in one further contribution to this tradition of Christian communism – apart from your garden-variety resuscitations of the assertion that Jesus of Nazareth was in some senses a revolutionary. It comes from Julia Kristeva in one of her more Marxist moments, or rather, when Marx emerges from the dark corner in which she hides him all-too often.[121] Kristeva is of course enamoured with psychoanalysis, being one of the more faithful daughters of the father, Freud, but every now and then she breaks from this commitment to offer a profoundly collective point, moments when she becomes for a day or so a Marxist feminist. One of those moments is her suggestion that the new collective, the *ekklesia* proposed and established by the Apostle Paul, offers a new way to deal with psychic distress and psychosis (schizophrenia and paranoia).[122] To be sure, this is not the early communism of the Book of Acts, but it provides another angle on that ideal image.

This move contrasts with the tendency of Kristeva to focus on the private individual, even in her treatments of Paul,[123] let alone the Protestant tendency to emphasise the introspective and individualist Paul, or indeed the great polemic of the Enlightenment in which the private individual is the point from which one must consider any group or society. No, Kristeva sides firmly with the collective, with the *ekklesia*. It is '*une communauté des étrangers*', 'a community of foreigners', an 'ideal community', 'an original entity', a 'messianism that includes all of humankind'.[124] The language may be a little over the top, filled with too

119. Luxemburg 1970, p. 136; Luxemburg 1982, p. 24
120. Luxemburg 1970, p. 148; Luxemburg 1982, p. 40; translation modified.
121. See further Boer 2009b, pp. 121–54.
122. Kristeva 1991, pp. 77–83; Kristeva 1988, pp. 113–22. *Ekklesia* is conventionally translated as 'church', but Kristeva stays with the Greek term in order to wrest it away from the mutations that 'church' implies. In Greek, of course, it means simply a gathering.
123. Kristeva 1987, pp. 139–50; Kristeva 1983, pp. 135–47.
124. Kristeva 1991, p. 80; Kristeva 1988, pp. 117–18.

much prophetic fervour, but Kristeva sees in the *ekklesia* the foreshadowing of a transformed society.

The key to this new community – largely due to the political and 'psychological intuition of its founder'[125] – is that it answers psychic distress. Or rather, the *ekklesia* provides a context and a narrative for overcoming psychosis. How does it do so? Not only is the *ekklesia* a foreign collective, a commune of people split between two or more identities, it also answers the schizophrenic split of the foreigner. Yet Paul does not try to fit foreigners within an existing social body, with all manner of programmes for 'integration' and 'assimilation' – language courses, skills training, strict visa requirements and so on. Instead, the *ekklesia* embodies psychosis within itself. So Paul recognises the split within the foreigner between two countries (as any child of immigrants like myself will recognise only too readily) and provides a narrative and experience for passing between two psychic domains – between flesh and spirit, old self and new self, sin and forgiveness, death and life, crucifixion and resurrection in a 'body' which is simultaneously that of the group and Christ's body.[126] That is to say, what appears to be an external split becomes internal – to both the individual psyche and the very construction of the collective. Paul's *ekklesia* is, then, the way of soothing psychosis, offering the experience of the split as 'a transition toward a spiritual liberation starting from and within a concrete body'.[127]

I do find Kristeva's reading a little too enthusiastic, bordering on the celebrations of the church as a breakthrough egalitarian community, a collection of happy former psychotics, or indeed masochists or narcissists or whatever. By contrast, I would suggest that that collective is quite unstable and fragile, perhaps offering a glimpse of the new; the transition from one side to the other was not quite as successful as Kristeva might imagine. The problem is that Paul's *ekklesia* replicates too many of the structures of the Hellenistic society from which it arose – in terms of gender, hierarchy, relations of production (slaves and masters) and so on.[128] It is not entirely clear how new this *ekklesia* really is, for Paul draws upon the same language as the imperial cult. In doing so, the new community threatens to replicate precisely those structures. Further, the history of the church is not as uplifting as might be expected in light of its supposed origins, for it has too often been intolerant of foreigners, hierarchical, repressive of sexual and gender difference, denigrating the libidinal and expelling heretics. And then the passage from one state to another, from sin to forgiveness, from

---

125. Kristeva 1991, p. 82; Kristeva 1988, p. 120.
126. See Romans 12:4–5.
127. Kristeva 1991, p. 82; Kristeva 1988, p. 121.
128. See Kittredge 2000; Økland 2005.

flesh to spirit, from law to grace, from death to life is not always so clear. For Paul also distinguishes between Jew and Greek, barbarian and Greek, male and female, slave and free, sin and law, grace and law, the law of God and the law of sin in a way that does not always offer a clear transition.

A collective it may be, but it is a very unstable one – different yet similar to the politico-religious bodies on which it was modelled, wavering between egalitarian, segregated and hierarchical structures, providing an answer for and yet perpetuating pathologies. As I will spell out in more detail in the fourth chapter, the reason for this instability in the texts may be located in the troubled social formation in which the early Christians found themselves. They were in the midst of a tumultuous and violent transition from one social formation to another, from a sacred economy to a slave system. The writers of these works – whether the Acts of the Apostles or Paul's letters – could not help evincing traces of this brutal context in their texts. We might put the question as follows: what is the question to which Paul's letters or the Book of Acts provides an answer? We have the answer, but not the question. Yet the traces of the question leave their marks all over the answer, especially in the effort to describe those early Christian communities. They tried as much as they could to provide a picture, desperately idealised, of a community that responded to the brutal changes everywhere apparent in economic and political forms.

And that brings me back at last to the question of political myth. It would be too easy to argue that the images of Christian communism in the Book of Acts – upon which Luxemburg and Kautsky build their arguments – are not based on any historically verifiable fact. Equally, the image of the *ekklesia* in Paul's letters fails to distinguish itself clearly from other collective structures from which he drew his ideas and terminology. But I wish to take a different tack, suggesting that Luxemburg, Kautsky and Kristeva have embellished and enhanced a profound political myth of early Christian communism. In fact, I want to insist on the historical unreliability of this image in Acts and the idealisation of the *ekklesia* in Paul's letters. Rather than their effort to fix such a moment historically (in this respect they merely share a desire with so many New Testament scholars), I prefer to argue that these images function far better as a 'founding myth'. Here we face a delightful contradiction: the less historically reliable such a story is, the more powerful it is as a political myth. Indeed, as long as the belief holds that Acts or Paul presents what was once a real, lived experience, then we will find efforts to restore such an original moment. However, if we insist that the communal life of the early church is myth, that it projects a wish as to what might be, that it gives us a powerful image of what may still be achieved, only then are we able to overcome the reactionary desire to return to the early church in the Book of Acts. It might then be possible to reclaim it as a radical rather than a reactionary myth. In this light we may understand the continued influence of this political myth of early Christian communism throughout history: the Franciscan order within the Roman Catholic Church; the communist efforts of Gerrard Winstanley and the Diggers in seventeenth-century England;[129] the Icarian communes of Étienne Cabet (1788–1856) in the USA; the various Christian communes that exist today.

Conclusion

I have skirted a continent or three in this argument for political myth. Myth, I argued, requires Bloch's discernment not only to identify the subversive moments in the midst of the depressing commonality of jack-booted terror, but also to appreciate myth's cunning in slipping away from the police actions and thereby preserving those invaluable insurrections. From there, I sought to toughen up the anticipatory and utopian elements of myth with the help of a grab-bag of proposals: Sorel's irrefutable motivation, Althusser's suggestion that myth may well be a totality that has yet to attain its concept, the ontological argument's 'that than which nothing greater can be conceived', Badiou's forcing of a truth, Deleuze and Guattari's reverse causality, and the analogical argument's effort to change perspectives so that the utopia is the privileged perspective. Myth, then, pushes to the edge of language and thought, speaking in other modes that attempt to switch perspective so that the utopian moment will have been true, so that its impending reality impinges on the contours of, and thereby reshapes, our situation. Finally, I traced the way utopia turns up in three very different myths, that of Barthes's dreamed-of pure denotation, Jameson's wary engagement with apocalyptic and Christian communism.

Let me close with what was my deepest engagement – the long history of the political myth of Christian communism – by bringing to bear the theoretical elaboration in which I plundered Bloch and company. In each case, the key terms I scavenged fit remarkably well, with a little sawing, hammering and sanding, into a larger whole: as an anticipatory myth, Christian communism is a 'totality which has not yet achieved its concept' (Althusser); 'that than which nothing greater can be conceived' (the ontological argument); a situation that will have been true at some future point (Badiou, who has his own version of

129. In Winstanley's own words: 'And when the Son of man, was gone from the Apostles, his Spirit descended upon the Apostles and Brethren, as they were waiting at *Jerusalem*; and Rich men sold their Possessions, and gave part to the Poor; and no man said, That ought that he possessed was his own, for they had all things Common, *Act.* 4.32'. Winstanley, Everard, Goodgroome, Palmer, Starre, South, Hoggrill, Courton, Sawyer, Taylor, Eder, Clifford, Bickerstaffe, Barker, Taylor and Coulton 1649.

Christian communism as a militant and faithful group). Why not go the whole way? I would go so far as to suggest that the political myth of Christian communism may well operate in terms of reverse causality. Speaking the language of myth – since we fall short of the language appropriate to what has not yet been experienced or what may be known – that communism functions as a constituent resistance (Negri) to which the various churches continually respond in an effort to block its possibility, curtailing currents within that perpetually break out and thereby generate in their very resistance the continued possibility of Christian communism. But is this not the case with the 'broad church' of communism itself?

Chapter Three
Ambivalence

> Religion is a big rip-off in itself, but it can also be a great instrument of liberation.[1]

My concern in this chapter is ambivalence, the political ambivalence of theology. The argument may be stated quite simply: a religion such as Christianity may be oppressive or liberating, a dreadful instrument for state-sanctioned terror or the source of inspiration for one revolutionary movement after another. Christianity is an exercise in delusion by self-serving priests, a woeful validation of the power of despots and oligarchs, says one; no, Jesus was a revolutionary and Christianity began as an anti-imperial movement, says another. Neither is entirely correct, it seems to me, for both options – as well as variations on them – are entirely possible.

The argument has three steps. I begin by drawing on one or two historical examples. The field of such examples passes well beyond the horizon, but I have chosen a few lesser-known instances that continue to intrigue and entice me. From history, I move to theoretical reflection with the help of sundry Marxists, corralling together those who have recognised in some way the political ambivalence of Christian theology. In this section, I draw upon and extend various moments in the earlier volumes of the *The Criticism of Heaven and Earth*, for political ambivalence became a consistent theme, especially in *Criticism of Theology*, where I traced it through the work of Max Horkheimer,

1. Negri and Scelsi 2008, p. 205.

E.P. Thompson, G.E.M. de Ste. Croix, Michael Löwy, Roland Barthes, Deleuze and Guattari, and Antonio Negri. Others will turn up in the following pages. Although they all give voice to this ambivalence to some extent, some are more astute than others, so I have distinguished between the unwitting and the witting – that is, in some cases the political ambivalence of Christian thought and practice emerges inadvertently in their work, while in other cases it is explicitly foregrounded. One question is left hanging: why is Christianity so riven with contrary political directions? So I close by outlining some of the preliminary theoretical questions that will set the scene for the full, gritty detail of a historical proposal that must await the next chapter.

Scandal and folly

No better illustration of the ambivalence of Christianity may be found than in the history of the last two millennia. Immediately I am faced with a problem of oversupply, for the examples could be piled up in an interminable, multivolume work; an encyclopaedia perhaps, one section known as the Christian Black Book and the other as the Christian Red Book, each competing with entries to outdo the other. Nonetheless, I restrict myself to a few key examples. On the negative side, the usual suspects include the infamous conversion of Constantine in 312 CE, with the subsequent legalisation, sponsorship and eventual declaration – by Theodosius I in 380 CE – that Christianity was to be the sole religion of the empire, as well as the Crusades, the pursuit of heretics, the Inquisition and the wars of religion in Europe after the Reformation. Some are desperately ludicrous, such as the admission by the Roman Catholic Church that it had erred in declaring Galileo's heliocentric positions heretical – in 1992! Others are barbaric, such as the pogroms against Jews in the Middle Ages or the rise of Islamophobia in the twenty-first century.

Papal power

Rather than express faux horror with the bloodiest examples to be found, I prefer to give a couple of lesser known but equally pertinent examples: the rise of papal power, the treatment of heretics, and the California missions of the nineteenth century.[2] On papal power: over the period of half a millennium, from 1000 to 1500 CE, papal power was to rise to unheard-of heights only then to begin a long decline. We can trace a number of key features of this period. During its peak,

2. I provide these examples for readers not familiar with such material. Those who know the stories may pass on without loss to the section 'Folly to the Rich'.

princes, kings and emperors would submit and kneel before the pope; by its end, they would use him as a pawn in their wider power struggles. At the beginning of this period, the feudal order of society was firmly in place and provided the sense of a unified and ordered Europe; by its end that order was beginning to become unstuck as the towns grew and a new economic and social order was showing its face. A major feature of the rise of papal power was a complex system of benefices and law which governed all aspects of daily life; decline set in when that system became bogged down in its own complexity. In the early years, kings and emperors would hand over heretics to be put on trial and executed by the church; in later years, these rulers would protect dangerous new thinkers as allies in their own struggles with the pope.

The rise of papal power was due to a new theory of that power, energetic popes, European politics, and changing social landscapes. The story begins with a forgery that expresses the dream of papal power: the *Donation of Constantine*. Although the *Donation* presents itself as a letter written by the Emperor Constantine to Pope Sylvester I on 30 March, 315 CE, it was actually written after 750. What does it claim? Apart from speaking of Constantine's conversion and baptism, and claiming to have been placed on the body of St Peter, it offers the pope control over all churches, especially the great centres of Antioch, Alexandria, Jerusalem, and Constantinople, the Lateran palace in Rome and the imperial insignia, as well as the transfer of all earthly power in Rome, Italy and the provinces of the West. It may not be a genuine document, but the forgery speaks a deeper truth, which was to spell out the basic claims of the medieval papacy. Here, we find the pope as universal bishop following in St Peter's footsteps, teacher and godfather of the emperor, Christ's agent on Earth and lord of the West.

The ideal took a while to come to fruition. Until the eleventh century, the pope's limited power was based on the fact that people looked towards Rome and Peter's tomb; the pope did not exercise any power himself. In theory, the fictional claim to be in a direct line from St Peter should have given the pope massive power – derived from the fact that Peter is supposed to have been a disciple of Christ, the one to whom the commission to establish the Church was given and to whom were granted the keys of Heaven (Matthew 16:19). Peter had at least died in Rome, so it became easy to produce the myth – first propounded in the third century CE – that he had been the first bishop, establishing a direct line of succession for all subsequent bishops of Rome (the reality is quite different, for the first bishop of Rome with some claim to credibility was Linus, c. 67–78 CE and only in 153 CE did Hyginus call himself 'pope'). Pope after pope took care to remind everyone that they spoke in the name of Peter. For three hundred years, this power remained a dream rather than reality. By the reign of Pope Gregory VII

(1073–85), all that had changed. These years are often called the papal revolution in both theory and practice. Gregory asserted the independent power of the papacy in all areas of life: in law, the first independent body of church (or canon) law developed; in politics, the pope strenuously asserted the right to appoint and depose rulers; in the church, the pope's own agents (legates) had the final say over all clergy; in the everyday life of common people, the pope became the ultimate feudal lord at the top of the pyramid.

There was also a vital shift in the source of the pope's power. No longer did the Vatican lawyers feel happy with the idea – embodied in the *Donation of Constantine* – that the emperor had given the pope all that power. No earthly ruler could grant anything to Christ's representative on Earth, for only Christ could do that. So the theory of papal power was deepened and strengthened: it came from none other than Christ, that is, God. No text better expresses the height of papal power than a statement in one of Gregory VII's letters:

> The pope can be judged by no one;
> The Roman church has never erred and never will err till the end of time;
> The Roman church was founded by Christ alone;
> The pope alone can depose and restore bishops;
> He alone can make new laws, set up new bishoprics, and divide old ones;
> He alone can translate bishops;
> He alone can call general councils and authorize canon law;
> He alone can revise his own judgments;
> He alone can use the imperial insignia;
> He can depose emperors;
> He can absolve subjects from their allegiance;
> All princes should kiss his feet;
> His legates, even though in inferior orders, have precedence over all bishops;
> An appeal to the papal court inhibits judgments by all inferior courts;
> A duly ordained pope is undoubtedly made a saint by the merits of St Peter.[3]

A series of energetic popes after Gregory VII, especially Innocent III (1198–1216) and Boniface VIII (1294–1303), put this theory into practice. Through astute diplomacy, they ensured that they were indispensable to medieval society at every level, gathering around them multiple allies who extended their rule into all walks of life. The backward nature of Western European politics, which paled by comparison with the Byzantine Empire in the East and the Muslim world, ensured that the popes were able to climb to the pinnacle of power. Warring princes, constant territorial conflict, and the perpetual search for strategic alliances meant that the pope became a useful ally for any prince seeking to gain

3. Southern 1970, p. 102.

influence for himself. Within the feudal system, the pope claimed he was the highest feudal lord, at the peak of the pyramid. Since he spoke God's word on Earth, all should obey them.

Even with all these developments, the pope was still called the 'Vicar of St Peter'. For many centuries, this had been sufficient. The problem was that it looked backwards, tracing a direct line to the Apostle Peter and thereby to Christ. But the papacy was now looking forward, so a new title was needed. At the end of the twelfth century, Innocent III (pope from 1198 to 1216) took on the title 'Vicar of Christ'. As he put it, 'We are the successor of the Prince of the Apostles, but we are not his vicar, nor the vicar of any man or Apostle, but the vicar of Jesus Christ himself'. It was an unambiguous claim to universal authority. Innocent opined, in all modesty, that although he was lower than God, he was higher than any human being. He occupied a place between God and human beings and was the mediator between them. It was the high point of the theory of papal power. From there it was a long and slow way down.

All this power could not be asserted merely on paper; power must be wielded in real terms. The popes did so by developing a highly complex system of benefices and a legal system. To those who came to Rome and kissed the pope's feet, the pope gave an extraordinary range of benefits. It might be the legal claim to land for a monastery, order or bishop, the confirmation of their customs, freedom from jurisdiction by a local lord, or honours such as the use of papal insignia. The popes showered their increasing number of supporters with these material benefits and signs of status. In this way, they ensured an ever greater number of allies. Further, the papacy created the most effective legal system of the Middle Ages. At its centre was the recovery of absolute private property, which had been forgotten after its invention by the Romans.[4] By adapting Roman law to feudalism, the murky area of property was clarified. The popes of the period from the eleventh to the thirteenth century developed a system in which everyone sought the opinion of the papal courts. Land claims were cleared up, due process for every minute aspect of daily life was established, litigants streamed to Rome for decisions, the pope's legal representatives (legates) were everywhere, and papal power spread. This achievement of the 'lawyer popes' in this papal revolution was the beginning of the legal system now dominant in the West.[5]

But to assert power, popes also need armies. They fostered support from princes by handing out benefits, which usually generated prestige and wealth for the recipients, providing an indispensable legal system, and through astute diplomacy between warring princes. As a result, the pope could call on some princes and their armed forces to further his agenda. And at times, especially

4. Gianaris 1996, p. 20; Miéville 2004, pp. 195–6.
5. See Berman 1983; Berman 2006.

when Italian princes themselves (such as the Borgias) became popes, they had their own standing armies. As Stalin once retorted when criticised by the pope many years later, 'how many divisions does the pope have?' In the years of papal power the answer was, 'very many'.

Heresy

My second example comes from the heretics, especially since – to gloss Ernst Bloch – the most notable feature of both Christianity and Marxism is that it continues to produce heretics. Although sexual misdemeanours – altar boys, orphans, cathedral pets – have replaced heresy in our own day, the standard term with which to dismiss and threaten an opponent in the Middle Ages was 'heretic'. The Greek *hairesis,* of course, means 'choice' – choosing a different position in a debate, but such choice became a little more risky after Christianity became the sole religion of the empire in the fourth century. The problem was determining which of the myriad versions of theology was the 'correct' one. For the trouble with heresy is that one's enemy is always a heretic; you are, of course, orthodox. Everyone claims to represent truth, so that whoever disagrees is heretical. In the end, those with favour at the imperial court, able to command the resources of army, secret service and imperial police, would triumph. They became 'orthodox', while those who lost were branded and burnt as 'heretics'. As the great Doctor Angelicus, Thomas Aquinas put it, 'Heresy is a sin which merits not only excommunication but also death, for it is worse to corrupt the Faith which is the life and soul than to issue counterfeit coins which minister to the secular life. Since counterfeiters are justly killed by princes as enemies to the common good, so heretics also deserve the same punishment'.[6] In fact, many heretical movements, especially in the Middle Ages, were born out of the perpetual desire to recover the perceived simplicity and authenticity of the early church – the effect of what I called in the previous chapter the political myth of early Christianity. They looked at the church of the day and saw little that resembled the narratives of the New Testament: the church had become massive, highly structured and wealthy. The church's response was simple: absorb them or crush them. Establish a new order – Franciscans, say – and channel the new ideas, or excommunicate and condemn them to death.

One colourful example is the Bogomils, now part of the unique legacy of the Balkans. Beginning in Bulgaria under the leadership of Bogomil in the ninth century, they spread rapidly from the eleventh century onwards and influenced deeply the development of the like-minded Cathari in Italy and France (also

6. Aquinas 1969, 2, 2, qu. xi, art. 3.

called Paterenes and Albigensians – the heritage of as important a Marxist as Henri Lefebvre). In the thirteenth century, the Cathari were perceived to be such a threat to the 'orthodox' church that the word 'heretic' actually came to be synonymous with Cathari. Both Bogomils and Cathari believed in dualism: the world and the human body are the work of Satan, while only the soul is made by God; the New Testament and Psalms are the only true scripture, for the rest was the work of Satan; Christ had only the appearance of a human body, his true soul leaving the body at his death; like Christ, salvation for the believer meant that the soul was freed from its evil body. Above all, they rejected the authority of the church and regarded its sacraments as evil. Naturally, they thought everyone else was a heretic, while the church treated them likewise. Unfortunately, they did not have the forces of the state at their beck and call and were mercilessly persecuted for centuries. Even a crusade was called to hunt them down.

Other groups suffered similar fates, such as the Waldensians (who still exist in Italy), the Beguines (a lay woman's movement in the Netherlands and Belgium), the followers of Geert de Groote (also from the Low Countries), as well as witches and even sodomites (a blanket term that covered same-sex relations, sex with animals and any other type of sex that was officially frowned upon). With the increasing plethora of 'enemies of the church', more extensive policing was required: the Inquisition was established in 1232.

By contrast, other 'enemies of God' such as the Jews were relatively privileged. It was a privilege most people would rather not have. Jews were not to be converted by force; their children could not be removed from parental care in order to be brought up as Christians; they could practise their religion as long as they refrained from proselytising. But that was all. They were allowed to survive, but only in the barest circumstances. Often reviled and attacked, Jews were widely accused of having 'sinned' through their 'unbelief', of having killed Christ and of having brought on the Black Death. Another heresy was Islam, which during the eighth century had overcome large stretches of territory under Christian sway. Palestine, Syria, North Africa and Spain all fell under the sway of these 'enemies of God'. As the Muslims were slowly being expelled from Spain a few centuries later, the Spanish Inquisition was established in 1478 and then in Portugal in 1536. Although the Inquisition originally pursued all forms of heresy, it turned its attention increasingly to 'Moriscos' (superficial converts from Islam, often done under duress) and then 'new Christians' (those with Jewish ancestry). Perceived to be an increasing problem after the forced mass conversions in the late fifteenth century, the Moriscos and new Christians were tried and executed if found to be insincere about the Christianity they had adopted – which usually meant the presence of secret Jewish or Muslim rites.

Missions, of the Californian variety

Finally, a little off the beaten track, my third example is that of California missions. These missions were a response by Philip V, king of Spain, to the long reach of the Russian empire. By 1741, it was clear that the Russians were heading south from their base in Alaska, down the west coast of North America. By 1812, they had reached present-day Sonoma County in California, establishing Fort Ross as a fur-trading, scientific and agricultural settlement. To counter this threat, Philip ordered the colonial headquarters in Mexico City to secure the holdings of 'New Spain' as far into northern or 'Alta California' as possible (in contrast to 'Baja California' in what is now Mexico).

The solution: Franciscan missionaries were to convert the heathen and establish mission stations all the way up the coast. The result: a 966 kilometre string of mission stations, each roughly fifty kilometres apart. The southernmost station was San Diego de Alacalá, first established in 1769, while the northernmost point was San Francisco Solana (in Sonoma), finally formed in 1823. Between these two dates is the period commonly known as the mission period in Californian history. Each station was placed as close as possible to the coast, partly because these were the most fertile regions and partly because heavy items could be transported only by sea. Eventually, it came to be known as the 'mission trail', maintained with the explicit purpose of providing safe rest stops for travellers overland; each mission was a long day's ride on horseback apart. As was so often the case, colonial expansion and missionary activity went hand in hand. The task of colonisation in Alta California was entrusted to the Franciscans, while the Dominicans were given control of Baja California after the Jesuits were thrown out by Charles III in 1767. The monks set out on foot, travelling in twos, partly in obedience to Jesus's command to the disciples to travel in pairs (Mark 6:7–13) and partly for companionship. Needless to say, they also had a company of soldiers with them, should the need arise to offer the natives some incentive to convert.

The problem for the Franciscan monks was how to convert the indigenous population. Preaching out aloud in Spanish and calling for people to admit their sins and turn to God was not a favoured option, largely because it did not seem to work. Instead, baptism was the key, for Christ is supposed to have said, 'Go therefore and make disciples of all nations, baptising them in the name of the Father and of the Son and of the Holy Spirit' (Matthew 28:19). However, according to church practice, baptism of adults required catechism first, a teaching in the basics of the Christian faith. The missionaries might have cut the course of catechism to a few basic principles, but they stuck with the accepted pattern. The next problem was how to encourage the local people to stay long enough to be taught. The solution was the mission station. The mission served to draw the locals into one place, so much so that at the high point of the missionary endeavour (in 1806) more than twenty thousand indigenous people lived at the missions. The layout included a chapel, accommodation for the monks, for single males and single females, for married couples, barracks for the soldiers, fields for cultivation and cattle, and workshops, since everything had to be made on site. The missions also supplied – in provisions and other 'services' – a nearby garrison [*presidio*] if there was one. The land around about grew crops of cereals and fruit (orange, apple, pear, peach, figs), olives, grapes for wine and even tobacco. And they farmed animals such as cows, sheep, goats, mules and pigs – all brought up from Mexico.

It takes little imagination to determine who actually did the work on the mission stations. Conversion obviously meant far more than committing one's life to God. The names given to the settlements are revealing: missions were known as *reducciónes* [reductions] or *congregaciónes* [congregations] and their purpose was to 'reduce' the heathen natives from their 'unfree' and 'uncivilised' status to the state of Christian belief, 'civilisation' and 'freedom'. If you were a local, that meant learning European ways, European dress, work rhythms, foods and customs – it was unimaginable that one could become a Christian without these necessary appurtenances. Did the people leave once baptised? Not at all, for after baptism they became 'neophytes', a euphemism for losing their freedom. They were expected to work six hours per day, the periods carefully regulated by bells, without pay on the farms or in the workshops or in building programmes. Many became disillusioned and fled the mission; the monks had limited success in finding them. If you were single, then you lived in male-only or female-only quarters. And if you were interested in a boy or girl, then you would conduct courtship on a Spanish model: under the watchful eye of the monk, you would talk with your prospective partner through bars, just in case those barbaric instincts got the better of you. To crown such a wholesome life, unhygienic European living conditions brought European problems and diseases. For example, in 1806, a quarter of the mission population died during a measles epidemic. Further, unsanitary conditions in the living quarters led to regular deaths; most of the monks too died in the mission field. In short, they were little better than prison camps. Finally, in 1833 the missions were secularised (that is, confiscated) by the Mexican government, the Franciscans were expelled and the work came to an end.

Many, many more examples of Christian cruelty could be gathered. Indeed, I could make this into a life's task, gathering all the evil effects of a religion such as Christianity – psychically, socially, politically, environmentally and on and on – as indeed the 'new old atheists' have tried to do recently. I do not wish to repeat my criticisms of such an approach here, since I have done so in Chapter One;

my point here is that it tells only one side of the story, and a rather lopsided one at that. For the other side, I trace three very different examples.

Folly to the rich

As with the previous section, with its brief selection of the less salubrious examples of the dirty deals between state power and Christianity, I will limit the revolutionary examples to three. I see little point in repeating the analysis I have provided elsewhere of Thomas Müntzer and the peasant revolution of 1525 (a common name in this roll call ever since Engels wrote of him),[7] Gerrard Winstanley and the Diggers in the seventeenth century, and the guerrilla priest, Camilo Torres Restrepo, in the context of liberation theology.[8] Nor do I wish to give a rendition of the long engagement with liberation theologies – Latin American, feminist, black and queer – that may be found in *Criticism of Theology*.[9] Plenty of other examples might make the list, such as Anglo-Catholic Socialism;[10] the Society of Sacramental Christians;[11] the International League of Religious Socialists,[12] with over two hundred thousand members in 21 countries; or indeed the Christian Socialists of the UK,[13] although I must admit the sheen has worn off this last group since the former Labour prime ministers of the UK, Tony Blair and Gordon Brown, were members. On the scholarly register, I might include Richard Horsley, the New Testament scholar who is developing a comprehensive picture of the economic and political climate in which the revolutionary Jesus movement took shape, or Gerald West, who has been deeply influential in South Africa as both a biblical scholar and activist, or Gale Yee, also a biblical scholar and activist who has been instrumental in bringing Marxist and feminist approaches together in her biblical work.[14] However, I limit my examples to three: Wilhelm Weitling, Thomas J. Hagerty, and the biblical scholar Norman Gottwald. Three very different characters and rather less well-known. Weitling is usually known through Marx and Engels, a communist before them, activist, founder of the League of the Just that Marx and Engels joined and turned into the Communist League, and signatory to early statements by the executive of the First International. Hagerty, one of the

7. Engels 1850a; Engels 1850b. Kautsky would provide the most complete treatment of Müntzer, at least until Ernst Bloch's famous description of him as 'theologian of the revolution'. See Kautsky 1979; Kautsky 1947a; Bloch 1969.

8. See Boer 2007b, pp. 105–27.

9. Boer 2010a.

10. <http://anglocatholicsocialism.org>.

11. <http://sacramentalsocialists.wordpress.com>.

12. <http://ilrs.org>.

13. <http://thecsm.org.uk>.

14. See Boer 2007b, pp. 47–9.

central figures in establishing the Industrial Workers of the World in 1905, seems to have slipped off the radar, with nary an entry on the Marxist Internet Archive and absent from the IWW website. And Norman Gottwald will be known only to biblical scholars and members of the Democratic Socialists of America. I have deliberately chosen them not because they provide nice, soft examples of philanthropic ventures such as meals on wheels or working bees at the local parish church, important though they are. Each of them was and is a revolutionary socialist.

Wilhelm Weitling

'The founder of German Communism' is how Engels describes Wilhelm Weitling.[15] A fascinating figure, Weitling was a man with impeccable revolutionary credentials: poor working-class background, journeyman tailor, autodidact, in touch with the assumptions and ways of working people, lifelong activist and one who found inspiration in the Bible for his early version of communism.[16] Here is Weitling:

> Christianity is the religion of freedom, moderation and enjoyment, not of oppression, extravagance and abstinence. Christ is the prophet of freedom.
>
> The christian has no right to punish the thief because as long as the theft exists christianity is not realised among us.
>
> Take courage, disinherited sinners. A beautiful kingdom is prepared for you. Look at the sloping fields, the trees laden with fruit, the fair streets and buildings, the ships on the sea, rivers and lakes, the roads and the railways... Look at all the cattle in the meadows, the shops, the birds in the air, the fish in the water, the plants in the high Alps and the precious minerals under the earth, all this by God and by right is our common property.[17]

Weitling stands between the tradition of Christian communism and the foundation of modern communism, an organiser, activist, revolutionary and for many years a militant on the run. However, he is usually remembered for coming out the worse for wear in the protracted struggle with Marx in 1846–7. The issue: a draft party programme for the League of the Just [*Bund der Gerechten*], an organisation Marx and Engels had only recently joined. For over a decade, however, Weitling had already been one of the leaders of the League, which was

15. Engels 1843c, p. 402. For a detailed if somewhat light and entertaining biography, see Wittke 1950. See also Haefelin 1986; Hüttner 1985; Knatz 1984.
16. Unfortunately, the collection edited by Knatz and Marsiske (2000) studiedly avoids the biblical dimensions of Weitling's activism, touching on it only in passing (pp. 50–1, 90, 96, 227–8).
17. Weitling 1969, pp. 10, 119, 115–16.

really the first international communist organisation with branches in Germany, France, Switzerland, Hungary and Scandinavia.[18] He had been actively at work, writing, editing journals, fomenting revolution (including the abortive Paris uprising in 1839), escaping police and prison and living on the run. The struggle with Marx took place after Weitling, disappointed with the poor reception of his ideas in London, turned up in Brussels in early 1846. Marx himself had arrived from Paris, banished due to pressure on the French by the Prussian government. The two went head-to-head: Weitling argued for a direct and violent overthrow of the state and the immediate establishment of communism based on the model of the first Christians in the New Testament. To Marx, all this was sentimental, backward-looking rubbish. After all, argued Marx, what was needed first was the full development of capitalism and bourgeois democracy before communism could take root. Weitling, the self-taught journeyman tailor, was no match for Marx's fierce intellect and university training. By June of 1847, the newly named Communist League endorsed Marx's programme, although by now the league was based in London, whither Marx had fled from the Brussels police. A year later, *The Manifesto of the Communist Party* was published, but by this time Weitling had emigrated to the USA.[19]

As they part ways, let us follow Weitling rather than Marx – a path less trodden and covered with weeds and overgrowth. In North America, after some years of activism, organisation of the Workingman's League and the commune called Communia in Iowa that eventually failed, Weitling called it a day in 1855. He married Dorothea Caroline Louise Toedt, a German immigrant like himself, settled in New York, fathered six children, resumed his work as a tailor and busied himself with inventions related to his trade, improvements to the sewing machine which came into general use, astronomy and the development of a universal language. The obituary in the *New York Times* of 27 January 1871 makes no effort to conceal his revolutionary and communist activities in Europe – he even returned to Paris to fight in the 1848 Revolution, coming back to North America in 1849. But I am interested in a passing comment in the obituary, one that observes he was largely self-taught and an 'active thinker'.[20]

This restless mind, full of plans, inventions, and ideas to improve the lot of the working class, also produced four books – an astonishing achievement by an autodidact, given that he often worked twelve hours a day earning a living.[21] These texts are full of the history of modern society with its private property, money and class antagonisms, and plans, constitutions and suggestions for organising

18. K. Taylor 1982, p. 187, puts the total membership at about 1,300.
19. Marx and Engels 1848c; Marx and Engels 1848d.
20. *The New York Times* 1871, p. 4.
21. Weitling 1845; Weitling 1955; Weitling 1969; Weitling 1967; Weitling 1846.

communist society, blueprints for the revolutionary and communal efforts he would undertake. But a key feature of these books, especially *The Poor Sinner's Gospel*, is the invocation of biblical texts in order to criticise the corrupt priest-craft, abuse of power and exploitation of workers. Already in his earlier *Die Menschheit* (from 1839–40), Weitling resorts to the Bible in the opening chapter.[22] His favourite texts are those sayings of Jesus where he tells the disciples not to lord it over others but serve them, comments on the inability to obey both God and mammon and the command to seek not treasure on Earth but in Heaven, for where your treasure is, there your heart will be also.[23] Indeed, he uses a text that would become a favourite of Marx: 'where moth and rust consume and where thieves break in and steal'.[24] And, of course, he resorts to the image of early Christianity in the Book of Acts with its *Gütergemeinschaft*, the community of goods, the condition of entry being the sale of all one's possessions and sharing with the poor. So seriously, observes Weitling, was this condition taken that failure to do so had the divine penalty of death – as the story about Ananias and Sapphira in Acts 5:1–11 makes clear.[25] Apart from urging a return to original Christianity (as is the wont of all religious reformers), he listed among his exemplars Thomas Müntzer, peasant leader and theologian of the revolution, Jan van Leyden (or Beukelszoon), a leader in the anabaptist Münster Revolution (1534–5), and Hugues Felicité Robert de Lamennais (1782–1854), the radical priest.

All this was only a warm up for *The Poor Sinner's Gospel*, written in Zurich in the first half of 1843. The book had an immediate impact, although not from the quarters that Weitling had expected. Midway through printing, Weitling was arrested on the street by the Zurich authorities and charged with sedition, inciting to riot, public nuisance and blasphemy. His defence that in a Reformed canton, one in which Zwingli had worked no less, the free interpretation of the Bible was the right of all, had no effect whatsoever.[26] Not a bad way to publicise the book, but the cost was high: Weitling served ten months in prison, suffered deep emotional turmoil[27] and was then banished from Switzerland for five years. Even though the authorities destroyed the plates of the book, a manuscript was preserved, printed and then later revised by Weitling himself. These experiences brought Weitling to observe that one day the persecutions of the communists

22. See also the treatment in Knatz 1984, pp. 112–17.
23. In sequence: Matthew 20:25–7; 6:24; 6:19 and 21. See Weitling 1845.
24. Matthew 6:19.
25. 'Die Bedingung der Aufnahme in das Christentum war der Verkauf der Güter des neu Aufzunehmenden und die Vertheilung derselben unter die Armen. Die Uebertreter dieses Gesetzes wurden schwer gestraft, und wir finden in der Bibel auf einen solchen Fall selbst die Todesstrafe. Vgl. Apostelgeschichte 5, 1–11' (Weitling 1845, p. 12).
26. Weitling 1969, pp. 187–97.
27. See Wittke 1950, pp. 85–9, who, based on Weitling's diaries, provides a haunting account of Weitling's mental instability while in prison.

would come to an end in the same way that they had for the early Christians (and, indeed, witches). But what did the conservative burghers of Zurich find so objectionable about the book?

Although the book shows all the marks of an autodidact – especially with the regular polemic against philosophers and their craft[28] but also with a vividness of writing for the common readers he knew so well – Weitling was no fool. Despite his liking for Christian love (he would not be the first on the Left to fall for this idea) and morals, he presents a relatively sophisticated view of communism, one that includes the paradox of communists despite themselves, a plurality of communisms, a call for putting aside disputes over detail and the assertion of freedom of religion. Weitling read the Bible carefully, often providing long lists of texts to back up his positions, and shows an awareness of critical issues relating to the text – issues that were novel then but are common parlance now. He was also able to identify a picture of a rebel Jesus that comes remarkably close to the image traced by liberation and political theologians in our own day, let alone the softer, mainstream image of a radical Jewish peasant by the likes of Jon Dominic Crossan.[29] Weitling finds a very human, earthy and earthly Jesus, born in the usual manner, one who was a 'sinner' and preferred the company of other 'sinners',[30] who struggled against imperialism and oppression, both external (Roman) and internal (Jewish). He presents such an image by situating Jesus and the early followers within an oppressive social and economic context, very much in the way Engels, Kautsky and Luxemburg would do after him. However, what interests me most is the way in which Weitling deals with contradiction. For much of the book, he uses contradictions and ambiguities – in terms of history, narrative, morality and doctrine – to undermine the platitudes of theologians. His strategy is to seek Jesus's core principles behind and around these contradictions, principles that he lays out in the key chapter of the book (one that comprises more than a quarter of the whole text)[31]: the gospel is preached to the poor; it entails Christian freedom and equality; action and not faith alone is necessary for the kingdom of God; all have equal responsibilities and duties; the abolition of property and community of goods, of inheritance and of money; abolition of the family for the sake of freedom; the value of the love feast. In sum, core teachings of

28. '"Avoid the quarrelsome debates which are falsely called knowledge", says Paul. But as he wrote this he must have forgotten that he was quite accomplished in this art himself… The bible is as full of such ambiguities as the writings of many modern philosophers' (Weitling 1969, p. 64).

29. Crossan 1993, 1995.

30. 'All the people that today we call wicked, outcast, debauched, immoral, common, etc., were called in those days plain sinners. These publicans and sinners who were despised by all were the very people sought out by Jesus and he ate and drank with them' (Weitling 1969, p. 131).

31. Weitling 1969, pp. 75–126.

the Bible 'can best be put into practice by the most perfect form of communism'.[32] Should there be any doubt, Weitling supports each proposition with long lists of biblical quotations, often followed by brief expositions. However, at some points Weitling explores a more dialectical approach to the ambivalences of the Bible, none more so than with this concluding observation:

> Now they ['Pharisees', capitalists, rulers] will read this book and say one can make whatever one likes of the bible. Too true, for they have made it a gospel of tyranny, oppression and deceit. I wanted to make it a gospel of freedom, equality and the community of faith, hope and love, if that is not what it already was. If they were wrong, they were wrong out of self-interest. If I am wrong, it is for love of mankind.[33]

Both options may resort to the text and find their positions validated; both too may find that they are wrong. So Weitling shifts the focus to the motivation for such readings, although he does hold out the possibility that his reading has a substantial basis in the texts he has painstakingly gathered.

For this revolutionary firebrand, there was no rupture between communism and Christianity, at least in the line he traced from the Bible to his own thought. He was, of course, not the first to do so, for he follows in a long train that includes the various movements for simple communal living in the Middle Ages, such as the Beguines and Beghards of the Netherlands in the twelfth century, the Waldensians, who derive from the twelfth century and still exist today in Piedmont, or the Bohemian (Moravian) Brethren from the fifteenth century, heirs of Jan Hus, who stressed personal piety, a focus on the world to come through their worship and communal life, and who settled under the protection of Count Zinzendorf at Herrnhut (sixty kilometres east of Dresden) in 1721. And he was also able to make use of the earlier works by Saint-Simon, Fourier, Cabet and Owen, which comprised a fledgling socialist literature. But what is unique about Weitling is how closely he tied the tradition of Christian communism to a sustained criticism of capitalism and the need for a communist revolution, in contrast to Saint-Simon, Cabet and Owen, who felt that a peaceful transition was eminently possible and practicable. Marx was to transform these criticisms and dismiss much of Weitling's thought in the process,[34] but not before Marx had praised Weitling's 'brilliant writings' and observed that *Guarantees of Harmony and Freedom* was a '*vehement* and brilliant literary debut of the German

---

32. Weitling 1969, p. 17.
33. Weitling 1969, p. 186.
34. See, for example: 'Then Weitling took the floor and proceeded to prove that Jesus Christ was the first communist and his successor none other than the well-known Wilhelm Weitling' (Marx 1853b, p. 296; Marx 1853c, p. 229).

workers'.[35] Not only did Marx and Engels inherit the hard work of Weitling with the League of the Just, but the initial effort by Engels to construct a history of Christian revolutionary activity before Marxism as well as the wholesale reconstruction of that history by Kautsky could not have happened without Weitling sowing the seeds.[36]

Father Thomas J. Hagerty

A very different story is that of Father Thomas J. Hagerty, but the underlying drive is the same, namely, a melding of Christian commitment and radical communism.[37] At the height of his activism in 1903 and 1904, Hagerty was an electrifying orator. In the words of Eugene Debs, Socialist Party and later IWW leader:

> Tall, massive, erect, he would command attention anywhere. On the rostrum he is a striking figure, and when aroused is like a wounded lion at bay. He has ready language, logic, wit, sarcasm, and at times they roll like a torrent and thrill the multitude like a bugle call to charge.[38]

Yet, the story of Father Hagerty is a somewhat sad one, a short incandescent burst of radical activity for some three years – 1902–5 – before disappearing into obscurity. His origins are similarly cloudy: he studied theology before becoming a pugnacious and active priest in New Mexico from 1895, serving in a number of parishes, saying mass, hearing confession, baptising children, burying the dead, before turning into a full-time militant in 1902. Addressing rallies for the Socialist Party, editing newspapers, writing articles, he put all of his formidable energy into grassroots activism. His crowning achievement was a direct and central role in the formation of the Wobblies, the Industrial Workers of the World. Hagerty had been one of the original six who had met in the autumn of 1904 to send out invitations to labour radicals to form a militant union and was at the centre of the conference in June 1905 that launched the IWW in Chicago. He was secretary of the union's constitution committee, helped frame the Industrial Union Manifesto, designed the most comprehensive diagram – Hagerty's Wheel of Fortune – mapping out the various trades and their relation, and he edited and wrote most of *The Voice of Labor*, the official newspaper of the American Labor

35. Marx 1844e, p. 201; Marx 1844f, pp. 404 and 405.

36. Engels 1843c; Kautsky 1947b; Kautsky 1947c; Kautsky and Lafargue 1977.

37. Since there is relatively little material available on Hagerty, I am reliant on the excellent article by Doherty 1962.

38. Debs 1903, quoted in Doherty 1962, p. 48. According to Clarence Smith, Secretary of the American Labor Union, 'Father Hagerty is without a doubt the brainiest and certainly one of the most eloquent speakers in the labor and Socialist movement in the world' (Clarence Smith, 'Reverend Father Hagerty's Lecture Tour', *American Labor Union Journal*, 1 January 1903, quoted in Doherty 1962, p. 48).

Union for the six months of its frantic existence. Indeed, Hagerty is credited with writing the preamble to the IWW constitution, with its slogan that rang around the world, 'The working class and the employing class have nothing in common'.

As quickly as he had come, he was gone. By the middle of 1905, Hagerty dropped out of political activism altogether and gave up his identity as a priest, a status he had never lost during his militant years, despite church disapproval. One or two old comrades caught up with him in Chicago many years later and found him living in deep poverty, eventually reliant on soup kitchens, a few cents from passers-by, missions for a bed and free concerts to keep up his cultural interests.

But what is so appealing about Father Thomas J. Hagerty? I am less interested in his usefulness as a priest who could persuade Roman Catholic workers to join the movement, and more in his effort to bridge the antagonism between the church and socialist leaders. He argued consistently in his speeches and articles that the church hierarchy had no business telling workers how to think and act politically. In line with this position, he would often write that religion and socialism dealt with different spheres of life, that religion and politics had no truck with one another: 'It is as much beyond the scope of Socialism to deal with divine revelation as it is beyond the range of the Republican Party to advance a new exegesis of the Davidic Psalms'.[39] 'Socialism', he wrote elsewhere, 'is an economic science, not a system of dogmatic beliefs'.[40] Given these two spheres, there was no problem in combining his Roman Catholic faith and radical socialism. However, at other moments he sought to bring these two realms together in a somewhat different fashion, drawing on the church fathers – Basil, Chrysostom, Gregory, Jerome – to show that socialism was consistent with their teaching. And in response to yet another round of condemnations from the church hierarchy, he responded that any priest who might vote for the capitalist system would make it perfectly clear that 'he has voted for the continuance of the very things against which his Master of yore thundered in the highways of Palestine'.[41]

---

39. Hagerty 1902a, p. 44, quoted in Doherty 1962, p. 41.

40. Hagerty 1902b, p. 229, quoted in Doherty 1962, p. 44.

41. Thomas J. Hagerty in the *Social Democratic Herald*, 8 August 1903, quoted in Doherty 1962, p. 50. In line with this sentiment, let me quote a hymn that Hagerty may well have known. It comes from the 1900–30 era of Christian Socialist gatherings – processions, rent strikes and May Day masses – in England, led by Father Conrad Noel (the 'Red Vicar of Thaxted'), Percy Dearmer and Basil Jellicoe. If he had, I am sure he would have sung along lustily. It is called 'God is the Only Landlord to Whom Our Rents Are Due'.

1. You faithful saints and martyrs / Who fought for truth and right, / We ask your prayers and blessings / To aid us in our fight. / Your faith shall be our watchword, / Your cause shall be our own – / To fight against oppression / Till it be overthrown. [Refrain:]

Was Hagerty's thought inconsistent? In one respect, yes, in the sense that the tension in his thought may well have played a role, along with sheer burn-out, in leading him out of both socialist activism and the church. The fact that he fell out with the bulk of the IWW and fellow socialists by the sheer radicalism of his positions did not help matters, for he advocated immediate revolution, disdained democracy, the ballot box and those he called the 'slowcialists'. In another respect, the answer must be no; his two positions are not so inconsistent. They may have been in his own mind, but they do reflect an uncompromising honesty in Hagerty's effort to work through the relation between Christianity and politics. Let me put it this way: in many respects the wavering back and forth between complete separation of the two spheres of socialism and theology and his effort to see their connections embodies the ambivalence that is the topic of this chapter. For Hagerty could see that his own tradition lent itself all too readily to reaction and the support of exploitation; at these moments he sought to separate his socialist and Christian commitments. But he could see equally well that the two had a good deal in common. It is a shame he was not able to resolve the tension.

Norman Gottwald

The final figure in my trinity of progressive appropriations of theology and indeed the Bible is Norman Gottwald. I have written about Gottwald on a number of occasions and will do so again in the next chapter, but these engagements have been mostly with his historical and social-scientific proposals regarding ancient Israel. An American Marxist biblical scholar (more than one jarring juxtaposition in that epithet!), Gottwald has in many respects both established social-scientific approaches to the Hebrew Bible with his monumental (if flawed) *Tribes of Yahweh*

Lift up the people's banner / And let the ancient cry / For justice and for freedom / Re-echo to the sky.

2. In many a golden story, / On many a golden page, / The poets in their poems / Have sung the golden age, / The age of love and beauty, / The age of joy and peace, / When everyone lived gladly / And shared the earth's increase. / [Refrain]
3. Today the tyrants triumph / And bind us for their gains, / But Jesus Christ our Saviour / Will free us from our chains, / And love, the only master, / Will strive with might and greed, / Till might is right no longer, / And right is might indeed. / [Refrain]
4. God is the only Landlord / To whom our rents are due. / God made the earth for everyone / And not for just a few. / The four parts of creation – / Earth, water, air, and fire – / God made and ranked and stationed / For everyone's desire. / [Refrain]
5. God made the earth for freedom / And God alone is Lord, / And we will win our birthright / By truth's eternal sword; / And all the powers of darkness / And all the hosts of pride / Shall pass and be forgotten / For God is by our side. / [Refrain]
6. Christ blessed the meek and told them / That they the earth should own. / And he will lead the battle / From his eternal throne. / O have no fear, my comrades, / Cry out in holy mirth! / For God to us has promised / His Kingdom here on earth. / [Refrain].

and opened up some space for credible Marxist analysis of biblical texts. My own work, at least in biblical studies, could not have taken place without the pioneering work of Gottwald. But there is another side to Gottwald – the long-time activist – that is my focus, here.[42]

Gottwald is at pains to point out that the various phases of his scholarship are inseparable from his experiences of activism of more than half a century. He is one of the few remaining radical biblical scholars who were immersed in the heady excitement of the 1960s. But even before then Gottwald had become involved as a young seminary lecturer in the fledgling anti-nuclear movement in the late 1950s which fed into the Vietnam War protests, as well as the first stirrings that were to explode into the Civil Rights movement of the 1960s. Already with an interest from earlier work on the prophetic literature of the Bible, he and his students began to see the way those texts spoke to their own situation: exploitation, abuse of power, grinding down of the weak and poor, these and more were the targets of prophetic invective. Time and place may have differed, but the situations were sufficiently analogous to see that the prophetic texts were more than relevant.

During the critical mass and urgency of the 1960s, with free speech, Vietnam, nuclear issues, feminism and racial discrimination all coming together, with myriad groups forming, reforming and coalescing into popular fronts, with calls to 'speak truth to power', Marx too was in the air. So Gottwald read Marx and read some more, discovering – or perhaps it would be better to say re-discovering – the way prophetic and Marxist critiques overlapped with one another. Note well: this pipe-smoking, pock-faced seminary professor with shaggy hair and a serious look did not resort to the Book of Acts or the sayings placed in the mouth of Jesus in the gospels. No, he saw the connections with the Hebrew prophets. I wrote *re*-discovery, since Gottwald was by no means the first to see that prophetic criticisms of wealth, latifundia, debt-bondage and exploitation of the vulnerable applied to his own time. To cull two examples from a very long list, Gerrard Winstanley and Thomas Müntzer had done it many centuries before. And since the nineteenth century Christian socialists had also made the connection between Marx and the prophets, Brooke Foss Westcott (1825–1901) – Old Testament scholar, Regius Professor of Divinity at Cambridge and then Bishop of Durham (UK) – being but one of the most notable.[43]

42. What follows is drawn from an interview I conducted with Gottwald in Amherst, Massachusetts, at the Rethinking Marxism Conference of 2000. See Boer 2002.

43. See Westcott's speech, simply called 'Socialism', delivered to the Christian Social Union (of which he was president) in 1890 at Project Canterbury (Westcott 1907). Westcott was one of the most significant biblical scholars of the late eighteenth and early twentieth centuries. See, more generally on Victorian Christian socialism, the study by Edward R. Norman (2002).

The difference for Gottwald, however, was the way that his political commitments and activism informed his scholarship and vice versa. Unlike Westcott, who carried on his impeccable scholarly work in Hebrew linguistics in strict separation from his political convictions (although I wonder whether he was really able to do so, for the two must have influenced one another, even if indirectly), Gottwald saw the importance of Marx for both his scholarly and political work. It is difficult for those who were not involved at the time to gain a sense of the sheer excitement and novelty of Marx, whose work had lain dormant for too long, the preserve of much-maligned communists and the atheistic totalitarianism of the Soviet Union. For Gottwald, in the same way that Marxism provides a way to overcome the splintering of politics into interest groups, it also provides the means for moving past the Taylorisation of academic work and thereby seeing social, political, economic and ideological issues as part of a larger whole. The *Radical Religion* journal came into being, edited by a collective in the late sixties and early seventies, and then *Tribes of Yahweh*,[44] with its proposal for an internal Canaanite revolution that comprised the origins of ancient Israel (1250–1050 BCE), followed by the widely used *The Hebrew Bible: A Socio-Literary Introduction* with its explicit focus on political matters and sustained critique of class dynamics in the reception and interpretation of the Hebrew Bible.[45]

Political involvement remained a continuous part of Gottwald's life – local elections in Berkeley, campaigns to turn electricity production and distribution over to public ownership, opting for a teaching post in New York on the wrong side of the tracks (is that not most of New York?), and then in retirement becoming involved with the Democratic Socialists of America, working on immigration, globalisation, healthcare and labour relations. In the meantime, Gottwald's scholarly work has been taken up by radical religious groups around the world, including Korea, the Philippines, South Africa and South America.

Enough, perhaps more than enough, examples of the way theology and the Bible seem to lend themselves to reaction and revolution, although there are myriad possibilities within such a simple opposition. Papal power, heresy and California missions are very different examples, but they all tend to be variations on the brutality of theology's ready embrace of earthly powers. While they might somewhat charitably be seen as efforts made in the interest of Christianity, that interest itself becomes questionable in the light of their outcomes – much like a passionate belief in bestiality. As for Weitling, Hagerty and Gottwald, I was interested in some lesser-known examples of the effort to link Marxism and Christianity. More seamless in the cases of Weitling and Gottwald and more problematic for Hagerty, but I would suggest that the point of unity came with

44. Gottwald 1999.
45. Gottwald 1985.

their political activism. And despite their flaws and limits, there is enough to show a revolutionary dimension to that same tradition which has also spawned more than its share of twitching, tortured corpses.

Towards a Marxist theory of political ambivalence

Reactionary or revolutionary, conservative or progressive, or, when it comes to identity politics, patriarchal or egalitarian, racist or inclusive, homophobic or polyamorous and on and on – all these are struggles fought within and over Christianity, the churches, the Bible and, of course, the Left. Anyone who surveys these brawls soon gains the impression that the favoured mode of engagement is 'proof-texting': a particular biblical text that supports one's own position is uttered with a triumphant flourish only to crumple when a counter-text comes straight back. For example, the biblical text from Galatians 3:28, 'There is neither Jew nor Greek, there is neither slave nor free, there is neither male nor female; for you are all one in Christ', finds its immediate counter in Paul's letter to the Corinthians, 'Every one should remain in the state in which he was called',[46] as well as the enlightened observation that 'the head of every man is Christ, and the head of a woman is her husband'.[47] This approach gets us nowhere, with one side claiming the upper hand through bibliometric means – my collection of proof-texts is bigger than yours – or perhaps by mounting up more examples of atrocities over philanthropic acts.

I do not wish to play this game. So let me clear the air with a few basic assumptions: the Bible contains texts that are both reactionary and revolutionary; there are tendencies within theology to move in either direction, or indeed in a multitude of directions that may be more of one than the other; revolutionary movements have found as much inspiration within the Bible and Christianity as many a brutal tyrant may have done. In its own way, the previous section has established as much. So, rather than arguing until I am hoarse for either side (although my preferences should be clear), the far, far more intriguing question is how to make sense of this situation. In other words, in good dialectical fashion I ask what the conditions for this ambivalence might be rather than wield cudgels in defence of one or other proposition. Nonetheless, given the nature of this study, I do not wish to trawl through various proponents of the religious Left or Right; instead, I turn to that motley collection of erstwhile Marxists to see what might be made of this political ambivalence within religion.

---

46. 1 Corinthians 7:20.
47. 1 Corinthians 11:3.

A good number of Marxists have been willing to acknowledge and even explore in some depth the rebellious, revolutionary possibilities of a religion such as Christianity – they are, after all, the subject of this study. I have always been struck by the fact that they are not oddballs in the Marxist pantheon, slightly off the mark since they do not regard religion as a potent mix of mystification, ignorance, musty priestcraft, sordid sexploitation and justifications for the blood and gore of oppression. There are far too many of these 'religion-positive' (the allusion to 'sex-positive' in relation to pornography and sex work is no accident) Marxists to relegate them to some institution for the deranged. However, it is one thing to say that religion can indeed be a factor in genuine liberation and quite another to acknowledge that it is simultaneously oppressive and liberating, that the two are intrinsic to the way that a religion such as Christianity functions. In this section I am interested in this latter group, although they are by no means uniform. So I begin with a rough distinction between the unwitting and the witting, between those who stumble across the political ambivalence of Christianity and those who zero in on this ambivalence as a central feature. To the former belong Rosa Luxemburg, some elements of Karl Kautsky's work, E.P. Thompson, Louis Althusser, G.E.M. de Ste. Croix, and some aspects of the thought of Max Horkheimer; among the witting we find Marx to some extent, Engels far more, Kautsky in a way that builds on Engels, Ernst Bloch (as we would expect by now), but also Max Horkheimer, Michael Löwy and, perhaps surprising to some, Antonio Negri. I would like to stop by the way for a few moments, sit in a quiet spot under the trees, boil a billy and make a cup of tea, light a smoke and first ask the unwitting what they might have to say; the witting will come soon enough.

The unwitting

Immediately it becomes clear that the unwitting are by no means a uniform group, so I distinguish further between the implicit, the broken and the fallen; or rather, between those for whom the political ambiguity of Christianity is implicit, for whom the connection between reaction and revolution is broken, and those who see the relation between them in terms of a fall, inevitably as a betrayal of a purported rebellious core.

The implicit

By an implicit recognition of the political ambivalence of Christianity I mean the effort to emphasise the revolutionary credentials of Christianity as a counter to its apparent default position of propping up the status quo. Rosa Luxemburg stands out in this respect, for she is fully conscious of the church's self-interest in terms of money and power. For instance, she provides some statistics regarding the property and capital of the Roman Catholic churches in Austria, Spain, Italy and France, and then draws on crime statistics to argue that ignorance, drunkenness and crime rise when the church enjoys extensive power.[48] In short, the church joins the worst of those who exploit labourers for profit, having adjusted very well to capitalism after the church's domination of feudal society. As if to counter these sordid details, Luxemburg develops an argument for early Christian communism, the details of which I outlined in the previous chapter. Here is a religion focused on the poor, condemning those who ride on their backs, advocating the abolition of wealth (or at least its even distribution), offering succour to the needy and outcast. Now, while Luxemburg makes the most of early Christian communism, she does not develop any dialectical argument for these two vastly different modes in which Christianity operates; instead, she pulls out a fall narrative to account for the drastic change from early Christianity to the glittering cathedrals and well-endowed clergy of the later church. I will have more to say about that narrative soon enough, but my point here is that a theory of the political ambivalence of Christianity is implicit in Luxemburg's account: both the church engaged in capitalist exploitation and early Christian communism are parts of the same whole. That approach would make far more sense of her argument than some putative fall narrative, but such a dialectical reading remains well concealed, never to show its face in her account.

Much the same could be said about Karl Kautsky's *Foundations of Christianity*, or at least most of it. He too waxes forth about the corrupt and grubby dealings of the Christian churches while developing an argument very similar to Luxemburg for early Christian communism. And he too relies on a fall narrative to account for the eye-popping shift between these two elements of Christianity. But Kautsky is, as we shall see, a jack-of-all-trades who is able to turn his hand to a range of positions on religion. So he also comes around to argue for the dialectical connection between reaction and revolution, but in a side alley – monasticism. I will save monasticism for my treatment of the witting, since in the main argument of *Foundations* Kautsky walks hand-in-hand with Luxemburg: two great and irreconcilable versions of Christianity are juxtaposed with one another and yet there is no comprehensive effort to account for why they are part of one and the same phenomenon. Or rather, the reason remains buried in his account.

Broken connection

In some respects, Luxemburg and Kautsky draw nigh to what I have called the broken connection: two (or even more) perceptions of Christianity jostle for

48. Luxemburg 1970; Luxemburg 1982.

space in their works, but they see little, if any, connection between them. Yet they differ from the genuine broken-connection group – E.P. Thompson and Louis Althusser – on one critical issue: Thompson and Althusser shift between enthusiastic censure of the evils of Christianity and equally enthusiastic advocacy of its revolutionary possibilities. It is either one or the other, with little middle ground. The reason: the shift is biographical, for at one point in their lives they were ardent opponents of religion, while at another point they pushed the radical potential of religion as hard as they could. Yet their biographical trajectories move in contrary directions, Althusser from a positive assessment of Christianity in his early life to one that was far more negative later, Thompson in reverse. Althusser began as a critical member of the Catholic Left in France, a keen advocate of radical, if somewhat fringe, groups within the Roman Catholic Church, seeking a politics of alliance with the socialists,[49] but then he passed through an under-documented conversion from Christianity and into Marxism. From that moment, religion became the bogey that he constantly sought to excise from his life and thought.[50] Thompson's biographical connection with religion went in exactly the opposite direction, although he spared himself Althusser's time of commitment. So we find the shift in his work from thoroughgoing denunciation of the psychic terror of Methodism in *The Making of the English Working Class* to the deep appreciation and even advocacy – much to the vocal chagrin of his comrades on the Left – of revolutionary Christianity in William Blake and sects such as the Muggletonians.[51] Perhaps because of these seismic shifts during their lives, the two ends of their approaches to religion do not connect. The radical moments of Christianity – from Althusser's early and Thompson's later years – fail to relate to its brutally conservative moments. As with two electrical wires that are too short, the soldering iron cannot attach them to one another.

---

49. See especially the early essays, 'The International of Decent Feelings', 'A Matter of Fact', 'On Conjugal Obscenity', the theological moments of his thesis on Hegel and his letter to Jean Lacroix. They may be found in Althusser 1997; Althusser 1994.

50. Although he was not able to rid himself of religion entirely, since it remained an absent cause of much of his later work. See Boer 2007a, pp. 107–62.

51. Thompson 1966; Thompson 1993. However, it is possible to find the seeds of that later reassessment of Christianity in *The Making of the English Working Class*. See Boer 2010a, pp. 57–102. I must admit that my narrative of Thompson's shift is troubled a little by the virtually unknown poetry collection, *Infant and Emperor*, which turns the infancy stories of Jesus into a secularised polemic against the Herods of nuclear armament. In the process, those apparently sweet stories of the baby Jesus become potent political pieces. Yet, despite the potential represented by the poems, Thompson does not bring the reactionary and revolutionary elements of Christianity together in any meaningful whole. See Thompson 1983.

The fall

At least Thompson and Althusser do not become ensnared in what I have called a fall narrative. A deceptively simple trap, with a lost golden age and banishment from paradise, it seems to catch many: Luxemburg and Kautsky are guilty, as are G.E.M. de Ste. Croix and Max Horkheimer. If you wish to make an argument for early Christian communism, then you must account for why Christianity is no longer like that; a narrative of the fall is one of the most convenient ways to deal with the loss. For Luxemburg and Kautsky (when he is engaged with this particular trade) the fall involves size and survival. As Christianity grew in size it could no longer maintain the community in which everything was held in common. And as it spread, wealthy patrons and community leaders also became Christians; it became increasingly unviable to ask them to give all they had to the poor, especially when Christianity became more and more respectable. I have already broached the issue of survival: an ever larger movement needed structure, a recognised leadership, and so the old communitarian impulse began to fade with offices such as priest and bishop. Of course, the great symbol of the fall is the conversion of Emperor Constantine in 312, his adoption and enthusiastic fostering of Christianity and then the eventual legislation that made Christianity the sole religion of the Empire.

Two comments need to be made here. First, Luxemburg and Kautsky have bought into one of the most common themes in the history of Christian reform movements. The church has lost its way, claims one movement after another; the priests have become lax and self-serving, the church wealthy and worldly. So we will base ourselves on the words of Jesus and go back to the model of early Christianity in the New Testament, seeking a simple faith in community (and often in poverty). The Reformation was only the high point of a series of such reform movements and they continue today, making the same claims. The second point is that Luxemburg and Kautsky inadvertently make use of a 'flawed crystal' argument. It opens with the question: how could such a fall happen? The paradigmatic story of the Garden of Eden offers multiple answers: the people are responsible (the man and woman disobey and eat from the tree); a third agent is at fault (the serpent); God is responsible, for he set them up to fall in the first place. How? By putting a tree or two (and there are two in the Genesis account, one of life and one of the knowledge of good and evil) in the garden from which one is forbidden to eat. This third option is the one that Luxemburg and Kautsky take, albeit in modified form. Early Christian communism was flawed, as we saw in the previous chapter, for it was a communism of consumption and not production. Such a system actually maintains the status quo, for it requires some at least to continue generating wealth outside the commune in order to keep redistributing goods. And it gives way too easily to a system of alms, in which the (very necessary) well-heeled members of the church can assuage their guilt at being wealthy by giving alms to the church (for its clergy) and to the poor (cared for by the church).

Terry Eagleton, G.E.M. de Ste. Croix and Max Horkheimer are caught in the same snare, although in a manner that differs from Luxemburg and Kautsky. Eagleton offers very little in the way of specifics in *Reason, Faith and Revolution*,[52] but he subscribes wholeheartedly to the argument that somewhere along the line, Christianity lost its radical, almost revolutionary edge. In a rambling, hodge-podge book (one gains the feeling that he has lost his edge since he gave up beer and smokes), he loosely distinguishes between the scriptural form of Christianity and the ideological, the former of course being the radical core and the latter its betrayal into an ideology of power, wealth and influence. So, in a classic move (his theology is in fact very conventionally Roman Catholic, with many references to Thomas Aquinas), he argues that the earliest is the more authentic and what followed is a bowdlerised and fallen version of Christianity.

In contrast to Eagleton's rambling prose and search for one-liners, Ste. Croix is detailed and careful. Yet he, too, opts for a narrative of fall and betrayal. For him it comes very early indeed, almost immediately after Jesus had spoken his words and challenged all with his provocative acts.[53] By the time one gets to the Apostle Paul, the rot has set in: members of the propertied class are given privileged status, slaves are told in no uncertain terms to stay where they are and women are relegated to inferior positions. The early Christian theologians hammered home the message: be conformed to this world, for we need to secure our place within it. A close reading of Ste. Croix's array of data reveals a few anomalies in this pile of evidence, church 'fathers' who questioned the massive property rapidly being accumulated by the church or who realised that slavery was not the appropriate lot for so many human beings,[54] but the overwhelming opinion offered no relief. Now Ste. Croix was no apologist for Christianity, for he was in polemical rejection of the British Israelite God of his youth (his mother belonged to this off-beat and very British strain of Christianity), so it is all the more remarkable that he could approve of Jesus. In theological terms, Ste. Croix did not mind the son, but could not abide his bloodthirsty brute of a father. But

52. Eagleton 2009a, pp. 47–108. This book recycles many of Eagleton's thoughts on theology – the intrinsic nature of key doctrines and of God, the ability to see the best and worst of human beings, the possible contributions to Left-thought and action – found not only in his return to theology (Eagleton 2001; Eagleton 2003c; Eagleton 2003a; Eagleton 2006; Eagleton 2007), but also in his early days as an amateur theologian of the Catholic Left. See Eagleton 1966a; Eagleton 1967a; Eagleton 1967b; Eagleton 1968a; Eagleton 1968b; Eagleton 1968c; Eagleton 1969; Eagleton 1970.

53. Ste. Croix 1981, pp. 103–11, 418–25, 433–8; Ste. Croix 2006, pp. 328–71. At the beginning of a very different argument, Goodchild makes a very similar point to Ste. Croix. See Goodchild 2009, pp. 2–7.

54. See the detailed treatment in Boer 2011a, pp. 103–58.

the only way he seems to be able to deal with the glaringly obvious way Christianity failed to live up to the teachings of its founder was through a version of the fall narrative.

Horkheimer, too, would draw upon a very similar version of the fall, namely the betrayal of the founder's words by those who professed to follow him.[55] Words of implacable criticism, dangerous doctrine and inflammatory words – all these come from the mouth of Jesus, and yet Christians have betrayed them again and again. Of course, the problem with such an argument (this comment applies also to Ste. Croix) is that the words of Jesus, if not his life as a whole, are virtually impossible to recover. That he existed is generally, although not universally,[56] admitted. What he said and did has been the subject of intense and ongoing quests for the historical Jesus, with no assured results. Ste. Croix depends far more on such historical data (as do Luxemburg and Kautsky), but not so Horkheimer. Instead Horkheimer espies key elements of authentic Judaism and Christianity that continue to be betrayed: the utopian longing for a totally other, the uncompromising allegiance to that other and the refusal to be conformed to or bent by any power in this world, and the commitment to perpetual resistance to all that corrupts and oppresses. By contrast, whenever Christianity or Judaism have become cosy with the state (Horkheimer was therefore an unrelenting critic of Zionism and the state of Israel), whenever theology makes its compromises with the ways of the world (he has liberal theology of the early- to mid-twentieth century in mind), it is a perversion of authentic religion.

In much of his writings on religion, Horkheimer falls prey to the desire for a pure core of religion that has been betrayed and distorted. Yet he differs from Luxemburg, Kautsky and Ste. Croix on two crucial matters. The first is that he sees no one moment of a fall – usually placed at some time after the Jesus of the gospels, sometimes sooner (Ste. Croix), sometimes later (Luxemburg and Kautsky) – but a perpetually repeating pattern of falling. A little like the beginning cyclist who keeps running off the road, Christianity and Judaism repeat the

---

55. Since Horkheimer had a liking for writing aphorisms and essays, his comments on religion are scattered through many different writings. They may be found in Horkheimer 1978; Horkheimer 1982; Horkheimer 1993; Horkheimer 1996; Horkheimer 2004; Horkheimer 1985a; Horkheimer 1985b; Horkheimer 1985c; Horkheimer 1985d; Horkheimer 1985e; Horkheimer 1985f; Horkheimer 1985g; Horkheimer 1985h; Horkheimer 1985i; Horkheimer 1985j; Horkheimer 1985k; Horkheimer 1985l; Horkheimer 1985m; Horkheimer 1985n; Horkheimer 1985o; Horkheimer 1985p; Horkheimer 1985q; Horkheimer 1985r; Horkheimer 1987a; Horkheimer 1987b; Horkheimer 1987c; Horkheimer 1987d; Horkheimer 1987e; Horkheimer 1988a; Horkheimer 1988b; Horkheimer 1988c; Horkheimer 1988d; Horkheimer 1988e; Horkheimer 1988f; Horkheimer 1988g; Horkheimer 1988h; Horkheimer 1988i; Horkheimer 1988j; Horkheimer 1989a; Horkheimer 1989b; Horkheimer 1991a; Horkheimer 1991b; Horkheimer and Adorno 1985; Horkheimer and Adorno 2002; Horkheimer and Adorno 2003. A full discussion with specific references may be found in Boer 2011a, pp. 11–56.

56. See Thompson and Verenna 2012.

same mistakes over and over again. It may be a small improvement on the arguments of Luxemburg, Kautsky and Ste. Croix, but the quite unoriginal schema of authentic kernel and corrupted outer shells is not much of an improvement. I did indicate that there is a second difference in Horkheimer's account, but for that we need to join the witting, since he, a little like Kautsky, is a jack of at least two trades.

The witting

Perhaps it is not so generous to refer to the various approaches – which I have just discussed – to the political multivalence of religion as unwitting, but they do give the impression that they were not quite as aware as they should have been of the connections between the reactionary and revolutionary strains of Christianity. Their falling short, however, shows up more clearly when we consider those who did realise the ambivalence I seek. Even here, I must make a distinction between glimpses and the startling clarity of full awareness, as when the mists clear in a mountain forest and one can find the path which has remained hidden until now.

Glimpses

Horkheimer turns up first, largely because we left him negotiating the troubled narrative of a fall from the unsettling and radical statements of Jesus and the early Christians. Like Kautsky, Horkheimer has the distinction of holding more than one position, for he can present a stark and irreconcilable contrast between resistance and compromise, or opt – problematically – for a version of the fall narrative, but also break through to a more dialectical understanding. These insights do not crowd Horkheimer's texts, appearing in passing in the aphoristic reflections of which he was fond.

Three of them are worth mentioning, each of them turning on the dialectical need for both resistance and betrayal. To begin with, Horkheimer observes far too briefly that the 'indwelling protest [*innewohnenden Widerspruch*]'[57] of religion – he means Judaism and Christianity – is actually nurtured by the inevitable tendency for religion to compromise with those accustomed to wielding wealth and power with disgusting ease. More than mere survival – in which Christianity had to betray its ideals in order to avoid coming to a swift and gory end – Horkheimer suggests that survival itself was the means by which the desire

57. Horkheimer 1978, p. 185; Horkheimer 1991a, p. 330. For an informed and sensitive engagement with Horkheimer, see Siebert 2001, pp. 131–46; Siebert 2003, pp. 185–96; Ott 2001.

for resistance and renewal was sustained, ready to cry out yet again when protest regained its voice. Here, we come close to the awareness that the tension between resistance and betrayal, between authentic and inauthentic religion, is an inescapable feature of Christianity.

Further, in a brief interpretation of Psalm 91 (a variation on verse 9 of the Psalm is etched on his gravestone), Horkheimer observes that the endless procession of brutal acts such as the Crusades and the Inquisition were all justified in the name of God. More often than not, Horkheimer would go on to argue that these acts were distortions and betrayals of the truth of Christianity. Not here, for the possibility of resistance springs out of these sustained moments of cruelty: 'its own love for the truth, its contempt for manipulation by unscrupulous cliques, finally even that faith *owes itself to that which it denounces* [*sich verdanken, den er denunziert*]'.[58] Not a bad dialectical insight, for even though betrayal constantly haunts authentic resistance, that authentic form cannot operate without such betrayal. Resistance arises from and responds to betrayal and compromise. Horkheimer is not done: 'Still through bitter disdain, with which *it disavows its own manifestation* [*mit dem er die Erfüllung leugnet*], it unconsciously recognises a homesickness that cannot refrain from the thought of paradise'.[59] No longer does he argue that the authentic core of religion has been betrayed, for all that Horkheimer finds so abhorrent about religion actually comes from within. Indeed, it is because of that manifestation from within that we find the yoking of bitter disdain *and* the recognition of homesickness, a longing for the other – they are one and the same feeling. A profound dialectical sense of the ambivalence of Judaism and Christianity, is it not? We may come across one form or the other, resistance and betrayal, authenticity and unauthenticity (the terms are Horkheimer's), but they cannot be divorced from one another in the schema of truth and its distortion that appears so frequently elsewhere in his thoughts on religion.

Finally, Horkheimer offers a glimpse of this dialectic in his comments on the origins of theology: he argues that theology came into being as a compromise between the demands of the gospels and power.[60] Note the point: theology did not betray itself when the church found itself padding along the halls of power; it was born of this compromise. This is a vital insight: theology is an exceedingly ingenious discipline, for it embodies the effort to bring into an embrace both the uncompromising words of Christ and the right of the stronger, the attempt to bring the laws of earth and heaven into touch with one another. Far more than mere survival in a sinful and corrupt world, theology sought a way for all people – poor and rich, Jew and Greek, slave and free, men and women, ruling

58. Horkheimer 2006, p. 117; Horkheimer 1985n, pp. 208–9; emphasis added.
59. Horkheimer 2006, p. 117; Horkheimer 1985n, p. 209; emphasis added.
60. Horkheimer 1996, p. 36; Horkheimer 1985g, pp. 174–5.

and oppressed classes – to find their place in the new order. Rather than fulsome praise, it is a grudging awareness of theology's *Realpolitik*. Without it, some of the great achievements of human culture would not have been, such as literature, art, architecture, the ingenious efforts of Thomistic scholasticism that offered a complete picture of one's place in the cosmos, even the Reformation which gave a huge impetus to human rights, civil liberty, reason and the importance of the individual.[61] Yet the compromise was costly, for each one of these achievements is built upon the sheer misery of the mass of the voiceless poor.

Let us take this insight into theology's inherent tension a little further. Horkheimer presents that tension as a devious and (grudgingly) brilliant effort at *Realpolitik*, but there are also matters of form and content that broadcast such a tension at all levels. In its effort to apply systematic categories, derived in part from Greek philosophy, to the narratives of that new genre, the gospel, theology enacted a compromise in form and content. In form, there is the tension between story and system, between variant narratives and coherent doctrine, while in content there was the obvious tension between outright resistance, especially by Christ, and the statements found elsewhere that one should obey the rulers of this world (Romans 13:1–2), obey the powers, principalities and magistrates (Titus 3:1), submit to kings and governors (1 Peter 2:13) and offer prayers and intercessions for all in authority (1 Timothy 2:1–2). Or, as Horkheimer observes, the utterances of the biblical prophets stand side by side with what he calls 'biblical patriotism', embodied above all in the stories of Joshua's campaigns to conquer the land of Canaan.[62]

Horkheimer is but the first of those who glimpse at various moments the political ambivalence of Christianity. For two other key examples, I roll back the years and focus on Marx and Engels, the former offering a more grudging awareness, the latter coming close to a full-blooded insight into the dialectic of revolution and reaction. As for Marx, there is a well-worn foothold in his texts, a passing comment or two where he recognises the potential ambivalence in religion. He writes:

> *Religious* suffering is, at one and the same time, the *expression* of real suffering but also the *protest* against real suffering. Religion is the sigh of the oppressed creature, the heart of a heartless world, just as it is the soul of soulless conditions. It is the *opium* of the people.[63]
>
> Das *religiöse* Elend ist in einem der *Ausdruck* des wirklichen Elendes und in einem die *Protestation* gegen das wirkliche Elend. Die Religion ist der Seufzer

61. Horkheimer 1996, p. 37; Horkheimer 1985g, p. 175.
62. Horkheimer 1996, p. 115; Horkheimer 1985f, p. 171.
63. Marx 1844c, p. 175 (translation modified).

> der bedrängten Kreatur, das Gemüt einer herzlosen Welt, wie sie der Geist geistloser Zustände ist. Sie ist das *Opium* des Volkes.[64]

As many have observed, to say that religious suffering is a protest against real suffering, or to allow that religion may provide some heart and soul in heartless and soulless conditions is to allow some ambiguity within religion. Yet, these admissions never pass over the basic point in Marx's treatment of religion, namely that it is a sign of the alienated conditions of human existence, conditions that need to be addressed and overturned. I often have the sense that commentators pin far too much on these statements, even if they come from a crucially important manifesto-like document, the published Introduction to Marx's unpublished critique of Hegel's *Philosophy of Law*.[65]

More intriguing is the most well-known of Marx's slogans on religion – 'Sie ist das *Opium* des Volkes', 'It is the opium of the people'. Much of the ambivalence surrounding religion in Marx's thought is contained in this one phrase. Even if we bracket out Marx's own complex intentions in penning the sentence (intentions that are as difficult to pin down as jelly to a wall), opium bears within it the contradictions I seek. For as McKinnon has shown so well, opium – both drug and idea – was overloaded with contradictory associations in nineteenth-century Europe.[66] A widespread medicine and pain reliever, especially for the poor, it was used, along with reputable products such as creosote and arsenic, for pains, aches, fevers, pustules, sniffles, hacking coughs and even for putting children to sleep while their parents worked. But it was also condemned as a dangerous placebo that could do more harm than good. Even more, opium was also a drug of choice in the nineteenth century for artists and writers, those seeking the realm of the muses through the age-old artistic practice of substance abuse. Add to this the economic importance of opium, particularly for the British Empire (most notably the wars fought with the Chinese over the opium trade), and it becomes a term overrun with opposed associations.[67] In short, opium was blessed medicine, recreational curse, and economic foundation all rolled into one. Of course, Marx himself used it for his many complaints brought on by over-writing, poor diet, chain-smoking and endless pots of coffee. His letters are full of reports and debates with Engels and others over what is best for his well-known carbuncles, but also his toothaches, liver problems, bone-rattling coughs and eye problems. In these letters opium appears very often indeed.

---

64. Marx 1844d, p. 378.
65. Marx 1843c; Marx 1843d.
66. McKinnon 2006.
67. McKinnon traces a shift from a generally benign view of opium at the beginning of the nineteenth century to its increasing condemnation, especially through government committees and studies, by the end of the century.

Unstable, shifting and somewhat volatile, opium stands in quite well as a metaphor for the political ambivalence of theology. But this is by no means the only time Marx lets slip a begrudging awareness of the revolutionary possibilities of theology. He may have commented in a letter to Lasalle, 'so specific is my aversion to Christianity [*so spezifisch ist mein Widerwille gegen das Christentum*]',[68] but that did not stop him noting that it may well have a moment or two that were far closer to his own preferences. Some of these moments may be found in the multitude of biblical and theological references and allusions that pepper his writings. Most of these deal with efforts to outwit the censor (especially in his early years of journalism with the *Rheinische Zeitung*), attacks on the ruling classes, whether a fading aristocracy or energetic bourgeoisie, critiques of the default tendency for clergy to creep into the same hole as a corrupt ruling class and polemic against political opponents, mostly on the Left.[69] However, at a few points we find Marx struggling with biblical contradictions in his youthful essay on the gospel of John,[70] touching on the revolutionary undercurrent of the Garden of Eden narrative in Genesis 2–3,[71] noting that the saints are often on the side of the poor,[72] systematically using New Testament texts on mammon and power to undermine the claims by the Prussian 'Christian state' to be based on the Bible[73] and referring to the 'divine inspiration from below' of the English Revolution when Charles I found his torso relieved of its head.[74]

---

68. Marx 1862a, p. 377; Marx 1862b, p. 627.

69. See the first chapter of Boer 2012, where I have gathered and assessed all of these theological allusions.

70. Marx 1835a; Marx 1835b.

71. In response to an effort by the speaker of the Rhine Province Assembly to appropriate the text for his own conservative position, Marx retorts that 'the devil *did not lie to us then*, for God himself says, "Behold the man is become as one of us, to know good and evil"' – thereby touching on a subversive tradition in which the serpent (the narrative does not have a devil) and thereby Eve stand up to the tyrant God. See Marx 1842k, p. 168; Marx 1842l, p. 156.

72. Marx 1842m, p. 253; Marx 1842n, p. 227.

73. Here is this full and delightful text: 'Do you consider it wrong to appeal to the courts if you have been cheated? But the apostle writes that it is wrong. If you have been struck on one cheek, do you turn the other also, or do you not rather start an action for assault? But the gospel forbids it. Do you not demand rational right in this world, do you not grumble at the slightest raising of taxes, are you not beside yourself at the least infringement of your personal liberty? But you have been told that suffering in this life is not to be compared with the bliss of the future, that passive sufferance and blissful hope are the cardinal virtues. Are not most of your court cases and most of your civil laws concerned with property? But you have been told that your treasure is not of this world. Or if you plead that you render unto Caesar the things that are Caesar's and to God the things that are God's, then you should regard not only golden Mammon, but at least as much free reason, as the ruler of this world, and the "action of free reason" is what we call philosophising.' (Marx 1842i, pp. 198–9; Marx 1842j, p. 186.)

74. Marx 1842k, p. 156; Marx 1842l, p. 144. For more detailed treatments of these texts, see Chapter Eight of Boer 2012.

I am wary of making too much of these glimpses within Marx's own texts, for he felt that theology and religion more generally were set to a reactionary default. With religion full of distinctly unhelpful ideas and focused on the heavens, he would rather concern himself with earthly matters. Nevertheless, occasionally he glimpses the radical undercurrents of theology and registers, despite his own inclinations, that theology cannot so easily be locked in. Engels, however, is a different story. On this matter of political ambivalence, he offered a position that recovered in some ways the brilliance that characterised him in the period before he became Marx's lieutenant.

I cannot press hard enough on this difference between Marx and Engels. It is not merely that Engels took a certain point from Marx, who was notoriously unable to finish a project in his last years, and gave it some substance. Further, Engels certainly did not get the nod from Marx to explore the revolutionary potential of Christianity or to point to its political ambivalence – even if they kept up lively commentary in their letters concerning the vital role of religion in geopolitics. No, this is Engels's own line. Much has to do with his upbringing in a Reformed (Calvinist) home in Elberfeld (Wuppertal), but I do not wish to dwell on that youth here, except to indicate that Engels's lifelong reflections on religion – especially 'Bruno Bauer and Early Christianity', 'The Book of Revelation' and 'On the History of Early Christianity'[75] – may be seen as his effort to come to terms with that background.

I have written enough in the previous chapter of Engels's argument for the radical, revolutionary nature of the early Christian movement, as well as his efforts to identify the recurrence of that seditious undercurrent in moments such as Thomas Müntzer and the peasant revolution. Now I shift my focus, interrogating Engels on the pattern of ambivalence that keeps recurring in his work. We must tread carefully here, for it is not always an explicit awareness. Often the ambivalence I seek appears more as a contradiction in his work. So we find variously a jostling crowd of statements concerning the obfuscation and deception of religion, or the way the working classes have taken up (at least in England) an increasingly anti-church position, or the narrative of world history that involves a desperate struggle against the evils of religion, which will be overcome only with communism.[76] In sharp contrast, Engels also argues again

75. Engels 1882a; Engels 1882b; Engels 1883a; Engels 1883b; Engels 1894–5c; Engels 1894–5d.

76. For example, 'We too attack the hypocrisy of the present Christian state of the world; the struggle against it, our liberation from it and the liberation of the world from it are ultimately our sole occupation' (Engels 1844a, p. 462; Engels 1844b, p. 544). Further: 'The prisoner in solitary confinement is driven insane; the model gaol in London, after only three months of existence, had already three lunatics to transfer to Bedlam, to say nothing of the religious mania which is still usually regarded as sanity' (Engels 1844e, p. 510; Engels 1844f, p. 589). See further Engels 1843a, pp. 385–6; Engels 1843b, pp. 460–1;

and again for the revolutionary potential of Christianity. I have noted a few of these already, but the moment this argument emerges in first bloom is in his 'Progress of Social Reform on the Continent', where he produces the first survey of radical movements and leaders inspired by Christianity – among them Thomas Müntzer, Étienne Cabet and Wilhelm Weitling (from whom he seems to have drawn the idea of a revolutionary Christian tradition).[77] Perhaps the best summary appears in an unexpected place, an 'Introduction to Karl Marx's *The Class Struggles in France*':

> It is now, almost to the year, sixteen centuries since a dangerous party of overthrow was likewise active in the Roman empire. It undermined religion and all the foundations of the state; it flatly denied that Caesar's will was the supreme law; it was without a fatherland, was international; it spread over the whole empire, from Gaul to Asia, and beyond the frontiers of the empire. It had long carried on seditious activities underground in secret; for a considerable time, however, it had felt strong enough to come out into the open. This party of overthrow . . . was known by the name of Christians.[78]

All the same, such a contradiction between condemnation and appreciation could not be maintained without some awareness that Engels was actually speaking of the same tradition. A few such moments occur, among which two stand out, one from his 'Letters from London' in 1843 and the other from 'Progress of Social Reform on the Continent' from the same year. In the former text, he differentiates between the abysmal state of the established Church of England and the revolutionary origins of Christianity. While the church is rusted onto the aristocrats and Tories, full of those seeking personal gain, petty politics, outright bigotry and useless theological debates, the 'lower classes' may at times of revolutionary upheaval become progressive and draw on Christianity for inspiration: 'In general, this is a feature of every revolutionary epoch, as was seen in particular in the religious revolution of which the outcome was Christianity'. The

---

Engels 1844c, pp. 469–76, 486; Engels 1844d, pp. 550–7, 567; Engels 1844a, pp. 446–7, 450; Engels 1844b, pp. 527–8, 531; Engels 1844g, p. 212; Engels 1846a, pp. 412, 421, 556, 569; Engels 1846b, pp. 343, 352–3, 480–1, 492–3; Engels 1845; Engels 1874–5a, pp. 15–16; Engels 1874–5b, pp. 531–2; Engels 1889, p. 539; Engels 1844e, pp. 501–4, 512; Engels 1844f, pp. 580–3, 591; Engels 1892, pp. 283–300. See also the myriad comments on religion in *Anti-Dühring* and *Dialectics of Nature*: Engels 1877–8a, pp. 16, 22, 26, 40–1, 62, 67–8, 79, 86, 93–9, 125–6, 130, 144, 232, 244, 300–4; Engels 1877–8b, pp. 16, 20–1, 25, 39–40, 62, 66–8, 79, 86–7, 93–100, 126–7, 131, 143–5, 230, 239, 294–8; Engels 1873–82a, pp. 318–20, 325, 423, 474, 480–1, 498–500, 551–2, 565; Engels 1873–82b, pp. 311–13, 318, 415, 465, 470–1, 486–9, 535–6, 547.

77. Engels 1843c.

78. Engels 1894–5a, p. 523; Engels 1894–5b, p. 526. With Engels's pushing, Marx too would admit a similar point in a letter written close to his death; Marx 1881a, p. 67; Marx 1881b, p. 161.

source is none other than the Bible, which among other texts observes: 'blessed are the poor, for theirs is the kingdom of heaven and, however long it may take, the kingdom of this earth as well'.[79] The text of course comes from the Sermon on the Mount (Matthew 5:3).

Better still is the comment on Étienne Cabet's Icarian socialism, which, Engels notes, is far more Christian than any English socialism. With their motto, '*le christianisme c'est le communisme*', Cabet's movement drew heavily on what I called in the previous chapter the political myth of Christian communism. Then Engels offers a crucial sentence: 'But all this shows only, that these good people are not the best Christians, although they style themselves so; because if they were, they would know the bible better, and find that, if some few passages of the bible may be favourable to Communism, the general spirit of its doctrines is, nevertheless, totally opposed to it, as well as to every rational measure'.[80] It is, I must admit, a grudging admission of political ambivalence – 'some few passages' – but it is enough: Engels recognises the ambivalence that I seek in the Bible and in the practice of Christianity. Dominant oppression may be, but glimpses emerge despite it all to show a more restless, revolutionary line – glimpses Engels would develop over the next fifty years into a full-blooded argument for the radically revolutionary nature of early Christianity.

Full throttle

Marx, Engels and Horkheimer each offer hints of a more thoroughgoing theory of the inherent ambivalence of Christianity on political matters. Passing comments and occasional sentences threaten to break through to sustained deliberations on precisely why this ambivalence is so pervasive. Yet they do not take the next step and construct a comprehensive theory as to why Christianity should be so two-faced, or even many-faced, concerning politics. Some, such as Michael Löwy, have tried to make precisely this argument, especially in respect of Marx.[81] After brief comments on the famous opium passage, Löwy suggests that Marx (and Engels following him) did indeed understand religion as a complex, ambiguous phenomenon, one given to protest and compromise. Löwy then marches on to offer a sympathetic and influential treatment of one notable instance of the protest dimension of religion, namely, the Latin American version of liberation theology. In one sense, Löwy seeks to complete Marx's passing insight, but he could well have done with further engagement with some of the Marxists with whom

79. Engels 1843a, p. 380; Engels 1843b, pp. 451–2.
80. Engels 1843c, p. 399.
81. Löwy 1996, pp. 5–8.

I deal here.[82] Löwy is less sympathetic to Engels, which is unfortunate since Engels would have given him far more theoretical resources. In fact, Engels came closest to a full-scale theory of the political ambivalence of religion. Much of his thought on religion operates as though such a theory lay in the background; as we saw above, extensive passages denouncing the hypocrisy of conniving priests and the sordid history of the Christian churches come up against equally sustained proposals concerning the revolutionary origins of early Christianity and the history of religiously-inspired revolutionary movements, especially that of the peasants and Thomas Müntzer. Yet Engels does not quite arrive at his destination; for that we need to turn to Karl Kautsky, Ernst Bloch and Antonio Negri.

Towards the end of Engels's life, he and Karl Kautsky engaged in an often intense correspondence. They wrote about all manner of topics – the rapid development of the Social Democrats in Germany, the legacy of Marx, the growth of worldwide communism, personal details, health and so on – but also about the nature of Christianity. In many respects, Kautsky took on the mantle Engels had left behind. So, instead of a brief survey of revolutionary movements inspired by Christianity, Kautsky set out to write his four-volume *Vorläufer des neueren Sozialismus*, running through from the Middle Ages and the Reformation into the verge of the modern era.[83] So vast was the project, he did not manage to finish it himself, with the third volume completed by Paul Lafargue and the fourth written by Hugo Lindemann and Morris Hillquit. While Engels wrote long essays on early Christianity and Thomas Müntzer, Kautsky wrote a whole book on the first and hundreds of pages on the second.[84]

If Engels is usually regarded as Marx II, one who kept the ship (basically Marx's family) afloat but who was not quite Marx's intellectual equal, then Kautsky, it is usually assumed, has even less depth than Engels. Although he was a crucial Marxist intellectual in the generation that followed Marx and Engels, he was – at least according to the standard narrative – a lightweight. Like Melanchthon to Luther, he filled out the gaps and tried to complete the tasks that Engels left hanging. The evidence does not support such a narrative, at least as far as religion is concerned. For much of the time, Kautsky did operate with the same grand divide as Engels – between a corrupt, decadent church that was a shrill defender of powerful privilege, and what may be called an encyclopaedia of revolutionary Christian movements – without seeing the intrinsic connection between

82. In the opening pages of *The War of Gods*, Löwy does engage with Bloch, Goldmann and others, but in order to show that Marxism and religion have a longer history of interaction than many of his readers might imagine. Needless to say, I miss the emphasis on the multi-faceted politics of Christianity in Löwy's analysis.

83. Kautsky 1947b; Kautsky 1947c; Kautsky 2002; Kautsky and Lafargue 1977; Lindemann and Hillquit 1977.

84. Kautsky 2007; Kautsky 1977; Kautsky 2002, pp. 105–98; Kautsky 1947c, pp. 7–103.

these two mounds of evidence. Not for nothing have we encountered Kautsky at earlier points among the unwitting, for he seems to take up nearly all possible positions in relation to religion. Yet Kautsky also strikes out much further than Engels, since he did come to realise that reaction and revolution are part and parcel of the same history of Christianity.

The key lies not – contrary to expectation – with the various revolutionary movements Kautsky tracks in *Vorläufer des neueren Sozialismus*, but with monasticism. In two texts monasticism plays an underhand but vital role. The first is in the closing pages of *Foundations of Christianity*, where Kautsky argues that the initial communitarian impulse of Christianity survived in monasticism. As mainstream Christianity enthusiastically embraced its new status as religion of the Empire in the fourth century CE, thereby betraying its initial ideals, the earliest practices of communal life were not entirely dumped overboard. They found a new expression in the rise of the monastic movement, first in Egypt with the desert fathers, but then later spreading further and further afield. This monasticism went beyond the initial communism of consumption of the early Christians (due to their urban context, suggests Kautsky), for they developed a communism of production. They had little choice, for in the rural areas and harsh environment of the deserts, survival required careful attention to growing what crops could be managed, husbanding animals and securing a reliable water supply. But the breakthrough for Kautsky is that monasticism was a response to the unwelcome – at least for those attracted to monasticism – turn taken by the church. That is to say, Kautsky undermines his own earlier narrative of the fall of Christianity from its early communistic practice: instead, Christianity may have opted for compromise with the Imperial apparatchiks, but that act produced a radical response. The two face off against one another within the same arena. While priests began to wear robes that resembled those of high Roman officials, began to have their churches (originally basilicas) built with state funds and began to live at the state's expense, others (men mostly but also women) became sick of the direction of the church and retreated to remote areas to establish communities that they felt were truer to the words of Jesus and the gospels.

Did monasticism, too, succumb to the temptations of easy living? Individual monastic communities would inevitably do so, becoming established orders within church structures, but their impetus renewed itself again and again. For Kautsky, monasticism was the vital conduit that kept alive the early ideal of Christian communism, inspiring one movement after another. And that brings us to the second crucial moment when monasticism appears in Kautsky's texts – the study of Thomas More.[85] For Kautsky, More is the crucial intersection

85. Kautsky 1979; Kautsky 1947a.

between the older religious motivations for communism and modern socialism, a man who uniquely holds both elements together and thereby enables the transition from one to the other. More stands at the gate of modern socialism with his vociferous criticism of the economic exploitation in Henry VIII's England, where the early outbreaks of capitalist economic and social relations were beginning to be felt (Kautsky neglects another stream that would have fed into More's critique: older prophetic denunciations of economic depredation in the Hebrew Bible). But More also drinks deeply from the stream of Christian communism (for Kautsky a manifestation of primitive communism), with his great love of the common meal, communal living and having all things in common. What was More's source? He found it in both the *Volkskatholizmus* (feudal, popular Catholicism rather than the hierarchy) and in the communal structures of the monasteries. They had kept this tradition alive in their own flawed way and More was, at least for Kautsky, the last in a long line – last because Kautsky also nominates More as the first modern socialist and his *Utopia* as the first socialist and materialist text before Marx and Engels.[86]

I am less interested in the validity of Kautsky's reconstruction (for example, I would argue that the stream of Christian communism did not dry up with More) as in the theoretical insight into the political nature of Christianity. The radical elements of monasticism did not operate in a vacuum-sealed jar, for they functioned as perpetually renewed responses to an otiose and self-absorbed church. As I pointed out earlier, the church's policy was as simple as it was effective: if you cannot absorb them, crush them. Time and again, a grassroots movement would begin with one or two seeking the simple life of poverty and communal living of the New Testament (as far as they saw it); the movement would attract followers; be sanctioned or condemned by the hierarchy; money and support would flow, monasteries built, coffers stuffed; another movement would begin. Benedictines, Premonstratensians, Augustinian canons, Dominicans, Franciscans and many others followed comparable paths, while others stayed on the fringes – Beguines and Beghards, or the followers of Geert de Groote – tolerated or condemned or both, while others were simply condemned and hunted down – Waldensians, Bogomils, Albigensians, Lollards, Hussites and so on. Of course, political and economic factors were vital in the changing fortunes of such groups (as with the Hussites in Bohemia), but one further point is worth emphasising:

86. 'We believe that we have disclosed the most essential roots of More's Socialism: his amiable character in harmony with primitive communism; the economic situation of England, which brought into sharp relief the disadvantageous consequences of capitalism for the working class; the fortunate union of classical philosophy with activity in practical affairs – all these circumstances combined must have induced in a mind so acute, so fearless, so truth-loving as More's an ideal which may be regarded as a foregleam of Modern Socialism' (Kautsky 1979, p. 128; Kautsky 1947a, pp. 228–9).

these movements not only challenged the church hierarchy, they also embodied the struggle between resistance and compromise, between communal traditions and hierarchies of power within themselves.

Nevertheless, even this insight from Kautsky is found in a back room to his main arguments – the fall from early Christian communism, the long roll-call of revolutionary movements inspired by Christianity, and the door to modern socialism in Thomas More. In order to find an author who has dragged it from that room and placed it in a spot where one cannot help but stumble over it, we need to (re)turn to Ernst Bloch. However, before picking up Bloch, a brief word on Negri is in order, especially since Negri assumes Bloch's position (inadvertently I suspect) without developing it further. Negri is responsible for the epigraph with which I began this chapter: 'Religion is a big rip-off in itself, but it can also be a great instrument of liberation'.[87] The rip-off appears often enough in Negri's texts, with persistent comments on the harsh rule of the church (by which he invariably means the Italian Roman Catholic church).[88] But Negri also occasionally explores the liberating side of religion, such as the creative labour of Job, which must pass through immeasurable suffering to find the desire and power to create anew,[89] or the role of political love: drawn directly from the Bible, he invokes the pre-modern, especially Jewish and Christian idea and practice of love as public, political, generous and constitutive of the multitude.[90]

However, Bloch is arguably the greatest proponent of the political ambivalence of Christianity and, indeed, Judaism. Nothing captures this awareness better than two phrases which I have quoted more than once: the Bible is 'often a scandal to the poor and not always a folly to the rich',[91] but it is also 'the Church's bad conscience'.[92] The Bible has often been and continues to be read as a friend of the rich and powerful *and* it has been and continues to be an inspiration for revolutionary groups seeking to overthrow those same powerful fat cats.

As for being a scandal to the poor, the Bible is claimed time and again by religious institutions that are on far too comfortable terms with powerful and wealthy rulers, if they themselves are not obscenely well-heeled. I need only mention the Emperor Constantine, Charlemagne, Queen Victoria and Ronald Reagan in order to illustrate such an observation. Bloch does not have in

---

87. Negri and Scelsi 2008, p. 205.
88. For example, 'Italy is a Catholic country, and therefore a cruel country. And a hypocritical one'. (Negri and Dufourmantelle 2004, p. 20; see also p. 24.)
89. Negri 2009. See further Boer 2011a, pp. 271–310.
90. Hardt and Negri 2004, pp. 351–2, 356, 358. Negri also invokes love in his treatment of Job and draws the theme of love from Spinoza. See Hardt and Negri 2000, pp. 78, 186; Negri and Dufourmantelle 2004, pp. 146–7; Negri 2009, pp. 115, 127, 165; Negri and Casarino 2008, pp. 31–7, 44, 86–7, 149, 151, 156, 234; Negri and Scelsi 2008, pp. 82–3.
91. Bloch 1972, p. 25; Bloch 1968, p. 53.
92. Bloch 1972, p. 21; Bloch 1968, p. 41.

his sights merely a string of venal popes, but even Luther – especially Luther – who sided with the powerful in suppressing the peasant revolt of Thomas Müntzer in sixteenth-century Germany. Luther made very good use of the Bible to call down authority from above and to urge the faithful to focus on their inner walk with God. Indeed, if we go back beyond the formation of the canon of the Bible (and the heavy hand of Roman emperors after Constantine), Bloch finds that those responsible for gathering the stories in the Bible were the scribes, themselves part of a small and specialised elite in service both to the priests and kings. So one would expect that the stories they gathered would support the ruling ideology. For, as Marx pointed out, are not the ruling ideas those of the ruling class? Thus, we find many, many stories of suppressed revolt, of insurrection brought to heel, beginning with the 'disobedience' of the first human beings in the Garden of Eden, running through the murmuring stories in the wilderness to the call for repentance of one's sins in the New Testament. Of course, those responsible for such rebellion are cast as sinners against God and against whatever tyrant happens to be in favour.

But then the Bible is also the church's bad conscience: it has an uncanny knack of undermining any position one might want to take. If the church wishes to preserve Western culture against the perceived threat of Islam, then it must dispense with well-known biblical statements such as 'love your enemies' (Matthew 5:44), or, 'to him who strikes you on the cheek, offer the other one also' (Luke 6:29), or indeed the account that Isaac and Ishmael are both sons of Abraham who played together when children (Genesis 21:9). If the church wishes to support a government that denies political asylum to those who seek it, then it will find texts that command one to 'love the foreigner' as God does (Deuteronomy 10:18–19), or the words of Jesus in Matthew 25:35, 'I was a stranger and you welcomed me', a little troublesome. On the other hand, if the church seeks to encourage peace, love and understanding, then the saying put in Jesus's mouth, 'I have not come to bring peace, but a sword' (Matthew 10:34), becomes problematic.

Throughout his great works on utopia – *The Spirit of Utopia* and *Principle of Hope*[93] – this ambivalence, or rather multivalence shows its face time and again. However, in the much neglected *Atheism in Christianity* it is at the forefront of Bloch's thought, particularly in relation to the Bible. He traces it in the story of Eden, with its oppressive God who treats the first humans as children only to find that they rebel; in the fatal conflict of Cain and Abel, where another face of God appears, the one who protects Cain with the well-known mark; in Jacob's wrestling with God (El in this case, not Yahweh) in Genesis 32; in the rebellion of the tower of Babel in Genesis 11; in the Nazirites, those enigmatic

93. Bloch 2000; Bloch 1985b; Bloch 1995; Bloch 1985a.

figures who vow not to cut their hair, drink strong drink and call the people back to their desert, Bedouin-like life in the wilderness; in the oppressive deity of Moses and Aaron who seeks to punish the people's constant murmur of rebellion in the wilderness; in the insurrections of Miriam, Moses's sister, and Korah against that authority; even in the two figures of Moses, who is both liberator of the slaves and theocratic tyrant in the wilderness; in the protests of Job against his inhuman treatment by this same Yahweh; in the prophetic denunciations of economic maltreatment and religious hypocrisy; in Jesus's stringent criticisms of the quislings who would accommodate the Roman colonisers; and in the fiery apocalyptic revolutionary protests of the Apocalypse against empire and its gods. Sometimes the bloodthirsty, vengeful God had the upper hand, but at others (admittedly less frequently) the rebels win out through cunning and ruse.

At times Bloch overdoes it, seeking a constant thread of both demonical rulers and resistance throughout the Bible, resistance that often ended up, he suggests, in militant sects which were systematically wiped out, such as the Ophites who saw the true God in the serpent of Eden and the creator God as a vile demiurge. I would prefer more scattered and disconnected resistances, local and by no means necessarily connected. At this point Bloch's valuable strategy of discernment, which I explored at some length in the previous chapter on myth, comes into its own: a process of judicious and dialectical judgement as to what is liberating and what seeks to crush such liberation. But vital for my argument, here, is Bloch's point that even God is split and ambivalent – after all he does have many names and identities, such as El, Yahweh, Adonai, El Elyon, El Shaddai, El Berit, El Olam, El Roi, Abir, Pahad, Shebaot, Adon and even Baal. God may appear as vengeful and terror-full, but then this same God turns out to be a champion of those who protest, fall and protest again. Bloch calls this the 'exodus out of Yahweh', a current which he argues is an early manifestation of what would later become atheism – hence 'atheism in the Bible'. This protest atheism, as I prefer to call it, is not merely crucial to Marxism or any insurrectionist tradition, but also to theology itself.

By way of conclusion

Two questions remain: first, is not the argument for ambivalence a counsel of despair and thereby an argument for inaction? Indeed, is not the resort to ambivalence as the final wisdom a reactionary position that may be usefully deployed to discourage liberation movements? The most direct answer is that Christianity historically exhibits both reactionary and revolutionary tendencies, as does the Bible itself. Too many have fallen into the trap of arguing that theology and the Bible are either thoroughly oppressive and thereby best tossed out the window or that they have a liberating core that has in some way been betrayed. I prefer an answer that is more political, dialectical and historical. Politically, the argument for ambivalence is not a counsel of inaction but a call to take sides.[94] On the dialectical register, I refer the reader back to the extensive argument of this chapter. As for history, that is the topic of the following chapter.

That chapter answers the second question that I wish to broach here: why is theology, or indeed Christianity as a whole, politically ambivalent? More specifically, why are its sacred texts so multivalent? The answer is deceptively simple and (one hopes) obvious: it is due to the social and economic conditions of its emergence.[95] Spinning out this answer is a little more complex, taking me eventually into the next chapter. Before I can do so, however, a number of theoretical questions demand attention, turning on the hoary distinction between idealism and materialism.

All the same, this distinction is not so grey and creaking with age, for – to my continued amazement and occasional annoyance – idealist approaches to Christianity still abound. Proponents of such approaches would answer my initial question in various ways. The crassest response would be to point out that many of the various interpretations of Christianity are wrong; they distort Christianity in various ways and so we must find its true core and adhere to that. Depending on one's perspective, that core may be a conservative one that sponsors the status quo and does not seek to shake its foundations, or it may be a more rebellious one that refuses to be conformed to this world, or it may be an entirely spiritual one with no concern for the earthly life, and so on. All too common, this truth-distortion or centre-periphery distinction occasionally ensnares even critics such as Max Horkheimer (whom I discussed above), or Terry Eagleton (who has of late been pushing in very unoriginal fashion a revolutionary Jesus)[96] or Slavoj Žižek (who seeks to recover that implacable resistance at the heart of Christian thought in Paul and the gospels). However, it is a ploy as old as Christianity, as one reform movement after another has sought to 'restore' Christianity to its authentic, original form. Even today, opponents will battle it out over what that central truth might be in relation to the role of women in the church, gays and lesbians, the response to climate change, environmental collapse and so on. But here a second feature emerges, often tacked onto the idea of a true centre

94. See Boer 2007b.

95. Contra the argument in the vein of Žižek, resorting to Lacan and arguing that yes, of course, (biblical) revolution is the necessary other of reaction, for without it revolution would not be. So if we opted for one side, it would fail the moment that we expelled the other, which would become its traumatic kernel, the impossible Real we cannot face. As one example among many, see his discussion of G.K. Chesterton in Žižek 2005b. The problem with the common pattern of Žižek's thought is that it lacks an adequate basis in historical analysis.

96. Eagleton 2007. See also Boer 2007a, pp. 275–333.

that has been corrupted: the key lies in a pure origin that must be recovered by recourse to the sacred texts. The catch, of course, is that those texts give by no means a uniform picture, a picture that is, it should be added, produced by a literary text rather than an actual window upon some historical reality.

A more sophisticated idealist answer to my question would admit that, yes, Christianity is a complex collection of ideas, and that many have been and continue to be mistaken in assuming that there is but one authentic form of Christianity and that all other forms are corruptions. Instead, the answer goes, these ideas have continued to motivate, to inform attitudes in regard to economics, social values, politics and personal life. Witness the continued effect of Christianity in shaping the ideas of so many today – however overt or covert, whether in the USA, Europe or Australia. But since it is complex and often contradictory, we can see the different channels it has formed, which then come into conflict with one another; Orthodox here, Roman Catholic there, Protestant elsewhere, each one with its myriad forms. Hence it is possible, according to this answer, to say that Christian ideas remain a historical force, whether for ill, as the 'new old atheists' would have it,[97] or for good, as the churches and their occasional sympathisers would argue. In sum, the political multivalence of Christianity is inherent.

A variation on this idealist argument would shift the focus to the Bible, for here is the source of the political multivalence of Christianity. We would begin with the agreed point that the Bible is deeply and thoroughly contradictory on political matters, given that it was narrated, written and collected over roughly a millennium. As a quick comparison, what would a collection of major English texts gathered over the last millennium look like? At the least, we would need to include Chaucer's *Canterbury Tales*, Shakespeare's plays, James Joyce's *Ulysses*, the Magna Carta, the American Declaration of Independence, the English translation of *The Manifesto of the Communist Party* and so on. It would be exceedingly difficult to avoid the conclusion that such a collection of key texts from the last millennium has a range of political, let alone theological, positions: so also with the Bible. The next step is to point out that since Christianity bases itself on its scriptures (no matter that the different confessions cannot agree on what precisely is in that canon), it cannot help being politically contradictory, inconsistent and ambivalent. Before we know it the text has gained a life of its own (in itself a deeply theological argument), influencing, directing, and setting in train a host of political ambivalences.

How seductive such arguments can be, especially since I agree with the key point: Christianity, is indeed, politically multivalent, as are its sacred texts (I

97. Dawkins 2006; Dennett 2007; Harris 2005; Harris 2006; Hitchens 2007. See the discussion in Chapter Six.

have argued as much in this chapter). However, I cannot agree with the idealist position that they have a direct effect through the force of their ideas alone, indeed that they motivate, inspire, refute, call one to rethink and change what one is doing purely by the force of the ideas themselves. Even though an intelligent idealism (to gloss Lenin once more) is preferable to a stupid materialism, at least two responses are possible. Firstly, and most obviously, a religion such as Christianity is not merely a collection of ideas and beliefs; it also includes social, institutional and economic elements, often difficult to separate clearly from one another in the manner favoured by our Taylorised academic disciplines and ways of thinking about the world. I should not need to make such a point in this day and age, but I keep coming across dolts who should know better. Secondly, ideas do nothing on their own; people who have ideas do. Or in a more dialectical formulation, people make ideas; ideas do not make people. Yet even this way of stating the issue remains within a Feuerbachian framework – the gods do not create us, for we create the gods. So let me invoke once again Marx's fourth thesis on Feuerbach: this is but the first step, for what is needed is an analysis of the conditions in which human beings create the gods and their myths in the first place.[98] We must move from the clouds down to earth, to explore the reality of life lived in its economic and social ground.

The attentive reader may begin to wonder whether I am now in outright contradiction with myself; did I not argue in the previous chapter on myth that it operates in an anticipatory and utopian fashion, a totality that awaits its concept, a mode of forcing the truth, or in terms of reverse causality? Is that not an idealist argument? There are two ways of dealing with this problem. One is to take up Engels's cue with his treatment of Thomas Müntzer and argue that theology or the Bible or myth are merely languages, ways of speaking about other realities, be they political, social or economic. Engels postulated that Müntzer used the most readily available language of his day, namely theology, especially Luther's theological challenge to the vested interests of Rome, in order to express what were at heart political grievances. Müntzer, of course, took this theological language much further, giving it an apocalyptic edge that saw the end of the world if not tomorrow then probably next week. But when Müntzer came close to speaking in directly political terms, he began to shed the theological trappings

98. 'Feuerbach starts out from the fact of religious self-estrangement [*der religiösen Selbstentfremdung*], of the duplication of the world into a religious world and a secular one. His work consists in resolving the religious world into its secular basis. But that the secular basis lifts off from itself and establishes itself as an independent realm in the clouds can only be explained by the inner strife and intrinsic contradictoriness of this secular basis. The latter must, therefore, itself be both understood in its contradiction and revolutionised in practice. Thus, for instance, once the earthly family is discovered to be the secret of the holy family, the former must then itself be destroyed in theory and in practice'. (Marx 1845b, p. 4; Marx 1845c, p. 6.)

and draw nigh to Engel's own preferred atheistic position. In other words, theology is the carapace, the outer clothing that may be shed when a proper understanding (Engels's own) of the issues becomes available.

For all my sympathies for Engels, this is not one of his better arguments, for it is given to a crass materialism that hobbles his insights. I prefer a more dialectical approach in which theology is neither the disposable coating for real historical and economic issues nor the central force of historical change. The relationship between ideas and their economic base is a two-way street, an interaction between theory and praxis in which they cannot be separated from one other. Or, to use the terms I invoked earlier, one may descend from the clouds to earth in order to investigate what is going on there among the everyday lives of people, but that does not mean one forgets the clouds; they do not dissipate, for they are still very much part of the total picture.

Chapter Four
History

History . . . represents life as continually disrupted.[1]

At last, it is history's turn to have a say. Political myths do not float in the ether and political multivalence is not intrinsic to a religion like Christianity – topics I explored in the previous two chapters. This chapter, then, offers a historical-materialist answer as to why Christianity is politically all over the place and why it should produce myths such as Christian communism. The bulk of my argument focuses on the meagre collection of letters by the most important ideologue in Christianity – the Apostle Paul (I dispense with the quaint 'saint', since either everyone is a saint or no-one is). It helps one's status immensely if you happen to have your correspondence enshrined in sacred scripture. Why Paul? It is partly because I have written elsewhere on Paul, partly because his few letters are the subject of some extended discussion among philosophers,[2] some from the Left, partly because Paul's position was to become so dominant, shaping not merely Christianity itself, but the ideology of an empire, but above all because he offers an imaginary resolution, or a literary and ideological mediation of competing social formations. Through a series of oppositions – law and grace, sin and faith and so on, all of which are clustered around the death and resurrection of Christ – Paul attempts a transition from

1. Adorno 2006b, p. 91; Adorno 2006c, p. 134.
2. Badiou 2003b; Badiou 1997; Agamben 2005; Taubes 2004; Žižek 2000; Žižek 2001b; Žižek 2003; Trigano 2004; Sichère 2003; Rey 2008.

one to the other, a transition that is also an effort to offer an ideological and cultural passage from an older economic system to the one that the Romans were brutally imposing in the ancient Near East. The problem is that Paul's transitions are neither neat nor complete, so he actually allows both sides of his many oppositions to continue. This ambivalence on his part enabled Christianity to take contrasting positions in relation to power, especially economic power, and it explains why Christianity so easily slipped into a seat at the table of empire. By contrast, a position such as Christian communism took one side, offering an idealised representation of a fading social formation. No transition or mediation, here; it was a desperate resistance to the new order of Roman power and for that reason failed to get any substantial grip.

That is my argument in brief; the rest of the chapter spins it out in some detail. In doing so, I engage in some historical reconstruction, stitching together the threads of various proposals I have made in earlier work concerning ancient economic history, but also pushing this reconstruction much further than I have done until now. Two epithets clarify what I mean by historical reconstruction: economic and ancient. My focus is on the ancient world, especially ancient Israel and early Christianity.[3] Apart from the fact that these are old stamping grounds that have a continuing fascination for me, they are also the eras in which the sacred texts of Judaism and Christianity (and indeed Islam in part) took shape. That is to say, they constitute the basis upon which the notorious political ambivalence of Christianity first was built, as well as the political myth of Christian communism. Now for the second epithet: I pursue an economic reconstruction, largely because such reconstructions are thin on the ground for the period in question. Apart from the persistent work of Richard Horsley,[4] which is thoroughly materialist but does not go far enough, one or two exist for the moment of the New Testament and early Christianity, although their influence is tangential, parts of much wider studies of the ancient Greek world (Ste. Croix and Wood) or as precursors to feudalism and the absolutist state (Anderson).[5] It goes without saying that I am interested in explicitly Marxist reconstructions,

3. One usually comes across 'early' Christianity, which carries its own ideological load, full of assumptions about pristine and authoritative origins.

4. Horsley and Hanson 1985; Horsley 1989; Horsley 1992; Horsley 1995; Horsley 1996; Horsley 2007; Horsley (ed.) 2008.

5. Ste. Croix 1981; Wood 1997; Wood 2008, pp. 36–42; Anderson 1974. In another place, I will engage with Wood more directly, since she challenges both Ste. Croix and Anderson regarding the dominance of slavery in the production of surplus. However, her argument is based on Athens as an exception to the Greek rule, one where free working peasants formed the basis of Athenian democracy in a long struggle with the 'aristocracy' (a term under-assessed in her work). The paradox is that precisely such a democracy required an increasing number of slaves to operate, which brings one to the obvious conclusion that the necessary economic motor of Athens at least included both slaves and peasants, a point to which Ste. Croix is open.

for that is what I too undertake. As far as ancient Israel is concerned, the situation is woeful. As Charles Carter, after a comprehensive survey of the available archaeological evidence, pointed out more than a decade ago, 'a new study of the economic patterns ... is still to be written'.[6] We do have piecemeal and misdirected efforts, the first being the under-appreciated work produced during the Soviet era in Russia, work that petered out by the 1980s,[7] and the second by scholars who either, for some reason that is beyond me, apply categories from capitalism to the ancient world or who get bogged down in the search for ever more modifications on modes of production.[8] The task of a systematic economic history still lies before us.

What follows is organised in three broad steps. First is a brief theoretical discussion that returns to Marx and Engels in their long engagement with Max Stirner. Second is an effort to locate the reasons for Christianity's political ambivalence in the letters of Paul by situating him in the conflicting economics of the province of Judaea during the period of Roman expansion. And third is a search for the roots of the myth of Christian communism, which entails moving back to unravel some of the economic issues of ancient Israel in what I call the sacred economy. I undertake this task not merely to take a step or two forward in a Marxist reconstruction of ancient economies, but also to provide a more comprehensive sense of how and why a political myth such as Christian communism may have arisen and why Christianity finds itself caught in a perpetual tension between reactionary and revolutionary political directions.

Method: search for an anti-fulcrum

Three comments on method are called for, two brief, one extensive. To begin with, and as should be obvious by now, I expand the reflection on ideas in the previous two chapters to include matters of economics. It is not simply a matter of texts and contexts, nor even of the ultimately determining instance of the economic, but the methodological point that ideas, texts and religious beliefs

6. Carter 1999; see also Grabbe 2006, pp. 190–2. In the authoritative collection *Civilizations of the Ancient Near East* by Sasson (Sasson (ed.) 2006), economics has only 123 pages out of 2,790; most attention is given to politics, society and religion. Indeed, there is no substantial economic history of ancient Israel or the ancient Near East that compares with Morris Finley's great work on Greece and Rome, *The Ancient Economy* (Finley 1999), or the even better work by Ste. Croix on class in ancient Greece (Ste. Croix 1981).

7. See especially D'iakonoff (ed.) 1969; D'iakonoff 1974; D'iakonoff (ed.) 1991; D'iakonoff 1999; Dandamaev 1984; Dandamaev, Gershevitch, Klengel, Komoroczy, Larsen and Postgate (eds.) 1982.

8. For example, see Hudson and Levine (eds.) 1996; Hudson and Levine 1999; Hudson and Mieroop (eds.) 2002; Hudson and Wunsch (eds.) 2004. See also Boer 2005b.

are part of a much larger whole that includes the shifting and interconnected mix of culture, ideology, politics, law, social relations and economics. But we can do better than this, for it is not as though we have these distinct zones, nicely Taylorised into disciplines and sub-disciplines, boxes and sections of boxes that must then be connected in some larger whole – what Adorno calls the 'virginity complex', in which the fake purity of each discipline is contained within its little box.[9] Instead of behaving like caged chickens, neatly arranged in rows above and below one another, plopping our eggs of knowledge into a tray to be collected by a faceless egg collector, I would rather begin from the other side, with the whole picture; the inter-relations are a given, the connections obvious, and one wonders how it became possible separate all those boxes from one another in the first place. In other words, literature, religion and ideas are inseparable elements in the total scene.

Perhaps the difference between a camera and the human eye can illustrate what I mean: as is well-known to camera operators, the camera sees differently to the eye. We see an item, automatically select it out from the surrounding material and focus on that item – a leaf on which the sun shines, the cockroach running across the footpath, the ship on the horizon. But raise a camera and take exactly the same scene, hoping to catch the leaf or cockroach or ship and the camera will record all the information that you did not realise was there: chairs, windows, carpets, grass, roadways, walls, and what have you. The camera has recorded all that is in range, most of them extraneous items that are there in the eye's view but excluded by the ability to zero in on one item. Yet, the camera presents a truth which the selective eye does not register: the total picture is always there, but we simply block it all out. So also with the relation between literature, structures of belief and ideas: we may think they are isolated, unique items, but they are really items jostling for space among many others, that cannot be understood without the total scene.

Further, I make use of a crucial piece of analytical apparatus called an 'imaginary resolution'. If we take the Bible – which as a sometime biblical critic I like to do – then the question that soon presses on my analysis is how this multifarious and contradictory text relates to its economic context. Here, I invoke a position that I have developed elsewhere,[10] namely that a text such as the Bible is a collection of literary texts that attempt imaginary resolutions, or more fully 'imaginary resolutions of real contradictions'. The idea originally comes from Claude Lévi-Strauss, although it is framed in Althusserian language and mediated by Fredric Jameson.[11] Let me explain: such a theory begins by noting the uncontroversial

9. Adorno 2000a, pp. 124–5; Adorno 2003q, pp. 209–11.
10. Boer 1996.
11. Lévi-Strauss 1989, pp. 229–56; Althusser 1971, pp. 127–86; Jameson 1981, pp. 77–80.

point that the search for an author's intention is a distraction, albeit one that continues to bedevil much interpretation, especially in biblical and theological research. Intention does count, but it is one minor element among many others. What this theory foregrounds is the role of unconscious forces, or in Freudian terms the far more powerful subconscious elements of our thought and lives. The core of the theory is that difficult and irresolvable social tensions will show up in the cultural products of a society, whether that is literature, art, film, television, or what have you. Those cultural products attempt to resolve the tensions in many possible fashions. Some may offer an alternative reality (as we find in science fiction or utopian works); others may present a story that violently breaks through the tensions (as in many works that solve the story's problems through a violent conflagration at the end); and others may do so through formal innovation (new genres in the mixture of old ones, new styles of painting, and so on).

As an example, let me use the famous one of Lévi-Strauss. In *Tristes Tropiques* (one of the best books that I have ever read) he offers a reading of facial art among different indigenous tribes in South America. His interest was drawn to the facial decorations of the tribes he visited, especially the Caduveo. Lévi-Strauss noticed that the Caduveo use facial decoration to ameliorate and repress the social tensions between social groups within the tribe. But those decorations indicate a tension, for they are based upon an axis at an oblique angle to the face. That is, rather than use the natural lines of nose, mouth and eyes, the Caduveo patterns follow another axis at an angle to these natural lines. There are, in other words, two axes in these face decorations. The reason: unlike the neighbouring Guana and Bororo, who have the social checks and balances of moieties to mitigate their caste system, the Caduveo have no such social solution. Their art then becomes another means of dealing with the social tensions. The catch is that in the very effort to deal with such a tension, the art shows up the tension at a formal level – hence an imaginary resolution of real social contradictions that reproduces those contradictions at another level.

So also with the political ambivalence of theology that I traced in the previous chapter; so also, therefore, with the Bible, which responds to its various contexts in all manner of unexpected ways.[12] More unconscious than conscious, unintended than intended, those responses often leave traces of that context in unexpected places in the text. Thus, if a text is produced in a conflict-ridden context, then that text may be seen as an effort to overcome those conflicts, provide a resolution through narrative, poem, song or letter. Yet that context will recur in the text indirectly, through formal features, in narrative tensions, in the structures of thought, in slips and breaks that betray the initial effort at resolution.

12. I choose 'respond' rather than 'reflect', for the latter term evokes the impression that the text represents realistic data concerning its context.

Now for the most extensive methodological point, for which I dip into Marx and Engels – not, however, the standard economic texts such as *Capital*, for I seek not the almost fully developed categories for the analysis of capitalism but the process of working itself, the way in which those categories emerge in the first place. So I explore the forbidding and tortuous pages – too readily neglected – of their polemic against Max Stirner in *The German Ideology*. Why? Here the immanent method of Marx and Engels is on full display, offering a close and intense engagement with Stirner in which the first pieces of the historical-materialist method began to surface. That is the feature of the method that interests me, its very working rather than the categories which are the result of the process.

So let us see what happens in those hundreds of pages on Stirner. Or rather, let us see what Stirner does first before turning to Marx and Engels's lengthy engagement. *The Ego and His Own* is a remarkable book – remarkably disorganised and haphazard.[13] It is a non-systematic gathering of Stirner's thoughts, which he admits have not been organised into any coherent whole. Indeed, they feel as though they were written at various moments as the thoughts came to him and then thrown into the basket that became the book. Stirner's book and indeed he himself (he was originally one of the Young Hegelians) would soon be forgotten, only to be revived by Nietzsche and then eventually claimed as one of the founding texts of anarchism.

Two features of Stirner's work stand out, at least for my purposes here: he attempts the modest task of reinterpreting world history and he does so in terms of the individual ego. In other words, it is not merely a celebration of the individual and a sustained diatribe against collectives that constrain this ego – state, family, Christianity, socialism and even liberalism (!) – but also a philosophical project of producing a schema of world history, however stumbling the effort might be. So the first half of the book is devoted to a series of loose historical stages: child through youth to man; negro through Mongol to Caucasian; ancients (really the ancient Greeks and Romans), moderns (roughly from the arrival of Christianity and the struggles between Roman Catholics and Protestants) and then the discovery of the ego in the present (which boils down to German philosophy in his own time). These various threefold schemas overlap and run into one another.

Yet there must be a lever of history, or better a pivot on which history turns. For Stirner, that is the individual ego, the focus of the second half of the book. This deep structure renders the book both thoroughly Hegelian and theological, despite Stirner's continued protests against both. The Hegelian echo is obvious, for Hegel's world spirit becomes the ego (as it became infinite self-consciousness

---

13. Stirner 2005; Stirner 1845. See also Boer 2012, pp. 109–25.

for Bruno Bauer), but theology? A key text comes towards the close of the book:

> Christ is the I of the world's history, even of the pre-Christian; in modern apprehension it is man, the figure of Christ has developed into the *figure of man*: man as such, man absolutely, is the 'central point' of history. In 'man' the imaginary beginning returns again; for 'man' is as imaginary as Christ is. 'Man' as the I of world history closes the cycle of Christian apprehensions.[14]

Stirner is not one to buy into the theological claims made for Jesus, but he does appropriate him as the paradigmatic ego, as an individual 'man' around whom history turns. Christ's value is that he is merely a man, one who stands proudly and independently and resists all that would subdue him. Stirner may have rejected the theological content, but it takes little mental work to see that he has taken up the form of a theological schema of history with not a little enthusiasm.

Marx and Engels devote hundreds of ponderous pages to this idiosyncratic book. More than one commentator has seen this as an act of sheer indulgence: is it really necessary to pull apart Stirner's text page by page, line by line, word by word? Surely there are more lucid sections of their work that provide us with clearer statements of their newly and roughly hewn method? And so most turn to the opening passages of *The German Ideology*, to the section ostensibly devoted to Feuerbach, even though Feuerbach himself makes few appearances. The catch is that some of the most significant pieces of that first section of the work were actually drawn from the treatment of Stirner. The process went as follows: as Marx and Engels worked their way through Stirner's text, they gradually found themselves called upon to offer answers to Stirner's comments on labour, property, money and competition. And as they did so they began to build more and more pieces of what was to become the historical-materialist method. Initially those chunks are smaller comments, a paragraph perhaps, dealing with the material, economic and relational factors in the 'family', the political factors that led to the collapse of the Roman Empire, the nature of worker rebellions and of revolutionary communists, the nature of private property, and the Christian dialectic of flesh and desire in relation to food.[15] But as the commentary goes on, especially when it enters the last hundred pages, these interventions grow in clarity and length: crime, society, private property, competition, revolution, labour, money, exploitation, class, contradiction, and even language, railways

---

14. Stirner 2005, p. 365; Stirner 1845, p. 427.

15. Marx and Engels 1845–6a, pp. 180–1, 187–8, 220, 226–7, 230–1, 247, 254–5; Marx and Engels 1845–6b, pp. 163–5, 170–1, 201, 207–8, 211–13, 229, 237–8.

and food. Since Marx and Engels cannot abide Stirner's take on these issues, they must provide a coherent response.

In the next crucial step they collect some of the more important and coherent interventions and move them to the chapter on Feuerbach, where they now appear as Sections III and IV. The result: the first comprehensive, if somewhat uneven, statement of historical materialism now appears in the chapter on Feuerbach, but it actually emerged in what is really the engine room of historical materialism – the long discussion of Stirner. And the topics are well known to Marxist analysis and those influenced by that analysis: division of labour (between the sexes, material and mental, town and country and then, with greater and greater complexity, in commerce and industry), private property, ideology (the 'ruling ideas' statement), individual and society (the legacy of Stirner is very clear on this matter), state, law, class and class conflict. Yet by far the most important theme is contradiction, for it runs through all of these items, becoming the pivot, the Archimedean point by which history shifts from one epoch to the other: the contradiction between productive forces and the 'intercourse of individuals' (later the relations of production) reaches a crisis point that can be resolved only through the appropriation of productive forces.[16]

Contradiction, the tension at the heart of a social formation, is then the answer to Stirner's fulcrum of history, to the ego that supposedly resists all forms of collective repression (Marx observes that Stirner actually gives voice to a fundamental piece of bourgeois ideology). But it is a curious answer, almost an anti-lever or anti-pivot; Marx and Engels focus on process rather than on an identifiable object or category, on the mechanisms of modes of production instead of a central item – perhaps great men of history, world spirit, infinite self-consciousness or even the ego. Yet my attention is drawn to another feature of this analysis: the process in which Marx and Engels come to this insight. They do not seek to impose a set of categories – as though they were following a car manual or perhaps a recipe for making bread. No, they develop their makeshift collection of categories through an immanent process – in this case a close reading of Stirner – in which the categories themselves – class, class-conflict, division of labour and so on – fade in importance. I cannot underscore this point enough: the process of analysis and discovery is vital. Thus, when one comes to dealing with the ancient world, the process is central, for through that process one comes to the categories of analysis. Those categories may bear some family resemblance to the ones moulded and beaten into shape by Marx, but that will be only as a result of the process of analysis itself, rather than any application of those categories from outside.

16. Marx and Engels 1845–6a, pp. 86–7; Marx and Engels 1845–6b, p. 67.

A caveat before I move on to an economic reconstruction: lest one be misled, I do not argue that one may develop a method operative only within the constraints of a time and place so distant from us – the ancient world. Too many are the dolts who believe that some methods are more appropriate, or 'emic' as the anthropologists like to put it, to a particular moment in history or to a specific collection of texts from such and such a time. So one comes across the obtuse argument that certain methods are inappropriate to the ancient world – poststructuralism say, or psychoanalysis or even Marxism – since they come from a different context; far better to use methods (and here I draw on examples from biblical criticism) more appropriate to the ancient world like 'historical criticism'. In response to such comments, often made in all scientific seriousness and without any appreciation of how ridiculous they are, I take the position that all methods are anachronistic, that they all derive from the untranscendable horizon within which we work. The same applies to my method; it, too, is anachronistic, but it has the advantage of being aware of such anachronism. Even the immanent approach of Marx, with its primacy of process rather than the resulting categories, is inescapably anachronistic. The twist is that this awareness gives it a better chance of competing for attention and viability.

Paul's shaky transitions

Let us reprise the task as hand: to fill out the picture and seek the reasons why Christianity is so riven with political ambivalence. Close behind comes the task of discerning what generated the political myth of Christian communism. I shall answer these question in sequence, focusing first on one who is arguably the crucial theologian who set in place the perimeters of Christian thought: the Apostle Paul, who happened to experience an author's dream (albeit posthumously) of having his works included in a collection of sacred scriptures.

In Romans 13:1, Paul writes, 'Let every person be subject to the governing authorities . . . anyone who resist the authorities resists what God has appointed'. This text and the few verses that follow it have raised the pulse of more than one rebel, revolutionary or even postcolonial critic, while at the same time warming the heart of not a few conservatives and other despots and megalomaniacs. Romans 13:1–7 raises an acute problem in the Bible itself: for every text of resistance and liberation, we can also find at least one of accommodation and oppression. By now, this problem is hardly unfamiliar, for I explored it at some length in the previous chapter. Nonetheless, here I consider that ambivalence at the roots of Christianity – in the letters of Paul. My exploration of the problem moves in three ever-wider circles, the first focuses on Romans 13 and the stumbling block that it poses for those who interpret the New Testament as an anti-imperial and anti-colonial collection of texts. From there I move on to connect this specific tension with the full run of political ambivalences and contradictions in Paul's letters. And finally I widen my scope to include socio-economic issues.

Anti- or pro-empire?

It is difficult to avoid the sense of Paul's exhortation in Romans 13. 'Let every person be subject [*hypotassesthō*] to the governing authorities [*exousiais hyperechousais*]' is quite clear: all of us must subordinate ourselves to those with power, authority, dominion and what have you. But this verse must be seen in the context of the full argument in Romans 13:1–7:

> 1 Let every person be subject to the ruling authorities. For there is no authority
> except from God, and those that exist have been instituted by God. 2 Therefore
> he who resists the authorities resists what God has appointed, and those who
> resist will incur judgement. 3 For rulers are not a terror to good conduct, but
> to bad. Would you have no fear of him who is in authority? Then do what is
> good, and you will receive his approval, 4 for he is God's servant for your good.
> But if you do wrong, be afraid, for he does not bear the sword in vain; he is the
> servant of God to execute his wrath on the wrongdoer. 5 Therefore one must
> be subject, not only to avoid God's wrath but also for the sake of conscience.
> 6 For the same reason you also pay taxes, for the authorities are ministers of
> God, attending to this very thing. 7 Pay all of them their dues, taxes to whom
> taxes are due, revenue to whom revenue is due, respect to whom respect is
> due, honour to whom honour is due.

Three points are worth noting in this text: a hierarchy of power, a concern with insurrection, and taxes. I will leave taxes alone (vv. 6–7), since the point flows on from the other two. As far as hierarchy is concerned, what runs through Paul's text is a chain of command (see v. 1b): God first, who bestows power and authority upon designated rulers, and then all the rest who must obey them. Here, it seems to be earthly rulers, but the same hierarchy applies to the spirit world (1 Corinthians 15:24). Now emerges the concern with sedition, which is really the main focus of this text, covering four of its seven verses. And it turns on a play with the term *tassō*. Originally designating the proper ordering of troops, *tassō* has come to mean the correct arrangement and order, the determined sequence of things. So Paul points out that authority has been ordered [*tetagmenai*; v. 1] by God and it requires one to 'be subordinate [*hypotassesthō*; vv. 1 and 5]' to that authority. However, what one must not do is undermine or go against that order [*antitassō*], or more strictly be a disruptor of order or 'a rebel [*ho antitassomenos*; v. 2]'. In other words, Paul is dead keen to counter any possibility of civil disobedience, sedition and insurrection. Woe to the 'one who resists the authorities [*ho antitassomenos exousiai*, v. 2]', he writes, for the wrath, judgement, terror, punishment and sword of the ruler and thereby of God will soon follow (vv. 2–5). Be afraid, be very afraid if you engage in such evil acts. I cannot help wondering why Paul is so eager to frighten his readers into obedience, into 'good conduct' in order to gain the approval of the authorities [*epainon ex autēs*; v. 3]. I suspect it is because he or those who took up his original message concerning a Judaean peasant known as Jesus saw the radical possibilities of that message and it frightened the hell out of him, but more of that later.

More than one conservative or reactionary has found a text such as Romans 13 extraordinarily useful. To cull a few more notable examples from a very long list, there is the dirty deal done with the state under Constantine and the resultant effort at 'catholic' orthodoxy, or the 'holy' Roman emperors who followed through the Middle Ages, the uncanny ability of monarchs to be, as Christ's representative on earth, both head of state and of the church, the class status of the church throughout feudalism, Luther calling on everyone and anyone to slaughter any rebel peasant they might encounter, the *sine qua non* of deep religious commitment by as many presidents of the United States as one cares to remember, and the grovelling support of wealthy and powerful rulers by any number of ecclesiastical bodies.

Romans 13 was not the only text called upon to justify such reactionary readings. For instance, John Calvin added to this flagship text Titus 3:1 on obeying the powers, principalities and magistrates, 1 Peter 2:13 on submission to kings and governors, and 1 Timothy 2:1–2 on prayers and intercessions for all in authority.[17] As I have argued elsewhere, Calvin gets himself into a massive knot, since he is too perceptive a student of the Bible not to see that there are a good many texts that advocate the overthrow of an ungodly ruler, a position which he ends up advocating, albeit with many qualifications.[18]

I will come back to this tension in a moment, but before I do so I wish to juxtapose Romans 13 with the positions taken by those who approach the New Testament from the perspective of 'empire' and postcolonial criticism. The fact that so many books published in the last few years on the New Testament have 'empire' somewhere in the title is an indication of a significant shift in scholarship. Four streams have come together to form what is now a wide and full

17. Calvin 2006, 4.20.23; Calvini 1957, 5.494.6–26. Stevenson 1999, pp. 143–4, heavily stresses this element in Calvin's political thought, drawing on letters that give direct advice on the matter. See also Calvin's commentaries on 1 Peter 2:13, 1 Timothy 2:1–2 and Titus 3:1 in Calvin 1855, pp. 79–80; Calvin 1856, pp. 51–3 and 324. I follow the standard practice of referencing Calvin's works. References to the English translation of *Institutes of the Christian Religion* use section, chapter and paragraph numbers, while references to the Latin edition of 1957 [1559], *Institutiones Christianae Religionis*, edited by P. Barth and G. Niesel, use volume, page and line numbers.

18. Boer 2009c.

river: older Marxist-inspired studies that have sought the historical conditions of a rebellious movement,[19] liberation-theological approaches to the Bible,[20] more recent postcolonial approaches[21] and the growing sense (not new in itself) that the New Testament cannot be understood without considering its place within the Roman Empire.[22] A significant feature of many of these studies is that they find deeply anti-imperial themes in the biblical texts. Or at least one can find, they argue, a consistent anti-imperial theme running through them. Invariably, the comparison is made with our own times, whether it is the imperialism of the United States, or the global ravages of transnational corporations, or the profound difference between the majority of impoverished peoples of the world and the small number of the obscenely rich.

These positions are a long way from Romans 13, so let us see what some of them make of that text.[23] As we will see in a moment, most of the efforts – by those who prefer a liberation and anti-imperial reading of the Bible – to deal with Romans 13 fall into standard patterns of interpretation when faced with a prickly and contrary text. On one matter they all agree: at some level, Paul must be consistent and coherent. Beyond that point, they deploy various strategies to neutralise or detoxify the text. Although some have toyed with the idea that Romans 13:1–7 is, without any evidence, an interpolation,[24] most fall back on the tried and not-so-true position that the text is a particular injunction limited to a specific time and place.[25] This argument has all manner of variations, such as a temporal one in which Paul advocated submission while the Romans seemed all powerful and resistance would have meant immediate annihilation,[26] or that he took up a standard theme and repeated it without reflecting too much,[27] or that he distinguishes between being forced to obey and willingly doing so.[28] The problem is that this position turns on a deeply theological and problematic distinction between universal and particular admonitions: the universal ones, of course, lay claim to divine origin, while the particular ones are simply human opinion. One cannot help notice that this distinction is more popular when there is a rather bad example of government in mind – the Nazis for German

19. Belo 1981; Belo 1975; Horsley 1989; Horsley 1992; Horsley 1995; Horsley 1996.

20. Gutiérrez 2001; Miranda 1974; Miranda 1982.

21. Marchal 2008; Segovia and Sugirtharajah (eds.) 2009.

22. Brett 2008; Carter 2001; Carter 2006; Elliott 1997; Elliott 2000; Elliott 2008; Horsley (ed.) 1997; Horsley 2003; Horsley (ed.) 2008.

23. This is a heavily interpreted text, as one would expect. See the survey of positions in Tellbe 2001, pp. 177–8, and especially Riekkinen 1980.

24. Kallas 1965.

25. As a small sample among many, see Käsemann 1980, pp. 338–47; Elliott 2008, p. 154; Tellbe 2001, p. 171; Ehrensperger 2007, pp. 173–4; Carter 2006, pp. 133–6.

26. Ehrensperger 2007, pp. 173–4.

27. Käsemann 1980, pp. 338–47.

28. Carter 2006, pp. 133–6.

critics or the USA for American critics. A less popular and indefensible line is to argue that Paul is being ironic, offering a subtle critique of Roman power.[29] Over against these various twists and turns, the very non-postcolonial Voelz actually offers a novel argument: the text is perfectly clear but it refers only to good governments – he explicitly mentions Nazi Germany as a situation where it would not apply.[30] Only one critic that I can find countenances the possibility that Paul may be thoroughly inconsistent and incoherent: in a remarkable work, Elliott argues that Paul does show signs of strain since he was under the influence of imperial ideological forces that produced ripples and disjunctions in his letters. With Romans 13, the argument that rulers derive their authority from God may well be read as an implicit counter to the Roman assumption that the emperor was God; yet at the moment Paul seeks to outfox the emperor, he also comes down on the side of obedience to such rulers. In other words, Elliott recognises a contradiction or two in Paul's texts, contradictions that arise from the 'material and ideological conditions in which the letter was written and which the letter was an attempt to resolve'.[31] I would like to take Elliott's suggestion further and argue that Paul is thoroughly contradictory and that his incoherence cannot be understood without considering his socio-economic situation.

Multivalence

We have arrived at the point where anti-imperial readings run up against and struggle with texts such as Romans 13, offering what are usually old exegetical responses. Barring Elliott's insight, none of these approaches dares to pursue the possibility that Paul may have been openly ambivalent on this matter, that there is a basic and irresolvable opposition in his thought. It should actually be no surprise that there is a tension or two in Paul's thought since his whole theoretical framework turns on them. Yet, the assumption by critics is that Paul has managed to work through them or overcome them. The trick for interpreters who assume that Paul must be coherent is to find out how he does so, for it is not always so clear. So let us explore these oppositions and tensions further.[32]

---

29. Jewett 2007, pp. 787–9; and in an earlier moment for Carter 2004.
30. Voelz 1999.
31. Elliott 2008, p. 156; see also Elliott 1997.
32. One or two critics have in argued that other parts of the New Testament are treacherous and highly ambivalent if one wishes to find a clear anti-imperial message. See the thorough discussions of the political ambiguities of the gospels of Mark, John and the Apocalypse in Moore 2006. However, Moore is content to identify the contradictions without offering any explanation for them. On the gospel of Mark see also Liew 1999.

Paul's letters are riddled with oppositions: Jews and Gentiles,[33] slave and free,[34] male and female,[35] flesh and spirit,[36] elect and damned,[37] Adam and Christ,[38] death and life,[39] grace and law,[40] grace and sin,[41] grace and works,[42] Christ and law,[43] Christ and sin,[44] righteousness through faith or works,[45] law of sin and law of Christ.[46] An extraordinarily persistent pattern of oppositions, is it not? Unlike cows in a field at night (in which they are all grey), not all oppositions are equal, at least as far as Paul is concerned. At times he approves one item – life, grace, Christ, righteousness through faith – at the expense of another – the damned, sin, law, works, righteousness through works. At other times, he reshuffles the oppositions: as is obvious from the list, both Christ and grace are fulcrums for many of those oppositions. In other words, Christ and/or grace also entail redemption, election, life and faith, all of them standing ground and seeking to overcome the evil alliance – once again sin, law, death, works and so on.[47] But at other times he sets up an opposition only to argue that the opposition itself is abolished (Aufhebung before Hegel, if you will) because of Christ. In this group are the contentious pairs of male and female, slave and free, Jew and Gentile of Galatians 3:28. Are they really abolished 'in Christ', as Paul would have it, or is this a way of ensuring that nothing changes in the real world? Do not worry about these, suggests Paul; in Christ they no longer exist, so you do not need to do anything about gender relations, or ethnic difference, or class conflict in this world. It is unclear precisely what Paul means.

That lack of clarity and even uncertainty becomes glaringly obvious when Paul begins to complicate, undermine and rearrange his oppositions. For example, precisely what the 'law' is remains problematic. Is it the law of Moses, the

---

33. Romans 2:8–10; 3:9, 29; 9:24; 10:12; 1 Corinthians 1:23; Galatians 2.
34. Romans 6; 1 Corinthians 7:20–2; 12:13; Galatians 3:28.
35. Galatians 3:28.
36. Romans 7:1; 1 Corinthians 6:16; 15:39, 50; Galatians 6:13; Philippians 3:1–4.
37. Romans 9:11; 11:7, 28.
38. Romans 5:11–13, 16–18; 1 Corinthians 15:22.
39. Romans 5–6; 7:10; 8:2, 6, 38; 2 Corinthians 2:16; 2 Corinthians 4:10–12; Philippians 1:20.
40. Romans 4:16; 5:20; 6:14–15; Galatians 2:21; 3:18; 5:4.
41. Romans 5:20–1; 6:1, 14–15.
42. Romans 11:6.
43. Romans 7:4, 25; 8:2; 10:4; 1 Corinthians 9:21; Galatians 2:16, 21; 3:1, 13, 24; 5:4; 6:2; Philemon 3:9.
44. Romans 5:21; 6:1, 9, 11, 23; 7:25; 8:2, 9–10; 13:14; 1 Corinthians 8:12; 15:3, 17; 2 Corinthians 5:19; Galatians 2:17; 3:22; 5:14.
45. Romans 1:17; 3:21–2; 4; 9:13; 10:6; Galatians 3:11; 5:5; Philemon 3:9.
46. Romans 7:25; 8:2.
47. At this point, we could extend this mixing in a way that would reveal some of Paul's more problematic assumptions. For example, what do the reshuffled oppositions of elect versus female, or law versus spirit, or indeed Jews versus life say about Paul's own deeper patterns of thought?

law of the Romans, any law of the land? Sometimes it joins the negative register, especially in opposition to Christ and grace. But then the law changes guise and obtains new documents, becoming the law of Christ (positive) over against its former self as the law of sin (negative). Law has been split, transformed and is supposed to overcome itself. And sometimes an opposition must deal with a third term, as with flesh and spirit; now we find that the body turns up, sometime ally with flesh and sin, and sometime ally with life. Does not Paul argue for the resurrection of the body? So the body, and thereby the flesh, is also on the side of resurrection, life, Christ and grace. In short, these tensions lead to a deep instability in Paul's thought.[48]

Rather than go through all of these oppositions in detail, let me focus on two of them, perhaps the most important of all – law and grace, and death and resurrection. As for law and grace, the key texts are Paul's letters to the Romans and the Galatians, where we find statements that have formed the battleground in more than one reform movement within Christianity, most notably the Reformation itself. Paul writes: 'you are not under law but under grace [*charin*]';[49] again, 'Law came in, to increase the trespass; but where sin increased, grace abounded all the more';[50] and in Galatians, 'I do not nullify the grace of God; for if justification were through the law, then Christ died to no purpose'.[51] But Paul never keeps his oppositions monogamous, so before we know it grace is coupled with sin and death: 'as sin reigned in death, grace also might reign through righteousness';[52] or with works, 'if it is by grace, it is no longer on the basis of works'.[53] And then faith comes in to operate in a tag-team effort with grace, over against works of the law, in Galatians, 'a man is not justified by works of the law but through faith in Jesus Christ';[54] and then again in Romans, 'For we hold that a man is justified by faith apart from works of the law'.[55] All the same, the operative distinction is between grace and law: the law (usually assumed to be of Moses, but there are no descriptors attached, so it may well be any law) has been abrogated by the coming of Christ; it has been annulled, negated and subsumed through God's grace – a free and undeserved gift.

The catch with these statements is that they have the propensity to follow various tracks, such as licence (if we are of the elect then nothing we do will

48. I draw this point, in part at least, from Agamben 2005, although he turns it into an argument for the difficult-to-pin-down remnant before trying to locate the key to Paul's thought in the moment of pre-law. See further Boer 2009b, pp. 181–204.

49. Romans 6:14.

50. Romans 5:20.

51. Galatians 2:21.

52. Romans 5:21.

53. Romans 11:6.

54. Galatians 2:16.

55. Romans 3:28.

change that), quietism (it is all up to God), activism (showing the fruits of grace), predestination (since we are completely reliant on God's grace we are also reliant on his decisions as to who will be saved and who damned), the Methodist tendency to Arminianism (God's grace is available to all but we can accept or reject it), puritanism (in response to grace we need to live lives acceptable to God), antinomianism (all law has been abrogated so we need pay no attention to it) and even political radicalism (grace is, after all, the theological version of revolution).

But what of Paul's own situation and these strange but important letters? Paul initially argued for freedom from the law through grace, but some of the groups to whom the letters were written and those which grew up around these letters took up the idea with far more gusto than he seems to have wished.[56] They interpreted freedom from the law in terms of sex, worship, Roman law, the role of women in worship and in the communities – so much so that one sometimes gains the impression of communes full of the slapping sounds of sex, leadership by anyone full of the spirit, flagrant civil disobedience and disregard for social customs (much like the weekend-long parties of the hippies next door, with their music and talk until dawn and smoke from the joints wafting in through our windows). Not quite, but Paul clearly saw problems springing up like mushrooms after the rain in the places where he had preached. As some major studies of the letters to – especially – the Corinthians and Galatians have observed, Paul runs around desperately mopping up the mess for which he himself was initially responsible.[57] While the Galatians erred on the side of abiding by the letter of the law, the Corinthians took Paul's arguments regarding the law to their logical conclusion. Women ecstatics were leading worship, throwing off the social codes of hair coverings; social mores regarding sex were tossed out the window; food offered to pagan idols was eaten freely; people uttered the slogan, 'all things are lawful for me'. This is the classic libertine and antinomian position: the law has been overcome, so what relevance has it for me? Or in a more theological vein, God has forgiven our sins in Christ, so I can act with impunity. And to give it an apocalyptic twist: the last days have begun with Christ and he will return soon, so this world is passing and no longer holds us in its thrall.

---

56. I frame the sentence in this way quite deliberately, since the letters may have been written to existing communities, but they also gathered new collectives around them after they were written and collected. For the sake of argument, I assume with the bulk of studies of Paul that his references to opponents and opposing positions actually reflect real opponents. It would be far more interesting (but a different study) to explore the possibility that Paul manufactures these opponents in a deft piece of rhetorical shadow-boxing. By doing so, he brings his readers onside by arraying himself against a range of imaginary opponents.

57. See Longenecker 1990; Martyn 2004; Matera 2007; Martin 1999; Thistleton 2000; Keener 2005; Fitzmyer 2008.

When he became aware of the outcomes of his teaching, Paul sat back with a shock: oh my God, what have I done? Although he had emphasised Christian freedom from the law in the letter to those sticklers for rules in Galatia, that message hit all the wrong buttons for his Corinthian readers. And to his own dismay, such developments could quite legitimately claim a beginning within his own thought; they were merely taking his teaching to its logical end. So he sets out to curb what he has inaugurated, desperately trying rope in grace, faith and freedom: he urges his readers not to dispose of the law entirely, for it is good – deep down; argues that there is another law, the law of Christ; bans the sexual licence that some saw in the idea; limits the freedom that women were taking in some of the churches; urges some concern for 'weaker' brethren in outward observance (meat given to idols and so on). The outcome: we find that the same person who wrote 'not under the law, but under grace'[58] and 'now we are discharged from the law, dead to that which held us captive'[59] also wrote the text with which I began my discussion, 'Let every person be subject to the governing authorities... anyone who resists the authorities resists what God has appointed'.[60] The same mouth that dictated 'all who rely on works of the law are under a curse'[61] also mentions that 'we uphold the law',[62] that the law is 'holy' and 'good'.[63] One more: to the Galatians he writes 'There is neither slave nor free... for you are all one in Christ Jesus',[64] while he tells the Corinthians, 'Every one should remain in the state in which he was called'.[65] Not a bad collection of tensions over such a vital question as the law.

Amidst the crush of jostling oppositions, one does stand out, going beyond that of grace and law. It is none other than the narrative of death and resurrection, focused on Christ. Obvious, one might say, for it is the core claim of Christianity – that this particular person at this particular time died and then rose from the dead. But we forget too easily that the reason it is so central is because Paul made it so.[66] The angle I seek comes initially from Julia Kristeva's argument concerning Paul, for she has a distinct insight (in the midst of much dross).[67] A heavy psychoanalytic bent pervades Kristeva's work – although one can detect a

---

58. Romans 6:14 and 15.
59. Romans 7:6.
60. Romans 13:1.
61. Galatians 3:10.
62. Romans 3:31.
63. Romans 7:11 and 16.
64. Galatians 3:28.
65. 1 Corinthians 7:20.
66. For example, see Romans 1:2–6; 3:21–6; 4:24–5; 5:6–11; 6:3–11; 8:11, 32; 10:9; 14:8–9.
67. Kristeva 1987, pp. 139–50; Kristeva 1983, pp. 135–47; Kristeva 1991, pp. 77–83; Kristeva 1988, pp. 113–22.

hidden Marx who peeks out every now and then[68] – and it brings her to argue that Paul was able, through this narrative of death and resurrection, to crucify many of the psychological pathologies – narcissism, masochism, fantasy, repression, death drive, oral sadism and above all psychosis.

In each case, argues Kristeva, Paul offers a way of traversing these pathologies, appropriating them or negating them through the death-resurrection narrative. Since I am enticed most by her argument concerning psychosis, only a summary of the other crucified pathologies is needed. Fantasy, repression and the death drive are each neutralised or negated in their own way. Paul neutralises fantasy by universalising Christ's death on the cross, a process that short-circuits fantasy since it snaps the identification between us and Christ. As for repression, the story of death and resurrection brings one's death to the fore; it can no longer be repressed and thereby idealised. The death drive is also avoided, since we are blocked from identifying with the Father on our own, of writing ourselves into the story, due to the collective nature of the story. The other pathologies – masochism, narcissism and oral sadism – follow a slightly different path, for in these cases Paul appropriates the pathology and thereby overcomes it. In the case of masochism Paul internalises the murder of the scapegoat (Christ) but then makes this masochism analogous rather than real – the believer dies in a manner analogous to Christ, not as Christ. Similarly, narcissism is appropriated and overcome: one accepts death as a way to achieve salvation (which is then the limit of negative narcissism), but then, just as narcissism seems to have achieved its goal, Paul transfers the death onto another, Christ, which overcomes the narcissism since it is focused not on the self but on an other, all of which is completed by the command to love one's neighbour rather oneself. And oral sadism, with its destructive hunger for the mother, is neatly overcome by Christ, who places himself between the hunger and its desire; he is the one eaten in the Eucharist, thereby satisfying the desire to eat but removing the sadistic satisfaction.

These various Pauline prescriptions really set the scene for psychosis, for there lies the hidden treasure of Kristeva's dealings with Paul. Simply put, Paul offers a passage from one identity to another, a bridge over the schizophrenic split of psychosis by means of that self-same narrative of Christ's death and resurrection. How does this work? To begin with, her discussion is decidedly collective: the *ekklesia*, or 'church', is the key. Further, that *ekklesia* is made up of foreigners, non-Jews who have become heirs to the promise of the Jewish God. They are Gentiles, potentially from every corner of the globe, and yet they are called to what began as a particular, local and ethnically restricted religion. Thus, by definition such a collective is split, caught between two identities. And the key

68. See Boer 2009b, pp. 123–9.

narrative of death and resurrection enables them to pass from one identity to another, to become dead to the old life and to be born into the new one – all of it mediated by Christ. Instead of trying to insert foreigners into an existing social body, Paul recognises the foreigners' split between two countries and transforms that split into the passage between and negotiation of two psychic domains – between flesh and spirit, life and death, crucifixion and resurrection in a body which is simultaneously that of the group and Christ's body.[69] Their external division becomes an internal one, internal to the collective's construction and the individual's psyche.

Kristeva's work, insightful though it is, always seems to fall short, without sufficient socio-economic context and hobbled by her commitment to psychoanalysis. So I would like to take her point much further, connecting it initially with the myriad oppositions I traced a little earlier. Let us see how they fare. The death-resurrection narrative is indeed one of transition, a long, rocky, overgrown path from one unknown place to another; or rather, it is a journey from one life to a very different life, negotiating perhaps the most challenging of obstacles in between. Many of Paul's other oppositions also signal a crossing: law to grace, works to grace, justification by the law to justification by faith, flesh to spirit, sin to redemption, damned to elect, from a life enslaved to sin to a life enslaved to Christ, and of course, for the believer, a transition from death to life. For Paul, Christ throws all these in a backpack and drags them with him in the long walk from death to resurrection. Other oppositions are transformed in the process – female and male, Jew and Greek, slave and free, and body and spirit – although some would argue that Paul effects a passage in some of these cases too, especially from female to male, given the history of Christianity.

Hesitating on the bridge

But does Paul really enable a transition? Let me reprise my earlier point concerning the instability of Paul's beloved oppositions. Is the passage as therapeutically successful as Kristeva would have us believe? Ambiguity haunts Paul's convoluted texts and practices, in terms of both the *ekklesia* that is supposed to enable the transition to a new identity as well as the transitions themselves. The *ekklesiae* Paul discusses in his letters replicates in many respects the gatherings of the imperial cult. Paul uses the same language as that cult, attempting to model a new collective in terms of the old. The trap is that it is never clear how much of a break his proposals offer, especially in light of the way Christianity has all-too readily affirmed existing structures of inequality.[70] In fact, from those crucial

69. See Romans 12:4–5.
70. See especially Kittredge 2000.

letters to the Corinthians, where Paul bends over backwards to curtail what he saw as antinomian excesses, he begins to reassert patterns of gender hierarchy in the structure of the *ekklesia*. In those letters, Paul demarcates the 'sanctuary space' of the *ekklesia* by means of a gender hierarchy of cosmic proportions, the model of the male body of Christ and women's dress and speech.[71] Paul seems to be stumbling, the innovation of the *ekklesia* muddied by its close connections with other collectives that existed around him.

As with the ambiguous *ekklesia*, so also with the transitions from one state to another, all of them clustered around the death and resurrection of Christ. Does one really pass from sin to salvation, from law to grace, from works to faith, from death to life? Even Paul is not so sure, as we saw earlier with his response to the Corinthians. The law is good, he says, and you should really obey those earthly rulers, for God has appointed them. Women should really not let freedom go to their heads, and as for sex, well, you had better be prudish, like me. Further, the theological problem arises in regard to sin and salvation: we may be dead to sin, Christ may have forgiven us, and we may have entered a new life, but for some reason we continue to sin, the new collective is split by strife and the cares of the world keep crouching by the door. In sum, the transition has not been as effective as Paul might have wished. Even more, if one has had the chance to speak intimately with a man or a woman of deep faith who is near death, then it becomes clear that the transition is by no means certain. Apprehension, uncertainty, denial and outright fear are all there, despite the depth of religious faith. I cannot help but wonder where the confidence has gone, especially if one is certain that Christ has cut a trail through death to life beforehand. The easy answer is to mutter about the fear of death that afflicts even the most devout believer, but I would suggest that Paul's ambivalence has much to do with it – a realisation, perhaps, that the crossing was not a clean one.

No certain passage, here, no bridge that may be dynamited after crossing; instead, Paul's narrative of passing from one state to another has become messy, fraught with uncertainty, wavering between two states. It is as though he is caught between the pull of his destination and homesickness, a desire for the road and a longing to stay in the old home as long as possible. But that is precisely why Paul's theology came to dominate and determine the shape of the Christianity that was to follow: *through his uncertainty he ensured that both conditions were preserved*. Without a clean break, caught in the messy state of transition, both sides of the oppositions have claimed a place in Christianity. So we have law *and* grace, works *and* faith, flesh *and* spirit, Adam *and* Christ, death *and* resurrection, and, most importantly, male *and* female, slave *and* free. Paul managed to craft

---

71. Økland 2005.

a contradictory system of thought and practice that preserved both moments, producing an ideology that was to resonate and become dominant after him. In this respect, Paul plays an anticipatory role, enabling Christianity to adapt to a series of contradictory positions. It is no wonder that Christianity became the religion of the propertied classes along with slaves and disenfranchised freemen, the religion of emperors and peasants and of all nations. There is no betrayal, here, no compromise as Luxemburg, Kautsky, Horkheimer, Ste. Croix and many others have argued, for the ability to develop these contrary positions is found in Paul's own thought and practice.

Between the sacred economy and slavery

By now, it should be obvious how my argument regarding Paul connects with my discussion of political ambivalence in the previous chapter. Soon I will want to ask why the myth of Christian communism was not successful by comparison with Paul, but before I do so, it is time at last to draw social and economic issues into the picture. Briefly put, the reason why Paul attempts the transitions I have traced is that he seeks to navigate at an intellectual and literary – or ideological – level the difficult passage from one socio-economic system to another.[72] That statement will take some unpacking.

Over against the garden-variety idealist solutions – so common in treatments of Paul and indeed early Christianity in general – I am after a materialist answer. A comment or two on those idealist approaches: they usually operate with two assumptions: Paul must be a consistent thinker and the solution is idealistic. But what if Paul is not consistent? What if the tensions in these few letters cannot be resolved? It seems to me that the contradictions in Paul *are* unresolvable, at least at the level of thought. Indeed, the effort to solve them and render Paul a consistent and systematic thinker is misguided, for there is enough evidence to draw the conclusion that Paul was a very inconsistent thinker. The question then becomes: why do these contradictions and paradoxes appear in Paul's letters in the first place? Further, many of these attempted solutions are resolutely idealistic.[73] One either takes one side in Paul's arguments – he was a guardian of the law, a conservative who felt that one should support the powers that be, or he was a radical antinomian who sought to undermine those same powers – and

72. The material that follows is analogous to Negri's argument for a 'Dutch anomaly' in relation to Spinoza's thought. See Negri 1991, pp. 3–21.

73. This idealistic affliction is the same, no matter what angle on Paul you prefer within that sub-sub-discipline of Pauline studies, whether the 'old perspective' with its introspective and theological Paul (loosely everything before 1980), the old 'new perspective' in which Paul must be understood in his Jewish context, or the new 'new perspective' where the Roman Empire becomes the key.

argues that the other position is an aberration; or one searches Paul's context and identifies some crucial third term outside his texts that provides the hidden key.[74] In other words, one set of ideas is supposed to provide the solution to the problems of another set of ideas. It is a little like trying to repair your bicycle's flat tyre by sitting down and thinking about it; or rather, it is as though I (the critic) join you (Paul) in thinking about your flat tyre while neither of us actually does anything about the tyre. To do so would be to take a materialist line.

In contrast to such idealist answers, I prefer to widen the scope by including socio-economic factors, specifically by means of the theory of 'imaginary resolution' I outlined earlier: Paul's contradictory texts function as a persuasive imaginary resolution of the seismic shifts taking place in society and economics at the time. The contradictions that show up in Paul's texts are creative and tension-ridden responses to socio-economic tension and tumult. So those well-known oppositions – grace and law, faith and works, Jew and Gentile, death and resurrection and so on – may be seen as perpetual efforts, at an intellectual and religious level, to resolve contradictions in the social formation in which Paul lived. And those contradictions turn on the clash between different social formations or modes of production. As New Testament scholars with an economic ear (all too rare among such scholars) have shown, Palestine at the time struggled with the imposition of a slave-based system over the top of a far older economic system that had been the status quo in the ancient Near East for centuries.

In reconstructing the economic situation of first-century Palestine – however brief that reconstruction must be for now – I focus on three areas: Roman economic practices in the Eastern Mediterranean, the brutal conquests and mass enslavements, and spatial analysis.[75] When the Roman legions began marching into the Eastern Mediterranean, they encountered an existing economic framework that had persisted for centuries, if not millennia, absorbing even the conquest by Alexander in the fourth century BCE. Despite significant urbanisation – the most notable being Alexandria, Antioch and Seleucia – of the coastal littoral and an orientation to the sea rather than the rivers, the economic patterns of the hinterland remained intact. I will have more to say about these patterns in a moment, but it is worth noting that what goes by the name of Hellenistic civilisation was the result of Greek conquest and adaptation in the Near East. As they

74. In biblical studies, this second option is studded with almost endless proposals. Some examples include the Stoics (Swancutt 2004; Engberg-Pedersen 2000), collective 'Mediterranean' notions of personality that must not be confused with 'Western' individualist notions in our understanding of Paul (Malina and Neyrey 1996), and Hellenistic perceptions of sexuality and the body that become the necessary background for reading Paul (Martin 1999).

75. In doing so I draw upon the lucid sketch of Anderson 1974, the detailed work of Horsley 1989, 1992, 1995, 1996, Horsley (ed.) 1997 and company, and the spatial analysis of Ste. Croix 1981.

settled in, produced hybrid states, built their cities and adapted their economic patterns to what the locals had done, the Greek rulers – Seleucids in Syria and Mesopotamia, the Lagid dynasty in Egypt (the Ptolemies) and the Attalids of Pergamum – soon eclipsed Greece in economic importance. The outcome was a concentration of political power, Hellenistic culture, Greek language and wealth in significant city-states in contrast to vast rural zones outside those cities, which themselves were focused on village communes in which older economic patterns continued with little change. When the Greeks first arrived, the only difference for the autonomous peasants and dependent tenants was that those who demanded tribute had changed.

The Romans took one look and decided they quite liked what they saw. Of course, they despatched the armies of the Hellenistic rulers and set up a system of client states, which now owed their continued existence to Roman 'goodwill' – at least, as long as the tribute kept flowing to Rome. Although the Romans were initially cautious about setting up provinces in the East, by the first century BCE they seemed to lose their reticence, enthusiastically conquering, plundering, enslaving and taking over the reins of power. This shift in approach must be underlined, with a thick pen and plenty of pressure, for it sets the scene for the first century CE when the first Christians began writing, Paul included. With the change in policy, economic approaches to the Near East began their seismic shift. Earlier, the Romans were content to leave the economic structures in place: peasant village communes and dependent tenants worked to the bone in order to keep the sparkling cities running and the coffers in Rome full – just as the Hellenistic rulers had done before them (minus the ships transporting sequestered goods to Rome) and as the Egyptian/Persian/Babylonian/Sumerian rulers had done before them. However, when the testosterone began flowing in the first century BCE, the Romans began to interfere more directly. What emerged was a significantly centralised economy, in which the cities were sites of the consumption of goods produced in the agricultural heartland (that is, they were certainly not sites of production), and in which much of what appeared to be trade was state-managed transport of goods to ensure that the armies could stay on the road and cities remained fed.[76]

In other words, the famed Roman roads were not built for the sake of the postal service or for wagons laden with trade; they were for rapid movement of armies, spatial control over the countryside and the movement of state-sequestered goods. The infamous *Pax Romana* (analogous to the *Pax Americana* of our own day) was actually spattered with the blood of systematic violence, destruction, enforcement and enslavement in order to expand and maintain the Empire.

76. See especially Horsley 1996, pp. 72–87, in contrast to Anderson 1974, pp. 64–5.

In the case of the province of Judea, which was riven with one insurrection and suppression after another, the Roman fist landed heavily, again and again. However, there is a particular text from Horsley that says more than he anticipates:

> During the first century B.C.E. Roman warlords took over the eastern Mediterranean, including Judea, where Pompey's troops defiled the Jerusalem Temple in retaliation for the resistance of the priests. The massive acts of periodic reconquest of the rebellious Judean and Galilean people included *thousands enslaved* at Magdala/Tarichaea in Galilee in 52–51 B.C.E., *mass enslavement* in and around Sepphoris (near Nazareth) and thousands crucified at Emmaus in Judea in 4 B.C.E., and the systematic devastation of villages and towns, destruction of Jerusalem and the Temple, and *mass enslavement* in 67–70 C.E.. In the area of Paul's mission, the Romans ruthlessly sacked and torched Corinth, one of the most illustrious Greek cities, slaughtered its men, and *enslaved* its women and children in 146 B.C.E.[77]

Horsley provides the building blocks of a more comprehensive economic picture, while baulking at undertaking the building programme. Note the word patterns: reconquest, sacking, torching, slaughter and, with great emphasis, *mass enslavement*. As Ste. Croix has shown in extraordinary detail, the production of surplus in the Greek world – a surplus that maintained the wealth and power of the ruling elite – was through unfree labour, primarily that of slaves.[78] While the Romans took a more direct hand in the ancient Near East and especially the province of Judea, they shifted from tapping into the existing economic system and sought to impose a slave-based system. What we witness, here, is a violent shift from one mode of production to another, one that gradually transformed the Roman Empire. The imposition of a different economic and social system took place in a consistent if piecemeal fashion through systematic violence and disruption, especially in the three or four centuries at the turn of the era.

One of the most obvious signs of this shift in social formations is a high level of violence, social unrest and conflict as the new system imposes itself on an older established one. Such troubled transitions produce displacement, tension and violence, in demographic, economic, social, political and psychological terms. The quotation from Horsley brings this out all too clearly: revolt after revolt cruelly crushed, until the Romans became so thoroughly sick and tired of all the trouble that they destroyed Jerusalem and its temple (67–70 CE) and banned Jews from entering the new city of Aelia Capitolana. One would have had to be

77. Horsley (ed.) 1997, pp. 10–11. Emphasis added.

78. Ste. Croix 1981. It is unfortunate that the excellent studies by Briggs 2000, Harrill 2006 and Glancy 2006 do not develop the full economic context of slavery for their studies of New Testament texts.

a hermit from the moment of birth to avoid such seismic shifts, to steer clear of any political opinion whatsoever, or not to want to resolve such tensions and conflicts in some fashion or other. Paul, and indeed all those involved in early Christianity, were in the thick of it.[79]

Space – in its (re)construction and use – is a tell-tale marker of economic tensions and shifts. I think, here, of the under-utilised insight by Ste. Croix into the tension between *polis* and *chora*.[80] In the initial spatial arrangement of these terms during the period of classical Greek civilisation, the *polis* designated a city or town (they are known well enough – Athens, Corinth, Sparta and so on) while the *chora* referred to the all-important fields [*agroi*] and villages [*komae*] under the city's control, fields that supplied the vital foodstuffs and myriad other agricultural goods that kept the city going. However, when the terms came to be used for the vast realms conquered by Alexander's armies and then controlled by his successors, these terms slipped to gain new senses. Or rather, the *polis* was still a city or town, built by the Greeks or perhaps taken over by them. By contrast, *chora* referred to all the territory outside the colonial city, cultivated or not, watered or arid.[81] Now the differences mount up, for in the *chora* the local language continued (Aramaic in the case of Judea and Galilee), while in the *polis* Greek was spoken. Peasant rhythms of agricultural production continued as before in the *chora*, but in the *polis* there was little by way of production, for they squeezed the peasants well beyond their thin margin of surplus for the sake of consumption. In contrast to the earthy culture and religion of the *chora*, tied in so closely to the patterns of agriculture and husbandry, the *polis* was consciously and overtly Greek in culture, dress, legal systems and modes of intellectual exchange. If the villages and farms of the *chora* had humble mud dwellings with at most four rooms, in which the domestic animals spent the night along with clan members, the *polis* had its amphitheatre, gymnasium, public buildings, market place, baths and fountains of water.

---

79. 'Jesus and his movement emerged at the end of series of developments that had a profound impact on life in Galilee. In successive generations, Galilee was incorporated into the temple-state by the Hasmonean high priesthood, invaded repeatedly by Roman armies, subjected by Herod, and finally ruled by Antipas, who (re)built two cities for his régime directly in Galilee. The impact of Antipas's massive city-building and Roman client-rule located in Galilee itself must have been sudden and dramatic. Jesus and his initial followers, who formed a movement rooted in villages, were from a generation struggling to adjust to and/or resist the dramatic changes that had so suddenly come upon their communities' (Horsley 1996, p. 178).

80. Ste. Croix 1981, pp. 9–19 and 427–30.

81. There is a shift in the relationship between *chora* and *polis* between the Greek and Roman periods: during the period of the kings who succeeded Alexander, the *chora* was administered directly by the royal bureaucracy; under the Romans much of the *chora*, especially the agricultural areas with their *komai*, villages, came under the administration of the *poleis*.

From the perspective of those in the *polis*, they inhabited islands of civilisation in a sea of barbarians; from the side of the *chora*, the *poleis* were alien and brutal parasites. In short, the exploiting ruling class of Palestine belonged to the *polis*; those upon whose backs they lived were in the *chora*. Given the vast differences between them, in terms of culture, language, architecture, power, and wealth, the interaction between the two zones was minimal, limited to the extraction of those vital goods – by enforced extraction – for the sake of the *polis*. That flow of goods, energy and power, is symbolised by two spatial features: the roads and aqueducts. The Roman roads effected not merely to link the *poleis* to one another, enabling the movement of troops and goods, but they also cut through the *chora*. They criss-crossed, dissected, parcelled into manageable lots, and provided a visual and experiential reminder of who was in charge. There was no doubt in the minds of peasants and tenant farmers what the roads signified. We might picture the situation in terms of Henri Lefebvre's rhythmanalysis:[82] the *chora* carries on its older rhythms, tied to the regular circadian rhythms of agriculture and festivals, with human beings moving in ways deeply infused with those cycles, back and forth to the fields, gathering for festivals, bartering and exchanging, along with the different patterns of rainfall, of animal herds, of famine and plenty. By contrast, the roads dissect these rhythms with that of armies on the march, convoys of tribute, the movement of food and other produce from *chora* to *polis* and from one *polis* to another. Whereas the rhythm of the roads is between *poleis*, cutting across the *chora*, that of the *chora* is internal, except for one feature that links them: the rhythm of resources and tribute to the *poleis* and that of armies and tax-collectors to the *chora*.

But the dominant rhythm is symbolised by the aqueduct, for the aqueduct symbolises the *polis*: 'siphoning off...the resources of the land into the urban centre, to feed the public baths where the imported water acts as focus of sociability and as a symbol of the "washed" and civilised way of life that rejects the stench of the countryman. Implicit in the aqueduct is a dynamic of power, flowing between town and country'.[83] What does all this mean for Paul's untidy oppositions and messy transitions? They may be regarded as the intellectual and literary efforts to deal with these massive and brutal economic realities. Above all, I would suggest that they should be read as a largely subconscious effort to map and overcome at an imaginary and ideational level the economic clash and transition between two modes of production. One after another, these oppositions roll out of Paul's texts, only to be treated in the various ways that I suggested

82. Lefebvre 2004; Lefebvre 1992. An extended engagement with rhythmanalysis would trace the disruption of rhythms, especially the counter-rhythms of rebel groups characteristic of Judaea at the time.

83. Horsley 1996, p. 87.

earlier. Each one is an alternative effort to deal with the fundamental socio-economic tension. For instance, siding with one side of the equation becomes an ethical decision for one or the other – life over death, grace over law, faith over works. This taking of sides is really the first option open to someone faced with a crushing opposition. But then Paul also suggests that 'in Christ' some of these oppositions are overcome – the famous trio of slave and free, Jew and Gentile, male and female. In this step, Paul makes a first effort at mediating the oppositions. One negates them by positing a greater and higher reality into which they are absorbed. A third option goes even further: in this case Paul narrates a passage from one to the other, from death to life, from law to grace, from works to faith and from sin to redemption. In the process the first term is appropriated and transformed: so death becomes part of resurrection, law is still needed within grace and works are transformed in faith. Even more, the effort to resolve these contradictions in some way ensures that they remain crucial elements of his texts. In this respect, they are significant traces of Paul's troubled and ruptured socio-economic context.

The risk of Paul's strategy is very high. On the one hand, a transformative story such as the death and resurrection of Jesus Christ – the key narrative that holds all the oppositions together – may offer a radical breakthrough. It seems as though some of those who first heard and read Paul caught a glimpse of that breakthrough and wanted to take it further. With sin, law, works, as well as gender, ethnic and economic divisions overcome by the story of Christ's death and resurrection, the possibility opened up for a very new world that might be realised here and now – sexually, communally, politically, economically. On the other hand, the way Paul replicates the socio-economic tensions in the structure of his arguments, especially in terms of the oppositions I have traced, means that they may come back with a vengeance. Add to that the sense one sometimes gets that Paul himself was genuinely troubled by the radical possibilities of his thought, and we have a real tendency towards reaction. So a transformed law may end up being a far more totalitarian law than the previous one, or reformed works may become an obsession with a whole new set of works, or proclaiming the end of gender, ethnic and economic tensions at a higher, theological level, may serve to divert attention from their very real presence in everyday life.

Paul is deeply ambivalent. Consciously, he tries to tone down the more radical effects of his thought, a move that exacerbates the tensions. Subconsciously, he offers the possibility of a transformative breakthrough: the transformation and overcoming of the oppositions in his thought, all of them linked to the story of the death and resurrection of Christ, open up radical possibilities. Yet these same tensions are far too closely tied to the socio-economic tensions of his context – between an older and highly resistant system (sacred economy) and the brutal new system based on slavery – so much so that the old realities of law, works, gender, ethnicity and economy come back with a vengeance.

Above all, the very presence of both sides of these constantly shifting oppositions, along with the lack of clarity about the transition between them, means that both sides – which are always multiple pairs – are preserved for what follows. From an economic perspective, try as he might, Paul was never going to resolve fundamental economic tensions at the level of thought. But in the effort to provide an ideological answer, in which the death and resurrection of Christ becomes a metaphor for the search for new life out of the destruction of the old economic world, Paul leaves open a range of ambivalent possibilities. The early church might appeal to the poor peasant or slave or tenant, but it also had much to say to the wealthy landlord or the powerful judge. It might offer new possibilities for women, but it also reasserts existing gender patterns in which men felt comfortable. It may have offered a new way of experiencing communal life, but it also ensured that such a life was hierarchical and unequal. In short, where grace appeared, so did law; where faith, so also works; where life, so also death; where resistance, so also compromise. And if it seemed to be in touch with the life of the village commune in the *chora*, it also felt at home in the Roman-administered *polis*, especially the one at the centre of the Empire.

The fate of Christian communism

Why was Paul's equivocating position so successful and others such as Christian communism less so? In short, Christian communism attempted not mediation but resistance to the conditions in which Christianity arose. More extensively, Christian communism embodies a utopian response to the situation I depicted above: Roman armies marching to crush yet another revolt, with grim cruelty, slaughter, mass enslavements, the onerous flow of resources to the bustling *poleis*, rebel movements by starving peasants, desperate efforts to maintain some sort of village and rural life amidst intolerable pressures of hunger, disease and disintegrating village life – in short, the brutalising effects of clashing economic and social systems. In the tension between the *chora* and the *polis*, Christian communism expresses the ideals of the former. It is an effort at resistance to the massive changes underway, an attempt to cling onto a way of life that was fading, and thereby an idealisation of that life.

In this light, the representation of Christian communism as one of consumption – astutely picked up by Luxemburg and Kautsky, and at the basis of their criticism – begins to make sense. As they point out, such a communism is unsustainable, for it requires the constant production of goods to be shared among its members. Once you have pooled all your resources and shared them out, then what do you do? Someone at least needs to go and produce more resources, for otherwise everyone would starve. However, in the rural situation of the village commune that is not an issue. Sheep keep producing wool, milk and meat, as do goats; the crops are planted, grown and reaped; water is gathered in cisterns or (in the north) from streams. Production is not an issue, for everyone contributes. But in the village commune, there was no private property in the sense first developed by the Roman jurors of the third century BCE, subsequently lost in the Middle Ages and only to be recovered with the 'Papal Revolution' of the eleventh century CE and then the Renaissance.[84] That sense of absolute and inalienable private property – which was to form the basic sense of property under capitalism – is completely foreign to the village commune. Instead, property was held in common by the village; resources, products and their consumption were shared, except that to put it in such a way assumes property in the first place. In this context, a communism of consumption operates side by side with a communism of production.

It may be objected that the depictions of Christian communism appear within the *polis* of Jerusalem, for the first Christians (at least in the fictional tale of Acts) meet in that city. The response to this objection has two steps. First, Jerusalem itself was a focus of turmoil between accommodation and resistance to the Romans, so much so that the Romans finally tired of the constant revolts and razed the city to ground. But this hardly goes far enough, so second: the representation of Christian communism in that city is displaced, out of its context within the *chora* and its villages, a situation that makes it only more idealistic and unrealisable. For this reason, it becomes a political myth.

All the same, I have scraped away only at the topsoil of this argument. In order to dig deeper, we need to take a wider historical view and make a few comments concerning economic patterns, before the Romans and indeed the Greeks appeared on the scene, in what I would like to call the sacred economy.[85] What the Greeks called the *chora* in the ancient Near East is actually the later manifestation of a much older feature – going back some four mellennia – of an overwhelmingly agricultural economy.[86] The sacred economy was shaped by five basic components, or institutional forms as the *Régulation* theorists describe

84. See Gianaris 1996, p. 20; Miéville 2004, p. 195; Anderson 1974, pp. 65–7; Jolowicz 1952, pp. 142–3, 426; Linklater 2000, p. 1432. A fuller discussion may be found in Boer 2013b.

85. For a full reconstruction, along with the references, see Boer 2013b. My proposal may, of course, be read as a comprehensive reworking of the Asiatic mode of production.

86. As obvious as this statement might seem, there is precious little that offers a systematic and sustained economic analysis of the agriculture of the ancient Near East. A basic start is offered by Borowski 1987.

them. These are the key elements, which combine in unique fashions, with one or more dominant during some periods, and then others in other periods.

The first institutional form is subsistence survival, which characterised the life of the vast majority, the 95 percent engaged in agriculture. Subsistence survival relates to both maintaining herds and cultivating crops. Recent zooarchaeological research has shown that the typical formation of herds involved two-thirds sheep and one-third goats.[87] Sheep provide vital fibres and high-yield meat, along with milk, while goats are hardy and versatile animals. Both reproduce quickly. Having the two types of animals ensures that should disease affect one type, the other type would remain to ensure survival. Herds were culled at regular intervals to maintain health and herd size. By contrast, bovines were few and the evidence indicates that they died at an advanced age. This meant that they were used as draft animals for ploughing, and not primarily for food.

The fields traversed by the bovines produced the necessary crops for subsistence survival (wheat, millet, barley, legumes, and occasional vegetables). The primary concern in relation to the land was usufruct and labour. Notions of private property or the permanence of land were irrelevant. Agricultural villages used a system of land shares – a practice widespread in societies focused on subsistence survival. This term refers not to a field or plot of land, which is demarcated in terms of land measurement, surveying and clear differentiation from neighbours. Instead, a land share is a moveable strip or strips of land that are constantly reallocated on the basis of use and need. The perpetual process of the reallocation of these land shares was undertaken by an authority, most often elders, a council, or the village commune as a whole.

Subsistence survival was notable for both its tenacity and its effectiveness in responding to the underlying reality of economic crisis. When the relatively short periods of economic stability succumbed once again to crisis, this institutional form persisted. Farmers worked to ensure survival in the face of the perpetual threat of chaos (disease, pests, taxes, attacks, droughts, and so on). This entailed production at a level below maximum capacity, so that something – in optimal conditions – was kept in reserve. Further, the processes of herd and crop management were infused with the sacred. 'Religion' was not a compartmentalised feature of life, an ideology distinct from the realities of agriculture. Rather, it was inescapably woven in with the birth of healthy sheep and goats, with the rains and full crop-yields, with the myriad determinations of the threats to that production. The gods gave and the gods took away.

A second institutional form was the kinship-household, an eminently collective form. It may be defined as a particular shape of collective life with

87. Sasson 2010.

ideological, social and economic dimensions. In its ideological dimension, the kinship-household functioned as an extra-economic form of compulsion, part of the mode of *régulation* crucial for any economic system to function. It ensured that most of the small population saw itself as part of the social whole and partook of the necessary functions to ensure survival. It did so by offering justifying narratives, such as genealogies and mythical stories of the ancestors, along with fostering customary assumptions, such as loyalty, behavior, association, and labour. Economically, the kinship-household determined who went out when to what field-shares, what animals would be taken out to the herds and back again, what equipment was used and to whom it should be given next, who would work the olive presses or cultivate the orchards, what foods, fibres, fuels, liquids, and other products were gathered, brought in and processed, where food was to be cooked and eaten and where it was to be taken, which animals would return, how waste was dealt with – these constant flows were determined by the social reality of the patriarchal kinship-household. So, too, were activities that required collective activity, such as harvesting, oil pressing, baking, beer and wine brewing, storage of surpluses for tough times.

The two institutional forms that I have discussed thus far are predominantly allocative or redistributive – what is produced by one is for all and vice versa. More ambivalent is a third institutional form, patronage. It may work primarily along allocative lines, or it may bend itself towards what may be called extractive lines: the appropriation of something from someone who has produced it by someone who has not. In terms of the former, patronage may work alongside the forms of subsistence survival and kinship-household. We see this in the structure of patronage: the patron has something that I want and need, such as security, shelter and food. But I have something he wants, namely my support, whether my ability with animals or crops, or perhaps with my fist and sword. The relationship is personalized and customary: I give allegiance and loyalty to my patron, while he protects me and ensures that I survive. This sounds reciprocal, an informal contract of sorts between equals, each bringing to the deal something the other needs. Indeed, the ideology of patronage seeks to give that impression, presenting the relationship as a reciprocal one. Nothing could be further from the truth, for patronage reminds us that allocatory economic systems are rarely festivals of equality. Patronage highlights the fact that allocation is all too often hierarchical, in which qualitatively different items pass between patron and client, in which the material balance heavily favors the patron.

At this point, the extractive potential of patronage reveals itself. While those who surrounded the powerful man – thugs, flunkies, sycophants, perpetual dinner guests, and whatnot – may have felt that they had never had it so good, the reality was that the patron extracted far more than he gave. Here, we need only remind ourselves that patronage is not peculiar to biblical societies, for it appears in ancient Rome, ancient China and today among politicians and gangsters at a more informal level. In the context of the sacred economy, the patron usually cut across clan lines, seeking clients in a way that challenged kinship organisation. Owing loyalty only to the patron, the clients enaged in protection rackets, enforced the patron's will, and lived by a code of honour and shame. A legendary biblical narrative that embodies the patterns of patronage is the account of David, before he becomes king. His band of followers cuts across clan lines, owes allegiance to him, fights for his cause, in return for security and the allocated products of plunder and agriculture.

The two remaining institutional forms are primarily extractive: estates and tribute-exchange. Rubbing up against the subsistence agriculture of the bulk of the small population was the system of agricultural estates. Given the needs of the non-labouring ruling class, some means was needed to ensure a supply of the necessary items of life. And given that the minimal surpluses of subsistence survival were not sufficient for such needs, agricultural estates were also established. The administration of such estates may have varied, ranging from directly appointed overseers to tenants and landlords, but the estates were a necessary item if the ruling class was to live in the manner to which it had quickly become accustomed. The purpose of the estates was to supply those who were not gainfully employed – priests, monarchs, and hangers-on – with food, alcohol, and textiles. Tax and tribute also played a role, here, but the estates were primarily organised to meet the increasing 'needs' of palace and temple.

A final, extractive institutional form, which has had more than its fair share of attention in ancient Near Eastern studies, is what I call tribute-exchange. Normally, these are distinguished from one another: tribute or tax is what a ruler demands from subjects and subjected peoples; trade is what entrepeneurs do outside government control. This convenient bifurcation of the sate and private enterprise simply misreads the situation in the ancient world. Simply put, they are variations on plunder. Tribute (for 'them') and taxation (for 'us') are really the politer and slightly more regulated faces of plunder. But how is exchange also a form of looting? The basic purpose of exchange in the ancient Near East was the acquisition of preciosities. The great expense and risk of long-distance trade ruled out the exchange of bulk goods. Royal courts and the small ruling class acquired exotic and expensive items, whether for useless decoration, clothing, weapons, lavish gifts offered to other rulers, or building materials for constructions by the state. The motive was acquisition, and one would reward handsomely a middle-man who took the risk to acquire items for pomp and glory. If one was in pursuit of the unnecessary items of life, then one used whatever means were available to get hold of them. If you had to give something in exchange, then so be it, for that was a necessary evil.

In outlining the five institutional forms of the ancient Near Eastern economy, my account has remained largely synchronic, but what of diachronic analysis? Here the key question concerns the means of achieving stability over against crisis. Such periods depended on different combinations of the institutional forms. One combination, with dominant and subordinate forms, may achieve relative stability for a longer or shorter time. When it succumbs to crisis, an effort may be made to restore the same combination or develop another. Each period of stability – or 'regime' – entails a set of compromises in order to achieve a modicum of continuity. In this light, I suggest we understand the well-known periods of expansion and contraction, or rather growth and collapse of economic and political power in the ancient Near East. From the first moment of the Uruk upsurge[88] in the fourth millennium to the collapse of the Persian empire a few centuries BC, different combinations of the these institutional forms may be identified.

For my purposes, here, three such combinations are relevant. Up to the sustained economic crisis at the end of the second millennium, the dominant form by which temple and palace supported themselves was the estate system. The type of management and labour may have varied over time and space, but it was the controlling extractive form for more than two millennia. By contrast, by the first millennium, there is a distinct shift to tribute-exchange as the preferred form. The Assyrians, Neo-Babylonians and Persians may have refined its workings, but they based imperial expansion by means of the many faces of plunder. In each case, a particular institutional form is dominant, while the others are subordinate. Or are they? I would suggest that the allocative forms were always present, often widespread, but that the nature of the records (palace, temple and landlord archives) do not always allow us to see them in action. They show up only in the archaeological record and are most obvious during prolonged periods of economic crisis, especially those of the third millennium and the centuries in the middle and at the end of the second millennium (the transition from Bronze Age to Iron Age). In these situations, subsistence survival, with its related kinship-household and patronage, are the dominant forms, the tried responses to times of troubles.

Christian communism will return in a moment, but first let me point out that the reconstruction I have outlined here is in many respects a thorough reshaping of debates over economics within biblical criticism. Most of those who work in the area – refreshingly informed by Marxist categories – assume at least two modes of production, a tributary one based in city-states and an oppositional

88. It seems as though human beings first gathered in settled communities to drink beer and then eat some bread. Bakeries and breweries were not separate affairs, but actually parts of the same building. Even more, about half of the total cereal crop, especially barley and wheat, was used for making beer. Braidwood 1953; Geller 1993; Protz 1995, pp. 201–3; Corran 1975, pp. 19–22; Boer 2006a.

communitarian or domestic or household mode based in the villages of the countryside.[89] We can, they argue, identify traces of the tensions between them in the biblical texts, so much so that early Israel – a thoroughly indigenous, Canaanite entity – may be seen as a communitarian/domestic/household mode of production set up in opposition to the tributary mode of the Canaanite city-states. I can see little reason to argue for distinct modes of production,[90] for what is variously described as tributary and domestic/household are really parts of one economic system. It is, as Deleuze and Guattari argue in a somewhat different context, a thoroughly internal affair,[91] which I prefer to analyse in terms of the régimes of allocation and of extraction within a sacred economy. After all, here is the basic tension that kept the system functioning in the first place.

In light of my reconstruction of the sacred economy, the pattern of *polis* and *chora* established by the Greek invaders was actually an accommodation to the prevailing economic situation. The changes they did bring about involved the construction of more cities, with the effect of burdening the village communes with ever more punitive demands for tribute. But this process may be understood as an effort to assert a greater role for the extractive rather than allocative institutional forms – to the detriment of the latter. Initially at least, the Romans took over the same system, adding a layer of extraction beyond the local *poleis*. However, the greater the extraction, the greater the resistance from the villages of the *chora*. Eventually, by the first century BCE, they were faced with the economic collapse of these older rural economic patterns along with the desperate resistance of those who saw their way of life being destroyed.

Christian communism, I would suggest, evokes the older patterns of allocative and social life based on subsistence survival and the village commune, which were later to become the *chora* of the Hellenistic era. A utopian and idealised effort to recover that older life, all that remained was a pattern of shared distribution and consumption, but its economic basis in agricultural patterns of subsistence survival and kinship-household, and a home-spun system of customary law was fading if not lost already. It did not help matters that the representation

---

89. Gottwald 1999; Gottwald 2001; Meyers 1988; Jobling 1991; Jobling 1998; Yee 2003. See the detailed analysis in Boer 2005b.

90. The multiplication continues, such as a 'patron-client' mode or even a 'Mediterranean' one. See Carter 1999 and T. Thompson 2000, pp. 177–81.

91. Deleuze and Guattari 1988, pp. 111–30; Deleuze and Guattari 1980, pp. 140–64; Deleuze and Guattari 1986. Yet their creative re-reading in terms of a central despotic signifying régime, with its multiple patterns of resistance from pre-signifying (tribal), counter-signifying (nomadic war machine) to post-signifying (the scapegoat Israelites themselves), is focused on the wrong place. The central economic engine of the system was with the village communes and agricultural production, rather than the temple-city complex of the despotic régime. See further Boer 2011a, pp. 271–310.

of Christian communism in the Book of Acts places it in Jerusalem, entirely divorced from any rural base.[92] Above all, it was never going to succeed as an image of the new movement, for it was based on a regressive resistance to the new economic and political system of the Romans. In this respect, Paul's much more ambivalent effort at providing a story of transition, based on the death and resurrection of Christ around which his overlapping oppositions clustered, would work much better. Yet as I argued above, it was precisely Paul's failure to offer a clean passage from one to the other, along with his political ambivalence and the lack of clarity as to how much his *ekklesia* was really a break, that enabled his approach to dominate and encompass conflicting positions in the Christianity that followed.

Here too we find the reason why the hard sayings of Jesus – at least those put in his mouth by the gospel writers – against wealth, exploitive landlords, privilege and power would become decidedly uncomfortable for the later church (as Ste. Croix has traced so well).[93] They too came from the realm of the *chora*, trailing its ancient history in the economic patterns of the village communes.[94] They too were forms of resistance against Roman domination and the *poleis* and for that reason caused more than a few headaches for those who wanted to file away the sharp points of his critique. As Horkheimer points out, the 'dangerous doctrine'[95] and 'inflammatory speeches'[96] of the founder of Christianity, his uncompromising attitude of mind, resistance to power and disdain for his own life,[97] were hardly the ingredients for a successful and long-lasting movement with its deep political ambivalence.

Conclusion

Paul's shaky transitions, Christian communism, and, indeed, the gospel representations of Jesus offer different responses – at a literary and ideological level – to

---

92. As Kautsky and Luxemburg astutely saw, albeit without the benefit of an adequate economic reconstruction; see Luxemburg 1970; Luxemburg 1982; Kautsky 2007; Kautsky 1977.

93. Ste. Croix 1981, pp. 103–11, 418–25, 433–8; Ste. Croix 2006, pp. 345–68.

94. Above all, see Horsley 1996, Horsley (ed.) 2008.

95. Horkheimer 1978, p. 222; Horkheimer 1991a, p. 394.

96. Horkheimer 1996, p. 49; Horkheimer 1985g, p. 185. See also Horkheimer 1991a, pp. 292–3; Horkheimer 1985m, p. 297.

97. Horkheimer 1996, pp. 35–6; Horkheimer 1985g, pp. 174–5. Also, 'he thought little of prevailing rules and customs; he acted contrary to accepted ways; he was much closer to the heretic than the orthodox'. See Horkheimer 1996, p. 156; Horkheimer 1985h, p. 277. See also Horkheimer's comments on Christianity coming into the world as a scandal to the prevailing norms and customs, in Horkheimer 1982, p. 283; Horkheimer 1988h, p. 430.

the deep economic and social tensions ripping their world apart. To that collection we may add the stern concern for order in the pastoral epistles (1 and 2 Timothy and Titus), or the Apocalypse with its bloodcurdling and lurid depictions of mayhem for all who oppose God. Arguably, the one that has been most influential is Paul's response for the reasons I have laid out in this chapter. It is not for nothing that the key moments of disruption within the history of Christianity have turned on the interpretation of Paul's texts. For Paul's uncertainties left open the possibility of taking very different positions on the basis of his arguments, whether resistance, accommodation or somewhere in between. He may have offered an alternative story of transition, a new *ekklesia* not sanctioned by the status quo, but his was also a position that suited the Empire all-too well. Yet these tensions at a literary level would only be exacerbated by juxtaposing different responses together in one collection of texts in which the patterns of resistance, reaction and accommodation are themselves only exacerbated. From there on Christianity had no option but to struggle with the multivalence of the texts it decided to call sacred.

Chapter Five
Kairós

Last of all, as to one untimely born . . .[1]

This chapter marks a transition in the structure of my study, moving from historical explanations to promising forays, from a relatively tight sequential argument to extensive reconnaissance missions into new territory. To recap, and thereby situate the shift: in the first part of this book, I charted a route from the preliminary concerns of atheism and theology and then through a sustained argument concerning myth, political ambivalence and economic history itself. However, in this second part, I broach three topics that may be seen as extensive forays into promising territory for the difficult love affair between Marxism and theology: time, ethics and fetishism.

I begin with time, or rather kairós, a term full of possibilities in the intersection between Marxism and theology and arguably one of the great organising categories for a spate of recent and not so recent efforts to rethink revolution. The narrative of this chapter has a number of twists, so let me outline it briefly before sinking into the detail. I begin with the agreed definition of kairós as the right or critical time, the opportune moment that must be seized. Under this meaning, with its heavy debt to the New Testament, I gather the efforts by a motley collection of Marxists to reshape our understanding of revolution. This is only the first (and not so spectacular) step, for kairós has much more to tell us. Yet, before I call kairós back

1. 1 Corinthians 15:8.

to the interrogation room for a few more questions, I seize the moment to lay to rest a few (quite erroneous) assumptions about the relationship between Marxism and Jewish and/or Christian eschatology. Marx and Engels make an appearance here, as do biblical genres and the figure of Ernst Bloch.

From this point, I open the investigation to wider usage and move back before the New Testament to ancient Greece, where it becomes clear that kairós refers not merely to time but also to space, with bodily and social senses. Now kairós becomes that which is in the right and proper place and time. Most importantly, the opposite of kairós in these texts is not ch/kronos, the ordered march of time, but ákairos, what is in the wrong time and place. In this light, it becomes clear that the efforts by the New Testament writers to appropriate kairós for their own agenda bear the traces of these earlier meanings. Thereby, subsequent efforts to develop a kairological politics by these Western Marxists also contain elements of this sense of kairós as the proper place and time for revolution. In response, I propose that a better term is ákairos, the untimely and out-of-place. Now Antonio Negri reappears on the scene, not so much for his uninspiring comments on kairós (they are quite run of the mill), but for an uncanny and unwitting insight into kairós and ákairos. I mean, here, his working distinction of measure and immeasure, which I read in terms of the biblical themes of created order and chaos.

By this time, I have thrown my lot in with ákairos, immeasure and chaos. In that company, I turn in the conclusion to reconsider the connection between the theological doctrine of grace and revolution. Here, Alain Badiou joins the discussion, especially his effort to 'laicise' the Pauline doctrine of grace as a version of his own event, which in its turn is a thorough attempt to provide a solid philosophical theory of revolution. In my perpetual effort to relativise theology, I understand grace not as a doctrine that needs to be laicised or 'secularised', but as one (passing) shape that revolution may take.

At the crossroads of time

I begin with a basic exercise in examining the semantic cluster surrounding the word kairós. In our current usage, kairós refers almost exclusively to time, designating both a point in time as well as a period of time. On this score, the New Testament bears heavy responsibility.[2] In that collection of texts, kairós may mean the period when fruit becomes ripe and the harvest is ready (Mark 11:13; 12:2; Luke 20:10), a season such as autumn or spring (Galatians 4:10), the present (Luke 12:56; 18:30; Romans 3:26; 8:18; 2 Corinthians 8:14), a designated period

2. See Kittel, et al. 1985, pp. 389–90; Barr 1969.

that is more often signalled by the plural, kairoí (Matthew 16:3; 21:41; Acts 1:7). But the term also identifies a specific moment, often in the dative 'at the right time', which may be opportune or favourable, or it may be dire and risky (Luke 4:13; 12:42; John 5:4; Romans 5:6; 9:9; Galatians 6:9). Increasingly the word takes the definite article, 'the time' (o kairós), and in this form its sense is the time that is fulfilled, or of crisis or the last times. Indeed, o kairós is one of the New Testament's major eschatological terms, specifying variously the time of Christ's appearance (Mark 1:16) or his own death (Matthew 26:18; John 7:6, 8), the fulfilment of his words (Luke 1:20), eternal life after death (Mark 10:30), the time of salvation (2 Corinthians 6:2), the longed-for, albeit troubled, time of final conflict, the end of history, the reign of the Evil One and Christ's return to vindicate the faithful (Matthew 8:29; 13:30: Mark 13:33; Luke 19:44; 21:8, 24; Romans 13:11; 1 Corinthians 4:5; 7:29; Revelation 1:3; 11:18; 12:12, 14; 22:10). In all this, a crucial distinction operates within the biblical sense, between the unexpected and the expected. The New Testament stresses again and again that o kairós will occur at a moment we, from our perspective, do not expect. And yet, when seen from God's perspective, that time is specifically appointed, occurring at the right and proper time that God has designated. This distinction will become vital in the later treatment of ákairos, which opposes this sense of the correct time. In various ways, these senses dominate, for good or ill, our sense of kairós, holding up and, as I will argue later, restricting kairós as a term devoted to time and gathering the semantic field around that point.

But let me stay with this sense of kairós for a while, for towards this point in time converges a significant number of thinkers of revolution with a Marxist bent, especially Walter Benjamin, Giorgio Agamben, Antonio Negri, Slavoj Žižek, Fredric Jameson, Alain Badiou and Ernst Bloch. At a critical, rather biblical crossroad I await not the devil and his desire for my soul but a disparate crew of thinkers of revolution. They are not so much 'political theologians', a title imposed after the fact and troubling for its implication, but rather kairological thinkers.[3]

To begin with, the bumbling Walter Benjamin offers variations on kairós, or *Jetztzeit*, the 'now-time', as he prefers to call it.[4] Poking around inside the baleful myth and dreadful nightmare of capitalism, especially in the context of an apparently unstoppable fascism before the Second World War, Benjamin tried to find different ways to break through its suffocating hold. For him capitalism, especially in the late nineteenth and early twentieth centuries, was a mix of both fascination

3. This exclusive focus on the temporal dimension of kairós also afflicts the recent work of Marramao 2007.

4. Benjamin 2003, p. 395; Benjamin 1982a, p. 702.

and fear.[5] The efforts to break out are determined by the biblical heritage not merely of kairós, but of o kairós, as both a moment and a period of imminent and final crisis. As far as the moment itself is concerned, he prefers not to invoke the conventional Marxist category of revolution, but to seek his answer in one image after another. It may be waking from a dream, with appropriate dialectical debts to the surrealists.[6] Or it may be the enigmatic dialectic at a standstill,[7] or perhaps the flash of a camera, a 'flash with the now',[8] a 'posthumous shock' that overcomes the merely temporal relation between past and present.[9] Fascinated by the techniques of recording images, Benjamin tries to explore this break through a theory of the image, through what is suddenly emergent, like a flash, in language itself. Another metaphor draws upon the explosive terms of birth in order to rethink history – the well-known 'monad' reduced and concentrated in the bowels of history which must then undergo a violent expulsion from the continuum of the historical process.[10] The image is one of a bomb, in which the monad (the historical object) explodes to open up the possibility of a new era, a new life. In other words, history – understood as a homogenous course, a continuous passage from past to future – becomes the barrier that must be blown apart in order to pass into a new moment that is thus opened up in the breach. As I have argued elsewhere, this terminology of giving birth is both heavily maternal (seen from a male perspective in which germination and birth seem to happen simultaneously) and thoroughly mythical, but it provides Benjamin with his beloved

---

5. Thus, in the great *Arcades* project (Benjamin 1999; Benjamin 1982c) he writes of the mythic landscape of hell that runs beneath the booming commercial city above.

6. 'Accordingly, we present the new, the dialectical method of doing history: with the intensity of a dream, to pass through what has been, in order to experience the present as the waking world to which the dream refers!' Benjamin 1999, p. 838; see also pp. 845, 854–5, 863, 883; Benjamin 1982c, pp. 1006, 1012, 1023, 1033, 1057–8. As Cohen 1993 and Pensky 1996 point out, the influence of surrealism is more obvious in the earlier drafts of *The Arcades Project*. Benjamin differed from the Surrealists in emphasising not so much the dream itself as waking from the dream. If the dream is one way of characterising the mythic world of nineteenth-century capitalism, then the rupture is the stunned moment of awakening. See Benjamin 1999, pp. 831and 261–4; Benjamin 1982c, pp. 998 and 577–80.

7. Benjamin 1999, p. 431; Benjamin 1982c, pp. 575–6.

8. Benjamin 1999, p. 432; Benjamin 1982c, p. 576.

9. Benjamin 1973, p. 132.

10. 'If the object of history is to be blasted out of the continuum of historical succession, that is because its monadological structure demands it. This structure first comes to light in the extracted object itself. And it does so in the form of the historical confrontation that makes up the interior (and, as it were, the bowels) of the historical object, and into which all the forces and interests of history enter on a reduced scale. It is owing to this monadological structure that the historical object finds represented in its interior its own fore-history and after-history' (Benjamin 1999, p. 475; Benjamin 1982c, p. 594). This text is of course the forerunner of the more well-known one on the monad from the theses 'On the Concept of History'. Benjamin 2003, p. 396; Benjamin 1982a, Volume 1, p. 703.

shocks, arrests, blasts, and explosions – all of which try to rip apart the thick blanket that keeps history from opening out to a new moment.[11]

Benjamin also invokes the seasonal, periodic sense of kairós with his much-discussed messianism. Here we find the explicitly theological idea of (weak) messianic or fulfilled time, which is set over against the humdrum mechanical version. And lest one misses the explicitly biblical tones of Benjamin's usage, he points out that 'the idea of fulfilled time is the dominant historical idea of the Bible: it is the idea of messianic time'.[12] There is no need to delve into the intricate and at times tense debate over Benjamin's use of messianic categories, suffice to point out, here, that both his efforts to pinpoint the rupture in business-as-usual capitalism and to find an intensified messianic time that breaks up the monotony of mechanical time fit easily within the two senses of kairós – as a purely temporal category.

Hard on the heels of Benjamin comes Giorgio Agamben, who expressly sets out to expand and systematise Benjamin's scattered insights. Like Benjamin, Agamben draws heavily on the Bible for his approach on kairós, although now the letters of Paul in the New Testament provide the crucial insights. Paul redefines, in Agamben's eyes, the messianic era as an in-between time; it is 'the time that is left us'.[13] Kairós becomes a suspended moment – really o kairós – between an instant of chronological time and its fulfilment. For Paul, this is the stretch between the first advent of the messiah – 'Jesus Messiah' in Agamben's translation – and his final return (Christ has come and will come again).[14] While the time of chronos, the regular beat of ordinary chronological time, leaves us powerless and weak, messianic or 'operational' time is that moment and period which we seize and bring to an end of our own making.[15] Indeed, Agamben names this time that remains kairós, which is the storming of a moment of chronos that enables its fulfilment.[16]

---

11. See also Benjamin 1999, pp. 857, 862, 863; Benjamin 1982c, pp. 1026–7, 1032, 1033.

12. Benjamin 1996, pp. 55–6; Benjamin 1982b, p. 134. For a detailed discussion and critique, with all the references, of Benjamin's use of the 'messianic', see Boer 2007a, pp. 96–103.

13. Agamben 2005, p. 68.

14. Of course, in Paul's letters and indeed in Agamben's reading of those letters, this kairological moment is inescapably Christological, for Christ comes once, dies and is resurrected, is therefore present with us from that moment on, even when he has gone, and yet remains to complete that presence on his return. The kairós is then Christ's life and death, one that seizes a moment of *chronos*, but one that can come to fulfilment only with his return.

15. Even more, this heightened moment is conversely a period of deactivation, when the law (Agamben's other great motif in his interpretation of Paul) is deactivated so that its potentiality may be pumped up, awaiting its fulfilment. Like the scribe whose full potentiality is manifested when he does not write (suffering perhaps from writer's block), *energeia* [act] becomes disengaged so that *dynamis* [potentiality] may flourish.

16. See also Agamben 1999, p. 168. My purpose here is merely to identify those who cluster under the umbrella of kairós. For a sustained critique of Agamben, see Boer 2009b,

Close to Agamben is Negri's treatment of kairós, although the initial impression is that little connects it with its biblical heritage. In an effort to recast the whole theory of time, he defines kairós as the 'moment when the arrow of Being is shot' and as 'the immeasurability of production between the eternal and the *to-come*'.[17] Yet the biblical distinction between kairós as moment and as period of time is clear, as also the resolutely temporal focus. On the first count, kairós is a rupture at the right time, the 'exemplary temporal point'.[18] It is an opening up in time that is eminently creative; it is the edge of time when Being is created. In the passionate and rigorous Kairós, *Alma Venus, Multitudo*,[19] Negri does his best to block the theological undertones of his take on kairós. However, at other moments when he invokes kairós he is more willing to acknowledge the biblical and theological traces in his position. For instance, in the conversations with Anne Dufourmantelle, he observes that with kairós we are always at the point of creativity; it is the moment each day when, 'one creates God': everything one does is a creation of God, since 'to create new Being is to create something that, unlike us, will never die'.[20] Further, this process of creativity is marked by naming, especially the common name. 'Whatever thing I name exists',[21] states Negri in Kairós, *Alma Venus, Multitudo*, without comment on the connections with God's naming of the various items of creation or Adam's naming of the animals in the early chapter of Genesis, but later he is happy to agree that naming 'is at once the Bible and what makes epistemology possible'.[22]

Kairós as a period of time – between the eternal and the *to-come* – constitutes Negri's opposition to the measurable piling up of time as past, present and future, in which our present is a moving point between the fixed detritus of the past (to be collated, measured and studied by historiography, to be celebrated in triumph or mourned as disaster) and the future (as a repeat performance of the past). In their place, he proposes that the 'before' should be understood as the sign of eternity – time rests in the eternal – and that the 'after' must be recast as the 'to-come'. Once again, it is not difficult to pick up a theological undertone: kairós operates not merely *sub specie aeternatis*, for it is part of eternity; from that context, kairós, as a perpetual moment of creativity, looks towards an eschatological 'to-come'. In its passage, kairós gathers more and more features:

---

pp. 181–204. For a trenchant criticism of Agamben and Badiou, see Ojakangas 2009. For a comprehensive assessment of and effort to move the debate further concerning Paul and political philosophy, see Blanton and De Vries (eds.) 2013.

17. Negri and Defourmantelle 2004, p. 104, and Negri 2003, pp. 154, 180. See also Negri 2008, p. 97; Hardt and Negri 2004, p. 357.
18. See Negri and Dufourmantelle 2004, pp. 104–6.
19. Negri 2003, pp. 139–261.
20. Negri and Dufourmantelle 2004, pp. 146–7.
21. Negri 2003, p. 147.
22. Negri and Dufourmantelle 2004, p. 119.

it is immeasurably productive, the home of living labour, restlessly in motion, multiple, common, the source of joy, corporeal and material, and thereby resists domination and oppression. It is not difficult to see the connection with Negri's exegesis of Job, for whom kairós is the point of contact between Job's lived time of pain and divine epiphany, the creative labour of suffering opening out to liberation.[23]

Despite all this compelling energy, Negri still rests with a very temporal kairós, opposing it to chronological time and then attempting to reshape it in terms of revolutionary creativity and desire.[24] Indeed, the reading of Job that I mentioned above shows how regular Negri's approach to kairós really is. For Negri, Job provides an energetic counter to the idea that time is empty, static and measured. This sense of time came into its own only with neo-Platonic thought, when time became abstract, a form of being, transcendent and dominating – precisely when Christianity became the dominant ideological force of empire. By contrast, in Job one finds that time is concrete, lived, painful, common, immanent and – most importantly for my purposes here – filled with theophany. A stark contrast with abstract and dominating time, is it not? More specifically, Negri argues that in Job, time is both being towards death (he quotes Job 7:4, 6–8 and 9:25–6) and a fullness and state of happiness (now it is 29:2–6). As content and part of existence, this time in Job is the point of contact between lived, concrete time and the linear movement of divine epiphany – here, Earth and Heaven touch as Job pulls God down to Earth, bends transcendence to immanence,[25] and forces God to answer his insistent questions. This ontology of time is nothing less than the 'immeasurable opening of kairós'.

Equally biblical but more Benjaminian is Žižek. He has been enthused by the possibilities opened up not only by Paul, but also by the gospels and elements of the Hebrew Bible, especially the law. Yet the Bible and theology constitute one dimension of a search for a truly radical break, a genuine kairós that brings him closer to Benjamin.[26] The nagging problem for Žižek is that he is caught in an irresolvable tension: on the one hand, he holds to the argument (most forcefully put in Lacanian terms) that any revolution will run into the mud, since it still operates with the same coordinates as those which it seeks to overthrow; on the

23. Negri 2009.

24. For an incisive critique of this conventional, albeit troubled distinction, see Marramao 2007, p. 40.

25. See also Negri and Fadini 2008, pp. 666–8.

26. Žižek 2000; Žižek 2001b; Žižek 2003; Žižek 2006, pp. 69–123; Žižek and Milbank 2009. See further Boer 2007a, pp. 334–90 and the lucid survey by Kotsko 2008.

other hand, he voices a desire for a genuine revolution, which is cast in various terms, whether theological, Leninist, good old communist or what have you.[27]

In more detail: Žižek is ever wary of available options for revolution, whether perversion, protest, acts of sabotage, support of the hungry and poor, since each of them fits within the logic of capitalism. The reason is that there is always an underside to any revolutionary moment, when the Real comes back with a vengeance and the revolution runs into the mud. Since all social systems operate in basically the same way, there is little point in following conventional patterns of revolution and overthrow, for the new system will merely be a variation on the same. So the problem is: how does one make a genuine break, shake up and change the very coordinates themselves so that we will not follow the same pattern of disappointed revolutionary aspirations? Or as Žižek puts it, 'it is easy to suspend the big Other by means of the act *qua* real, to experience the "non-existence of the big Other" in a momentary flash – however, what do we do *after* we have traversed the fantasy?'[28] The search for an answer to that question sends Žižek on a path that includes: the feminine formula of sexuation or the non-all; the Jewish law which is deprived of the law's usual fantasmatic support (that is, which feeds off its own transgression);[29] the moment of grace (following Badiou) as an incalculable and undeserved irruption beyond human agency; the Christian realisation of the Jewish rupture of the traumatic kernel through the cross (God or the big other really is impotent); Lenin's unique effort to shift the coordinates by which we live with the assertion of actual freedom (in which one chooses to change the conditions of formal or limited freedom). In each case Žižek seeks a radical kairós that must be sustained, a thoroughly radical break, a crack through which all the lost causes may pour through. And yet, he always hesitates, never sure whether the cause will run into another dead end, wondering whether refusism is not the best answer.[30]

---

27. I cannot help wondering whether this tension, to which Žižek returns again and again, marks the trauma of the failed revolution in Slovenia, in which he was a full participant? See also Boer 2007d.

28. Žižek 1996, p. 133.

29. For an excellent survey of Žižek's changing positions regarding the Jewish law, see Kotsko 2008, pp. 88–93.

30. 'This is how we pass from the politics of "resistance" or "protestation," which parasitizes upon what it negates, to a politics which opens up a new space outside the hegemonic position *and* its negation. We can imagine the varieties of such a gesture in today's public space: not only the obvious "There are great chances of a new career here! Join us!" – "I would prefer not to"; but also "Discover the depths of your true self, find inner peace!" – "I would prefer not to"; or "Are you aware how your environment is endangered? Do something for ecology!" – "I would prefer not to"; or "What about all the racial and sexual injustices that we witness all around us? Isn't it time to do more?" – "I would prefer not to." This is the gesture of subtraction at its purest, the reduction of all qualitative differences to a purely formal minimal difference' (Žižek 2006, pp. 382–3).

In this wake of Benjamin belongs Fredric Jameson as well, who invokes a kairological rupture as a key to utopia, except that he keeps such a rupture relatively low-key.[31] For example, in a curious effort to recover the abolition of money as a political programme, he writes:

> Thus the revival of the old Utopian dream of abolishing money, and of imagining life without it, is nothing short of precisely that dramatic rupture we have evoked. . . . The lived misery of money, the desperation of poorer societies, the pitiful media spectacles of the rich ones, is palpable to everyone. It is the decision to abandon money, to place this demand at the forefront of a political program, that *marks the rupture and opens up a space into which Utopia may enter, like Benjamin's Messiah, unannounced, unprepared by events, and laterally, as if into a present randomly chosen but utterly transfigured by the new element.*[32]

Less an exploding bomb or violent rupture, this break is a mild if insistent political demand that would, Jameson hopes, lead to the complete reshaping of the whole economic system. Thus, the abolition of money may lead to replacing the wage relationship by means of labour chits and work certificates, alternatives to market exchange and consumption and so on. Or the call for full employment at a living wage would raise not merely issues directly related to labour, but also host of other issues, such as 'crime, war, degraded mass culture, drugs, boredom, the lust for power, the lust for distraction, the lust for nirvana, sexism, racism',[33] all of these being symptoms of unemployment or alienated labour. By this time, so many things will need to be changed that the system makes a qualitative leap and becomes something very different. In all this, the rupture itself clearly falls into the category of kairós, although it is not some violent, cathartic bloodbath out of which utopia will emerge, but a relatively modest collection of non-violent proposals to get things moving.

By contrast, Badiou's rereading of kairós is much more spectacular and more obviously biblical (here he is closer to Agamben and Žižek), for the Apostle Paul provides an illustration of a system he had developed beforehand. Yet it is far more than an illustration, for Paul emerges in Badiou's thought as exemplary instance of the event and its procedures of truth.[34] Paul identifies and names

---

31. Low – key despite his various statements – the future as 'radical and systemic break' (Jameson 2005, p. 228) and disruption as 'the name for a new discursive strategy' (Jameson 2005, p. 231).

32. Jameson 2005, p. 231; emphasis mine.

33. Jameson 2005, pp. 147–8.

34. Badiou 2003b; Badiou 1997; Badiou 2006a; Badiou 1988. Alongside love, art, science and politics, one can trace the ghostly presence of a fifth, theological procedure of truth in Badiou's thought. See further Boer 2009b, pp. 155–204. For an astute engagement from New Testament studies, see Welborn 2009.

an event – the resurrection of Jesus of Nazareth – which becomes for him the truth. Around this truth forms a militant movement made up of subjects called by the event and characterised by fidelity to the truth Paul names. Badiou offers two unique developments to the notion of kairós we have encountered thus far. To begin with, an event can never be apprehended directly, for it becomes a truth only if it is named as such (although the two are inseparable). Thus Paul comes after the 'fact' of Christ's resurrection,[35] identifies it as something unique and extra-numerary, and thereby establishes that truth-event. As with any event in the four zones of politics, science, art and love, it leaves in its wake linguistic traces, like the strange and wonderful detritus after a roadside picnic, or what Badiou calls procedures of truth.[36] In other words, the event itself may be a specific moment of kairós, but its procedures becomes the new, intensified kairological period that follows. The second development will have ramifications for the discussion of ákairos below, for the event itself is unexpected and incalculable, crashing into our mundane reality to rearrange the very coordinates of that reality. One cannot earn an event through hard work and planning, predict it through careful calculation, assume it is inevitable or indeed that history will be on one's side. Does not this unexpected dimension of the event break from the biblical heritage of o kairós as the designated time of the end? Although one may identify a potential excess that does threaten to break away, in Badiou's formulation that unexpectedness fits in rather well with the biblical adage to keep watch, for one knows not the day or hour (Matthew 25:13).

I have left Ernst Bloch until last, for he offers one of the most sustained reflections on kairós and tries to push beyond the biblical heritage of the term. He does so in two ways. The first is via a dialectical relation between *novum* and *ultimum*, while the second concerns his focus on realised eschatology and the miracle. As for *novum* and *ultimum*, which together function as a succinct definition of his approach to utopia, a few crucial pages of *The Principle of Hope*[37] outline what he means. The semantic cluster of *novum* concerns what is new, fresh, unheard of, novel and revolutionary. Bloch's own definition comes in his usual thought-twisting style: 'the still unbecome total goal-content [*noch ungewordenen totalen Zielinhalts*]'.[38] Let me exegete this statement for a moment.

35. I write 'fact' here within quotation marks, for the problematic feature of Badiou's engagement with Paul is that the crucial event of the resurrection is for him a 'fable'.

36. The pure event – or 'events' since the event is multiple and not one – can never be apprehended directly. It can be identified only via the proclamation of a truth, that is, via its consequences. So also with Badiou's other key moments – May '68, the mathematical discoveries of Cohen, Gödel and Fraenkel, the breakthrough of Galileo, the poetry of Mallarmé, or the simple words 'I love you' – are always inadequate names for an event that has been.

37. Bloch 1995, pp. 200–5; Bloch 1985a, pp. 230–5.

38. Bloch 1995, p. 202; Bloch 1985a, p. 233.

Out of the two crucial elements in the *novum* – possibility and finality – the first is embodied in the curious phrase 'still unbecome'. Possibility is, then, the opening up of the future, which is not merely still coming, nor indeed has it become reality: it is incomplete, has not yet become reality, has still to become such a real future. Thus it is open and unbecome. As for finality, the phrase 'total goal-content' captures the sense of fixing on a goal in that opened-up future, or as Bloch puts it, the 'goal determination of the human will'.[39] Bloch characterises the *novum* as both possible and final, open to the future and fixed on a goal for which it strives again and again, in order to contrast it with innovation for its own sake, the endless, repetitive and frenzied parade of fashions, each one claiming to be revolutionary – like those toothbrushes that are 'revolutionary' in design and yet all seem to be the same. And that is Bloch's point, especially against Bergson: change for the sake of change is but more of the same and falls into the logic of capitalist marketing, the need for perpetual turnover, built-in obsolescence and the generation of artificial needs (such as shoes for every conceivable activity). Against the pseudo-*novum*, the genuine *novum* is nothing other than the horizon of utopia.

However, the most effective way to overcome such a pseudo-*novum* of endless and meaningless repetition is to link the *novum* with the *ultimum*. For Bloch, the *ultimum* designates what is last and highest, consistent with its basic Latin meaning. *Ultimum* includes within its semantic field what is furthest, the most remote, the last and the end, but also what is the highest and greatest, as well as the goal. On its own, the *ultimum* has had quite a career, designating not merely the traditional category of ontological transcendence, but also the doctrine of the last thing, whether that is Jewish and Christian eschatology, the Heraclitean and Stoic doctrine of world conflagration or indeed Hegel. It becomes, then, either the self-sufficient prime mover that is beyond the world or it evokes the eschatological end of history. The catch with the first is that the *ultimum* is removed from history; with the second, the invocation of the last thing becomes a reversion to the first thing. Bloch is perpetually on his guard against such reactionary senses of the end of history, where we just return to where we began; the omega becomes the alpha and the whole cycle begins again. For these reasons, the *ultimum* needs the *novum*.

Now the two terms converge on temporal kairós, especially when they become the 'the highest newness [*höchste Neuheit*]'.[40] The perpetual search for the new comes to its last and highest point in the *ultimum*; the possibility opened up by the *novum* realises its goal in the *ultimum*. In dialectical terms, if the *ultimum* releases the *novum* from repetition, then the *novum* frees the *ultimum* from a

39. Bloch 1995, p. 202; Bloch 1985a, p. 232.
40. Bloch 1995, p. 203; Bloch 1985a, p. 233.

reactionary return to origins and the retreat into the un-moved mover. Or as Bloch puts it, 'the newness in the Ultimum really triumphs by means of its total leap out of everything [*totalen Sprungs aus allem*] that has previously existed'.[41] Not a bad definition of kairós – a complete leap out of all that has gone before into something entirely new.

As far as the biblical terminology of kairós is concerned, Bloch stresses that it both a realised eschatology and embodied in the miracle, all of which relies on the fact that kairós is inseparable from the message and mission of Jesus of Nazareth. Kairós is the urgency not merely of apocalyptic anticipation, but of the reality of apocalypse brought about in Jesus himself. Bloch explicates the core New Testament sense of kairós as 'the measure is full, the time complete'[42] here and now: 'Jesus preached of Kairós, of time which is fulfilled and which is consequently mediated by and through history'.[43] This kairós is at the forefront of Jesus's message, full of apocalyptic and thereby utopian realisation, and in his miracles, which embody such a rupturing kairós within them at each moment they are enacted.[44] Indeed, in terms that anticipate both Benjamin and later Jameson, miracle is a concrete definition of kairós and thereby of how Christ might be understood. Miracle is a 'blasting apart of the accustomed status quo', a 'formal point of interruption' that is absolutely good, and, in a convergence of Bloch's comments on utopia as *novum* and *ultimum*, a leap 'which stems from explosive religion [*den vom Sprengglauben herstammenden*]'.[45] For Bloch at least, kairós leads us straight to the core of utopia. Yet, this kairological utopia also bears a strong element of unexpectedness and unnacountability (more than Badiou). That is, the *novum et ultimum*, the eschatological miracle, may in some respects be seen as untimely, one that is out of place with the accumstomed coordinates of existence. This dimension will become vital in the treatment of ákairos.

We are all children of kairós, it would seem, even if the specific ways of articulating kairós vary from one to the other. Blast, flash, time that remains, creative tip of the arrow of time, the moment of bending transcendence to immanence, fulfilment, apocalypse, rupture, event as laicised grace, *novum* and *ultimum,* miracle – they are all variations on a persistent biblical motif. Three key elements run through each of the proposals considered: kairós is resolutely temporal, and it designates both a specific moment of ruptural crisis and a period of opportune, revolutionary time. Some also (Benjamin, Agamben, Negri) emphasise the contrast with abstract, mechanical time, cast in terms of ch/kronos

41. Ibid.
42. Bloch 1972, p. 135; Bloch 1968, p. 181.
43. Bloch 1995, p. 1264; Bloch 1985a, p. 1492.
44. Bloch 1995, pp. 1303–11; Bloch 1985a, pp. 1540–50.
45. Bloch 1995, pp. 1306–7; Bloch 1985a, pp. 1544–5.

versus kairós. Only with Bloch did we note a possibility of breaking from this biblical dependence.

Eschatology

At this point I would like to reinterrogate kairós, for it has not yet told us everything. But before doing so, I need to make a slight excursus in order to deal with eschatology. There are two reasons for doing so: to fill in some of the background to kairós (as a temporal term); and to deal with the perennial problem of the relation between Marxism and eschatology, a problem that has caused more than one hard-nosed Marxist to squirm and shuffle.

As we saw earlier, o kairós, 'the time', is the preferred New Testament term for the end times with its trials and tribulations; others include 'day of judgement', 'armageddon', 'the millennium' and so on. However, that term has its own background in the Hebrew Bible (Old Testament) themes of eschatology, messianism and apocalyptic; more of those in a moment. As far as Marxism is concerned, how often do we hear the charge that it is a secularised Jewish and/or Christian eschatology? From the time of Nikolai Berdyaev and Karl Löwith at least, the claim has grown in authority from countless restatements.[46] It has become such a commonplace that as soon as one raises the question of Marxism and religion in a gathering, at least one person will jump at the bait and insist that Marxism is a form of secularised eschatology (or messianism, the term so many use erroneously). These proponents argue that Jewish and Christian thought has influenced the Marxist narrative of history, which is but a pale copy of its original: the evils of the present age with its alienation and exploitation (sin) will be overcome by the proletariat (collective redeemer), who will usher in a glorious new age when sin is overcome, the unjust are punished and the righteous inherit the Earth. Most of the time, the argument is used as ammunition in the hands of conservative and liberal critics, but apostate Marxists such as Berdyaev and Kolakowski add to the chorus of voices proclaiming that there is a dreadfully smelly theological corpse under the floorboards. Unfortunately, the response of Marxists to such criticism has been to increase the distance between Marxism and its Jewish or Christian heritage, to expunge any last vestiges of that

46. Berdyaev 1937; Löwith 1949; see also Kolakowski 1981, pp. 372–5, and, from a virulent right-wing perspective, see Rothbard 1990. For a more Jewish angle, see Fischman 1991, pp. 94–108. The most dreadful and perhaps honest version of this argument is that, since religious belief was so fundamental to people's worldviews at the time, Marx and Engels were hedging their bets in case Christianity proved to be right. This came as a comment to a paper I had delivered on Christian communism in the work of Rosa Luxemburg and Karl Kautsky.

dreaded religious heritage. That response is wrong-headed, it seems to me, for it allows the enemy to determine the field of battle.

I would rather choose my own battleground, and in doing so, I make three points. First, eschatology is first and foremost a genre of biblical literature, where we find that it must be distinguished from messianism and apocalyptic. Second, Marx and Engels did not derive historical materialism from any Jewish or Christian form of eschatology, or indeed from messianism or apocalyptic. Third, the explicit connection between Marxism and eschatology comes later, especially at the hands of Ernst Bloch. I shall deal with each point in turn.

As far as eschatology is concerned, I need to do some basic ground-clearing, for there is a woeful tendency in much recent philosophical writing to mangle terms that are quite distinct – eschatology, messianism and apocalyptic are assumed to mean roughly the same thing, namely, the destruction of this age and the inauguration of a new one.[47] In light of this situation, we need to pause for a few moments and offer some terminological clarity, for they are distinct categories, with their own characteristics, although seeping into each other at the edges.[48] And I stress that although they are taken as theological and philosophical categories,[49] if not worldviews and social phenomena (although 'millenarianism' usually does its duty, here), eschatology, apocalyptic and messianism are primarily literary categories, genres of biblical and extra-biblical literature in their own right.

---

47. Walter Benjamin, Ernst Bloch, Giorgio Agamben and Slavoj Žižek are all guilty of gleefully mixing these terms, as are their numerous commentators. Throw in the phenomenologists of the 'theological turn' in France – Michel Henry, Jean-Luc Nancy, Jean-Luis Chrétien, Jean-Luc Marion and so on – and we have an epidemic.

48. The following discussion fills out the brief outlines in Boer 2007a, pp. 99–101 and Boer 2009b, pp. 189–91.

49. The most significant efforts to construct theological systems on eschatology come from those hangovers of German theological dominance, Wolfhart Pannenberg and Jürgen Moltmann. They have tried to argue that eschatology is not about the future from the standpoint of the past or present, but that it is about the future from the standpoint of the future. So, present and past are drawn into the future rather than the future becoming a result of the past and present. While Moltmann's theology is one of hope, Pannenberg's seeks an eschatological ontology in which God's being cannot be separated from his rule. Given that assumption, if the kingdom is an eschatological reality, then God must be understood in an eschatological fashion. Perhaps the best way of explaining Pannenberg's take is as follows: imagine a huge library representing your life with each book a narration of that life from a specific point in time; you can pick up any book and read your story 'from that point'. That is the eschatological rationality. We can know it only in the future but it turns out to be retroactively applied throughout time. In short, such an eschatological perspective is 'ontologically' retroactive. Needless to say, both Moltmann and Pennenberg are a long way from biblical categories. See Moltmann 1965; Moltmann 1974; Moltmann 1996; Moltmann 1999a; Moltmann 1999b; Moltmann 2000b; Pannenberg 1969; Pannenberg 1991–3; Pannenberg 2002. See also Mostert 2002, pp. 129, 152–82. Many thanks to Mark Crees for guidance on these matters.

Some rapid definitions:[50] the word *eschatology* was an invention of German biblical scholarship of the nineteenth century[51] and it designates a distinct category of literature and thought. Out of our three terms, it is both the broadest category and probably the earliest. Its concern is with the transition in the near future from the present undesirable age to another that is qualitatively better, a shift from hardship to peace and plenty. In all cases, it is Yahweh, the main god of the Hebrew Bible, who brings in the better world. Even though we might describe the well-known feature of the promised land as an eschatological motif (and in many circumstances it has functioned in precisely this fashion), it is only with the prophetic literature that eschatology emerges as a distinct genre.

A few examples, from Isaiah 35, 42 and 61:

> Behold, the former things have come to pass,
> and new things I now declare;
> before they spring forth I tell you of them.[52]
>
> Then the eyes of the blind shall be opened,
> and the ears of the deaf unstopped;
> then shall the lame man leap like a hart,
> and the tongue of the dumb sing for joy.
> For waters shall break forth in the wilderness,
> and streams in the desert;
> the burning sand shall become a pool,
> and the thirsty ground springs of water.[53]
>
> The Spirit of the Lord God is upon me,
> because the Lord has anointed me
> to bring good tidings to the poor;
> he has sent me to bind up the broken-hearted,
> to proclaim liberty to the captives,
> and the opening of the prison to those who are bound;
> to proclaim the year of the Lord's favour,
> and the day of vengeance of our God.[54]

---

50. The literature on these terms is rather large, to say the least, but good starting points are Reventlow (ed.) 1999 and Braaten and Jenson (eds.) 2002.

51. See Caird 1980, who gives a good account of the history and uses of the term, although his suggestion that it is a metaphorical way of providing a theological interpretation of history betrays his own heavy and lamentable theological tendencies. See also Schweitzer 1998, the classic New Testament study from a century ago which argues that Jesus should be understood as an apocalyptic figure. This argument, picked up by theologians such as Moltmann and Pannenberg, leads directly, I would suggest, to the near-cult status of eschatology as a theological framework for contemporary theology.

52. Isaiah 42:9.

53. Isaiah 35:5–7.

54. Isaiah 61:1–2.

Stretches of texts such as these appear throughout the various prophetic texts in the Hebrew Bible, and the generic markers are quite clear: Yahweh's agency, the word of the prophet, an emphasis on the process of ending social, economic and bodily ills, the emergence of a new age of freedom and plenty and an unavoidable use of figurative language, or, as I have argued elsewhere, the inescapable use of mythological language.[55]

Messianism, too-often regarded as a defining feature of eschatology, is usually assumed by biblical scholars to be a subset of eschatology. In this case a particular individual, divinely appointed and directed, brings about the transition from old to new. The messiah, or 'the anointed one', is in the earlier material mostly a royal figure based around the figure of King David, but then later, especially at Qumran in the Dead Sea Scrolls, we find royal, priestly and possibly a prophetic messiah for whom Moses, Aaron and Elijah become the models. Of course the Christians will claim Jesus as messiah as well, but by this stage messianic eschatology is much more highly developed and depends very much on the saviour figure.

One more example:

> There shall come forth a shoot from the stump of Jesse,
> and a branch shall grow out of his roots.
> And the spirit of Yahweh shall rest upon him,
> the spirit of wisdom and understanding,
> the spirit of counsel and might,
> the spirit of knowledge and the fear of Yahweh.
> He shall not judge by what his eyes see,
> Or decide by what his ears hear;
> But with righteousness he shall judge the poor,
> And decide with equity for the meek of the earth;
> And he shall smite the earth with the rod of his mouth,
> And with the breath of his lips he shall slay the wicked.[56]

A distinct logic connects eschatology and messianism, for if God brings about the eschaton, then he may as well delegate the task to a chosen individual. And yet, I want to hold on to the difference, for it seems to me that one of the distinct problems with religions such as Christianity and Judaism is their reliance on messiahs or saviour figures, or what has become known as the cult of personality.[57] In other words, I can see some value in eschatology, but far less in messianism.

---

55. Boer 2009d.
56. Isaiah 11:1–4.
57. See Boer 2007a, pp. 433–5.

The final genre is *apocalyptic*. Although it also has at base the move from old to new, here we have a body of revealed knowledge [*apocalyptein*, in Greek] about the end times; efforts at very specific calculations of the end, usually through calendars and numerology; a dualism between good and evil, between God and the devil and a host of angels and demons; an esoteric method of interpreting the sacred scriptures to find hidden messages; the destruction of the present age and the inauguration of a completely new one (the 'New Jerusalem'); and an overly metaphoric language that provides a coded narrative of the end times.

Although there is one full apocalyptic text in the Hebrew Bible, the Book of Daniel, and one in the New Testament, the Apocalypse or Revelation, we find a plethora of this literature in extra-canonical texts, at Qumran and in the period of the New Testament. While apocalyptic is intriguing as a genre of literature and at times of political action, I am as sceptical about its benefits as I am concerning messianism, if only because of the reactionary crackpots who engage in apocalyptic speculation today. A deeper reason lies in the radical dependence of apocalyptic on divine intervention and the absolute necessity of the saviour or redeemer figure. All the same, apocalyptic is not completely without virtue, for it cranks up the expectation of the end, rendering it imminent rather than off in a somewhat distant future. Yet, while such fervour for the end means you cannot get comfortable in the present age, it is also notorious for failed predictions and futile political action that expects God to arrive with his chariots and horsemen.

On one level, we can understand eschatology as the base category, the primary genre of which messianism and apocalyptic are both derivatives and sub-genres that developed subsequently.[58] Or, at least, this is the case with the Hebrew Bible (Old Testament), for by the time of the New Testament – from where the dominant perception of kairós begins its influential career – the apocalyptic element had come to the fore, sweeping up eschatology and messianism within itself in the figure of Jesus.

58. One might object that I have fudged the meaning of eschatology: does the term not signal a concern with the end, with the *eschaton*? In this sense it comes closer to apocalyptic. The snare lies, however, in the mix of Hebrew and Greek terms. Eschatology and apocalyptic are derived from Greek, whereas messianism is a Hebrew term (*mashiakh*). To be consistent, either we need Hebrew terms for all three – perhaps the genres of the *nabi, messiah*, and *ro'eh*, or prophet, messiah and seer – or we need Greek terms, such as eschatology, Christology and apocalyptic. If it came to the crunch, I would prefer the Hebrew terms, not least because Christology (*Christos* is the closest Greek term to *mashiakh*) is just a little too overloaded. Yet, the 'prophetic' has a host of other associations that would take too much labour to overcome, so I will stay with the accepted terminology, save to emphasise that 'eschatology' designates not so much speculation about the time after the end, as the process itself, albeit figuratively.

I have stressed that these are literary genres first, that they refer to types of literature. Genres, of course, do not exist in isolation, the mere whim of writers' imaginations. They relate in all manner of complex patterns to worldviews, or rather, to ideological frameworks that both generate and give voice to the aspirations of various groups, political movements and even classes that overlap and bleed into one another – so also with eschatology, messianism and apocalyptic. With an influential text such as the Bible, the situation becomes even more delectably complex: although in their initial forms, these genres of literature may transmit the ideological frameworks of certain groups and classes (who are now lost in the fog of history, even though biblical scholars carry on their unending and often fruitless task of trying to identify what these groups might have been), they have also had the effect of gathering collectives around the texts, generating a host of subsequent religious and political movements with real historical effect. For whatever enlightened or misguided reasons, these figurative and mythological texts have had and continue to have historical repercussions, inspiring one after another group to claim that the messiah has arrived or will arrive tomorrow, or to proclaim that Armageddon will happen on Tuesday next week.

I have given these matters some attention, since some clarity is sorely needed, especially in Marxist engagements with these categories. But that leads me to my second topic, the alleged influence of biblical and theological eschatology on Marx and Engels. Like so many others, did Marx and Engels take some of the strands of this influential tradition and weave them into their own work? Despite all the smug assertions that they did, the answer to that question is a resounding negative. Let me summarise the main points of that answer:[59] Marx actually studied the key prophetic Book of Isaiah – a major eschatological biblical text – in 1839 under Bruno Bauer at the Friedrich Wilhelm University. The previous year Bauer had written an extensive work on the Hebrew Bible,[60] but the last thing Bauer would have been teaching Marx was an eschatological understanding of Isaiah. Both the developing tradition of critical German biblical scholarship and Bauer's own growing argument concerning the false particularity of religion (over against free self-consciousness) forestalled any eschatological interpretation – which was, after all, the traditional one of the church. As for Engels, he had been a devout Reformed (Calvinist) Christian in his youth, read the New Testament in Greek, and was keenly interested in the raging debates over biblical interpretation. Even more, he was fascinated by the Book of Revelation in the New Testament. However, a close reading of his engagements with that text show that he systematically negated the apocalyptic reading of history that such a text has generated from generation to generation. Instead, Engels deals with it

59. For the detail of the argument presented here in summary, see Boer 2012, pp. 124–5, 284–92, 317–18.

60. Bauer 1838.

playfully,[61] appropriates it satirically,[62] and uses its language to express his own growing self-awareness that he was leaving behind the faith of his youth.[63] The telling piece of evidence that Engels was not the conduit for eschatological or apocalyptic themes in Marxism is his later engagement with the Book of Revelation. By the 1850s, Engels, following Bauer, argued that it was a purely historical text, giving us a window into early Christianity before the elaborate theological formulae and high-sounding ideas. Indeed, he dismisses any historical residue of the text: 'All this has now lost its interest, except for ignorant persons who may still try to calculate the day of the last judgment'.[64]

All this is very well, it may be argued; Marx and Engels may not have consciously appropriated an eschatological perspective on history, but they may still have absorbed such a perspective by osmosis, as it were. The trap with that objection is that Marx and Engels consciously set themselves against the prevailing form of socialism at the time, which was decidedly religious and deeply eschatological. That socialism, which they first encountered as it filtered across the border from France, was, as we saw earlier (in Chapter Two) of a distinctly Christian type. These early socialists argued that the original form of Christianity was communist – as found in the legendary accounts of Acts 2:44–5 and 4:32–5 where the early communities had 'all things in common' – and sought to transform Christianity's teachings into codes of ethics without all the supernatural trappings.

So we find Saint-Simon's critique of capitalism tied in with an argument that both the Protestant Reformation and medieval Catholicism had distorted the nature of early Christianity, which was really a religion of brotherly love and not a dualistic one that elevated heaven and debased earth. Despite the inevitable fractions in the movement after Saint-Simon's death, defections to Fourier and ill-fated efforts to usher in the new age, this type of early socialism heavily influenced some German radicals, such as Heinrich Heine, August von Cieskowski and Moses Hess.[65] As we saw earlier, it also influenced some of the early leaders of the German communist movement, much to Marx's and Engels's chagrin – Hermann Kriege, Karl Grün, Gottfried Kinkel and Wilhelm Weitling. In reply, Marx and Engels consciously opposed the apocalyptic flavour of this early communism, especially as it entered Germany through Moses Hess. In his *Die Heilige Geschichte der Menschheit* and *Europäische Trierarchie*, Hess both

61. Engels 1839c; Engels 1839d; Engels 1841a; Engels 1841b.
62. Engels 1842a; Engels 1842b.
63. Engels 1842c, pp. 238–40; Engels 1842d, pp. 312–14.
64. Engels 1883a, p. 117; Engels 1883b, p. 15. See further Boer 2010b.
65. See especially Breckman 1999, pp. 131–76.

introduced communism to Germany and gave it a distinctly apocalyptic tone.[66] His widely read *Europäische Trierarchie* proposed that the fusion of the Young Hegelian criticism of theology, French socialist politics and English industrial materialism would bring about the total collapse of the existing order and usher in a new age. For Marx and Engels, this approach to communism was off with the pixies and had nothing to do with the realities of political organisation.

How then did the connection between Marxism and eschatology take place? Moses Hess soon faded from view in the history of Marxism, so it was left to none other than Ernst Bloch to make explicit a connection with which Walter Benjamin was playing in his own idiosyncratic fashion.[67] Bloch drew from the Bible the various eschatological, messianic and apocalyptic strains into what he called 'warm Marxism'. For Bloch, they gave expression to a deep utopian longing, a hope for a better world no matter how forlorn that hope may be. Any reader of his magnum opus, *The Principle of Hope*,[68] or that fascinating Marxist interpretation of the Bible, *Atheism in Christianity*,[69] will soon come across myriad biblical references, allusions and extended treatments of texts. And the reader will also meet the argument that biblical eschatology is the forerunner of Marxism, the atheism of which is the logical and historical outcome of the deep impetus of the Bible itself. Let me be perfectly clear: Bloch does not recognise the underlying biblical eschatology of Marxism and seek to make it a virtue; instead he is the first to make this connection in an extraordinary tour de force, thereby setting that connection on its path.[70]

I have tarried with eschatology for a time and soon we will be able to resume our journey with kairós. But what I have sought to do is fill out some of the background to the way kairós came to designate the end times in the New

66. Hess 1837, 1841, 2004. See the excellent discussion of Hess in Kouvelakis 2003, pp. 121–66.

67. A precursor to Bloch's warm Marxism may be found in Anatoly Lunacharsky, comrade of Lenin, God-builder and first Commissar for Enlightenment after the Russian Revolution. God-building proposed a place for enthusiasm, feeling, the gods as utopian ideals of potential human achievement and appropriation of the Christian socialist tradition, all of which was embodied in the Revolution. However, since Lenin had condemned God-building in his debate with Lunacharsky in the first decade of the twentieth century, the latter's project fell into official disrepute and his two-volume *Religion and Socialism* (1908, 1911) was not republished – 'officially', since at an unofficial level Lunacharsky held to most of his positions after the Revolution. Due to this publishing non-history, the works disappeared from view and Bloch had to rediscover many of the themes proposed by Lunacharsky all over again. For a full discussion, see Boer 2013a.

68. Bloch 1995; Bloch 1985a.

69. Bloch 1972; Bloch 1968.

70. The embarrassment over Bloch's overt appropriation of eschatological themes has contributed to the avoidance of Bloch by many hard-nosed Marxists. The exception here is Daniel and Moylan 1997, although Peter Thompson's new Bloch centre at the University of Sheffield will hopefully overcome the continuing neglect of Bloch.

Testament – that is, through the connection with eschatology, messianism and apocalyptic. At the same time, I have taken the opportunity to debunk some misconceptions about the supposed debts of Marx and Engels to a secularised form of Jewish and/or Christian eschatology, as well as indicate where the explicit connection was in fact made. That point was, of course, Ernst Bloch; his work opened up the possibility of appropriating kairós into Marxist thought.

Ákairos

But now it is time to return to kairós itself, which needs to be subjected to a few more searching questions. Despite the strength of the biblical kairological tradition, this provides a limited picture of the dimensions of kairós. In particular, the biblical heritage serves to conceal a range of class and economic traces that are associated with the term. So in order to identify those traces, I shall take a step beyond this biblical legacy and widen our search to consider the Greek context of kairós.

When I first began chasing down kairós, so that, puffing and cornered, it would finally tell me the full story, I undertook the simplest of exercises. I began with a comprehensive lexicon of New Testament Greek, where of course the temporal senses of kairós we encountered earlier were laid out with an impressive range of examples. But then I reached across to a lexicon of classical Greek, its page corners darkened with finger oils from many years of leafing through its pages. A cursory glance seemed to confirm the familiar sense I had uncovered earlier: kairós appears initially as a temporal term, designating the right, critical and proper time or season. But now the deeper implications and associations of the word's semantic cluster began to emerge. For the word has deeper economic undertones, which come to the surface with difficulty: in a largely agricultural economy, kairós indicates the right season for planting or reaping, with a particular emphasis on the time that the fruit is ripe, so much so that kairós also bears the sense of fruitfulness and advantage.

All the same, we are still in familiar territory, dealing with time and its permutations. Along with philosophical commentary, biblical exegesis and theological elaboration, this delving into classical Greece seems to confirm the sense that kairós designates the right time and a time of crisis. But now my search, moving deeper into this territory, began to bump into one surprise after another. The first of these was that kairós is not only a term of time but also of *place*, indeed that the spatial sense is earlier.[71] And in this spatial sense, kairós designates what is in or at the right place, particularly in terms of the body. Kairós and especially

71. Rickert 2007, pp. 72–3.

its adjective, kaírios, designate a vital part of the body. For example in Homer's *Iliad*, the adjective is used to mark the right place on the body for an arrow to find its mark. And in the works of Pindar, Aeschylus and Euripides, the word means a target, especially on the body in battle: it is the point where a weapon can inflict the most damage.[72]

So now we have an extended sense of kairós, one that goes well beyond time. Even more, both temporal and spatial meanings of the term find their basis in the sense of measure, proportion or fitness. As time, kairós is then a distinct measure or the appropriateness of time – the exact, critical and opportune time. As place, it becomes measured space, as well as the way space is proportioned, preferably 'correctly' when one refers to the body where everything is in its right place. Given the distinctly masculine dominance of Greek culture, especially of elite, ruling class males, it takes little imagination to see that such a kairological, that is, properly proportioned body, would be a male body, athletic, warlike and virile. One gains a distinct sense that kairós actually refers to what is in its *right place and time*, duly measured, appropriate and opportune. Indeed, although kairós takes on a range of meanings – convenience, decorum, due measure, fitness, fruit, occasion, profit, proportion, propriety, symmetry, tact, wise moderation, as well as opportunity, balance, harmony, right and/or proper time, opening, timeliness – the semantic cluster coalesces around the idea of what is duly measured and proportional; in short, the right time and right place.[73]

Not quite the sense of kairós to which we have become accustomed, for its deeper sense concerns measure, proportion and harmony. However, I am interested in uncovering the economic and class dimensions of kairós. In order to identify those features we must follow a path through two further dimensions of kairós, namely, the expansion of its sense to a universal category or law, and its concern with the harmony of opposites. As for expansion, let us begin with Hesiod, in which agriculture unfolds to include economics. In that agricultural text par excellence, *Works and Days*, Hesiod writes: 'Observe due measure, and proportion (kairós) is best in all things'.[74] Here, kairós means the right season of the year for planting, cultivating and harvesting crops and fruit. But it also indicates the right place, due to soil, landform and amount of moisture, for planting a particular crop or orchard. However, note that kairós inescapably bears an economic sense, for the business of agriculture is not merely concerned with soils and seasons and the right practice, but also and fundamentally with economics.

---

72. See Onians 1973, pp. 343–7; Rickert 2007, p. 72.

73. See further Rickert 2007; R. Thompson 2000, p. 75; Kinneavy 1983; Carter 1988; Untersteiner 1954; Enos 1976, p. 44; Sipiora 2002.

74. Hesiod 1973, p. 81; cited in Rickert 2007, p. 72.

Two further examples illustrate a far greater expansion of kairós. Thus, Plato writes in *The Laws*:

> Pleasure and pain, you see, flow like two springs released by nature. If a man draws the right amount from the right one at the right time, he lives a happy life; but if he draws unintentionally at the wrong time [*ektos tōn kairōn*], his life will be rather different. State and individual and every living being are on the same footing here.[75]

As with Hesiod, due measure and proportion are invoked here, now in terms of a harmony of opposites, in which one draws appropriately from pleasure and pain in relation to individual happiness. The key, however, lies with the last sentence, for Plato indicates that kairós applies not merely to individual life, but also to the state and 'every living being', an expansion that includes medicine, navigation, sex and universal harmony.[76] A further example comes a little earlier from the Pythagoreans, for whom kairós embodies a universal law in which opposites, 'bound together by harmony, give life to the universe'.[77] Kairós has expanded its sense considerably, for now it is a law of the universe, if not crucial to the creation of that universe in the resolution of the tension between form and matter.[78]

Already we have moved to the question of conflict and resolution, the second step on the path to the economic and class dimensions of kairós. As we have just seen, in both Plato and those upon whom he relied, the Pythagorans, kairós involves a doctrine of the harmony of opposites. While Plato speaks of pleasure and pain, Pythagoreans such as Empedocles were concerned with the opposites of form and matter, odd and even, right and left, limited and unlimited – all of them embodied in the fundamental conflict of monad and dyad. The universe could be generated only through the resolution of this conflict.[79]

So kairós now involves a universal principle focused on the balance or harmony of opposites. Yet, given this fuller meaning, a question lurks in the shadows of this classical kairós: what is its opposite? Not chonos, and thereby chronological, measured and dominating time – the position emphasised in Benjamin, Agamben and Negri, and indeed a standard opposition in most philosophies of time. In classical Greek, merged chronos-kronos became a byword for an old fool or dotard, especially in the comedies of Aristophanes. As a proper name, Kronos is, as is well known, the father of Zeus; but he also designates that period before the current era, the

75. Plato 1970, p. 62; *Laws* I: 636d–e. See also Foucault 1985, pp. 57–9.
76. Eskin 2002.
77. Untersteiner 1954, pp. 110–11.
78. Carter 1988, p. 102.
79. Carter 1988, pp. 101–2; Gorman 1979, pp. 135–41; Untersteiner 1954, p. 111.

distant past which may be either a golden age or the dark ages, depending on one's perspective.

Instead of chronos-kronos, the opposite of kairós is determined by a series of prepositions: in the text from Plato quoted above, we have already seen that the opposite of kairós is *ektos tōn kairōn*, without or far from kairós, or simply wrong. Other prepositional opposites include *apó kairoû*, away or far from kairós; *parà kairón*, to the side of or contrary to kairós; *pró kairoû*, before kairós or prematurely; *kairoû péra*, beyond measure, out of proportion and unfit. These senses all bear the weight of what is outside the zone of kairós, untimely and out of place. And all of them may be gathered under ákairos. If kairós designates the well-timed, opportune and well-placed, then ákairos means the ill-timed, inopportune and displaced. I cannot emphasise enough how important this opposite of kairós is: over against measure we have beyond measure; timely versus untimely; in the right place versus the wrong place. One who is ákairos is in the wrong place at the wrong time.

Kairós has by now considerable expanded from its temporal sense, now designating space, universal law in which the resolution of opposites is crucial, and being opposed by ákairos. In light of these developments, it becomes possible to identify the economic and class dimensions of kairós and ákairos. In order to do so, we must ask: due measure, timeliness, harmony and universal law for whom and for what purpose? The answer begins with Wood, who has made clear in regard to Plato that he embodies the thought of an aristocratic and anti-democratic elite, in short a ruling class ideology.[80] A characteristic feature of such an ideology is the claim that its own particular perspective is applicable to all, that it is a universal law. A further dimension in our search for the class dimensions of kairós involves an unwitting insight by Kinneavy, who was instrumental in recovering kairós as a term in recent debates over ethics and rhetoric. Asked whether kairós is a political term, Kinneavy responds:

> In its origins it was. As a matter of fact, you may remember that the symbolic reference was to kairos as a god. He was a god in Greece, and he was represented as a young man, a student at the two-year, kind of junior-college preparation they had for policing and for war.[81]

But what kind of young man does this god represent? Here Aristotle, true to the spirit of his teacher Plato, provides the best definition. Such education is appropriate not for persons of low tastes, who are the vast majority: 'The utter vulgarity of the herd of men comes out in their preference for the sort of existence a

80. Wood 1997, pp. 142–3; 2008, pp. 50–98.
81. R. Thompson 2000, p. 79; see also Kinneavy 1983, p. 93.

cow leads'.[82] In other words, only ruling class males, precisely Plato's and Aristotle's students, if not of every philosopher-teacher,[83] are capable of philosophical reflection, rhetorical training and political leadership, thereby excluding slaves, peasants, artisans and women. Yet this particular ideology is assumed to be universal, applicable also to those members of the vulgar herd.

At this point a connection opens up between kairós-ákairos and a wider series of moral, class and economic oppositions, each of which favours one term over another. As Ste. Croix has shown, the apparently innocent Platonic question, 'what is good [*agathós*]?' is far from innocent. It has distinctly class assumptions, in which 'good' designates the values of the ruling, propertied class and 'bad' [*kakós*] those of the ruled. Overlapping with good vs. bad are a host of other terms that reveal the intersections between politics, class, ethics and even physical appearance: wealthy vs. poor, noble vs. ignoble, brave vs. cowardly, well-born vs. ill-born, blessed vs. cursed, lucky vs. unlucky, upright vs. lowly, elite vs. masses, pillars of society vs. dregs, beautiful vs. ugly.[84] Within this constellation the opposition of kairós and ákairos finds its home, if not the organising principle itself.[85] Thus, the harmony of opposites is a harmony from the perspective of the ruling class in which an apparent harmony is actually the domination of one term over another. The universal law of kairós becomes the claim of a particular perspective to universal status at the expense of others.[86]

It has become apparent that kairós has a rather unsavoury class sense. The body out of proportion, one that is 'ugly', is also the body of the poor, exploited majority of Greek society – what, following Negri, we might call the

---

82. Aristotle 1955, p. 30; *Eth. Nic.* 1.5; see also pp. 309–10; *Eth. Nic.* 10.9.

83. For the importance of kairós as a principle of teaching such students, see the discussion of Isocrates in Sipiora 2002, p. 14.

84. See Ste. Croix 2006, pp. 338–9, who provides a host of related terms: *oi tas ousias echontes, plousioi, pacheis, eudaimones, gnōrimoi, eugeneis, dunatoi, dunatōtatoi, kaloi kagathoi, chrēstoi, esthloi, aristoi, beltistoi, dexiōtatoi, charientes, epieikeis* – all for the 'good' propertied classes; for the 'bad' unpropertied classes we have *oi penētes, aporoi, ptōchoi, hoi polloi, to plēthos, o ochlos, o dēmos, oi dēmotikoi, mochthēroi, ponēroi, deiloi, to kakiston*. See also Ste. Croix 1972, pp. 371–6. One might gather a similar collection of terms with such moral, class and economic overlaps in our own day: uneducated, trailer-trash, bogan (an Australian with a similar sense), rabble, low culture, unfashionable, and so on.

85. Sipiora 2002, p. 3.

86. A contemporary example of the way kairós offers a ruling class perspective may be found in the work of Kinneavy, who seeks to provide a universal code of ethics based on kairós: 'My code is based upon five principles: respect for life, respect for family, respect for property, respect for truth, and respect for liberty' (R. Thompson 2000, p. 84). Kinneavy goes on to argue that this universal kairological code provides the basis for the United Nations Declaration of Human Rights, albeit used appropriately. Thus, if someone attacks him or his family, the kairological response would be to a defence that entails extinguishing someone else's right to life. He remains blind to the fact that such a code is the expression of a specific, bourgeois ideology that claims universal validity.

monstrous.[87] From here kairós may also, in connection with this cluster of other terms, apply to social measure and order. A kairological social order has everything in its proper place – aristocratic elites, exploited peasants, driven slaves, women and so on. Such a proportioned and fit society, one characterised by 'eugenia', ensures that the ruling elite remains precisely where it is. Disorder and immeasure, what is contrary to kairós and thereby ákairos, designate an unfit and unhappy society, one in turmoil and on the rocks, when time is out of joint and events take place outside their proper time and season.

To take but one example, is not the wildcat strike an excellent example of ákairos? For the ferociously independent Georges Sorel, the strike was as much a potent political weapon as it was a myth.[88] This great admirer of action over against contemplation saw in the general strike the most forceful weapon in the war of socialism against capitalism. More recently, for Antonio Negri and his comrades the industrial involvement of the 1960s and 1970s, with its ongoing battles and wildcat strikes, was a key component in the development of workerism, or *operaismo*. And both Negri and Sorel still have a point, given the way business and the owners of capital seek to curtail the possibility and effectiveness of the strike. While we still see the use of scab labour to replace striking workers, in our own time the big end of town prefers to pressure governments to enact more and more legislation in order to restrict the strike to an 'appropriate' time, carefully measured and portioned out. They say: you may strike only at this point (kairós) in the process of negotiating a new award; before or after is illegal and you will be charged. The untimely, ákairos strike must be brought to order, allotted its place and time.

Kairós has turned out to be far more multifaceted than its biblical heritage has suggested. Not content to be restricted to a temporal register, it has now spilled out to include agricultural and bodily spaces, the sense of measure and then blurted out its potential class allegiances. The implications for my earlier gathering of kairological theories of revolution should be obvious, but some care is needed. To begin with, a key term such as kairós inescapably carries with it the rich and at times unwanted dimensions of its semantic cluster. This is so for both the distinctive biblical appropriations of kairós as it is for the Marxist efforts to rethink revolution in light of that category. Further, a crucial dimension of that legacy is the opposition in which kairós is located. As we have seen, the opposition is not, as many have argued, between chronological and kairological time, between the mechanical march of time and the opportune moment; rather, the

87. Negri and Casarino 2008, pp. 193–218.

88. Sorel 1961. For Sorel the myth of the general strike, with its collective, motivational and irrefutable nature, was as necessary and as powerful as the act itself. See further my discussion of myth in the second chapter.

opposition is between kairós and ákairos, between timely and untimely, well-placed and out of place. In this light, kairós begins to show its true colours. Not quite a shift in sides to that of mechanical, abstract time, yet the word now becomes associated with moral, economic and class associations that stress order over chaos, proper functioning society over against the improper, the right time and place against the wrong.

What of the shift into biblical usage? Is that not a change in direction, indicating the opportune time of crisis, the unexpected end time? The full picture provides us with two elements in that appropriation, with a distinct emphasis on the temporal. First, the sense of a right and proper time is indeed found in the Bible, with respect to the seasons and harvest, which take place at the appointed time. However, the minor role this sense has indicates a more systematic avoidance of the ordered class and economic dimensions of kairós. Or rather, they are not so much avoided as occluded, conveniently relegated to another sphere, hidden and thereby unknown. Let us put it in terms the unexpected, for kairós is clearly represented as such in the Bible. Here, we need to take into account a tension between human and divine perspectives. From our earthly perspective, we may not know the day or hour of the Lord's return and thereby must be prepared for the unexpected. Yet from a divine perspective, that kairós has already been appointed by the one who knows precisely when it will occur. For us, it may be unexpected and certainly unannounced, but for God it will occur at the right and proper time.

All of which has distinct implications for the appropriations of kairós in order to recast revolution. Initially, it may seem that the emphasis on the undeserved and unexpected dimensions of kairós – as blast, rupture, event and miracle – signals that some dimensions of ákairos have crept into the Marxist appropriations of kairós. Thus, revolution has a spontaneous, unseasonable, immeasurably creative element that cannot be predicted or planned. The rupture or event or miracle crashes through the door without a polite knock, or perhaps like a thief in the night; we should be always alert, for we know not the day or hour, as the New Testament would have it. Apart from the fact that this dimension is contained within the biblical notion of kairós, as I have just indicated, it also resonates a little too uncomfortably with certain elements of capitalism. For instance, the emphasis on the unexpected nature of kairós sounds like 'good' business practice, as when one seizes an unexpected turn in the market to one's advantage. Opportunity, innovation, creativity – these are watchwords for 'successful' business. The catch, here, is not merely that one may also see a greater plan beneath the unexpected, in which the biblical God becomes Adam Smith's famous 'invisible hand', but that the leaders of business and of wealthy nations are always well-positioned – in the right place and time – to take maximum advantage of such apparently unexpected turns. In other words, the sense of kairós as an unexpected moment still assumes the right and opportune time, the crucial flashpoint that will kick-start the revolution.

Thus, the Marxists I considered in the first part of this argument risk an unwitting connection with those associations, thereby providing a bulwark for the status quo they seek to oppose and overthrow. Does not Benjamin's fulfilled messianic time sound uncomfortably close to Fukuyama's argument for the end of history with the 'end' of communism in Eastern Europe?[89] Does not Agamben's time that is seized out of chronos and brought to fulfilment lend itself a little too easily to astute business practice? Is not Negri's infinitely creative moment at the tip of the arrow of being too close to the bourgeoisie's attribution of supernatural creative power to labour, as Marx pointed out in *Critique of the Gotha Programme*?[90] Does not Žižek's tension between a search for the genuine shift in the coordinates of existence and refusism echo the business executive caught between the big break-through and throwing it all in for a cottage in the woods? Is not Jameson's growing rumble of a low-key rupture too much like a social-democratic reform program that has made its peace with capitalism? Is not Badiou's event comparable to an unexpected stock market crash that enables one to buy bankrupt businesses at basement prices? And does not Bloch's miraculous leap into the highest newness risk veering towards Schmitt's counter-Reformation notion of the miracle as the constitutive exception that supports, *sub specie aeternitatis*, the status quo?[91]

All of them run the danger of siding unwittingly with the well-proportioned over against ill-fashioned bodies, ruling elites rather than downtrodden peasants and slaves; in short, with the interweaving of moral, economic and biological factors, kairós sides with the good, beautiful, well-born, wealthy and educated aristocrats. But is there nothing retrievable from these various efforts at a kairological revolutionary politics? I hinted earlier that the point where they may break out of the heritage of kairós lies in their emphasis on the undeserved, unannounced and unexpected dimension, with a particular emphasis on Bloch's miracle as the *novum et ultimum*, now on a radical political trajectory in which miracle is but one, theological code, for revolution. However, what is needed is a push that will take this element of kairós out of the spatial, social and economic

89. Fukuyama 1992.

90. 'The bourgeois have very good grounds for falsely ascribing *supernatural creative power* to labour; since precisely from the fact that labour depends on nature it follows that the man who possesses no other property than his labour power must, in all conditions of society and culture, be the slave of other men who have made themselves the owners of the material conditions of labour. He can only work with their permission, hence live only with their permission' (Marx 1891a, p. 81; 1891b, p. 17).

91. Schmitt 2005, p. 36.

dimensions that trail the term from its Greek and thereby biblical heritage, a shove that will take it away from its associations with the well-proportioned ruling elites and towards the ill-proportioned and untimely, that is, to the bad boys and girls, ugly bodies, poor peasants, cowardly slaves, ill-born labourers, cursed, unlucky and lowly masses, in short, to ákairos. The catch is that the opposition itself is one determined by the ruling classes, a way of asserting their own right and proper role and of marginalising those who would oppose them. If we were to shift to an akairological perspective, then the very terminology would shift and the opposition itself would be cast aside.

Measure and immeasure (Negri)

Now that we have thrown in our lot with ákairos, I would like to return to Negri, not to reprise or even adapt his rather ordinary comments on time but to mine a central concept that is full of inadvertent promise – the opposition between measure and immeasure [*misura* and *dismisura*]. I am intrigued: measure-immeasure immediately connects with my earlier discussion of the basic sense of kairós-ákairos; yet Negri makes nothing of the link (I can only assume that he does not know of the semantic cluster of kairós). So I seek to do what Negri does not and bring the two together.

However, before I make the connection, I need to ask what Negri makes of measure and immeasure. This opposition may be regarded as a substantial realignment of some old philosophical distinctions, especially those between eternity and contingency, universal and particular. And in Negri's commentary on the biblical Book of Job (my focus in what follows),[92] measure-immeasure also becomes the way of reorganising a significant number of topics: pain, time, ontology, value, labour, power, evil, creation, theodicy and cosmogony. I have no need to dig deep into each topic here,[93] for the importance of that opposition lies elsewhere, at least for my purposes. Briefly put, measure and immeasure take on different values; they intersect with the themes of chaos and creative order; and they overlap (unbeknownst to Negri) with kairós. Let us explore each point in some more detail.

To begin with, Negri (through Job) dismisses all forms of measure and comes out as a champion of immeasure. However, this is only the beginning; although Negri wants to dispense with a negative, retributive measure in favour of a creative immeasure, that chaotic moment is only a transition to a new, positive form of measure. That is, by the time Negri has finally worked his way through the Book

92. Negri 2009.
93. See the last chapter of Boer 2011a.

of Job, the values attached to measure and immeasure have shifted: initially, measure is a negative feature and immeasure takes on a positive sense; but then immeasure shifts to a negative register and a new, creative measure emerges.

One example of the baleful effects of measure suffices for my purposes – the pervasive doctrine of retribution, which is expounded with impressive sophistication by Job's supposed lawyer 'friends', Eliphaz, Bildad, Zophar, as well as the late addition of Elihu. The logic of retribution is well known: if I perform an act, whether good or evil, I will be rewarded or punished for it. Retribution assumes a vast universal balance: evil in one place or moment is balanced by good in another time and place, and vice versa. But the doctrine means far more than this, for evil also brings with it an appropriate punishment: laziness brings hunger and penury, greed brings retribution and so forth. So also with goodness, for a beneficial act leads to the appropriate and carefully measured reward. The wallet returned will rebound in the universal calculus with an unexpected recompense. How pervasive such an approach remains! At a religious level, it is astonishing how many still believe that a reasonable collection of good works will earn them some reward in the afterlife (salvation by works-righteousness) or perhaps that their evil works will come back to haunt them in some unforeseen way. Funeral eulogies invariably wheel out the list of stellar achievements of the dead person in question, no matter how cranky, grumpy and malicious that person may have been. So also in the Book of Job: his friends opine that Job's suffering must be due to some evil he has done, however unknown or unwitting it might have been. He had better search far and wide, they advise, to recall what evil he has done. In this moral universe, evil and good appear in measured quantities. The other items on our earlier list fall under the same pervasive logic. Thus justice becomes a quantifiable category; it involves matching the appropriate reward or punishment with whatever act has been committed. Ethics, too, becomes a calculation of benefits and drawbacks of this or that act. As does labour, for capitalism operates on the basis of determining how much labour is spent on a job, how overtime is to be calculated, what the right wage is for the labour-time given and so on. The operation of retributive measure seems so commonsensical, working its way into the smallest mundane acts: the cost of a loaf of bread, whether I should reciprocate that invitation from people whom I cannot stand, the grades that a child receives at school – the *lex talionis* of everyday life.

Through his reading of the Book of Job, Negri dismisses these variations on measure as restrictive and exploitative. Yet, just when it seems as though he has granted measure a negative value and, by default, immeasure has taken a positive sense, the terms begin to shift in his hands. Immeasure – that which is outside of and beyond measure – turns out to be more multifaceted than initially appeared to be the case, so let us track that change carefully. As the chaotic excess that measure tries to control, immeasure may seem like a fundamental challenge to the ordering efforts of measure, but then we find that the exploitation of labour becomes immeasurable, as does evil itself.[94] Even more, God joins this gaggle of excessive oppressors; indeed, he is their great mentor, representing all that is immeasurable, imbalanced and disproportionate: 'God is the seal of the clearest, fiercest, deepest of social injustices'.[95] No measured God of the scholastic theologians here, no ordered being with static attributes,[96] for this God is an immeasurably oppressive one.

How to oppose both the deadening effect of measure and the endless evil of exploitation? At this point, a more positive sense of immeasure emerges in Negri's interpretation of Job: exploitation, evil and even God find themselves opposed by the immeasurable nature of pain and suffering – the central topic of the Book of Job. Negri argues that the only way to overcome the immensity of evil is through the immeasurability of pain. Dialectically put: only through the depths of undeserved and guiltless suffering are we able to glimpse something worthwhile, which is nothing less than power, the creative power of labour. In other words, not only do we have two types of immeasurability – endless suffering and pain versus immeasurable evil and exploitation – opposed to one another, but the creative possibility of labour-power emerges from the midst of the pain of exploitation.

Soon enough, I will stitch this sense of immeasure in with what I have called ákairos, but before I do, there is one last step in Negri's narrative, namely, the revaluing of measure. It, too, becomes more complex, for it is not restricted to the dreadful patterns of payback, in which reward and punishment are appropriate to the initial act. Measure may take on a more positive hue, dismantled and reshaped for a new task. Negri speaks of 'an immensely powerful, creative ontology that emerges from chaos',[97] which I take to be, as it were, a return to the chaotic immeasure that precedes creation so that the world may be re-created from the beginning. In other words, through the two types of immeasure, one evil and oppressive and the other creative and powerful, a new measure emerges, the creation of a very different and just order.

Let me summarise the moves as follows: negative measure → negative immeasure → positive immeasure → positive measure. In sum, if we think that a retributive system of carefully measured patterns of labour, time and value are bad enough, then we are in for a shock; immeasurable labour and exploitation are far worse. Yet, in the midst of this untold pain and suffering, a new creative

94. Negri 2009, pp. 8–9.
95. Negri 2009, p. 43; see also pp. 28–9.
96. Negri and Dufourmantelle 2004, p. 80.
97. Negri 2009, p. 73.

power emerges, one that leads to a thoroughly new measure, a new order that has nothing to do with the old.

That is all very well, but is not the far more interesting moment that of immeasure? I must confess to being drawn to immeasurability rather than some search for a new measure, particularly because Negri's terminology overlaps significantly with that old mythological (and biblical) pattern of chaos and created order. The bare narrative sequence of the story of creation is deceptively simple and perhaps too well known: out of chaos comes the careful ordering of creation in which every thing finds its place. We might fill out this bare structure with all manner of detail – chaos may be the destructive force of older, cranky gods, as in the Mesopotamian creation myth, *Enuma Elish*, or it may be the formless and void state of the 'deep', the *tehom*, in the account of Genesis 1, or it may be the pure absence of apparent form and clear demarcation, the proverbial primaeval swamp. In response to such chaos, creation involves victory over chaos (variously a monster, the sea, a serpent, woman, an older opponent from an earlier generation of the gods), the demarcation of Heaven and Earth, planets in their paths, seasons at the right time, and the careful ordering of created life, usually in some form of hierarchy that places humans at the top or, as is more often the case, subordinates human beings to the gods. Or we might turn to the flood narrative of Genesis 6–9 for another version of the same story: the initial creation (measure) has turned out to be flawed, characterised by extraordinary evil and exploitation. In order to begin again, God makes use of a beneficial chaos (the flood) to wipe out the old and begin again with a new, created order. Or, in Negri's own take on this narrative, when 'measure fades into the disorder of the universe and evil is reflected in chaos, in the immeasurable',[98] we need 'the collective creation of a new world' that 'is able to reconstitute a world of values'.[99]

Negri is not shy about these cosmological connections, evoking the creative power of labour, the bringing into being of which human beings are capable, and above all – for my purposes at least – 'a great chaos, a great immeasurableness'[100] (this from the commentary on Job) that makes it clear enough that the connection is not at all forced. As I argued earlier, this immeasurable chaos may be one of endless exploitation or it may be the highly productive one of depthless pain and suffering.

One feature of this cosmological chaos is worth emphasising, for too often it slips by without notice, camouflaged behind the screen of natural chaos: it is also, if not primarily, a political chaos. Once again, Negri unwittingly brings the

98. Negri 2009, p. 49. See Job 28:23–7.
99. Negri 2009, p. 14.
100. Negri 2009, p. 52.

connection to the fore,[101] although now in his opposition between eugenics and the monster, the one a favoured theme from the Greeks onwards (meaning to be well-born, good and beautiful – in short, the myriad overlaps of moral, biological and class terms I noted earlier) and the other a marker of what resists. In the creation myths, the monster is the one that must be overcome through the creation of order. These stories of creation are usually depicted, as we explored in my discussion of political myth, as cosmogonic (creation of the natural world), theogonic (creation of the gods), and anthropogonic (human beings come into the picture). Nice and neat, but far too limited, for these myths are also what I have called poligonic.[102] They deal with the origins of, and thereby provide ideological justification for, the current political and social order. As we saw earlier, the Mesopotamian myth *Enuma Elish* is keen to point out that the Babylonian king is a direct descendent of Marduk, the warrior and creator god, and the myth spends a good deal of time with the ordering of society, the construction of Babylon and the establishment of the state. Similarly, the creation story in the Bible does not end with the seven days of Genesis 1 or indeed the alternative story of Genesis 2 with its more earthy narrative of the garden. It runs all the way through the stories of the patriarchs and matriarchs (Abraham and Sarah, Isaac and Rebekah, Jacob and Leah and Rachel, and then the twelve sons and one daughter, Dinah), the migration to Egypt, Moses and the Exodus, wilderness wandering and formation of a state in waiting, and then ends with the conquest of the promised land. In other words, it is primarily a political myth of creation. So, if created order means political order, then the chaos against which that order continually struggles is as much political as it is natural. Primaeval abyss and catastrophic flood are inseparable from disobedience regarding the tree of good and evil in the garden, from murmuring and insurrection in the wilderness, from the perpetual challenges to the divinely given power of Moses and so on.

Now, at last, I can come back to the matter of kairós, which begins to look rather different from my initial foray into Negri's treatment of that theme. Two lines intersect at this point: the extraordinary way measure slots into kairós, immeasure into ákairos; and the way in which chaos and order have an inescapably political dimension. As for the first line, recall that the basic sense of kairós is indeed measure and that the temporal and spatial senses of the term are modifications on this basic sense. Kairós is both the properly proportioned body (physical, political and social) and the right or opportune time. It takes little imagination to see that the myths of creation – especially in their poligonic dimension – express this double sense of kairós: they provide narratives as to how everything finds its spatial (from the heavenly bodies through the creation

101. Negri and Casarino 2008, pp. 193–218.
102. See further Boer 2005–6.

of human beings to the seat of power in the city) and its temporal (days, months, seasons and their proper relations) order.

What then is contrary to kairós, is outside it or far away from it, or indeed beyond kairós? Immeasure, obviously, or as I have called it earlier, ákairos – the ill-timed, unseasonable, and out of place. Negri, as we saw, wants to find a retooled measure and indeed kairós, but he tarries long with immeasure, with the monstrous and thereby with ákairos. Here the very political nature of chaos comes into play, for if chaos marks the constitutive resistance to oppressive power, then we need to dwell in the midst of that chaos. Among others in the innovative *operaismo* movement in Italy, Negri should be the one to identify most closely with such resistance; as he has argued repeatedly, state and economic power are not givens to which people resist; no, that resistance is primary and to it oppressive political and economic power must constantly respond and adapt. So it is with the narratives of chaos, which have already been joined by our comrades, immeasure and ákairos – the fathomless, ill-timed and displaced. We see it again and again in those creation myths where chaos – disobedience, murmuring, insurrection, challenges to divinely appointed leaders – is the constitutive force that must be countered in ever new ways. But we also see it in our own day with the running riots in Paris in 2006 and in Greece in 2008 and then again in 2010, in the 'hooligans' and disaffected youth who burn cars and smash shop fronts, the brazen disregard for police, the massed protests in Seattle, Genoa, Copenhagen and countless other moments of anti-capitalist protest. All of these are dubbed as chaotic and monstrous, threats to social order and the state, the result of outsiders breaching the borders, the work of thugs and criminals. They are, I would suggest, manifestations of ákairos.

By way of conclusion: political grace

It is time to review my argument thus far. By now the conventional and rather biblical understanding of kairós – as the right season and opportune moment – has little credence, even if it allowed me, initially and temporarily, to gather together some of the major thinkers of revolution (Benjamin, Agamben, Badiou, Žižek, Bloch, Jameson and Negri). On the way, another standard assumption concerning Marxism's secularised eschatology was also shown the door. But it was only when I explored the other senses of kairós, uncovering its quite unattractive spatial, moral and economic dimensions, that I could side with ákairos, enriching it with Negri's immeasure and not his measure, with the monstrous rather than eugenics. Here the various lines came together, especially in the immense possibilities of immeasure, which is not only cognate with ákairos, but also intersects with the theme of chaos as a distinctly political motif. In short, I have sided quite clearly with those who are untimely, not in the right place, chaotic and beyond measure. Indeed, I prefer the akairological and the immeasurable over the kairological.

However, I would like to finish on a slightly different note, offering a few observations on a connection that has always captivated me: the relation between grace and revolution, a translation between a theological doctrine and a political praxis. Needless to say, this connection is a prime instance of ákairos. In order to bring out the akairological dimension of both grace and revolution, I beckon to the shaggy head of Alain Badiou, for I wish to interrogate his theory of the event in light of ákairos. Why? Not only is Badiou quite explicit about his effort to laicise Paul's doctrine of grace,[103] to offer a militant rereading of grace in terms of the event and its truth, but that event is itself the most rigorous effort to rethink the possibility and nature of revolution.[104] It will be objected that Badiou began this chapter in the camp of kairós. True enough; in my earlier discussion I did locate him in that camp, but it seems to me that Badiou and his thought are most amenable to cross over and warm their hands by the fire of ákairos.

Before I question him more closely, let me reprise the continual need to relativise theology and biblical themes. A 'no road' sign bars the way to any fruitful progress in thought if we continue to think – as so many argue – of theology or the Bible as the *fons et origo* of political thought, philosophy and what have you. In what follows, I do not assume that grace is in some way the ultimate source – hidden perhaps under the dense undergrowth of secularism – of any idea of revolution; rather, revolution (in the way Badiou articulates it) and the doctrine of grace (in a certain Protestant inflection) are two forms, however momentary and incomplete, that such thought may take.

As we saw earlier, for Badiou Paul's identification and elaboration of an event as well as the building of a faithful, militant group is an exemplary case of the truth-event. I am less interested, here, in the event, its inseparable naming, the procedures of truth, conventionally and somewhat arbitrarily identified as science, art, love and politics (although one may also glimpse a ghostly fifth procedure in theology), or indeed the fidelity, confidence, and collective nature (faith, hope and love, of course) of the militant group that forms in the wake of the event. Or rather, I am interested in that naming or identification of the event, but not in light of those four procedures: it is Badiou's own 'naming', if I may

103. Badiou 2003b; Badiou 1997. See also his treatments of Pascal and Kierkegaard in Badiou 2006a, pp. 212–22; Badiou 1988, pp. 235–45; Badiou 2009, pp. 425–36; Badiou 2006b, pp. 447–57.

104. A point emphasised in an informed and insightful essay by Alberto Toscano (Toscano 2004).

put it that way, of how the event itself works that is the most seductive aspect of his theory.

Badiou is perfectly clear: like grace, the event is supernumerary; it cannot be anticipated or planned within the way things are, or what he calls the order of being, the state of the situation or the 'there is'; the event is therefore entirely unexpected and one certainly does not earn the event as a reward for this or that revolutionary good work; it smashes its way into the ordinary run of collective life, after which nothing can be the same. Or, to use Negri's terms, the event cannot be measured in any known way, for it is immeasurable and incommensurable. Now it becomes possible to rearrange Badiou's theory in terms of kairós and ákairos – in the full senses that I have developed above. The 'there is' or the order of being becomes the realm of kairós or measure (to keep Negri in the picture). Seasons and times have their correct place; right moments appear in good time; bodies, both physical and social, are properly ordered; entrepreneurs seize the moment when it comes in order to make a killing; the good, the beautiful, the upright and the well-born ensure that the ugly, the bad, the lowly and the ill-born know their place – all is measured and measurable, in its due time and place; in short, kairós. But then an event crashes the party, contrary to kairós, beyond measure, untimely and distinctly out of place. Like the old bum in smelly clothes who sits at a fine table in a restaurant and pulls out his scavenged cigarette butts and soiled burger found in a bin, this event is ákairos.

As with this theory of revolution, so also with its translation into the doctrine of grace in its raw, unadorned form – the reason why it appeals so much to Badiou. Grace, too, does not compute, does not fit the expectations of priests obsessively poring over their holy books, does not meet the expectations of a people longing for military deliverance, makes no sense even to the closest of followers, bursts in without human agency or anticipation.[105] In theological terms, grace simultaneously suspends, completes and therefore dispenses with law, ethics, and any notion of love that is tied to the law.[106] In its *form*, the doctrine of

105. Lest this comment on human agency be misread, let me point out that 'God' in the doctrine of grace should be understood as a placeholder for non-human agency. Examples of non-human agency in revolutions include nature – witness the role of environmental factors such as rainfall patterns, flooding, seismic events, disappearance of fish stocks and even the seasons – and the irrational, especially given that human agency is assumed to be rational agency. Still useful in thinking about the revolt of nature is Horkheimer's essay of the same name. See Horkheimer 2004, pp. 63–86; Horkheimer 1991b, pp. 105–35. In theological terms, such a restriction to rational human agency classes as salvation by works. Indeed, the primacy of human agency becomes a sign of arrogance, a hubristic assumption that human beings can save the world on their own, or at least make that world a better place.

106. Žižek's engagement with Badiou and then Christianity's revolutionary core is an excellent negative example of avoiding the traps of law, ethics and love. Žižek follows a tortuous path through Paul and the New Testament to Lenin. On the way, he is

grace is an instance of Badiou's event, but the catch is that its *content* troubles him: God becomes a man in the person of Jesus of Nazareth, dies and is then raised from the dead. A 'fable', says Badiou, which does not concern him at all, at least as far as the content is concerned. As I have argued in the chapter on myth, the fabulous nature of the story is not to be avoided, for it is crucial to the role of such a fable.

But what interests me is the raw form of the doctrine of grace, which is something that frightened even its first theorist, Paul in the New Testament, and produced all manner of ambivalences that are still with us. After emphasising the radical freedom of grace in relation to the law with respect to the Galatian church, Paul found – as we saw in Chapter Four – that he had to try and rope grace back in, for it kept sparking radical fires in the early churches. No, he wrote to the Corinthians and the Romans, grace does not mean that women may participate freely in worship, nor does it mean sexual freedom or a complete disregard of the law. No, he argues, for the law is good, or there is another law, the law of Christ that we must follow. No, he points out, we cannot live in the full freedom of grace since we must show concern for those not as strong as we are, ensuring that our outward observance is suitable and law-abiding. In trying to tighten the reins on grace, Paul found himself in all sorts of knots. Similarly in the Roman Catholic Church, grace became restricted to the walls of the church itself – *extra ecclesiam nulla salus*, no salvation outside the church. Grace had its designated roles, in the sacraments (which were slowly limited to seven by the fifteenth century in the conflict with the Orthodox churches) or in priestly ministration. Or grace becomes a partner, as in Molinism,[107] with human striving and obedience to God's law in the process of salvation. Even John Calvin, who kept seeing the radical possibilities of grace and taking dreadful fright from it, sought to channel

---

perpetually waylaid by love (which he elides with grace) and ethics. But it is only when he realises, towards the end of *The Puppet and the Dwarf*, the full import of grace that he is able to see Lenin's point: only through grace, with its absolute suspension of the law and ethics, does Lenin's actual freedom make sense, the over-riding of any and every ethical and political code that there might have been. See Žižek 2000; Žižek 2001b; Žižek 2003. See my detailed discussion in Boer 2007a, pp. 335–90. By contrast Agamben simply gets lost in the law when reading Paul: Agamben 2005; see Boer 2009b, pp. 181–204.

107. Luis de Molina (1535–1600) argued in his *Concordia liberi arbitrii cum gratiae donis* of 1588 that human works and obedience to the divine commandments have a complementary role along with grace. Opposing the Reformers' emphasis on grace alone, Molina argued that freely chosen human cooperation with the gift of grace was the ultimate cause of the efficacy of grace. This effectiveness, which means the ability of human beings genuinely to obey God, comes not from grace itself, but from the human decision to obey. Thus, in opposition to the Protestant position on the total depravity of human beings, who can do no good on their own, Molinism attributes to human beings as much involvement as possible in ensuring their own salvation. Molinism attempts to escape espousing self-earned salvation by arguing that the free act of human beings to cooperate with God is itself foreknown by God.

it along carefully constructed channels: Christian freedom means only spiritual and not temporal freedom; grace follows a two-step programme of redemption and sanctification, kept firmly in the pocket of the Holy Spirit; above all, grace does not mean the revolutionary doctrine that those frightful anarchist anabaptists took it to mean, with their liking for seizing control of cities (Münster in 1534–5), or that firebrands such as Thomas Müntzer and the peasant revolution of 1525 took it to mean.[108] Perhaps the most mundane instance of grace's domestication is the way it has become a term for the prayer before a meal.

In contrast to these continual efforts to contain grace and tie it down, I prefer a grace that is unrestrained and unrefined, is untimely and out of place; ákairos, in the same way that Badiou's event is. Nonetheless, I do not argue that grace and the event are identical, or indeed that the theological idea of grace is the source of Badiou's event or indeed any other comparable theory. Grace is, I would suggest, the theological shape that idea and practice may take. So also, Badiou's event is another, more philosophical and political shape it may take. Or indeed, Negri's immeasurable multitude may be seen as yet another possibility. Yet grace, event and immeasure are not the partial manifestations of a pure type of revolution, for they exist only in these particular shapes, constructed ad hoc for the purpose in question, translated and rearticulated in different languages.

I have reshaped much in the argument of this chapter. Kairós has given way to ákairos; timely, well-placed and ordered proportionate measure has given way, especially in light of its moral and class connections, to the unruly, chaotic and immeasurable. But then the unearned, even unworthy, doctrine of grace had added to this sense of ákairos, albeit in interaction with its translation as revolutionary event. All the same, thus far I have opted for relativising theology, for the contingency of different positions, and I have suggested the metaphor of translation: grace and revolution may be translated into one another, with the usual losses and gains, overlapping but not exact semantic fields and so on. Instead of this minimal option, what if we took a stronger, dialectical one? On this register, I would suggest that through this materialist translation can the doctrine of grace realise its political potential. Restrained within the confines of theology, it continues to under-perform, unsuited to its strange role. But as a revolutionary doctrine, it is full of the gunpowder of political change and overthrow.

108. See further Boer 2009c.

Chapter Six
Ethics

> Morality itself is a special case of immorality.[1]

The second reconnaissance mission deals with ethics, which may be defined here as the means of greasing or oiling social relations so that they work more smoothly. More specifically, ethics assumes multiple others with whom and between whom social relations are problematic, thereby seeing its task as overcoming those problems in order to make social relations operate in a more improved manner. By defining this as greasing social relations, it should be clear that I am profoundly suspicious of ethics, a suspicion shared by Marx for whom ethics is a mystifying ideology that justifies that status quo and keeps the ruling class in position. That suspicion that is aroused whenever I encounter a certain cluster of unthinking phrases. It may be a discussion over global warming or environmental politics and someone will say, 'ethically speaking....' Or it may be the question of asylum seekers and refugees and another will say, 'if we approach this ethically....' Or I may suggest an ambit claim, an overdone proposal in order to make what I really want to propose seem perfectly reasonable; a moral warrior will look at me sourly and pronounce, 'that's not ethical'. Or I may be talking with an apostate lefty over a beer, and she will suggest I become involved in that oxymoron, 'ethical investment'. The invocation of 'ethical' effectively seeks a closure to argument and an unassailable position with which we

1. Nietzsche 1968, p. 254, §462.

must agree, for it really seems to mean what is 'good', or more often 'I think this is correct and you had better not disagree, for my position invokes a higher order before which your position counts for nothing'. After all, who does not want to be ethical? All such approaches, I suggest, are actually moralising, telling people what they should or should not do.

Why the negative reaction? Is not politics inherently ethical? And does not the Left seek to take a better ethical approach to economics, society and politics? Do we all not want apply the oil can to our social relations, and indeed our sense of connectedness to nature, so that they may work better than they do? As will become clear soon enough, the reasons for this suspicion are both political and theological: among a good number on the Left, ethics has sidled up to politics, absorbing it in the process into a bloated hybrid; theologically, as ethics pushes to the front, other items become sidelined, especially the doctrine of grace, which, as I argued in the preceding chapter, may be seen as a theological version of the theory of revolution. In its place comes an emphasis on salvation by works, good deeds that will smooth the path to (social) salvation.

So I mount an argument against ethics, or rather, against 'ethics' as a lubricator for social relations, which then becomes a marker for that which is 'good'. For some reason, the critical corner of ethics is crowded to overflowing, with voices raised, feet trodden upon and books produced at a furious rate. It seems especially the case among those on the Left (both mild and militant): Gayatri Spivak, Luce Irigaray, Michel Foucault, Judith Butler, Terry Eagleton, Slavoj Žižek and Alain Badiou are only some of those crowding the scene. And when I pick up a work by one of them, a trail of other names appears, although each one chooses a different collection with whom to deal. Turtles all the way down, except that in each the turtles are not the same. Since I do not wish to produce a heavy tome on ethics, I need to be even more judicious in my choice of sparring partners, drawing out the key elements of my critique and proposal from dialogue partners on the Left. In the following discussion, I begin with some definitions and then critique the two bleached forms ethics takes today – care of the self (Foucault) and relations to the 'other' (Butler and Eagleton), usually designated as the stranger or the neighbour or some such term. From that moment, I draw out my criticisms, using as a springboard Badiou's outright dismissal of the 'ethical ideology' of the other as an apology for the 'state of the situation', for the way things are (although I am less enthused by his solution in which ethics becomes both encouragement and warning in post-evental militancy), as well as Žižek's effort to exacerbate the alien nature of the other by smashing his way through the imaginary and symbolic other to the unknowable, traumatic and obscene other. I share their suspicions of ethics as it is parleyed about in these times, especially in the way it easily becomes moralising, offering advice as to how we should live our lives, but I take a different track.

My critique begins by asking a preliminary question: how is the 'other', a given of so much ethics, produced in the first place? Is it needed for the formation of the self or is the discourse of ethics itself responsible for producing the 'other'? The answer is that the discourse of ethics does so, but in the process it obfuscates its arrogation of other discourses that also produce others, as well as concealing the socio-economic connections that enable such productions. The result is that ethics gives the impression that the other is a given upon which ethics may set to work. However, that concealment requires further interrogation, specifically in terms of its biblical and class dimensions. On the biblical side, the 'other' trails the dust of the pernicious theme of the chosen people. The process of claiming to be chosen requires the production of all manner of 'others', of strangers who are not part of that select group. By this time, someone may well object that ethics is not so much an issue of self, other, stranger, neighbour, social relations or chosen people, but actually of goodness. In response, I tackle goodness in terms of its problematic theological associations and then its Greek heritage (Socrates and Plato).

Once I connect that proposal of an ethereal goodness for which we must strive with class assumptions concerning good and evil, I focus on my main objection, focussing on Aristotle, arguably the founder of the classical philosophical tradition of ethics. Not only was Aristotle clear that ethics pertains to the male ruling class elite (ethics are simply not appropriate for the herds), but also the very terminology of *ta ethika* bears those class assumptions. Thus, the Greek *ethos* and Latin *mos* (the basis of ethics and morals) refer to custom, habit, the known status quo in terms of social relations. They certainly should not be disrupted, particularly if you happen to belong to the ruling, propertied class. In response to these structurally inescapable connections, I ask whether the term can be appropriated, emptied and refilled by those opposed to the ruling classes. In the end that may be impossible, so I suggest that a position opposed to ruling class custom and habit be pursued, that is, *aēthēs* and *praeter morem*, unethical and unmoral. That is, I seek not an amoral position, which dispenses with ethics, but one that seizes ruling class ideology and turns it against itself. In the end, even these terms should be understood as place-holders for an entirely other terminology that may be more appropriate.

Ethics, morality and moralising

I shall not spend a great deal of time mapping the vast and varied terrain of ethics. However, it can be argued that reflections on ethics are caught in the bind of moralising. Either one commits to a version of moralising or one attempts to escape the bind by refusing to moralise. The problem with moralising is that it is a version of preaching in which the congregation is told what wrongs to avoid and what the right behaviour should be. The scene is all-too well-known. The priest, minister or pastor thunders from the pulpit against fornication, sloth, murder, slander, idol-worshipping, bestiality, poisoning the neighbour's hedge, fighting over the flower roster, necrophilia and harbouring evil thoughts against the Conservative Party (all without distinction); by contrast the upright items include not lusting after one's neighbour's spouse (or indeed one's neighbour), not stealing, keeping the Sabbath, telling the truth, supporting one's community, stoning one's child should they give cheek and giving handsomely to the priest's Mercedes Benz fund.[2]

At a philosophical level, such moralising may take two forms: the care of the self and how we should react to and behave towards the 'other'. How should I care for my body, my mind and soul? What is required to stay healthy, vigorous, sensitive and tolerant? Or at a more sophisticated level, what is required in the construction of a self that is by no means a given. Ethics, then, comes down to the assumption – asserted explicitly or implicitly – that the way I live or construct my life, or at least would like to live my life, is the way you should live yours. As for the 'other', the question becomes: what is the appropriate way to respond to the stranger in our midst, the refugees from that country where our government sent the army, the immigrants with a vastly different cultural, social and religious background to the one with which we are accustomed? And how should we respond to that greatest 'other' of all, the non-human, or as it is sometimes called, the 'more-than-human other'? Or, on a more mundane level, how do we deal with the neighbour in our own small social network, attempting to find ways in which we can all get on. In these cases, ethics becomes the process of producing a code of acceptable conduct for relating to those 'others'. I will have more to say on both the care of the self and the response to the 'other' soon enough, but they are both regarded as central categories of ethics. And both are forms of moralising, a favoured pastime that has not escaped the ubiquity of television programmes (Oprah Winfrey has much to answer for), self-help manuals, the desire for makeovers and the obnoxious need to 'sell' oneself in order to make any headway in the world.

What I have called moralising has a more reputable philosophical pedigree, variously designated as normative ethics or an ethics of good or of responsibility. One identifies a desirable end or purpose and devises an ethics that will enable people to attain that end. For example, in medical ethics the purpose of medicine is to cure a patient (which includes preventative measures). On the basis of this purpose, we can then argue for patient-doctor confidentiality, since that will

2. See, for example, Romans 1:29–31; 1 Corinthians 6:9–11; Galatians 5:19–24.

encourage the patient to trust the doctor and thereby provide more information so that the doctor may come up with a more accurate diagnosis. By analogy, the same principle applies to a society, the relations to others or the care of the self. The key is to identify what the chief end might be, which is itself based on various arguments concerning the human condition – human nature, the relation between God and human beings, the greater good of society and so on. Once these basic elements are established, we can then determine what the appropriate moral action might be, even if it seems contradictory, to achieve that end. A classic example is war. We may conclude that a desirable good is peaceful existence, without the threat of conflict, destruction and enslavement. However, to ensure that end, it may be necessary to go to war in order to preserve that possibility of peace – for our society at least.

This type of ethical reflection leads us to a distinction between reflection and action, reasoned consideration and the appropriate acts that embody those considered conclusions. Yet they are intimately related, the one leading to the other and then back again. In other words, ethics is normative, involving the investigation of moral principles and their justification in terms of basic principles. If we follow Aristotle's approach, then this is an inevitable connection: ethics as careful reflection and as practical advice are two parts of a whole. Ethics is, as far as Aristotle is concerned, a form of practical knowledge (and thereby a branch of politics) which sought on the basis of reasoned deliberation upon chosen acts to enable upright and well-born citizens to conduct their lives and those of their communities well, that is, towards the end of happiness (a poor translation of *eudaimonia*) by means of the famous prudence – *phronēsis* or 'mean' – in relation to the virtues.[3] Or, as I would put it, the business of normative ethics (in its various forms of virtue ethics, deontology and consequentialism) is to engage in moralising.

However, this version of ethics faces a profound contradiction, namely, that between the specificity of any society or group and the search for universal norms for ethics.[4] This contradiction is really the other side of the problem with

---

3. Aristotle 1955, pp. 25–7, 55–6; *Eth. Nic.* 1.1–2 and 2.1. Despite all their differences, the ethics of such varied thinkers as Aquinas, Spinoza, Hobbes, Hume and J.S. Mill are also normative.

4. A contradiction brought to the fore in the useful, if somewhat flawed, history of ethics in MacIntyre 1998. As MacIntyre puts it in the Preface to the revised edition: 'these philosophical attempts to present rationally justifiable universal claims to moral allegiance, claims upon human beings as such, claims about human nature as such, in the local and particular terms which each culture provides for its moral philosophers as their starting-point, had generated for each major moral philosophy its own particular difficulties and problems, difficulties and problems sometimes acknowledged and sometimes not. The subsequent history of each such moral philosophy revealed the extent to which each possessed or lacked the resources necessary to become aware of and to resolve those difficulties and problems – each by its own particular standards. And

which I began this section: to moralise or not to moralise, or in the terms in which I am now operating, to connect universal norms with a specific context or to refuse such a connection. The problem is both obvious and simple: the ethical norms determined for one group will be limited by ethnicity, gender, age, religion, sexuality and economics; any universal principles will be a projection of that particularity. As Adorno puts it, 'the more you admit empirical conditions, the more you rule out the possibility of any objective definition of the good life and of moral action'.[5] In order to avoid the dreaded bogey of relativism, a favoured path has been to divorce utterly the connection between ethical reasoning and practical advice. It may take different forms, such as restricting oneself to critiquing and assessing the moral principles of other ethical systems (a good example here is utilitarianism), or it may seek to develop a system by means of a radical refusal of empirical knowledge, intentions or human ends (the sheer formalism of Kant), what Adorno calls an ethics of conviction,[6] or it may retreat as far as possible from any threat of relativising through moralising into the realm of meta-ethics. In this case, there is a retreat from content, principles, let alone advice, into the exploration of the logical consistency or otherwise of ethical thought. For example, a meta-ethical approach argues that one must first determine whether ethical positions rely on objective and universal truths or are the result of the specific concerns of a group or even an individual. Without deciding on this matter, one cannot determine what argument is appropriate in order to develop and defend an ethical system. Meta-ethics, however, especially in its claim to constitute ethics as such, preserves the universal applicability of reasoned reflection, craftily identifying relativity as an item for analysis rather than considering the nature of that analysis as subject to the same concerns.

As I pointed out earlier, these efforts to dig out and deepen the abyss between practical advice and reasoned reflection are responses to the perceived problems of the initial connection of reflection and advice in ethics, a connection I have dubbed moralising. At least two replies have been made against such a drastic retreat into the rarefied air of pure thought, replies convinced that the remove from the immediacy of ethics and moralising is at best fictional. One is to return to the Aristotelian approach, facing the contradiction of universal precepts and specific advice and seeking to dress up moralising as desirable and necessary.

---

by *this* standard the major claimants in modern moral philosophy . . . seem to me . . . to fail' (MacIntyre 1998, pp. xvi–xvii). At the same time, MacIntyre goes on to defend a revamped and cleaned-up Aristotelian approach.

5. Adorno 2000c, p. 107.

6. As Adorno points out so well, Kant knew that any concession to intention or subjective human ends or goals would compromise the universal nature of his argument. The catch is that it faces insuperable contradictions. See Adorno 2000c, pp. 127–45.

Some of those I consider below fall into this group, such as Foucault, Eagleton and Butler. By contrast, I prefer another path, one that is indebted to Adorno, for he persistently locates the inconsistencies of any moral philosophy (Kant is his main target), the contradictions and problems that render any ethics highly problematic. However, since Adorno runs the risk of following a meta-ethical approach, I wish to give him a push, for I want not to dispense with moral philosophy, but to undermine it from within, seeking to take a position against ethics through ethics itself.

Before I proceed, a few basic words on usage are needed. As is reasonably well known, 'ethics' as a term (in the plural) was coined by Aristotle: *ta ethika*, 'the ethical matters', a word that then set in motion a sub-discipline of philosophy and then later theology. However, as Aristotle himself explicitly recognises in *The Nicomachian Ethics*,[7] its basis lies with the Greek term *ethos*, a lowly word that speaks of custom and habit. And since, argues Aristotle, these community habits are not natural, one needs practice and training in order to develop the correct habits. I will have much more to say about this etymological background to the term, save to point out here that the Latin translation is *mos*. But we know that word almost exclusively in its plural, as *mores*, the habits, unwritten codes and patterns of behaviour of a society or an individual. Both words, *ethika* and *mores*, ethics and morals (or preferably moral philosophy) are interchangeable, at least etymologically, and that will be my practice here. I do so for two reasons: first, to run against the tendency to see ethics as one rung above morals, the former speaking of extended and systematic philosophical reflection of a social nature and the latter dealing with the codes by which individual human beings live – sexual morals or religious morals and other such private matters. The second reason why I equate the terms is due to the fact that it is only lately that ethics has attained this higher status, largely through repetition. It is worth recalling that the terms have not always been arranged in this way. Take for example Adorno's lectures, published as *Problems of Moral Philosophy*:[8] Adorno finds ethics a little trendy for his liking, far too close to the slick advertising (or so it seemed back then) that began to invade Europe in the wake of the American invasion at the end of the Second World War. Indeed, it comes close to the moralising he abhors – a sense that I obviously share with him. And so Adorno prefers moral philosophy as the proper task of philosophical reflection, although he seeks to show how such a philosophy is riven with contradictions, so much so that it is difficult to produce such a philosophy in the first place.

7. Aristotle 1955, p. 55; *Eth. Nic.* 2.1.
8. Adorno 2000c.

Care of the self

Much of contemporary ethics, especially on the Left, concerns the stranger, foreigner or 'other', in itself a move to get beyond the sense that ethics applies to our group, our society. On the other side of the equation is the one who cares for the other, a self that also needs care. Enter a large chain bookshop, perhaps like Borders, and the self-help shelves loom before you, a vast obstacle you need to negotiate in order to get anywhere else in the shop. Here are books with glossy covers, bristling with images of ageless authors, impossibly white teeth, wrinkles smoothed out – all speaking of the value of precisely the book in question. If you follow my advice, the image wants to say, you can be just like me – youthful, successful, happy, with internal plumbing like a twelve-year-old and a libido like a woman of forty.[9]

To my dismay, I find them broken down into ever more subgenres, such as the spirituality section with its formulae for inner peace, happiness and endless orgasms; or the fitness books, packed with advertisements for plastic tubs of brown powder with all those supplements necessary for bulging muscles, popping veins, paper-thin skin and shrunken libidos;[10] or the cookbooks for cleansing one's liver, or weaning oneself off carbohydrates, or perhaps curing everything from the common cold to AIDS by drinking copious amounts of water; or books full of advice on how to repair relationships, become a loving, trusting and randy partner; not to speak of that trusty line of works for whom the cursed Dale Carnegie is responsible, namely, how to win friends and influence people.

It should come as no surprise whatsoever that our bookshops are crammed with such self-help works, for if we turn on the television every now and then or have children to send to school, then we are bombarded with graphic and gruesome advice that smoking is bad for you (a man with tubes in his nose talks about seeing his grandchildren but then dies soon afterwards); or that driving while under the influence puts your life in grave danger (a teenager relates through sobs that he has just killed his best friend); or that obesity is at epidemic proportions (so coin-shaped contestants with slabs of fat larger than the Ross Ice Shelf of Antarctica compete to see who can lose the most weight); or that we really should exercise more to keep us trim and taut for that unexpected moment when the clothes must come off (three women – for these television shows come on mid-morning when the men have gone to work – of different sizes, graded from fat to firm offer an aerobic routine to help you move from one to the other, hopefully firm rather than fat); or the need to watch that cursed sun and its rays, slipping on a shirt, slopping on sunscreen and slapping on a hat.

9. See, for instance, Žižek's comments in Žižek 2005b, pp. 55–6.
10. See further Boer 2009e.

But let us return to our bookshop, where we will find, sadly, that one or two philosophers may be found on the self-help shelves too... such as Alain de Botton, with his cute books (transformed into audio books, DVDs and television shows), on love, status, travel, happiness and work.[11] Alongside his own smooth and self-indulgent reflections, he rips out chunks of text from their contexts, dripping blood and gore and odd pieces of gristle, from philosophers, artists and writers in order to offer advice as to how to make life more pleasant and... nice. So we find Van Gogh, Ruskin, Huysmans, Wordsworth and Flaubert on travel, Christopher Wren, Le Corbusier and Norman Foster on the architecture of home, and Socrates (on unpopularity), Epicurus (on lack of money), Seneca (on frustrations), Montaigne (on inadequacy), Schopenhauer (on broken hearts) and Nietzsche (on difficulties) and so on. Self-help for the thinking woman and man, philosophical soufflé, philosophy as a 'school of life' – the actual name for de Botton's new institution, which teaches courses on careers, relationships, politics, travels, families, offers psychotherapy in a way that one might get a haircut and has – no surprise here – a shop selling the necessary accoutrements of a soothed life.

Not quite so banal but of the same ilk was the later Foucault. His acolytes may find my locating him – this ethereal solver of all our philosophical and political problems – in such company a deep affront. Is not his challenge to ethics like no other, dismissing concerns of social greasing, questioning the very basis of ethics in human nature and the subject and for that reason focusing on the construction of the human subject in the first place? Granted to some extent, for Foucault clearly – in fact, clearer than most – saw the problems I have mentioned in the previous section, specifically the tension between universal precept and particular origin, as well as the concomitant problem of moralising, but he chose to deal with those problems by what he and his followers thought was a radical turn, questioning the basic assumption of a human subject. To my mind, this turn by Foucault was drastically mistaken, devolving in his late work to what he calls, in the third volume of *The History of Sexuality*, the care of the self.[12] That third volume was actually an effort to bring together the two different directions of the previous two,[13] the first concerned more directly with sex and the second with the self, especially the argument that the ancient Greeks were not so much interested in moral codes or even a hermeneutics of the subject but techniques of existence, modes of subjectivation, processes that require a

11. Botton 1994, 2001, 2003, 2005, 2006, 2009.
12. Foucault 1986.
13. Foucault 1981; Foucault 1985.

Greek 'to act upon himself, to monitor, test, improve and transform himself'[14] as an open-ended programme; the third was then an effort to mediate the two, focused on an 'intensification of the relation to oneself by which one constituted oneself as the subject of one's acts'[15] in the first two centuries of our era, all of which comprises an attempt to produce a genealogy of ethics through which we constitute ourselves as moral agents, defined by our relation to sexual activity. Equally revealing are his posthumously published lectures, course outlines and interviews, especially those which speak about 'technologies of the self', where he maps out the project that came to be the incomplete *History of Sexuality*.[16] These 'technologies' – one of those arresting and fuzzy terms so beloved by Foucault – are the specific practices used by individuals in constructing their own selves. Or in Foucault's words, these practices 'permit individuals to effect by their own means, or with the help of others, a certain number of operations on their own bodies and souls, thoughts, conduct, and way of being, so as to transform themselves in order to attain a certain state of happiness, purity, wisdom, perfection, or immortality'.[17]

In the perpetual effort to map his changing patterns of thought, this technology of the self marks a shift in the last years of his life from the interest in power, domination and what he came to call 'governmentality', to the actions an individual exercises in constructing his own self (the pronoun is quite deliberate, for the model in the end is Foucault as his own project). He does so by making a troubled classicist move, turning to the perceived roots of the West in ancient Greece and Rome, specifically the first and second centuries CE, as well as the ascetic Christian practices of the third and fourth centuries. And so we come across a diverse and changing collection of practices: reflection, writing, listening, letters to friends and self-disclosure, examination and review of self and conscience, *ascesis* as an act of mastery over oneself in order to acquire truth (Stoics) and then later renunciation (Christian),[18] interpretation of dreams, *exomologesis* as the recognition of the fact of sin leading to repentance through

14. Foucault 1985, p. 28. See also his comment concerning 'a stylization of attitudes and an aesthetics of existence' (Foucault 1985, p. 92).

15. Foucault 1986, p. 41.

16. See especially Foucault 2000, pp. 223–51, 269–80.

17. Foucault 2000, p. 225. See also Foucault 1985, p. 28: 'the individual delimits that part of himself that will form the object of his moral practice, defines his position relative to the precept that he will follow, and decides on a certain mode of being that will serve his moral goal'. Foucault delineates this technology as the fourth type, the others being technologies of production, sign systems and power, which he acknowledges – in a rare moment of attributing the source of an idea – come from Habermas (see Foucault 1985, p. 177).

18. I find the interest by the later Foucault in asceticism not so much a personal agenda for the construction of his own self as the appeal of a way of life rather different from his own (earlier) drinking, drug-taking and sexual practices.

renunciation of the self, *exagoreusis* as a dual process of obedience and contemplation that achieves its goal through verbalising and thereby renouncing your will to a master. These various practices carry through, flowing together and then running off into different channels, from the probably spurious Platonic dialogue *Alcibiades I*, through the Stoics and on to the early Christians.

More extensively, Foucault offers four categories for the care of the self, modalities providing a full range of ethical concerns that are summed up in four words: *what*, *why*, *how* and *end*.[19] 'What' concerns ethical substance, the material of ethics, which he describes as the will to truth, or, more prosaically, that aspect or part of oneself which is concerned with moral conduct. 'Why' deals with the mode of subjectification, the form it is given or the mode of self-stylisation: it explores the way in which one recognises one's moral obligations, establishing a relation to the rule and recognising that it needs to be put into practice. 'How' is the ethical work itself, entailing critical activity, thought interacting with experience, the work performed to change oneself into the ethical subject of one's own behaviour; in short, the process of self-formation. And 'end' or *telos* entails, obviously, the purpose of ethics, the being to which one aspires by behaving in a moral way. For Foucault, this is nothing less than disassembling the self, of releasing oneself from oneself – his curious definition of freedom that emphasises the specific practices of freedom rather than liberation of a given human nature from its constraints.[20]

The overwhelming focus is on the ethical subject: out of what, for what reason, in what way and to what purpose is that subject constructed? However, in developing this fourfold schema, Foucault works in his characteristic fashion, plundering the thought of others without attribution, reshaping categories to suit his own wishes. In this case, he has, with a wink to those in the know, taken on Aristotle's four causes – material, formal, efficient and final. With trademark audacity, Foucault welds together the usual starting point for ethical reflection – Aristotle's *Nicomachean Ethics* – with the *Metaphysics*. For Aristotle, as is well-known, the material cause is 'that from which, as its constitutive material, something comes, for example the bronze of a statue . . .'.[21] In Foucault's appropriation, it becomes the ethical substance, a more intangible matter than Aristotle's bronze used for a statue, or, to add an example of my own, perhaps the old wood one might retrieve in order to make a bookshelf for all those philosophical self-help books, or indeed a bicycle from old parts in order to carry them home. The formal cause, for Aristotle, is the account of what the statue or bookshelf is – perhaps that bust of Lenin that I place on top of the bookshelf or the bicycle with

19. See Foucault 2000, pp. 262–9; Foucault 1985, pp. 26–7.
20. Foucault 2000, pp. 282–3.
21. Quotations in this paragraph come from Aristotle 1989, Book 5, Section 1013a.

its two wheels, handlebars, chain, seat and carry-rack. Yet, both can arise only from some idea, a plan that gives shape to the material at hand. For Foucault, this formal cause becomes the mode of subjectification, the constitution of a subject into which the 'material' sources of ethics are to be shaped. And then we find the efficient cause (in English, 'cause' properly refers to this category), which is 'the source of the first beginning of change'. Aristotle uses the example of the father being the cause the child, but in the case of our statue or indeed bookshelf and bicycle, the crucial element is an agent which brings about the transformation, producing something with the statue mould, the hammer, nails, sandpaper and dowelling, or the spanner, Allen keys and cable cutters. This agent brings about change in the matter in order to produce the form of the object. So, too, with Foucault's interest in how the ethical subject comes about; it is not a given but requires work, yet once again understood intangibly, as critical reflection, thought on experience, the process of self-formation by reflecting and acting in light of the books on ethics that I now have on my new shelf.

Finally (quite literally) comes Aristotle's famous end or purpose, 'that for the sake of which' something is done – deliberately, unintentionally or blindly. Walking may be for health (Aristotle's example – the first moment of ethics as self-help?), the statue may be for adoration or as an ironic nod, the bookshelf for books, which I have bought to make me healthy, wealthy and wise, and the bicycle to transport those books, although it now may have other ends, such as getting me to the shops or as a way to travel long-distance. And for Foucault, the purpose of ethics is the constitution of the moral subject, one who acts in a moral way. Now, Foucault's effort to link ethical categories with the modes of causality is not without warrant in Aristotle's work, for the latter's modes of causation are woven in with the main features of his thought – form and matter, for instance, or agency, or the outcome of physics where there is no conscious purpose. But what has happened in Foucault's appropriation is a de-substantialisation of the four causes for the sake – paradoxically – of Foucault's central concern, namely, the self.

Why is Foucault interested in all this? To begin with, he wishes to recover a nearly forgotten dimension of ancient practices, that of care of the self, rather than the dominant memory of the 'know thyself' of the Delphic oracle. The key phrase is *epimeleisthai sautou*, which Foucault translates in a curious moment of repetition as 'to take care of yourself', to take 'care of the self', 'to be concerned, to take care of yourself'.[22] He argues that for the Greeks and especially those of the Hellenistic era the latter was far more important than the oracle's brief

22. See Foucault 2000, p. 226. On p. 269 he uses *epimeleia heautou*, while in the third volume he interchanges these two words. See the important discussion in Foucault 1986, pp. 43–68.

statement from Delphi. But the repetition of definitions is telling, for it marks not so much an unresolved trauma as an obsession with the care of the self. Why? He seeks not to return to an archaic age, but to see what can be recovered for the present for his own project of constructing the self. He wishes to overturn the way in which morality has become based on external law, whether theological or secular (he actually identifies this external law as secular, which is a curious slip), as well as beat a path away from 'knowing oneself', especially since that has, since Descartes at least, become the basis for the philosophy of knowledge. Above all, he wishes to challenge the overwhelming concern of ethics with the other by focusing on the self. Nonetheless, this self is a subject that is not a given, not an essential unity upon which one gives due attention with the aim of improving oneself. Rather, Foucault's concern was with the self as a problem, requiring production and manipulation and thereby becoming a basis for ethics.

So rather than a code, provisional or absolute, rather than reflection as the basis for action or an effort to resolve the moralising tension, and rather than a concern with the other, the project of the self becomes the basis for morality or ethics. It is an ingenious move, but one fraught with problems. I find myself wanting to criticise his comments on theology: the deeply and unacknowledged Roman Catholic nature of his take on Christianity shows up all too readily, especially when he suggests that salvation is the passing from death to life by means of a set of rules of behaviour to transform the self. His abiding interest in confession, in self-knowledge as a basis for purity of the soul, in perpetually slipping by the Reformation and preferring the Counter-Reformation as the major path, in replicating the conservative theological argument for Christian exceptionalism, all represent strange twists that hover between illumination and obfuscation. But the major problem with this 'turn to the self' is not only the content of these late interviews, lectures and written texts. In them we find a constant process of self-reflection, of critiquing his own earlier work, identifying where he has changed direction and trying to make sense of it; is this not one of the tell-tale signs of an intellectual becoming self-obsessed and self-indulgent?[23] The very act of turning to the self leaves its mark in the material that tries to account for such a turn in his project. In fact, Foucault relished the inability of people to locate where he stood politically, in their accusations that he has changed his mind: 'I am not interested in the academic status of what I am doing because my problem is my own transformation'.[24]

However, a deeper and more persistent problem bedevils this project – that of class. I will have more to say later about the associations between *ethos*, *mos* and

23. For example, see Foucault 1985, pp. 3–13.
24. Foucault 2000, p. 131.

class, especially in connection with my earlier discussion of kairós and ákairos, but the examples Foucault gives of the care of the self are telling: one of Plato's contested dialogues – *Alcibiades I* – in which Socrates instructs the young Athenian leader from the ruling elite; Stoics such as Marcus Aurelius; Christian fathers pondering the ascetic life. All of these come from a small and literate elite, precisely those who had the time and leisure to be able to write, to think and retreat and undergo self-examination and self-construction. The possibility of doing so depended, as Ste. Croix has shown so well, on the surplus produced by slaves and indentured peasants. Now, Foucault recognises this problem, pointing out that the possibility of living the beautiful life was restricted to very few among an elite, that Greek society in particular was a 'disgusting' virile and dominating one in which women and slaves were passive objects of pleasure and in which boys were a problem (since they would grow up to be men).[25] But that is it. The point does not make him ask further questions, especially to explore the nature of ancient morality and its class and economic associations. Even when he discusses *ethos*, describing it in terms of a way of behaviour, clothing, appearance, gait, calmness – all for the sake of 'freedom' – he fails to ask what these various elements of *ethos* actually mean on the level of class and economics, especially when they entail the glaring class signals of terms such as goodness, beauty and honour.[26] Instead, ethics turns inward, becoming nothing less than a relationship to oneself, a *rapport à soi*.[27]

Greasing the other

Defenders of Foucault will be quick to point out that in these same later texts he does in fact concern himself with issues beyond the self. He devotes attention to friendship (among gay men), to social, sexual and psychological outsiders, to the inevitable turn towards others that the Greek *ethos* entails, even if that relation was a form of mastery that followed from mastery of the self.[28] Yes, of course, one can find comments of this sort in these reflections, especially in the interviews when Foucault was explicitly asked about ethics and the other. But let me change focus for a moment, away from the texts of Foucault which

---

25. Foucault 2000, pp. 254, 257–8. In *The Uses of Pleasure* one struggles to find an adequate discussion of class and economic issues. In the section designated 'Economics' (pp. 143–84) precious little appears, while in the chapter entitled 'The Object of Pleasure' (pp. 215–25) the brief comments on class in relation to sex with boys are very weak. The same applies to the chapter called 'The Political Game' in Volume 3 of *The History of Sexuality*. Foucault 1986, pp. 81–95.

26. Foucault 2000, p. 286.

27. Foucault 2000, p. 263.

28. Foucault 2000, pp. 170–1, 287.

draw one's attention. When reading the interviews, the eye skips far too rapidly by the questions posed, preferring to absorb, appropriate and perhaps critique the words of the master; but the questions themselves are worth a look. For instance, in the group session that was published as 'The Ethics of the Concern of the Self as a Practice of Freedom',[29] the interviewers show a distinct nervousness concerning Foucault's extended deliberations on the care of the self. Yes, they say, but that implies others, does it not? Of course, replies Foucault, and promptly moves on. They press him, ever so gently, to include the other within his exploration of this relationship with the self. He is willing to admit that these matters are important, but only if one begins with the self as the basis of such relations with others.

Thus far, I have argued that Foucault is responding to the impasse within ethics, between specific instance and universal norm, between the urge for and resistance to moralising, by problematising the human subject that has, he feels, been the basis of prior ethical thought. However, another way of considering his response is in terms of the bright Hegelian room in which the self is constituted as a secondary procedure in a dialectic with the other. Once you grant these terms, no matter how constructed, how lacking in an essential nature the self or other may be, you are left with prioritising one or another of the terms. Foucault has opted to go one way, through the self, while many would find that this care of the self is a very limited form of ethics; a little self-indulgent perhaps. Instead, ethics really deals with the stranger, the neighbour, or the 'other'. In short, it provides us with guidelines for relating to 'others', for adding a few drops of lubricant to rusted and creaking social relations.

But who exactly are the 'others'? They turn out not to be the physical, biological distinctions between bodies (animal or plant), but what I am tempted to call 'ontological' others. They may be the neighbours in a literal sense, those next door with whom one must live. Easy enough to get on with the genial, helpful neighbour (who is thereby 'ethical'), but the real test comes with the annoyingly repressed neighbour, the one who calls the police or fire brigade at the slightest and, wishes to govern the whole street as a petty fiefdom. Or they may be the hippies next door with their all-weekend parties, rave music and clouds of smoke from inhaled illegal substances wafting in through the windows. Of course, this sense of the neighbour is far too restricted for such ethics. The 'other' is actually a collective category. Men and women, constructed in terms of different genders within a distinct social formation, become 'othered'. Ethnicity, now the preferred term for the out-of-favour 'race', becomes another mode of otherness. Class too is a collective form of the other, whether one claims in futile desperation to

29. Foucault 2000, pp. 281–301.

belong to an aristocracy of an age now past, or sees the bourgeoisie or working class as one's class other. While blinkered Marxists, feminists and ethnic lobbies argue with one another concerning the primacy of these forms of otherness – what question does a parent ask of a child first? what form of oppression is the foundation of all the others? will the solution to one solve the other forms? – two newer forms of otherness have stolen the show: religious and environmental others.

Muslims, Jews, Shintos, Scientologists, Christians, the John Frum religion (of Vanuatu) – these and more become religious others. So, argue some in Australia, Muslims should not be permitted in Australia since they are so different from Australia's Christian heritage. So, argue some in the Middle East, Israel should be wiped off the face of the map. And so, some courts argue, Scientologists are crackpots and do not count as a religion at all. Alongside the renewed primacy of religious others come the environmental others, displacing disabled others, subcultural others (bikies, ferals, Chardonnay socialists, surfies...), homeless others, poor others... The donkey in the field, the endangered Tasmanian Devil in the forests, the Horny Owl in the hollow tree, the snake in the grass, the tomato in the vegetable patch – all these have become the non-human other, the more-than-human other or perhaps the other-than-human other, in a rather clumsy eco-critical excess of language.

A bewildering array of others, is it not? And it is certainly a rich field for ethics. Everywhere I turn others confront me. On the train I meet women, hear half a dozen languages, occasionally encounter a businessman or woman in a power suit talking assuredly on the phone, may need to give up my seat for an elderly or disabled passenger, avoid the feral kids drinking and smoking in the toilets and watch the non-human other pass by through the window or in the collection of plants which the woman holds on her lap in the seat opposite. In short, nearly everyone apart from me is an overlapped alien to me, an other with whom I must learn to relate. That train carriage, with its ad hoc collection of others, is a burgeoning microcosm for ethics – as it is understood by some.

We may define such ethics simply: it involves reflection upon and directions for the ways in which I should relate to these myriad others. Its purpose: to change the social relations within the world for the better. Before laying out my criticisms of this approach to ethics, I restrict myself to two initially different but ultimately quite similar examples of such an ethics – those of Terry Eagleton and Judith Butler. The palpable reason for concerning myself with them is that they do not make easy targets, offering not versions of bourgeois ethics (of which the worst form must be business ethics, generated by philosophy and theology departments in universities to forestall the bean counters in administration from slashing such departments or closing them altogether) but coming from the Left and seeking to challenge such bourgeois ethics.

Quailing before the Real: Terry Eagleton

Terry Eagleton has joined the rush of the Left to offer opinions on ethics in a recent lopsided work called *Trouble with Strangers*.[30] His argument is as straightforward as is to be expected in these days of his recovered role as a Left theologian: Christian theology and socialism offer a far more profound sense of both the depravity of human beings and the capacity for ground-shaking renewal. After all, is this not the point of the narrative of Christ's death and resurrection? It leads one to what should be an entirely disinterested obligation to sympathy, compassion, understanding and obligation to one's fellow men and woman. But why is this position expected? In most of Eagleton's works after the turn of the millennium,[31] he has offered variations on the same, rather traditional Roman Catholic form of theology: the intrinsic nature of God, who had no need to create the world but did so out of love (God, therefore, does not depend upon creation for existence); the power of simple, intrinsic virtues in constructing a metaphysical response to the equally intrinsic and apparently insurmountable forces of evil (capitalism, selfishness, mayhem, bloodshed, cruelty and what have you); the centrality of ethics and love as the process of selfless giving; the need for forgiveness, especially political forgiveness; the role of genuine hope, especially through and for the *anawim* (the poor, dispossessed and downtrodden), a term dragged out of retirement from his early theological works. Through it all, ethics sounds a regular beat as a central feature of that theology. In work after work we find the same potted theology, with occasional references to Thomas Aquinas and an old mentor, Herbert McCabe. And in work after work, Eagleton ritually opines in his preface that Christianity may be responsible for some of the most bloodthirsty acts in the last two thousand years, but is one of the few systems of ideas that may offer some viable resources for the Left – to whom of course he feels obliged to apologise for dipping into such a theology once again while also castigating his comrades for their studied ignorance, indolence and hostility to theology.[32]

The recent work of Eagleton has settled upon a three-legged stool: Marxism, Lacanian psychoanalysis and theology provide largely the same message concerning the depths of human depravity and the possibility of overcoming it.

30. Eagleton 2009b. Loaded with quotation and exposition (perhaps to show that Eagleton does read every now and then), it is an odd collection that includes Francis Hutcheson and Aristotle, Shakespeare and Adam Smith, Heinrich von Kleist and Kierkegaard.

31. Eagleton 2001, 2003a, 2003b, 2003c, 2005, 2006, 2007, 2009a, 2009b, 2010. Often scattered in various reflections throughout these works, the most complete statement of what I no longer hesitate to call Eagleton's theology may be found in Eagleton 2009a, pp. 5–32, which he is 'reluctant to label ... liberation theology', even though he sees the connection (p. 32). See the detailed discussion in Boer 2007a, pp. 275–333.

32. Eagleton 2009b, p. vi; Eagleton 2009a, pp. xi–xii; Eagleton 2005, p. vi.

Or rather, while psychoanalysis might provide an excellent description of our fallen state, Christianity and Marxism have by far the best solution. But this triangulation explains the choice of Lacan's imaginary, symbolic and Real as a grid for *Trouble with Strangers* – a decision that initially seems like window-dressing for some rather ordinary arguments concerning ethics but then turns out to be quite forced. By the later stages of the book, the grid looks decidedly lumpy, with Eagleton struggling to bend and stretch it to fit yet more ethical positions: Shakespeare in the symbolic, Kierkegaard's aesthetic, ethical and religious as imaginary, symbolic and Real, and then the leftovers gathered at the end from Aristotle to Kant.

However, the trap with using these categories, particularly in the way Eagleton presents them, is that they fall into a developmental pattern. Although Eagleton notes Lacan's dialectical reading of the imaginary, symbolic and Real, he takes them either as stages in a child's development, a potted historical narrative of bourgeois fortunes, and, of course, as a progressive narrative structure in which Christianity holds the trump card. The effect is obvious, for the imaginary is an immature form, caught in the primitive mirror stage, and an ethics that falls into this category is focused on the self. The symbolic is a step forward with its negotiation of the self and the other, but even this falls short of the terrible place of the Real: the traumatic, indescribable kernel that keeps us all going but threatens to destroy our world at any moment. Only at this point do we reach the Christian doctrine of sin, which is not only the springboard for a theological solution, but also the moment where Marxism's profound pessimism about the status of exploited and alienated human beings comes into its own. Or, as Eagleton puts it, the Lacanian Real is 'a psychoanalytic version of Original Sin'.[33] So psychoanalysis gets us to our fallen, sinful state, but from there we need theology and Marxism. The problem now is that Eagleton simply assumes, without offering any extensive analysis, that Marxism drinks deeply at the well of Jewish and Christian thought.

What has all this got to do with ethics? One keeps anticipating a breakthrough, a deep and thorough transformation of ethics in light of the traumatic and terrible Real. If we need to have a Lacanian structure, then let us make the most of it. Does the passion narrative of Christ's death allow us to stare that beast in the face? Does it provide a narrative of transition, the ultimate psychoanalytic cure? In the despairing cry of dereliction and abandonment – 'My God, my God, why have you forsaken me?' – does the narrative take us through and beyond the Real? Do we finally get past the subjective concerns of the imaginary and

33. Eagleton 2003b, p. 205.

the interpersonal obsessions of the symbolic to a moment when the over-riding desire of ethics is to help us get on better with our fellow man and woman?

The simple answer is no: Eagleton does not deliver. All we find are some observations on disinterested goodness and virtue: Christ overcomes death and despair basically through being nice and not expecting to be rewarded for it – like lending my shovel to a neighbour and not expected anything in return. According to Eagleton, Christian theology offers a number of simple, unprepossessing virtues that may actually overcome the depths of evil (and Eagleton does not shy away from admitting that he seeks to recover a full-blooded 'metaphysics'). Kindness, love, justice, humility, modesty, meekness, vision, courage, dedication, selflessness and endurance – all of these and more are marshalled again and again to do battle with evil in a starkly dualistic universe.[34] But the greatest virtue is love, which he takes not as the lusty desire for getting one's clothes off and connecting the plumbing, but as an indifferent, unconditional, impersonal and, especially, a public and political law of love that has its benchmark in the love for enemies and strangers. For Eagleton, this is the key to ethics, a self-less and disinterested – as in not expecting anything in return – obligation to care for the 'stranger'. The echoes of the biblical injunction to show kindness to the stranger in our midst, for we too were strangers in Egypt, runs through Eagleton's text.[35] In the end, ethics is at the core of the Christian message, found on the cross of Christ as an ethical act. And its concern is that other to whom we must show self-less love, a banal goodness that will overcome evil.

At a theological level, as I have argued elsewhere, Eagleton's overriding concern with ethics betrays the worst of his Roman Catholic background. It is a short step from ethics to the law, for ethics in Eagleton's account is really a code of life for the religious Left. Follow these guidelines – the law of love – which happen to be much the same in both Christianity and socialism, and you are on the path to salvation. For Eagleton, this is a 'scriptural' theology, one tied into the Bible, rather than an 'ideological' one, which turns out to be that of the later Christian church. In making this facetious distinction, Eagleton subscribes, as I argued in Chapter Three, to a fall narrative: the 'scriptural' theology is a more genuine, radical one, but at a specific moment the church betrayed those roots, took a sinister turn and offered a reactionary 'ideology' that was welcomed by the overlords of this world.

The snare with this popular narrative of a theological fall (one shared with, Eagleton might be interested to note, any reformer within the history of theology) is that there is no uniform pattern of thought in the biblical texts upon which Eagleton claims to base his theology. This odd collection of texts is, as I

34. Eagleton 2003b, p. 120; Eagleton 2003c, p. 74.
35. Exodus 22:21; 23:9; Leviticus 19:34; Deuteronomy 10:19.

argued in Chapter Three, thoroughly and deeply ambivalent, at cross-purposes with itself, loaded with competing ideas, approaches and political possibilities. To Eagleton's argument for self-sufficient and disinterested evil and good (which are then opposed to one another in a dualistic system – with no sense of contradiction with his argument for the intrinsic nature of good and evil), I can simply pick up those texts, especially Isaiah, Ezekiel and Job, where God is the source of both good and evil – as any thoroughly consistent monotheism needs to argue. Or, as an alternative counter to the argument for disinterested evil, I could pick up the contradictory and persistent theme that evil is an affront to God, an affront of which human beings seem particularly prone. As with anyone who wishes to construct some type of consistent theological system he must pick and choose, opting for certain lines and ignoring others. And those lines tend to be ones that come out of Eagleton's own Roman Catholic tradition.

As far as ethics itself is concerned, Eagleton's smooth prose slides towards the themes of law and love, the ultimate law being to love one's neighbour as oneself.[36] In such an amorphous collection like the Bible, many texts might be marshalled to favour his position. I will fill a few in here, since Eagleton's works are remarkably free of actual biblical references. For instance, we find that Christ came to fulfil the law; he does not remove one jot or tittle (as the Authorised Version of King James would have it); the law is good, upright and just, and on and on.[37] And there are enough texts on love – *agape*, Christian love, which is supposed to be more political, social and spiritual than *eros* and goes much further than *philia* – to suggest that love is meant to save. Is not love stronger than hope and faith, as Paul argues in 1 Corinthians 13? In the ethical text par excellence, at least for Eagleton, did not God so love the world that he gave his only son (John 3:16)? But it is a truncated theology, one that favours texts concerning love, law and ethics, caught in the end in the vicious cycle of the law – the result is, as we find in Eagleton, a code of behaviour for a much more spiritual Left.

I am far less enthused with both ethics and love, partly due to their popularity today, but also for theological reasons. To begin with, the word 'ethics' hardly appears in the New Testament at all. Or rather, *ethikos* and *ethika* cannot be found. *Ethos* does appear, but it is a lowly word, preferred by that very urbane author of Luke and Acts.[38] Its meaning: the customs and law, whether of the priests, the Jews, Moses or the fathers. At this level, it strikes me as passing strange that Eagleton can claim that ethics is an inescapable feature of 'scriptural'

---

36. Eagleton 2009b, pp. 291–2. Eagleton 2009b, pp. 195–6, 272, 323.
37. For example, Matthew 5:18; Romans 7:12; 10:4.
38. See Luke 1:9, 2:42, 22:39; Acts 6:14, 15:1, 16:21, 21:21, 25:16, 26:3, 28:17. Only two occurrences appear outside this collection, one in John 19:14 and the other in Hebrews 10:25.

theology. But one may object that ethics appears implicitly in the law and love. Let us grant that position for a moment. The problem is, as we saw in Chapter 4, that law and love, as well as the body, flesh, Jews and Gentiles, male and female, Jew and Greek and so on, are actually transformed, especially in those texts conveniently ignored by Eagleton. Christ is the end – *telos* – of the law,[39] since he negates it and thereby overcomes it – Hegel's Aufhebung before Hegel. Elsewhere, we find that we are 'not under the law, but under grace', that we are freed from captivity to the law since the only way for true justice to be done (theologically termed 'justification') is not through the law but through faith in Christ.[40] The theological term for this banishment and thorough reshaping, negation and overcoming is grace – *charis* in Greek – and it works through faith, which is itself given by God as an act of grace. Grace as rupture, unexpected and undeserved, unable to be won through any ethical act, any obedience to a law, leaves ethics in tatters – as Eagleton presents it. Grace does not institute a new law code, slightly more enlightened and benevolent, calling on us to be good and loving; it simply dispenses with any such code. On one point I agree with Eagleton: theology does have a thoroughly dismal view of human beings. In my own tradition (Calvinism), it is known as total depravity – which makes much sense of the piles of corpses from warfare, starvation, disease and grinding poverty of the majority over, say, the last few thousand years. But that means no-one can do any good on their own, let alone earn salvation. That is purely for grace, for here – on a theological register at least – we do pass through the Real.

Two caveats. First, the position I have espoused is one possible line of interpretation, favouring one position in a collection of texts that is notoriously two-faced (as I argued in Chapter Three). One may simply point out that Eagleton differs from me (even without too many explicit references to texts) and prefers another theological stream that is filled with ethics, love, virtues and so forth. One may well support either position, or a range of others depending on the texts chosen. Nothing new in that point, although it does mean that Eagleton's claim to have a 'scriptural' foundation for ethics, as though there were one, proper foundation, is special pleading. Nevertheless, he does face a deeper problem, for it is impossible to find any explicit discussion of ethics as such in the New Testament; for that we must resort to the law. Second caveat: as I argued earlier, that key theologian, the Apostle Paul, equivocates within his own thought. At times he crashes through to a new insight, but then he holds back, fixes the breaches in the wall and sends out the search party in order to find that fearful and dangerous insight he has let loose. So Paul himself, as with the rest of the Bible, is in two or more

39. Romans 10:4.
40. See Romans 3:28; 6:14 and 15; 7:6; Galatians 2:16.

minds – a signal in itself of the contested social formations within which he thought and wrote.

At a philosophical level, Eagleton is ultimately unable to slip past the idea that ethics concerns the proper relations with one's others, or, as I prefer to put it, greasing the mechanisms of society so that they run more smoothly. To his credit, he sees little mileage in the care of the self and has questions for inter-personal relations. And yet he cannot get beyond that point, for Christian theology ends up offering a better way for us to relate to all those real, pulsing, throbbing others out there. It may be disinterested love and goodness, with no expectation of a reciprocal deal, but he is locked into the assumption that ethics concerns the way you and I act in relation to others. Such a position is caught on at least three snags: the idea of a chosen people to whom everyone else is 'other'; the creation of the category of 'other' as a process of the self; and the role of ethics as a discourse that creates and perpetuates the other. I will deal with each objection after I have grappled with Butler, Badiou and Žižek.

Ultimately, Eagleton falls into a tired – no, well and truly buried – argument that was common in the nineteenth century. Ethics, it was argued, or a moral code for society, can only be based on Christian theology. Casting anxious looks at the swelling mobs of anti-clerical protesters and openly secular social movements, church and political leaders opined that with the decline of Christianity so would the social glue of morals disappear. For all his trumpeting of a more radical ethics based on love and the death and resurrection of Christ, Eagleton makes largely the same argument (shared, incidentally, by conservative Muslims). Values have been dropped by the wayside, he argues, as capitalism and its empty consumerism have gained sway. We no longer have a robust metaphysical framework and ethics is left to wander about, thirsty and hungry, in a moral wasteland. The solution is, then, a recovery of the Christian message. I have argued elsewhere that this narrative has a distinct autobiographical resonance, covering what may now seem to an older man as the morally vacuous years of smoking, drinking, flitting about the world as the proponent of the latest phase of high literary theory and other items that cannot be mentioned in polite company. But since the turn of the millennium, the explicit theological tone in Eagleton's works has sounded ever more loudly, so that now he writes openly of old themes, such as the need for a bodily resurrection of Christ (for otherwise the message is meaningless), the power of the resurrection of Christ and the nature of God, and – a topic on which he has been a little cagey until recently – the solidarity of the sacrificial meal and love feast of the Eucharist. Not only is this an adequate replacement for self-sacrifice, should we miss the grand opportunity to give our lives in service for others, but it is a pure blast from Eagleton's past, when he used to argue for the value of the Eucharist.[41] The only item missing is the old argument that the priesthood might become the Leninist vanguard.[42] It is no wonder the Archbishop of Canterbury reads him with approval.

The ethics of ethical failure: Judith Butler

I have less to say about Butler, largely because her position is more coherent (paradoxically, it will turn out) than that of Eagleton. More inspired by Foucault than Marx, Judith Butler's Amsterdam lectures from 2002 seek to produce what she calls an 'account of oneself'.[43] This account is not merely a self-serving exercise, a means of coming to an awareness of one's self through, say, the writing of letters. Instead, the subject is not the ground of ethics but a problem for ethics – since all of these discussions concerning the self, ego, first person and so on actually concern the subject.[44] For all her creative engagement with Foucault, here she goes beyond him, arguing that every account takes the form of an address, directed not merely to someone, but to you in particular. Ethics is therefore a thoroughly relational activity: 'the scene of address, what we might call the rhetorical condition for responsibility, means that while I am engaging in a reflexive activity, thinking about and reconstructing myself, I am also speaking to you and thus elaborating a relation to an other in language as I go'.[45] Ethics arises not in the account itself, whether it suffices or not, but in the dialogue. Are both parties to this duality sustained by the interaction? Are they altered in the process, hopefully coming to a greater understanding of one another in the act of addressing each other?

Within the perimeters set by the discourse of ethics, this position is already a step beyond Foucault. But the key to Butler's argument is that the accounts given are of necessity limited, lacking and broken, containing incoherencies and remaining incomplete – her creative reworking of the poststructuralist argument that the subject is divided, ungrounded and incoherent. This opacity, and indeed apparent failure, is where ethics really begins. If my account is limited and incoherent, if the way I give an account is not quite the way I would like it, then that should lead me to exercise patience with an interlocutor caught in the same

41. Eagleton 2009b, pp. 195–6, 272, 323. Compare Eagleton 1966a, pp. 69–84; Eagleton 1970, pp. 39–40; Eagleton 1968a; Eagleton 1968b.

42. Eagleton 1970, pp. 75–93.

43. Butler 2005. For a defence of Butler, see Loizidou 2007.

44. Butler 2005, p. 110, argues that both Foucault and Adorno effectively make this move, yet she clearly moves beyond Foucault, taking a few scattered hints much further.

45. Butler 2005, p. 50.

bind. Patience, tolerance and an effort to understand – these flow precisely from the awareness that both interlocutors struggle with comparable incoherencies. The paradox is that Butler's own account is very accessible and coherent, a situation that appears to trouble her as the account wears on, page after page. So we find that the deadpan beginning, with its short sentences and simple syntax, gives way to notes about slips of the typing finger and a noticeably lyrical style in the midst of the second, long chapter on psychoanalysis. But she never explicitly mentions that she is aware of the question posed to her own account; instead, that troubling matter is shunted off into an extraordinary examination of Foucault's interviews towards the end of his life, the 'ethical' that period we explored a little earlier. Here Butler notes the inconsistencies, the lack of connections and prevarications when Foucault is asked to give an account of himself.[46] All the same, that is not a shortcoming on his part, engaged in discussion as he is, but of the very nature of ethical engagement.

In making this argument, Butler wishes to counter at least two positions. The first one comes from Nietzsche, for whom the awareness of oneself – which for Butler implies giving an account – comes from a violence suffered, a punishment inflicted, an allegation or an accusation made, to which one must respond. Butler disagrees, arguing that an account, partial and halting as it is, need not arise from violence. That point leads to her second countermove: she seeks to negate ethical violence, which eventuates when one believes that one's own position is inviolable, true and clear, thereby enabling one to judge others who do not measure up. This strategy is Butler's response to the perennial tension, which I have already mentioned on a number of occasions, between universal precept and particular situation. For Butler, when the universal seeks to force itself upon the particular, rather than – in similar dialogic fashion – relating to, negotiating with and altering in light of the particular, then it engages in the violence of imposed indifference.

Negotiation, relation, dialogue, mutuality – these are the keys to Butler's ethics, which may be seen as a reconditioned Hegelian dialectic. They produce a modesty of ethical accounts, seek to negate the violence of imposed absolutes and universals, and become the workings of the subject, democracy, justice, patience, responsibility, agency, hope, politics and the very definition of what it means to be human. Much hangs, it seems, on the frail task of ethics. Above all, ethics is the relation between a self and an other, I and you, 'whether conjured or existing',[47] which is the particular shape that the relation of the self and its social

46. Butler 2005, pp. 111–38. She focuses on the interview, 'How Much Does It Cost for Reason to Tell the Truth?'. See Foucault 1989.

47. Butler 2005, p. 21. She is keen to distance herself from those, like Levinas and Laplanche, who prioritise the 'Other'. See Butler 2005, pp. 84–101.

context must take. Neither conditions the other in terms of absolute cause, for they are semi-autonomous. They need each other, but do not cause each other.

If one grants the premises of ethics – self, other and the relations between them – Butler's account is one of the most persuasive and thought-provoking, not the least gain being an extraordinary unpicking of the inconsistencies in Levinas's Zionism.[48] But those premises are the issue. Ethics, for Butler, involves the betterment of society, the greasing of social relations so that the creaking, rusty parts may run more smoothly. And who does not want justice, tolerance, responsibility, understanding and democracy, even if they do rely on the idea of conscious and relatively free agents? Ethics is the stuff of interpersonal relations, social interaction and a political desire to change the world – gradually and patiently – for the better. But this version of ethics is really one of reform, a counsel against revolution, for that would be, according to Butler, the violent imposition of an absolute moral code and indifferent universal.

In the end, Butler comes quite close to Eagleton with his simple and modest virtues of goodness, justice, courage and responsibility. These values may be a little banal, unexciting even, but they are the stuff of ethics. I would suggest that Eagleton's quailing before the Real, his failure to deliver on a radical ethics, brings him into the same camp as Butler and other social reformers. On Butler's part, that moment explicitly comes when she argues that the most difficult ethical response to violence is that one must not respond with violence, exercising patience and restraint rather than suddenly believing you are in the right to seek revenge.[49] This is an argument that Eagleton would love, for it is merely a secularised version of Jesus's saying to turn the other cheek should someone strike you.[50] Ethics seems to take an inevitable theological turn even in Butler.

Blasting away the other

Self, other, and mediation between the two – these seem to be the options available within the 'ethical ideology', as Badiou calls it, which dominates recent discussions. All of them wish to wash away the rusty accretions of a creaking social machine, spray on the latest Teflon lubricant and get the parts working more smoothly. And inevitably they tend to slip into versions of moralising, one perhaps a little more gentle than the other, but moralising all the same. I have already made it clear enough that I am less than enthused by these projects, but before I outline my own responses, I shall pass through two who seek to take a wrecking ball to contemporary debates on ethics: Slavoj Žižek and Alain Badiou.

---

48. Butler 2005, pp. 90–6.
49. Butler 2005, pp. 100–1.
50. Matthew 5:39; Luke 6:29.

Despite their common ground – they both negotiate the work of Lacan – their approaches to ethics are diametrically opposed. In the wake of Levinas, Laplanche, Irigaray, even Spivak and a host of dimmer stars, the other reigns supreme, at least in the domain of ethics. While Badiou argues that the problem is not the other but the same, Žižek pushes the other to its psychoanalytic extreme. For Badiou the other, alterity, difference, or whatever name it is called, is the way things are; it describes the coordinates of the status quo: 'what we must recognise is that these differences hold no interest for thought, that they amount to nothing more than the infinite and self-evident multiplicity of humankind, as obvious as the difference between me and my cousin from Lyon as it is between the Shi'ite "community" in Iraq and the fat cowboys of Texas'.[51] We are all different, others to one another – so what! Ethics with its concern for the other becomes a convenient ideology for that status quo, making us believe that there is a problem and that we simply need to readjust a few things here and there in order to make it all work more smoothly, with greater understanding, tolerance and patience. We must learn, so the advice goes, to celebrate our differences, live harmoniously in multicultural societies. Or, in the terms I have been using thus far, ethics assists in oiling the parts of a social system that is not working so well.

Take, for example, the tendency in some universities today to establish centres for social inclusion and wellbeing.[52] Much money is available for such centres, both from liberal philanthropists keen to assuage their guilty consciences and from governments which find themselves facing the downsides of aggressive immigration policies. Ethics is, of course, central to these centres, which seek to find strategies and offer advice – moralising again – so that all of us may feel as though we belong to a more harmonious society and thereby feel good about ourselves and our fellow men and women.

Thus far I can agree with Badiou, but I am not so sure of his solution. That turns on what is by now his well-known, if problematic, event and its truth, in which an event tears through the social fabric rather than smoothing it over, risking all to start again. The appeal of Badiou's argument is that it runs against common sense. Is not truth singular, universal and thereby totalitarian and absolute, rendering everything the same? Far better, then, to argue against such truth in the name of multiplicity, difference and contingency. In reply, Badiou brilliantly deploys mathematics to argue that universals are multiples, that sameness is not

---

51. Badiou 2002, p. 26; Badiou 2003a, p. 51. For insightful if preliminary engagements with Badiou's ethics, see Critchley 2000; Barker 1992, pp. 130–48; Hallward 2003, pp. 255–69, Laclau 2004.

52. As has, indeed, happened at the university that pays me a little money for food, clothing and shelter. Macquarie University (Sydney) had a similar centre.

uniformity but may also be multiple, happening in contingent and unexpected events. Through such an event, a truth appears, not singular but multiple, with multiple claims to be universal and thereby the same.[53]

What happens to ethics in the face of such an event? As a liberal ideology of the status quo, ethics is tossed aside as so much useless garbage, but as an ethics of the event it lays claim to the basic ethical division between good and evil in an entirely new fashion. The good designates what pertains to the event, marked by fidelity to that truth; ethics is thereby what is needed to provide courage to keep going, to keep the faith to that original truth. Evil, however, is what leads one to: delusion, in which one confuses a simulacrum of an event for a real one and becomes the terrorising follower of a false event (as with the Nazis); betrayal of the truth through exhaustion and renunciation, giving up on a truth in the name of one's own concerns; disaster, or the effort to impose a truth in an authoritarian manner, in the arrogance and hubris that comes from feeling that one has all the answers.[54] On this last point, the nagging doubt raised by Butler's critique of the violence of absolutes is laid to rest. So ethics – or rather, the ethic of a truth[55] – becomes a handmaiden to truth, offering discernment so that one does not confuse a simulated truth for the real thing (be careful!), courage so that one is consistent and does not flag (keep going!), and temperance or discipline so that one does not seek to impose a total truth (you're not perfect!).[56]

I do not wish, here, to question Badiou's description of the truth-event, for others have begun to do so.[57] However, the Badiouean invocation of good and evil is problematic, not merely for the theological residue, but especially because they reinstate the primary schema for ethics. It is the absolute code, the one that

---

53. Eagleton simply misses the point of Badiou's event, especially its sound theological pedigree in the doctrine of grace, when he opines, 'Nothing is more traditionally modernist than the dream of such an ineffable rupture with the actual' (Eagleton 2009b, p. 261).

54. Badiou 2002, pp. 72–87, 91; Badiou 2003a, pp. 104–23, 126.

55. For Badiou there is no ethics as such, but only an ethic-of. See Badiou 2002, p. 28; Badiou 2003a, p. 53.

56. Here lies much of the appeal for Badiou, for one gets the distinct sense that he has spent many years being an outsider and not fitting in; hence the call to keep on going, not being tempted or impressed by awards or recognition or status.

57. The various objections to Badiou's perpetually modified position enhance the contingent nature of his own argument for the event, no matter how absolutely he presents it. For example, one may object that Badiou's theory smacks of a certain Romanticism (Critchley 2000), or that it is difficult to distinguish an event from a pseudo-event such as the Nazi moment or perhaps 9/11 (Surin 2009, p. 198; Žižek 1999, pp. 138–40), or that the high-minded 'perspective of the Last Judgement' leads one to eschew getting one's hands dirty in gradual politics or state formation (Žižek 2006, pp. 321–3; Žižek 2008, pp. 389–92), or that Badiou's thought has totalitarian tendencies (Sharpe 2008), or that no such extraneous irruption actually exists, for the paradigmatic events Badiou names can actually be thickly analysed in order to show that they were, in some sense, possible within the matrix of social and economic life.

has been betrayed by all those apologists for capitalism and its pernicious ideology and one that Badiou wishes to restore to its rightful place. Two counts may be registered against the schema, here (another will follow in my discussion of good and evil below): first, the Platonism bursts through, where the good remains an absolute value, one to which we must look up, although for Badiou it is the truth of revolution. What has always bothered me about Plato is that, as Ste. Croix argues, he was the anti-democratic ideologue par excellence of the ruling class in ancient Athens, the small propertied class which generated its surplus from slave and indentured labour. So I am left puzzled by the way Badiou can favour Plato and his creation, Socrates. More substantially, it is not that good and evil have been bowdlerised by betrayal, deceit and simulation, and that what one must do is restore them to their proper status, but that goodness itself is a problem. As I will argue below, I am far more interested, for both political and theological reasons, in what challenges the good, what is designated evil, especially because I want to know who decides what is evil and for what reason.

Žižek begins at a similar point to Badiou, namely that difference is part of the status quo and that multiculturalism and tolerance are integral to an obnoxious liberalism. Yet Žižek takes a different tack to Badiou, pushing the other to its obscene and traumatic extreme rather than seeking to overturn it by the event. In order to understand what Žižek does with the other, we need to track through the three Lacanian categories of the imaginary, symbolic and Real, for which ethics stands as the true 'Borromean knot' that ties them all together.[58] In the imaginary the other is the person, mirror-like, who is like me, with whom I enter into relationships, compete, love, hate, and so on. This is the status quo, the way things are now and that upon which most ethics focuses. However, in the symbolic, the other becomes the 'big Other', the impersonal rules of conduct, whether the law, state, school, or unwritten moral assumptions, which theologians are apt still to attribute to God in some way. But Žižek really hankers for the Real, where the other is inhuman, the traumatic and terrifying thing with which I cannot enter into any contact. It is a monster that cannot be pacified through dialogue or given a partial account in patience and mutual respect, for if we did recognise this other, everything would fall apart. Lest we assume some radical separation between the three realms, Žižek insists that they are entwined with one another: the other at the level of the imaginary or symbolic, my partner or the customary law of my town, always hovers on the edge of this traumatic

---

58. Žižek 2005a, p. 4. A longer version of the same argument appears in Žižek, Santner and Reinhard 2006, pp. 134–90. See also Žižek 2001a, pp. 160–73; Žižek 2008, pp. 46–7. Note the difference with Eagleton's approach to the Lacanian triad, which I discussed a little earlier.

other of the Real. In effect, Žižek says: you want the other? Then here it is in all its ontological monstrosity!

So when ethics tries to deal with the other, it does so at an imaginary level, thinking that the other is one whom I must engage in dialogue, narrating our accounts, trying to understand one another in patience, show some love and trust and courage. But this approach forgets two points. First, there is always a forgotten third in this ideal dyadic relation: the symbolic, which marks not only the nameless and faceless others of the social network, but also the big Other of the law. Second, beneath the calm exterior of my partner, colleague or drinking mate lurks the traumatic other of the Real, which is mediated by the symbolic. With this obscene, abyssal other no reciprocity is possible, no dialogue or engagement. We gain the impression that we can do so only because the symbolic intervenes to render my other as a quarrelsome partner, demanding boss, annoying employee or drunk at the bar. One can read here the situation Žižek faced in the Balkans, where such a theory was all too traumatically real: the neighbour down the street, whether Serb or Croat or Bosnian, Muslim or Orthodox or Roman Catholic, with whom my children played and went to school, became overnight my sworn enemy, burning with hatred, threatening death, dismemberment and rape, ready to slit my throat at the first opportunity. Here was the Real bursting forth with obscene urgency. One gets the sense that Žižek's perpetual return to such an issue, his obsession with the Real and the repeated stories and jokes from the 'former Yugoslavia', are all part of a failed effort to deal with that trauma – even in Slovenia, which suffered relatively little in the Balkan War.[59]

What is the proper ethical response to such a situation? One does not engage with the imaginary other, but engages the hidden third partner, the mediating symbolic, by going straight for the Real other.[60] How? You smash the other's face, seeking to break through the mirror, so that we confront directly the traumatic other with whom no dialogue is possible. Facing the monster, the abyss and even God (who belongs very much to the Real) is the first step to a truly radical break with the status quo which is undergirded by the Real. To my mind, Žižek provides an answer to Eagleton's failure, for Žižek does not quail before the Real and asks what ethics might look like in that situation. Ethics requires,

---

59. See, for example, his sustained reflections in Žižek 2002, pp. 117–26. See also Boer 2007c.

60. 'The true ethical step is the one *beyond* the face of the other, the one of *suspending* the hold of the face, the one of choosing *against* the face, for the *third*. This *is* justice at its most elementary. Every pre-empting of the Other in the guise of his or her face relegates the Third to the faceless background' (Žižek 2005a, p. 12; Žižek, Santner and Reinhard 2006, p. 183).

as Žižek urges provocatively, that we engage in ethical violence, smashing all the known codes of ethics.

An immediate upshot of Žižek's argument is its connection (one that he does not pursue) with the ban on images of the second commandment in Exodus 20/ Deuteronomy 5.[61] I will have more to say on the ban in the next chapter, but in this case the image becomes the marker of the imaginary, the face of the other with whom I am supposed to enter into cooperative dialogue in order to sort out our differences. The response to images – and thereby idols – is to smash them into pieces, grind them into dust and throw them into Gehenna, the disgusting pit of fire, garbage, offal and carcases outside Jerusalem. Better still, one should simply not have images in the first place: no symbols of the divine, no finger pointing to God, no mediation between God and me. Instead I need to deal directly with the Real, with God, who is the unbearable, unknowable and unfathomable other.

The ban on images, in its utopian starkness, has for me extraordinary appeal. But I would like to read Badiou and Žižek in a different vein: I would suggest that their varying takes on the ethics of otherness – seeking to break it up in the name of an irruptive event for which ethics becomes a demoted assistant, or calling on us to confront the obscene other, to grab the beast from our shoulder and stare it down – are expressions of a desire for ethical insurgency. Badiou challenges the ethics of the 'there is', the state of the situation, with a revolutionary ethics (for which the event is perhaps the most thorough and rigorous formulation we have seen for some time). Žižek seeks to undermine the ethics of otherness by taking it to its disgusting extreme to render ethics inoperable as it is understood – and thereby make it revolutionary.[62] I wish to take this insurgent impulse, including its challenge to the obsession with the other, on a slightly different path. And that is a path towards an approach that undermines ethics from within, an insurrectionist counter to ethics that perpetually disrupts ethics as it is known.

Towards ethical insurgency

Thus far, I have limited myself to tracing the positions of some key thinkers on ethics, moving towards Badiou and Žižek in their efforts to blast away the 'other' which dominates contemporary treatments of ethics. But now I will outline my own misgivings, before arguing for what I call unethical insurgency. They concern:

---

61. See Žižek, Santner and Reinhard 2006, p. 141.

62. 'We can now precisely locate the ethical act – or, rather, the act *as such* – with respect to the reign of the "reality principle": an ethical act is not only "beyond the reality principle"...; rather, it designates an intervention that *changes the very co-ordinates of the "reality principle"*' (Žižek 2001a, p. 167).

the production of the 'other' through the discourse of ethics; the troubling connection of ethics with the biblical theme of the chosen people; and the connection with the theological concern with good and evil. As for insurgency, I seek an unethical and unmoral politics. If ethics, as it has developed in current debates, concerns not merely the way we must learn to relate to our myriad others but especially the way to make society run more smoothly, then I am not interested – hence the unethical.

Producing the other

A crucial but curiously unaddressed question is how the other is produced in the first place.[63] Here the alignments are somewhat different, for now Eagleton and Badiou draw closer together in assuming the other as a given. For Badiou the myriad others are unremarkable and therefore need no account of their production, while for Eagleton they are givens and thereby constitute the key problem for ethics. By contrast, Butler prevaricates, suggesting that self and other may be seen as either 'conjured or existing'.[64] For one who has consistently argued that bodies and sexes are discursively and performatively constructed, this is a curious moment of wavering. One would expect that the other is produced discursively, in the broken and limited accounts that human beings give to one another, but she does not take that option. Instead, she falters, loosening her rigorous discursivity and allowing space for a preexisting other. Only Žižek, then, provides a theory concerning the other's production, and that is a psychoanalytic one that plays off against one another the Lacanian triad of imaginary, symbolic and Real.

But how is the other produced *in ethics*? I would begin by observing that without an other – male or female, Muslim or Shinto, African or Indonesian, refugee or citizen, animal or plant – ethics would be out of business. In this situation it needs to be asked: who or what tells me they are 'others'? Instead of ethics prescribing the way one should relate to a preexisting category of other, does not the discourse of ethics create the other in the first place? I cannot see why a person from China or Serbia or Greenland is alien, a stranger to me. I do not see why the tree out my window, the chillies on the veranda or the kangaroos I meet are foreign to me – unless, of course, there is a discourse that constructs them as such.

63. On this matter, Foucault was both correct and mistaken: he assumed that the radical question was to attack the givenness of the self; I suggest that the first step is to question the givenness of the other.

64. Butler 2005, p. 21.

Such a discursive production, however, never takes place in isolation, even though a strictly discursive approach would like to give that impression. To begin with, other discourses also produce others, such as the gendered other of feminism, the colonial other of (post)colonial discourse, the class other of political economy, or the sexual other of queer theory. In each case a specific discourse produces an other as part of that discourse's own operation. Of course, no discourse operates in pure isolation, especially in terms of those I have just mentioned. Each is usually aware of the many overlaps between them, producing complex and multifaceted others. The problem with ethics is that it tends to conceal those overlaps, thereby arrogating non-ethical discursive productions of the other. Žižek provides an explicit example in his deployment of Lacanian psychoanalysis, for the dialectic of the Lacanian triad provides him with a specific construction of alterity that is then appropriated by ethics. It must be said that he deploys that triad to undercut the conventional ethical concern with improving one's relations with the other, pointing out that the other is not quite what it seems. Nonetheless, he draws that other from an alternate discourse and assumes its pre-given status as far as ethics is concerned.

A further aspect of the connectedness of discourse concerns its relations with its socio-economic context. At this point I need to introduce what may be called the discursive link. By discursive link I mean the connection between a discourse and its socio-economic context, which the traditional Marxist category of ideology renders explicit. Here the discourse of class is instructive, for the production of class takes place at the intersection between socio-economic and discursive factors. That is, the various others of class – working class and bourgeoisie, lord and serf, slave and master – never emerge without both the interaction of socio-economic conditions and discourses (or, more traditionally, ideologies) that enable both those discourses themselves and the production of class others. Or to use traditional Marxist terminology, objective and subjective conditions are both necessary for the production of these others. Another example is the construction of sexual identities. As Peter Drucker has argued, the construction of older lesbian and gay identities cannot be understood without the development of capitalism, as also the more recent rise of alternative sexual identities among disadvantaged and working-class young people – known as LGBT (lesbian, gay, bisexual and transgender) or 'queer' – has taken place with the unwinding of Fordism and the dominance of neoliberal economic practices.[65] One may designate such a discourse as a political discourse, a term that also applies to postcolonial, feminist and environmental discourses, insofar as they are explicitly aware of the discursive link in the process of producing others.

65. Drucker 2011.

The question remains as to why the ethical proposals from the Left that I have considered do not make explicit this process of the production of alterity, preferring either to assume the other as a given or borrow its production from another discourse? I would suggest that the fault lies with ethics itself, for it systematically conceals both the relations with other discourses, arrogating their others, and the discursive link with its socio-economic contexts. And the reason is the distinctly logocentric focus of ethical discourse. Two factors have played a role in this matter: first, the Foucauldian shift from ideology to discourse, a shift that was meant to breathe life into the supposedly tired category of ideology but had the effect of effacing ideology's connectedness with socio-economic factors; second, the 'linguistic turn' in which language becomes the prime factor and discourse becomes logocentric. The outcome is that the Marxist heritage, which provided the springboard for such analysis, was discarded. That is, the ladder which enabled discursive construction was kicked away, so much so that any mention of Marxist analyses of class, gender or sexuality is dismissed as so much 'essentialism'.[66] Ethics thereby conceals its own process of producing the other, giving the impression that others are givens so that ethics may get to work.

Chosen people

Nonetheless, is it not common sense that there are selves and others? Is this not the way the world works? And should we not try to find ways for our selves and others to get on better than we do? Let me continue to trouble this natural assumption by connecting it with the theme of the chosen people.[67] As is reasonably well known, a persistent theme throughout the Hebrew Bible is that the children of Israel are God's chosen people. Out of all the peoples of the earth, they are the chosen ones, whom God opts to assist, punish, love and save.[68] A narrative construction, to be sure, but it sets up a pattern of us and them, the favoured people and all the others, who then become the stranger, the alien, the *ger* so beloved by Levinas. That theme of the chosen people has been a remarkably popular one, recycled by one group after another, whether a faithful revolutionary remnant, the British Israelites or a stumbling superpower such as the United States.

---

66. The essentialism in question is usually a caricature, designating an unchanging and thereby fixed 'essence', without considering, for instance, Marx's early argument concerning species-essence, which is itself changed by socio-economic circumstances.

67. See also Žižek 2008, pp. 53–5, where he points out that the more radical the attempt at inclusion, the more radical its exclusion of anyone who does not fit in or accept the terms of the chosen.

68. See especially Genesis 13:14–17; 15:1–20; 17:1–21.

We might object that the idea of a chosen people has been misinterpreted in such recycling, that it has been abused rather than used, for the Israelites chosen in the Hebrew Bible are the least of all peoples, the most undeserving and often the most sinful. Further, the task of the chosen people is to be a light to the nations,[69] offering themselves humbly to the task of enlightening all peoples and bringing them to God. Does this not undermine the theme of a chosen people, or at least turn it on its head? The trap with this theological response is that it is based on a mythical narrative, a political myth that works overtime to develop a collective self-understanding of a distinct identity. It matters little how lowly such a chosen people might be, they are still chosen. Further, such a theme appears to be imposed over an unruly collection of texts that show, upon closer analysis, a profound anxiety about the identity of the chosen people. In narrative after narrative, it turns out to be a mishmash of different groups – they are in fact the strangers whom that overarching narrative tries to externalise.[70] Add to this the historical consensus that Israel as an ethnic identity is quite late and that it arose as an indigenous grouping within Palestine – that is, that they are Canaanites or what we would now call Palestinians – and the theme of the chosen people becomes a matter of special pleading and brazen ideological construction. In sum, through the effort to create a subjective identity as a chosen people, this discourse too constructs others.

I give but one example of the way that the narrative of the chosen people unravels within the biblical texts in question, showing how the other is produced. It comes from a relatively unknown story, the deception of the Gibeonites in Joshua 9. Here we find the Israelites under Joshua rampaging through the land of Canaan in that mythical account of the conquest. The Gibeonites hear of the exploits of Joshua and company at the walls of Jericho (as well as the sacking the city of Ai); they know that they are next. So they equip some messengers with worn-out, torn and mended sacks, wineskins, sandals and clothes, and find some mouldy and dry provisions. The messengers set out on the short distance to meet Joshua (for his army is just around the corner). When the messengers arrive, apparently weary and dusty, they say: 'we have come from far, far away, and we have heard much about your prowess in war; so make a covenant with us'. Just to reinforce the point, they say, 'Here is our bread; it was still warm when we took it from our houses as our food for the journey, on the day we set forth to come to you, but now, look, it is dry and mouldy; these wineskins were new when we filled them, and look, they are burst; and these garments and shoes of ours are worn out from the very long journey'.[71] We can imagine them swooning from hunger

69. Isaiah 51:4.
70. See Boer 2008, pp. 109–34.
71. Joshua 9:12–13; my translation.

and thirst as they speak and the Israelites rushing to make a covenant with them, assuring them of an alliance and assistance, giving them food, water, wine and a place to rest.

Three days later, the army comes upon the cities of Gibeon and the leaders of the Israelites, their stupid faces turning slightly red, confront the Gibeonites, 'But you said you came from far away!' The Gibeonites merely smile. Caught in a covenant, Joshua and the Israelites cannot kill the messengers or destroy their cities. In frustration, they make the Gibeonites hewers of wood and drawers of water. Apart from the difficulty of extracting a moral from this story – the inestimable value of a good lie, a tall story that will get you what you want – the story shows despite itself a nervousness about what constitutes the chosen people and what the other. Are the Gibeonites strangers or members of the chosen? Is the chosen people a collection of disparate others, a situation that breaks down the very category of otherness? And why produce the category of stranger or foreigner except to produce a subjective identity?

Good and evil

A third objection picks up an old point from Fredric Jameson (with a heavy debt to Nietzsche): ethics cannot avoid the theological opposition between good and evil and should therefore be avoided.[72] Usually made in passing, Jameson has been castigated more than once for giving up valuable ground that the Left might want to claim.[73] All the same, after reading someone like Eagleton, for whom goodness and disinterested neighbourliness are the keys to ethics, all of which is based on a retrieved theology, Jameson may have a point: running through all the complexities of ethical decisions, in which competing claims struggle with one another, is the basic distinction between what is good and evil, or at least between what is better and worse. And given the intellectual heritage of these terms, especially in Western thought and practice, theology always seems to lurk in the background.

However much I agree with Jameson's suspicion of ethics, I am not sure that this is his best argument. All I need to do is deploy the relativisation of theology to show that the opposition between good and evil is not restricted to theology, that the theological shape of that argument is but one shape it may take. So why raise the issue in the first place? The reason is that I would like to criticise the purveyors of ethics who find they must fall back on theology, the numbers

---

72. Jameson 1981, pp. 114–17, 234–6; Jameson 1990, pp. 86–7; Jameson 1991, pp. 289–90; Jameson 2005, pp. 58, 250. Jameson's comments tend to be brief, noting the regressive nature of ethics and citing Nietzsche, Sartre and Freud as having shown the reactionary ideological function of ethics in which evil becomes all that is other.

73. For example, see West 1982; Eagleton 2003a, p. 143.

of whom seem to be swelling of late.[74] So let us consider theology more closely, for we will soon find that the question of good and evil becomes rather murky. For instance, in the Bible, three options may be found, two of which have been taken up by subsequent theological reflection: good and evil are embodied in two entities, God and the devil, along with their cohorts; good is what God does and is, evil is what human beings bring about through the exercise of free will; and God is the source of both good and evil.

The first is found almost only in the New Testament, which came together after an extraordinarily creative period of theological imagination. Spirits, good and evil, angels and demons, began rushing into heavenly and hellish spaces in the last couple of centuries BCE, racing for the last available berths in what would become an overpopulated part of the cosmos. Once there, they began a vigorous and vicious competition with one another and for human hearts, a struggle that spills over into the New Testament (you will not find them in the Hebrew Bible). On this score, good and evil fall into two camps, the sons of light and the sons of darkness. For human beings, it is a relatively straightforward matter of determining whence evil and good derive, albeit with some nagging questions: what is the origin of Satan and those deliciously evil spirits (hence the late, extra-biblical and retrofitted myth about the fall of Lucifer through pride)? How do you know it is an evil or a good spirit? And so on. Needless to say, this spiritual universe found itself elaborated upon, extended and then preserved, so that it remains a vibrant element of Christian theology, at least in some conservative quarters, not to mention its extraordinary resourcefulness for literature, film and popular culture.[75]

Equally popular in subsequent theology, especially today among those urbane liberals who find all this talk of spiritual warfare between angels and demons a little quaint, if not deeply embarrassing, is the argument that human beings are responsible for evil. In the Bible it turns up in the story of the fall in Genesis 2–3 (at least on a certain reading of that story), in the pronouncements by a prophet such as Jeremiah or Ezekiel that we are responsible for our sins,[76] and in the call to *metanoia* in the New Testament. In this case, God is the repository of good, but evil enters the world because God created human beings with the capacity to choose, with the free will to decide whether to opt for God or not, to obey or disobey God's commands. And so when human beings choose to disobey, to turn their face from God and go their own way, sin and evil enter the world. On an ethical front, this approach has more traction than the first with its flitting and

74. Apart from Eagleton's wholesale embracing of theological ethics, see also Milbank 1999.
75. See the excellent study by Wray and Mobley 2005, especially pp. 27–74.
76. Jeremiah 31:29–30; Ezekiel 18.

cackling spirits warring over our souls. God may be the repository of good, the arbiter of absolute morality, but human beings have the option to act 'ethically' or not. For the Eagletons of this world, this situation opens up a whole swathe of complex ethical situations – how can I know that this choice will be the good one? what if my choice for goodness, love, justice and courage actually has some negative side-effects? and is it not possible that even a choice for evil may work for good? – but it is still tied to a problematic theological framework.

A third option, which runs deeply in the Bible, is far less popular, for reasons that will become obvious. If one argues that there is but one God, that this God created all there is, then the conclusion must be that God is the source of both good and evil. It is a common theme in the Hebrew Bible, before the spirits began colonising heaven and burrowing out hell. Here we find, in the stories of King Saul, in prophets such as Jeremiah and Ezekiel, in the stories of the wilderness wandering of Exodus through to Deuteronomy, or in the bewildering suffering of Job, that God brings evil upon people as much as he might bring good fortune. Perhaps the most notable in this collection is Joshua 23:15: 'But just as all the good things which the Lord your God promised concerning you have been fulfilled for you, so the Lord will bring upon you all the evil things, until he have destroyed you from off this good land which the Lord your God has given you'.[77] Now, this is a far more interesting approach to ethics, one that we might want to retrieve in our own way. It leads in the end to what can only be described as – in the conventional patterns of ethical thought – an unethical and unmoral position.

To begin with, as the 'new old atheists' are fond of reciting, the God of the Hebrew Bible is a proper bastard. He is vindictive, jealous, petty, partisan, capricious and unmerciful, given to outbursts of mayhem and destruction without apparent reason. Hardly the one upon whom to base an ethics committed to the good, let alone that dreadful collection of moralising platitudes known as 'family values'. But that is only an initial and rather crude step; to go further, I draw once again upon Ernst Bloch. Yes, Bloch points out, this God is guilty as charged, but it is a Yahweh of the rulers and powerful, of theocratic tyrants, depots and kings. His fuming, contorted face, red with anger, is usually directed at those who rebel against those rulers; those who murmur and protest, who 'disobey' and go their own way, who win through by a ruse, are felled by plague, fire, snakes, yawning chasms, floods, and marauding armies eager for rape, plunder

77. Note also Genesis 2:9: 'And out of the ground the Lord God made to grow every tree that is pleasant to the sight and good for food, the tree of life also in the midst of the garden, and the tree of the knowledge of good and evil'. See also 1 Samuel 16:14–15, 23; 18:10; 19:9; Job 1:6–12; Ecclesiastes 6:2; Ezekiel 20:1–31, especially verse 25: 'I gave them statutes that were not good and ordinances by which they could not have life'.

and gore. Yet there is another Yahweh who sides with the rebels and outcasts, who blesses Cain with his mark, who goes with the man, Adam, as he leaves the garden,[78] who blesses the poor and condemns the rich. Eventually, Bloch argues, this side of God becomes an 'exodus out of Yahweh', a protest that will unfold as atheism. On this matter, Bloch is to my mind a far better theological thinker than someone like Eagleton, let alone the sundry intellectuals who make theology the source of their bread and butter. Ethics, however, struggles for traction on this rocky ground, for God is the focus of what is both ethical and unethical, both good and evil. Precisely what constitutes the good in this picture becomes almost impossible to determine, for rulers will prefer the God of order, measure and stability, one who ensures obedience and subservience, but the rebels will prefer a very different God. Who is to say what is ethical and what not? Ruler or rebel, tyrant or revolutionary? Ethical becomes unethical while unethical becomes ethical.

Towards the unethical and the unmoral

A little earlier, I pointed out that the word ethics – *ethikos* in the singular, *ethika* in the plural – does not appear in the Bible; all that we find is the homely *ethos*, designating custom and habit. Now I would like to extend that analysis, in order to answer a question left begging in my earlier argument concerning the production of others by ethics. If ethics seeks to conceal its process of producing others, both in terms of its connections with related discourses and in terms of its discursive link, then does it not have reasons for doing so, reasons that will turn out to have unsavory class dimensions? In dealing with this question, I dip once again into a classicist moment of etymology, not so much to reinforce the assumption that all Western thought derives from those parts of Eastern and Southern Europe (Greece and Rome), but to turn that classicism – once again – on its head.

Ethics derives from the Greek *ethikos*, the adjective which means 'of morals' or 'for morals'. As I noted earlier, Aristotle is the guilty party in this matter, for his treatises on morals, *ta ethika*, ensured that the word became fixed ever afterwards and a discipline of reflection was spawned. The adjective *ethikos* is actually part of a larger semantic cluster around the substantive *ethos* and the verb *ethō*, which bear the basic sense of custom and habit. Other items of this cluster include the meanings of an accustomed place, an animal's lair (Homer), and then the disposition, character and manners (in the plural) of human beings (Hesiod, Herodotus and Thucydides). At this point, the overlap with the Latin *mores* (plural) becomes obvious, for that becomes the translation of *ethoi*

78. Eve, curiously, is not mentioned along with Adam when he exits the garden. See Genesis 3:23–4.

(plural, too), especially in the sense of character and manners. At the centre of this Latin semantic cluster we find *mos*, which comes close indeed to the basic sense of *ethos*. For *mos*, too, means habit, custom, common usage and then even law, although it can also designate a slightly more capricious sense of humour and will.

By now my suspicions are properly aroused. They gain strength when Aristotle, early in the *Nicomachean Ethics*, opines that his detailed reflections on ethics are not for those of low taste. To return to a text that I quoted earlier: 'The utter vulgarity of the herd of men comes out in their preference for the sort of existence a cow leads'.[79] He means, of course, the slaves, peasants, artisans and women who made up the vast bulk of the Greek polis. Needless to say, those sympathetic to Aristotle's practical ethics, to his wish not to shirk practical matters but make them central to ethics, find this move problematic. For example, MacIntyre, who is usually quite astute on these matters,[80] tries to purge, or claims that the Aristotelian tradition has already purged, these 'inessential and objectionable elements'.[81] I disagree, for such a move on Aristotle's part is utterly essential to his ethics. In order to explain, let me pick up my reflections on kairós and ákairos in the previous chapter, where the one designates what is according to measure and the other to what is against and beyond measure. As a measured time and space, the timely and the well-proportioned, kairós also speaks of what goes according to expectation, the social assumptions of classes and class-difference, which should be kept in their proper, accustomed place and not be disrupted – of course, in terms established by the ruling classes. Further, in that discussion I connected with kairós the myriad terms for good, beautiful, well-born, wealthy, noble, brave, blessed, lucky, upright, elite and the pillars of society, while their opposites began the slide towards ákairos, such as bad, poor, ignoble, cowardly, ill-born, cursed, unlucky, lowly, masses and the dregs of society. Moral, economic, social, temporal and spatial terms overlap and merge into one another to provide a complete discourse, a class consciousness that is voiced again and again in the classical Greek and Roman texts.[82]

So if *ethos* and *mos* designate what is habitual and customary, the appropriate character and manners for human beings, they begin to attach themselves to kairós, namely what is in due measure, timely and well-placed. And once they have done so, they begin to mingle with all those class assumptions from the

79. Aristotle 1955, p. 30; *Eth. Nic.* 1.5. See also Aristotle 1955, pp. 309–10; *Eth. Nic.* 10.9. For an excellent analysis of Plato's and Aristotle's class assumptions and a defence of Protagoras as a democrat and sophisticated political theorist, see Wood 1997, pp. 142–3; Wood 2008, pp. 50–98.

80. MacIntyre 1998, pp. 83, 98–9

81. MacIntyre 1998, p. xviii.

82. Ste. Croix 2006, pp. 338–9; Ste. Croix 1972, pp. 371–6.

Greek and Roman worlds, where moral, social and economic terms work together to designate one's place among the powerful ruling classes or in one's customary place among the slaves, impoverished peasants and indentured labourers. The connection becomes stronger when I mention that what is customary and habitual at a social level, what is expected of one in such circumstances, is not to disrupt social 'harmony', but rather to follow all those ethical and moral expectations, assumptions and laws that keep the social fabric together. Once again, Aristotle reveals the truth of the matter when he points out that, yes, ethics does derive from *ethos*, habit, and since such habits come not from nature, one must undertake training and practice so that one may learn the 'correct' habits.[83] In this light, it becomes well-nigh impossible to separate Aristotle's proposed ethics from the class assumptions that structure them, not merely because of Aristotle's own oligarchic leanings but because the terminology of ethics is inescapably a class terminology.

Perhaps ethics has good reason to conceal these connections; or rather, in a universalizing move characteristic of ruling ideologies, it systematically effaces its specific location and claims to apply to everyone. So what is to be done with ethics? One option is to divest the term of its pernicious class associations and then fill it with new content. This has been the preferred option for those who wish to maintain the term for feminist ethics, environmental ethics, queer ethics, or indeed working class, revolutionary or Marxist ethics. Ethics would then be appropriated for very different purposes. The trap here is that one cannot distinguish form and content so easily, for a form inevitably trails the dust of its former associations. That is, the enmeshing of form and content ensures that a term such as ethics is never quite free of its ruling class dimensions. To put it slightly differently, the framework of ethics as it has been classically conceived sets the terms of debate and one cannot simply divest a term such as ethics from that ruling class framework.

For those reasons, in the same way that I prefer ákairos to kairós, what is untimely and out of place to what is timely and well-placed, so also I prefer a focus on what is opposed to the class assumptions of the semantic cluster of ethics – *ethikos, ethos, ethika, mos, mores*. That entails deploying the terminology of *aēthēs* (or *aētheia*), what is unaccustomed, unusual, unwonted and unexpected – unethical. Or in its Latin form, I prefer what is *praeter morem*, contrary to custom, and *sine more*, against custom – in short, unmoral. Undesirable terms in classical writers such as Thucydides, Aeschylus, Euripides, Virgil and Terence, but this is precisely why the terms are so appealing, for they voice the position of those outside the restricted zone of ruling class ethics. Note care-

83. Aristotle 1955, p. 55; *Eth. Nic.* 2.1.

fully: I do not argue for an amoral position, beyond ethics. The universe may well be amoral, for there is nothing good or bad about a piece of rock floating in space, as Darko Suvin once put it.[84] It may be objected that these terms too are part of ruling class discourse, designating the class other, that they are still within that framework. In response, I would suggest that the valorisation of the realm of those opposed to the ruling class then becomes an act of subverting the very discourse of ethics and its class associations. That is, such a position may be regarded as a taking of sides, for these terms indicate what is disruptive, unwelcome, what shakes up the customary and comfortable social order – an unethical and unmoral politics.

Conclusion

I have passed from self-help books to *aēthēs*, tarrying with Foucault, Butler, Eagleton, Badiou and Žižek in order to construct some of the elements of an unethical and unmoral position. In a way comparable to my treatment of kairós, in which we ran up against and opposed the implicit social, economic and moral overtones of the word, so also have I come to oppose *ethos* and *mos*, the customary and habitual that dresses itself up as ethics. In this sense, what is unethical and unmoral becomes a political position, one that undermines custom, habit and social order. But let me backtrack a little: I quickly dispensed with moralising, which bedevils far too much ethical discussion today. Indeed, I argued that any effort to provide specific guidelines on the basis of deliberation upon universal or even relative precepts is by definition moralising. But then I found that much of what passes for ethics is predicated on the interwoven care of the self and especially concern for the other, an other that is constructed by ethics itself, a discursive construction necessary for ethics itself to get moving in the first place. Ultimately, however, the concern of ethics is to make it possible for us all to live together a little more harmoniously, to grease social relations within which multiple selves and others might actually get on. I simply want to challenge that desire of ethics, for I seek a disruption of those relations, a breakdown of the social and its given power structure. Add to that the inescapable connections with a chosen people (or indeed person), as well as the profound difficulties of any resource to a grounding in theology, and ethics as it is understood struggles to maintain any worthwhile place.

Does this mean that I opt for ethical nihilism? Four possibilities might be distinguished: ethical absolutism (a code that in some way relies on absolute sanction, whether religious, social or political); ethical relativism (you in your culture can

84. Suvin 1979, p. 2.

do what you want and I will respect that, as long as you respect mine – we may think possums are cute and you may use them as sacrifices, but let us carry on all the same); ethical agnosticism (the situation is far too complex to make any viable ethical judgements); ethical nihilism (ethics should be abolished as a stupid and debilitating subservience to custom and habit). I must admit that at times I come close to the last option, especially with its Nietzschean traces,[85] enjoying the challenge to ethics as a problem in and of itself. In the end, however, I prefer to give ethics a distinct spin in terms of class and class consciousness. For I share Marx's profound suspicion of ethics as a mystifying ideology, a cultural dimension which justified that status quo and keeps the ruling class in its position as the ruling class. Where the church provides the moral glue for such a structure, it too comes in for full condemnation. So I suggest a fifth term, one that is not amoral but unmoral, an unethical and unmoral politics. Of course, if the masses silenced in the elite literature of ethics were to be asked, they may offer a very different terminology.

85. Nietzsche is the name that is usually conjured with in connection with this last position, but his approach to ethics is two-faced. To begin with, ethics is itself a problem, a blockage to the will to power, a sign of the herd, tyranny, slavish conformism and the unnatural code of priests out to control the mob. Fully aware of its etymological roots as custom and habit, Nietzsche excoriates ethics as mindless obedience to custom, an ignorant and barbaric code for social life among the masses. But in response he seeks to recover what strikes one as the ideal Homeric world, with its larger-than-life heroes of the ruling class, who speak strong and violent '*mythoi*', act passionately and throw themselves into life and battle (see my discussion of myth in Chapter 2). In his perpetual return to the problem of morality, Christianity was crucial. The history of morality was the battleground of the sick against the healthy, the unnatural against the natural. The Christian 'soul' emerged from a slave revolt in morality with a disastrous outcome: the old and noble distinction between good and bad was replaced by a herd morality in which humility and 'bad conscience' (sin, guilt) triumphed, with the result that the need for redemption came to lie at the core of subjectivity. Even the much-vaunted Christian love arose from hatred in what he calls 'the vindictive cunning of powerlessness' (Nietzsche 1994, p. 29 (I.13)), marking the long and persistent revenge against its pagan enemy. For this ethics, unnatural, destructive and diseased, he has no time, as also the moral philosophy of his own day, but for one of life, instinct, vitality, passion and power he has much time. As he admits, there is a deep morality in his immorality. See Nietzsche 1994; Nietzsche 1990, pp. 52–6; Nietzsche 1973, pp. 90–109; Nietzsche 1968, pp. 146–219; Nietzsche 1982.

Chapter Seven
Idols

> It is an enchanted, perverted, topsy-turvy world, in which Monsieur le Capital and Madame la Terre do their ghost-walking as social characters and at the same time directly as mere things.[1]

> Capitalist production first develops the conditions of the labour process on a large scale . . . but developing them as powers which dominate the *individual worker* and are *alien* to him. Thus capital becomes a very mysterious being.[2]

In our third foray, fetishism comes to the fore as Marxism and theology continue to rub up against one another, at times intimately and at others fractiously. Let me state my basic argument at the outset, which seeks to flush out the underlying connections between fetishism and idolatry.[3] By focusing on fetishism rather than idolatry, Marx and then Adorno brought about a shift: instead of the signifying link between idol and god characteristic of the critique of idolatry, Marx and Adorno focused on the transferring relation between object produced and the human being who produced it. The rest of the chapter will unpack this way of

1. Marx 1894a, p. 817; Marx 1894b, p. 838.
2. Marx 1861–3, p. 459.
3. Marx's interactions with fetishism are diverse and fecund, generating various types of critical response. I have produced three overlapping but also distinct reflections, of which the following is the second in a series. Each has their own rhetorical integrity, each their own flaws and, I would hope, insights. For the other two readings, please consult Boer 2012, pp. 177–206; 2011a. The latter piece focuses on Marx's elaboration of fetishism in the second and third volumes of *Capital*, where he speaks of '*Kapitalfetisch*'.

describing Marx's approach to fetishism, but I do need to clarify the terms I use before going any further.

By *critique of idolatry*, I refer primarily to the polemic found in some biblical texts, although it may also include the more elaborate theological category of idolatry in the later tradition. *Fetish* is a term that was first used by the Portuguese when they encountered African social and religious practices on the West-African coast in the fifteenth century. They preferred *fetisso*, since 'idol' did not capture the nature of the amulets, small objects and even food items used by the Africans. Subsequently, 'fetish' became an overarching category for analysing supposedly earlier stages of religion among 'primitives'. By *signifying link* I refer to the relation between the object and the deity or superhuman power to which it refers. The critiques of idolatry sought to break that link, arguing that no god exists and that the worshipper – stupidly – serves a mere object of wood, stone, metal, or perhaps animal or human. So, as a recognisable shorthand I will call the signifying connection and the effort to break it the *idol link*. Finally, the *transferring relation* is different: it takes place between human beings and the products of their labour. In Marx's hands, fetishism tends to deal with the transferring relation, or what I prefer to call the *fetish transfer*, for he wished to find out why there seems to be a transfer of powers between a range of elements within capitalism – commodity, money, value, capitalist, profit, wealth and so on – and the human beings who produce those elements. The theory of fetishism provided him with an answer – a mutual transfer of powers between human beings (who lost out) and the products of their labour – that would later gain philosophical rigour with Georg Lukács's elaboration of reification: the tendency in capitalism for living relations to become thing-like while things themselves seem to have life breathed into them. Let me be clear: that is not how Marx (or, as we will see a little later, Adorno) describes the process. Instead, it is my own take on what is going on behind the scenes, for I am interested in the theological implications of Marx's breakthrough, especially in terms of the way idol and fetish interact.

I have already provided an outline of my argument for the first half of this chapter, where I explore the way Marx brings about a shift from the signifying link characteristic of idolatry to the transferring relation of the fetish, or from the idol link to the fetish transfer. I also trace the way Marx reshaped the idea of the fetish to deal with the alienation of labour, money, commodities and eventually every facet of capitalist economic activity, so much so that capitalism itself becomes the religion of everyday life. In the process, Marx also assumed that fetishism, which was originally a term conceived to bypass the perceived shortcomings of a theologically overloaded idolatry, subsumed idolatry within itself. There idolatry acts like an agent under cover, opening up a covert exchange between Marx's thought and theology.

The second part of the chapter argues that Latin American liberation theology's appropriation of Marx's idea of fetishism fails to notice the shift Marx brought about. Instead, these theologians regard Marx's fetishism as a useful and promising extension of the critique of idolatry. As an extension, fetishism remains within the theological framework of idolatry, although it does enable them to argue that issues such a foreign debt, gross domestic product and theories of underdevelopment are also idols. By contrast, Theodor Adorno appreciates Marx's breakthrough with fetishism and thereby undertakes a dialectical reading in which idolatry and fetishism move to a new level. By applying the ban on images – a central feature of the critique of idolatry from the second commandment – to the transferring relation of fetishism, Adorno develops a comprehensive strategy for blocking the reifying effects of fetishism in philosophy, utopian thought, music and art, theology and even student politics.

That hideous pagan idol: Marx and fetishism

The tale of how Marx brings about the shift from the idol link to the fetish transfer (the transferring relation of fetishism) is a long one, although I will do my best to keep it brief. Marx's theory of fetishism is paradoxically one of the most well known and least known features of his thought. The section on 'The Fetishism of Commodities and the Secret Thereof' in *Capital* is like an iconic landmark – Uluru in the centre of Australia, perhaps – which rears up from the surrounding landscape and draws the eye. Here is the mature statement of Marx's theory of fetishism, or so goes the assumption, one that provides a unique insight into capitalism, let alone religion.[4] The trap is that, with our wondering gaze directed at the landmark, we miss the surrounding landscape, with its myriad subtle features. So it is with Marx, for there is much more concerning fetishism for the patient reader: his youthful reading of key works in the history of religions pertaining to fetishism among African peoples of the west coast, or his repeated use of the idea through his journalistic pieces, or the continual modifications in his other economic pieces, or indeed his notes on ethnography in the last years of his life are far less known, if at all. To be content with the section on fetishism in *Capital* is to do a disservice to Marx, let alone the full complexity of the idea itself. In order to provide a more complete picture of the way that fetishism works its way through Marx's œuvre, I will rummage around in the dusty corners of Marx's writings for a while, especially since these texts reveal precisely what Marx does with fetishism once he gets his hands on it.

4. So, for example, in the detailed study by Hinkelammert 1986.

A number of important points emerge from these texts. First, the key to Marx's early thoughts on the fetish are tantalisingly lost in the missing manuscript called *A Treatise on Christian Art*. However, since one's thoughts are never restricted to one text, I pursue hints and comments on fetishism in other writings of the time. From there I move on to focus on the texts Marx was reading in the early 1840s, especially one by Charles de Brosses on fetishism and ancient Egypt. De Brosses effectively subsumed idolatry within fetishism, which was now the overarching category within which idolatry became a subset. Even more, De Brosses made extensive use of the Bible for 'evidence' of ancient Egyptian fetishism and read the references to Egyptian idolatry as fetishism. Further, once he has appropriated fetishism, Marx constantly tinkers with the idea, adding a little here, filing away there, rearranging the parts so that he can put it to ever new uses. In the process, he gives priority to the fetish transfer and begins to transform the idol link. Finally, in the famous treatment of the fetishism of commodities in *Capital* Marx attempts to think through a dialectical transformation of fetishism that has profound implications for what I call political iconoclasm.

The idol link

Before all of this, however, I should explain in more detail what I mean by the idol link and the critique of idolatry. One of the best expressions of that critique is found in a biting passage I have used on more than one occasion. It comes from the biblical Book of Isaiah:

> 9 All who make idols are nothing, and the things they delight in do not profit;
> their witnesses neither see nor know. And so they will be put to shame.
> 10 Who would fashion a god or cast an image that can do no good? 11 Look,
> all its devotees shall be put to shame; the artisans too are merely human. Let
> them all assemble, let them stand up; they shall be terrified, they shall all be
> put to shame.
>
> 12 The blacksmith fashions it and works it over the coals, shaping it with ham-
> mers, and forging it with his strong arm; he becomes hungry and his strength
> fails, he drinks no water and is faint. 13 The carpenter stretches a line, marks
> it out with a stylus, fashions it with planes, and marks it with a compass; he
> makes it in human form, with human beauty, to be set up in a shrine. 14 He
> cuts down cedars or chooses a holm tree or an oak and lets it grow strong
> among the trees of the forest. He plants a cedar and the rain nourishes it.
> 15 Then it can be used as fuel. Part of it he takes and warms himself; he kindles
> a fire and bakes bread. Then he makes a god and worships it, makes it a carved
> image and bows down before it. 16 Half of it he burns in the fire; over this
> half he roasts meat, eats it, and is satisfied. He also warms himself and says,

'Ah, I am warm, I can feel the fire!' [17] The rest of it he makes into a god, his idol, bows down to it, and worships it; he prays to it and says, 'Save me, for you are my god!'

[18] They do not know, nor do they comprehend; for their eyes are shut, so that they cannot see, and their minds as well, so that they cannot understand. [19] No-one considers, nor is there knowledge or discernment to say, 'Half of it I burned in the fire; I also baked bread on its coals, I roasted meat and have eaten. Now shall I make the rest of it an abomination? Shall I fall down before a block of wood?' [20] He feeds on ashes; a deluded mind has led him astray, and he cannot save himself or say, 'Is not this thing in my right hand a fraud?'[5]

As far as the critique is concerned, it gives the impression, on the surface at least, that idol-worshippers are simply deluded, for they worship an oddly shaped block of wood, a chiselled piece of stone or perhaps a polished metal icon. That inanimate object or perhaps animal itself has no powers whatsoever and anyone who worships it is deceived and deceiving. However, if we shift perspective from the polemicist to the so-called worshipper of the idol, then the idol turns out to be a mere symbol or pointer to the deity, a tangible, earthly marker of the god's connection to this world. The idol worshipper does not think of this statue or that icon as the god itself; no, it is a finger pointing to the deity. Consider the first and second commandments together, for they reveal this precondition of the critique of idolatry.

You shall have no other gods before me.
You shall not make for yourself a graven image, or any likeness of anything that is in heaven above, or that is in the earth beneath, or that is in the water under the earth; you shall not bow down to them or serve them.[6]

The second commandment forbids the making and worshipping of any graven images, while the first commands one not to have any other god before Yahweh. These two commandments are not discrete items, for they flow into one another: one should have neither other gods nor idols, for they are intimately connected. In other words, there is an idol link between god and idol, deity and representation, and the one who shows reverence for the idol does so in order to honour his or her god to whom the idol directs one's attention.

The polemicist steps in and breaks the signifying link between object and god: that piece of wood points to nothing, for there is no god to whom it refers. Ergo, all you are worshipping is that block of wood, which – I would like to remind you – comes from a tree, half of which you used to make that shelf and half that

5. Isaiah 44:9–20. See also Isaiah 40:19–20; 41:7; 42:17; 45:16–17 and 46:1–2, 5–7; Romans 1:21, 23, 25.
6. Exodus 20:3–5. See also Deuteronomy 5:7–9.

silly object you worship. Can you not see how stupid it is to worship a clump of wood or stone? It does nothing, says nothing, thinks nothing. It just sits there and you worship it. In other words, the critic of idolatry snaps the signifying link between representative object and deity. If the deity no longer exists, then there is no link and so one worships what now becomes an idol.

Was Marx aware of such a critique of idolatry? On this matter there are no definitive answers, but one or two pieces of circumstantial evidence suggest that it is highly likely. A little before he began his research on fetishism, religion and art for the lost treatise on Christian art (which I discuss in a moment), Marx studied the Book of Isaiah with none other than Bruno Bauer in the summer term of 1839.[7] With Bauer, one of the leading biblical scholars and Young Hegelians of his day, who was soon to lose his post at Berlin for his radical positions, Marx worked through Isaiah, a major prophetic book of the Bible – precisely that text in which the most trenchant and sophisticated critiques of idolatry may be found, texts that suited Bauer's argument for the false particularity of religion, a particularity made false by claiming to be universal.

Further, among the last material he wrote, Marx made some notes on the work of John Lubbock on ancient religions.[8] Marx has little time for the pious Lubbock's schema of religious development (from primitive atheism, through fetishism to higher forms), but when Lubbock discusses fetish sacrifice he refers to the Bible. In Marx's notes the following biblical texts appear: the sacrifice of Jephthah's daughter in Judges 11, prescriptions for Israelite sacrifice of animals in Leviticus 7, Paul's comments on the origin of idolatry in Romans 1:23, Christ's sacrifice, and, most significantly, an extended quotation of the polemic against idolatry found in the deutero-canonical book known as the Wisdom of Solomon. Marx quotes the full text of chapter 14:12–20, ostensibly to deride Lubbock's use of the text to provide a theological judgement on fetishism – as a turning-away from God by deluded minds. Even more, the text from the Wisdom of Solomon is a rather poor pastiche of arguments found in the Book of Isaiah, where the polemic is sharper. In other words, Marx seems to have known of the biblical critiques of idolatry, which he read as texts referring to fetishism. One further piece of evidence is that Marx was fond of alluding to biblical texts concerning the Ammonite idol, Moloch, the one who demanded child sacrifice, as the

7. An entry in Marx's certificate from the Friedrich Wilhelm University reads: 'V. In the summer term 1839: 1. Isaiah with Herr Licentiate Bauer, attended' (*Leaving Certificate from Berlin University* 1841, p. 704).

8. Marx 1974. Written in a mix of German, English and French, with plenty of colloquialisms and crude terms, the work also includes notes on L.H. Morgan (the basis for Engels's *Origin of the Family*), John B. Phear and Henry Maine.

embodiment of the rapacity of capitalism.[9] And in a wonderful text, Marx sees capitalism itself as an idol: 'When a great social revolution shall have mastered the results of the bourgeois epoch, the market of the world and the modern powers of production ... then only will human progress cease to resemble that hideous, pagan idol, who would not drink the nectar but from the skulls of the slain'.[10] Enough evidence, I would suggest, to assume that Marx was aware of biblical idolatry and the polemic against it. But I am more interested in what Marx made of the idol link, particularly via his theory of fetishism.

In search of a lost treatise

In the early 1840s, Marx had a good deal to say about fetishism, mainly because he was working on a text that is now lost, *A Treatise on Christian Art*. In a classic case of a tantalisingly lost manuscript, one that would have provided a much fuller picture of Marx's views on religion and art, we are left with the fragments and overflows of his thought at the time. As happens with the processes of reading, thinking and writing, ideas are not contained within one zone, restricted purely to the manuscript in preparation. They flow out, sparking all manner of other connections and insights, becoming applicable to topics not within the original scope of research.

So it is with the lost treatise, although I must admit that searching for those glimpses requires a reasonable amount of educated guesswork. I am, of course, interested in the comments on fetishism rather than those that deal with art and aesthetics.[11] A few tell-tale comments appear in material from 1842 and soon afterwards – precisely when Marx was working on the treatise. They exhibit two lines of argument: first, common ideas of religious progress are rubbish; second, fetishism involves a transfer of properties between the object fetishised and human beings, with human beings diminished to mere objects and the fetish itself gaining human properties. We see both lines in a piece that constitutes perhaps Marx's most extensive early reflection on theology (with the grand title of 'The Leading Article in No. 179 of the *Kölnische Zeitung*'). Here, Marx takes on Herr Hermes, government agent and editor of a major conservative Roman Catholic rag, and pulls him to pieces line by line. On fetishism, Marx writes:

9. Marx 1864, pp. 10–11; Marx and Engels 1845a, p. 21; Marx and Engels 1845b, p. 21; Marx 1845a, p. 226; Marx 1882a, p. 234; Marx 1882b, p. 54; Marx 1855a, p. 95; Marx 1855b, pp. 132–3; Marx 1859a, p. 294; Marx and Engels 1848a, p. 264; Marx and Engels 1848b, p. 251; see also Engels 1846a, p. 474; Engels 1846b, p. 405; Engels 1893c, p. 234; Engels 1893d, p. 171.

10. Marx 1853a, p. 222.

11. For studies on the aesthetic dimension of this lost treatise, see Lifshitz 1973, Lifshitz 1984 and Rose 1984.

> And now, indeed 'fetishism'! Truly, the erudition of a penny magazine! Fetishism is so far from raising man *above* his sensuous desires that, on the contrary, it is 'the *religion of sensuous desire*'. Fantasy arising from desire deceives the fetish worshipper into believing that an 'inanimate object' will give up its natural character in order to comply with his desires. Hence the crude desire of the fetish-worshipper *smashes* the fetish when it ceases to be its most obedient servant.[12]

Hermes had proposed a rather conventional schema that moves from sensuous animal worship, through fetishism to the highest form of Christianity, which by some strange coincidence was precisely the form of Christianity in Germany at the time. In response, Marx points out that there is no progress at all, that fetishism is no advance on animal worship, for both fall into the same category (and so, presumably, does Christianity). Fetishism, too, is saturated with sensuous desire, a desire that produces a fantasy that this inanimate object actually has all manner of magical and superhuman powers. However, when the fetish no longer provides what the worshipper wants – recovery from illness, favourable outcomes in battle, a good harvest, or success in seducing that sexy woman or a man from the next tribe – he smashes it in disgust. Behind Marx's argument lies a crucial assumption: with fetishism we have not two but three steps. Instead of sacralised fetish → de-sacralised object, he postulates three steps: profane object → sacralised fetish → de-sacralised object once again. The first and third stages frame the fetish itself, one as a point of origin and the other as a point of return to that state. The fetish itself is the anomaly, the break in the profaneness of the object. Now, Marx recognises – through the quotation marks around 'inanimate object' in the quotation above – that this is really his own perspective and not that of the fetish user, for he or she would see the object as inherently sacred in the first place.

This three-fold schema has at least one important ramification that goes beyond the specific instance of fetishism. I am thinking in particular of narratives of secularisation: according to one quite popular assumption, secularisation follows the two-stage schema. Once upon a time we lived in a predominantly sacred world, but then the process (either celebrated or excoriated) of secularisation set in and that world lost its dominant position. Disenchantment, banishment of superstition, the flight of the gods, a coming down to earth – all these and more designate the loosening of sacred categories in a world come of age. But it also means that one assumes the origin of all these terms – freedom, sovereignty, hope, love, morality, the political subject and so on – is resolutely theological, so much so that one cannot understand them without recourse to that theological

---

12. Marx 1842i, p. 189; Marx 1842j, p. 177.

past which still clings to their garments.[13] However, if we open the scene up with the threefold schema, then the sacred slips from its absolute throne to become relative and contingent. It is but one phase through which the profane may pass, except that now the term 'profane' is not so appropriate given that it emerges as an opposition to the sacred. The theological shape of an idea, a practice or a position becomes a momentary shape, a possible but by no means necessary path that it may take. I would go a step further and suggest that for Marx secularisation itself is not the problem, but sacralisation. The idea of fetishism raises a prior question: how was this idea or this practice sacralised in the first place?

All of which is an elaboration of the first argument in this short text, namely that any idea of progress, from a primitive religious state to one of refinement, is so much garbage. As for the second argument – the transferring relation – Marx writes: 'an "inanimate object" gives up its natural character'. In other words, it ceases to be a mere object – a piece of wood, stone, metal, star or perhaps tree – and becomes something else, a god or fetish with powers it never had before. It thereby gains a whole series of attributes – able to affect human interaction, redirect nature, produce miraculous results – which it did not have before. This surrender of the object's natural properties is but one side of the inversion – as Marx would soon come to argue – for human beings too change in the process; they give up their nature as human beings to become abject worshippers and fetish users, more and more resembling lifeless objects.

Marx would take both arguments – concerning the transferring relation and the inversion of the narrative of progress – and use them to polemical effect. For example, a couple of years later in *The Economic and Philosophic Manuscripts*, he comments on the French who are 'still dazzled by the sensuous glitter of precious metals, and are therefore still fetish-worshippers of metal money, and are not yet fully-developed money-nations'.[14] In this case, he assumes the narrative of progress, only to turn it against the vaunted sophistication of the French: you might think you are advanced, but you are really still savages, worshipping precious metals. The bite of this argument comes through more strongly in a jibe at the Rhine Province Assembly (a pseudo-democratic gathering restricted to the nobles):

> The *savages of Cuba* regarded gold as a *fetish of the Spaniards*. They celebrated a feast in its honour, sang in a circle around it and then threw it into the sea.

13. The proponents of radical orthodoxy go a step further and argue that the theological past of contemporary secular thought must be rejuvenated, retrained and sent into battle as the shock troops of a post-secular, or rather resacralised, world. Needless to say, I see little gain in such a regressive utopian approach. See, for example, Milbank 1990 and many of the essays gathered in Davis, Milbank and Žižek (eds.) 2005.

14. Marx 1844g, p. 312; Marx 1844h, p. 552.

> If the Cuban savages had been present at the sitting of the Rhine Province Assembly, would they not have regarded *wood* as the *Rhinelanders' fetish?* But a subsequent sitting would have taught them that the worship of animals is connected with this fetishism, and they would have thrown the *hares* into the sea in order to save the *human beings*.[15]

For these cultured nobles, the Cubans would indeed be seen as savages – hence the emphasis in Marx's text: 'savages of Cuba' was the nobles' phrase. But now Marx inverts the whole relation, for he purports to write from the perspective of the Cubans. To them, the mad search for gold by the Spaniards – so much so that Columbus threatened to cut off the hands of any inhabitant of Hispaniola who did not bring him gold – was much like the worship of fetishes. Well then, Marx imagines the Cubans saying, let us recognise its fetish character and toss it into the sea; hopefully the Spanish too will go, perhaps diving into the sea in order to find their precious fetish. By the time the Cubans have crossed the Atlantic and sit at the Rhine Province Assembly, the relation of savage-civilised has been fully inverted. The Cubans are now the calm, rational observers and what do they see? The nobles obsess about wood laws, especially the move to ban the ancient practice of peasants gathering fallen wood for their cooking and heating fires. Surely wood must be their fetish, then, since they wish to preserve it. Or, indeed, in relation to hares, which the nobles wish to preserve from the peasants' snares, the Cubans could only conclude that the nobles are also into animal fetishism. The proper response: in order to save human beings from such terrible developments, the hares too should be thrown into the sea. And why is fetishism so deleterious for human beings? Once again the transferring relation appears: the fetish humanises – or rather, super-humanises – animals and objects while it dehumanises human beings.

I have run ahead of myself, exploring possible arguments from the treatise before recounting the fate of the treatise itself. It arose from the confluence of at least three streams: the nature of public debate in Germany at the time, which was deeply theological, or rather, biblical; the close friendship and early collaboration with Bruno Bauer, Marx's one-time biblical teacher in Berlin; the search for research topics and employment after Marx had finished his PhD thesis in 1841.

---

15. Marx 1842m, pp. 262–3; Marx 1842n, p. 236. See also his observations concerning the Assembly of the Estates of the Rhine Province, which has a tendency to 'canonise individuals' and to 'demand that we should bow down before the holy image of certain privileged individuals' (Marx 1842k, p. 169; Marx 1842l, p. 157) and the polemic against Louis Napoleon: 'And the cast-down, broken idol can never be set on its pedestal again. He may recoil before the storm he has raised, and again receive the benedictions of the Pope and the caresses of the British Queen' (Marx 1859b, p. 273).

As for German public debate, the conservative nature of Prussian politics – pushed by the new king, Friedrich Wilhelm IV and his desire for a 'Christian state' – brought theology to the fore in public debate. Not for nothing was David Strauss's *Das Leben Jesu* with its democratic Christ (we may all become Christs) the most debated work of the time.[16] And Bruno Bauer, for a while leader of the Young Hegelians, caused a furore with a radical biblical criticism which arrived at a position of atheism in the name of a free and infinite self-consciousness for which any religion, but especially that form of Christianity identified with the state, was a hubristic and brutalising particularity that claimed universal status.[17] Both Strauss and Bauer were to be denied teaching positions as the climate became unfriendly to their radical positions. Obviously Marx, who had tied his hopes for a university position in with Bauer, was going to fare no better.

Given that Bauer was a biblical scholar and sometime theologian, and given that Marx set out in the first months after completing his thesis on Epicurus to collaborate with Bauer, Marx's path veered towards theology, albeit of a radical type. They had grand plans: a journal called *Archiv des Atheismus*, a critique of Hegel's *Philosophy of Religion*, and a series of book reviews, one at least on K. Fischer's book called *Die Idee der Gottheit*[18] and another on *Die menschliche Freiheit in ihrem Verhältnisse zur Sünde und zur göttlichen Gnade*, written by the Hegelian biblical critic and theologian Wilhelm Vatke (this one for Arnold Ruge's *Deutsch-Französische Jahrbücher*).[19] None of these projects came to anything much, largely because the collaboration was a rocky one and because Marx's own interests began to change.

The closest they came to producing anything together was a two-volume work, to be called *Die Posaune*, or *Trumpet of the Last Judgement*. The outcome, however, was two works in Bauer's name, the first with the agreed-upon title and the second called *Hegels Lehre von der Religion und Kunst*.[20] Although Marx had a light hand in the first volume, the second one was to be truly collaborative. Again, nothing came of it. So what happened? In a series of letters to Arnold Ruge in 1842, we find comments by Marx on the collapse of the collaboration and his plans to produce his part of the second volume as a separate publication. It was to be called *A Treatise on Christian Art*. From Marx's other writings of the period, it seems that work would have moved from a study of the religious and fetishist art of Asia and Greece to the Christian art of the Romantics, showing

16. Strauss 1902; Strauss 1835.
17. Bauer 1838, 1839, 1840, 1841, 1842a, 1842b, 1843, 1850–1, 1852.
18. Fischer 1839
19. See Marx 1842a; Marx 1842b. Vatke (1806–82) was one of the significant contributors to the developing theories about sources in the Hebrew Bible (Old Testament). See also Marx 1842g; Marx 1842h.
20. Bauer 1983; Bauer 1967.

how the two are connected.[21] Each time Marx mentions the manuscript in the letters to Ruge, it is one step away from completion, needing a few corrections and the writing up of a fair copy; but then, no, he had decided to expand it and include a section on Romanticism; then it had become two volumes, one on Christian art and the other to be called *On the Romantics*; after that we hear nothing more of the treatise.[22] Marx had clearly not learnt how to finish a manuscript (a problem that stayed with him),[23] although it did not help that he was in Trier for three months, sitting by his future father-in-law's deathbed. Herr Ludwig von Westphalen died on 3 March 1842; within a couple of months, Marx's manuscript went the same way.[24]

One other piece of evidence has turned up regarding this manuscript. Apart from the letters to Ruge and the scattered comments on religion, fetishism and art from the same period, we also have a collection of reading notes from works that Marx read as he was writing the manuscript. In the Bonn Notebooks of 1842, we find excerpts from the following works:

Karl Friedrich von Rumohr, *Italienische Forshungen*. Bonn, 1842.
Johann Jakob Grund, *Der Malerey der Grieschen oder Enstehung, Fortschritt, Vollendung und Verfall der Malerey. Ein Versuch*. Dresden, 1810.
Charles de Brosses, *Du culte des dieux fétiches ou Parallèle de l'ancienne religion de l'Egypte avec la religion actuelle de Nigritie*. German translation by Pistorius, Berlin and Stansrund 1785. French, 1760.
C.A. Böttinger, *Ideen zur Kunstmythologie*. 2 vols. Dresden and Leipzig, 1826–36.
Christoph Meiners, *Allgemeine kritische Geschichte der Religionen*. 2 vols. Hannover, 1806–7.
Benjamin Constant, *De la religion*. Paris, 1826.
J. Barbeyrac, *Traité de la Morale des Pères de l'Église*. Amsterdam, 1728.

Clearly, he was studying a significant number of works on religion as well as art, especially when we add Gibbon, Hegel and Feuerbach, whom he was reading

21. We can also find a hint in Marx's comment to Ruge on 20 March 1842, where Marx mentions that the revised manuscript disagrees with Feuerbach's concept of religion, a disagreement that has actually turned up in the *Theses on Feuerbach*. As Marx points out in the letter, he disagrees not with the principle (projection) but the conception. It would seem that Marx was already arguing that religion is a projection of the worst in human beings rather than the best, that religion is an expression of alienation and not hope and love.

22. Marx 1842c; Marx 1842d; Marx 1842e; Marx 1842f; Marx 1842g; Marx 1842h.

23. Marx comments to Ruge that 'the work has steadily grown into almost book dimensions, and I have been drawn into all kinds of investigations which will still take a rather long time' (Marx 1842g, p. 387; Marx 1842h, p. 402).

24. 'The fact is that my future father-in-law, Herr von Westphalen, lay on his deathbed for three months and died the day before yesterday. During this period, therefore, it was impossible to do anything properly' (Marx 1842c, p. 383; Marx 1842d, p. 397).

on the same topics. But let us zero in on a few of them, especially the books by Böttinger and Grund, as well as Feuerbach's discussion of *Bildlichkeit* in *The Essence of Christianity*,[25] which Marx was reading at the time. Among the notes Marx took, there appears the argument that, in the same way as the Greeks idealised men as gods and anthropomorphised men (especially from Böttinger), so also did Christian art produce a fetishistic anthropomorphisation of the divine while it alienated human sensuality (from Feuerbach). In short, Christianity took over the thoroughly fetishistic and pagan nature of the culture it thought it was transforming.[26] Not a bad argument against conventional narratives of Christian progress!

However, I am less interested in Marx's arguments concerning art or Christianity, the connections between them, or the possible links with Marx's other polemic against state censorship at the time,[27] and far more drawn to what he might have read in terms of fetishism. On this matter, the work by De Brosses stands out in the collection,[28] for it sought to develop a comprehensive theory of fetishism in order to understand the religion of ancient Egypt. How did De Brosses go about his task? He drew upon studies of fetishism in Western Africa and applied them – in a process that would become standard among historians and anthropologists – to the ancient world. Here too are primitives, went the argument, living in our own day and time; surely their religious practices would be similar to those of other primitives, even if they lived millennia before our civilised society?

The crucial moment in De Brosses's work is when he begins searching for evidence of ancient Egyptian religious practice. There was, of course, some scattered material available in the mid-eighteenth century – a pyramid or two, a tomb opened, an inscription and some Greek sources. But the primary source for De Brosses is the Bible, which he took as a reliable historical source (the full sceptical brunt of biblical criticism had not had an impact as yet). So all of the various stories concerning Egyptians and their gods, magicians and beliefs, especially those clustered around the accounts of Joseph, Israelite slavery and escape under Moses, became evidence for ancient fetishism. And where there were accounts of Canaanite practices, in which the Israelites engaged with alarming

25. Feuerbach 1989, pp. 74–9; Feuerbach 1924, pp. 94–100.
26. See Rose 1984, pp. 65–9.
27. Rose 1984, p. 61. Rose, especially on pp. 1–70, also offers an excellent contextual analysis of the artistic and very political struggles in Germany at the time between Hellenes and conservative Nazarenes on the question of religious art.
28. Marx 1842o.

and frequent ease when they had settled in the land,[29] these too provided data regarding fetishism.

Idolatry goes underground

Fetishism? Why not idolatry, as traditional interpreters of the Bible would have it? De Brosses simply subsumed idolatry within an overarching category of fetishism. Thus, the idolatries of the Egyptians, the Canaanites and even the Israelites on many occasions, were actually instances of fetishism. In order to appreciate De Brosses's move – and of course Marx's appropriation of the idea of fetishism – let us backtrack a little, assisted by the exhaustive studies of Pietz.[30] When the Portuguese began pushing down the West-African coast in their tiny caravels in search of a way to the 'East' that circumvented the Muslim-dominated lands of the Middle East, they encountered local people with their own cultures and religious practices. As the Portuguese established forts, refuelling stations and slaving posts, they also made a desperate effort, with few resources upon which to draw, to understand cultures that were so vastly different from their own. In particular, the crucial amulets and objects, endowed with super-human powers and keys to social exchange, had to be understood. And the term 'idolatry' was not adequate. Why? It had become an elaborate term in the theological tradition. Church fathers, heresiarchs and theologians had developed a complex understanding of idolatry that went far beyond its initial biblical framework: idolatry had become a mirror of 'true religion', requiring a cultic practice, ecclesial structure, clergy, collection of sacred objects, architecture and tradition. Clearly this was not at all adequate to the practices of the West Africans. And so the Portuguese used the term *fetisso*, the etymology of which is still disputed.[31] But they played a double game: on the one hand, the term was used to indicate that these primitive Africans were entirely irrational, for they attributed super-human and magical powers to simple objects of wood, stone or metal; on the other hand, the Portuguese also would swear by and even consume a fetish (where needed) to ensure a commercial exchange. In short, they derided the

29. Twentieth-century work in biblical scholarship would come to dispense with any historicity for the Exodus, pointing out that Israel (where it can be discerned) emerged from within Canaan and that its early religious practices were polytheistic.

30. Pietz 1985, 1987, 1988.

31. The word has suffered many efforts to trace its etymology. It is an English translation of the pidgin *Fetisso*, connected to the Portuguese *feitiço*, which in the late Middle Ages designated 'magical practices' or 'witchcraft'. However, efforts have been made to derive the word from the Latin *fatum*, signifying both fate and charm (De Brosses and Marx following him), *factitius*, linking the magic arts and the work of art (Edward Tylor) or *facere*, designating the false representation of things sacred, beautiful, or enchanting.

claim that the fetish had powers in social networking and yet they recognised those powers in their everyday interactions with the Africans.

The fetish was in, the idol out. The term certainly caught on, so much so that Dutch, French and English Protestants used it to describe Roman Catholic sacramental objects. And Enlightenment intellectuals used it in the eighteenth century as the basis for a general theory of religion.[32] At this moment, De Brosses comes back into the picture, for he takes the whole argument a step further. He may have derided fetishism as a 'stupid' and 'ridiculous' practice,[33] but by turning to the Bible for evidence of ancient Egyptian religious practices (there described as idolatry) and by subsuming them within a general theory of fetishism, he re-inserted idolatry into discussions. Further, as a subset of fetishism, idolatry could also mean fetishism, although not vice versa. So whenever De Brosses read the word 'idol' in the Bible, he assumed 'fetish'.

This connection, I would suggest, is the one Marx that took over from De Brosses. The evidence: one of the passages Marx cites with interest is a key section concerning the nature of fetishism in ancient Judah.[34] Marx notes that De Brosses distinguishes between two types of fetish, the private and the public. As for the public, national fetishes, four appear: serpents, trees, the sea and 'a small, filthy clay image [*Bild*]' which presided over councils.[35] The key term here is *Bild*, for it translates De Brosses's *idole*. Marx goes on to make further notes from these pages by De Brosses on the roles of these four types of fetish – or idols or images – in Judah. But the elision has taken place: Marx appropriates the link between idol and fetish and in the process the idols of ancient Judah become instances of the broader category of fetishism.

Before I explore what Marx did with the idea after taking it over from De Brosses, two points demand attention. To begin with, the idolatry in question was a stripped-down version, the one found in various biblical texts rather than the elaborate version that came out of the theological tradition. It is as though idolatry had to spend some time in the wilderness, on a simple diet and in a tent so that it could shed all its accretions and then return, fit and trimmed down, in order to resume its place in discussions. Secondly, there is a natural ideological fit between those who use the term idol or fetish: both come from a particular

32. For example, for Auguste Comte fetishism becomes the first stage (followed by polytheism and monotheism) of his first great period of human history. Comte used the term in his *Système de politique positive* (1851–4). After the theological age, of which fetishism is the first stage, we have the metaphysical and scientific stages.

33. Brosses 1760, pp. 10 and 11.

34. Marx 1842o, pp. 321–2. See the original passage in Brosses 1760, pp. 27–30.

35. From the translation by Pistorius, Marx quotes: 'die Schlange, die Bäume, das Meer und ein kleines schmutziges Bild von Thon, das in den Rattsammlungen den Vorstiz hat' (Marx 1842o, p. 321). In the original by De Brosses it reads: 'le serpent, les arbres, le mer, & une vilaine petite idole d'argille qui préside aux Conseils' (Brosses 1760, p. 27).

perspective, after the fact, creating a category and simultaneously making a theological and moral judgement. In the case of the biblical 'idol', the very use of the term comes much later, creating a category of religious practice that, in the very process of being created, critiqued and dismissed that category. The designation 'idol', apart from the polemic often associated with the term, was in itself a condemnation. With 'fetish' the situation is similar: the category is developed to describe what others do, imposed after the fact by an external observer. But it also contains critique and judgement, for the fetishist is mistaken, deluded, ridiculous and stupid. Marx too would take a similar line, for 'fetish' may occasionally be a descriptive term, but more often than not it bears a negative weight: to describe something – money, commodity, capital itself – as a fetish is to imply critique on Marx's part and delusion on the part of the fetishist.

In the tinker's thinking shed

I have come back to my starting point, namely, Marx's early comments on fetishism which I discussed above. There too the delusion of the fetish worshipper is clear; there too describing an item as a fetish – gold, wood or hares – acts as a criticism; there too the crucial transferring relation between fetish and human being is central. Since we have come back to Marx's fetishistic polemic, I can now note another connection with De Brosses. Recall the example of the Cubans and the Spanish fetish for gold, which Marx applied to the Rhine Province Assembly. The inversion actually comes from De Brosses, which Marx cites, evidently with some interest, for his own use.[36] De Brosses, it seems, had become a crucial source that sparked Marx's interest on the question of fetishism.

But what did Marx do with the term after he drew it into his critical arsenal? It became an extraordinarily fruitful idea, appearing throughout his work from the earliest journalistic pieces with the *Rheinische Zeitung* to the great economic manuscripts of the 1860s. He would constantly tinker with the fetish, reshaping it for analysing alienation, labour, money as mediator, the commodity form and then capital as a whole, but it would always keep its core concept: the transferral of powers from human beings to the object in question, to the detriment of one and the gain of the other.

For example, with alienation and labour Marx argues in *The Economic and Philosophic Manuscripts of 1844* that the more the worker puts into the product of his labour, the greater it becomes while the worker diminishes. The key passage

36. 'Die *Wilden von Cuba hielten* das *Gold* für den Fetisch der Spanier, sie feierten ihm ein Fest, tanzten und sangen um ihn und warfen es dann ins Meer, um es zu entfernen' (Marx 1842o, p. 322; emphasis in original). This is an abbreviation of the account in Brosses 1760, pp. 52–3.

is worth quoting in full, for its basic argument would remain the same, even if the terms themselves would change:

> All these consequences are implied in the statement that the worker is related to the *product of his labour* as to an *alien* object. For on this premise it is clear that the more the worker spends himself, the more powerful becomes the alien world of objects which he creates over and against himself, the poorer he himself – his inner world – becomes, the less belongs to him as his own. It is the same in religion. The more man puts into God, the less he retains in himself [*Es ist ebenso in der Religion. Je mehr der Mensch in Gott setzt, je weniger behält er in sich selbst*]. The worker puts his life into the object; but now his life no longer belongs to him but to the object... The *alienation* of the worker in his product means not only that his labour becomes an object, an *external* existence, but that it exists *outside him*, independently, as something alien to him, and that it becomes a power on its own confronting him. It means that the life which he has conferred on the object confronts him as something hostile and alien.[37]

These alien objects take on lives of their own, becoming greater than me, ruling my life. The products of everyday labour swell into alien and powerful creatures because of this transferral of powers and relations. But note the analogy, for here the theological secret agent I mentioned earlier makes an appearance: 'It is the same in religion', Marx writes, and then goes on to draw the analogy: 'The more man puts into God, the less he retains in himself [*Es ist ebenso in der Religion. Je mehr der Mensch in Gott setzt, je weniger behält er in sich selbst*]'.

Note carefully what has happened here: Marx actively subsumes theology, with its signifying relation between heaven and earth, to the transferring relation between the worker and her product. Theology does not determine or set the framework for Marx's analysis; it is now subject to that analysis. Further, in doing so, Marx also begins to go beyond Feuerbach, as he claimed he would in the famous fourth thesis,[38] for Feuerbach remains with the signifying relation between God and human beings. By arguing that the gods are really the projections of what is best in human beings and that in order to realise our full potential we need to reclaim those 'divine' properties, Feuerbach offers a version of the critique of idolatry, except that now he directs the critique not

37. Marx 1844g, p. 272; Marx 1844h, p. 512. So also: 'Every self-estrangement of man, from himself and from nature, appears in the relation in which he places himself and nature to men other than and differentiated from himself. For this reason religious self-estrangement necessarily appears in the relationship of the layman to the priest, or again to a mediator, etc., since we are here dealing with the intellectual world' (Marx 1844g, p. 279; Marx 1844h, p. 519). See also Marx 1857–8b, pp. 209–10.

38. Marx 1845b, p. 4; Marx 1845c, p. 6.

at false gods and idols, but at the heart of Christianity itself.[39] In other words, Feuerbach remains within the signifying link between God and human beings, seeking to break the link and allow human beings to hold their own leash. By contrast, Marx shifts focus since he is concerned with human beings and the products of their labour. This transferring relation now becomes the category within which Feuerbach's critique may be understood.

The pattern of invoking fetishism and then using a theological analogy would remain remarkably consistent as Marx tinkered with the fetish. For example, in notes written at the same time on the French translation of James Mill's *Elements of Political Economy*, Marx uses a similar argument in connection with money. The difference now is that it is not money per se that is the issue, but the mediatory role of money: this mediating activity 'is *estranged* from man and becomes the attribute of money, a *material thing* outside man'.[40] The analogy this time is with Christ, the mediator between heaven and earth. Like Christ, money as mediator acquires human properties of social interaction at the expense of those very human properties. And in the process of making the analogy, Marx once again shifts the theological emphasis on the idol link to his materialist one of the fetish transfer. So also with the commodity relation, where my brief narrative touches on a text over which many have pored and pondered: the famous section called 'The Fetishism of Commodities and the Secret Thereof' in *Capital*. I do not propose to spend a great deal of time on this text, since I have done so elsewhere, except to press hard on the following point.

Towards political iconoclasm

By now Marx has established the priority of the transferring relation characteristic of fetishism. But in this text from *Capital* he attempts a dialectical leap: he argues that the transferral of powers in the commodity-form – the notion that everything, no matter how different, may be exchanged in terms of its value – is both illusory and real, both mystified and concrete. Perhaps the best way to see how Marx attempts his massive leap is to exegete a central passage:

> There [with commodities] it is a definite social relationship between men, that assumes, in their eyes, the fantastic form of the relation between things. In order, therefore, to find an analogy, we must have recourse to the

39. Feuerbach 1989; Feuerbach 1926. Although he was to become critical of Feuerbach's work, Marx was initially very enthusiastic about Feuerbach's achievement. See especially Marx 1843e; Marx 1843f; Marx 1844k; Marx 1844l.

40. Marx 1844a, p. 212; Marx 1844b, p. 446. Marx would continue this line in other works. See Marx 1844g, pp. 325–6; Marx 1844h, pp. 565–7; Marx 1857–8a, pp. 154, 164, 257; Marx 1857–8c, pp. 148, 158, 250; Marx 1857–8b, pp. 216; Marx 1859a, p. 359; Marx 1867a, pp. 142–3; Marx 1867b, pp. 146–7.

> mist-enveloped regions of the religious world. In that world the productions of the human brain appear as independent beings endowed with life, and entering into relation both with one another and the human race. So it is in the world of commodities with the product of men's hands. This I call the Fetishism which attaches itself to products of labour, so soon as they are produced as commodities, and which is therefore inseparable from the production of commodities.[41]

Initially, Marx assumes the position on fetishism with which he has worked until now: the fetish signals a transferral of attributes from human social relation to the fetish (now the commodity-form) and vice versa. In earlier texts, he has used this argument in relation to labour, alienation and money. The first sentence in the quotation makes the same point: the social relation between men assumes a fantastic form in the relation between things.[42] Into this pattern he has repeatedly drawn theological analogies, effectively subsuming and transforming the signifying relation central to theology. But now he faces at least two problems: is this transference real or illusory? And what does one do with the fetish transfer? The first question really asks how the fetish transfer takes place, while the second asks the political question as to how we might respond.

An initial response to the question concerning illusion and reality would argue that we suffer from a mistaken belief that the products of labour, like the fetish, gain such powers. In this case the political response is straightforward: all one need do is indicate why those beliefs are mistaken, show what the object really is – a product made by human hands – and the task is done. At times Marx seems to take this line, sprinkling his text on the fetishism of commodities with phrases such as 'grotesque ideas', 'mystical character', 'mysterious thing', 'fantastic form', 'mist-enveloped', 'abstraction', 'social hieroglyphic', 'incarnation of abstract human labour', 'magic and necromancy', 'mystical veil', 'unsubstantial

41. Marx 1867a, p. 83; Marx 1867b, pp. 86–7. In an otherwise provocative study of the theology of money, Goodchild, for some unaccountable reason, does not pursue the theological question of fetishism. He quotes this and other passages from the crucial section on commodity fetishism in *Capital* and yet is content to describe fetishism as the 'exotic other' – all of which is relegated to the endnotes. See Goodchild 2009, p. 264, n. 21; p. 271, n. 34. Similarly, in an earlier and longer discussion of Marx and the commodity form, in the apocalyptic *Capitalism as Religion*, fetishism receives barely a mention. See Goodchild 2002, pp. 80–7.

42. Or more fully, this transferral is a 'mysterious thing, simply because the social character of men's labour appears to them as an objective character stamped upon the product of that labour; because the relation of the producers to the sum total of their own labour is presented to them as a social relation, existing not between themselves, but between the products of their labour' (Marx 1867a, pp. 82–3; Marx 1867b, p. 86. See also Marx 1861–3, p. 450).

ghost', 'superstition' and 'illusions'. Commodification has become a gnostic, unreal appearance of what is actually going on.[43]

The problem with this argument is obvious, for it would make commodities, labour, money, exploitation, suffering, indeed capitalism as a whole, a grand delusion. One puff and it dissipates on the wind. Is Marx then misguided in his use of the idea of fetishism, especially in light of its religious ties? Some would suggest so, for they argue that the understanding of how powers are transferred to the fetish is illusory, a product of the imagination, but those gained by the commodity are real.[44] What Marx was really doing was to show that the perception of how those attributes are passed over to commodities is mistaken; he sets out to correct the mistake. Marx would have done better – so the argument goes – to have used an analogy other than fetishism. Politically, the option now is to dispense with religious trifles and focus on the real issue at hand: human exploitation through capitalism.

This criticism has a point, but Marx's comments begin to make more sense if we keep in mind what I have called the idol link and the fetish transfer. He seems to slip too easily between them, creating apparent confusion. So, in order to illustrate the fetish transfer, he moves to the mist-enveloped regions of the religious world, where the human brain creates beings which interact with one another and with human beings. But this analogy actually operates in terms of the idol link, which seeks to break the signifying connection between the gods and human products. However, Marx has fused the two, I would suggest, since he wants to set up a nocturnal border-crossing from idol link to fetish transfer. He may have little time for the reality of the religious products made by human beings, but what interests him is the form of the idol transfer, namely the way those products – the gods – gain powers at the expense of human beings. Similarly, at the level of the fetish transfer, an exchange of properties takes place: human beings belittle themselves while the products of their hands increase. At this level the products are perfectly real, as are the powers they gain. In short, the form of the interaction at each level is what interests Marx, even though the products of human minds (the gods) are illusory while those of human hands (commodities) are quite real.

But how exactly does the transfer take place between fetish and human beings? Let me put it this way: Marx may well argue that workers, processes of material production, social relations and the product made are real; indeed, he argues that the powers transferred and thereby gained by the product are also real and materially grounded, which then means that the effects on human beings – exploitation, suffering, ruined bodies – are equally real. But what of

43. So argues Ward 2005, pp. 333–4.
44. See the widely quoted observation of Geras 1983, p. 165.

the perceptions of this process held by workers? Are they illusory? Are those who labour deluded? No, for the transferral of powers between commodities and human beings appear to those producers as 'what they really are, material relations between persons and social relations between things'.[45] They know perfectly well, especially in their bodies, what is going on. And yet their perception of how this process works is illusory and mystified: commodities do not have this power in themselves, for it comes from the labour-power of those who produce commodities. It is both/and and not either/or. Marx works overtime, pushing at the edge of language, to explain what is going on. For instance, the qualities of the products of labour 'are at the same time *perceptible and imperceptible* by the senses'.[46] Once again: although one may reveal the process of transferral and thereby show how value appears in the product of labour, that value appears 'just as real and final, as the fact that, after the discovery by science of the component gases of air, the atmosphere itself remained unaltered'.[47] In order to get through what he is trying to argue, Marx formulates a curious phrase to express this dual character of social relations and the transferred relations between commodities: 'socially valid as well as *objective thought forms* [*gesellschaftlich gültige, also objektive Gedankenformen*]'.[48] And this applies to the theories of bourgeois economists! In other words, the process of transferral is a thought-form that has become objective, utterly real. The commodity-form and the value of abstracted labour it attracts are both products of thought *and* objective, imaginary *and* real, mysterious *and* concrete. This is how the fetish transfer happens.

What, then, of the political response? Here I must move beyond Marx and anticipate my discussion of Adorno below. Recall once again my distinction between the idol link and the fetish transfer as well as the porous borders between them, for a political response also emerges in their interaction. In the same way that the critique of idolatry (as embodied, for example, in Feuerbach's argument) snaps the signifying connection between idol and god, so also does the critique of the fetish take an axe to the transferring relation between fetish and human beings. Marx may have sought to describe this fetish transfer, but that is merely the first step, for he wants to destroy the transfer itself and thereby free human beings from their enslavement to the fetish.

In this light, let me turn finally to Marx's wider observations on the fetishism of capitalism, where the fetish transfer is extended to the whole of capitalism.

45. Marx 1867a, p. 84; Marx 1867b, p. 87.
46. Marx 1867a, p. 83; Marx 1867b, p. 86; emphasis mine.
47. Marx 1867a, p. 85; Marx 1867b, p. 88.
48. Marx 1867b, p. 90; my translation and emphasis. The English translations try various formulations, such as 'forms of thought expressing with social validity' (Marx 1867a, p. 87) and 'forms of thought which are socially valid, and therefore objective' (Marx 1976, p. 169). My thanks to Jan Rehmann for this insight (personal communication).

Towards the close of the exceptional *Economic Manuscripts of 1861–63*, Marx deploys the same logic of transfer, but now we find a full list of the abstractions from the social process of labour: the capitalist as a personification of capital, the productive powers of capital, use-, exchange- and surplus-value, the application of the forces of nature and science, the products of labour in the form of machinery, wealth, the conversion of production relations into entities, interest, rent, wages and profit. All of them face the labourer as objective, alien realities that rule his life. In other words, capital as a whole has become both a multitude of fetishes and one massive conglomerate fetish, a power to which the worker is subject. All its components 'stand on their hind legs vis-à-vis the worker and confront him as capital'.[49] In this sense should we understand the comment that capital itself 'becomes a very mysterious being',[50] that it becomes the 'religion of everyday life [*diese Religion des Alltagslebens*]'.[51] Is this not what Marx wished to break, the fetish transfer that is so destructive of human beings? It may best be described as a form of political iconoclasm.

Time to sum up: fetish and idol carry on a covert liaison within Marx's multiple recastings of the fetish. From first encountering fetishism while reading material for his lost treatise on Christian art, Marx would use the idea in many ways: criticisms of wood (or indeed hare) theft laws and smug assertions concerning religious superiority; the development of his early theory of the alienation of labour; the identification of the mediatory role of money in social relations; and eventually in respect of commodities, value (use, exchange and surplus), wealth, profit, the capitalist – in short, every conceivable dimension of capitalism. At each moment a mystifying transfer takes place, in which the product, commodity-form or money relation gains mysterious properties while those human beings responsible for their production lose out and suffer. But the idol carries out a covert operation throughout Marx's different uses of the fetish. Much like a secret agent, the (biblical) idol disappears from the scene only to reappear in a different guise, as a subset of the fetish. Again and again, Marx's theological allusions hint at the hidden presence of the idol link, as do his invocations of Moloch, the god of the biblical Ammonites, his late notes on John Lubbock and his early study of the Book of Isaiah under Bruno Bauer. The main task of this secret agent was to provide the form of Marx's argument regarding

49. Marx 1861–3, pp. 457–8. See also the description of wealth as a fetish in Marx 1859a, p. 387.

50. Marx 1861–3, p. 459.

51. Marx 1894a, p. 817; Marx 1894b, p. 838. Apart from Walter Benjamin's oft-noted fragment, 'Capitalism as Religion' (Benjamin 1996, pp. 288–91), the theme has been developed in a very different direction from that of liberation theology or Marxism by a group of what may be called 'economic theologians' such as Cobb 1999, Meeks 1989, Loy 1996 and especially Goodchild 2002.

the fetish transfer: in the same way that the gods produced by the human imagination draw their powers from human beings, so also do the products of human labour within capitalism gain power at the expense of those human beings. As he made this argument, Marx developed the dialectical idea of the 'objective thought-form' in an effort to describe how the transfer took place, but it also led him to what I called political iconoclasm. Just as the critique of fetishism seeks to break the signifying link between idol and god, so also does the critique of fetishism aim to smash the transfer between fetish and human beings.

On graven images: from liberation theology to Theodor Adorno

This fusion of the idol link and the fetish transfer was to have significant repercussions well beyond its operation in Marx's texts, showing up particularly in two inheritors of Marx's critique: Latin American liberation theology and Theodor Adorno. For the liberation theologians, Marx's breakthrough in regard to fetishism became an extension of the critique of idolatry. So they appropriated that breakthrough within a theological framework and argued that the various elements of capitalism too are idols which demand service, blood and sacrifice. In other words, they drew the fetish transfer back into the idol link, a move that is regressive, for it retreats from Marx's insight rather than taking it further. By contrast, Adorno picks up from where Marx left off, and by means of the *Bilderverbot* develops the fusion of the idol link and the fetish transfer much, much further.

In order to situate both contributions, let us recall my earlier comments on the polemic against idolatry found in texts such as Isaiah 44. The polemicist in question is not so much a conqueror of the neighbouring tribe, scoffing at the god of the vanquished for he or she was little use in the battlefield or in successful seduction, but is more likely to be either a monotheist or atheist (the two share more ground than they care to admit).[52] Both may in fact say that the piece of wood or stone or metal points to nothing, for no god exists. And so all the idolater does is worship some inanimate or perhaps animate object. However, the monotheist and atheist do of course differ on one point, for the monotheist argues that all gods apart from one's own are unreal delusions, while the atheist points out that the monotheist's claim falls under the same logic. Thus the atheist observes that the monotheist must be consistent: if you are going to break the signifying link of all others, then you must carry that logic through to your own religion. Those images in your church, the crucifix on the altar, the

52. It is of course quite possible for a polytheist to make this argument as well, selecting one or two gods out of a larger collection for the argument that follows. But it is a more difficult position to hold, for the polytheist by definition recognises a multiplicity of gods.

Bible you read, or indeed the belief that Christ is God's presence on earth, are all forms of idolatry. You set up a signifying link between them and your God, whether Bible or Christ as revelation, icon or crucifix as symbols of your God, or even the word 'God' or 'Yahweh' itself. But your God does not exist, cannot be experienced or verified, heard or encountered in any real sense, so you too are an idolater, worshipping a text, human being or nicely polished object. You are, the atheist goes on, no better than the teenager who lovingly polishes his first car and spends all his money on it, or those who look up to flawed leaders to bring them victory and the promised land.

The fallback position for the monotheist, especially in Judaism, Christianity or Islam, is iconoclasm – or rather (since iconoclasm assumes an existing image to be smashed) a ban on images in the first place. For this reason, the mythical second commandment (for it comes from a political myth)[53] is so powerful: one is not permitted to make any image whatsoever, not of anything on the earth, in the seas, or in the heavens. Without such a representation, there is no hook-up for the signifying link, no possibility to set up a connection between earthly object and super-human being. Instead, one must direct one's attention to God alone. And without a signifying link it becomes impossible to break such a link. One can hardly pull out the chain-cutters to sever a chain that does not exist. So, responds the monotheist, your argument has no bite; I am not an idolater.

Of course, the monotheist would have to admit that there have been more than a few slip-ups in the ban of images. Witness the synagogue with its symbols – menorah or Star of David – or the church with its crucifixes, stained-glass windows and iconography. And one cannot escape the reliance on holy scriptures, which are felt to varying degrees to be the revelation of God or – at a minimal level – the written experiences of those human beings who have experienced God. The histories of Judaism, Christianity and Islam are overflowing with moments when people became enamoured with an earthly representation of God, but the monotheist could respond in a way that is consistent with the critique of idolatry: these are examples of disobeying the command against graven images, which is an exceedingly difficult command to follow consistently.

Liberation theology

At this point I would like to introduce the liberation theologian, especially the Latin American variety,[54] who lays a strong claim to being the monotheist in

53. Boer 2009d.

54. The specificity is important, for too often Latin American liberation theology is assumed to be the only form of liberation theology, thereby neglecting feminist, black and queer liberation theologies which arose independently and at the same time – out

this little dialogue. Up until now the default position for the monotheist was the Hebrew prophet – like the one we encountered in the text from Isaiah. But a liberation theologian or two fit the position equally well. A long line, I must admit, stretches from Hebrew prophet to liberation theologian, but it is a line both inspired by those biblical texts and supported along the way by the odd compiler and editor of the Bible (who had such a strong hand shaping the ideological framework of the text that has come down to us) and the occasional reformer out to shake up a corrupt and otiose church. But let us tarry with the liberation theologians for a while, and see how they develop the position of the monotheist.

Latin American liberation theologians deploy two variations of the critique of idolatry, one that may be called the ontological reserve and another that is an appropriation of Marx's development of the idea of fetishism. The basic move of the ontological reserve is the precept that a Christian should not identify completely with any political movement, position or person. To do so would involve going to the theological toolshed and constructing one's own idols, and thereby having other gods besides God. An old theological strategy, this ontological reserve is deployed by the Latin American liberation theologians in an unexpected fashion, for they direct it at Marxism. How so? These theologians made a name for themselves by dipping into the Marxist toolbox in order to analyse what was and is going on in Latin America. Seeing that the various economic fashions – colonialism and the supply of raw materials for Europe, independence and the desire to emulate the United States, and development policies in which Latin America seeks to catch up with overdeveloped economies – had landed Latin America in ever-worse economic predicaments, the liberation theologians made use of Marxist analysis. They sought to understand why Latin America remained in a state of economic dependency, why a small and powerful elite held most of the wealth, why the beggars and street children grew in number, why trade union leaders were imprisoned or simply disappeared, why even the most basic welfare was a pipe dream, and why the Roman Catholic Church said and did nothing about it, being all-too comfortable in the warm bed of the big capitalists.[55]

It was all relatively straightforward economic analysis, but it was a shock for the Roman Catholic hierarchy and their intimate friends in the ruling class to have theologians, religious orders and priests criticising them in the name of Marx. It did not help matters that Marxist rebel organisations were quite

of the turmoil of the 1960s. For a detailed engagement with liberation theology on these issues, see Boer 2011a, pp. 170–98.

55. Gutiérrez 2001, pp. 106–10. In his extensive notes, Gutiérrez refers almost exclusively to Spanish and Portuguese texts from Latin America.

active across Latin America. It seemed that the liberation theologians had sided with these enemies of society and the state. Partly due to pressure from the hierarchy – accustomed to stressing the great evils of extra-marital sex and contraception – and partly due to the theological tradition (so important to Roman Catholicism), liberation theologians kept Marxism at arm's length.[56] Theologians such as Gustavo Gutiérrez, Leonardo and Clodovis Boff, Rubem Alves, Juan-Luis Segundo and others made use of what are really rather mild forms of Marxist analysis in order to interpret the economic and social situation of Latin America, especially in solidarity with the poor. But they abruptly cut Marx off when offering a solution. They might use terms such as 'liberation' and 'revolution', but they understood the terms primarily in a theological sense. In short, some liberation theologians offered a critical assessment of capitalist economics, often using the tools of Marxist analysis, but they reserved the central matters of being and salvation for God alone. The reason: to identify with Marx, or any rebel group or leader, or indeed the poor (who replaced the working class as a focus of analysis and action), would betray the ontological reserve, replacing God with an idol as the only agent of salvation.

In sum, most liberation theologians have been and continue to be solidly focused on what I have called the idol link, although now formulated in terms of an ontological reserve. They are faithful to the critique of idolatry, in which the idol link is snapped and the object made signifies not a god but merely itself. And they are faithful to the ban on images from the second commandment, wishing to ensure that no signifying link between God and any image is established in the first place, so that it may not be subsequently broken and fall to the logic of the critique of idolatry. In other words, the ontological reserve ends up quarantining God and theology from the critique of idolatry. All of which has two ramifications. First, no approach to salvation, whether capitalist or Marxist, should substitute for a Christian one. Second, since the idol link is the primary category with which they work, their framework is resolutely theological.

This theological orientation has a profound and limiting effect on their engagement with Marx's critique of fetishism. That engagement has the potential to be immensely fruitful, but it remains hobbled by prioritising the idol link at the expense of the fetish transfer. These theologians, as well those involved in the Marxist-Christian dialogue of the 1960s and 1970s, made a direct, albeit sometimes superficial, connection between Marx's use of fetishism and the traditional

56. See especially Kee 1990, who argues that liberation theology mistakenly preserves its own theology as a no-go zone for Marxist analysis. Turner 1999 agrees, although he wants to see a more sustained engagement with Marx's atheism via the mystifications of apophatic theology.

critique of idolatry.[57] They read Marx's critique of fetishism as an extension of the polemic against idolatry, which they now appropriated within a theological framework. So idolatry is not restricted to the false gods of other religions, or to the materialism of modern life, but it also applies to the elements of capitalism: its many parts, such as the foreign debt, gross domestic product, current account balance and growth, are all parts of a destructive cult that worships these idols as gods. And the economic theories that explain, justify and support these idols are false theologies which demand endless sacrifices. In short, like the idols of the Hebrew Bible, they are false gods that demand blood and destroy their worshippers.

I cannot deny that this revitalisation of theology via Marx's idea of fetishism constitutes a significant step forward in developing a theological critique of capitalism. Nonetheless, it falls short of the mark in one important respect: they read fetishism as an extension of idolatry into new areas of analysis – capitalism and its attendant theories and justifications – without noticing what has happened within the complex development of Marx's own thought. A major reason is the tendency to focus on Marx's comments concerning commodity fetishism in *Capital*, without realising that this is one moment in a much longer history of Marx's appropriation and reshaping of the idea. However, when we do consider that longer view, it becomes clear that Marx, as I argued earlier, subsumed theology and made it a subset of fetishism (in fact, he followed De Brosses in this regard). From that position theology acted as a secret agent, or to shift the metaphor, as leaven for what was really a new argument. He dispensed with what I have called the idol link and directed his attention to the fetish transfer: the signifying link between idol and God – characteristic of the critique of idolatry – went by the way while Marx focused instead on another relationship, namely, that between fetish and human being. Liberation theologians remain caught in the first relation, assuming that Marx's fetish transfer easily applies to the idol link, indeed that the idol link is primary and the fetish transfer a subsidiary that can easily enhance the idol link. In the end, this is a regressive step, for it fails to make use of Marx's breakthrough. Marx appropriated the formal nature of the idol link in order to explain how the fetish transfer works – a transfer of powers between human beings and commodity fetishes – and he thereby developed a political iconoclasm.

---

57. Hinkelammert 1986, especially pp. 5–42; Sobrino 2004a, pp. 57, 146, 165–7; Sobrino 2004b, pp. 59, 99; Dussel 1993; Dussel 2001, pp. 298–9; Sung 2007; Assmann and Hinkelammert 1989; Scott 1994, pp. 75–109; Löwy 1996, pp. 56–7; Evans 1984, pp. 146–8; Lischer 1973, pp. 554–5; Suda 1978; Thiemann 1985. See more recently Ward 2005, pp. 333–4.

Adorno: barricading the fetish transfer

By contrast, Adorno takes Marx's insight much further, picking up the covert operation between the idol link and fetish transfer and developing a distinct philosophical motif – the *Bilderverbot* – that runs throughout his work. We see it in the effort to produce a non-conceptual philosophy, or rather unlocking the non-conceptual through the conceptual; his central category of the non-identical; his refusal to speculate upon or represent utopia; his (appropriately) incomplete attempt at an aesthetic theory; the search for the possibility of resistance through modern music; his thoughts on the personality cult and secularised theology; as well as his sense that the student revolutions of the sixties were futile. In brief, his achievement was to extend the blockage of the signifying connection, characteristic of the idol link and embodied in the ban on images, to the fetish transfer between human beings and the various elements of capitalism.[58]

However, in order to situate Adorno's argument, let us return to the dialogue between our monotheist and atheist on the matter of idolatry. If the liberation theologians take sides with the monotheist, we might expect that Adorno would speak for the atheist who hoists the monotheist on his own petard. Not quite, for Adorno actually offers a dialectical move in which the critique of idolatry and Marx's fetish transfer rise to a completely new level, although Adorno does take the cue from Marx's own opening up of connections between the two. Adorno stretches and reshapes the critique of idolatry, not as the liberation theologians do by seeing the fetish transfer merely as an extension of the idol link, but by transforming the critique of fetishism by means of a bold appropriation of the ban on images from the critique of idolatry. He does so by applying the ban on images not to the idol link but to the transfer of powers characteristic of fetishism. In short, Adorno takes Marx's latent political iconoclasm to a new level.

To see how he does so, I need to backtrack a little and retell the story of those Portuguese who first began using *fetisso* to describe the West-African amulets and objects that were crucial for social exchange. The Portuguese may have felt that the term 'idol' was unsuitable, for here, among the Africans, there was no elaborate cult, priesthood, tradition of falsehood and wilful heresy. The catch here is that the underlying logic of the criticism of idolatry (especially the biblical version I outlined earlier) applied, in the minds of the Portuguese, to the fetish too: the Africans may think that these items enable supernatural power, that a spirit or two works through them to help one's crops, improve relations with those dreadful, warmongering neighbours and enhance the chances of

58. For example: 'It is the fact that the prohibition on graven images [*das Bilderverbot*] that occupies a position of central importance in the religions that believe in salvation, that this prohibition extends into the ideas and the most sublime ramifications of thought' (Adorno 2008, p. 26; Adorno 2007, p. 46).

getting laid, but they are mistaken. There is no signifying link, argue the Portuguese, to anything beyond the fetish; they simply believe there is, that the pieces of bone, wood or stone around their necks, or indeed the strange pieces of food they eat, have some magical power. They are merely bone, wood, stone or some indescribable part of an animal. For the Portuguese, the Africans are deluded, for they do not understand what is really going on. It is nothing less than a version of the critique of idolatry, although now thoroughly retooled – since the category of idolatry had become too encrusted with theological elaboration – in terms of the fetish.

The next step is to recognise that the fetishes do seem to have a power or two, but that such power is gained in a way different from what their makers and users believe. How, then, do the fetishes gain their power? In order to find an answer, I move beyond the Portuguese to the early theorists of the fetish and to Marx himself. That power comes, they argue, from a transfer between human beings and the objects made, in which human beings give up what is really their own and invest it in the fetish, which therefore becomes more powerful than human beings and indeed leads to the latter's belittlement. This argument becomes possible only on the assumption that there is no superhuman or spiritual being beyond the fetish, a being to which the fetish is connected. Indeed, the question itself – how do they gain their power? – arises precisely because that primary signifying link is broken; or rather, that it does not exist in the first place. In effect, one relation has replaced another. The idol link, initially applied to the fetish, has become the fetish transfer in Marx's sense: the signifying connection between fetish and spiritual being fades into the mist and in its place comes the transferring link between object produced and the human being who has made it. And yet the effect of that usurping connection is very real. The users of the fetish may not realise what is going on, but they act in a way that makes the powers of the fetish real enough. Social interaction is lubricated by the fetish; one will not do a deal without first invoking, touching, kissing or eating the fetish; a liaison will not happen without calling on the fetish; the very possibility of living at all in a social context relies on the fetish. In short, human beings have in effect divested themselves of their own social relations and granted them to the fetish. The transferral between fetish and human being is nothing less than an objective thought-form.

At this point Adorno returns, although he does so with the assumption of Georg Lukács's reification,[59] which may be read as a philosophically coherent elaboration of the fetish transfer in Marx's work achieved by combining it with Max Weber's notion of rationalisation. As the term implies, reification is the

59. Lukács 1988, pp. 83–110; see also Jameson 1991, pp. 95–6.

process by which living beings, thoughts, activities, relations and so on, become thing-like, especially when the 'thing' in question is the commodity. Conversely, that 'thing' acquires the properties which have so quickly been divested from those beings, thoughts, activities and relations.

Adorno's move is to pick up the biblical injunction against images from Exodus 20/Deuteronomy 5 and boldly slide it from the initial signifying link of the idol to the transferring connection between human being and object produced, from idol link to fetish transfer. The audacity of Adorno's move is comparable to Marx's initial effort to rework the idea of the fetish. In a way analogous to the barring of the passage from image to god, so also one blows up the bridge that connects the object produced and the human being who has produced it. In the same way that the ban on images removes any anchor for the signifying link between god and idol, so also does its application to the transferral of powers between product and human being chop off any foothold that such a transferral might gain. In Adorno's skilful hands, the ban on images becomes a way of preventing the fetish transfer from taking place in the first place. One difference between the targets of the two strategies does remain. The ban on images in the Bible is twofold, while its application to capitalist fetishism is singular: the former is designed to negate the possibility that the signifying link may be broken by preventing that link from being established in the first place, but the application to the fetish transfer of powers is more direct, for it simply seeks to prevent the transferring connection from taking place at all. However, even here the two strategies are analogous: one seeks to quarantine God from idolatry, while the other desperately wishes to protect human beings from the baleful effects of capitalist fetishisation.

Adorno sought a way to resist the persistent invasion of capitalism into the capillaries of everyday life. Its irrepressible ability to commodify every aspect of tangible and – increasingly – intangible reality and the seemingly inescapable reification that attends every act, thought and product means that any resistance had to be trenchant and radical. Adorno resolved not to allow even the smallest finger-hold for the reifying processes of capitalism. For as soon as one produced a concept, offered an image of a better world, or put one's trust in a leader, it (or he or she) would become reified and commercialised. Witness how in our day 'Ideology' or 'Politix' have become clothing labels, or the way Bob Dylan ended up doing car advertisements, or how Che's image made its way onto ice-cream labels and t-shirts for bourgeois teenagers. In other words, the ban on images became in Adorno's hands a grimly defended barricade against the persistent and permeating waves of capitalist commodification.

In order to understand this wielding of the ban on images – which is really a remoulding of the motif of fetishism – as a mode of resistance, we need to be aware of the context in which Adorno (and Horkheimer) worked. They voiced their opposition in terms of a profound dismay at the technological leaps of capitalism (if only they could have seen the cyber-technologies of today), the repressive state apparatuses of the police and the military and the lock-down of the Cold War, all of which produced a sense that capitalism had dug itself in and would not be dislodged. But at a deeper level they were caught in a double-bind. The first was the melancholy ambivalence over what Germany meant: Adorno hated the USA and his exile there during the Second World War, longing to return to Germany and to be able to express himself in German. Yet that return brought on a melancholy that came from the awareness of what had been perpetrated there in the very recent past. It would have been like the children of migrants, who inherit from their parents a profound ambivalence about home: the old country is far better than this primitive place to which we have emigrated, but then the old country is dreadful, since otherwise we would not have left in the first place. The second double-bind for Adorno was the cost of defeating fascism: it brought with it an unprecedented penetration (and I use the word deliberately) of American money and commercial practices into a now bankrupt and war-torn Europe. Was the cost worth it? Adorno was not so sure, since he espied the techniques of fascism within US-style commerce and propaganda.[60] It did not help matters that Stalin's ascendency in the East meant that hope had dissipated like fog before the burning sun. In the face of these onslaughts, Adorno resorted not to give the patterns of fetishism, commodification and reification any purchase within his philosophy.

I have sought to fill out the logic and background to Adorno's appropriation of the ban on images, but now let me briefly review a few of the instances when Adorno deploys the ban. One of the most controversial is his effort to produce a non-conceptual philosophy, the most significant manifestation of his effort to refuse philosophical systematising.[61] Over against the central role of concepts – ontology, immanence, transcendence, univocity, analogy, Dasein, truth, event and on and on – Adorno sought in his search for a negative dialectic to block the production of such concepts in the first place. He did not simply refuse to use concepts as such but sought to show how those concepts undermined themselves, turning them through an immanent method into a non-conceptual

---

60. See Adorno 2003b; Adorno 2003c; Adorno 2003n; Adorno 2009, pp. 469–76; Horkheimer and Adorno 2002, pp. 94–136; Horkheimer and Adorno 2003, pp. 144–96.

61. Apart from the extraordinary effort at working through such a non-conceptual approach in the formidable *Negative Dialectics* (Adorno 1973b; Adorno 2003k), see also his much more accessible comments in the lectures given at the time he writing this text: Adorno 2008, pp. 57, 62, 68–75, 94–5, 185–6; Adorno 2007, pp. 87, 95, 102–13, 139–40, 229–31. For reflection on philosophical systems, see Adorno 2008, pp. 22–43; Adorno 2007, pp. 40–54.

framework in which one never pins one's colours to one concept or another. An almost impossible process that produced a formidable mode of philosophising (in which each sentence is a discrete argument in itself so that one did not succumb to the pattern of logical argumentation),[62] its underlying drive is to prevent the possibility of any concept becoming reified and hijacking philosophy as it does so.

Another is the application of the ban to utopia. One must not, argues Adorno, spend months and years perfecting a blueprint of utopia, since that becomes an image, a fetish at the feet of which one lays all hope and expectation. It comes to replace utopia itself, standing in as an idol for what cannot yet be achieved. Or in the case of the personality cult, Adorno (and Horkheimer) argued that as soon as we recognise someone with charisma, who convinces us with stunning oratory or perhaps simple sayings of deep wisdom, who promises much if only we will trust him or her, we are lost. They do not merely mean that such leaders will disappoint, leading us to a mosquito-infested marsh or treacherous jungle to eke out a slave-like existence, or that they end up seducing the young boys and girls while owning a fleet of Rolls-Royces, or that the Swiss bank account will swell while we become penniless. Rather, they mean that the process of deification has already taken place, that the human being has become like God, an idol in whom we have invested our own powers and resources. That process, they suggest, has been enabled in a way not seen before by Christology: as Christ has become man and then returns to the heavens, human beings may now join him on the return journey, becoming deified in the process – or at least they become so in the eyes of their adorers. Being a god-human (according to traditional Christology) opens the door for others to reverse the equation and become a human-God.[63] In each case – non-conceptual philosophy, utopia and the personality cult – Adorno shows an extraordinarily rigorous adherence to the ban on images, to keeping the barricade in place to thwart the fetish transfer.

Conclusion

My argument in this chapter may be summarised in one sentence: by opening up the borders between the idol link and the fetish transfer, Marx (nocturnally) and then Adorno (in broad daylight) were able to move between the two and develop a political iconoclasm. By way of conclusion, I would like to ask but one question: is political iconoclasm really possible and viable? Recall the objections

62. Adorno's preference for micro-analysis (he notes his debts to Benjamin here) also plays a role in such sentences.

63. Horkheimer and Adorno 2002, pp. 145–7; Horkheimer and Adorno 2003, pp. 206–9. See Boer 2007a, pp. 433–5.

a little earlier from the atheist to the monotheist: no matter how rigorously one tries to follow an iconoclastic policy, some symbol, some image always bounces back. For example, churches in the north of the Netherlands, with their strong Calvinist heritage, may be bare of any stained-glass windows, images, crucifixes and symbols or ornamentation. Here, the effort to embody the second commandment is adhered to as rigorously as possible. The only focus in the church, with its bare, white walls, is the pulpit where the word of God is proclaimed. And yet pride of place is given to the Bible, read, interpreted, expounded, preached – one symbol that will not be erased. It is not for nothing that the Reformed heritage repeatedly suffers from what they call bibliolatry. It may be named as such, deliberated upon and sternly opposed, yet it keeps recurring. Or take the example of the Free Presbyterians in Scotland (a breakaway from the Church of Scotland), with their absence of musical instruments and any obvious formal liturgy. No prayers are read, no feasts of the Christian year are observed (not even Christmas and Easter), the Lord's Prayer is not recited. Everything in the service, often including the sermon, is expressed ex tempore, for only then does one communicate directly with God. Nothing that would even threaten to become an idol makes an appearance. Above all, anything that resembles a 'pattern' is shunned like the devil. And yet, the minister falls into regular turns of phrase in the sermon and in the prayers, the psalms take pride of place, and patterns establish themselves despite their best intentions.

On a different plane, Adorno, too, found the task of developing a non-conceptual philosophy exceedingly difficult. He was often challenged by his students and critics whenever it looked like he was using a concept. But he did not shy away from the issue, arguing that terms such as history and freedom turn out, when pushed hard enough, to undermine their status as concepts. The best instance of this process is of course the ban on images: it looks distinctly like a concept, applied across the various moments of his philosophy, and yet that concept is one that by definition blocks its own conceptual formation. But the task is difficult, for in the act of invoking concepts such as utopia, history, and even philosophy itself, Adorno risks the concept returning despite his best efforts at the barricades.

So how are we to view political iconoclasm? (I must admit that I have deep sympathies with this approach, but that has much to do with my own Calvinist background.)[64] Two responses to that question are possible. First, if we historicise, then the political and economic conditions of different moments of iconoclasm go some way to making sense of those moments. Thus, the iconoclasm of Dutch Calvinism had much to do with resistance to the Spanish and their lurid

64. See my effort to come to terms with that background in Boer 2009c.

Roman Catholicism, imposed with an iron fist on Belgium and the Southern Netherlands. Iconoclasm in worship was an act of defiance. And in Scotland, the fierce opposition to any pattern or liturgy in worship was a mark of resistance to the British colonial presence. Part of that colonial effort was the imposition of the Church of England, with its ambiguous relationship to its Catholic past, full of ornamentation, vestments and heavy reliance on the Christian calendar. In other words, the refusal of the idol link was also deeply political. In an analogous fashion, political iconoclasm may then be understood as a response to the pervasive fetish transfer of capitalism, a resolute stand that seeks to block the process of transfer itself. In other words, political iconoclasm will always be contingent, limited and piecemeal. Its ad hoc appearance in a given situation will inevitably be a temporary affair, needing to be pulled down and reconstructed elsewhere.

But this historicist response takes us only part of the way. So the second answer returns, surprisingly, to Roland Barthes.[65] As we saw in my treatment of political myth (Chapter Three), his effort to resist the baleful bourgeois mythologising of everyday life took the form of constructing a purely denotative world in which there was no signifying handhold which myth might grasp and thereby begin its work. However, when Barthes comes to construct such a world, especially in his extraordinary *Empire of Signs*, it is nothing other than a utopian myth.[66] In Barthes's case that myth is an imaginary Japan, where there is no master signifier, no leftover between word and object designated; in short, an iconoclastic utopia. That is to say, the possibility of a complete and thorough political iconoclasm remains, for now at least, a utopian project. For Adorno, of course, that utopia falls under the ban itself, except that now we can read this utopian iconoclasm dialectically: in the very act of invoking the ban on the fetish transfer in relation to utopia, in the process of barricading the possibility of utopia in which the fetish transfer functions no more, we open up the possibility of precisely such an iconoclastic utopia.

65. See further Boer 2011a, pp. 201–29.
66. Barthes 1982; Barthes 2002h.

Conclusion
On Secularism, Transcendence and Death

> The question about the elimination death is indeed the crucial point.[1]

I have followed a winding path, seeking to collect the various ideas and insights I had garnered in my engagements through the other four volumes of *The Criticism of Heaven and Earth* and to link them together in a reasonably coherent argument. In that respect the whole book has been an extended conclusion to the series. And as is the wont of conclusions, I found myself backtracking, summarising and reworking the most important of those various ideas and insights. In doing so, I became aware of how the destination (conventionally known as an 'aim') for this series has changed in the last decade of labour. Actually, the first idea of what I might do came to me in 1992. I was sitting in a small room out the back of a laundry in an old house in the country town of Armidale in Australia. Pondering my small collection of Marxist authors, I had become intrigued by the occasional references to the Bible and theology in their work. What would it be like, I wondered, to explore those references more systematically? I had no idea what that would entail and the idea simmered away for some seven years until I formulated it a little more clearly. At that time the aim was modest: to offer a critical commentary on the engagements by some of the leading Marxists with the Bible and theology. I would explore, assess and critique those interactions,

1. Bloch and Adorno 1988, p. 8; Bloch and Adorno 1975, p. 65.

but I would also see whether the allure of theology had implications for the wider thought of each critic, especially – as I soon found – since those theological engagements were often ignored by critics.

As the first book, *Criticism of Heaven*, grew in the writing (it was originally almost 300,000 words long, only to be 'trimmed' for publication), the scope of the project grew in my imagination. It became clear that, in order to do a reasonably proper job, I had more books to write. As the plan grew, other destinations emerged. One destination was to seek out new ideas and insights, which could be gathered and developed beyond the authors in question. So I began to identify possibilities and promising ideas, collating them in conclusions to earlier books in the series, awaiting a chance to elaborate upon them. Some were more obvious, such as the perennially important question of theism and atheism, especially via Marx and Engels, or the matter of economic history (Marx and Engels, Kautsky, Ste. Croix, Deleuze and Guattari). But others were far less expected, such as the importance of myth, its discernment, necessity and political promise, including the myth of Christian communism (Bloch, Althusser, Badiou, Deleuze and Guattari, even Barthes and Jameson), or the extraordinary importance of the political ambivalence of Christianity (Luxemburg, Kautsky, Thompson, Althusser, Ste. Croix, Horkheimer, Löwy, Eagleton, Negri, and, of course, Marx and Engels), or the question of fetishism in relation to idolatry (via Marx and Adorno). These are, of course, the topics of five of the seven chapters in this book.

What of the other two chapters, on kairós and ethics? These are the clearest indicators that I have sought to go beyond a mere summary, beyond cataloguing positions on major questions for an engagement of Marxism with theology. Thus, under kairós I initially gathered the contributions of Bloch, Benjamin, Badiou, Žižek, Jameson and Negri, only to turn the word on its head, seek out its moral, social and economic associations and thereby propose an akairological position, with a little unwitting help from Negri's distinction between measure and immeasure. Here, too, I explored the potential for a political reading of the Christian doctrine of grace. And with my discussion of ethics I pursued a similar approach, offering the possibility that ethics – as a means of care of the self or interacting with others as a way of greasing social relations – might be undermined by asking what would break the hold of custom and habit (*ethos* and *mos*). The result was an unethical and unmoral approach, ready to become comrades with the akairological. Some familiar names (at least from my earlier studies) appeared here, such as Eagleton, Badiou and Žižek, but so too did Foucault and Butler.

Were these two chapters the only real steps beyond a summary and catalogue of earlier insights? Not really, since in the other chapters I often read beyond and against the critics in question. Badiou and Jameson are not names that immediately come to mind concerning political myth, nor are those of Ste. Croix and Thompson on the political ambivalence of Christianity. And in other cases, I took my argument well beyond what I had found in the thought of others, such as the economic reconstruction of the context in which Christianity first arose, or the way the critique of idolatry and fetishism weave together in order to develop a political iconoclasm.

In other words, in this book I have gone well beyond the usual remit of conclusions; not so much a summary and wrapping-up as an opportunity to develop some ideas much further. As I did so, it became clear that I was really engaging in a dialectical exercise – a further destination along the long and winding path this project has taken me. Let me explain via a couple of metaphors. Instead of placing both feet firmly in the Marxist camp and seeking to deploy some old and well-oiled machinery for assessing religion, reprising tried and true arguments to adjudge what contribution, if any, theology might make to Marxism (Eagleton's approach), I preferred to have one foot in each camp. This situation opened up the possibility that Marxism and theology might have telling points to make against one another, either in criticism or by enhancing a contribution from the other. The other metaphor that I have used until now to describe this task is one of rubbing: Marxism and theology rub up against one another, both a sensual rubbing, one guaranteed to get the juices flowing, and a frictional one, since Marxism and theology have often been a fractious couple, arguing, disagreeing, separating for a while in mutual recrimination. In response to the earlier volumes, some have noticed what they felt to be a prevarication as to my own position, wanting me to indicate unequivocally where I stand in relation to Marxism and theology, to which audience I speak, offering a resolutely Marxist theory of religion or presenting a theological engagement with Marxism. Such a question misses the point, for what I have sought to do is open up an interaction in which neither Marxism nor theology remain the same – hence the metaphors of feet in camps and sensual-cum-fractious rubbing. Thus, if Marxism needs to be challenged from the perspective of theology, theology is not immune from facing a few unwelcome truths at the hands of some of Marxism's best minds. I think here of the viable place within theology of a protest atheism, or the need for Marxism seriously to consider the political myths it deploys, or the implications for understanding Christianity in light of its economic history, or the outcome for Marxism of Christianity's deep ambivalence between reaction and revolution, or the repercussions for both in terms of what I have argued in regard to fetishism/idolatry, kairós and ethics. What would an akairological, unethical and unmoral approach look like for Marxism and theology, along with a resolutely iconoclastic agenda, however utopian it might be? I hope to have given a few suggestions in the chapters that deal with those topics.

One destination remains and that is the possibility of revitalising the 'Marxism and religion' debate. I certainly did not begin with such a lofty aim when I began this book, let alone the series as a whole, and I am all-too aware of where it falls short. As I mentioned earlier, the project began – back with *Criticism of Heaven* – as a modest affair, as a critical commentary on some of the key Marxists who had written on the Bible and theology. I have remained true to that approach, at least until this book, since nothing surpasses careful exegesis. However, the project has also taken on a life of its own, so that it has grown into a comprehensive study of the rich and varied tradition of Marxist engagements with theology, even to the extent that I felt I could write a final book – this one – where I sought to outline some of my own responses to that tradition. In both respects, I hope that it may also contribute in some ways to a renewed and informed debate.

Secular and anti-secular

I would like to finish with three overlapping matters: secularism, transcendence and death. At first glance, Marxism is associated most clearly with the first, but transcendence and death? Are they not the business of theology rather than a very secular Marxism? In response, I will argue for three propositions: Marxism and theology are both secular *and* anti-secular programmes; transcendence means less the world above than a transgressive break out of this one; any body of thought and practice, especially Marxism, that ignores death does so at its own peril. Let me unpack these three propositions for a few moments.

Secular, secularism, secularisation: the terms conjure up immediate associations while they are also among the most contested in current debates.[2] As for the associations, they become the opposite of religion. A secular approach is one that does not use religious or theological categories. For example, a secular state is one that is not founded on religious principles and does not favour one religion over against others; indeed, in a tired old phrase, it marks the separation of church and state. Secularism is therefore the position taken in which religion does not figure at all, so much so that one will avoid terms such as 'belief', oppose the influence of church, synagogue, mosque or temple, and generally find that religion is a form of primitive superstition that human beings should have left behind when they first showed a modicum of civilisation. And secularisation is the long, rocky, hard-fought struggle to rid the world of religion; or rather, it is the gradual process, lamented or celebrated, in which society has gradually

2. Representative texts out of the flood of debate include Martin 1978; Bruce 2002; Beckford 2003; Swatos and Olson 2000; Berger, Davie and Fokas 2008; C. Taylor 2007; Asad 2003.

dismantled the theological framework of the world and replaced it with non-theological content.

This opposition between religion and secularism is also the foundation upon which some of the most influential of recent studies have based their counter-arguments. For example, Talal Asad argues that secularism is really another way for the state, especially in Muslim-majority states, to control religion, while Charles Taylor proposes that far from being an anti-religious move, the many strains of secularism are merely other ways of being religious.[3] In other words, secularism is not anti-religious or indeed the opposite of religion. To suggest so is a mismatch of terms, if not an outright obfuscation. However, we can go much further than either Asad or Taylor, although once again it requires some alternative etymology, a digging-out of repressed possibilities within the terms themselves in a way that undermines accepted meanings. It is instructive to revisit the man who invented the word 'secularism'. George Holyoake (1817–1906), nineteenth-century activist and occasional jailbird (for blasphemy), decided to draw upon the Latin word *saeculum* (the noun) and *saecularis* (the adjective) in order to define secularism. For Holyoake, the secular concerns issues that 'can be tested by the experience *of this life*'.[4] Holyoake was no fool, for the Latin term designates this generation, this age and this world. In other words, secularism takes its terms and principles for life from this world and this age, and not any world above or world to come.

Since then, of course, the term has been used – and at times restricted to – an opposition to religion, thereby becoming synonymous with atheism, the separation of church and state, the distinction between religious law and secular law, and the separation between theology and other disciplines. I have argued in detail elsewhere that each of these senses is a derivative and secondary meaning of secularism and that each of them faces significant contradictions.[5] For example, the opposition to religion and elision with atheism faces the problem of religious secularists, as well as Holyoake's own argument (in contrast to Charles Bradlaugh, leader of the Secular Society in Sheffield) that secularism should be indifferent to religion, since it is a side-issue. And crowding in amongst the religious

3. Asad 2003; C. Taylor 2007.

4. Holyoake 1896, p. 36; emphasis mine. Or more fully, 'Secularism is a form of opinion which concerns itself only with questions the issues of which can be tested by the experience of this life' (Holyoake 1896, p. 60). In *Principles of Secularism* he writes: 'Secularism is that which seeks the development of the physical, moral, and intellectual nature of man to the highest possible point, as the immediate duty of life – which inculcates the practical sufficiency of natural morality apart from Atheism, Theism or the Bible – which selects as its methods of procedure the promotion of human improvement by material means, and proposes these positive agreements as the common bond of union, to all who would regulate life by reason and ennoble it by service' (Holyoake 1860, p. 17).

5. Boer 2007b; Boer 2009a.

he included atheism: atheism, religion and the Bible were simply non-issues for secularists, who should be concerned for human flourishing in this life.

As another example, the separation of church and state – taken by the various secularist societies as the basic meaning of secularism – must deal not only with the simple point that the more secular a state is, the more religious it becomes (witness the USA), but also with Marx's argument that a secular state is the logical outcome of the Christian state. For Marx, the contradictions inherent within the idea and practice of a Christian state can only lead to its dissolution. Or rather, those contradictions lead to the simultaneous negation and realisation (Aufhebung) of Christianity.[6] However, as an effort to resolve the contradiction of the Christian state, the secular state – 'which relegates religion to a place among other elements of civil society [*der bürgerlichen Gesellschaft*]'[7] – is less a solution than another manifestation of those contradictions. It is not for nothing that Marx calls the secular state the fully-realised Christian state.

However, what I wish to stress here is that, in light of the definition of secularism I proposed earlier, anti-secularism becomes any approach, movement or mode of thought that looks towards and perhaps takes its terms from another world or age beyond this one. Theology is a more obvious candidate for this anti-secular stance, for it refers both to the heavens 'above' and the world to come. The problem, as I will argue more fully in my discussion of transcendence, is that theology has been largely banished to this anti-secular realm. It takes its marching orders, or so it seems, from God, who is definitely not of this world, and it looks to a new heaven and a new earth. This perception is a profound misreading of theology, which has been and remains concerned as much with this world as the next. The doctrinal concerns with creation, with human beings (the source of the term 'anthropology') and the human condition (harmatology, or the doctrine of sin), with history and society (ecclesiology) are distinctly this-worldly concerns. They clearly deal with this world and this age. Of course, theology is also concerned with the sense that this world is not as it should be and that – hopefully – something better awaits us. The upshot is that theology is both secular and anti-secular in its outlook.

What about Marxism? Surely it is a programme, political movement and formidable body of thought that is thoroughly secular? Human alienation, economic exploitation, class consciousness and class struggle, structures of the state, internal contradictions, patterns of opposition, revolutionary overthrow of a destructive social formation – all these and more concern this world and this age. And does not Marx, in that crucial fourth thesis on Feuerbach, decisively shift analysis from the clouds above and fix it squarely on this vale of tears in which we

6. Marx 1844i, pp. 156–8; Marx 1844j, pp. 357–9. See further Boer 2010a.
7. Marx 1844i, p. 156; Marx 1844j, p. 357.

live? No argument here, but I also suggest that Marxism has a strong anti-secular dimension to it as well. The premise of that argument is that Marxism is neither comfortable with the way things are nor does it seek a slight amelioration of the conditions of life; a tinker here, a nail hammered in there, a screw turned elsewhere. This world is thoroughly and deeply flawed, riven with systemic oppression. For that reason, it must be analysed, understood and overturned. By now the direction of my argument should be clear: since Marxism looks to a world beyond this one, an age to come that is qualitatively different, it also contains a deep anti-secular current. Marxism too is both secular and anti-secular.

Transgressive transcendence

All of which brings me to transcendence. Here I face an immense wall of opinion in which transcendence becomes either the oppressive bogey to be resisted at all costs or a category that will provide us with the answer to our problems. The framework within which transcendence must operate is known well enough: absolute versus contingent, a vertical relation versus a horizontal one (immanence), other-worldly versus this-worldly, anti-secular versus secular. In this light, we find that transcendence becomes an embattled term. Orthodox theologians (whether 'radical' or not) seek to recover a traditional theological doctrine of transcendence as an answer to our ills, or at least the shortcomings of materialism.[8] Phenomenologists of the 'theological turn' argue for an opening to transcendence within Heideggerian thought, neglecting to mention until late that they do so from a Roman Catholic perspective.[9] On the other side, materialist philosophers, from Spinoza through to Deleuze, Badiou and Negri, see transcendence as an oppressive category best opposed in the name of a liberating immanence.[10]

The beginning of resistance to this perception of transcendence may take two paths. One is to follow Horkheimer's 'totally other' of an authentic religion, one that resists any betrayal, compromise and identification with the state. This version of transcendence may give a religion such as Christianity a revolutionary

8. See, for example, Milbank 2005. See also Schwartz (ed.) 2004.

9. See Janicaud, Courtine, Chrétien, Henry, Marion and Ricœur 2000 and Schwartz (ed.) 2004.

10. In this company, the accusation of transcendence, or the ability to locate an inadvertent use of a transcendent category in a critic's thought, is felt to be a devastating criticism. Or, at least, it is taken as such if the critic in question operates within a radically immanent framework, or perhaps a Marxist or materialist one. For example, to accuse Deleuze of being a thinker of transcendence is really an accusation that all is not as it seems, that Deleuze has cheated us all these years – the argument, for instance, that Deleuze is a thinker of the One (Badiou 2000) or that he is ultimately a spiritual thinker of creation (Hallward 2006).

edge, which always lurks within Calvinism, for example. However, since I have discussed Horkheimer at length elsewhere,[11] here I follow another path, which begins by picking up an observation by Adorno: he says, in a corner I can no longer recall (but one that struck me forcefully when I read it, or was that my own thought bouncing off his?), that for some strange reason transcendence came to be associated with theology, while immanence became the stamping ground of history, society, economics and so forth. Marx is often, although not always, guilty of this assumption: theology as an other-worldly discipline has little to do with the this-worldly business of philosophy.[12] As should be obvious by now, I find this association wayward, but how did it come to be so?

Transcendence has had a rather unfortunate history in the dual homes of philosophy and theology, which themselves have often been separated only to reconcile for a time.[13] As a result of its chequered career – Plato's uncaused 'prime mover' (which must be outside the world), theology's appropriation of this same mover whom Plato and Aristotle called *o theos*, the fully transcendent God of speculative monotheism in which the object of divine thought can only be divine thought itself, the medieval transcendental concepts (such as *ens*, the existent, and the characteristics of unity, truth and goodness), Kant's transcendental as a new term to describe his attempt to determine the conditions of knowledge,[14] and 'the absolute' as a perennial topic in both philosophy and theology – transcendence has become a rather autocratic character. Along the way, it has attracted a host of less than desirable epithets such as domination, tyranny, the one, intolerance, sexism, homophobia, racism, speciesism, so much so that it is anti-human and anti-nature. By contrast, immanence has become the zone of equality and liberation, highly desirable over against the tyranny of transcendence.

---

11. Boer 2011a, pp. 11–56. For Horkheimer's conception of a 'totally other', see especially Horkheimer 1985p, as well as Horkheimer 1978, pp. 184–5; Horkheimer 1991a, p. 330; Horkheimer 1996, p. 50; Horkheimer 1985g, p. 186; Horkheimer 2006, pp. 116–17; Horkheimer 1985n, pp. 208–9; Horkheimer 1988j, pp. 510–11, 517; Horkheimer 1973, p. xxvi; Horkheimer 1985r, p. 431.

12. Marx 1842i; Marx 1842j.

13. How do philosophy and theology relate to one another? Are they in bed with one another or sworn enemies? It is far more interesting to ask why these positions are taken than seek some elusive truth on the matter. For instance, if one argues for the closest intimacy and attends conferences that assume their union as a given, then one is probably enamoured with Thomistic theology and its scholastic residue. On the other hand, if philosophy (Greek or otherwise) is a pagan pollution, then the chances are that Augustine is to be preferred to Aquinas and that Calvin and the Reformed tradition will feel familiar. I suspect the truth is somewhere in between, a narrative of fractious relations with occasional alliances against common foes or agreements to deal with shared issues, such as metaphysics and the absolute.

14. 'I call all cognition *transcendental* that is occupied not so much with objects, but rather with our *a priori* concepts of objects in general.' (Kant 1998, p. 133, A12.)

As a result, transcendence has had to make its home out on the street, a philosophical and political pariah, befriended by few. I would like to befriend transcendence, but not in the way it has been understood. As has been my practice on occasions, let me deploy some wayward etymology. The word 'transcendence' comes from the present participle *transcendens*, of the Latin verb *transcendo* (*trans* + *scando*), which means to climb or rise over. It is, if you like, a dead metaphor, a word whose original metaphoric function has been lost or deadened as it took on a life of its own. Not quite, since the spatial element of transcendence persists in another sense: climbing or rising over entails a spatial movement upwards and transcendence still invokes a vertical spatial movement. If something is transcendent, if it transcends something else, then it rises above that something: it is 'beyond', 'on high' or 'from above'.

Over against this austere sense of *transcendo*, another is far more heartwarming: it also means to pass over and then to violate or *transgress*. That is, within the semantic cluster of 'transcend' may be found the sense of 'transgress'. Still we find a spatial residue, for one passes over an obstacle – say, a river – by means of a device such as a bridge or a boat. One also passes over by neglecting or ignoring, such as an idea or a useful tool for a particular job. But I am most intrigued by the transgressive element of transcendence. As far as transgression is concerned, its contemporary usage is weighed down by a long history of theological abuse. At the fag-end of this tradition, transgression has a largely negative sense, where it designates the breaching of a norm, a custom or a law. Under theological pressure, transgression came to refer to human beings: it is what we do when rebelling and sinning against the one who occupies the transcendent realm, namely God. If God is transcendent, human beings transgress. Or rather, transgression is an affront to transcendence.

Thus far I have been concerned with the various meanings within the semantic cluster of *transcend*, one of which is transgression. What of the Latin *transgresso* itself, from which the English 'transgression' is derived? Here we find that the core idea of this term, *transgresso*, is to climb over, pass over or step across. It lends itself easily to notions of disobedience, rebellion and sin. But it is also rather close to *transcendo*, is it not? In sum, both terms, transcend and transgress, have closely overlapping semantic fields.

What is the outcome of this dip into etymology? Transcendence and transgression draw close to one another, bearing with them a distinct sense of the illegal, contraband and even criminal. Transcendence becomes less the authoritarian and oppressive word from above, the law one dare not disobey, the stern order that maintains the status quo. Instead, transcendence begins in this world and seeks to break out of, to step or pass over, in short, to transgress. The connection with the discussion of secular and anti-secular should be obvious: if anti-secular designates a focus on what is beyond this world and this age and if transcendence speaks of a transgressive crossing of the restrictions that keep us within this world, then transcendence becomes the way of realising the anti-secular element of both Marxism and theology.

Now I can add another term to my quiver of reworked terms that I have gathered from scattered places in this book: a transgressive transcendence joins ákairos, for what is untimely and out of place has also become distinctly transgressive; so too is transcendence unethical and unmoral, especially when ethical and moral (*ethos* and *mos*) designate what is customary and habitual; transcendence is also a-theistic, particularly in a protest sense, for when theism becomes the justification for a tyrannical status quo, we may transcend that situation in the name of protesting a-theism; and all of this becomes part of a political iconoclasm, in which we resist and seek to transgress/transcend the fetish transfer ubiquitous in our own situation. It is quite a collection: akairological, unethical, unmoral, a-theistic, iconoclastic, transgressive and transcendent.

Does Marxism too have its transcendent moment? Yes, but in a distinctly temporal and qualitative sense. It too involves a search for the way to climb over the boundary between our history and socialism, given that our own world and history is far from satisfactory. Indeed, does not Marxism seek the motor – the classic search for the ultimate contradiction that will bring a mode of production to its knees – of the end of this age and the emergence of the next? In this sense, I suggest we may speak of a temporal transcendence within Marxism.

Death

I finish, quite deliberately, with the question of death. It is partly because some of the leading Marxist figures alive today aver that they are interested in life, not death. Badiou has made it clear on more than one occasion that there is no point in talking about death, for he is interested only in life.[15] Negri, in all his enthusiasm and energy, is concerned with what may give life, in creative being, and not death.[16] Even Jameson is remarkably reticent to discuss the topic. By contrast, we need to remind ourselves of Adorno's comment that any Marxist approach fails if it does not deal adequately with death.[17] Indeed, in order to find some substantial reflections on death in the Marxist tradition, it is necessary to go back to Horkheimer, Adorno and Bloch.

15. Badiou 2002, pp. 35–9; Badiou 2003a, pp. 61–6; Badiou 2009, pp. 507–14; Badiou 2006b, pp. 529–37.
16. Negri and Casarino 2008, pp. 152–3, 155–6; Negri 2004, pp. 105–11.
17. Bloch and Adorno 1988, p. 8; Bloch and Adorno 1975, p. 65.

Their observations may be conveniently – and obviously – divided in terms of what happens before and after death. As we might expect, the former category is full to overflowing, while the latter enjoys a sparser collection of comments. Despite the significant overlap between Horkheimer and Adorno, especially in terms of the deleterious effects of capitalism, reified social relations and the pervasiveness of instrumental reason, they emphasise different aspects of the anticipation of death. For Adorno, the reification of death has at least two dialectically opposed outcomes. On the one hand, death has become a mechanical process of being snuffed out. Once the dignity of the individual is gone, each of us becomes replaceable, a stand-in ready to take our place. The degradation of human life leads to the degradation of death. Even the old, who die at the end of a full life, are no longer regarded as being full of sage advice, but become pathologised (gerontology!) and enter a second dependency. And so, in the very repression of a healthy approach to death, society itself has taken on the aura of death. The most telling example for Adorno is genocide, especially the mass murder of approximately six million Jews (as well as communists, gypsies and homosexuals) at the hands of the Nazis. In his work, Auschwitz becomes the keyword for genocide as such, leading him to argue that philosophy would never be the same after Auschwitz and that education must ensure that it never happens again. Indeed, the new categorical imperative is that human beings need to mobilise all their thoughts and acts to prevent anything similar from taking place in the future.[18] On the other hand, the dialectical outcome – on the other side of reification – of this technical banality of death is the cleavage between death and life, a casualty of the fragmentation of the unity of life. Death has become external and strange, outside the totality of life. It has become an incomprehensible interruption, an accident that comes in from outside. As a result, since death is now alien, it is a terrifying breach and one faces it with unaccountable panic.[19]

Although Horkheimer agrees to some extent, he differs in emphasis. They are both concerned with the repression of death, arguing that it equates to a forgetting of history,[20] with dire consequences for the nature of society: 'True humanity would repeat the rite according to which the life that seeks to forget death stands all the more certainly under its scourge'.[21] However, for Horkheimer the effect of that repression is an unfathomable terror that is conveniently blocked in whatever way possible. The frenzy of consumption and the absolute attachment

18. Adorno 1973b, pp. 361–8; Adorno 2003k, pp. 354–61; Adorno 1998a, pp. 89–103, 191–204; Adorno 2003h, pp. 573–94; Adorno 2003m, pp. 674–90; Adorno 1978, pp. 58–60, 165–6, 231–3; Adorno 2003d, pp. 65–7, 188–9, 264–6.

19. Adorno 1973b, pp. 368–73; Adorno 2003k, pp. 361–6; Adorno 2000b, pp. 106–7; Adorno 2006a, pp. 166–7.

20. Horkheimer and Adorno 2002, pp. 178–9; Horkheimer and Adorno 2003, pp. 245–7.

21. Horkheimer 1978, p. 211; Horkheimer 1991a, p. 374.

to the trash of industrial production are all part of the effort to deny the reality of death.[22] But Horkheimer also points out that death varies across different classes. For instance, the millionaire and the proletarian approach death in very different ways. The former, not having to worry about the wellbeing of dependents, is focused very much on his or her own condition and fate, while the latter knows that death will lead to hardship for her or his dependents.[23]

This emphasis on differing approaches to death actually stands in tension with the tendency by both Horkheimer and Adorno to make universal comments on death. At times, they stress that death itself varies not only within a particular age, but also over time and social context. Here the assumed narrative from precapitalist to capitalist societies plays a role, for the reification of death, with all its contradictions, is not as it has always been – death changes, but not always for the better. At other moments they begin to absolutise the experience of death. Adorno is particularly guilty here, arguing that death causes a rupture with which no-one is equipped to deal. It juts into life, generates futile efforts at metaphysics and threatens to be meaningless in any formulation since it is absolutely inaccessible. Here he is suspicious of older images of a meaningful and fulfilled death. For example, the biblical patriarch, sated with life and experience, who dies in peace, may express not so much the ideal of being reconciled to death as the longing for the relief from an intolerable burden.[24] This sense of absolute annulment is reinforced for Adorno in the death of an old, frail person: 'there is also something immeasurably sad in the fact that, with the decline of very old people, the hope of *non confundar*, of something which will be preserved from death, is also eroded, because, especially if one loves them, one becomes so aware of the decrepitude of that part of them which one would like to regard as the immortal that one can hardly imagine what is to be left over from such a poor, infirm creature who is no longer identical with itself'.[25]

What are we to make of the differing emphases and indeed tensions in the thought of Adorno and Horkheimer? Here Bloch offers a useful way through in what is perhaps one of the most honest and refreshing reflections on death from a Marxist.[26] He differentiates between the physical act of dying, which is really a part of life, and the state of death: 'the act of extinction is very different from the resultant state'.[27] The fear of dying is a far cry from the horror of death: while the former may generate an occasional apprehension, death as an ontological

22. Horkheimer 1978, pp. 210–11, 236; Horkheimer 1991a, pp. 373–4, 418–19.
23. Horkheimer 1978, pp. 38–9; Horkheimer 1987c, pp. 345–6.
24. Adorno 2000b, pp. 106, 130–4; Adorno 2006a, pp. 166, 202–10.
25. Adorno 2000b, p. 135; Adorno 2006a, p. 210.
26. Bloch 1972, pp. 255–63; Bloch 1968, pp. 335–44. These reflections are far better than those found in Bloch 2000, pp. 233–78; Bloch 1985b, pp. 291–346.
27. Bloch 1972, p. 255; Bloch 1968, p. 335.

status produces annihilating dread. The real issue is this second category, the horror of the complete pulverisation of any identity at death. Here Bloch finds plenty of room for his overriding concern with utopia, for in that context death is 'a highly inadequate end, generally breaking, only very rarely rounding off, the human life'.[28] It puts a damper on any effort to change the world, let alone the sense that any life is incomplete, that there was so much that could have been achieved.

That utopian element brings me to two final and pressing questions: what would an unalienated and dereified approach to death look like? And what can one say concerning what happens after death? In answer to the first question, Adorno and Horkheimer offer a few hints. Death would lose its bitterness and terror, becoming an inseparable element of life, a relativising of the life that removes the desperate clinging to life, indeed an enhancement of life, if not of death itself. The unity of a person's history includes both death and life even if that unity remains to be achieved rather than being lost in the past.[29]

In response to the second question, each has their own answer. Horkheimer professes an agnostic position: 'I don't know what comes *after* death, but what happens before it takes place in capitalist class society'.[30] Yet his tombstone has an edited text from Psalm 91:9: '*Denn du ewiger bist meine Zuversicht* [Because you, eternal one, are my confidence]'.[31] Even here Horkheimer equivocates, for the biblical text has been altered, removing *der Herr*, the Lord, and replacing it with *du ewiger*.[32] For his part, Adorno makes a valiant effort to deal constructively with death in an essay on Gustav Mahler, an essay that coincided with the death of his aunt, Agathe Calvelli-Adorno, who had lived with the family from the time Adorno was a child and to whom he had become much attached. But all he can do here is invoke the memory of the defenceless dead and suggest that love leads us to treat the dead as if they were children: 'uncomprehending love can only comprehend death as if the last farewell were that of children who will come home again' he writes; 'We can hope for the dead only as if for children'.[33] Of course, this is still the perspective of the living in relation to others who have died. What of ourselves? What happens then? Adorno, usually reticent to speak

28. Bloch 1972, p. 249; Bloch 1968, p. 329; see also the discussion in Bloch 2000, pp. 255–66; Bloch 1985b, pp. 318–31.

29. For Horkheimer, such a healthy approach to death would render euthanasia perfectly normal for the incurably ill and the doomed. Horkheimer 1978, pp. 230–1; Horkheimer 1991a, p. 410.

30. Horkheimer 1978, p. 39; Horkheimer 1987c, p. 346.

31. '*Denn der Herr ist deine Zuversicht*' from verse 9 ('Because the Lord is your confidence').

32. See the fuller discussion in Boer 2011a, pp. 14–15, 52–53, as well as Horkheimer's extended reflection on Psalm 91 in Horkheimer 2006; Horkheimer 1985n.

33. Adorno 2002b, pp. 612–13; Adorno 2003p, p. 236.

of what is beyond the experience of any human being, is pushed only when he engages in an extended discussion concerning utopia with Bloch.

However, let me lead into that discussion by returning to Bloch, for he is willing to go much further than either Horkheimer or Adorno. As I noted earlier, for Bloch even the sense of being unfulfilled, that there is something more to life than what we have experienced, becomes the signal of utopian longing for a fulfilled life. More importantly, he seeks a way to overcome the horror of the state of death. And his answer is that death should be viewed as a departure, the beginning of a journey, the destination of which is unknown and which can only be spoken of in mythical language.[34] Far more than a simple agnostic position, in which one avers that since no-one has experienced the other side of death and come back to inform us, it would be rash to make any statements, Bloch seeks to offer a utopian look to the *novum*. Death should not be the occasion for a regretful and longing retrospective of one's life, but rather an anticipation. What is on the other side, the destination of the journey? It is not a pre-fabricated place, postulated by the 'positive dogmatism' of Christian theology with its heaven and hell, or by the 'dogmatic negativity' of materialism, which asserts with equal confidence that death is an absolute end, with nothing to expect beyond the body's dissolution. Instead, the journey's destination remains an open question: 'the *status viae* lies far beyond death, which hardly represents an inflexibly formative *status termini*'.[35] The ones who dogmatically assert that they know have another, sinister agenda in the here and now.

Bloch wishes to do far more as he sets out on the journey, especially in terms of the 'life force [*Lebensmut*]' and of hunger, the former an irrepressible push out of dullness, oppression and any effort to close it down, the latter a desire for that which is better, a craving for his great category of the not-yet. But what is this life-force but the innate desire within each human being for a better world? Part of a wider agenda, the life-force is that within human life which has a potential beyond itself, a capability for a fuller realisation that is only partially fulfilled in an individual life. And what are its sources and signs? The ability to stand up straight, a moral independence, finality, understood as 'the courage to break free from this devil's guesthouse, this world',[36] and hope, especially the hope that does not disappear, that holds on in the worst of circumstances. For Bloch, human beings can come close to the realisation of their potential to which the life-force points only in a utopian, that is, a properly socialist environment, where the as-yet unimagined social and economic conditions will enable

34. See the tales recorded in Bloch's distinctive style in Bloch 2006, pp. 116–19, 171–3; Bloch 1985d, pp. 152–6, 218–20.
35. Bloch 2000, p. 265; Bloch 1985b, p. 330.
36. Bloch 1972, p. 252; Bloch 1968, p. 332.

a transformation of human beings themselves and thereby a transformation of death. In his perpetual tendency to dip into his theological storehouse, Bloch offers a materialist translation of resurrection and especially eternal life, which is not the dogmatic answer to death but the 'deep presence of something that has not yet appeared'.[37]

More than one commentator has begun to squirm at this point, feeling that Bloch's critics in East Germany were right in charging him with a little too much mysticism for comfort. Is not all this talk of journeys, life-forces and the transformation of death in socialism a load of prophetic mumbo-jumbo? Is it not a metaphoric overload that requires some of the sobriety of a Horkheimer or an Adorno to bring us back to earth? In response, let us pick up the dialogue between Bloch and Adorno called 'Something's Missing', for it contains a few surprises, especially with regard to Adorno. To begin with, they come to the rapid agreement that utopia can hardly be discussed without considering the question of death, for 'death depicts the hardest counter-utopia'.[38] But it is worth considering carefully Adorno's comments in the discussion, since they pick up exactly at the point where most of us would object to Bloch's arguments.[39]

Ever the dialectician, Adorno is interested in the resistance to utopia that shows up in the question of death, for this is the crux of utopia and anti-utopia. Suggest, he proposes, the elimination of death to someone who may be sympathetic to the idea of utopia. At least you will not get the knee-jerk response that you must be crazy. But the knee will certainly come up at another point: to eliminate death, says the interlocutor, would be dreadful. It would be absolutely terrible, boring and enervating, to face endless life. For Adorno, this is the moment of the most absolute resistance to utopia, since the strongest tie to the status quo is not social but an identification with and attachment to death. Given Adorno's commitment to the determinate negation and the need to maintain, even negatively, the hope of utopia, this resistance must be negated. How? Death must be eliminated if utopia is to have any meaning. The possibility of utopia is therefore predicated on a double position, for not only must death itself be eliminated, but so must the resistance to that elimination: 'Utopian consciousness means a consciousness for which the *possibility* that people no longer have to die does

37. Ibid. For a very different attempt to remove death's sting, in which death and immortality are actually expressions of the human need for survival in the face of death, see Hägglund 2008. Many thanks to Alex Andrews for alerting me to this work. See his unpublished paper, 'Sovereign Autoimmunity: Hägglund, Bataille and The Secular'.

38. Bloch and Adorno 1988, p. 9; Bloch and Adorno 1975, p. 66.

39. The following analysis follows closely the argument in Bloch and Adorno 1988, pp. 8–10; Bloch and Adorno 1975, pp. 65–9. For a comparable position, see Rose 1996, pp. 125–46.

not have anything horrible about it, but is, on the contrary, *that* which one actually wants'.[40]

We have reached the point at which the anti-utopian attachment to death must be negated and the way to do so is insist on the elimination of death. But what does Adorno mean? He accepts Bloch's distinction between dying and death. The former concerns the scientific, physical process of dying. In this he is not interested; or rather, he argues that utopia would not involve new scientific discoveries that enable us to pass over the threshold from organic to inorganic life. He is, however, very interested in death as an ontological state. Is this light, we can understand the following extraordinary observation:

> I believe that without the notion of an *unfettered life*, freed from death, the idea of utopia, the idea of *the* utopia, *cannot* even be thought at all.... There is something profoundly contradictory in every utopia, namely, that it cannot be conceived at all without the *elimination of death*; this is inherent in the very thought. What I mean is the *heaviness of death and everything that is connected to it*. Wherever this is not included, where the threshold of death is not at the same time considered, there can actually be no utopia.[41]

Note the emphases: the elimination of death involves eliminating the heaviness of death and all that is attached to it. In other words, the sheer terror and horror of death, the pure annihilation that such a state is supposed to entail, must pass for any utopia to have meaning. Awaiting the threshold should hold no dread for us; indeed, we may be able to look forward to it.

Not the Adorno to whom we are accustomed. To my knowledge, this is one of Adorno's most forthright statements concerning both utopia and death. He has been led to this point not merely by the arguments of Bloch, but also by the logic of his own position. Determinate negation is the key, for the attachment to death as it now exists is also an attachment to the status quo. That anti-utopian resistance must be met by the determinate negation, for 'death is nothing other than the power of that which merely *is*'.[42] Even here he remains to true to his position that one must heed the ban on images, or what I have called the political iconoclasm of the fetish transfer, for in arguing for the negation of the attachment to death, he remains within a negative argument. However, the dialectic can surprise even Adorno at times, for he finds himself making a positive statement. 'Excuse me', he says a little later, 'if I have taken the unexpected role of the attorney for the positive'.[43]

---

40. Bloch and Adorno 1988, p. 8; Bloch and Adorno 1975, p. 66.
41. Bloch and Adorno 1988, p. 10; Bloch and Adorno 1975, p. 68; except for 'the' and 'cannot', emphasis is mine.
42. Bloch and Adorno 1988, p. 10; Bloch and Adorno 1975, pp. 68–9.
43. Bloch and Adorno 1988, p. 13; Bloch and Adorno 1975, p. 71.

We are left with the position that dying in a physical sense may well continue; we will still die as we do now. But the horror of death as an ontological state may itself pass, so that one may look forward to the threshold of dying. Bloch, of course, agrees, for the moment of passing over becomes an open question, one of hope rather than despair, the beginning rather than the end of a journey. Couple that metaphor with Adorno's proposal and we have a thorough transformation of death. Is that not the ultimate transgression?

References

Adorno, Theodor W. 1973a [1964], *The Jargon of Authenticity*, translated by Knut Tarnowski and Frederic Will, Evanston: Northwestern University Press.

—— 1973b [1966], *Negative Dialectics*, translated by E.B. Ashton, New York: Seabury.

—— 1978 [1951], *Minima Moralia: Reflections from Damaged Life*, translated by Edmund Jephcott, London: Verso.

—— 1981 [1952], *In Search of Wagner*, translated by Rodney Livingstone, London: New Left Books.

—— 1989 [1933], *Kierkegaard: Construction of the Aesthetic*, translated by Robert Hullot-Kentor, Minneapolis: University of Minnesota Press.

—— 1991 [1968], *Alban Berg: Master of the Smallest Link*, translated by Juliane Brand and Christopher Hailey, Cambridge: Cambridge University Press.

—— 1992 [1960], *Mahler: A Musical Physiognomy*, translated by Edmund Jephcott, Chicago: University of Chicago Press.

—— 1998a [1963/9], *Critical Models: Interventions and Catchwords*, translated by Henry W. Pickford, New York: Columbia University Press.

—— 1998b [1963], *Quasi una Fantasia: Essays on Modern Music*, translated by Rodney Livingstone, London: Verso.

—— 1999 [1959], *Sound Figures*, translated by Rodney Livingstone, Stanford: Stanford University Press.

—— 2000a [1993], *Introduction to Sociology*, translated by Edmund Jephcott, edited by Christoph Gödde, Stanford: Stanford University Press.

—— 2000b [1998], *Metaphysics: Concept and Problems*, translated by Edmund Jephcott, edited by Rolf Tiedemann, Stanford: Stanford University Press.

—— 2000c, *Problems of Moral Philosophy*, translated by Rodney Livingstone, edited by Thomas Schröder, Stanford: Stanford University Press.

—— 2002a [1978], 'Wagner's Relevance for Today', in Adorno 2002c.

—— 2002b [1984], 'Marginalia on Mahler', in Adorno 2002c.

—— 2002c, *Essays on Music*, edited by Richard Leppert, Berkeley: University of California Press.

—— 2003a [1933], *Kierkegaard: Konstruktion des Ästhetischen*, in *Gesammelte Schriften*, Volume 2, Frankfurt am Main: Suhrkamp Verlag.

—— 2003b [1946], 'Anti-Semitism and Fascist Propaganda', in *Gesammelte Schriften*, Volume 8, Frankfurt am Main: Suhrkamp Verlag.

—— 2003c [1951], 'Freudian Theory and the Pattern of Fascist Propaganda', in *Gesammelte Schriften*, Volume 8, Frankfurt am Main: Suhrkamp Verlag.

—— 2003d [1951], *Minima Moralia*, in *Gesammelte Schriften*, Volume 4, Frankfurt am Main: Suhrkamp Verlag.

—— 2003e [1952], *Versuch über Wagner*, in *Gesammelte Schriften*, Volume 13, Frankfurt am Main: Suhrkamp Verlag.

—— 2003f [1959], *Klangfiguren*, in *Gesammelte Schriften*, Volume 16, Frankfurt am Main: Suhrkamp Verlag.

—— 2003g [1960], *Mahler: eine musikalische Physiognomik*, in *Gesammelte Schriften*, Volume 13, Frankfurt am Main: Suhrkamp Verlag.

—— 2003h [1963], *Eingriffe: Kritische Modelle 1*, in *Gesammelte Schriften*, Volume 10, Frankfurt am Main: Suhrkamp Verlag.

—— 2003i [1963], *Quasi una Fantasia: Musikalische Schriften II*, in *Gesammelte*

Schriften, Volume 16, Frankfurt am Main: Suhrkamp Verlag.

—— 2003j [1964], *Jargon der Eigentlich: Zur deutschen Ideologie*, in *Gesammelte Schriften*, Volume 6, Frankfurt am Main: Suhrkamp Verlag.

—— 2003k [1966], *Negative Dialektik*, in *Gesammelte Schriften*, Volume 6, Frankfurt am Main: Suhrkamp Verlag.

—— 2003l [1968], *Berg, der Meister des kleinsten Übergangs*, in *Gesammelte Schriften*, Volume 13, Frankfurt am Main: Suhrkamp Verlag.

—— 2003m [1969], *Stichworte: Kritische Modelle 2*, in *Gesammelte Schriften*, Volume 10, Frankfurt am Main: Suhrkamp Verlag.

—— 2003n [1975], *The Psychological Technique of Martin Luther Thomas' Radio Addresses*, in *Gesammelte Schriften*, Volume 9, Frankfurt am Main: Suhrkamp Verlag.

—— 2003o [1978], 'Wagners Aktualität', in *Gesammelte Schriften*, Volume 18, Frankfurt am Main: Suhrkamp Verlag.

—— 2003p [1984], *Komponisten und Kompositionen*, in *Gesammelte Schriften*, Volume 18, Frankfurt am Main: Suhrkamp Verlag.

—— 2003q [1993], *Einleitung in die Soziologie (1968)*, in *Nachgelassenen Schriften*, Section 4, Volume 15, Frankfurt am Main: Suhrkamp Verlag.

—— 2006a [1998], *Metaphysik: Begriff und Probleme (1965)*, in *Nachgelassenen Schriften*, Section 4, Volume 14, Frankfurt am Main: Suhrkamp Verlag.

—— 2006b [2001], *History and Freedom: Lectures 1964–1965*, translated by Rodney Livingstone, edited by Rolf Tiedemann, Cambridge: Polity.

—— 2006c [2001], *Zur Lehre von der Geschichte und von der Freiheit (1964/65)*, in *Nachgelassenen Schriften*, Section 4, Volume 13, Frankfurt am Main: Suhrkamp Verlag.

—— 2007 [2003], *Vorlesung über Negative Dialektik: Fragmente zur Vorlesung 1965/66*, in *Nachgelassenen Schriften*, Section 4, Volume 16, Frankfurt am Main: Suhrkamp Verlag.

—— 2008 [2003], *Lectures on Negative Dialectics: Fragments of a Lecture Course 1965/1966*, translated by Rodney Livingstone, edited by Rolf Tiedemann, Cambridge: Polity.

—— 2009, *Current of Music: Elements of a Radio Theory*, edited by Robert Hullot-Kentor, Cambridge: Polity.

Adorno, Theodor W. and Walter Benjamin 1994, *Briefwechsel 1928–1940*, Frankfurt am Main: Suhrkamp Verlag.

—— 1999 [1994], *The Complete Correspondence 1928–1940*, translated by Nicholas Walker, Cambridge, MA: Harvard University Press.

Adorno, Theodor W., Emil Blum, Emil Brunner, Martin Dibelius, Heinrich Frick, Max Horkheimer, Karl Mannheim, Carl Mennicke, Friedrich Pollock, Kurt Rietzler, Hermann Schafft, Hans Freiherr von Soden, Paul Tillich and Lilli Zarncke 1987 [1931], 'Diskussion über die Aufgabe des Protestantismus in der säkularen Zivilisation', in *Gesammelte Schriften*, Volume 11, Frankfurt am Main: Fischer Taschenbuch.

Agamben, Giorgio 1999, *Potentialities: Collected Essays in Philosophy*, translated by Daniel Heller-Roazen, Stanford: Stanford University Press.

—— 2005, *The Time That Remains: A Commentary on the Letter to the Romans*, translated by Patricia Dailey, Stanford: Stanford University Press.

Althusser, Louis 1971, *Lenin and Philosophy and Other Essays*, translated by Ben Brewster, New York: Monthly Review Press.

—— 1994, *Écrits philosophiques et politiques. Tome I*, Paris: Éditions Stock/IMEC.

—— 1995, *Sur la Reproduction*, Paris: Presses Universitaires de France.

—— 1997 [1994], *The Spectre of Hegel: Early Writings*, translated by G.M. Goshgarian, London: Verso.

Althusser, Louis and Étienne Balibar 1979 [1968], *Reading Capital*, translated by Ben Brewster, London: Verso.

Althusser, Louis, Étienne Balibar, Roger Establet, Pierre Macherey and Jacques Rancière 1996 [1968], *Lire le Capital*, Paris: Presses Universitaires de France.

Altizer, Thomas J.J. 1966, *The Gospel of Christian Atheism*, Philadelphia: Westminster.

—— 1985, *History as Apocalypse*, Albany: State University Press of New York.
—— 1990, *Genesis and Apocalypse: A Theological Voyage toward Authentic Christianity*, Louisville: Westminster John Knox.
—— 2003, *The New Gospel of Christian Atheism*, Aurora, CO: Davies Group Publishers.
—— 2006, *Living the Death of God: A Theological Memoir*, Albany: State University Press of New York.
Altizer, Thomas J.J. and William Hamilton 1968, *Radical Theology and the Death of God*, Harmondsworth: Penguin.
Anderson, Perry 1974, *Passages from Antiquity to Feudalism*, London: New Left Books.
Andrews, Alex [n.d.], 'Sovereign Autoimmunity: Hägglund, Bataille and The Secular', unpublished paper.
Aquinas, Thomas 1969, *Summa Theologiae*, edited by Thomas Gilby, Garden City, NY.: Image Books.
Aristotle 1955, *The Ethics of Aristotle*, translated by J.A.K. Thomson, Harmondsworth: Penguin.
—— 1989, *Metaphysics*, translated by Hugh Tredennick, London: Heinemann.
Asad, Talal 2003, *Formations of the Secular: Christianity, Islam, Modernity*, Stanford: Stanford University Press.
Assmann, Hugo and Franz J. Hinkelammert 1989, *A idolatria do mercado: ensaio sobre economia e teologia*, Petrópolis: Vozes.
Badiou, Alain 1988, *L'être et l'événement*, Paris: Éditions du Seuil.
—— 1997, *Saint Paul: la fondation de l'universalisme*, Paris: Presses Universitaires de France.
—— 2000 [1997], *Deleuze: The Clamor of Being*, translated by Louise Burchill, Minneapolis: University of Minnesota Press.
—— 2002 [1998], *Ethics: An Essay on the Understanding of Evil*, translated by Peter Hallward, London: Verso.
—— 2003a [1998], *L'éthique: essai sur la conscience du Mal*, Paris: Nous.
—— 2003b [1997], *Saint Paul: The Foundation of Universalism*, translated by Ray Brassier, Stanford: Stanford University Press.
—— 2004, *Theoretical Writings*, First Edition, edited by Ray Brassier and Alberto Toscano, London: Continuum.
—— 2005a [1998], *Handbook of Inaesthetics*, translated by Alberto Toscano, Stanford: Stanford University Press.
—— 2005b, 'Politics: A Non-Expressive Dialectics', available at: <http://blog.urbanomic.com/sphaleotas/archives/badiou-politics.pdf>.
—— 2006a [1988], *Being and Event*, translated by Oliver Feltham, London: Continuum.
—— 2006b, *Logiques des mondes*, Paris: Éditions du Seuil.
—— 2006c, 'The Subject Supposed to Be a Christian: On Paul Ricœur's *Memory, History, Forgetting*', *The Bible and Critical Theory*, 2, 3: 27.1–27.9.
—— 2006d, 'Lacan and the Pre-Socratics', *Lacanian Ink*, available at: <http://www.lacan.com/badpre.htm>.
—— 2008, *Conditions*, translated by Steven Corcoran, London: Continuum.
—— 2009 [2006], *Logics of Worlds: Being and Event II*, translated by Alberto Toscano, London: Continuum.
Baker, Anthony and Rocco Gangle 2005, 'Ecclesia: The Art of the Virtual', in Davis, Milbank and Žižek (eds.) 2005.
Barker, Jason 1992, *Alain Badiou: A Critical Introduction*, London: Pluto.
Barr, James 1969, *Biblical Words for Time*, Second Edition, London: SCM.
Barrett, Michèle 1991, *The Politics of Truth: From Marx to Foucault*, Stanford: Stanford University Press.
Barthes, Roland 1982 [1970], *Empire of Signs*, translated by Richard Howard, New York: Hill and Wang.
—— 1983 [1967], *The Fashion System*, translated by Matthew Ward and Richard Howard, Berkeley: University of California Press.
—— 1985 [1981], *The Grain of the Voice: Interviews 1962–1980*, translated by Linda Coverdale, Berkeley: University of California Press.
—— 1989 [1984], *The Rustle of Language*, translated by Richard Howard, Berkeley: University of California Press.
—— 1990 [1970], *S/Z*, translated by Richard Miller, Oxford: Blackwell.

—— 1991 [1982], *The Responsibility of Forms*, translated by Richard Howard, Berkeley: University of California Press.

—— 1993 [1957], *Mythologies*, translated by Annette Lavers, London: Vintage.

—— 1997 [1957], *The Eiffel Tower and Other Mythologies*, translated by Richard Howard, Berkeley: University of California Press.

—— 2002a [1957], *Mythologies, suivi de Le Mythe, aujourd'hui*, in *Œuvres complètes. Tome 1: Livres, textes, entretiens, 1942–1961*, Paris: Seuil.

—— 2002b [1959], 'Les deux salons', in *Œuvres complètes. Tome 1: Livres, textes, entretiens, 1942–1961*, Paris: Seuil.

—— 2002c [1959], 'New York, Buffet et la hauteur', in *Œuvres complètes. Tome 1: Livres, textes, entretiens, 1942–1961*, Paris: Seuil.

—— 2002d [1959], 'Tricots à domicile', in *Œuvres complètes. Tome 1: Livres, textes, entretiens, 1942–1961*, Paris: Seuil.

—— 2002e [1959], 'Wagon-Restaurant', in *Œuvres complètes. Tome 1: Livres, textes, entretiens, 1942–1961*, Paris: Seuil.

—— 2002f [1964], 'La Tour Eiffel', in *Œuvres complètes. Tome 1: Livres, textes, entretiens, 1942–1961*, Paris: Seuil.

—— 2002g [1967], *Système de la mode*, in *Œuvres complètes. Tome 2: Livres, textes, entretiens, 1962–1967*, Paris: Seuil.

—— 2002h [1970], *L'Empire des signes*, in *Œuvres complètes. Tome 3: Livres, textes, entretiens, 1968–1971*, Paris: Seuil.

—— 2002i [1970], ' "L'Express" va plus loin avec... Roland Barthes', in *Œuvres complètes. Tome 3: Livres, textes, entretiens, 1968–1971*, Paris: Seuil.

—— 2002j [1970], 'Musica Practica', in *Œuvres complètes. Tome 3: Livres, textes, entretiens, 1968–1971*, Paris: Seuil.

—— 2002k [1970], *S/Z*, in *Œuvres complètes. Tome 3: Livres, textes, entretiens, 1968–1971*, Paris: Seuil.

—— 2002l [1970], 'Sur "S/Z" et "L'Empire des signes" (avec R. Bellour)', in *Œuvres complètes. Tome 3: Livres, textes, entretiens, 1968–1971*, Paris: Seuil.

—— 2002m [1975], *Le bruissement de la langue*, in *Œuvres complètes. Tome 4: Livres, textes, entretiens, 1972–1976*, Paris: Seuil.

Bauer, Bruno 1838, *Kritik der Geschichte der Offenbarung: Die Religion des alten Testaments in der geschichtlichen Entwicklung ihrer Prinzipien dargestellt*, Berlin: Ferdinand Dümmler.

—— 1839, *Herr Dr. Hengstenberg: Ein Beitrag zur Kritik der religiösen Bewußtseins. Kritische Briefe über den Gegensatz des Gesetzes und des Evangeliums*, Berlin: Ferdinand Dümmler.

—— 1840, *Kritik der evangelischen Geschichte des Johannes*, Bremen: Karl Schünemann.

—— 1841, *Kritik der evangelischen Geschichte der Synoptiker*, two volumes, Leipzig: Otto Wigand.

—— 1842a, *Die Gute Sache der Freiheit und meine eigene Angelegenheit*, Zurich and Winterthur: Verlag des literarischen Comptoirs.

—— 1842b, *Kritik der evangelischen Geschichte der Synoptiker und des Johannes, Dritter und letzter Band*, Braunschweig: Fr. Otto.

—— 1843, *Das entdeckte Christentum. Eine Erinnerung an das 18. Jahrhundert und ein Beitrag zur Krisis des 19. Jahrhundert*, Zurich and Winterthur: Verlag des literarischen Comptoirs.

—— 1850–1, *Kritik der Evangelien und Geschichte ihres Ursprungs*, three volumes, Berlin: Gustav Hempel.

—— 1852, *Die theologische Erklärung der Evangelien*, Berlin: Scientia Verlag.

—— 1967 [1842], *Hegels Lehre von der Religion und Kunst von dem Standpunkte des Glaubens aus beurteilt*, Aalen: Scientia Verlag.

—— 1983 [1841], *Die Posaune des jüngsten Gerichts über Hegel den Atheisten und Antichristen: Ein Ultimatum*, Aalen: Scientia Verlag.

—— 2002, *Christianity Exposed: A Recollection of the Eighteenth Century and a Contribution to the Crisis of the Nineteenth Century*, translated by Esther Ziegler and Jutta Hamm, Lewiston: Edwin Mellen.

Beckford, James 2003, *Social Theory and Religion*. Cambridge: Cambridge University Press.

Bell, Daniel M. 2005, 'Only Jesus Saves: Towards a Theopolitical Ontotheology of Judgment', in Davis, Milbank and Žižek (eds.) 2005.

Belo, Fernando 1975, *Lecture matérialiste de l'évangile de Marc: Récit-Pratique-Idéologie*, Revised Edition, Paris: Les Éditions du Cerf.

—— 1981, *A Materialist Reading of the Gospel of Mark*, translated by M.J. O'Connell, Maryknoll: Orbis.

Benjamin, Walter 1973, *Charles Baudelaire: A Lyric Poet in the Era of High Capitalism*, translated by Harry Zohn, London: New Left Books.

—— 1982a, *Gesammelte Schriften*, Volume 1, Frankfurt am Main: Suhrkamp Verlag.

—— 1982b, *Gesammelte Schriften*, Volume 2, Frankfurt am Main: Suhrkamp Verlag.

—— 1982c, *Gesammelte Schriften*, Volume 5, Frankfurt am Main: Suhrkamp Verlag.

—— 1996, *Selected Writings. Volume 1: 1913–1926*, edited by Marcus Bullock and Michael W. Jennings, Cambridge, MA: Belknap.

—— 1999, *The Arcades Project*, translated by Howard Eiland and Kevin McLaughlin, Cambridge, MA: Belknap.

—— 2003, *Selected Writings. Volume 4: 1938–1940*, translated by Edmund Jephcott et al., edited by Howard Eiland and Michael W. Jennings, Cambridge, MA: Belknap.

Berdyaev, Nikolai 1937, *The Origin of Russian Communism*, translated by R.M. French, London: G. Bles.

Berger, Peter Ludwig, Grace Davie and Effie Fokas 2008, *Religious America, Secular Europe?: A Theme and Variations*, Aldershot: Ashgate.

Berman, Harold Joseph 1983, *Law and Revolution: The Formation of the Western Legal Tradition*, Cambridge, MA: Harvard University Press.

—— 2006, *Law and Revolution, II: The Impact of the Protestant Reformations on the Western Legal Tradition*, Cambridge, MA: Harvard University Press.

Bernal, Martin 1987–2006, *Black Athena: The Afroasiatic Roots of Classical Civilization*, three volumes, New Brunswick: Rutgers University Press.

Blanton, Ward and Hent de Vries (eds.) 2013, *Paul and the Philosophers*, New York: Fordham University Press.

Bloch, Ernst 1968, *Atheismus im Christentum: Zur Religion des Exodus und des Reichs*, in *Werkausgabe*, Volume 14, Frankfurt am Main: Suhrkamp Verlag.

—— 1969, *Thomas Münzer als Theologe der Revolution*, in *Werkausgabe*, Volume 2, Frankfurt am Main: Suhrkamp Verlag.

—— 1972 [1968], *Atheism in Christianity: The Religion of the Exodus and the Kingdom*, translated by J.T. Swann, New York: Herder and Herder.

—— 1985a [1959], *Das Prinzip Hoffnung*, in *Werkausgabe*, Volume 5, Frankfurt am Main: Suhrkamp Verlag.

—— 1985b [1964], *Geist der Utopie, Zweite Fassung*, in *Werkausgabe*, Volume 3, Frankfurt am Main: Suhrkamp Verlag.

—— 1985c [1965], *Literarische Aufsätze*, in *Werkausgabe*, Volume 9, Frankfurt am Main: Suhrkamp Verlag.

—— 1985d [1930/69], *Spuren*, in *Werkausgabe*, Volume 1, Frankfurt am Main: Suhrkamp Verlag.

—— 1988 [1974/5], *The Utopian Function of Art and Literature: Selected Essays*, translated by Jack Zipes and Frank Mecklenburg, Cambridge, MA: MIT Press.

—— 1995 [1959], *The Principle of Hope*, translated by Neville Plaice, Stephen Plaice and Paul Knight, Cambridge, MA: MIT Press.

—— 1998 [1965], *Literary Essays*, translated by Andrew Joron, Stanford: Stanford University Press.

—— 2000 [1964], *The Spirit of Utopia*, translated by Anthony A. Nassar, Stanford: Stanford University Press.

—— 2006 [1930/69], *Traces*, translated by Anthony A. Nassar, Stanford: Stanford University Press.

Bloch, Ernst and Theodor W. Adorno 1975, 'Etwas fehlt ... Über die Widersprüche der utopischen Sehnsucht', in *Gespräche mit Ernst Bloch*, edited by Reiner Taub and Harald Wieser, Frankfurt am Main: Suhrkamp Verlag.

—— 1988 [1975], 'Something's Missing: A Discussion Between Ernst Bloch and Theodor W. Adorno on the Contradictions of Utopian Longing', in Bloch 1988.

Blond, Phillip 2005, 'The Politics of the Eye: Toward a Theological Materialism', in Davis, Milbank and Žižek (eds.) 2005.

Boer, Roland 1996, *Jameson and Jeroboam*, Atlanta: Scholar's Press.

—— 2002, 'Political Activism and Biblical Scholarship: An Interview with Norman Gottwald', in *Tracking 'The Tribes of Yahweh': On the Trail of a Classic*, edited by Roland Boer, London: Continuum.

—— 2005a, 'A Level Playingfield? Metacommentary and Marxism', in *On Jameson:*

From Postmodernism to Globalization, edited by Caren Irr and Ian Buchanan, Albany: State University Press of New York.

—— 2005b, 'Women First? On the Legacy of "Primitive Communism"', *Journal for the Study of the Old Testament*, 30, 1: 3–28.

—— 2005–6, 'Phases of the Gonic: Re-Reading Genesis to Joshua as Myth', *Literary Newspaper (Bulgaria)*, 13, 21 December 2005–10 January 2006: 18.

—— 2006a, 'He/brew(')s Beer, or H(om) ebrew', in *The Recycled Bible: Autobiographical Criticism, Cultural Criticism, and the Space Between*, edited by Fiona C. Black, Atlanta: Society of Biblical Literature.

—— 2006b, *Novel Histories: The Fiction of Biblical Criticism*, Atlanta: SBL.

—— 2006c, 'An Un-Original Tale: Utopia Denied in *Enuma Elish*', *Arena Journal (New Series)*, 25/6: 136–52.

—— 2007a, *Criticism of Heaven: On Marxism and Theology*, Historical Materialism Book Series, Leiden: Brill.

—— 2007b, *Rescuing the Bible*, Oxford: Blackwell.

—— 2007c, 'The Search for Redemption: Julia Kristeva and Slavoj Žižek on Marx, Psychoanalysis and Religion', *Filozofija i Društvo [Philosophy and Society]*, 32, 1: 153–76.

—— 2008, *Last Stop Before Antarctica: The Bible and Postcolonialism in Australia*, Second Edition, Atlanta: Society of Biblical Literature.

—— 2009a, 'The Antinomies of Secularism and Religion', in *Religion and Civil Society*, edited by Natalia Gavrilova, Sebastopol: Taurida National University.

—— 2009b, *Criticism of Religion: On Marxism and Theology II*, *Historical Materialism* Book Series, Leiden: Brill.

—— 2009c, *Political Grace: The Revolutionary Theology of John Calvin*, Louisville: Westminster John Knox.

—— 2009d, *Political Myth: On the Use and Abuse of Biblical Themes*, Durham, NC: Duke University Press.

—— 2009e, 'Skin Gods: Circumcising the Built Male Body', *Journal of Men, Masculinities and Spirituality*, 1, 1: 35–44, available at: <http://www.jmmsweb.org/issues/volume1/number1/pp35-44>.

—— 2010a, 'Marx and the Christian Logic of the Secular State', *The Hobgoblin*, 7 March, available at: <http://www.thehobgoblin.co.uk/journal/2010_Roland_Boer.htm>.

—— 2010b, 'Revelation and Revolution: Friedrich Engels and the Apocalypse', *Interdisciplinary Journal of Research on Religion*, 6, 2: 1–23, available at: <http://www.religjournal.com/articles/article_view.php?id=41>.

—— 2011a, *Criticism of Theology: On Marxism and Theology III*, *Historical Materialism* Book Series, Leiden: Brill.

—— 2011b, '*Kapitalfetisch*: "The Religion of Everyday Life"'. *International Critical Thought* 1, 4: 416–26.

—— 2012, *Criticism of Earth: On Marx, Engels and Theology*, *Historical Materialism* Book Series, Leiden: Brill.

—— 2013a, *Lenin, Religion, and Theology*. New York: Palgrave Macmillan.

—— 2013b, *The Sacred Economy*. Louisville: Westminster John Knox.

—— 2013c, 'The Privatisation of Eschatology and Myth: Ernst Bloch versus Rudolf Bultmann', in *The Privatisation of Hope: Ernst Bloch and the Future of Utopia*, edited by Peter Thompson, Durham, NC: Duke University Press.

Boothman, Derek 2008, 'The Sources of Gramsci's Concept of Hegemony', *Rethinking Marxism*, 20, 2: 201–15.

Borowski, Oded 1987, *Agriculture in Iron Age Israel*, Winona Lake: Eisenbrauns.

Bottomore, Tom (ed.) 1983, *A Dictionary of Marxist Thought*, Oxford: Blackwell.

Botton, Alain de 1994, *Essays in Love*, London: Picador.

—— 2001, *The Consolations of Philosophy*, Harmondsworth: Penguin.

—— 2003, *The Art of Travel*, Harmondsworth: Penguin.

—— 2005, *Status Anxiety*, Harmondsworth: Penguin.

—— 2006, *The Architecture of Happiness*, London: Hamish Hamilton.

—— 2009, *The Pleasures and Sorrows of Work*, London: Hamish Hamilton.

Braaten, Carl E. and Robert W. Jenson (eds.) 2002, *The Last Things: Biblical and Theological Perspectives on Eschatology*, Grand Rapids: Eerdmans.

Bracht, Heinrich, Peter Brückner, Max Horkheimer, Alexander Mitscherlich and Hans Götz Oxenius 1989 [1963], *Das Ende einer Illusion? Religionskritik heute [Eine Diskussion über Horkheimers 'Theismus-Atheismus']*, in *Gesammelte Schriften*, Volume 13, Frankfurt am Main: Fischer Taschenbuch.

Braidwood, Robert J. 1953, 'Did Man Once Live by Beer Alone?', *American Anthropologist*, 55, 4: 515–26.

Breckman, Warren 1999, *Marx, the Young Hegelians, and the Origins of Radical Social Theory*, Cambridge: Cambridge University Press.

Brenner, Athalya 1994, 'Introduction', in *A Feminist Companion to the Bible: Exodus to Deuteronomy*, edited by Athalya Brenner, Sheffield: Sheffield Academic Press.

Brett, Mark G. 2008, *Decolonizing God: The Bible in the Tides of Empire*, Sheffield: Sheffield Phoenix.

Briggs, Sheila 2000, 'Paul on Bondage and Freedom in Imperial Roman Society', in Horsley (ed.) 2000.

Brosses, Charles de 1760, *Du culte des dieux fétiches ou Parallèle de l'ancienne religion de l'Égypte avec la religion actuelle de Nigritie*, Paris: n.p.

Bruce, Steve 2002, *God is Dead: Secularization in the West*, Oxford: Blackwell.

Bultmann, Rudolf 1948, *Theologie des neuen Testaments*, two volumes, Tübingen: J.C.B. Mohr (Siebeck).

—— 1951 [1941], 'Neues Testament und Mythologie: Das Problem der Entmythologisierung der neutestamentlichen Verkündigung', in *Kerygma und Mythos*, edited by H.W. Bartsch, Hamburg: Herbert Reich-Evangelischer Verlag.

—— 1952 [1948], *Theology of the New Testament*, Volume 1, translated by Kendrick Grobel, London: SCM.

—— 1984 [1941], 'New Testament and Mythology: The Problem of Demythologizing the New Testament Proclamation', in *The New Testament and Mythology and Other Basic Writings*, edited by Schubert M. Ogden, Philadelphia: Fortress.

Butler, Judith P. 2005, *Giving an Account of Oneself*, New York: Fordham University Press.

Caird, George B. 1980, *The Language and Imagery of the Bible*, London: Duckworth.

Calvin, John 1855, *Commentaries on the Catholic Epistles*, translated by John Owen, Edinburgh: Calvin Translation Society.

—— 1856, *Commentaries on the Epistles to Timothy, Titus, and Philemon*, translated by William Pringle, Edinburgh: Calvin Translation Society.

—— 2006 [1559], *Institutes of the Christian Religion*, translated by Ford Lewis Battles, Louisville: Westminster John Knox.

Calvini, Johannes 1957 [1559], *Institutiones Christianae Religionis*, edited by Petrus Barth and Guilelmus Niesel, three volumes, Monachii in Aedibus: Chr. Kaiser.

Carter, Charles E. 1999, *The Emergence of Yehud in the Persian Period: A Social and Demographic Study*, Sheffield: Sheffield Academic Press.

Carter, Michael 1988, '*Stasis* and *Kairos*: Principles of Social Construction in Classical Rhetoric', *Rhetoric Review*, 7, 1: 97–112.

Carter, Warren 2001, *Matthew and Empire: Initial Explorations*, Harrisburg: Trinity Press International.

—— 2004, 'The Irony of Romans 13', *Novum Testamentum*, 46, 3: 209–28.

—— 2006, *The Roman Empire and the New Testament: An Essential Guide*, Nashville: Abingdon.

Cobb, John 1999, *The Earthist Challenge to Economism: A Theological Critique of the World Bank*, Basingstoke: Palgrave Macmillan.

Cohen, Margaret 1993, *Profane Illumination: Walter Benjamin and the Paris of Surrealist Revolution*, Berkeley: University of California Press.

Corran, H.S. 1975, *A History of Brewing*, London: David and Charles.

Critchley, Simon 2000, 'Demanding Approval: On the Ethics of Alain Badiou', *Radical Philosophy*, 100: 16–27.

Crossan, John Dominic 1993, *The Historical Jesus: The Life of a Mediterranean Jewish Peasant*, San Francisco: Harper.

—— 1995, *Jesus: A Revolutionary Biography*, San Francisco: Harper.

Csapo, Eric 2005, *Theories of Mythology*, Oxford: Blackwell.

Cunningham, Conor 2005, 'Nothing Is, Something Must Be: Lacan and Creation from No One', in Davis, Milbank and Žižek (eds.) 2005.

Curtis, Richard 2007, *What Is Religion? On the Nature of the Human Mind and the Role of Religion (With or Without God)*, Seattle: Dialectical Books.

Dandamaev, Muhammad 1984, *Slavery in Babylonia: From Nabopolassar to Alexander the Great (626–331 BC)*, DeKalb: Northern Illinois University Press.

Dandamaev, Muhammad, I. Gershevitch, Horst Klengel, G. Komoroczy, M.T. Larsen and J.N. Postgate (eds.) 1982, *Societies and Languages of the Ancient Near East: Studies in Honour of I.M. Diakonoff*, Warminster: Aris and Phillips Ltd.

Daniel, Jamie Owen and Tom Moylan (eds.) 1997, *Not Yet: Reconsidering Ernst Bloch*, London: Verso.

Davis, Creston, John Milbank and Slavoj Žižek (eds.) 2005, *Theology and the Political: The New Debate*, Durham, NC: Duke University Press.

Davis, Creston and Patrick Aaron Riches 2005, 'Metanoia: The Theological Praxis of Revolution', in Davis, Milbank and Žižek (eds.) 2005.

Dawkins, Richard 2006, *The God Delusion*, Boston: Houghton Mifflin Harcourt.

Debs, Eugene V. 1903, 'A Valiant Foeman', *Social Democratic Herald*, 15 August.

Debray, Régis 1983, *Critique of Political Reason*, translated by David Macey, London: New Left Books.

—— 2004, *God: An Itinerary*, translated by Jeffrey Mehlman, London: Verso.

Deissman, Adolf 1929, *The New Testament in the Light of Modern Research*, Garden City, NY.: Doubleday, Doran and Company.

—— 1978 [1908], *Light From the Ancient East*, Grand Rapids: Baker Book House.

DeLanda, Manuel 2002, *Intensive Science and Virtual Philosophy*, London: Continuum.

Deleuze, Gilles and Félix Guattari 1980, *Mille Plateaux: Capitalisme et Schizophrénie*, Paris: Les Éditions de Minuit.

—— 1986, *Nomadology: The War Machine*, translated by Brian Massumi, New York: Semiotext(e).

—— 1988, *A Thousand Plateaus: Capitalism and Schizophrenia*, translated by Brian Massumi, London: Athlone Press.

Dennett, Daniel C. 2007, *Breaking the Spell: Religion as a Natural Phenomenon*, Harmondsworth: Penguin.

Dever, William G. 2001, *What Did the Biblical Writers Know and When Did They Know It? What Archaeology Can Tell Us about the Reality of Ancient Israel*, Grand Rapids: Eerdmans.

D'iakonoff, Igor M. 1974, 'The Commune in the Ancient East as Treated in the Works of Soviet Researchers', in *Introduction to Soviet Ethnography*, edited by Stephen P. Dunn and E. Dunn, Berkeley: Copy Centers of Berkeley.

—— 1999, *The Paths of History*, Cambridge: Cambridge University Press.

D'iakonoff, Igor M. (ed.) 1969, *Ancient Mesopotamia: Socio-Economic History. A Collection of Studies by Soviet Scholars*, Moscow: 'Nauka' Publishing House.

—— (ed.) 1991, *Early Antiquity*, Chicago: Chicago University Press.

Dixon, Thomas 1999, 'Theology, Anti-theology and Atheology: From Christian Passions to Secular Emotions', *Modern Theology*, 15, 3: 297–330.

Doherty, Robert E. 1962, 'Thomas J. Hagerty, The Church, and Socialism', *Labor History*, 3, 1: 39–56.

Drucker, Peter 2011, 'The Fracturing of LGBT Identities Under Neoliberal Capitalism'. *Historical Materialism* 19, 4: 3–32.

Dupré, Louis 1983, *Marx's Social Critique of Culture*, New Haven: Yale University Press.

Dussel, Enrique 1993, *Las metáforas teológicas de Marx*, Estella (Navarra): Editorial Verbo Divino.

—— 2001, 'From Ethics and Community', in *The Postmodern Bible Reader*, edited by David Jobling, Tina Pippin and Ronald Schleifer, Oxford: Wiley-Blackwell.

Eagleton, Terry 1966a, *The New Left Church*, London: Sheed and Ward.

—— 1966b, 'The Roots of the Christian Crisis', in *'Slant Manifesto': Catholics and the Left*, edited by Adrian Cunningham, Terry Eagleton, Brian Wicker, Martin Redfern and Lawrence Bright, London: Sheed and Ward.

—— 1967a, 'The Slant Symposium', *Slant*, 3, 5: 8–9.

—— 1967b, 'Why We Are Still in the Church', *Slant*, 3, 2: 25–8.

—— 1968a, 'Language, Reality and the Eucharist (1)', *Slant*, 4, 3: 18–23.
—— 1968b, 'Language, Reality and the Eucharist (2)', *Slant*, 4, 4: 26–31.
—— 1968c, 'Politics and the Sacred', *Slant*, 4, 2: 18–23.
—— 1969, 'Priesthood and Leninism', *Slant*, 5, 4: 12–17.
—— 1970, *The Body as Language: Outline of a 'New Left' Theology*, London: Sheed and Ward.
—— 1991, *Ideology: An Introduction*, London: Verso.
—— 2001, *The Gatekeeper: A Memoir*, Harmondsworth: Penguin.
—— 2003a, *After Theory*, New York: Basic Books.
—— 2003b, *Figures of Dissent: Critical Essays on Fish, Spivak, Žižek and Others*, London: Verso.
—— 2003c, *Sweet Violence: The Idea of the Tragic*, Oxford: Blackwell.
—— 2005, *Holy Terror*, Oxford: Oxford University Press.
—— 2006, 'Lunging, Flailing, Mispunching', *London Review of Books*, 28, 20: 32–4, available at: <http://www.lrb.co.uk/v28/n20/terry-eagleton/lunging-flailing-mispunching>.
—— 2007, *Jesus Christ: The Gospels (Revolutions)*, London: Verso.
—— 2009a, *Reason, Faith, and Revolution: Reflections on the God Debate*, New Haven: Yale University Press.
—— 2009b, *Trouble with Strangers: A Study of Ethics*, Oxford: Wiley-Blackwell.
—— 2010, *On Evil*, New Haven: Yale University Press.
Eagleton, Terry and Nathan Schneider 2009, 'Religion for Radicals: An Interview with Terry Eagleton', *The Monthly Review*, 61, 4, available at: <http://mrzine.monthlyreview.org/2009/eagleton200909.html>.
Ehrensperger, Kathy 2007, *Paul and the Dynamics of Power: Communication and Interaction in the Early Christ-Movement*, London: T. & T. Clark.
Elliott, Neil 1997, 'Romans 13:1–7 in the Context of Imperial Propaganda', in Horsley (ed.) 1997.
—— 2000, 'Paul and the Politics of Empire: Problems and Prospects', in Horsley (ed.) 2000.
—— 2008, *The Arrogance of Nations: Reading Romans in the Shadow of Empire*, Minneapolis: Fortress.
Engberg-Pedersen, Troels 2000, *Paul and the Stoics*, Louisville: Westminster John Knox.
Engels, Friedrich 1839a, 'Letters from Wuppertal', in Marx and Engels 1975–2005, Volume 2.
—— 1839b, 'Briefe aus dem Wuppertal', in Marx and Engels 1975–, Section 1, Volume 3.
—— 1839c, 'To Friedrich Graeber, Bremen, February 19, 1839', in Marx and Engels 1975–2005, Volume 2.
—— 1839d, 'An Friedrich Graeber, 19. Februar 1839', in Marx and Engels 1956–1990, Volume 41.
—— 1839e, 'To Friedrich Graeber, Bremen, April 8, 1839', in Marx and Engels 1975–2005, Volume 2.
—— 1839f, 'An Friedrich Graeber, 8.–9. April 1839', in Marx and Engels 1956–1990, Volume 41.
—— 1839g, 'To Friedrich Graeber in Berlin, Bremen, about April 23–May 1, 1839', in Marx and Engels 1975–2005, Volume 2.
—— 1839h, 'An Friedrich Graeber, um den 23. April–1. Mai 1839', in Marx and Engels 1956–1990, Volume 41.
—— 1839i, 'To Wilhelm Graeber in Berlin, Bremen, about April 28–30, 1839', in Marx and Engels 1975–2005, Volume 2.
—— 1839j, 'An Wilhelm Graeber, um den 28.–30. April 1939', in Marx and Engels 1956–1990, Volume 41.
—— 1839k, 'To Wilhelm Graeber in Berlin, Bremen, May 24–June 15, 1839', in Marx and Engels 1975–2005, Volume 2.
—— 1839l, 'An Wilhelm Graeber, 24. Mai–15. Juni 1839', in Marx and Engels 1956–1990, Volume 41.
—— 1839m, 'To Friedrich Graeber in Berlin, Bremen, June 15, 1839', in Marx and Engels 1975–2005, Volume 2.
—— 1839n, 'An Friedrich Graeber, 15. Juni 1839', in Marx and Engels 1956–1990, Volume 41.
—— 1839o, To Friedrich Graeber in Berlin, Bremen, July 12–27, 1839', in Marx and Engels 1975–2005, Volume 2.
—— 1839p, 'An Friedrich Graeber, 12.–27. Juli 1839', in Marx and Engels 1956–1990, Volume 41.

—— 1839q, 'To Wilhelm Graeber in Berlin, Bremen, July 30, 1839', in Marx and Engels 1975–2005, Volume 2.

—— 1839r, 'An Wilhelm Graeber, 30. Juli 1839', in Marx and Engels 1956–1990, Volume 41.

—— 1839s, 'To Wilhelm Graeber in Berlin, Bremen, October 8, 1839', in Marx and Engels 1975–2005, Volume 2.

—— 1839t, 'An Wilhelm Graeber, 8. Oktober 1839', in Marx and Engels 1956–1990, Volume 41.

—— 1839u, 'To Wilhelm Graeber in Berlin, Bremen, October 20–21, 1839', in Marx and Engels 1975–2005, Volume 2.

—— 1839v, 'An Wilhelm Graeber, 20./21. Oktober 1839', in Marx and Engels 1956–1990, Volume 41.

—— 1839w, 'To Friedrich Graeber, Bremen, October 29, 1839', in Marx and Engels 1975–2005, Volume 2.

—— 1839x, 'An Friedrich Graeber, 29. Oktober 1839', in Marx and Engels 1956–1990, Volume 41.

—— 1839y, 'To Wilhelm Graeber in Berlin, Bremen, November 13–20, 1839', in Marx and Engels 1975–2005, Volume 2.

—— 1839z, 'An Wilhelm Graeber, 13.–20. November 1839', in Marx and Engels 1956–1990, Volume 41.

—— 1839–40a, 'To Friedrich Graeber in Berlin, Bremen, December 9, 1839–February 5, 1840', in Marx and Engels 1975–2005, Volume 2.

—— 1839–40b, 'An Friedrich Graeber, 9. Dezember 1839–5. Februar 1840', in Marx and Engels 1956–1990, Volume 41.

—— 1840a, 'Reports from Bremen: Ecclesiastical Controversy', in Marx and Engels 1975–2005, Volume 2.

—— 1840b, 'Korrespondenz aus Bremen: Kirchlicher Streit', in Marx and Engels 1975–, Section 1, Volume 3.

—— 1840c, 'Reports from Bremen: Rationalism and Pietism', in Marx and Engels 1975–2005, Volume 2.

—— 1840d, 'Korrespondenz aus Bremen: Rationalismus und Pietismus', in Marx and Engels 1975–, Section 1, Volume 3.

—— 1840e, 'Reports from Bremen: Theatre. Publishing Festival', in Marx and Engels 1975–2005, Volume 2.

—— 1840f, 'Korrespondenz aus Bremen: Theater. Buchdruckerfest', in Marx and Engels 1975–, Section 1, Volume 3.

—— 1840g, 'To Wilhelm Graeber in Barmen, Bremen, November 20, 1840', in Marx and Engels 1975–2005, Volume 2.

—— 1840h, 'An Wilhelm Graeber, 20. November 1840', in Marx and Engels 1956–1990, Volume 41.

—— 1841a, 'To Friedrich Graeber, February 22, 1841', in Marx and Engels 1975–2005, Volume 2.

—— 1841b, 'An Friedrich Graeber, 22. Februar 1841', in Marx and Engels 1956–1990, Volume 41.

—— 1841c, *Schelling on Hegel*, in Marx and Engels 1975–2005, Volume 2.

—— 1841d, *Schelling über Hegel*, in Marx and Engels 1975–, Section 1, Volume 3.

—— 1842a, *The Insolently Threatened Yet Miraculously Rescued Bible or: The Triumph of Faith, To Wit, the Terrible, Yet True and Salutary History of the Erstwhile Licentiate Bruno Bauer; How the Same, Seduced by the Devil, Fallen from the True Faith, Became Chief Devil, and Was Well and Truly Ousted in the End: A Christian Epic in Four Cantos*, in Marx and Engels 1975–2005, Volume 2.

—— 1842b, *Die frech bedräute, jedoch wunderbar befreite Bibel. Oder: Der Triumph des Glaubens. Unter Mitwirkung von Edgar Bauer*, in Marx and Engels 1975–, Section 1, Volume 3.

—— 1842c, *Schelling and Revelation: Critique of the Latest Attempt of Reaction against the Free Philosophy*, in Marx and Engels 1975–2005, Volume 2.

—— 1842d, *Schelling und die Offenbarung. Kritik des neuesten Reaktionsversuchs gegen die freie Philosophie*, in Marx and Engels 1975–, Section 1, Volume 3.

—— 1842e, *Schelling, Philosopher in Christ, or the Transfiguration of Worldly Wisdom into Divine Wisdom: For Believing Christians Who Do Not Know the Language of Philosophy*, in Marx and Engels 1975–2005, Volume 2.

—— 1842f, *Schelling, der Philosoph in Christo, oder die Verklärung der Weltweisheit zur Gottesweisheit*, in Marx and Engels 1975–, Section 1, Volume 3.

—— 1843a, 'Letters from London', in Marx and Engels 1975–2005, Volume 3.
—— 1843b, 'Briefe aus London', in Marx and Engels 1975–, Section 1, Volume 3.
—— 1843c, 'Progress of Social Reform on the Continent', in Marx and Engels 1975–2005, Volume 3.
—— 1844a, 'The Condition of England: *Past and Present* by Thomas Carlyle, London, 1843', in Marx and Engels 1975–2005, Volume 3.
—— 1844b, 'Die Lage Englands. I. "Past and Present" by Thomas Carlyle', in Marx and Engels 1956–1990, Volume 1.
—— 1844c, 'The Condition of England. I. The Eighteenth Century', in Marx and Engels 1975–2005, Volume 3.
—— 1844d, 'Die Lage Englands I. Das achtzehnte Jahrhundert', in Marx and Engels 1956–1990, Volume 1.
—— 1844e, 'The Condition of England II: The English Constitution', in Marx and Engels 1975–2005, Volume 3.
—— 1844f, 'Die Lage Englands II. Die englische Konstitution', in Marx and Engels 1956–1990, Volume 1.
—— 1844g, 'Continental Socialism', in Marx and Engels 1975–2005, Volume 4.
—— 1845, '"Young Germany" in Switzerland (Conspiracy against Church and State)', in Marx and Engels 1975–2005, Volume 4.
—— 1846a, *The Condition of the Working-Class in England*, in Marx and Engels 1975–2005, Volume 4.
—— 1846b, *Die Lage der arbeitenden Klasse in England. Nach eigner Anschauung und authentischen Quellen*, in Marx and Engels 1956–1990, Volume 2.
—— 1850a, 'The Peasant War in Germany', in Marx and Engels 1975–2005, Volume 10.
—— 1850b, 'Der deutsche Bauernkrieg', in Marx and Engels 1956–1990, Volume 7.
—— 1856a, 'Engels to Marx in London, Manchester, 23 May 1856', in Marx and Engels 1975–2005, Volume 40.
—— 1856b, 'Engels an Marx 23. Mai 1856', in Marx and Engels 1956–1990, Volume 29.
—— 1865a, 'The Prussian Military Question and the German Workers' Party', in Marx and Engels 1975–2005, Volume 20.
—— 1865b, 'Die preußische Militärfrage und die deutsche Arbeiterpartei', in Marx and Engels 1956–1990, Volume 16.
—— 1867a, 'Engels to Ludwig Kugelmann in Hanover, Manchester, 8 and 20 November 1867', in Marx and Engels 1975–2005, Volume 42.
—— 1867b, 'Engels an Ludwig Kugelmann 8. und 20. November 1867', in Marx and Engels 1956–1990, Volume 31.
—— 1870a, 'Engels to Marx in London, Manchester, 21 April 1870', in Marx and Engels 1975–2005, Volume 43.
—— 1870b, 'Engels an Marx 21. April 1870', in Marx and Engels 1956–1990, Volume 32.
—— 1871a, 'Account of Engels' Speech on Mazzini's Attitude towards the International', in Marx and Engels 1975–2005, Volume 22.
—— 1871b, 'Engels to Carlo Cafiero in Barletta, London, 1–3 July 1871', in Marx and Engels 1975–2005, Volume 44.
—— 1871c, 'On the Progress of the International Working Men's Association in Italy and Spain', in Marx and Engels 1975–2005, Volume 23.
—— 1872a, 'The Congress at The Hague (Letter to Enrico Bignami)', in Marx and Engels 1975–2005, Volume 23.
—— 1872b, 'Der Haager Kongreß [Brief an Bignami]', in Marx and Engels 1956–1990, Volume 18.
—— 1873–82a, *Dialectics of Nature*, in Marx and Engels 1975–2005, Volume 25.
—— 1873–82b, *Dialektik der Natur*, in Marx and Engels 1956–1990, Volume 20.
—— 1874–5a, 'Refugee Literature', in Marx and Engels 1975–2005, Volume 24.
—— 1874–5b, 'Flüchlingsliteratur', in Marx and Engels 1956–1990, Volume 18.
—— 1877–8a, *Anti-Dühring: Herr Eugen Dühring's Revolution in Science*, in Marx and Engels 1975–2005, Volume 25.
—— 1877–8b, *Herrn Eugen Dührings Umwälzung der Wissenschaft (Anti-Dühring)*, in Marx and Engels 1956–1990, Volume 20.
—— 1880a, *Socialism: Utopian and Scientific*, in Marx and Engels 1975–2005, Volume 24.
—— 1880b, *Die Entwicklung des Sozialismus von der Utopie zur Wissenschaft*, in Marx and Engels 1956–1990, Volume 19.
—— 1882a, 'Bruno Bauer and Early Christianity', in Marx and Engels 1975–2005, Volume 24.

—— 1882b, 'Bruno Bauer und das Urchristentum', in Marx and Engels 1956–1990, Volume 19.

—— 1883a, 'The Book of Revelation', in Marx and Engels 1975–2005, Volume 26.

—— 1883b, 'Das Buch der Offenbarung', in Marx and Engels 1956–1990, Volume 21.

—— 1884a, 'Engels to Eduard Bernstein in Zurich, London, July 1884', in Marx and Engels 1975–2005, Volume 47.

—— 1884b, 'Engels an Eduard Bernstein Juli 1884', in Marx and Engels 1956–1990, Volume 36.

—— 1888a, 'Engels to August Bebel in Berlin, London, 25 October 1888', in Marx and Engels 1975–2005, Volume 48.

—— 1888b, 'Engels an August Bebel 25. Oktober 1888', in Marx and Engels 1956–1990, Volume 37.

—— 1889, 'The Ruhr Miners' Strike of 1889', in Marx and Engels 1975–2005, Volume 26.

—— 1892, 'Introduction to the English Edition of *Socialism: Utopian and Scientific*', in Marx and Engels 1975–2005, Volume 27.

—— 1893a, 'Engels to Franz Mehring in Berlin, London, 14 July 1893', in Marx and Engels 1975–2005, Volume 50.

—— 1893b, 'Engels an Franz Mehring 14. Juli 1893', in Marx and Engels 1956–1990, Volume 39.

—— 1893c, 'Engels to Natalie Liebknecht in Berlin, London, 1 December 1893', in Marx and Engels 1975–2005, Volume 50.

—— 1893d, 'Engels an Natalie Liebknecht 1. Dezember 1893', in Marx and Engels 1956–1990, Volume 39.

—— 1894–5a, 'Introduction to Karl Marx's *The Class Struggles in France*', in Marx and Engels 1975–2005, Volume 27.

—— 1894–5b, 'Einleitung zu Karl Marx' "Klassenkämpfe in Frankreich 1848 bis 1850" (1895)', in Marx and Engels 1956–1990, Volume 22.

—— 1894–5c, 'On the History of Early Christianity', in Marx and Engels 1975–2005, Volume 27.

—— 1894–5d, 'Zur Geschichte des Urchristentums', in Marx and Engels 1956–1990, Volume 22.

Enos, Richard Leo, 1976, 'The Epistemology of Gorgias' Rhetoric: A Re-examination'. *The Southern Speech Journal* 42: 35–51.

Eskin, Catherine R. 2002, 'Hippocrates, Kairos, and Writing in the Sciences', in *Rhetoric and Kairos: Essays in History, Theory, and Praxis*, edited by P. Sipiora and J.S. Baumlin, Albany: State University Press of New York.

Evans, C. Stephen 1984, 'Redeemed Man: The Vision Which Gave Rise to Marxism', *Christian Scholar's Review*, 13, 2: 141–50.

Farrer, Austin 1979, *Finite and Infinite: A Philosophical Essay*, New York: Seabury.

Feuerbach, Ludwig 1924 [1841], *Das Wesen des Christentums*, Leipzig: Friedrichs & Bley.

—— 1989 [1841], *The Essence of Christianity*, translated by George Eliot, Amherst: Prometheus Books.

Finley, Morris I. 1999, *The Ancient Economy*, Berkeley: University of California Press.

Fischer, Karl Philipp 1839, *Die Idee der Gottheit: Ein Versuch den Theismus speculativ zu begründen und zu entwickeln*, Stuttgart: Liesching.

Fischman, Dennis K. 1991, *Political Discourse in Exile: Karl Marx and the Jewish Question*, Amherst: University of Massachusetts Press.

Fitzmyer, Joseph A. 2008, *First Corinthians: A New Translation with Introduction and Commentary*, New Haven: Yale University Press.

Flood, Christopher G. 2002, *Political Myth: A Theoretical Introduction*, London: Routledge.

Fontana, Benedetto 1993, *Hegemony and Power: On the Relation between Gramsci and Machiavelli*, Minneapolis: University of Minnesota Press.

Foucault, Michel 1981 [1976], *The History of Sexuality, Volume 1: An Introduction*, translated by Robert Hurley, New York: Pantheon.

—— 1985 [1984], *The History of Sexuality, Volume 2: The Uses of Pleasure*, translated by Robert Hurley, New York: Vintage.

—— 1986 [1984], *The History of Sexuality, Volume 3: The Care of the Self*, translated by Robert Hurley, New York: Vintage.

—— 1989, 'How Much Does It Cost for Reason to Tell the Truth?', in *Foucault Live*, edited by Sylvère Lotringer, New York: Semiotext(e).

—— 2000 [1994], *Ethics: Subjectivity and Truth*, translated by Paul Rabinow, Harmondsworth: Penguin.

Friedman, Milton 2002, *Capitalism and Freedom: Fortieth Anniversary Edition*, Chicago: University of Chicago Press.

Frye, Northrop 1982, *The Great Code: The Bible and Literature*, New York: Harcourt Brace Jovanovich.

—— 1990, *Words With Power, Being a Second Study of 'The Bible and Literature'*, New York: Harcourt Brace Jovanovich.

Fukuyama, Francis 1992, *The End of History and the Last Man*. New York: Free Press.

Geller, Jeremy 1993, 'Bread and Beer in Fourth-Millenium Egypt', *Food and Foodways*, 5, 3: 255–67.

Geras, Norman 1983, 'Fetishism', in Bottomore (ed.) 1983.

Gianaris, Nicholas V. 1996, *Modern Capitalism: Privatization, Employee Ownership, and Industrial Democracy*, Westport: Greenwood.

Glancy, Jennifer A. 2006, *Slavery in Early Christianity*, Philadelphia: Fortress.

Goodchild, Philip 2002, *Capitalism as Religion: The Price of Piety*, London: Routledge.

—— 2009, *The Theology of Money*, Durham, NC: Duke University Press.

Gorman, Peter, 1979, *Pythagoras: A Life*, London: Routledge & Kegan Paul.

Gottwald, Norman K. 1985, *The Hebrew Bible: A Socio-Literary Introduction*, Minneapolis: Fortress.

—— 1999 [1979], *The Tribes of Yahweh: A Sociology of the Religion of Liberated Israel 1250–1050 BC*, Sheffield: Sheffield Academic Press.

—— 2001, *The Politics of Ancient Israel*, Louisville: Westminster John Knox.

Grabbe, Lester 2006, *A History of the Jews and Judaism in the Second Temple Period*, Volume 1, London: T. & T. Clark.

Gramsci, Antonio 1971, *Selections from the Prison Notebooks*, translated by Quintin Hoare and Geoffrey Nowell Smith, London: Lawrence and Wishart.

—— 1992 [1975], *Prison Notebooks*, Volume 1, translated by Joseph A. Buttigieg and Antonio Callari, New York: Columbia University Press.

—— 1995, *Further Selections from the Prison Notebooks*, translated by Derek Boothman, Minneapolis: University of Minnesota Press.

—— 1996 [1975], *Prison Notebooks*, Volume 2, translated by Joseph A. Buttigieg, New York: Columbia University Press.

—— 2007 [1975], *Prison Notebooks*, Volume 3, translated by Joseph A. Buttigieg, New York: Columbia University Press.

Gutiérrez, Gustavo 2001 [1969], *A Theology of Liberation*, translated by Caridad Inda and John Eagleson, London: SCM.

Haefelin, Jürg 1986, *Wilhelm Weitling. Biographie und Theorie. Der Zürcher Kommunistenprozess von 1843*, Bern: Lang.

Hagerty, Thomas J. 1902a, *Economic Discontent and Its Remedy*, Terre Haute, IN.: Standard Publishing Co.

—— 1902b, 'Thomas J. Hagerty to A.M. Simons', *International Socialist Review*, 3: 229–30.

Hägglund, Martin 2008, *Radical Atheism: Derrida and the Time of Life*, Stanford: Stanford University Press.

Hallward, Peter 2003, *Badiou: A Subject to Truth*, Minneapolis: University of Minnesota Press.

—— 2006, *Out of This World: Deleuze and the Philosophy of Creation*, London: Verso.

Hardt, Michael and Antonio Negri 2000, *Empire*, Cambridge, MA: Harvard University Press.

—— 2004, *Multitude: War and Democracy in the Age of Empire*, Harmondsworth: Penguin.

—— 2009, *Commonwealth*, Cambridge, MA: Belknap.

Hamer, Dean H. 2005, *The God Gene: How Faith Is Hardwired into Our Genes*, New York: Anchor Books.

Harrill, Albert J. 2006, *Slaves in the New Testament: Literary, Social and Moral Dimensions*, Minneapolis: Fortress.

Harris, Sam 2005, *The End of Faith: Religion, Terror and the Future of Reason*, New York: W.W. Norton.

—— 2006, *Letter to a Christian Nation*, New York: Knopf.

Haught, John F. 2007, *God and the New Atheism: A Critical Response to Dawkins, Harris, and Hitchens*, Louisville: Westminster John Knox.

Hayek, Friedrich von 1960, *The Constitution of Liberty*, Chicago: University of Chicago Press.

Hedges, Chris 2009, *When Atheism Becomes Religion: America's New Fundamentalists*, New York: Simon and Schuster.

Heinlein, Robert A. 1991 [1961], *Stranger in a Strange Land*, New York: Ace Books.

Hesiod 1973, *Hesiod and Theognis*, translated by Dorothea Wender, Harmondsworth: Penguin.

Hess, Moses 1837, *Die heilige Geschichte der Menschheit*, Stuttgart: n.p.

—— 1841, *Die europäische Trierarchie*, Leipzig: n.p.

—— 2004, *The Holy History of Mankind and Other Writings*, edited by Shlomo Avineri, Cambridge: Cambridge University Press.

Hinkelammert, Franz J. 1986 [1977], *The Ideological Weapons of Death: A Theological Critique of Capitalism*, translated by Phillip Berryman, Maryknoll: Orbis.

Hitchens, Christopher 2001, *Letters to a Young Contrarian*, New York: Basic Books.

—— 2007, *God Is Not Great: How Religion Poisons Everything*, New York: Twelve Books.

Holyoake, George 1860, *The Principles of Secularism*, London: Austin & Co.

—— 1896, *English Secularism: A Confession of Belief*, Chicago: Open Court.

Horkheimer, Max 1973, 'Foreword', in *The Dialectical Imagination: A History of the Frankfurt School and the Institute of Social Research, 1923–1950*, edited by Martin Jay, Berkeley: University of California Press.

—— 1978, *Dawn and Decline: Notes 1926–1931 and 1950–1969*, translated by Michael Shaw, New York: Seabury.

—— 1982 [1972], *Critical Theory: Selected Essays*, translated by Matthew J. O'Connell et al., New York: Continuum.

—— 1985a [1943], 'Plan des Forschungsprojekts über Antisemitismus', in *Gesammelte Schriften*, Volume 12, Frankfurt am Main: Fischer Taschenbuch.

—— 1985b [1943], 'Zur Psychologie des Antisemitismus', in *Gesammelte Schriften*, Volume 12, Frankfurt am Main: Fischer Taschenbuch.

—— 1985c [1945], 'New Yorker Notizen 1945', in *Gesammelte Schriften*, Volume 12, Frankfurt am Main: Fischer Taschenbuch.

—— 1985d [1957], 'Zum Begriff des Menschen', in *Gesammelte Schriften*, Volume 7, Frankfurt am Main: Fischer Taschenbuch.

—— 1985e [1960/1967], 'Zur Ergreifung Eichmanns', in *Gesammelte Schriften*, Volume 8, Frankfurt am Main: Fischer Taschenbuch.

—— 1985f [1961], 'Über die deutschen Juden', in *Gesammelte Schriften*, Volume 8, Frankfurt am Main: Fischer Taschenbuch.

—— 1985g [1963], 'Theismus – Atheismus', in *Gesammelte Schriften*, Volume 7, Frankfurt am Main: Fischer Taschenbuch.

—— 1985h [1965], 'Bedrohungen der Freiheit', in *Gesammelte Schriften*, Volume 8, Frankfurt am Main: Fischer Taschenbuch.

—— 1985i [1966], 'Letzte Spur von Theologie – Paul Tillichs Vermächtnis', in *Gesammelte Schriften*, Volume 7, Frankfurt am Main: Fischer Taschenbuch.

—— 1985j [1967], 'De Anima', in *Gesammelte Schriften*, Volume 7, Frankfurt am Main: Fischer Taschenbuch.

—— 1985k [1967], 'Erinnerung an Paul Tillich [Gespräch mit Gerhard Rein]', in *Gesammelte Schriften*, Volume 7, Frankfurt am Main: Fischer Taschenbuch.

—— 1985l [1967], 'Religion und Philosophie', in *Gesammelte Schriften*, Volume 7, Frankfurt am Main: Fischer Taschenbuch.

—— 1985m [1968], 'Christentum, Marxismus und studentische Protestbewegung. Gespräch mit Dagobert Lindlau', in *Gesammelte Schriften*, Volume 7, Frankfurt am Main: Fischer Taschenbuch.

—— 1985n [1968], 'Psalm 91', in *Gesammelte Schriften*, Volume 7, Frankfurt am Main: Fischer Taschenbuch.

—— 1985o [1969], 'Die Funktion der Theologie in der Gesellschaft. Gespräch mit Paul Neuenzeit', in *Gesammelte Schriften*, Volume 7, Frankfurt am Main: Fischer Taschenbuch.

—— 1985p [1970], 'Die Sehnsucht nach dem ganz Anderen [Gespräch mit Helmut Gumnior]', in *Gesammelte Schriften*, Volume 7, Frankfurt am Main: Fischer Taschenbuch.

—— 1985q [1971], 'Bemerkungen zue Liberalisierung der Religion', in *Gesammelte Schriften*, Volume 7, Frankfurt am Main: Fischer Taschenbuch.

—— 1985r [1971], 'Zur Zukunft der Kritische Theorie [Gespräche mit Claus Grossner]', in *Gesammelte Schriften*, Volume 7, Frankfurt am Main: Fischer Taschenbuch.

—— 1987a [1926–31], *Notizen zur Dämmerung*, in *Gesammelte Schriften*, Volume 11, Frankfurt am Main: Fischer Taschenbuch.

—— 1987b [1930], 'Anfänge der bürgerlichen Geschichtsphilosophie', in *Gesammelte Schriften*, Volume 2, Frankfurt am Main: Fischer Taschenbuch.

—— 1987c [1934], *Dämmerung: Notizen in Deutschland*, in *Gesammelte Schriften*, Volume 2, Frankfurt am Main: Fischer Taschenbuch.

—— 1987d [1944/6], 'Antisemitismus: Der soziologische Hintergrund des psychoanalystischen Forschungsansatzes', in *Gesammelte Schriften*, Volume 5, Frankfurt am Main: Fischer Taschenbuch.

—— 1987e [1945], 'Zur Klassifikation jüdischer Einwanderer', in *Gesammelte Schriften*, Volume 5, Frankfurt am Main: Fischer Taschenbuch.

—— 1988a [1934], 'Zum Rationalismusstreit in der gegenwärtigen Philosophie', in *Gesammelte Schriften*, Volume 3, Frankfurt am Main: Fischer Taschenbuch.

—— 1988b [1935], 'Gedanke zur Religion', in *Gesammelte Schriften*, Volume 3, Frankfurt am Main: Fischer Taschenbuch.

—— 1988c [1935], 'Zum Problem der Wahrheit', in *Gesammelte Schriften*, Volume 3, Frankfurt am Main: Fischer Taschenbuch.

—— 1988d [1936], 'Zu Theodor Haecker: *Der Christ und der Geschichte*', in *Gesammelte Schriften*, Volume 4, Frankfurt am Main: Fischer Taschenbuch.

—— 1988e [1938], 'Montaigne und die Funktion der Skepsis', in *Gesammelte Schriften*, Volume 4, Frankfurt am Main: Fischer Taschenbuch.

—— 1988f [1939], 'Die Juden und Europa', in *Gesammelte Schriften*, Volume 4, Frankfurt am Main: Fischer Taschenbuch.

—— 1988g [1940], 'Die gesellschaftliche Funktion der Philosophie', in *Gesammelte Schriften*, Volume 4, Frankfurt am Main: Fischer Taschenbuch.

—— 1988h [1941], 'Neue Kunst und Massenkultur', in *Gesammelte Schriften*, Volume 4, Frankfurt am Main: Fischer Taschenbuch.

—— 1988i [1949–69], *Nachgelassene Schriften*, in *Gesammelte Schriften*, Volume 14, Frankfurt am Main: Fischer Taschenbuch.

—— 1988j [1950–70], 'Späne. Notizen über Gespräche mit Max Horkheimer, in unverbindlicher Formulierung aufgeschrieben von Friedrich Pollock', in *Gesammelte Schriften*, Volume 14, Frankfurt am Main: Fischer Taschenbuch.

—— 1989a [1961], 'Paul Tillich [Zum 75. Geburtstag]', in *Gesammelte Schriften*, Volume 13, Frankfurt am Main: Fischer Taschenbuch.

—— 1989b [1963], 'Skepsis und Glaube [Ein Brief an Götz Harbsmeier]', in *Gesammelte Schriften*, Volume 13, Frankfurt am Main: Fischer Taschenbuch.

—— 1991a, *Notizen, 1949–1969*, in *Gesammelte Schriften*, Volume 6, Frankfurt am Main: Fischer Taschenbuch.

—— 1991b [1967], *Zur Kritik der instrumentellen Vernunft*, in *Gesammelte Schriften*, Volume 6, Frankfurt am Main: Fischer Taschenbuch.

—— 1993, *Between Philosophy and Social Science: Selected Early Writings*, translated by G. Frederick Hunter, Matthew S. Kramer and John Torpey, Cambridge, MA: MIT Press.

—— 1996, *Critique of Instrumental Reason*, translated by Matthew J. O'Connell et al., New York: Continuum.

—— 2004 [1947], *Eclipse of Reason*, London: Continuum.

—— 2006 [1968], 'Psalm 91', in *Marx, Critical Theory, and Religion: A Critique of Rational Choice*, translated by Michael R. Ott, edited by Warren S. Goldstein, Leiden: Brill.

Horkheimer, Max and Theodor W. Adorno 1985 [1943], 'Diskussion zu den 'Elementen des Antisemitismus' der Dialektik der Aufklärung', in *Gesammelte*

Schriften, Volume 12, Frankfurt am Main: Fischer Taschenbuch.

—— 2002 [1947], *Dialectic of Enlightenment: Philosophical Fragments*, translated by Edmund Jephcott, Stanford: Stanford University Press.

—— 2003 [1947], *Dialektik der Aufklärung*, in *Gesammelte Schriften*, Volume 5, Frankfurt am Main: Fischer Taschebuch.

Horsley, Richard A. 1989, *Sociology and the Jesus Movement*, New York: Crossroad Publishing Company.

—— 1992, *Jesus and the Spiral of Violence: Popular Jewish Resistance in Roman Palestine*, Philadelphia: Augsburg Fortress.

—— 1995, *Galilee: History, Politics, People*, Philadelphia: Trinity Press International.

—— 1996, *Archaeology, History and Society in Galilee: The Social Context of Jesus and the Rabbis*, Philadelphia: Trinity Press International.

—— 2002, *Jesus and Empire: The Kingdom of God and the New World Order*, Minneapolis: Augsburg Fortress.

—— 2003, *Religion and Empire: People, Power, and the Life of the Spirit*, Minneapolis: Augsburg Fortress.

—— 2007, *Scribes, Visionaries, and the Politics of Second Temple Judea*, Louisville: Westminster John Knox.

—— 2008, 'Jesus and Empire', in *In the Shadow of Empire: Reclaiming the Bible as a History of Faithful Resistance*, edited by Richard Horsley, Louisville: Westminster John Knox.

Horsley, Richard A. (ed.) 1997, *Paul and Empire: Religion and Power in Roman Imperial Society*, Philadelphia: Trinity Press International.

—— (ed.) 2000, *Paul and Politics: Ekklesia, Israel, Imperium, Interpretation. Essays in Honor of Krister Stendahl*, Philadelphia: Trinity Press International.

—— (ed.) 2008a, *In the Shadow of Empire: Reclaiming the Bible as a History of Faithful Resistance*, Louisville: Westminster John Knox.

Horsley, Richard and John S. Hanson 1985, *Bandits, Prophets, and Messiahs: Popular Movements in the Time of Jesus*, Philadelphia: Trinity Press International.

Hudson, Michael and Baruch A. Levine (eds.) 1996, *Privatization in the Ancient Near East and Classical World*, Cambridge, MA: Peabody Museum of Archaeology and Ethnology, Harvard University.

—— (eds.) 1999, *Urbanization and Land Ownership in the Ancient Near East*, Cambridge, MA: Peabody Museum of Archaeology and Ethnology, Harvard University.

Hudson, Michael and Marc van de Mieroop (eds.) 2002, *Debt and Economic Renewal in the Ancient Near East*, Bethesda: CDL.

Hudson, Michael and Cornelia Wunsch (eds.) 2004, *Creating Economic Order: Record-Keeping, Standardization, and the Development of Accounting in the Ancient Near East*. Bethesda: CDL.

Hüttner, Martin 1985, *Wilhelm Weitling als Frühsozialist*, Frankfurt am Main: Haag und Herchen.

Jameson, Fredric 1971, *Marxism and Form: Twentieth-Century Dialectical Theories of Literature*, Princeton: Princeton University Press.

—— 1981, *The Political Unconscious: Narrative as a Socially Symbolic Act*, Ithaca: Cornell University Press.

—— 1986, 'Religion and Ideology: A Political Reading of Paradise Lost', in *Literature, Politics and Theory: Papers from the Essex Conference 1976–84*, edited by Francis Barker, London: Methuen.

—— 1987, 'Foreword', in *On Meaning: Selected Writings in Semiotic Theory*, by A.J. Greimas, Minneapolis: University of Minnesota Press.

—— 1990, *Late Marxism: Adorno, or, the Persistence of the Dialectic*, London: Verso.

—— 1991, *Postmodernism, or, the Cultural Logic of Late Capitalism*, Durham, NC: Duke University Press.

—— 1996, 'On the Sexual Production of Western Subjectivity, or, Saint Augustine as a Social Democrat', in *Gaze and Voice as Love Objects*, edited by Renata Salecl and Slavoj Žižek, Durham, NC: Duke University Press.

—— 2005, *Archaeologies of the Future: The Desire Called Utopia and Other Science Fictions*, London: Verso.

Janicaud, Dominique, Jean-François Courtine, Jean-Louis Chrétien, Michel Henry, Jean-Luc Marion and Paul Ricœur 2000 [1991/2], *Phenomenology and the 'Theological Turn': The French Debate*, New York: Fordham University Press.

Janz, Denis R. 1998, *World Christianity and Marxism*, Oxford: Oxford University Press.

Jewett, Robert 2007, *Romans*, Minneapolis: Fortress.

Jobling, David 1991, 'Feminism and "Mode of Production" in Ancient Israel: Search for a Method', in *The Bible and the Politics of Exegesis: Essays in Honor of Norman K. Gottwald on His Sixty-Fifth Birthday*, edited by David Jobling, Peggy L. Day and Gerald T. Sheppard, Cleveland: Pilgrim Press.

—— 1998, *1 Samuel*, Collegeville: Liturgical Press.

Jolowicz, Herbert Felix 1952, *Historical Introduction to the Study of Roman Law*, Cambridge: Cambridge University Press.

Kallas, James 1965, 'Romans XIII:1–7: An Interpolation', *New Testament Studies*, 11: 365–74.

Kant, Immanuel 1998 [1781/7], *Critique of Pure Reason*, translated by Paul Guyer and Allen W. Wood, Cambridge: Cambridge University Press.

Käsemann, Ernst 1980, *An die Römer*, Tübingen: J.C.B. Mohr (Paul Siebeck).

Kautsky, Karl 1947a [1888], *Thomas More und seine Utopie: mit einer Historischen Einleitung*, Third Edition, Berlin: J.W.H. Dietz.

—— 1947b [1895–7], *Vorläufer des neueren Sozialismus I: Kommunistische Bewegungen im Mittelalter*, Berlin: J.H.W. Dietz.

—— 1947c [1895–7], *Vorläufer des neueren Sozialismus II: Der Kommunismus in der deutschen Reformation*, Berlin: J.H.W. Dietz.

—— 1977 [1908], *Der Ursprung des Christentums: Eine Historische Untersuchung*, Stuttgart: J.H.W. Dietz.

—— 1979 [1888], *Thomas More and His Utopia*, translated by Henry James Stenning, London: Lawrence and Wishart.

—— 2002 [1897], *Communism in Central Europe in the Time of the Reformation*, translated by J.L. Mulliken and E.G. Mulliken, available at: <http://www.marxists.org/archive/kautsky/1897/europe/index.htm>.

—— 2007 [1908], *Foundations of Christianity*, translated by H.F. Mins, London: Socialist Resistance.

Kautsky, Karl and Paul Lafargue 1977 [1922], *Die Vorläufer des neueren Sozialismus III: Die beiden ersten grossen Utopisten*, Stuttgart: J.H.W. Dietz.

Kee, Alistair 1990, *Marx and the Failure of Liberation Theology*, London: SCM.

Keener, Craig S. 2005, *1–2 Corinthians*, *New Cambridge Bible Commentary*, Cambridge: Cambridge University Press.

Kiernan, J.G. 1983, 'Religion', in Bottomore (ed.) 1983.

Kinneavy, James 1983, 'Kairos: a Neglected Concept in Classical Rhetoric', in *Rhetoric and Praxis: The Contribution of Classical Rhetoric to Practical Reasoning*, edited by Jean Dietz Moss, Washington, DC.: Catholic University of America Press.

Kittel, Gerhard, Gerhard Friedrich and Geoffrey William Bromiley (eds.) 1985, *Theological Dictionary of the New Testament*, Grand Rapids: Eerdmans.

Kittredge, Cynthia Briggs 2000, 'Corinthian Women Prophets and Paul's Argumentation in 1 Corinthians', in Horsley (ed.) 2000.

Knatz, Lothar 1984, *Utopie und Wissenschaft im frühen deutschen Sozialismus: Theoriebildung und Wissenschaftsbegriff bei Wilhelm Weitling*, Frankfurt am Main: Peter Lang.

Knatz, Lothar and Hans-Arthur Marsiske (eds.) 2000, *Wilhelm Weitling: ein deutscher Arbeiterkommunist*, Hamburg: Ergebnisse.

Kolakowski, Leszek 1981, *Main Currents of Marxism*, Volume 1, translated by P.S. Falla, Oxford: Oxford University Press.

Kotsko, Adam 2008, *Žižek and Theology*, London: T. & T. Clark.

Kouvelakis, Stathis 2003, *Philosophy and Revolution: From Kant to Marx*, translated by G.M. Goshgarian, London: Verso.

Kristeva, Julia 1983, *Histoires d'amour*, Paris: Éditions Denoël.

—— 1987 [1983], *Tales of Love*, translated by Leon S. Roudiez, New York: Columbia University Press.

—— 1988, *Étrangers à nous-mêmes*, Paris: Gallimard.

—— 1991 [1988], *Strangers to Ourselves*, translated by Leon S. Roudiez, New York: Columbia University Press.

Laclau, Ernesto 2004, 'An Ethics of Militant Engagement', in *Think Again: Alain Badiou and the Future of Philosophy*, edited by Peter Hallward, London: Continuum.

Larrain, Jorge 1983a, 'Ideology', in Bottomore (ed.) 1983.

—— 1983b, *Marxism and Ideology*, Basingstoke: Palgrave Macmillan.

Leaving Certificate from Berlin University 1841 [1926], in Marx and Engels 1975–2005, Volume 1.

Lefebvre, Henri 1992, *Éléments de rythmanalyse*, Paris: Éditions Syllepse.

—— 2004, *Rhythmanalysis: Space, Time and Everyday Life*, translated by Stuart Elden and Gerald Moore, London: Continuum.

Lefort, Claude 2006, 'The Permanence of the Theologico-Political?' in *Political Theologies: Public Religions in a Post-Secular World*, edited by Hent de Vries and Lawrence E. Sullivan, New York: Fordham University Press.

Lemche, Niels Peter 1998, *The Israelites in History and Tradition*, London: SPCK.

Lenin, Vladimir Ilyich 1976 [1922], 'Political Report of the Central Committee of the R.C.P. (B.), March 27', in *Lenin: Collected Works*, Volume 33, Moscow: Progress Publishers.

Lévi-Strauss, Claude 1966, *The Savage Mind*, London: Weidenfeld and Nicolson.

—— 1968, *Structural Anthropology*, translated by Claire Jacobsen and Brooke Grundfest Schoepf, Harmondsworth: Penguin.

—— 1989, *Tristes Tropiques*, translated by John Weightman and Doreen Weightman, London: Pan.

—— 1994, *The Raw and the Cooked: Introduction to a Science of Mythology*, London: Pimlico.

Liew, Tat-siong Benny 1999, 'Tyranny, Boundary and Might: Colonial Mimicry in Mark's Gospel', *Journal for the Study of the New Testament*, 73: 7–31.

Lifshitz, Mikhail 1973 [1933], *The Philosophy of Art of Karl Marx*, translated by Ralph B. Winn, New York: Pluto.

—— 1984, *Collected Works*, Moscow: Progress Publishers.

Lincoln, Bruce 2000, *Theorizing Myth: Narrative, Ideology, and Scholarship*, Chicago: University of Chicago Press.

Lindemann, Hugo and Morris Hillquit 1977 [1922], *Vorläufer des neueren Sozialismus IV*, Stuttgart: J.H.W. Dietz.

Linklater, Andrew 2000, *International Relations: Critical Concepts in Political Science*, London: Routledge.

Lischer, Richard 1973, 'The Lutheran Shape of Marxian Evil', *Religion in Life*, 42, 4: 549–58.

Loizidou, Elena 2007, *Judith Butler: Ethics, Law, Politics*, Oxford: Routledge-Cavendish.

Longenecker, Richard N. 1990, *Galatians*, Waco: Word Books.

Löwith, Karl 1949, *Meaning in History: The Theological Implications of the Philosophy of History*, Chicago: University of Chicago Press.

Löwy, Michael 1996, *The War of Gods: Religion and Politics in Latin America*, London: Verso.

Loy, David 1996, 'The Religion of the Market', *Journal of the American Academy of Religion*, 65, 2: 275–90.

Lukács, Georg 1966, *Der junge Hegel: Über die Beziehungen von Dialektik und Ökonomie*, in *Georg Lukács Werke*, Volume 8, Third Edition, Neuwied and Berlin: Hermann Luchterhand.

—— 1968, *Geschichte und Klassenbewusstsein*, in *Georg Lukács Werke*, Volume 2, Neuwied and Berlin: Hermann Luchterhand.

—— 1971 [1920], *Theory of the Novel: A Historico-Philosophical Essay on the Forms of Great Epic Literature*, translated by Anna Bostock, Cambridge, MA: MIT Press.

—— 1975 [1966], *The Young Hegel: Studies in the Relations between Dialectics and Economics*, translated by Rodney Livingstone, London: Merlin.

—— 1988 [1968], *History and Class Consciousness: Studies in Marxist Dialectics*, translated by Rodney Livingstone, Cambridge, MA: MIT Press.

—— 1994 [1920], *Die Theorie des Romans: Ein geschichtsphilosophischer Versuch über die Formen der grossen Epik*, Munich: Deutscher Taschenbuch Verlag.

Lunacharsky, Anatoly 1908, *Religiia i sotsializm: Tom 1*, Moscow: Shipovnik.

—— 1911, *Religiia i sotsializm: Tom 2*, Moscow: Shipovnik.

Luxemburg, Rosa 1970 [1905], 'Socialism and the Churches', in *Rosa Luxemburg Speaks*, edited by Mary-Alice Waters, New York: Pathfinder Press.

—— 1982 [1905], *Kirche und Sozialismus*, Frankfurt am Main: Stimme-Verlag.

MacIntyre, Alasdair 1998, *A Short History of Ethics: A History of Moral Philosophy from the Homeric Age to the Twentieth Century*, Second Edition, Notre Dame: University of Notre Dame Press.

Mack, Burton L. 2008, *Myth and the Christian Nation: A Social Theory of Religion*, London: Equinox.

Malina, Bruce J. and Jerome H. Neyrey 1996, *Portraits of Paul: An Archaeology of Ancient Personality*, Louisville: Westminster John Knox.

Marramao, Giacomo 2007, *Kairós: Towards an Ontology of 'Due Time'*. Aurora: The Davies Group.

Marchal, Joseph A. 2008, *The Politics of Heaven: Women, Gender, and Empire in the Study of Paul*, Philadelphia: Fortress.

Marin, Louis 1984, *Utopics: Spatial Play*, translated by Robert A. Vollrath, Basingstoke: Macmillan.

Martin, Dale B. 1999, *The Corinthian Body*, New Haven: Yale University Press.

Martin, David 1978, *A General Theory of Secularization*. Oxford: Blackwell.

Martyn, J. Louis 2004, *Galatians*, New Haven: Yale University Press.

Marx, Karl 1835a, 'The Union of Believers with Christ According to John 15:1–14, Showing Its Basis and Essence, Its Absolute Necessity, and Its Effects', in Marx and Engels 1975–2005, Volume 1.

—— 1835b, 'Die Vereinigung der Gläubigen mit Christo nach Johannes 15, 1–14, in ihrem Grund und Wesen, in ihrer unbedingten Notwendigkeit und in ihren Wirkungen dargestellt', in Marx and Engels 1975–, Section 1, Volume 1.

—— 1842a, 'To Arnold Ruge in Dresden, February 10, 1842', in Marx and Engels 1975–2005, Volume 1.

—— 1842b, 'Marx an Arnold Ruge in Dresden, den 10ten Februar 1842', in Marx and Engels 1956–1990, Volume 27.

—— 1842c, 'To Arnold Ruge in Dresden, March 5, 1842', in Marx and Engels 1975–2005, Volume 1.

—— 1842d, 'Marx an Arnold Ruge in Dresden, den 5ten März 1842', in Marx and Engels 1956–1990, Volume 27.

—— 1842e, 'To Arnold Ruge in Dresden, March 20, 1842', in Marx and Engels 1975–2005, Volume 1.

—— 1842f, 'Marx an Arnold Ruge in Dresden, den 20ten März 1842', in Marx and Engels 1956–1990, Volume 27.

—— 1842g, 'To Arnold Ruge in Dresden, April 27, 1842', in Marx and Engels 1975–2005, Volume 1.

—— 1842h, 'Marx an Arnold Ruge in Dresden, den 27. April 1842', in Marx and Engels 1956–1990, Volume 27.

—— 1842i, 'The Leading Article in No. 179 of the Kölnische Zeitung', in Marx and Engels 1975–2005, Volume 1.

—— 1842j, 'Der leitende Artikel in Nr. 179 der "Kölnische Zeitung"', in Marx and Engels 1975–, Section 1, Volume 1.

—— 1842k, 'Proceedings of the Sixth Rhine Province Assembly. First Article: Debates on Freedom of the Press and Publication of the Proceedings of the Assembly of the Estates', in Marx and Engels 1975–2005, Volume 1.

—— 1842l, 'Die Verhandlungen des 6. Rheinischen Lantags. Erster Artikel: Debatten über Preßfreiheit und Publikation der Landständischen Verhandlungen', in Marx and Engels 1975–, Section 1, Volume 1.

—— 1842m, 'Proceedings of the Sixth Rhine Province Assembly. Third Article: Debates on the Law on Thefts of Wood', in Marx and Engels 1975–2005, Volume 1.

—— 1842n, 'Verhandlungen des 6. Rheinischen Lantags. Dritter Artikel: Debatten über das Holzdiebstahlsgesetz', in Marx and Engels 1975–, Section 1, Volume 1.

—— 1842o, 'Exzerpte aus Charles de Brosses: Ueber den Dienst der Fetischengötter', in Marx and Engels 1975–, Section 4, Volume 1.

—— 1843a, 'Comments on the Latest Prussian Censorship Instruction', in Marx and Engels 1975–2005, Volume 1.

—— 1843b, 'Bemerkungen über die neueste preußische Zensurinstruktion', in Marx and Engels 1975–, Section 1, Volume 1.

—— 1843c, *Contribution to the Critique of Hegel's Philosophy of Law*, in Marx and Engels 1975–2005, Volume 3.

—— 1843d, *Zur Kritik der Hegelschen Rechtsphilosophie. Kritik des Hegelschen Staatsrechts*, in Marx and Engels 1956–1990, Volume 1.

—— 1843e, 'To Ludwig Feuerbach in Bruckberg, Kreuznach, October 3, 1843', in Marx and Engels 1975–2005, Volume 3.

—— 1843f, Marx an Ludwig Feuerbach in Bruckberg, 3. October 1843', in Marx and Engels 1956–1990, Volume 27.

—— 1844a, 'Comments on James Mill, *Éléments d'économie politique*', in Marx and Engels 1975–2005, Volume 3.

—— 1844b, 'Auszüge aus James Mills Buch "Éléments d'économie politique". Trad. Par J.T. Parisot, Paris 1823', in Marx and Engels 1956–1990, Volume 40.

—— 1844c, 'Contribution to the Critique of Hegel's Philosophy of Law: Introduction', in Marx and Engels 1975–2005, Volume 3.

—— 1844d, 'Zur Kritik der Hegelschen Rechtsphilosophie. Einleitung', in Marx and Engels 1956–1990, Volume 1.

—— 1844e, 'Critical Marginal Notes on the Article "The King of Prussia and Social Reform. By A Prussian"', in Marx and Engels 1975–2005, Volume 3.

—— 1844f, 'Kritische Randglossen zu dem Artikel "Der König von Preußen und die Sozialreform. Von einem Preußen"', in Marx and Engels 1956–1990, Volume 1.

—— 1844g, *Economic and Philosophic Manuscripts of 1844*, in Marx and Engels 1975–2005, Volume 3.

—— 1844h, *Ökonomisch-philosophische Manuskripte aus dem Jahre 1844*, in Marx and Engels 1956–1990, Volume 40.

—— 1844i, *On the Jewish Question*, in Marx and Engels 1975–2005, Volume 3.

—— 1844j, *Zur Judenfrage*, in Marx and Engels 1956–1990, Volume 1.

—— 1844k, 'To Ludwig Feuerbach in Bruckberg, Paris, August 11, 1844', in Marx and Engels 1975–2005, Volume 3.

—— 1844l, 'Marx an Ludwig Feuerbach in Bruckberg, 11. August 1844', in Marx and Engels 1956–1990, Volume 27.

—— 1845a, 'Draft of an Article on Friedrich List's Book *Das Nationale System der Politischen Oekonomie*', in Marx and Engels 1975–2005, Volume 4.

—— 1845b, 'Theses on Feuerbach (Original version)', in Marx and Engels 1975–2005, Volume 4.

—— 1845c, 'Thesen über Feuerbach', in Marx and Engels 1956–1990, Volume 3.

—— 1847, 'Minutes of Marx's report to the London German Workers' Educational Society on November 30, 1847', in Marx and Engels 1975–2005, Volume 6.

—— 1851a, 'Marx to Joseph Weydemeyer in Frankfurt am Main, London, 27 June 1851', in Marx and Engels 1975–2005, Volume 38.

—— 1851b, 'Marx an Joseph Weydemeyer 27. Juni 1851', in Marx and Engels 1956–1990, Volume 27.

—— 1852a, *The Eighteenth Brumaire of Louis Bonaparte*, in Marx and Engels 1975–2005, Volume 11.

—— 1852b, *Der achtzehnte Brumaire des Louis Bonaparte*, in Marx and Engels 1956–1990, Volume 8.

—— 1853a, 'The Future Results of British Rule in India', in Marx and Engels 1975–2005, Volume 12.

—— 1853b, 'Marx to Engels in Manchester, London, 22–23 March 1853', in Marx and Engels 1975–2005, Volume 39.

—— 1853c, 'Marx an Engels 22./23. März 1853', in Marx and Engels 1956–1990, Volume 28.

—— 1855a, 'Agitation Against Prussia. – A Day of Fasting', in Marx and Engels 1975–2005, Volume 14.

—— 1855b, 'Agitation gegen Preußen – Ein Fasttag', in Marx and Engels 1956–1990, Volume 11.

—— 1857–8a, *Economic Manuscripts of 1857–58* (*First Version of Capital*) [*Grundrisse*], in Marx and Engels 1975–2005, Volume 28.

—— 1857–8b, *Outlines of the Critique of Political Economy* (*Rough Draft of 1857–58*) [Second Instalment], in Marx and Engels 1975–2005, Volume 29.

—— 1857–8c, *Ökonomische Manuskripte 1857/1858* [*Grundrisse*], in Marx and Engels 1956–1990, Volume 42.

—— 1859a, *A Contribution to the Critique of Political Economy*, in Marx and Engels 1975–2005, Volume 29.

—— 1859b, 'A Historic Parallel', in Marx and Engels 1975–2005, Volume 16.
—— 1861–3, *Economic Manuscripts of 1861–63 (Conclusion): A Contribution to the Critique of Political Economy*, in Marx and Engels 1975–2005, Volume 34.
—— 1862a, 'Marx to Ferdinand Lassalle in Berlin, London, 16 June 1862', in Marx and Engels 1975–2005, Volume 41.
—— 1862b, 'Marx an Ferdinand Lasalle 16. Juni 1862', in Marx and Engels 1956–1990, Volume 30.
—— 1864, 'Inaugural Address of the Working Men's International Association', in Marx and Engels 1975–2005, Volume 20.
—— 1867a, *Capital: A Critique of Political Economy, Volume I*, in Marx and Engels 1975–2005, Volume 35.
—— 1867b, *Das Kapital. Kritik der politischen Ökonomie. Erster Band Buch I: Der Produktionsprozeß des Kapitals*, in Marx and Engels 1956–1990, Volume 23.
—— 1868, 'Remarks on the Programme and Rules of the International Alliance of Socialist Democracy', in Marx and Engels 1975–2005, Volume 21.
—— 1871a, *The Civil War in France*, in Marx and Engels 1975–2005, Volume 22.
—— 1871b, *Der Bürgerkrieg in Frankreich: Adresse des Generalrats der Internationalen Arbeiterassoziation*, in Marx and Engels 1956–1990, Volume 17.
—— 1871c, 'Record of Marx's Interview with *The World* Correspondent', in Marx and Engels 1975–2005, Volume 22.
—— 1872, 'Declaration of the General Council of the International Working Men's Association Concerning Cochrane's Speech in the House of Commons', in Marx and Engels 1975–2005, Volume 23.
—— 1875a, 'Marx to Engels in Ramsgate, Karlsbad, 21 August 1875, Germania, Schlossplatz', in Marx and Engels 1975–2005, Volume 45.
—— 1875b, 'Marx an Engels 21. August 1875', in Marx and Engels 1956–1990, Volume 34.
—— 1879, 'Account of Karl Marx's Interview with the *Chicago Tribune* Correspondent', in Marx and Engels 1975–2005, Volume 24.
—— 1881a, 'Marx to Ferdinand Domela Nieuwenhuis in the Hague, London, 22 February 1881, 41 Maitland Park Road, N.W.', in Marx and Engels 1975–2005, Volume 46.
—— 1881b, 'Marx an Ferdinand Domela Nieuwenhuis 22. Februar 1881', in Marx and Engels 1956–1990, Volume 35.
—— 1882a, 'Marx to Engels in London, Algiers, 8 April (Saturday) 1882', in Marx and Engels 1975–2005, Volume 46.
—— 1882b, 'Marx an Engels 8. April 1882', in Marx and Engels 1956–1990, Volume 35.
—— 1891a, 'Critique of the Gotha Programme', in Marx and Engels 1975–2005, Volume 24.
—— 1891b, 'Kritik des Gothaer Programms', in Marx and Engels 1956–1990, Volume 19.
—— 1894a, *Capital: A Critique of Political Economy, Volume III*, in Marx and Engels 1975–2005, Volume 37.
—— 1894b, *Das Kapital. Kritik der politischen Ökonomie. Dritter Band Buch III. Der Gesamtprozeß der kapitalistischen Produktion*, in Marx and Engels 1956–1990, Volume 25.
—— 1974 [1880–2], *The Ethnological Notebooks of Karl Marx*, edited by Lawrence Krader, Second Edition, Assen: Van Gorcum.
—— 1976 [1867], *Capital: A Critique of Political Economy, Volume One*, translated by Ben Fowkes, Harmondsworth: Penguin.
—— 2002, *Marx on Religion*, edited by John Raines, Philadelphia: Temple University Press.
Marx, Karl and Friedrich Engels 1845a, *The Holy Family, or Critique of Critical Criticism*, in Marx and Engels 1975–2005, Volume 4.
—— 1845b, *Die heilige Familie oder Kritik der kritischen Kritik*, in Marx and Engels 1956–1990, Volume 2.
—— 1845–6a, *The German Ideology: Critique of Modern German Philosophy according to Its Representatives Feuerbach, B. Bauer and Stirner, and of German Socialism according to Its various Prophets*, in Marx and Engels 1975–2005, Volume 5.
—— 1845–6b, *Die deutsche Ideologie. Kritik der neuesten deutschen Philosophie in ihren Repräsentanten Feuerbach,*

B. Bauer und Stirner und des deutschen Sozialismus in seinen verschiedenen Propheten, in Marx and Engels 1956–1990, Volume 3.

—— 1846a, 'Circular Against Kriege', in Marx and Engels 1975–2005, Volume 6.

—— 1846b, 'Zirkular gegen Kriege', in Marx and Engels 1956–1990, Volume 4.

—— 1848a, 'The Civic Militia Bill', in Marx and Engels 1975–2005, Volume 7.

—— 1848b, 'Der Bürgerwehrgesetzentwurf', in Marx and Engels 1956–1990, Volume 5.

—— 1848c, *The Manifesto of the Communist Party*, in Marx and Engels 1975–2005, Volume 6.

—— 1848d, *Manifest der Kommunistischen Partei*, in Marx and Engels 1956–1990, Volume 4.

—— 1850a, 'Review (May to October 1850)', in Marx and Engels 1975–2005, Volume 10.

—— 1850b, 'Revue, Mai bis Oktober 1850', in Marx and Engels 1956–1990, Volume 7.

—— 1852a, *The Great Men of the Exile*, in Marx and Engels 1975–2005, Volume 11.

—— 1852b, *Die großen Männer des Exils*, in Marx and Engels 1956–1990, Volume 8.

—— 1873a, 'The Alliance of Socialist Democracy and the International Working Men's Association. Report and Documents Published by Decision of The Hague Congress of the International', in Marx and Engels 1975–2005, Volume 23.

—— 1873b, 'Ein Komplott gegen die Internationale Arbeiterassoziation. Im Auftrage des Haager Kongresses verfaßter Bericht über das Trieben Bakunins und der Allianz der sozialistichen Demokratie', in Marx and Engels 1956–1990, Volume 18.

—— 1956–1990, *Marx-Engels-Werke*, 43 volumes, Berlin: Dietz.

—— 1975–2005, *Marx and Engels Collected Works*, 50 volumes, London: Lawrence and Wishart.

—— 1975–, *Marx-Engels-Gesamtausgabe*, 114 volumes (projected), Berlin: Akademie Verlag.

—— 1976, *On Religion*, Moscow: Progress.

Matera, Frank J. 2007, *Galatians*, Collegeville: Liturgical Press.

McKinnon, Andrew M. 2006, 'Opium as Dialectics of Religion: Metaphor, Expression and Protest', in *Marx, Critical Theory and Religion: A Critique of Rational Choice*, edited by Warren S. Goldstein, Leiden: Brill.

McLellan, David 1987, *Marxism and Religion: A Description and Assessment of the Marxist Critique of Christianity*, New York: Harper and Row.

—— 1995, *Ideology*, Minneapolis: University of Minnesota Press.

Meeks, M. Douglas 1989, *God the Economist: The Doctrine of God and Political Economy*, Minneapolis: Fortress.

Meyers, Carol 1988, *Discovering Eve: Ancient Israelite Women in Context*, Oxford: Oxford University Press.

Miéville, China 2004, *Between Equal Rights: A Marxist Theory of International Law*, *Historical Materialism* Book Series, Leiden: Brill.

Milbank, John 1990, *Theology and Social Theory: Beyond Secular Reason*, Oxford: Blackwell.

—— 1999, 'The Ethics of Self-Sacrifice', *First Things*, March, available at: <http://www.firstthings.com/article/2009/02/004-the-ethics-of-self-sacrifice-20>.

—— 2005, 'Materialism and Transcendence', in Davis, Milbank and Žižek (eds.) 2005.

Miranda, José P. 1974, *Marx and the Bible: A Critique of the Philosophy of Oppression*, translated by John Eagleson, Maryknoll: Orbis.

—— 1982, *Communism in the Bible*, translated by Robert R. Barr, Maryknoll: Orbis.

Moltmann, Jürgen 1965, *Theology of Hope: On the Ground and the Implications of a Christian Eschatology*, translated by James W. Leitch, London: SCM.

—— 1974, *The Crucified God: The Cross of Christ as the Foundation and Criticism of Christian Theology*, translated by R.A. Wilson and John Bowden, London: SCM.

—— 1996, *The Coming of God: Christian Eschatology*, translated by Margaret Kohl, London: SCM.

—— 1999a, 'Liberating and Anticipating the Future', in *Liberating Eschatology: Essays in Honor of Letty M. Russell*, edited by Margaret A. Farley and Serene James, Louisville: Westminster John Knox.

—— 1999b, 'The Liberation of the Future and Its Anticipations in History', in

God Will Be All in All: The Eschatology of Jürgen Moltmann, edited by Richard Bauckham, Edinburgh: T. & T. Clark.

—— 2000a, 'Godless Theology', *Christian Century*, 117, 36: 1328–9.

—— 2000b, *Is the World Coming to an End or Has Its Future Already Begun?*, edited by David Fergusson and Marcel Sarot, London: T. &. T. Clark.

Molyneux, John 2008, 'More Than Opium: Marxism and Religion', *International Socialism*, 119, available at: <http://www.isj.org.uk/index.php4?id=456&issue=119>.

Moore, Stephen D. 2006, *Empire and Apocalypse: Postcolonialism and the New Testament*, Sheffield: Sheffield Phoenix.

Morgan, Lewis Henry 1877, *Ancient Society, or, Researches in the Lines of Human Progress from Savagery through Barbarianism to Civilization*, Chicago: C.H. Kerr.

Moroziuk, Russel P. 1974, 'The Role of Atheism in Marxian Philosophy', *Studies in Soviet Thought*, 14, 3/4: 191–212.

Mostert, Christiaan 2002, *God and the Future: Wolfhart Pannenberg's Eschatological Doctrine of God*, London: T. & T. Clark.

Negri, Antonio 1991 [1981], *The Savage Anomaly: The Power of Spinoza's Metaphysics and Politics*, translated by Michael Hardt, Minneapolis: University of Minnesota Press.

—— 2003 [1997/2000], *Time for Revolution*, translated by Matteo Mandarini, London: Continuum.

—— 2004 [1985–98], *Subversive Spinoza: (Un)contemporary Variations*, translated by Timothy S. Murphy, Michael Hardt, Ted Stolze and Charles T. Wolfe, Manchester: Manchester University Press.

—— 2008 [2003], *The Porcelain Workshop: For a New Grammar of Politics*, Los Angeles: Semiotext(e).

—— 2009 [2002], *The Labor of Job: The Biblical Text as a Parable of Human Labor*, translated by Matteo Mandarini, Durham, NC: Duke University Press.

Negri, Antonio and Cesare Casarino 2008, *In Praise of the Common: A Conversation on Philosophy and Politics*, Minneapolis: University of Minnesota Press.

Negri, Antonio and Anne Dufourmantelle 2004, *Negri on Negri*, translated by M.B. DeBevoise, New York: Routledge.

Negri, Antonio and Gabriele Fadini 2008, 'Materialism and Theology: A Conversation', *Rethinking Marxism*, 20, 4: 665–72.

Negri, Antonio and Raf Valvola Scelsi 2008, *Goodbye Mr. Socialism*, translated by Peter Thomas, New York: Seven Stories Press.

Nietzsche, Friedrich 1968 [1901], *The Will to Power*, translated by Walter Kaufman and R.J. Hollingdale, New York: Vintage.

—— 1973 [1886], *Beyond Good and Evil*, translated by R.J. Hollingdale, Harmondsworth: Penguin.

—— 1982 [1881], *Daybreak: Thoughts on the Prejudices of Morality*, translated by R.J. Hollingdale, Cambridge: Cambridge University Press.

—— 1990 [1888], *Twilight of the Idols* and *The Anti-Christ*, translated by R.J. Hollingdale, Harmondsworth: Penguin.

—— 1994 [1887], *On the Genealogy of Morality*, translated by Carol Diethe, Cambridge: Cambridge University Press.

Noll, Kurt L. 2009, 'The Ethics of Being a Theologian', *Chronicle of Higher Education*, 27 July, available at: <http://chronicle.com/article/The-Ethics-of-Being-a/47442/>.

Norman, Edward R. 2002, *The Victorian Christian Socialists*, Cambridge: Cambridge University Press.

Ojakangas, Mika 2009, 'Apostle Paul and the Profanation of the Law', *Distinktion*, 18: 47–68.

Økland, Jorunn 2005, *Women in Their Place: Paul and the Corinthian Discourse of Gender and Sanctuary Space*, London: T. & T. Clark.

Onians, Richard Broxton 1973, *The Origins of European Thought*, New York: Arno Press.

Ott, Michael R. 2001, *Max Horkheimer's Critical Theory of Religion: The Meaning of Religion in the Struggle for Human Emancipation*, Lanham: University Press of America.

Pannenberg, Wolfhart 1969, *Theology and the Kingdom of God*, Philadelphia: Westminster.

—— 1991–3, *Systematic Theology*, translated by Geoffrey William Bromiley, three volumes, Grand Rapids: Eerdmans.

—— 2002, 'The Task of Christian Eschatology', in *The Last Things: Biblical and*

Theological Perspectives on Eschatology, edited by Carl E. Braaten and Robert W. Jensen, Grand Rapids: Eerdmans.

Pensky, Max 1996, 'Tactics of Remembrance: Proust, Surrealism, and the Origin of the Passagenwerk', in *Walter Benjamin and the Demands of History*, edited by Michael P. Steinberg, Ithaca: Cornell University Press.

Peterson, Gregory R. 2007, 'Why the New Atheism Shouldn't Be (Completely) Dismissed', *Zygon: Journal of Religion and Science*, 42, 4: 803–6.

Pickstock, Catherine 2005, 'The Univocalist Mode of Production', in Davis, Milbank and Žižek (eds.) 2005.

Pietz, William 1985, 'The Problem of the Fetish, I', *Res: Anthropology and Aesthetics*, 9: 5–17.

—— 1987, 'The Problem of the Fetish, II', *Res: Anthropology and Aesthetics*, 13: 23–45.

—— 1988, 'The Problem of the Fetish, III', *Res: Anthropology and Aesthetics*, 16: 105–23.

Plato 1970, *The Laws*, translated by Trevor J. Saunders, Harmondsworth: Penguin.

Poincaré, Henri 1892, *Les Methodes Nouvelles de la Mécanique Celeste*, Paris: Gauthier-Villars.

Pritchard, James B. (ed.) 1955, *Ancient Near Eastern Texts Relating to the Old Testament*, Princeton: Princeton University Press.

Protz, Roger 1995, *The Ultimate Encyclopedia of Beer*, London: Carlton.

Reventlow, Henning Graf (ed.) 1999, *Eschatology in the Bible and in Jewish and Christian Tradition*, Sheffield: Sheffield Academic Press.

Rey, Jean-Michel 2008, *Paul ou les ambiguïtés*, Paris: Editions de l'Olivier.

Rickert, Thomas 2007, 'Invention in the Wild: Locating Kairos in Space-Time', in *The Locations of Composition*, edited by Christopher J. Keller and Christian R. Weisser, Albany: State University Press of New York.

Ricœur, Paul 1970 [1965], *Freud and Philosophy: An Essay on Interpretation*, translated by Denis Savage, New Haven: Yale University Press.

Riekkinen, V. 1980, *Römer 13: Aufzeichnung und Weiterführung der exegetischen Diskussion*, Helsinki: AASF.

Roberts, Christopher J. 2005, 'On Secularization, Rationalization, and Other Mystical Things: The Unfinished Work of Marx's Religious Criticism', *Iowa Journal of Cultural Studies*, 7, 1: 15–34.

Roberts, John 2008a, 'The "Returns to Religion": Messianism, Christianity and the Revolutionary Tradition. Part I: "Wakefulness to the Future"', *Historical Materialism*, 16, 2: 59–84.

—— 2008b, 'The "Returns to Religion": Messianism, Christianity and the Revolutionary Tradition. Part II: The Pauline Tradition', *Historical Materialism*, 16, 3: 77–103.

Rose, Gillian 1996, *Mourning Becomes the Law: Philosophy and Representation*, Cambridge: Cambridge University Press.

Rose, Margaret A. 1984, *Marx's Lost Aesthetic: Karl Marx and the Visual Arts*, Cambridge: Cambridge University Press.

Rothbard, Murray N. 1990, 'Karl Marx: Communist as Religious Eschatologist', *The Review of Austrian Economics*, 4: 123–79.

Sasson, Aharaon 2010, *Animal Husbandry in Ancient Israel: A Zooarchaeological Perspective on Livestock Exploitation, Herd Management and Economic Strategies*. London: Equinox.

Sasson, Jack M. (ed.) 2006, *Civilizations of the Ancient Near East*, four volumes, Peabody: Hendrickson.

Schmitt, Carl 2005 [1922], *Political Theology: Four Chapters on the Concept of Sovereignty*, translated by George Schwab, Chicago: University of Chicago Press.

Schwartz, Regina (ed.) 2004, *Transcendence: Philosophy, Literature, and Theology Approach the Beyond*, London: Routledge.

Schweitzer, Albert 1998 [1910], *The Quest of the Historical Jesus: A Critical Study of Its Progress from Reimarus to Wrede*, Baltimore: Johns Hopkins University Press.

Schweitzer, Steven 2007, *Reading Utopia in Chronicles*, London: T. & T. Clark.

Scott, Peter 1994, *Theology, Ideology and Liberation*, Cambridge: Cambridge University Press.

Segovia, Fernando F. and R.S. Sugirtharajah (eds.) 2009, *A Postcolonial Commentary on the New Testament Writings*, London: T. & T. Clark.

Sharpe, Matthew 2008, 'Resurrecting (Meta-) Political Theology, or the Abstract Passion of Alain Badiou', *Arena Journal*, 29/30: 273–303.

Sichère, Bernard 2003, *Le jour est proche: la révolution selon Paul*, Paris: Desclée de Brouwer.

Siebert, Rudolf J. 2001, *The Critical Theory of Religion: The Frankfurt School*, Lanham: Scarecrow Press.

—— 2003, *From Critical Theory to Critical Political Theology: Personal Autonomy and Universal Solidarity*, Revised Edition, New York: Peter Lang.

Sipiora, Phillip, 2002, 'Introduction: The Ancient Concept of *Kairos*', in *Rhetoric and Kairos: Essays in History, Theory, and Praxis*, edited by P. Sipiora and J.S. Baumlin, Albany: State University Press of New York.

Sobrino, Jon 2004a [1982], *Jesus in Latin America*, Eugene: Wipf and Stock.

—— 2004b [1985], *The True Church and the Poor*, Eugene: Wipf and Stock.

Sorel, Georges 1961, *Reflections on Violence*, translated by T.E. Hulme and J. Roth, New York: Collier.

Southern, Richard William 1970, *Western Society and the Church in the Middle Ages*, Harmondsworth: Penguin.

Stark, Rodney 1996, *The Rise of Christianity: How the Obscure, Marginal Jesus Movement Became the Dominant Religious Force in the Western World in a Few Centuries*, Princeton: Princeton University Press.

Ste. Croix, Geoffrey Ernest Maurice de 1972, *The Origins of the Peloponnesian War*, London: Duckworth.

—— 1981, *The Class Struggle in the Ancient Greek World: From the Archaic Age to the Arab Conquests*, Ithaca: Cornell University Press.

—— 2006, *Christian Persecution, Martyrdom, and Orthodoxy*, edited by Michael Whitby and Joseph Streeter, Oxford: Oxford University Press.

Stevenson, William R. 1999, *Sovereign Grace: The Place and Significance of Christian Freedom in John Calvin's Political Thought*, Oxford: Oxford University Press.

Stirner, Max 1845, *Der Einzige und sein Eigentum*, Leipzig: Philipp Reclam.

—— 2005 [1845], *The Ego and His Own: The Case of the Individual against Authority*, translated by Steven T. Byington, Mineola: Dover Publications.

Strauss, David Friedrich 1835, *Das Leben Jesu, kritisch bearbeitet*, Tübingen: C.F. Osiander.

—— 1902 [1835], *The Life of Jesus: Critically Examined*, translated by George Eliot, London: Swan Sonnenschein.

Suda, Max Josef 1978, 'The Critique of Religion in Karl Marx's Capital', *Journal of Ecumenical Studies*, 15, 1: 15–28.

Sung, Jung Mo 2007, *Desire, Market, and Religion*, London: SCM.

Surin, Kenneth 2005, 'The Ontological Script of Liberation', in Davis, Milbank and Žižek (eds.) 2005.

—— 2009, *Freedom Not Yet: Liberation and the Next World Order*, Durham, NC: Duke University Press.

Swancutt, Diana 2004, 'Sexy Stoics and the Reading of Romans 1.18–2.16', in *A Feminist Companion to Paul*, edited by Amy-Jill Levine and Marianne Blickenstaff, London: T. & T. Clark.

Swatos, William A. and Daniel V.A. Olson 2000, *The Secularization Debate*, Lanham: Rowman and Littlefield.

Taubes, Jacob 2004, *The Political Theology of Paul*, translated by Dana Hollander, Stanford: Stanford University Press.

Taylor, Charles 2007, *A Secular Age*, Cambridge, MA: Belknap.

Taylor, Keith 1982, *The Political Ideas of the Utopian Socialists*, London: Frank Cass.

Taylor, Mark C. 1975, *Kierkegaard's Pseudonymous Authorship: A Study of Time and the Self*, Princeton: Princeton University Press.

—— 1984, *Erring: A Postmodern A/Theology*, Chicago: University of Chicago Press.

—— 1986, *Deconstruction in Context: Literature and Philosophy*, Chicago: University of Chicago Press.

—— 1987, *Altarity*, Chicago: University of Chicago Press.

—— 2000, *Journeys to Selfhood: Hegel and Kierkegaard*, New York: Fordham University Press.

—— 2001, *The Moment of Complexity: Emerging Network Culture*, Chicago: University of Chicago Press.

—— 2004, *Confidence Games: Money and Markets in a World without Redemption*, Chicago: University of Chicago Press.

—— 2007, *After God*, Chicago: University of Chicago Press.

Tellbe, Mikael 2001, *Paul between Synagogue and State: Christians, Jews and Civic Authorities in 1 Thessalonians, Romans and Philippians*, Stockholm: Almqvist & Wiksell.

The New York Times 1871, 'Wilhelm Weitling – An Inventor of Prominence – A Remarkable Career', 27 January: 4.

Thiemann, Ronald F. 1985, 'Praxis: The Practical Atheism of Karl Marx', *Journal of Ecumenical Studies*, 22, 3: 544–9.

Thistleton, Anthony C. 2000, *The First Epistle to the Corinthians*, Grand Rapids: Eerdmans.

Thomas, Peter 2009, *The Gramscian Moment: Philosophy, Hegemony and Marxism*, *Historical Materialism* Book Series, Leiden: Brill.

Thompson, Edward Palmer 1966, *The Making of the English Working Class*, Second Edition, New York: Vintage.

—— 1983, *Infant and Emperor: Poems for Christmas*, London: Merlin.

—— 1993, *Witness against the Beast: William Blake and the Moral Law*, Cambridge: Cambridge University Press.

Thompson, Thomas L. 2000, *Early History of the Israelite People: From the Written and Archaeological Sources*, Leiden: Brill.

Thompson, Thomas L., Thomas S. Verenna (eds.) 2012, *'Is This Not the Carpenter?' The Question of the Historicity of the Figure of Jesus*, London: Equinox.

Thompson, Roger, 2000, '*Kairos* Revisited: An Interview with James Kinneavy', *Rhetoric Review* 19, 1/2: 73–88.

Tillich, Paul 1951–63, *Systematic Theology*, three volumes, Chicago: University of Chicago Press.

—— 1952, *The Courage to Be*, New Haven: Yale University Press.

Toscano, Alberto 2004, 'Religion and Revolt', *Slash Seconds*, 4, available at: <http://www.slashseconds.org/issues/001/004/articles/04-atoscano/index.php>.

—— 2009, 'Rethinking Marxism and Religion', *Marx au XXI siècle: l'esprit & la lettre*, available at: <http://www.marxau21.fr/index.php?option=com_content&view=article&id=5:rethinking-marx-and-religion&catid=65:sur-la-religion-et-la-laicite&Itemid=88>.

Trigano, Shmuel 2004, *L'E(xc)lu: Entre Juifs et chrétiens*, Paris: Denoël.

Troeltsch, Ernst 1992 [1911], *The Social Teaching of the Christian Churches*, two volumes, Louisville: Westminster John Knox.

Turner, Denys 1999, 'Marxism, Liberation Theology and the Way of Negation', in *The Cambridge Companion to Liberation Theology*, edited by Christopher Rowland, Cambridge: Cambridge University Press.

Untersteiner, Mario 1954, *The Sophists*, translated by Kathleen Freeman, Oxford: Basil Blackwell.

Vattimo, Gianno and John D. Caputo 2009, *After the Death of God*, New York: Columbia University Press.

Voelz, James W. 1999, 'A Self-Conscious Reader-Response Interpretation of Romans 13:1–7', in *The Personal Voice in Biblical Interpretation*, edited by Ingrid Rosa Kitzberger, London: Routledge.

Ward, Graham 2005, 'The Commodification of Religion, or the Consummation of Capitalism', in Davis, Milbank and Žižek (eds.) 2005.

Weitling, Wilhelm 1845 [1838–9], *Die Menschheit. Wie Sie ist und wie sie sein sollte*, Berne: n.p.

—— 1846, *Ein Nothruf an die Männer der Arbeit und der Sorge, Brief an die Landsleute*, Berne: n.p.

—— 1955 [1842], *Garantien der Harmonie und Freiheit*, Berlin: Akademie-Verlag.

—— 1967 [1845], *Das Evangelium eines armen Sünders*, Leipzig: Reclam.

—— 1969 [1843], *The Poor Sinner's Gospel*, translated by Dinah Livingstone, London: Sheed and Ward.

Welborn, Larry L. 2009, '"Extraction from the Mortal Site": Badiou on the Resurrection in Paul', *New Testament Studies*, 55, 3: 295–314.

Wellmer, Albrecht 1990, 'Metaphysics at the Moment of Its Fall', in *Literary Theory Today*, edited by P. Collier and H. Geyer-Ryan, Ithaca: Cornell University Press.

—— 1997, 'Adorno, Modernity, and the Sublime', in *The Actuality of Adorno: Critical Essays on Adorno and the Postmodern*, edited by Max Pensky, Albany: State University of New York Press.

West, Cornell 1982, 'Fredric Jameson's Marxist Hermeneutics', *Boundary 2*, 11, 1/2: 177–200.

Westcott, Brooke Foss 1907, 'Socialism', available at: <http://anglicanhistory.org/england/westcott/socialism.html>.

Williams, Raymond 1958, *Culture and Society 1780–1950*, London: Chatto and Windus.

—— 1960, *Border Country: A Novel*, London: Chatto and Windus.

—— 1961, *The Long Revolution*, London: Chatto and Windus.

—— 1978, *Second Generation*, London: Chatto and Windus.

Winstanley, Gerrard, William Everard, Richard Goodgroome, John Palmer, Thomas Starre, John South, William Hoggrill, John Courton, Robert Sawyer, William Taylor, Thomas Eder, Christopher Clifford, Henry Bickerstaffe, John Barker, John Taylor and John Coulton 1649, *The True Levellers Standard Advanced: or, The State of Community Opened, and Presented to the Sons of Men*, available at: <http://www.rogerlovejoy.co.uk/philosophy/diggers/diggers2.htm>.

Wittke, Karl Frederick 1950, *The Utopian Communist: A Biography of Wilhelm Weitling, Nineteenth-Century Reformer*, Baton Rouge: Louisiana State University Press.

Wood, Ellen Meiksins 1997, *Peasant-Citizen and Slave: The Foundations of Athenian Democracy*, London: Verso.

—— 2008, *Citizens to Lords: A Social History of Western Political Thought from Antiquity to the Late Middle Ages*, London: Verso.

Wray, T.J. and Gregory Mobley 2005, *The Birth of Satan: Tracing the Devil's Biblical Roots*, Basingstoke: Palgrave Macmillan.

Yee, Gale A. 2003, *Poor Banished Children of Eve: Woman as Evil in the Hebrew Bible*, Minneapolis: Fortress.

Yu, Jian-xing and Jun-guo Chu 2001, 'A Reconsideration of Marx's Idea of "Association of Free Individuals"', *Journal of Zhejiang University – Science A: Applied Physics & Engineering*, 2, 3: 348–55.

Zipes, Jack 1979, *Breaking the Magic Spell: Radical Theories of Folk and Fairy Tales*, London: Routledge.

—— 1988, *Fairy Tales and the Art of Subversion: The Classical Genre for Children and the Process of Civilization*, London: Routledge.

Žižek, Slavoj 1996, *The Indivisible Remainder: An Essay on Schelling and Related Matters*, London: Verso.

—— 1999, *The Ticklish Subject: The Absent Centre of Political Ontology*, London: Verso.

—— 2000, *The Fragile Absolute: Or, Why is the Christian Legacy Worth Fighting For?*, London: Verso.

—— 2001a, *Did Somebody Say Totalitarianism? Five Interventions in the (Mis)use of a Notion*, London: Verso.

—— 2001b, *On Belief*, London: Routledge.

—— 2002, *Welcome to the Desert of the Real*, London: Verso.

—— 2003, *The Puppet and the Dwarf: The Perverse Core of Christianity*, Cambridge, MA: MIT Press.

—— 2005a, 'A Plea for Ethical Violence', *Bible and Critical Theory*, 1, 1: 1–15.

—— 2005b, 'The Thrilling Romance of Orthodoxy', in Davis, Milbank and Žižek (eds.) 2005.

—— 2006, *The Parallax View*, Cambridge, MA: MIT Press.

—— 2008, *Violence: Six Sideways Reflections*, New York: Picador.

Žižek, Slavoj (ed.) 1994, *Mapping Ideology*, London: Verso.

Žižek, Slavoj and John Milbank 2009, *The Monstrosity of Christ: Paradox or Dialectic?*, Cambridge, MA: MIT Press.

Žižek, Slavoj, Eric L. Santner and Kenneth Reinhard 2006, *The Neighbor: Three Inquiries in Political Theology*, Chicago: University of Chicago Press.

Index

www.ingramcontent.com/pod-product-compliance
Lightning Source LLC
Chambersburg PA
CBHW060021030426
42334CB00019B/2127